Vikings

- Sailed over one-third of the globe and were the first northern Europeans to harness the technology of long-distance seafaring.
- Spoke Old Norse, the source of many English words and the parent of modern Scandinavian languages: Icelandic, Danish, Swedish, Faroese, and Norwegian.
- Told their myths, legends, and sagas wherever they went. Today these are the basis of Tolkien's *Lord of the Rings*, Wagner's *Ring Cycle*, and a host of fantasy writing and gaming.

THE VIKING LANGUAGE SERIES

Viking Language 1 & 2 are a comprehensive course in Old Norse language, runes, Icelandic sagas, and Viking history and Culture

Viking Language 1: Learn Old Norse, Runes, and Icelandic Sagas (the first book in the Viking Language Series) is an introduction to Old Norse and Icelandic. The beginner has everything in one book: Reading passages, graded lessons, vocabulary, grammar, exercises, and pronunciation. A full complement of maps, runic inscriptions and culture sections explore the civilization and myths of the Vikings. The book follows an innovative method that speeds learning. Because the grammar of Modern Icelandic has changed little from Old Norse, the learner is well on the way to mastering Modern Icelandic.

Viking Language 2: The Old Norse Reader (the second book in the Viking Language Series) immerses the learner in Old Norse and Icelandic. It offers readings of complete sagas, poems of the Scandinavian gods and heroes, and runic inscriptions and includes a large vocabulary, a full reference grammar, and an answer key to the exercises in *Viking Langauge 1*.

Visit our website www.vikingnorse.com

ABOUT THE AUTHOR

Jesse Byock received his Ph.D. from Harvard University. He is Distinguished Professor of Old Norse and Medieval Scandinavian Studies at the University of California, Los Angeles (UCLA). An archaeologist, he is professor at UCLA's Cotsen Institute of Archaeology and directs the Mosfell Archaeological Project (MAP) in Iceland excavating a Viking Age chieftain's hall. He writes about the Viking Age, sagas, archaeology, Icelandic society, and feud.

BOOKS BY JESSE BYOCK

STUDIES

Viking Age Iceland. Penguin Books

L'Islande des Vikings. Flammarion, Editions Aubier

La Stirpe Di Odino: La Civiltá Vichinga in Islandia. Oscar Mondadori

Джесси Л. Байок. Исландия эпохи викингов. Corpus Books

Feud in the Icelandic Saga. University of California Press

サガ ノ シャカイカイシ チューセイアイスランド ノ シュウコッカ. Tokai University Press

Medieval Iceland: Society, Sagas, and Power. University of California Press

Island í sagatiden: Samfund, magt og fejde. C.A. Reitzel

アイスランド サカ Tokai University Press

TRANSLATIONS FROM OLD NORSE

Grettir's Saga. Oxford University Press

The Prose Edda: Norse Mythology. Penguin Books.

The Saga of the Volsungs: **The Norse Epic of Sigurd the Dragon Slayer.** Penguin Books

The Saga of King Hrolf Kraki. Penguin Books

Sagas and Myths of the Northmen. Penguin Books (a short introductory book)

THE VIKING LANGUAGE SERIES

Viking Language 1: Learn Old Norse, Runes, and Icelandic Sagas. Jules William Press

Viking Language 2: The Old Norse Reader. Jules William Press

www.vikingnorse.com
www.vikingoldnorse.com

VIKING LANGUAGE 1

LEARN OLD NORSE, RUNES, AND ICELANDIC SAGAS

JESSE L. BYOCK

Jules William Press

www.vikingnorse.com

Jules William Press
www. vikingnorse.com

Copyright © 2013, Jesse L. Byock
Maps Copyright © 2013, Jesse L. Byock

All rights reserved. No part of this copyrighted book may be reproduced, transmitted, or used in any form or by any means graphic, electronic, or mechanical, including internet, photocopying, recording, taping, pdf, or any information storage and retrieval systems without written permission from Jesse L. Byock.

Cataloging-in-Publication Data
Byock, Jesse L., 1945-
Viking Language 1 : Learn Old Norse, Runes, and Icelandic Sagas / Jesse Byock. - 1st ed.
        v. cm. - (Viking language series)
Contents: v. 1. Viking language 1 : Learn Old Norse, runes, and Icelandic sagas. v. 2.
Viking language 2 : The Old Norse reader.
Summary: Old Norse Icelandic language introductory textbook with readings from sagas, runes, and the Viking Age in Scandinavia.
Includes bibliographical references, vocabulary, appendices, and student´s guide.
ISBN-13: 978-1480216440 (v. 1, pbk.)
ISBN-10: 1480216445 (v. 1, pbk.)
1. Old Norse language-Grammar. 2. Old Norse language-Readers. 3. Vikings-Language. 5. Sagas-Icelandic. 6. Runes-Scandinavian. I. Title.
PD2235.B9 2012/v.1
439/.6/v.1-dc   2012921210 (LCN)

Printed in Calibri
Cover Picture Permission: Cf24063_C55000_100_VSH: Vikingskipshuset, det akademiske dyrehodet fra Oseberg © Kulturhistorisk museum, Universitetet I Oslo / Ove Holst

DEDICATION

This book is dedicated to my teachers of Old Norse: Einar Haugen at Harvard University; Kenneth Chapman and Eric Wahlgren at the University of California, Los Angeles (UCLA); and Gösta Holm at Lunds Universitet. They were great scholars with deep learning in different aspects of Old Norse. It was an honor and a pleasure to learn with them. I believe this book would please them.

ACKNOWLEDGMENTS

Viking Language was long in the making, and I am indebted to many for their help. I thank the students and post docs who worked with me during the many phases of this project. I especially thank Kevin Elliott, a brilliant student in Indo-European Studies with an extraordinary knowledge of Old Norse. So also, I thank Randall Gordon, Marcin Krygier, Colin Connors, and Davide Zori for their insights and critique. It is a professor's joy to have such astute students. I also thank the undergraduates in my Old Norse classes at UCLA.

A good part of this book was written in Iceland, where for several years I was affiliated with the Medieval Studies Program at the University. I thank Professors Torfi Tulinius, Helgi Þorláksson, Ármann Jakobsson, and Ástráður Eysteinsson for providing me with an office and assistance. I warmly thank my friends Aðalsteinn Davíðsson, Gunnlaugur Ingólfsson, and Kristján Jóhann Jónsson for their assistance. These specialists in Old Icelandic cast their sharp eyes over the manuscript. Camilla Basset, Chad Laidlaw, Miriam Mayburd, Rabea Stahl, and Arngrímur Vídalín Stefánsson, excellent graduate students at the University of Iceland, read the advanced draft. Their attention to detail and the additional suggestions by Sigrid Juel Hansen, Ilya Sverdlov, and Brett Langenberger were a boon for the last phases of the project.

Guðmundur Ólafur Ingimundarson, Jean-Pierre Biard, Robert Guillemette, and Ilya Sverdlov worked with me in making the charts and maps, and I warmly thank them for their great skill. I also thank Gayle Byock for her careful reading of the manuscript and constant cheerful support. David Lasson and J. Sebastian Pagani read portions of the manuscripts and contributed many useful suggestions. Any errors that remain are my own.

I am grateful to the Arcadia Foundation, Menntamálaráðuneyti (the Icelandic Ministry of Education, Science, and Culture), the Alcoa Foundation, the Institute for Viking and North Atlantic Studies, the Gelsinger Memorial Fund, the UCLA Center for Medieval and Renaissance Studies, and the UCLA Academic Senate. Their support made this project possible.

Finally, I thank the President of Iceland, Ólafur Ragnar Grímsson, for his constant support for this long project and Björn Bjarnason, the former Minister of Culture.

ORGANIZATION AND NOTES FOR USING
VIKING LANGUAGE 1

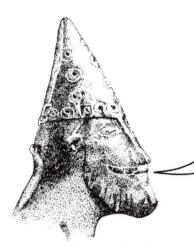

This book has two narratives. One is the tale of teaching Old Norse language, especially the Icelandic variant in which the sagas are written. The other is the story of the people who spoke Old Norse, traveled widely, and carved runes. Both tales are extraordinary.

Figure 1. Viking Age head carved on elk-horn found in Sigtuna, Sweden.

The Book Includes

Table of Contents – a comprehensive listings so that all readings and grammatical information can be easily located.

Introduction – defines the sources and culture for learning Old Norse / Icelandic and runes.

Discussions, Lists, and Features
     Old Norse / Icelandic Alphabet and Spelling.
     List of Abbreviations.
     Extensive Grammar Index telling where to find grammatical explanations and rules.
     A list of Sagas and their locations on a map of Iceland.
     Maps, Charts, and Illustrations.

Lessons – include Old Norse / Icelandic language, runic writing, and the history, mythology, and literature of the Viking Age. Each lesson focuses on an aspect of language and life. The Old Norse reading passages and cultural sections in the first and second lessons concentrate on the settlement of Iceland and Greenland. Succeeding lessons turn to different locations in the Viking world including Denmark, Sweden, Norway, the British Isles, Europe, the Baltic region, Russia, Byzantium, the East. An extensive series of maps visualize the seafaring and travels of the Viking Age.

All lessons include grammar and exercises.

Runes are taught in almost all lessons.

Grammar Toolboxes. Special review sections defining basic parts of speech are strategically located in the lessons. They offer overviews of core grammatical elements for those readers wishing to brush up their grammar while learning Old Norse.

Appendix A – Quick Guide to Old Norse Grammar is a study resource offering the most important tables of nouns, pronouns, adjectives, and verbs.

Appendix B – The Most Frequent Words in the Sagas. *Viking Language* is designed with a word frequency strategy to speed learning. Each lesson has a word frequency section and the symbol ❖ marks each of the 246 most common words in the sagas. Two listings in Appendix B give the 70 most frequent words in the sagas and the 246 most frequent words.

Appendix C – Pronunciation of Old Icelandic. In addition to this appendix, www.vikingnorse.com offers an audio learning section with Icelandic speakers pronouncing reading passages from the early lessons.

Vocabulary. The rear of the book contains a comprehensive Vocabulary. So also, the reading passages in the first 7 lessons have their own specific vocabularies. These small vocabularies free the learner to concentrate on mastering the grammar of the early lessons. For those interested in word stems, the vocabulary entries offer all necessary information.

CONTENTS

INTRODUCTION
    Icelandic Sources
    Scandinavian Runes
    Old Norse Language
        Cognates and Borrowings
    Iceland Where the Sagas Were Written
        The Viking Age
        The Rus
    End of the Viking Age

TOOLS FOR USING *VIKING LANGUAGE*
        Old Norse/Icelandic Alphabet and Spelling
        Anglicizing Old Norse Personal Names
        List of Abbreviations
        Grammar Index

LESSON 1: SAILING WEST TO ICELAND, GREENLAND, AND NORTH AMERICA
      1.1 Culture – Atlantic Seafaring
      1.2 The Letters Þ and Ð
      1.3 Reading – Ingolf Gives Land to Herjolf (*Grœnlendinga saga*)
      1.4 Grammar Toolbox. Nouns and Personal Pronouns
      1.5 Gender of Nouns and Pronouns – Masculine, Feminine, Neuter
      1.6 Case of Nouns and Pronouns – Nominative, Accusative, Dative, Genitive
      1.7 Exercise – Case: Nominative, Accusative, Dative, and Genitive
      1.8 Apposition – Case Agreement of Nouns
      1.9 Word Frequency – The Most Common Words in the Sagas
         Word Frequency Vocabulary – List 1. The Most Frequent Words in the Sagas

in each part of speech
Exercises 1.10 to 1.17
1.18 Culture – Gudrid Travels from Vinland to Rome

LESSON 2: NORSE SETTLERS IN GREENLAND AND VINLAND

2.1 Culture – Norse Greenland
2.2 Reading – 'Land-taking' in Greenland (*Landnámabók*)
2.3 Exercise – The Reading Selection from *Landnámabók*
2.4 Culture – Vinland (*Vínland*)
2.5 Grammar Toolbox. Definite and Indefinite Article
2.6 Proper Nouns
2.7 Grammar Toolbox. Verbs
2.8 Verbs, Infinitives
2.9 Linking Verbs – *Vera*, *Verða*, and *Heita*
2.10 Culture – The Family and Sturlunga Sagas
2.11 Culture – Saga Genres
2.12 Grammar Toolbox. Adjectives
2.13 Old Norse Word Paradigms
2.14 Word Frequency Vocabulary – List 2. The Most Frequent Words in the Sagas
Exercises 2.15 to 2.22

LESSON 3: DENMARK: RUNESTONES AND THE FIRST VIKING STATE

3.1 Culture – Runes
3.2 Reading – The Small Runestone at Jelling, Denmark
3.3 Culture – The Elder and Younger Runic Alphabets
3.4 Runic Letters Which Spell More Than One Sound
3.5 Runic Spelling Variations and Standardized Old Norse
3.6 Exercise – Runic Script
3.7 Reading – Gorm and Thyri (*Óláfs saga Tryggvasonar in mesta*)
3.8 Culture – Gorm the Old and the Danish Jelling Dynasty
3.9 Personal Pronouns – 1st and 2nd Persons
3.10 Exercise – Personal Pronouns – 1st and 2nd Persons
3.11 Personal Pronouns – 3rd Person
3.12 Exercise – Personal Pronouns – 3rd Person
3.13 Nouns – Strong and Weak
3.14 The Verb *Vera* 'to be' – Present and Past
3.15 Exercise – The Verb *Vera*
3.16 Culture – *Son* and *Dóttir* in Names
3.17 Exercise – *Son* and *Dóttir*
3.18 Word Frequency Vocabulary – List 3. The Most Frequent Words in the Sagas

Exercises 3.19 to 3.26

LESSON 4: KINGS AND HEROES

4.1 Reading – The Large Runestone at Jelling
4.2 Exercise – Reading the Large Runestone at Jelling.
4.3 Grammar Toolbox. Vowels and Consonants
4.4 *U*-Umlaut
4.5 Exercise – *U*-Umlaut
4.6 Strong and Weak Verbs
4.7 Exercise – Strong and Weak Verbs
4.8 Weak Verbs in the Present Tense
4.9 Word Frequency – Weak Verbs
4.10 Exercise – Weak Verbs in the Present Tense
4.11 The Reflexive Possessive Pronoun *Sinn*
4.12 Exercise – The Pronoun *Sinn* and Personal Pronouns
4.13 Reading – Midfjord-Skeggi (*Landnámabók*) and Hrolf Kraki's Sword
4.14 Exercise – The Reading Selection from *Landnámabók*.
4.15 Culture – Harald Bluetooth Forges a Viking Age State
4.16 Word Frequency Vocabulary – List 4. The Most Frequent Words in the Sagas
Exercises 4.17 to 4.27

LESSON 5: SWEDEN: A FAMILY RUNESTONE

5.1 Culture – Lands of the Swedes (Svíar) and Goths (Gautar)
5.2 Reading – Sigurd the Dragon-Slayer on the Ramsund Runestone
5.3 Culture – Sigurd the Dragon Slayer
5.4 Short and Long Vowels –Stressed and Unstressed
5.5 The Two Special Stem Rules
5.6 Verbs and the Special Stem Rules
5.7 Exercise – Special Stem Rules
5.8 Words with Stem Endings -*j*- and -*v*-
5.9 Strong Nouns – Introduction
5.10 Strong Nouns – Type 1 Masculine
5.11 Exercise – Strong Nouns – Type 1 Masculine
5.12 The Nouns *Maðr* and *Sonr*
5.13 Exercise – *Maðr* and *Sonr*
5.14 The Weak Verb *Hafa* in the Present Tense
5.15 Exercise – *Hafa*
5.16 Grammar Toolbox. Prepositions
5.17 Reading – A Man of Moderation (*Gunnlaugs saga ormstungu*)
5.18 Word Frequency Vocabulary – List 5. The Most Frequent Words in the Sagas

Exercises 5.19 to 5.30

Lesson 6: Sacral Kingship in Ancient Scandinavia

6.1 Culture – The Ynglings in Sweden and Norway
6.2 Reading – Domaldi Sacrificed for Better Harvests (*Ynglinga saga*, from *Heimskringla*)
6.3 Culture – The Temple at Uppsala and Human Sacrifice
6.4 Strong Nouns – Type 1 Feminines and Neuters
6.5 Exercise – Strong Nouns, Type 1 Feminines and Neuters
6.6 Past Tense of Weak Verbs
6.7 Vowel Sounds and Assimilation
6.8 *I*-Umlaut
6.9 Identifying The Four Weak Verb Conjugations
6.10 Exercise – Identifying Weak Verb Conjugations
6.11 Verbs – Voice, An Introduction
6.12 Culture – Snorri Sturluson and *Heimskringla*
6.13 Reading – Halfdan the Black's Body in Four Parts (*Hálfdanar saga svarta*, from *Heimskringla*)
6.14 Word Frequency Vocabulary – List 6. The Most Frequent Words in the Sagas
Exercises 6.15 to 6.25

Lesson 7: Norway's Harald Fairhair and His Son Eirik Bloodaxe

7.1 Culture – Harald Fairhair
7.2 Reading – Harald Fights His Way to the Throne (*Grettis saga Ásmundarsonar*)
7.3 Culture – Harald Fairhair
7.4 Reflexive Pronouns
7.5 Exercise – Reflexive Pronouns
7.6 Strong Nouns – Type 2
7.7 Exercise – Type 2 Strong Nouns
7.8 Weak Nouns
7.9 Exercise – Weak Nouns
7.10 Nouns Whose Stems End in a Long Vowel
7.11 Reading – Eirik Bloodaxe, the King's Son, Receives a Ship (*Egils saga Skalla-Grímssonar*)
7.12 Culture – Eirik Bloodaxe – A Viking King in England
7.13 Reading – A Cruel King, a Cunning Wife, and Their Promising Children (*Haralds saga ins hárfagra*, from *Heimskringla*)
7.14 Word Frequency Vocabulary – List 7. The Most Frequent Words in the Sagas
Exercises 7.15 to 7.25

LESSON 8: HARALD HARDRADI IN CONSTANTINOPLE

8.1 Culture – Harald and the Varangians

8.2 Reading – Harald Hardradi Leads the Varangian Guard (*Haralds saga Sigurðarsonar*, from *Heimskringla*)

8.3 Exercise – Translating from *Haralds saga Sigurðarsonar*

8.4 Culture – The Rus Across Russia and Further

8.5 Nouns – Kinship Terms in *-ir*

8.6 Nouns Whose Stems End in *-nd-*

8.7 Present Tense of Strong Verbs

8.8 Past Tense of Strong Verbs

8.9 Exercise – Principal Parts of Strong Verbs

8.10 Past Tense Ending *-t* of Strong Verbs

8.11 Exercise – Past Tense Ending *-t* of Strong Verbs

8.12 Reading – Harald Hardradi Sends Famine Relief to Iceland (*Haralds saga Sigurðarsonar*, from *Heimskringla*)

8.13 Grammar Toolbox. Verb Mood

8.14 Commands and the Imperative Mood of Verbs

8.15 The Present Subjunctive of Verbs

8.16 Culture – Harald Hardradi, A Violent End

8.17 Word Frequency Vocabulary – List 8. The Most Frequent Words in the Sagas

Exercises 8.18 to 8.30

LESSON 9: RAIDING IN THE WEST

9.1 Reading – Onund Tree-Foot Raids in the West (*Grettis saga Ásmundarsonar*)

9.2 Exercise – Reading *Grettir's saga*

9.3 Culture – Western Norway

9.4 More on the Definite Article

9.5 Strong Nouns – Type 3

9.6 Strong Nouns – Type 4

9.7 Demonstrative Pronouns *Þessi* and *Sá*

9.8 Clauses – Independent, Dependent, and Relative

9.9 Exercise – Main and Dependent Clauses

9.10 Verbs – The Past Subjunctive

9.11 Exercise – The Past Subjunctive of Verbs

9.12 Reading – Murder, Fosterage, and a Widow's Resourcefulness (*Grettis saga Ásmundarsonar*)

9.13 Culture – Vikings in the British Isles and Western Europe

9.14 Word Frequency Vocabulary – List 9. The Most Frequent Words in the Sagas

Exercises 9.15 to 9.25

Lesson 10: Beached Whales in Iceland

10.1 Culture – Competition for Resources

10.2 Reading – A Whale Washes Ashore (*Grettis saga Ásmundarsonar*)

10.3 Exercise – *Grettir's Saga*

10.4 Strong Adjectives

10.5 Exercise – Nouns and Strong Adjectives

10.6 Strong Adjectives of Two Syllables

10.7 Strong Adjective Endings

10.8 Exercise – Strong Adjectives

10.9 Verbs – Past Participles Introduction

10.10 Past Participles of Strong Verbs

10.11 Present and Past Perfect of Verbs

10.12 Verbs – Passive Voice

10.13 Reading – The Whale Dispute Turns Deadly (*Grettis saga*)

10.14 Exercise – From *Grettir's Saga*

10.15 Culture – Resources and Subsistence in Iceland

10.16 Word Frequency Vocabulary – List 10. The Most Frequent Words in the Sagas

Exercises 10.17 to 10.25

Lesson 11: The Endless Battle

11.1 Reading – The Battle of the Hjadnings (*Skáldskaparmál*, from *The Prose Edda*)

11.2 Exercise – Close Reading of The Battle of the Hjadnings

11.3 Weak Adjectives

11.4 Exercise – Nouns with the Definite Article and Weak Adjectives

11.5 Strong Verbs – Guidelines for Distinguishing Strong Verb Classes

11.6 Strong Verbs – Class I

11.7 Strong Verbs – Class II

11.8 Exercise – Strong Verbs, Class I and II

11.9 Verbs Taking Dative and Genitive Objects

11.10 Exercise – Verbs Taking Dative or Genitive Objects

11.11 Reading – The Battle of the Hjadnings Continues (*Skáldskaparmál*, from *The Prose Edda*)

11.12 Possessive Pronouns

11.13 Verbs – Impersonal Constructions

11.14 The Indefinite Pronoun *Engi*

11.15 The Indefinite Pronoun *Annarr*

11.16 Direct and Indirect Speech

11.17 Grammar Toolbox. Adverbs

11.18 Word Frequency Vocabulary – List 11. The Most Frequent Words in the Sagas

Exercises 11.19 to 11.28

Lesson 12: Feud in Iceland's East Fjords

12.1 Reading – Helgi Earns his Nickname (*Vápnfirðinga saga*)

12.2 Culture – Norse Farmsteads

12.3 The Indefinite Pronoun *Nökkurr*

12.4 Pronouns – *Hverr* and *Hvárr*

12.5 The Indefinite Pronoun *Einnhverr*

12.6 The Pronoun *Hvárrtveggi*

12.7 Strong Verbs – Class III

12.8 Verbs – Present Participles

12.9 Reading – The Outlaw Svart Steals Old Thorstein's Sheep (*Vápnfirðinga saga*)

12.10 Culture – Icelandic Chieftains, *Goðar*

12.11 Word Frequency Vocabulary – List 12. The Most Frequent Words in the Sagas

Exercises 12.12 to 12.19

Lesson 13: Spike-Helgi Kills a Thief in Weapon's Fjord

13.1 Reading – Spike-Helgi Hunts Down Svart (*Vápnfirðinga saga*)

13.2 Culture – Assemblies and Courts in Iceland, Background to the Sagas

13.3 Strong Verbs – Classes IV and V

13.4 Preterite-Present Verbs

13.5 Preterite-Present Verbs – Modals With and Without *at*

13.6 Exercise – Preterite-Present Verbs

13.7 Comparative and Superlative Adjectives

13.8 Comparative Adjective Endings

13.9 Superlative Adjective Endings

13.10 Usage of Comparative and Superlative Adjectives

13.11 Exercise – Comparative and Superlative Adjectives

13.12 Comparative and Superlative Adverbs

13.13 Reading – Brodd-Helgi's Relationship to Geitir (*Vápnfirðinga saga*)

Exercises 13.14 to 13.20

Lesson 14: Norse Mythology and The World Tree Yggdrasil

14.1 Culture – The World Tree

14.2 Reading – Gangleri Asks About Yggdrasil (*Gylfaginning*, from *The Prose Edda*)

14.3 Reading – Norns, Well of Fate, and Baldr (*Gylfaginning*, from *The Prose*

    Edda)

14.4 Strong Verbs – Class VI

14.5 Verb Middle Voice – Introduction and Formation

14.6 Verb Middle Voice – Meaning and Use

14.7 Cardinal Numbers 1 to 20

14.8 The Past Subjunctive of Preterite-Present Verbs

14.9 Two-Syllable Nouns – Syncopated Stems

14.10 Exercise – Vowel Loss in Two-Syllable Nouns

Exercises 14.11 to 14.16

LESSON 15: THE SAGA OF KING HROLF KRAKI

15.1 Reading – Bodvar Rescues Hott from the Bone Pile (*Hrólfs saga kraka*)

15.2 Culture – *The Saga of King Hrolf Kraki* and *Beowulf*

15.3 Enclitic Pronouns

15.4 Strong Verbs – Class VII

15.5 Verbs – Subjunctive Middle

15.6 Verbs – Subjunctive and Indirect Speech in Main and Dependent Clauses

15.7 Past Infinitives of the Verbs *Mundu*, *Skyldu*, and *Vildu*

15.8 Cardinal Numbers Above 20

15.9 Ordinal Numbers

15.10 Exercise – Ordinal Numbers

15.11 Reading – Bodvar Kills the Monster (*Hrólfs saga kraka*)

15.12 Culture – Legendary Lejre (Hleiðargarðr)

15.13 Reading – Hrolf Gets The Nickname Kraki (*Skáldskaparmál*, from *The Prose Edda*)

15.14 Culture – Berserkers

Exercises 15.15 to 15.22

APPENDIX A: QUICK GUIDE TO THE OLD NORSE GRAMMAR

APPENDIX B: THE MOST FREQUENT WORDS IN THE SAGAS

A. The 70 Most Frequent Words in the Sagas

B. The 246 Most Frequent Words in the Sagas (by part of speech)

C. THE 246 MOST FREQUENT WORDS IN THE SAGAS (in alphabetical order)

APPENDIX C: PRONUNCIATION OF OLD ICELANDIC

VOCABULARY

FIGURES

1. A Viking Age Head
2. Helmet Nose-Piece, Sweden
3. The Skivum Runestone from Denmark
4. Indo-European Languages Arriving at Proto Old Norse
5. Proto Old Norse (North Germanic) and Its Descendant Languages
6. Scandinavian Settlement in England
7. Norse Settlement in Normandy
8. Sailing Distances from Iceland
9. The World of the Vikings, West
10. The World of the Vikings, East
11. Beads Excavated by the Mosfell Archaeological Project (MAP) in Iceland
12. The Norse Cross the Atlantic
13. The Travels of Gudrid Thorbjarnardottir
14. The Eastern Settlement (*Eystribyggð*) of Norse Greenland (*Grœnland*)
15. Locations of Major Family and Sturlunga Sagas
16. The Runestone, front and back, of King Gorm the Old (Gormr inn gamli) at Jelling, Denmark
17. Runic and Latin Equivalents
18. Viking Age Denmark (*Danmörk*)
19. Eirik the Red's Family Tree
20. The Large Jelling Runestone, Denmark
21. Sides B and C of the Jelling Runestone
22. Dental Consonants
23. The Ramsund Runestone, Sweden
24. Viking Age Sweden (Svíaland or Svíþjóð)
25. The Swedes Kill Their King Domaldi
26. The Vowel Space Chart and the Vocal Tract
27. Pronunciation of the Vowel *i*, as in English 'see'
28. The Vowel *i*
29. Old Icelandic Vowel System
30. *I*-Umlaut of Old Icelandic Vowels
31. Snorri Sturluson
32. King Halfdan's Sleigh Falls Through the Ice
33. The Sea Battle at Hafrsfjord
34. The Negative Prefix *ó*
35. Viking Age Norway (*Noregr*)
35. Ships Riding at Anchor in a Fjord
37. The Route Probably Taken by Haraldr Harðráði
38. The Ed (Boulder) Inscription from Uppland, Sweden

39. Raids and Battles of the 9th-Century Norwegian Viking Onund Tree-Foot

40. The Fläckebo (Hassmyra) Runestone from Västmanland, Sweden

41. The Strands in Iceland's West Fjords (*Grettir´s Saga*)

42. The Väsby Runestone from Uppland, Sweden.

43. The Tingsflisan Runestone from Öland, Sweden

44. A Gotland Picture Stone

45. A Swedish Picture Stone from Lärbrö Hammars

46. Reconstruction of an Icelandic Turf Hall (*Skáli*) Worthy of a Chieftain

47. The Sites of a Tenth-Century Feud in *Vápnfirðinga saga*

48. The Long House (*Skáli*) at *Stöng*, Iceland

49. Short Vowel Placement in the Mouth

50. The Bro Church Runestone from Uppland, Sweden

51. Archaeological Site Map of an Icelandic Turf Hall (*Skáli*) at Hrísbrú in the Mosfell Valley, Iceland

52. The Icelandic Althing

53. The World Tree Yggdrasil

54. The Altuna Church Runestone, Sweden

55. Reconstruction of the Ninth-Century Great Hall at Lejre, Denmark

56. End-View of the Ninth-Century Great Hall at Lejre

57. Interior of the Reconstructed Ninth-Century Great Hall at Lejre

INTRODUCTION

Icelandic Sources. At the end of the eleventh century, Icelanders mastered writing. They adopted a slightly altered Latin alphabet that included the consonants '*þ*' (called thorn) and '*ð*' (called eth). With writing at their disposal, Icelanders soon began capturing on skin manuscripts their laws, genealogies, histories, sagas, legends, and myths. These medieval writings, many of which have survived, provide much of what we know from native Old Norse sources of the history and personalities of the Viking Age.

Figure 2. Helmet Nose-Piece, Sweden.

In composing their prose sagas and histories (among the latter, the most important are *The Book of Settlements [Landnámabók]* and *The Book of the Icelanders* [*Íslendingabók*]), Icelanders recognized that the origins of their community were not timeless or very distant. Instead they saw their personal roots and those of their island-wide community encapsulated in the relatively recent, memorable events of the Viking Age. Keeping these memories alive, they composed the family sagas (*Íslendingasögur*) about Icelanders and the kings' sagas (*konungasögur*) about the rulers and history of Norway, Denmark, and Sweden. These two groups of sagas (there are others, as discussed in this book) form a large literature of quasi-historical prose stories focusing on private and public life and Viking Age conflicts. With often great social detail, the sagas recount moments of honor and deceit as well as the banality and humor of everyday life.

Icelanders also wrote mythic-legendary sagas (*fornaldarsögur*). These 'sagas of ancient times' captured Viking Age stories of ancient heroes such as Sigurd the Dragon Slayer (Siegfried in the German Nibelung tradition) and King Hrolf Kraki. Other Icelandic writings such as *The Prose Edda* preserved Old Norse mythology, legends, and poetry. They recount tales of the Norse gods from their origins in the great void of Ginnungagap to their demise at the final battle of Ragnarok. Each of these sources of writing is included in the reading passages of this book.

In the medieval period immediately following the Viking Age, when the texts were written down, the Icelanders continued speaking Old Norse, as did Norwegians and other Scandinavians.

RUNES. Runic inscriptions are the second of the two major groups of native sources for learning the language and history of the Viking Age. Runes were an alphabetic writing system. The letters are made from short straight strokes carved on wood, bone, bark, wax tablets, and stone. Sometimes runes were engraved, inlaid, or etched onto steel objects such as sword blades. At other times, they were carved on household artifacts such as spindle whorls and bone combs.

Many of the longer runic inscriptions were carved as memorials on stones. Such stones with their runes and sometimes pictorial ornamentation are called runestones. Runes were also used for everyday messages and grafitti. Many inscriptions had a magical context, and some are found on wooden healing sticks. The majority of runic finds are from mainland Scandinavia, but examples of runes have been found in many areas where the Northmen traveled or lived.

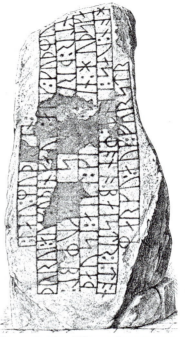

Figure 3. The Skivum Runestone, Denmark.

The runic alphabet is called the 'futhark' after the first six runic letters ᚠᚢᚦᚨᚱᚲ. Runes pre-date the Viking Age by many centuries, offering an efficient way of sharing and preserving information. The oldest runes date from the first century A.D., when writing in runes first caught on among Germanic peoples, spreading to Goths, Frisians, Anglo-Saxons, and the northerners who became the Northmen (*Norðmenn*) of the Viking Age.

Over the centuries there were several different futharks. The earliest from the first century is called the elder futhark with twenty-four characters.

ᚠᚢᚦᚨᚱᚲᚷᚹ ᚺᚾᛁᛃᛇᛈᛉᛊ ᛏᛒᛖᛗᛚᛟᛞ

With variations, the elder futhark was in use into the late eighth century. At the beginning of the Viking Age, the elder futhark was replaced by the younger futhark, a shortened runic alphabet with sixteen characters.

ᚠᚢᚦᚬᚱᚴ ᚼᚾᛁᛅᛋ ᛏᛒᛘᛚ

The younger futhark was used throughout the Viking world, including Iceland, where archaeologists have found a small stone spindle whorl from the time of Iceland's settlement with runes naming a woman as its owner. Runic inscriptions provide our most direct link to the speech of the Vikings.

Together the two major sources for Old Norse language – texts from Iceland and Viking Age runes – offer an extraordinary window into the language of the Vikings.

Old Norse Language. Old Norse is the parent language of modern Icelandic, Norwegian, Swedish, Danish, and Faroese. During the Viking period, Old Norse speakers from different regions within Scandinavian and in overseas Norse settlements readily understood each other with few dialectical differences. For several centuries after the end of the Viking Age, Old Norse was spoken in Scandinavia and the Norse Atlantic settlements, such as Iceland, with relatively small changes in grammar, vocabulary, and phonetics.

Medieval Scandinavians called their language the Danish tongue, *dönsk tunga*. No one is quite sure why this was so. Perhaps it was because Denmark was the first of the Scandinavian lands to become a powerful, centralized kingdom, and the speech of the influential Danish court became for a time the accepted standard. It may also have been because the Danes were closest to the Frankish Empire and the rest of Europe. The Danish tongue may have distinguished Scandinavians from speakers of other Germanic languages on the continent or in England.

Several questions concerning Old Norse arise. One is, How close was Old Norse to Old English? Old Norse was related to but different from the language spoken in Anglo-Saxon England. With a little practice, however, Old Norse and Old English speakers could understand each other, a factor that significantly broadened the cultural contacts of Viking Age Scandinavians. The two languages derived from a similar Germanic source, which had diverged long before the start of the Viking Age (see the accompanying Indo-European language tree). Another question is, Does learning Old Norse/Old Icelandic help in learning Modern Icelandic? The answer is that the two languages are quite similar. The Old Norse of the medieval Icelanders, especially the language of the sagas, remains the basis of Modern Icelandic with relatively few changes. Most of the grammar and vocabulary taught in this book are current in Modern Icelandic.

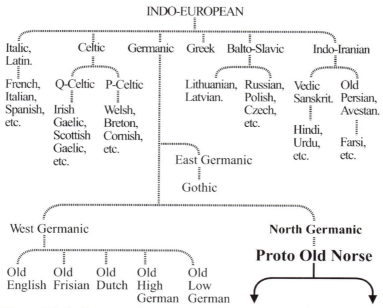

Figure 4. Indo-European Languages Arriving at Proto Old Norse.

As a distinct language, Old Norse has a traceable history. It is the most northerly and most westerly medieval member of the large Indo-European family of languages. The Indo-European language family tree offers an overview of the placement of Proto Old Norse (the ancestor of Old Norse) in the Germanic branch of Indo-European. Old Norse shares a close relationship with early Germanic languages such as Old English, Gothic, and Old High German, while the relationship with other Indo-European languages, such as Latin, Greek, and Sanskrit, is more distant.

At the start of the Viking Age, there were two closely related varieties of Old Norse. East Old Norse was spoken in Denmark, Sweden, and the Norse Baltic region. West Old Norse was spoken in Norway and the Atlantic Islands. Toward the end of the Viking period, around the year 1000, Old West Norse split into Old Icelandic and Old Norwegian.

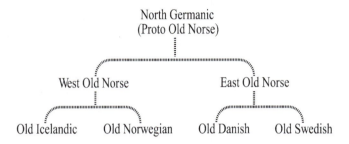

Figure 5. Proto Old Norse (North Germanic) and Its Descendant Languages.

Icelandic and Norwegian share an especially close kinship, since Iceland was settled largely by Norwegian speakers. Today, we call the language of the sagas and the other written Icelandic sources Old Norse (ON) or more precisely Old Icelandic (OI). Old Icelandic is a branch of Old West Norse that developed in Iceland from the Old Norse speech of the first settlers. By the twelfth century, the differences between Old Icelandic and Old Norwegian was noticeable but still minor, resembling to some extent the present-day distinctions between American and British English. At roughly the same time, East Old Norse diverged into Old Swedish and Old Danish. Still the four languages remained similar and mutually intelligible until about 1500 A.D., and all the Old Norse sources, from either the Atlantic or the Baltic regions, are accessible with training in Old Norse.

By the modern period, Norwegian, Swedish, and Danish changed considerably from Old Norse. These languages were strongly influenced by Low German dialects, and English. They dropped numerous aspects of Old Norse grammar and changed many sounds. Modern Icelandic, however, remained faithful to the older language and underwent remarkably few alterations. Today speakers of modern mainland Scandinavian languages can easily understand one other, but they cannot understand Icelandic without training. Old Icelandic grammar underwent relatively few changes on its way to Modern Icelandic. The most noticeable diversion from the medieval language to the modern is a series of sound shifts, spelling modifications, and the adoption of new words and meanings.

The most noticeable spelling difference between Old and Modern Icelandic is the addition of the vowel -u- before the consonant r in many Modern Icelandic words. For example, the Old Icelandic words *maðr* 'man,' *fagr* 'beautiful,' and *fegrð* 'beauty' are spelled in Modern Icelandic *maður*, *fagur*, and *fegurð*. The addition of the -*u*- first appeared in manuscripts around the year 1300 and became standard in later Icelandic. Most alterations from Old to Modern Icelandic are small and systematic, and an Icelander today can read the sagas much as English speakers can read Shakespeare.

COGNATES AND BORROWINGS. Many words in Old Norse resemble English words in pronunciation and meaning. For example, Old Norse *dalr* is similar to English 'dale,' and *taka* has its counterpart in English 'take.' Such words are classified as either cognates or borrowings.

'Cognate' is a Latin term meaning 'related by having the same ancestor' and is used to refer to words that derive from a common parent language. Old Norse and English both originate from (Proto) Germanic, which was spoken in parts of northern Europe between 500 BC and 100 A.D. This early language split into dialects, with words retaining similarities. For example, the word 'father' is *fadar* in Gothic, *fæder* in Old English, *fader* in Old Saxon, *fater* in Old High German, and *faðir* in Old Norse. Many of the most common words in Old Norse have cognates in English as evidenced in the following:

NOUNS	*ADJECTIVES*	*VERBS*
sonr - son	*lítill* - little	*koma* - to come
skip - ship	*smár* - small	*bera* - to bear
konungr - king	*góðr* - good	*segja* - to say
vápn - weapon	*fár* - few	*vilja* - to will
hönd - hand	*fyrstr* - first	*hafa* - to have
bróðir - brother	*víss* - wise	*gefa* - to give
land - land	*dauðr* - dead	*láta* - to let
dagr - day	*langr* - long	*ríða* - to ride

Numerous cognates deriving from the ancient parent language have been lost in Modern English. Among archaisms there are many words no longer used such as 'quoth' (ON *kveða* 'to say') and 'sooth' (ON *sannr* 'true'). Others only survive in compounds, as in English black*mail*, where the second element is cognate with Old Norse *mál* 'speech.' 'Borrowings,' loan words taken from one language into another, are usually the result of close cultural contact. During the Viking Age, Scandinavian trade, conquest, and settlement in Western, Central, and Eastern Europe resulted in the adoption of Norse words into local languages. Some borrowed words are still present in the modern speech of different regions. Two contrasting examples of Old Norse influence on modern languages are found on either side of the English Channel. One is from the Danelaw, the area in northeastern England that saw widespread Scandinavian settlement, and the other from Normandy in northern France.

The closeness of Old Norse with Old English facilitated extensive adoption of everyday Old Norse words, and there were many borrowings into local English dialects. Such borrowings included basic grammatical words such as 'they' (*þeir*), 'their' (*þeira*), and 'them' (*þeim*). In addition, most words in English that begin with *sk-* or *sc-* are borrowings from Old Norse (e.g., sky, scrape, skill), while those beginning with *sh-* are of English origin (e.g., short, shape, shell). Sometimes both the Old Norse borrowing and its Anglo-Saxon cognate survive in Modern English, as for example 'skirt' and 'shirt.'

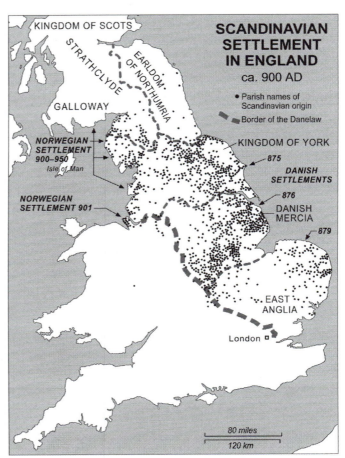

Today there are at least nine hundred words in contemporary English borrowed from Old Norse. Among these are common words such as 'cast' (*kasta*), 'hit' (*hitta*), 'low' (*lágr*), 'egg' (*egg*), 'same' (*samr*), 'want' (*vanta*), 'wrong' (*rangr*), 'law' (*lög*), 'outlaw' (*útlagi*), 'viking' (*víkingr*), 'fjord' (*fjörðr*), and 'husband.' 'Husband' comes from ON *húsbóndi*, a compound word composed of *hús* + *bóndi* ('house' + 'farmer' or 'landowner'), meaning 'the master of the house.'

In the area of the Danelaw, the local speech today retains many borrowings. These include words such as *garth* for 'yard,' *beck* for 'stream,' and *mickle* for 'much' (ON *garðr, bekkr,* and *mikill*). Many place names in the Danelaw contain Norse elements such as *-by* and *-thorpe*, derived from ON *bær*

Figure 6. Scandinavian Settlement in England. Viking raids began in England in the 790s and eventually brought change to the vocabulary and structure of English. Serious Norse settlement began in 865, when the Great Army, consisting mostly of Danes, arrived in East Anglia. York was conquered in 866 and became the Viking Kingdom of York (Jórvík). Alfred the Great defeated the 'Danes' in the late 800s, who then withdrew north of the line on the map and settled among the Saxon population. As the map shows, the Vikings were most active in the north and east (K. Cameron, *Scandinavian Settlement*). The last Viking King of York Eirik Bloodaxe was killed in 954. The English re-conquered the Danelaw, and the Norse settlers were integrated into the English Kingdom.

and *þorp*, meaning 'farmstead.' The town of York derives its name from Old Norse Jórvík, the Scandinavian adaptation of Eoforwic, the older Anglo-Saxon name for the town. Many parish names in the areas of Scandinavian settlement are of Norse origin.

English words of Old Norse origin often have an interesting history. For example, in Yorkshire the word 'riding' was officially used until 1974 to denote each of the shire's three parts. Most people assume the word relates to horses, but 'riding' comes from ON *þriðjungr*, meaning the third (*þriði*) part of an assembly or of a geographically defined region. The Old Norse word was adopted into Old English as *þriðing*. The word continued as *thriding,* with *-riding* as its core, into middle English, where *thriding* continued to define the Northern, Eastern, and Western districts of Yorkshire. *Thriding* was adopted into medieval Latin as *tridingum*. Finally in its modern English form, the intitial *th-* was dropped, and the word became 'riding.' In this modern form, 'riding' was taken to Canada by British colonial administrators, where today it is used in parts of the country to denote a parliamentary constituency.

The relative ease with which large numbers of Old Norse words were taken into English contrasts to what occurred in other languages. Only a few Scandinavian loan words have survived in Gaelic-, Irish-, and Russian-speaking areas, despite significant Scandinavian settlements during the Viking Age.

We have a good deal of information on what happened linguistically in Normandy. The Viking incursions in Normandy started in the 800s with

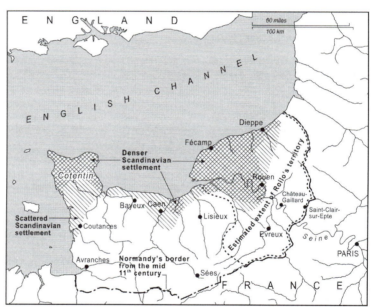

Figure 7. Norse Settlement in Normandy. In 911 the Frankish King Charles the Simple ceded land at the mouth of the Seine around Rouen to the Viking chieftain Rollo. Rollo became a vassal of the Frankish King and undertook the region's defense against future Viking incursions. Rollo's descendants expanded their territory, forming the duchy of Normandy, a powerful feudal state.

small settlements, but in 911, a Viking army under the leadership of the chieftain Rollo (*Hrólfr*) took possession of the lands around Rouen at the mouth of the river Seine. The settlers and their descendants rapidly established an aggressive new state, the duchy of Normandy, which became a powerhouse in tenth- to twelfth-century France. In the early years, Rollo's Norse followers were joined by small Viking warbands and probably some mixed Anglo-Scandinavian settlers. The Scandinavian colonists in the more westerly

Cotentin region appear to have been principally Norwegian, perhaps arriving from the Viking encampments in Ireland.

While politically dominant, the Viking contingents in Normandy were never large. The Scandinavian settlers retained relations with the Old Norse world until the beginning of the eleventh century, but they had, by a half century after 911, lost most of their own language. In place of Old Norse, they adopted the local Old French dialects of *langue d'oïl* derived from Vulgar Latin.

Many traces of Old Norse still exist in local place names in Normandy such as *La Londe* 'grove,' (ON *lundr*) and *Bricquebec* 'slope' (ON *brekka*). Many words and terms remained in the local Norman dialects into the mid-20th century, when such local speech mostly died out. These dialects, however, never had a great influence on Modern French. Normandy remained distant from the center of French power and culture, and Modern French favored the dialects from the more inland regions. Today the traces of Old Norse in Modern French are principally concerned with the sea, a Norman specialty. Words of Old Norse origin include *vague* 'wave' (ON *vágr*), *crique* 'creek' (ON *kriki*), and *equiper* 'equip' (ON *skipa* 'fit out a ship').

ICELAND WHERE THE SAGAS WERE WRITTEN. The Viking Age began in the late 700s, and by the 800s Norse seafarers had discovered Iceland far out in the North Atlantic. Reports of Iceland's large tracts of available land circulated throughout the Scandinavian cultural area, including the Viking encampments in neighboring Celtic lands. The result was the rapid ninth- and early tenth-century settlement of Iceland, a period called the *landnám* (the land-taking).

Icelandic sources also tell of voyages further to the west of Iceland. At the end of the tenth century, Icelanders and Norwegians sailed from

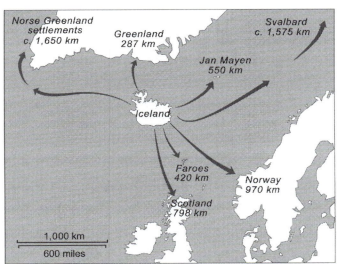

Figure 8. Sailing Distances from Iceland. If somewhat isolated, Iceland was also well placed in the center of the Northern seas. Navigation across the North Atlantic was based on land sightings, astronomical observations, as well as knowledge of currents, bird-life, sea mammals, and light reflected from glaciers. In bad weather, when the sun in its east-west trajectory was obscured, mariners often lost their way. The sagas tell us that some seafarers sailed as far off course as North America.

Iceland into the far North Atlantic where they discovered and settled Greenland. About the year 1000, they reached the North American continent, which they called Vinland (Vínland, Land of Vines or Wineland), and Viking Age archaeological remains have been excavated at

L'Anse aux Meadows on the northern tip of Newfoundland.

Early Iceland, with its writings about the Viking Age settlement, is a laboratory for exploring Old Norse language, history, and social forces of the Viking Age, as well as the development of narrative. In most places, Norse colonists took land by force from indigenous populations. Iceland was different. It was uninhabited except for a few Celtic monks, who, seeking solitude, had earlier sailed there in small skin boats. The majority of Viking Age immigrants to Iceland were free farmers. The settlers came with their families, laborers, craftsmen, slaves, livestock, house equipment, and farm implements. They also brought their language Old Norse, the language of Scandinavia during the Viking Age.

From the Icelanders' medieval histories and sagas, we know a great deal about the men and women who settled Iceland. They were a predominantly Norse culture group with numbers of Celts, often women as determined by DNA studies. Among the colonists were small-scale chieftains who in Iceland came to be called *goðar* (singular *goði*, a term which carries the meaning of priest chieftain). Some of these leaders are said in the medieval Icelandic sources to have left Viking Age Norway because they had troubles with the centralization of royal power there. Iceland's settlers seized the opportunity to bring their families, their wealth, and their livestock nearly 1,000 kilometers (600 miles) over the North Atlantic in search of land. During the *landnám* perhaps ten thousand or more people immigrated to Iceland.

Far out in the North Atlantic, Iceland developed in semi-isolation without national or regional commanders powerful enough to lead disputes with other countries over dynastic claims, territorial dominance, trade, or wealth. The task facing the immigrants to this new land was to prosper on a empty island with only a limited habitable area. Iceland is two-thirds the size of England and Scotland together, but much of the island is uninhabitable, as only the coast is warmed by a northern arm of the Gulf Stream.

Beginning in the tenth century with the close of the *landnám* (ca. 930), Icelanders established a general assembly, the Althing, and a system of regional and national courts. With this basic governance structure sufficient for regulating feud, Iceland functioned as a single island-wide polity.[1] In the year 1000, Icelanders peacefully converted to Christianity by agreement at the Althing. In this decision, as in many decisions made at Icelandic assemblies, compromise played a large role, and for a time after the conversion, pagans were allowed to continue practicing the old religion in the privacy of their property.

During more than three centuries of independence, Iceland was never invaded nor to our knowledge mounted an attack against another country. In many ways, Viking Age Iceland was a decentralized, stratified society. It was kingless and operated with a mixture of pre-state features and state institutions. The island was an inward-looking country that was aware of, and at times influenced by, the cultures of other medieval lands, but which depended on its own institutions and leaders to maintain viability and stability. Iceland maintained its independence from the ninth-century settlement until the years 1262-1264,

---

[1]   Jesse Byock, *Viking Age Iceland*. London and New York: Penguin Books. See also, *Feud in the Icelandic Saga*. Berkeley: University of California, Press.

when by agreement of the farmers, that is the property owners, at a series of local Icelandic assemblies, the Icelanders granted the king of Norway leadership of the country.

The Viking Age. Vikings were people of the ship, the first northern Europeans to harness and exploit a full technology of long-distance water travel. Their era, called the Viking Age, was an epoch of sea-borne expansion. It began in the late 700s A.D., when Scandinavia was a land of pagan chieftaincies. As part of their late Iron Age warrior culture, Vikings sailed from Scandinavia in all compass directions. Scandinavian shipwrights had advantages over most of their contemporaries. They could draw on native resources of high quality woods, tar, iron and salt-water resistant sea mammal hide for ships' ropes.

The navigational skills of the Northmen were prodigious. They reached four different continents, making their presence felt in Europe, Asia, the Middle East, North America, and Africa. Their voyages generated wealth for the Viking world from places as distant from Scandinavia as Ireland, the Byzantine Empire, and the Caliphate of Baghdad. Depending on the opportunities offered by different places, Northmen traded, raided, explored, and colonized. The distinction between Viking raiders and merchants was often unclear. Some sailors were mostly raiders, and others were mostly merchants, but all were armed. Depending on the defenses they met on the shores, Norse seamen might engage in raiding or commerce.

Wherever Scandinavians went, they brought with them their legends, myths, and language. Especially in Iceland, the Faroe Islands, Britain, and Ireland, Vikings settled and brought their families. In some of these regions, as in parts of England, Viking customs and language had a lasting effect. In other regions, such as in Normandy (*Normandie,* meaning 'Northmen's Land,' from Old Norse) in northern France, the influence of the *Norðmenn* diminished.

The term Viking is not a modern invention. The early Scandinavians used *víking*, although they did not, as is done today, employ it in an ethnic sense. Almost surely they would have understood the concept of a Viking Age, but calling Scandinavian society a 'Viking society' would have been a misnomer to them. Throughout medieval Scandinavia, *víkingr* meant pirate or freebooter, and *víkingar* (plural) were bands who raided from ships. The term applied to those who sailed the seas to steal and conquer as well as to mariners who robbed neighbors at home in Scandinavia. *Víkingar* also referred to non-Norse pirates, such as the Slavic Wends, who harassed shipping and raided in the Baltic Sea.

Although the meaning of the term *víkingr* is clear, its origin is not. Probably it relates to the word *vík*, meaning 'inlet' or 'bay'— places where *víkingar* lived and lay in wait. A raid was called *víking*, and men were said to 'go raiding' (*fara í víking*). Viking plundering, extortion, and kidnaping differed little from the war practices of petty chieftains throughout Western Europe in the Early Middle Ages. Northern Europeans, mostly Christian by that time, made much of the fact that the Scandinavian raiders were pagan outsiders who did not respect holy sanctuaries. They called these raiders Northmen, Danes, and Vikings. In the East, Scandinavian warriors and traders were called Rus and Varangians.

Viking boats were the result of a long Scandinavian ship-building tradition, which saw the development of a variety of specialized warships and commercial craft. Archaeologists can trace Scandinavian boat building back to the bronze age, that is into prehistory. In contrast to ships of Mediterranean construction, Northmen built their vessels from the outside inward. First they formed a flexible outer hull of overlapping planks held together with iron rivets. Then into this 'clinker' built hull, they inserted the ship's rigid internal wooden skeleton. Built with this clinker method, the hull was both flexible and strong, an innovative combination suitable for the rough seas of the North Atlantic. With their single mast and square sail, Norse vessels were swift. With the sail was down, the boats were easily rowed.

Designed with a shallow draft, Scandinavian ships offered exceptional mobility, and they could be beached without harbors. This feature allowed Norse seafarers, whether in war, commerce, or exploration, to sail a wide variety of ocean and inland waterways. Vikings tended to attack when and where they detected weakness. Speed at landing their ships and then withdrawing increased the terror of Norse raiders. If they miscalculated, and the defenses of those attacked proved too strong, Vikings returned to their ships and sailed off in search of weaker prey.

Seagoing Viking Age ships carried between twenty and fifty tons of cargo, and Viking merchants were major traders. They transported and traded furs, slaves, fish, walrus-tusk ivory, amber, honey, wheat, grains, iron, weapons, wool, wood, tin, and leather. In return, they bought slaves, cloth, weapons, silver, silk, spices, wine, jewelry, beads, glass, luxury goods, and pottery. In Viking graves and at Viking Age trading sites, archaeologists have found numbers of small folding scales. These were likely used for weighing pieces of silver and coins, either whole or cut into pieces. Silver was by far the most precious metal during the Viking Age, although there was some gold.

Viking activity continued for three centuries, with Vikings targeting settlements, monasteries, towns, and sometimes kingdoms. Foreign leaders, who faced repeated Viking attacks became accustomed to paying the Northmen to leave them in peace. In England, the Vikings were mostly Danes, and these payments were called 'danegeld.' In many regions, Vikings served as catalysts for social, commercial, and political transformations. In western Europe, the need to respond to Viking attacks contributed to the consolidation of the kingdoms of England and France and to a lesser extent the German Empire. In the East, the Scandinavian Rus gave their name to Russia and played a crucial role in the early formation of the Russian state.

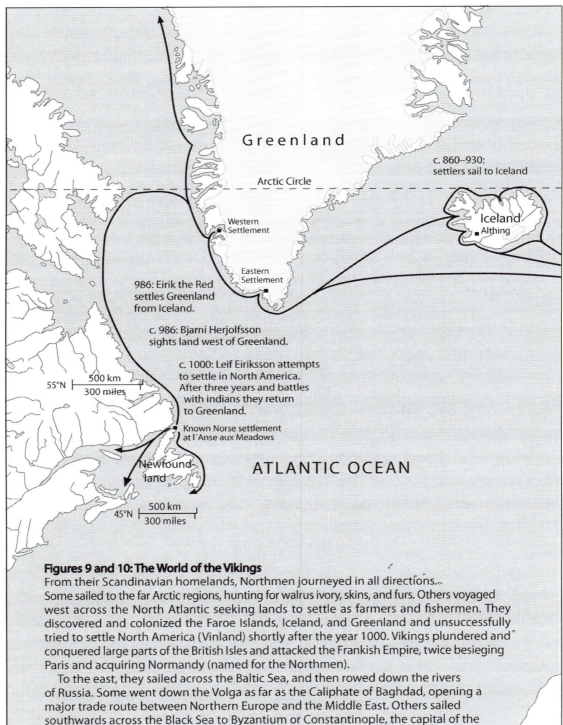

Figures 9 and 10: The World of the Vikings

From their Scandinavian homelands, Northmen journeyed in all directions. Some sailed to the far Arctic regions, hunting for walrus ivory, skins, and furs. Others voyaged west across the North Atlantic seeking lands to settle as farmers and fishermen. They discovered and colonized the Faroe Islands, Iceland, and Greenland and unsuccessfully tried to settle North America (Vinland) shortly after the year 1000. Vikings plundered and conquered large parts of the British Isles and attacked the Frankish Empire, twice besieging Paris and acquiring Normandy (named for the Northmen).

To the east, they sailed across the Baltic Sea, and then rowed down the rivers of Russia. Some went down the Volga as far as the Caliphate of Baghdad, opening a major trade route between Northern Europe and the Middle East. Others sailed southwards across the Black Sea to Byzantium or Constantinople, the capital of the Greek speaking Byzantine Empire. From there, as merchants, raiders, and bodyguards to the Greek Emperors, they journeyed throughout the Near East and Mediterranean.

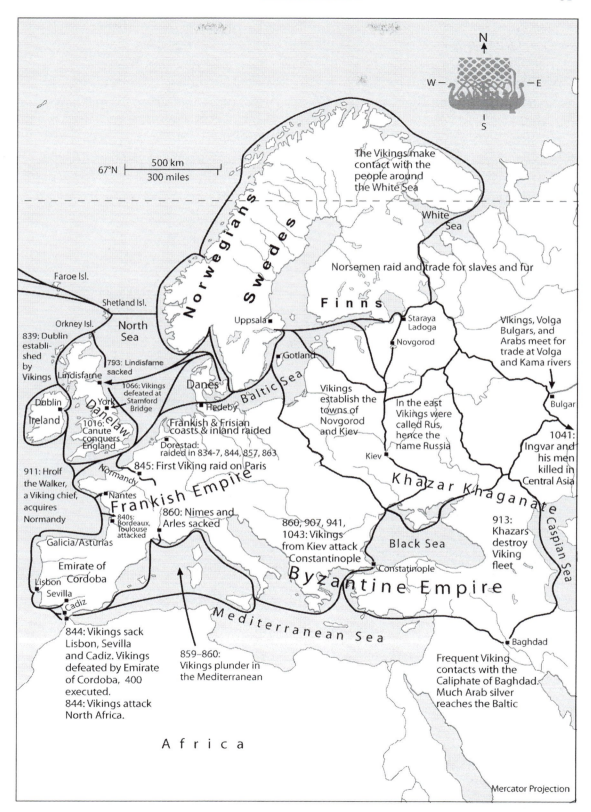

N
W — E
S

67°N |— 500 km —|
300 miles

The Vikings make contact with the people around the White Sea

Norsemen raid and trade for slaves and fur

White Sea

Finns

Norwegians

Swedes

Faroe Isl.

Shetland Isl.

Orkney Isl.

North Sea

839: Dublin established by Vikings

793: Lindisfarne sacked

Lindisfarne

Dublin

Ireland

York

Danelaw

1066: Vikings defeated at Stamford Bridge

1016: Canute conquers England

Danes

Hedeby

Baltic Sea

Uppsala

Gotland

Staraya Ladoga

Novgorod

Vikings, Volga Bulgars, and Arabs meet for trade at Volga and Kama rivers

Vikings establish the towns of Novgorod and Kiev

In the east Vikings were called Rus, hence the name Russia

Bulgar

1041: Ingvar and his men killed in Central Asia

Frankish & Frisian coasts & inland raided

Dorestad: raided in 834-7, 844, 857, 863

845: First Viking raid on Paris

911: Hrolf the Walker, a Viking chief, acquires Normandy

Normandy

Nantes

Frankish Empire

840s: Bordeaux, Toulouse attacked

860: Nimes and Arles sacked

Galicia/Asturias

Emirate of Cordoba

Lisbon

Sevilla

Cadiz

Kiev

860, 907, 941, 1043: Vikings from Kiev attack Constantinople

Khazar Khaganate

Black Sea

Constatinople

Byzantine Empire

913: Khazars destroy Viking fleet

Caspian Sea

Baghdad

844: Vikings sack Lisbon, Sevilla and Cadiz. Vikings defeated by Emirate of Cordoba, 400 executed.
844: Vikings attack North Africa.

859–860: Vikings plunder in the Mediterranean

Mediterranean Sea

Frequent Viking contacts with the Caliphate of Baghdad. Much Arab silver reaches the Baltic

Africa

Mercator Projection

THE RUS. Contemporaries of the Vikings, from places as distant as the British Isles and the lands of the Caliphate of Baghdad, recorded their impressions of the Northmen. Three aspects of culture – seafaring, religion, and language – distinguished Vikings from others with whom they came into contact. Among the most detailed accounts is a description by an Arab diplomat and traveler named Ibn Fadlan, whose account of tenth-century Scandinavian traders called 'Rus' is preserved in Arabic sources. Ibn Fadlan encountered Rus traders in the year 922 while in Russia on a diplomatic mission to the Turkic-speaking Khazars and Bulgars. At the time, these Scandinavian merchants and warriors had been in contact with the Muslim world for more than a century.

The Bulgars were horsemen living in northern Russia on the upper Volga River. Their territory at the confluence of the Volga and Kama rivers controlled the rich Volga trade route. Between the Bulgars in the North and the Caliphate in the South lay the Khaganate of the Khazars, whose territories stretched across the steppes between the Rus city state of Kiev and the Ural mountains. The Khazars adopted Judaism, and their empire controlled the trade routes on the lower reaches of the Volga River and the north Caspian Sea.

The Rus traveled up and down the Volga River between the Baltic Region and the Middle East. They bought, bartered, and sold slaves, furs, glass beads, weapons, and silver. While at the Bulgars' winter encampment, Ibn Fadlan encountered a party of Rus, who arrive by ship and set up an encampment. Ibn Fadlan offers an eye-witness account, which is unlike any of the western Latin descriptions of the Vikings, which were mostly written by clerics. As a secular diplomat, Ibn Fadlan shaped his account in the manner of a report describing the behavior of the Rus, their dress, hygiene, customs, religious practices, table manners, trade, and sexual activities. One passage gives the views of a Rus on mortuary practices and tells how Ibn Fadlan spoke with these travelers.[2]

> [One of the Rus was standing beside me] and I heard him speak to my interpreter. I asked the latter [what he had said.] He replied:
> 'You Arabs are fools!'
> ['Why is that? I asked him.]
> He said:
> 'Because you put the men you love most, [and the most noble among you,] into the earth, and the earth and the worms and insects eat them. But we burn them [in the fire] in an instant, so that at once and without delay they enter Paradise.'

---

[2]   This and the following translation of Ibn Fadlan's report is from *Ibn Fadlan and the Land of Darkness: Arab Travellers in the Far North*. Transl. Paul Lunde and Caroline Stone. London: Penguin Classics, 2012, pp. 45-49 and p. 54. I have changed the descriptive headins. See also Johannes Brønsted, *The Vikings*. Baltimore: Pelican Books, 1973, pp. 266-267.

Ibn Fadlan's description of the use of Arabic silver coins (dirhams) and glass trade beads agrees with modern archaeological finds in Russia, the Baltic, and as far away as Iceland. Coin hoards of dirhams struck in the Caliphate's mints have been found throughout the Baltic and especially on the island of Gotland. The sometimes enormous size of the Gotland coin hoards of Arabic silver, some weighing up to eighty kilos, attest to the extent

Figure 11. Beads Excavated by the Mosfell Archaeological Project (MAP) in Iceland. The Viking love of ornamental beads noted by the Arab traveler Ibn Fadlan is well attested archaeologically. Beads were valuable trade goods, and both men and women wore them. These beads were found buried as a set of four in a pit inside the Hrísbrú longhouse in the Mosfell Valley in Iceland. They are of a type that originated in Central Asia on the eastern shore of the Caspian Sea. Called 'eye beads,' each bead has clear glass rods in the centers, with colored circular surroundings, giving the impression of a bloodshot eye. The bead on the

of the money economy and the Volga trade described by Ibn Fadlan in the following passages from his report.

The Rus Arrive in Their Ships

I saw the Rus, who had come for trade and had camped by the river Itil [the Volga]. I have never seen bodies more perfect than theirs. They were like palm trees. They are fair and ruddy. They wear neither coats nor caftans, but a garment which covers one side of the body and leaves one hand free. Each of them carries an axe, a sword and a knife and is never parted from any of the arms we have mentioned. Their swords are broad bladed and grooved like the Frankish ones. From the tips of his toes to his neck, each man is tattooed in dark green with designs, and so forth.[3]

The Rus – Women

All their women wear on their bosoms a circular brooch made of iron, silver, copper or gold, depending on their husband's wealth and social position. Each brooch has a ring in which is a knife, also attached to the bosom. Round their necks, they wear torques of gold and silver, for every man, as soon as he accumulates 10,000 dirhams, has a torque made for his wife. When he has 20,000, he has two torques made and so on. Every time he increased his

---

[3]   The translation of the first two paragraphs of Ibn Fadlan's report are from *Ibn Fadlan and the Land of Darkness: Arab Travellers in the Far North*. Transl. Paul Lunde and Caroline Stone. London: Penguin Classics, 2012, pp. 45-46. The remaining translation is from

fortune by 10,000, he adds another torque to those his wife already possesses, so that one woman may have many torques round her neck.

The most desirable ornaments they have are green ceramic beads they keep in their boats. They will pay dearly for them, one dirham for a single bead. They thread them into necklaces for their wives.

Hygiene

They are the filthiest of God's creatures. They do not clean themselves after urinating or defecating, nor do they wash after having sex. They do not wash their hands after meals. They are like wandering asses.

The Rus – Men

When they arrive from their land, they anchor their boat on the Itil, which is a great river, and they build large wooden houses on the banks. Ten or twenty people, more or less, live together in one of these houses. Each man has a raised platform on which he sits. With them, there are beautiful slave girls, for sale to the merchants. Each of the men has sex with his slave, while his companions look on. Sometimes a whole group of them gather together in this way, in full view of one another. If a merchant enters at this moment to buy a young slave girl from one of the men and finds him having sex with her, the man does not get up off her until he has satisfied himself.

More Hygiene

Every day without fail they wash their faces and their heads with the dirtiest and filthiest water there could be. A young serving girl comes every morning with breakfast and with it a great basin of water. She proffers it to her master, who washes his hands and face in it, as well as his hair. He washes and disentangles his hair, using a comb, there in the basin, then he blows his nose and spits and does every filthy thing imaginable in the water. When he has finished, the servant carries the bowl to the man next to him. She goes on passing the basin round from one to another until she has taken it to all the men in the house in turn. And each of them blows his nose and spits and washes his face and hair in this basin.

Gifts to the Gods for Favorable Trading Terms

As soon as their boats arrive at this port, each of them disembarks, taking with him bread and meat, onions, mild and *nabidh*, and he walks until he comes to a great wooden post stuck in the ground with a face like that of a man, and around it are little figures. Behind these images there are long wooden stakes driven into the ground. Each of them prostrates himself before the great idol, saying to it:

'Oh my Lord, I have come from a far country and I have with me such and such a number of young slave girls, and such and such a number of sable skins...' and so on, until he has listed all the trade goods he has brought. [Then he adds:] 'I have brought you this gift.' Then he leaves what he has with him in front of the wooden post [and says:]

'I would like you to do the favour of sending me a merchant who has large quantities of *dinars* and dirhams and who will buy everything that I want and not argue with me over my price.'

Then he departs.

If he has difficulty selling and his stay becomes long drawn out, he returns with another present a second and even a third time. If he cannot get what he wants, he brings a present for each of the little idols and asks them to intercede, saying:

'These are the wives of our Lord and his daughters and sons.'

Thus he continues to make his request to each idol in turn, begging their intercession and abasing himself before them. Sometimes the sale is easy and after having sold his goods he says:

'My Lord has satisfied my needs and it is fitting that I should reward him for it.'

Then he takes a certain number of sheep or cows and slaughters them, distributing part of the meat as gifts and carrying off the rest to set before the great idol and the little figures that surround it. Then he hangs the heads of the sheep or cows on the wooden stakes which have been driven into the ground. When night falls, the dogs come and eat all this, and the man who has made the offering says:

'My Lord is pleased with me and has eaten the gift that I brought him.'

Treatment of the Sick

If one of them falls ill, [the others pitch a tent from him] in a place distant from them. They leave him some bread and water, but they neither go near him nor speak to him. [They do not even come to visit him] during all the days of his illness, particularly if he is a poor man or a slave. If he recovers and gets well, he comes back to them; if he dies, they burn him. If he is a slave, they leave him where he is, and the dogs and birds of prey devour him.

Punishment of Thieves

If they catch a thief or a brigand, they lead him to a great tree, tie a stout rope round his neck and hang him [from the tree, and there he remains] until he drops to pieces [from exposure] to the wind and the rain.

End of the Viking Age. While the Viking Age is most known for voyages and raiding, only a small proportion of the Scandinavian population sailed on Viking journeys. Most people stayed home and farmed. The climate in northern Europe and the North Atlantic during the Viking centuries was a few degrees warmer than the average over the past thousand years, and in Scandinavia, the Viking Age was a time of population growth. Archaeology and landscape studies tells us that the amount of land devoted to agriculture increased. To bring more land into production, woodlands were cleared, wetlands drained, and the use of highland pastures expanded. At the end of the Viking period, there were more farms, communal settlements, and cemeteries than at the start.

It is hard to calculate the exact end of the Viking Age, but around A.D. 1100 the raids on European countries mostly came to an end. At home in Scandinavia, the more than three centuries of the Age saw extensive social and economic changes. Socially and economically the societies became more complex. As signs of change, warfare by the eleventh century had in many ways moved from the local to the state level, and the older regional chieftaincies evolved into national kingdoms. By the twelfth century Scandinavia was firmly divided into the kingdoms of Denmark, Norway, and Sweden. Sweden in the Baltic Sea region, more distant from Western Europe than either Norway or Denmark, was the last of the Scandinavian kingdoms to abandon the worship of the Norse gods and become Christian.

The passing of the Viking Age saw little change in the lives of the majority of the Scandinavian population. Most people continued living their traditional farm life and went on speaking variants of their Old Norse language.

– Jesse Byock, University of California, Los Angeles (UCLA)

TOOLS FOR USING *VIKING LANGUAGE*

OLD NORSE/ICELANDIC ALPHABET AND SPELLING. The Latin alphabet adopted by the Icelanders in the eleventh century was probably modeled on Anglo-Saxon writing, where the Icelanders may have learned the letters *þ* ('thorn', upper case, *Þ*) and *ð* ('eth', upper case, *Ð*). Old Norse writers, whether they wrote runes or manuscripts, did not follow a standardized spelling. Scholars addressed this issue more than a century ago by adopting a standardized Old Norse/Icelandic spelling and alphabetic order. Reading passages and vocabularies in the book generally follow standardized Old Norse spelling as found in the Icelandic *Íslenzk fornrit* saga editions.

The Old Norse vowels *ǫ* and *ø* coalesced in the medieval period into the single vowel *ö*, which is still used in Modern Icelandic. This book maintains the distinction between *ǫ* and *ø* but uses the modern letter *ö* in place of *ǫ*. A primarily reason for adopting *ö* in the lessons is that it is included in almost all modern digital fonts. That said, *ö* is not a bad choice, because it is found in many manuscripts. Where the phonological distinction between *ö* and *ǫ* remains important, especially in pronumciation charts, *ǫ* is used.

Modern Icelandic has lost the distinction between *æ* and *œ* and employs *æ* for both letters. This book retains the original medieval distinction. Overall, the spelling differences between Old and Modern Icelandic are minor.

In the Old Norse/Icelandic alphabet, long vowels are distinguished from short vowels by an accent (for example, long *é* and short *e*). The long vowels *æ*, *œ*, *ø* and umlauted *o* (*ö/ǫ*) are listed at the end of the Icelandic alphabet. The letters *c*, *q*, and *w* are occasionally found in manuscripts but have not been adopted into the standardized alphabet.

> *a, á, b, d, ð, e, é, f, g, h, i, í, j, k, l, m, n, o, ó, p, r, s, t,*
> *u, ú, v, x, y, ý, z, þ, æ, œ, ö(ǫ), ø*

ANGLICIZING OLD NORSE PERSONAL NAMES. Rendering Old Norse and Icelandic names into English is always a problem. This book employs a set of rules. The Icelandic vowels *ö* and *ø* are written as *o*, hence, Björn becomes 'Bjorn.' The long vowels *œ* and *æ* are retained, hence, Æsir remains 'Æsir.' Accents over long vowels are omitted in personal names when spelled in English, hence, Sigrún becomes 'Sigrun.' The letters *þ* and *ð* are spelled *th* and *d* in English, and Old Norse case endings are dropped, hence Þórðr (with case ending *r*) becomes 'Thord' and Önundr becomes Onund. The exception is weak masculine and feminine names that end in vowels and keep their endings, hence Bjarni and Gyða are 'Bjarni' and 'Gyda.'

Many names in Old Norse easily translate into English, as for instance, *Laxárdalr* = *Lax* 'salmon' + *ár* 'rver' + *dalr* 'valley' . Others prove more difficult and some appear impossible. The Icelandic name of the Irish king Mýrkjartan does not easily lend itself to translation. Older translators choose Moorkjartan from the word *mýri* ('moor,' 'swamp') and the name Kjartan. In most of such instances, I give the original Old Norse name in English without accents, hence Myrkjartan. In some instances, where it seems best, the book uses the Old Norse name.

List of Abbreviations

1dual, 2dual	1st person dual, etc.
1pl, 2pl, 3pl	1st person plural, etc.
1sg, 2sg, 3sg	1st person singular, etc.
acc	accusative
adj	adjective
adv	adverb
art	article (definite)
aux	auxiliary (verb)
comp	comparative (adjective or adverb)
conj	conjunction
conjug	conjugation
dat	dative
def	definite (article)
defect	defective
dem	demonstrative (pronoun)
esp	especially
etc	etcetera
ex	example
f	feminine
fig	figurative
gen	genitive
impers	impersonal (verb)
indecl	indeclinable
indef	indefinite (pronoun)
indic	indicative
inf	infinitive
interrog	interrogative (adverb or pronoun)
intrans	intransitive (verb)
leg	legal usage
lit	literally
m	masculine
mid	middle voice
neg	negative
n	neuter
nom	nominative
num	number
obj	object

OE	Old English
OI	Old Icelandic
ON	Old Norse
ord	ordinal (number)
pl	plural
poet	poetical usage
poss	possessive (pronoun)
ppart	past participle
pref	prefix
prep	preposition
pres	present
pres part	present participle
pret-pres	preterite-present (verb)
pron	pronoun
refl	reflexive (verb or pronoun)
rel	relative (pronoun or particle)
sb	somebody
sg	singular
sth	something
str	strong (adjective or verb)
subj	subject
subjunct	subjunctive
superl	superlative (adjective or adverb)
trans	transitive (verb)
transl	translation
usu	usually
var	variant
vb	verb
w	with
wk	weak (adjective or verb)
=	equals
~	Alternative or alternating (spelling)
=	equals

GRAMMAR INDEX
—Adjectives—

1.6	Case of Nouns, Pronouns, and Adjectives – Nominative, Accusative, Dative, Genitive
2.12	Grammar Toolbox Adjectives
10.4,6,7	Strong Adjectives
11.3	Weak Adjectives
13.7-13.10	Comparative and Superlative Adjectives

—Adverbs—

11.17	Grammar Toolbox. Adverbs
13.12	Comparative and Superlative Adverbs

—Articles—

2.5	Grammar Toolbox. Definite and Indefinite Article
9.4	More on the Definite Article

—Clauses—

9.8	Clauses – Independent, Dependent, and Relative
11.16	Direct and Indirect Speech
15.6	Subjunctive Verbs and Indirect Speech in Main and Dependent Clauses

—Gender—

1.5	Gender of Nouns and Pronouns – Masculine, Feminine, Neuter

—Nouns—

1.4	Grammar Toolbox – Nouns and Pronouns
1.5	Gender of Nouns and Pronouns – Masculine, Feminine, Neuter
1.6	Case of Nouns, Pronouns, and Adjectives – Nominative, Accusative, Dative, Genitive
1.8	Apposition – Case Agreement of Nouns
2.6	Proper Nouns
3.13	Nouns – Strong and Weak
5.9	Strong Nouns – Introduction
5.10	Strong Nouns – Type 1 Masculines
5.12	The Nouns *Maðr* and *Sonr*
6.4	Strong Nouns – Type 1 Feminines and Neuters
7.6	Strong Nouns – Type 2
7.8	Weak Nouns
7.10	Nouns Whose Stems End in a Long Vowel
8.5	Nouns – Kinship Terms in *-ir*
8.6	Nouns Whose Stems End in *-nd-*
9.5	Strong Nouns – Type 3
9.6	Strong Nouns – Type 4
11.4	Nouns with the Definite Article and Weak Adjectives
14.9	Two-Syllable Nouns – Syncopated Stems, vowel loss

—Numbers—

14.7   Cardinal Numbers 1 to 20
15.8   Cardinal Numbers Above 20
15.9   Ordinal Numbers

—Prepositions—

5.16   Grammar Toolbox. Prepositions

—Pronunciation and Spelling—

3.4   Runic Letters Which Spell More Than One Sound
3.5   Runic Spelling Variations and Standardized Old Norse
Appendix C: Pronunciation of Old Icelandic

—Pronouns—

1.5   Gender of Nouns and Pronouns – Masculine, Feminine,
                Neuter
1.4   Grammar Toolbox. Nouns and Personal Pronouns
1.5   Gender of Nouns and Pronouns – Masculine, Feminine,
                Neuter
1.6   Case of Nouns, Pronouns, and Adjectives – Nominative,
                Accusative, Dative, Genitive
3.9   Personal Pronouns: 1st and 2nd Persons
3.11   Personal Pronouns: 3rd Person
4.11   The Reflexive Possessive Pronoun *Sinn*
7.4   Reflexive Pronouns
9.7   Demonstrative Pronouns *þessi* and *sá*
9.10   The Past Subjunctive of Verbs
11.12   Possessive Pronouns
11.14   The Indefinite Pronoun *engi*
11.15   The Indefinite Pronoun *annarr*
12.3   The Indefinite Pronoun *nökkurr*
12.4   Pronouns *hverr* and *hvárr*
12.5   The Indefinite Pronoun *einnhverr*
12.6   The Pronoun *hvárrtveggi*
15.3   Enclitic Pronouns

—Runes—

3.1-3.3   Culture and Background of Runes
3.4   Runic Script
3.5   Runic Spelling Variations
3.4   Runic Letters Which Spell More Than One Sound
                See Lessons 4 and 6

—Speech—

11.16	Direct and Indirect Speech
15.7	Indirect Speech – Accusative Subject Plus Infinitive

—Special Stem Rules—

5.5-5.6	Special Stem Rules
5.8	Words with Stem Endings -*j*- and -*v*-

—Verbs—

2.7	Grammar Toolbox Verbs
2.8	Verbs, Infinitives
2.9	Linking Verbs *Vera*, *Verða*, and *Heita*
3.14	The Verb *Vera* 'to be' – Present and Past
4.6	Strong and Weak Verbs
4.8	Weak Verbs in the Present Tense
4.9	Word Frequency: Weak Verbs
5.14	The Weak Verb *Hafa* in the Present Tense
5.6	Special Stem Rules
6.6	Past Tense of Weak Verbs
6.9	Identifying the Four Weak Verb Conjugations
6.11	Voice – An Introduction
8.7	Present Tense of Strong Verbs
8.8	Past Tense of Strong Verbs
8.10	Past Tense Ending -*t* of Strong Verbs
8.13	Grammar Toolbox. Verb Mood
8.14	Commands and the Imperative Mood of Verbs
8.15	The Present Subjunctive of Verbs
9.10	Past Subjunctive
10.9	Past Participles
10.10	Past Participles of Strong Verbs
10.11	Present and Past Perfect of Verbs
10.12	Verbs – Passive Voice
11.13	Impersonal constructions
11.5	Strong Verbs
11.6	Strong Verbs – Class I
11.7	Strong Verbs – Class II
11.9	Verbs Taking Dative and Genitive Objects
11.13	Impersonal Constructions
12.7	Strong Verbs – Class III
12.8	Verbs – Present Participles
13.3	Strong Verbs – Classes IV and V
13.4-13.5	Preterite-Present Verbs & Modal Auxiliaries
14.4	Strong Verbs – Class VI

14.5	Middle Voice – Introduction and Formation
14.6	Middle Voice – Meaning and Use
14.8	The Past Subjunctive of Preterite-Present Verbs
15.4	Strong Verbs – Class VII
15.5	Subjunctive Middle
15.6	Subjunctive Verbs and Indirect Speech in Main and Dependent Clauses
15.7	Past Infinitives of the Verbs *Mundu*, *Skyldu*, and *Vildu*

—Vowels—

4.3	Vowels and Consonants
5.4	Short and Long Vowels – Stressed and Unstressed
6.7	Vowel Sounds and Assimilation

Umlaut/Vowel Shifts—

4.4	*U*-umlaut
6.7	Vowel Sounds and Assimilation
6.8	*I*-umlaut

—Word Frequency—

1.9	Word Frequency – The Most Common Words in the Sagas
	WF Vocabulary – List 1. The Most Frequent Words in the Sagas in Each part of Speech
2.14	List 2. The Most Frequent Words in the Sagas
3.18	List 3. The Most Frequent Words in the Sagas
4.16	List 4. The Most Frequent Words in the Sagas
5.18	List 5 The Most Frequent Words in the Sagas
6.14	List 6 The Most Frequent Words in the Sagas
7.14	List 7 The Most Frequent Words in the Sagas
8.17	List 8 The Most Frequent Words in the Sagas
9.14	List 9 The Most Frequent Words in the Sagas
10.16	List 10 The Most Frequent Words in the Sagas
11.18	List 11 The Most Frequent Words in the Sagas
12.11	List 12 The Most Frequent Words in the Sagas

LESSON 1

SAILING WEST TO

ICELAND, GREENLAND, AND NORTH AMERICA

Inn fyrsti fugl fær it fyrsta korn.
(The early bird gets the first grain.)

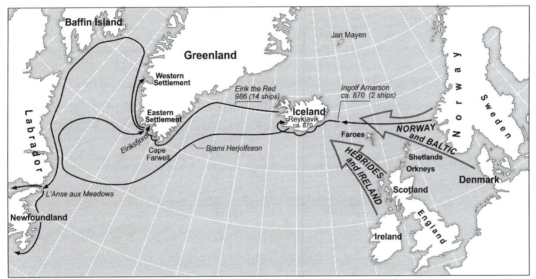

Figure 12. The Norse Cross the Atlantic. Routes taken by settlers to Iceland, Greenland, and North America (*Vínland*) from the ninth to eleventh centuries.

1.1 CULTURE – ATLANTIC SEAFARING

Medieval sailors followed the coast where possible, but Norse seafarers of the Viking Age were able to cross the open sea. *The Book of Settlements* (*Landnámabók*) records specific departure points from Norway for sailing to Iceland and Greenland. Weather permitting, an east-west course (one running along a line of latitude) could be fixed by noting the height of the sun at its midday zenith. Heading west, sailors corrected their course by sighting landmarks on the horizon such as Shetland and the Faroe Islands. Knowledge of geography was crucial. Without maps or navigational charts, mariners relied on personal experience and orally transmitted knowledge.

When land was out of sight, sun, winds, currents, and the north star served as directional indicators. Navigational experience was crucial. Weather conditions, sea animals, seabirds, cloud formations, wave patterns, changing currents, water color, and the movements of whales indicated when land was near. In the far North Atlantic, light reflected by glaciers was visible from considerable distances. Some Norse mariners may have relied on a navigational tool that utilized the sun's shadow as cast by a central pin onto a wooden disc with radial markings around the edge (similar to the degrees on a modern compass). Part of such a device was first found in Greenland in 1948, but its use is disputed. To avoid reefs and shallows a simple weighted rope was cast overboard to measure water depth.

Icelandic medieval writings are our major source for information concerning Norse exploration and settlement of the North Atlantic. Based on older oral traditions, Iceland's sagas and historical writings recount the events of the settlement or *landnám* ('land-taking') of Iceland, the Faroes, Greenland, and Vinland on the North American continent. Icelandic manuscripts offer valuable historical information. They tell of individuals, families, and conflicts in the first century and a half after the ninth-century *landnám*, but the narratives are not always factual. The manuscripts were written in the twelfth and thirteenth centuries, when writing became common among Icelanders.

Icelandic historical writings are far fewer than the sagas. The main ones are *Landnámabók* (*The Book of Settlements*), probably first composed in the early-to-mid-twelfth century, and *Íslendingabók* (*The Book of the Icelanders*). *Íslendingabók* was written around the year 1122 by the Icelandic historian, Ari the Learned (*Ari fróði*), a careful historian who names his sources. Iceland's extensive medieval law books called *Grágás* (*The Grey Goose Law*) are an additional source of information about the society.

Ingolf Arnarson (*Ingólfr Arnarson*), whose name appears in the reading passage below, was the first recorded settler or *landnámsmaðr* ('land-taking man,' a term which includes women). Around the year 860, he sailed west from Norway and sighted land in the southeast of Iceland. Eventually Ingólfr settled in Iceland's southwest at a site which he named *Reykjavík* because of the smoke or steam escaping from hot springs. The older form of the name, *Reykjarvík*, means Smoky Bay, literally the 'bay of smoke.' Today, *Reykjavík* is the capital of Iceland. Ingólfr initially claimed a large portion of land, much of which he distributed to other settlers.

1.2 THE LETTERS Þ AND Ð

- **The letter *þ* (upper case, Þ)** is called 'thorn' and pronounced like 'th' in the English word 'thought' or the name of the god Thor (*Þórr*).
- **The letter *ð* (upper case, Ð)** is called 'eth' and pronounced like 'th' in the English word 'breathe' or Othin (*Óðinn*), often spelled Odin in English.

1.3 READING – INGOLF GIVES LAND TO HERJOLF (*Grœnlendinga saga*)

The Old Norse reading passage below tells of Herjolf Bardarson, his wife Thorgerd, and their son Bjarni Herjolfsson. Bjarni's last name is derived from his father's first name plus *son* (the use of *son* and *dóttir* are discussed in a later lesson). *The Saga of the Greenlanders* (*Grœnlendinga saga*) was written in thirteenth-century Iceland. It was copied and preserved in a late fourteenth-century vellum (parchment) manuscript called *Flateyjarbók* (*The Book of Flatey*). This extensive compilation of Icelandic prose and poetry is so named because it was found on the island of Flatey (Flat Island) in Breiðafjörðr (Broad Fjord) in western Iceland.

Flateyjarbók consists of 225 large sheets, some of which are illustrated. The book is organized around the history of Norway's kings. It also includes many *þættir* (sg *þáttr* 'short story') and whole sagas such as *Grœnlendinga saga*. *Flateyjarbók* is the largest Icelandic manuscript. It contains written sources not preserved in other manuscripts and is one of Iceland's greatest treasures.

Grœnlendinga saga (2. kap)	*The Saga of the Greenlanders* (ch 2)
Herjólfr var Bárðarson	Herjolf was the son of Bard,
Herjólfssonar;	[who was]* the son of Herjolf;
hann var frændi Ingólfs	he was [a] kinsman of [the] settler
landnámsmanns.	Ingolf.
Ingólfr gaf Herjólfi land	Ingolf gave land to Herjolf
á milli Vágs ok Reykjaness.	between Vag and Reykjanes.
Herjólfr bjó fyrst á Drepstokki.	Herjolf lived first at Drepstokk.
Þorgerðr hét kona hans,	His wife was named Thorgerd,
en Bjarni sonr þeira,	and their son [was named] Bjarni,
ok var efniligr maðr.	and [he] was a promising man.

* Brackets [ ] indicate words needed for English translation but missing in the Icelandic.

VOCABULARY

❖**á** *prep* [*w dat*] on; upon; at; in; **á**

Drepstokki at Drepstokk

á milli *prep* [*w gen*] between

Bárðarson *m* the son of Bard

Bárðr <*gen* Bárðar> *m* Bard (*personal name*)

Bjarni *m* Bjarni (*personal name*)

bjó (*inf* ❖**búa**) *vb* lived

Drepstokkr <*dat* Drepstokki> *m* Drepstokk (*place name*)

efniligr *adj* promising

❖**en** *conj* but; and (*in a contrastive sense*)

❖**frændi** *m* kinsman

fyrst *adv* first

gaf (*inf* ❖**gefa**) *vb* gave

Grœnlendingr <*gen pl* Grœnlendinga> *m* Greenlander

❖**hann** *pron* he

hans *pron gen* his

Herjólfr <*gen* Herjólfs> *m* Herjolf (*personal name*)

Herjólfssonar *m gen* 'of the son of Herjolf'

hét (*inf* ❖**heita**) *vb* was named

Ingólfr <*gen* Ingólfs> *m* Ingolf (*personal name*)

Ingólfr landnámsmaðr *m* Ingolf the Settler (*personal name*)

❖**kona** *f* wife; woman

❖**land** *n* land

landnámsmaðr <*gen* landnámsmanns> *m* settler, *lit* land-take-man (the term refers both to women and men)

❖**maðr** <*gen* manns> *m* man; person, human being

nes *n* headland

❖**ok** *conj* and

papi *m* pope; priest

Reykjanes <*gen* Reykjaness> *n* Reykjanes (*place name*) Headland of Smoke

saga *f* what is said, story, saga, tale, legend,

history

❖**sonr** <*gen* sonar> *m* son

var (*inf* ❖vera) *vb* was

Vágr <*gen* Vágs> *m* Vag (*place name*) Bay

þeira *pron* (*gen pl of* ❖sá) their

Þorgerðr *f* Thorgerd (*personal name*)

1.4 GRAMMAR TOOLBOX. NOUNS AND PERSONAL PRONOUNS

- Nouns are words that name persons, places, things, or acts.
- Personal Pronouns, such as 'I/me, he/him, she/her, we/us, they/them, you, it' stand in the place of nouns. Nouns and personal pronouns function as subjects, objects, or complements (an example of a complement is 'it is I'). Pronouns are discussed in Lesson 3.
- To translate Old Norse, the learner needs to recognize noun endings.
- All nouns in Old Norse decline; that is, they take endings indicating the noun's case and role in the sentence. In most instances: the subject of a sentence is in the nominative case; the direct object is in the accusative case; the indirect object is in the dative case; and the possessor (of something) is in the genitive. Nouns following a preposition fall into different cases. They can be accusative, dative, or genitive depending on the preposition.
- Nouns in Old Norse distinguish between singular and plural. This category is called **number**.
- All nouns in Old Norse belong to one of three **genders**: masculine, feminine, or neuter. The gender of a noun can be determined by looking at its set of case endings. For example, many masculine nouns, such as *maðr* 'man; person' and *sonr* 'son,' have the ending *-r* in the nominative case. If the noun denotes a living being, its gender often matches the being's sex, for example, *faðir* 'father' (*m*) and *móðir* 'mother' (*f*). However, sex is not a sure indicator of gender, and nouns referring to abstract concepts and objects can have a gender that bears no relationship to the word itself.
- All nouns in Old Norse fall into one of two **declension types**: strong or weak. Weak nouns take simpler endings than strong nouns. A noun's declension type never changes. For example, *dagr* 'day' is always strong while *goði* 'chieftain' is always weak.

In summary, the endings of nouns are determined by

- their **declension type**: strong or weak
- their **case**: nominative, accusative, dative, or genitive
- their **number**: singular or plural
- their **gender**: masculine, feminine, or neuter

1.5 GENDER OF NOUNS AND PRONOUNS – MASCULINE, FEMININE, NEUTER

As noted above, Old Norse nouns and pronouns belong to one of three genders: masculine, feminine, and neuter. The same is true for pronouns which stand in the place of nouns, and adjectives modifying nouns and pronouns agreed in gender.

The gender of most nouns cannot be predicted. For instance, *hlutr* 'part' is masculine, *brú* 'bridge' is feminine, and *nes* 'headland' is neuter. Except in rare instances, a noun's gender never changes.

MASCULINE	FEMININE	NEUTER
konungr 'king'	*dróttning* 'queen'	*land* 'land'
frændi 'kinsman'	*kona* 'woman; wife'	*korn* 'grain, seed'

Masculine Nouns. The most common masculine ending in the nominative singular is -*r*, as in the noun *konungr*, the name *Herjólfr*, and the place *Drepstokkr*. Another masculine ending is -*i*, as in the name *Bjarni* and the noun *frændi* 'kinsman.' Generally speaking, masculine nouns and names (proper nouns) that end in -*r* are called strong nouns, while those that end in -*i* are called weak nouns. Later lessons address the distinction between strong and weak nouns.

Compound Words are formed from two or more root words, as in English *farmland* (farm + land). Old Norse frequently employs compound words such as *landnámsmaðr* 'settler,' built from three words: *land* ('land') + *náms* ('taking') + *maðr* ('man,' 'person'). Compound words always take the gender of the last noun. For example, *Herjólfsnes* (*Herjólfs* + *nes*) is neuter because *nes* is neuter.

1.6 CASE OF NOUNS AND PRONOUNS – NOMINATIVE, ACCUSATIVE, DATIVE, GENITIVE

Old Norse nouns, pronouns, and adjectives always appear in one of the following four grammatical cases: nominative, accusative, dative, or genitive. The word's role in the sentence determines which case is used; for example, the subject of a sentence typically takes the nominative case while a direct object takes the accusative. Compare the Old Norse pronouns *hann* and *hon* below with their English counterparts and note how these words take different forms depending on their usage in a sentence. Pronouns in Modern English are one area where the case system is preserved.

	OLD ICELANDIC		ENGLISH
CASE	PRONOUN	GRAMMATICAL ROLE	PRONOUN
nom	hann	*subject*	he, it
acc	hann	*direct object*	him, it
dat	honum	*indirect object*	him, it
gen	hans	*possessive*	his, its

CASE	OLD ICELANDIC PRONOUN	ENGLISH GRAMMATICAL ROLE	PRONOUN
nom	hon	*subject*	she, it
acc	hana	*direct object*	her, it
dat	henni	*indirect object*	her, it
gen	hennar	*possessive*	hers, its

Nominative. The subject of a sentence generally is in the nominative case. Words modifying the subject, such as adjectives (for example, *efniligr maðr* 'a promising man') or in apposition, that is equal to, other nouns are also in the nominative (*Leifr, sonr hans* 'Leif, his son'). The same is true for predicate nouns and adjectives, which are words connected to the subject by way of a linking verb such as *vera* 'to be,' *verða* 'to become,' and *heita* 'to be named; to be called.' Two examples from the reading are *Herjólfr var efniligr maðr* 'Herjolf was a promising man,' and *Þorgerðr hét kona hans* 'His wife was named Thorgerd.' 'Man' and 'Thorgerd' are predicate nouns because they refer to the same person, place, or thing.

Accusative. A noun which receives the action of the verb is a direct object and stands in the accusative case, as in the sentence, *Eiríkr nam **land*** 'Eirik took **land**.' The accusative case has some other functions, such as indicating the objects of certain prepositions (*eptir hann* 'after him').

Dative. The indirect object of a verb takes the dative case. For example, in the sentence *Ingólfr gaf **Herjólfi** land*, *Ingólfr* (subject) gave *land* (direct object) to *Herjólfr* (indirect object). A simple way to test if an object is indirect is to see if it can be translated into English with the preposition *to* or *for*. For example, the sentence above can be translated 'Ingolf gave Herjolf land' or 'Ingolf gave land to Herjolf.' One of the other common uses of the dative is with certain prepositions (*á Drepstokki* 'at Drepstokk,' in the reading passage of this lesson).

Genitive. The genitive case usually denotes possession. Two common genitive endings in Old Norse are *-s* (*Ingólf**s***) and *-ar* (*son**ar*** and *Barð**arson***). The English possessive ending *-'s* (*John's*), like the Old Norse endings, is a remnant of the older Germanic case system, inherited in turn from Indo-European. In English the possessive may also be expressed by the preposition *of* (*gates **of the city***). The genitive appears in other contexts, for example, as the object of some verbs as well as with a small number of prepositions such as *til* (*til Grœnlands* 'to Greenland,' in the reading passage of the next lesson).

CASE	MAIN FUNCTIONS
nominative	subject; predicate nouns and adjectives
accusative	direct object; object of certain prepositions
dative	indirect object (*to, for*); object of certain prepositions
genitive	possessive; object of certain prepositions

The following table gives the declension of *Herjólfr* in all four cases, with the case endings in bold. Whereas Old Norse relies heavily on case endings, English depends mostly on word order and prepositions to distinguish a word's role in the sentence.

Case	Old Icelandic	English	Noun Stem + Case Ending
nom	Herjólf**r** bjó á Drepstokki.	Herjolf lived at Drepstokk.	Herjólf + **r**
acc	Þorgerðr sá Herjólf.	Thorgerd saw Herjolf.	Herjólf
dat	Ingólfr gaf Herjólf**i** land.	Ingolf gave land to Herjolf.	Herjólf + **i**
gen	Þorgerðr hét kona Herjólf**s**.	Herjolf**'s** wife was called Thorgerd.	Herjólf + **s**

The charts below give the declensions in the singular of some frequently occurring nouns in the sagas. *Maðr, sonr, sök*, and *vík* have characteristics which are discussed in later lessons.

MASCULINE

Case	MAÐR	KONUNGR	SONR	HESTR	VÍKINGR	Endings
nom	ma**ð**r	konungr	sonr	hest**r**	víking**r**	**-r**
acc	mann	konung	son	hest	víking	—
dat	manni	konungi	sy**n**i	hesti	víkingi	**-i**
gen	mann**s**	konung**s**	sonar	hest**s**	víking**s**	**-s, -ar**

Transl: *maðr* 'man,' *konungr* 'king,' *sonr* 'son,' *hestr* 'horse,' *víkingr* 'viking'

FEMININE

Case	FERÐ	SÖK	LEIÐ	VÍK	HLÍÐ	Endings
nom	ferð	sök	leið	vík	hlíð	—
acc	ferð	sök	leið	vík	hlíð	—
dat	ferð	sök	leið	vík	hlíð	—
gen	ferð**ar**	sak**ar**	leið**ar**	vík**r**	hlíð**ar**	**-ar, -r**

Transl: *ferð* 'journey,' *sök* 'cause,' *leið* 'way, road,' *vík* 'bay,' *hlíð* 'slope'

NEUTER

Case	SKIP	LAND	MÁL	SVERÐ	ÞING	Endings
nom	skip	land	mál	sverð	þing	—
acc	skip	land	mál	sverð	þing	—
dat	skip**i**	land**i**	mál**i**	sverð**i**	þing**i**	**-i**
gen	skip**s**	land**s**	mál**s**	sverð**s**	þing**s**	**-s**

Transl: *skip* 'ship,' *land* 'land,' *mál* 'speech,' *sverð* 'sword,' *þing* 'assembly'

1.7 EXERCISE – CASE: NOMINATIVE, ACCUSATIVE, DATIVE, AND GENITIVE

A. Rearrange the following sentences, putting the pronouns in the correct case.

INCORRECT	CORRECT
Ex: *Us* invited a friend to go with *we*.	*We invited a friend to go with us.*
1. *Him* went with *his* to *he* house.	_____
2. *Her* gave a gift to *she*.	_____
3. *Them* are sitting in *they* ship with *their*.	_____
4. *Her* brought food for *he* and *I*.	_____

B. Identify the function of the italicized nouns in the sentences below, and state what case must be used in Old Norse.

Ex: A man was called Herjolf, *Bard's* son.   *possessor; genitive*
1. Eirik took Eirik's *Fjord* and lived at Brattahlíð.   _____
2. *Herjolf* was a kinsman of the settler Ingolf.   _____
3. Ingolf gave him *land*.   _____
4. Ingolf gave land *to her*.   _____
5. Herjolf's *wife* was named Thorgerd.   _____
6. *Herjolf's* wife was named Thorgerd.   _____
7. Eiríkr nam *Brattahlíð*.   _____
8. Dróttning gaf *Þorgerði* land.   _____

1.8 APPOSITION – CASE AGREEMENT OF NOUNS

When a noun follows another noun and refers to the same person, place, or thing, the second noun must be in the same case as the first. In the sentence below, *landnámsmanns* is in the genitive case as is *Ingólfs*.

Hann var frændi Ingólfs landnámsmanns.   *He was a kinsman of **Ingolf**, the **settler**.*
In grammatical terms, we say that *landnámsmanns* is in the genitive case because it is <u>in apposition</u> with *Ingólfs*. An appositive (like *landnámsmanns*) always matches the case of the noun it describes.

Ingólfr gaf Herjólfi landnámsmanni land.   *Ingolf gave land to **Herjolf**, the **settler**.*
In the above sentence, *landnámsmanni* is in apposition with *Herjólfi*, hence it too must be in the dative.

Eiríkr nam Eiríksfjörð ok bjó í Brattahlíð,   *Eirik took Eiriksfjord and lived at*
en Leifr sonr hans eptir hann.   *Brattahlid, and **Leif**, his **son**, after him.*
Here *sonr* [*hans*] is in apposition with *Leifr*. Both nouns are in the nominative case.

(Note that in English the appositive is often set apart by commas: ***Herjolf, the settler***)

1.9 WORD FREQUENCY – THE MOST COMMON WORDS IN THE SAGAS

Word frequency is the key to learning both Old and Modern Icelandic, and this book is designed with a word-frequency strategy. It concentrates on the 246 most common words in the sagas. In the vocabularies, these words are marked with the symbol ❖.

The total vocabulary of the sagas is surprisingly small.[4] Excluding names, there are only 12,400 different words in the corpus of the family sagas out of a total word count of almost 750,000. The 70 most frequently used words account for nearly 450,000 or 60% of the total word count. As one might expect this 70 contains the most frequently repeated prepositions, pronouns, conjunctions, verbs, and adjectives. The greatest benefit is found in learning the 246 most frequent words divided into parts of speech in groups of 50 each. This way the learner can concentrate on the 50 most frequent nouns, verbs, adjectives, etc.

Starting with List 1 below, the most frequent words are presented incrementally over the next twelve lessons. As one sees from the first list, *maðr* (man or person) is the most common noun in the sagas, and *konungr* (king) the second.

Appendix B: The Most Frequent Words in the Sagas, offers two lists. The first gives the 70 Most Common Words in the Sagas. The second list gives all 246 of the Most Common Words. These are divided by parts of speech into the 50 most common nouns, adjectives, pronouns, numerals, verbs, prepositions and adverbs, and conjunctions. The majority of the 246 entries remain among the most commonly used words in modern Icelandic.

The *Saga of the People of Weapon's Fjord* (*Vápnfirðinga saga,* see *Viking Language 2: The Old Norse Reader*) offers an example of the word frequency learning strategy. This short saga contains all 246 most frequent words except for the word *vísa* 'poetry' and a few numerals. *Vápnfirðinga saga* employs 1,000 different words and has a total word count of roughly 9,500 word entries. The 246 most frequent words make up about one quarter of the saga's vocabulary of 1000 distinct words, but because the words are frequently repeated and in compounds, they account for large percentage of the saga's total word count.

As in most sagas, the majority of the most frequent words appear early in *Vápnfirðinga saga*, and 175 of them occur in the first four chapters. These four first chapters from *Vápnfirðinga saga* are the readings in Lessons 12 and 13 in this book. The learner might want to finish the saga in *Viking Language 2* where there the saga is given with extensive maps and notes.

VOCABULARY – LIST 1 . THE MOST FREQUENT WORDS IN THE SAGAS IN EACH PART OF SPEECH

This first list gives the most common of the 246 most frequent words in the sagas. In their different forms, these words below comprise 34.43% of all words in the sagas.

---

[4]   *Íslendinga sögur orðstöðulykill og texti: Handbók.* Eds. Bergljót S. Kristjánsdóttir, Eiríkur Rögnvaldsson (chief editor), Guðrún Ingólfsdóttir and Örnólfur Thorsson. 2nd ed. Reykjavík: Mál og menning, 1998.

NOUNS	**ADJECTIVES**	**PRONOUNS**	**NUMERALS**
maðr – man, person	**mikill** – great	**sá** – that (one)	**einn** – one
konungr – king	**margr** – many	**hann** – he, it	
skip – ship	**góðr** – good		

VERBS	**PREPOSITIONS AND ADVERBS**	**CONJUNCTIONS**
vera – to be	**til** – to	**ok** – and
hafa – to have	**í** – in, into	**at** – that
segja – to say	**á** – on, onto	

EXERCISES

1.10 Genealogy. Most Icelandic sagas begin with genealogical information. Chart the genealogy from *Grœnlendinga saga* given in the first reading passage in this lesson by listing the Old Norse names (with accents) in the tree below. The connection with Ingolf Arnarson, who is mentioned as a kinsman, is unclear. Note that there are two men named Herjolf, a grandfather and his grandson (whose name has been entered in the proper place).

1.11 Nouns from *Grœnlendinga Saga*. Use the following nouns to complete the sentences below from the first reading and translate.

maðr   kona   var   efniligr   faðir   sonr   land   fugl   korn

Ex: Inn fyrsti _*fugl*_ fær it fyrsta _*korn*_.
   The first bird gets the first grain.

1.   Þorgerðr hét _____ hans, en Bjarni _____ þeira.

   _____

2.   Herjólfr hét _____, Bárðarson Herjólfssonar.

   _____

3.   Bárðr var _____ Herjólfs.

   _____

4. Bjarni _____ _____ maðr.

    _____

5. Ingólfr gaf Herjólfi _____.

    _____

1.12 Vocabulary. Match the nouns in each column with their English meanings by drawing a line between the two.

Ex:	korn		bird
	fugl		grain
1	maðr		bay
2	kona		daughter
3	víkingr		man, person
4	fjörðr		settler
5	vík		son
6	frændi		fjord
7	dóttir		country, land
8	konungr		viking
9	sonr		woman, wife
10	land		kinsman
11	landnámsmaðr		king

1.13 Translation. Translate the following reading passage from *Grœnlendinga saga* into Old Norse. Remember to include accent marks where needed.

Herjolf was the son of Bard,   *Herjólfr var Bárðarson* _____

[who was] the son of Herjolf;   _____

he was [a] kinsman of [the] settler Ingolf.   _____

Ingolf gave land to Herjolf   _____

between Vag and Reykjanes.   _____

Herjolf lived first at Drepstokk.   _____

His wife was named Thorgerd,   _____

and their son [was named] Bjarni,   _____

and [he] was a promising man.   _____

1.14 Gender and Meaning of Nouns. Complete the chart below with words from the lesson's reading passage.

	NOUN	GENDER	ENGLISH MEANING
Ex:	kona	*feminine*	*wife/woman*
1	_____	_____	story/history
2.	Vágr	_____	_____
3	_____	_____	land, country
4.	frændi	_____	_____
5	_____	_____	settler

The following words are the three most frequent nouns from *List 1. The Most Frequent Words in the Sagas in Each Part of Speech* given in this lesson. Their genders can be found in the *Vocabulary* at the end of the book.

	NOUN	GENDER	ENGLISH MEANING
6.	maðr	_____	_____
7.	konungr	_____	_____
8.	skip	_____	_____

1.15 Cases. Rewrite the following sentences so that they refer to *Haraldr* and *Eiríkr*, which decline the same as *Herjólfr*.

1. *Herjólfr* bjó á Drepstokki.   *Haraldr* _____
   Þorgerðr sá *Herjólf*.   _____
   Ingólfr gaf *Herjólfi* land.   _____
   Þorgerðr hét kona *Herjólfs*.   _____

2. *Herjólfr* bjó á Drepstokki.   *Eiríkr* _____
   Þorgerðr sá *Herjólf*.   _____
   Ingólfr gaf *Herjólfi* land.   _____
   Þorgerðr hét kona *Herjólfs*.   _____

1.16 Apposition. Fill in the correct form of *landnámsmaðr* (declines the same as *maðr*)in the spaces below and translate.

1. Hann var frændi Ingólfs _____.

   _____

2. Herjólfr gaf Ingólfi _____ land.

   _____

3. Maðr hét Ingólfr _____.

   _____

4. Þorgerðr sá Ingólf _____.

   _____

   Hint: *sá* comes from *sjá*, meaning 'to see'

1.17 Word Frequency. Using *List 1. The Most Frequent Words in the Sagas*, write below the most frequently used words in each part of speech and translate.

OLD NORSE	ENGLISH	OLD NORSE	ENGLISH
NOUNS		**ADJECTIVES**	
1 _____	_____	4 _____	_____
2 _____	_____	5 _____	_____
3 _____	_____	6 _____	_____

VERBS			**PREPOSITIONS AND ADVERBS**		
7	_____	_____	10	_____	_____
8	_____	_____	11	_____	_____
9	_____	_____	12	_____	_____

1.18 CULTURE – GUDRID TRAVELS FROM VINLAND TO ROME

Another example at the turn of the first millennium of a traveler from the far North Atlantic is Guðríðr Þorbjarnardóttir (Gudrid Thorbjorn's daughter). Gudrid lived and journeyed

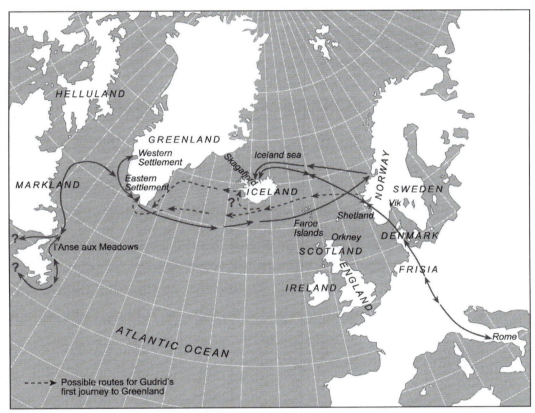

Figure 13. The Travels of Gudrid Thorbjarnardottir from *The Saga of the Greenlanders* and *The Saga of Eirik the Red* are indicated by dotted lines. Together the solid and dotted lines give the routes of the Viking period.

across the then known world, and she stands out as one of the most widely traveled Viking Age Icelanders. Her voyages are reported in the sagas in part because she was a respected ancestor of later Icelanders, including three twelfth-century bishops.

Grœnlendinga saga and Eiríks saga rauða (*The Saga of Eirik the Red*) describe Guðrun's life and travels. *Eiríks saga* is preserved in two manuscripts: the *Hauksbók* compilation from the early fourteenth century and *Skálholtsbók* from ca. (that is, *circa* or 'around' the year) 1420. Although *Grœnlendinga saga* and *Eiríks saga* are different in numerous ways, they are in general agreement about Gudrid's journeys, with *Grœnlendinga saga* recounting additional travels after Gudrid leaves Greenland.

Gudrid's North Atlantic journeys, a mixture of entrepreneurial trading voyages and pioneering attempts at colonization, are a medieval picture of the long-range sailings undertaken by the Norse. According to *Grœnlendinga saga*, Gudrid arrives in Greenland with her husband Thorir around the year 1000. The couple may have married in Norway, but it is more likely that Thorir, a Norwegian, first sailed to Iceland and there met and married Gudrid. With his wife on board, Thorir continues to Greenland, where his luck runs out. The two are shipwrecked on the Greenland coast and lose their boat. After they and their crew are rescued, Thorir dies of an illness during the winter in the Eastern Settlement.

A widow, Gudrid now marries Thorstein Eiriksson, the son of Eirik the Red (*inn rauði*) the settlement's leader. With her new husband, Gudrid moves north up the Greenlandic coast to a farm in the Western Settlement, but then Thorstein dies of illness. Widowed again, she returns to the Eastern Settlement, where she stays with her brother-in-law, Leif the Lucky (*inn heppni*), at the farm Brattahlid. Not long afterward, Gudrid marries Thorfinn Karlsefni, an Icelander recently arrived from Norway.

The next year (ca. 1010), Gudrid and Thorfinn Karlsefni set out in Karlsefni's ship in an ambitious attempt to settle Vinland (Vínland). The directions to the possible locations of Vinland are noted on the map by the two question marks with arrows leading west and southwest from l'Anse aux Meadows at the northern tip of Newfoundland. L'Anse aux Meadows is a modern English corruption of the French placename L'Anse aux Méduses (The Bay of Jellyfish). Accompanied by men and women in two other ships, they sail west to the North American continent and then south along the coast.

Reaching Vinland, they settle in, some using the cabins (*búðir*) built by Leif Eiriksson on his earlier Vinland voyage. Gudrid gives birth to a son named Snorri, the first European child born in North America. After a few years, the Vinland settlement fails. Gudrid and Thorfinn Karlsefni sail back to Greenland, spending the winter in the Eastern Settlement. The following spring the couple sails east to Norway. They sell the cargo they acquired in Vinland and Greenland and winter in Norway.

In the spring, Thorfinn and Gudrid sail back to Iceland, presumably with a shipload of valuable Norwegian goods. According to *Grœnlendinga saga,* the couple landed in Skagafjord, Thorfinn's home region. There they buy a farm called Glaumbær, and after a successful life together, Thorfinn Karlsefni dies. *Eiríks saga rauða* also places Thorfinn Karlsefni and Gudrid in Skagafjord, but at Reynines.

Eiríks saga rauða stops at this point. *Grœnlendinga saga*, however, says that Gudrid, a widow for the third time, manages the farm with the help of her son Snorri, the child born in Vinland. When Snorri marries, Gudrid, now a woman of advanced age, sets off on a pilgrimage south to Rome. Surviving this arduous and dangerous journey, she returns to Iceland. There she lives out the rest of her life in solitude as one of Iceland's first Norse anchorites, or independent nuns, dying about the year 1050. She outlived three husbands and saw the world from Vinland to the Mediterranean.

Was Gudrid unique? The medieval visitors' book at the Swiss monastery of Reichenau hints about the travels of other Icelandic women. This register, used mainly to record names of pilgrims heading south, contains a page with the heading *Hislant terra* (Iceland). It lists eight Icelandic men and four Icelandic women (Vigdis, Vilborg, Kolthera and Thurid), who probably stopped at the monastery in the eleventh century.

LESSON 2
NORSE SETTLERS IN
GREENLAND AND VINLAND

Eigi fellr tré við fyrsta högg
(A tree does not fall with the first blow)

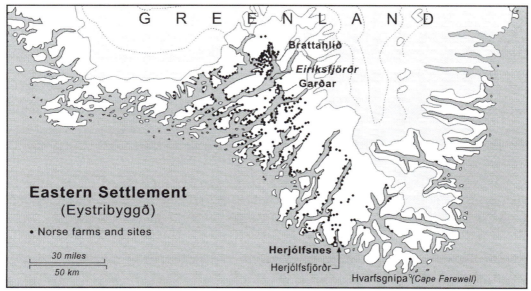

Figure 14. The Eastern Settlement (Eystribyggð) of Norse Greenland (Grœnland). The farm Herjólfsnes of Herjolf Bardarson is in Herjolfsfjörðr ('fjord'). Eirik the Red settled at Brattahlíð (Steep-Slope) in Eiriksfjörðr. The original settlers converted to Christianity around the year 1000. After the year 1124, Garðar became the seat of Greenland's bishop.

2.1 CULTURE – NORSE GREENLAND

Within a century of its settlement, Iceland was already crowded. New settlers, as well as established Icelandic families, looked to Greenland, the new land that Eirik the Red had discovered to the west of Iceland around the year 985. The family of Herjolf Bardarson, who appears in this and the preceding reading passage, sailed with Eirik to Greenland and settled at Herjólfsnes (Herjolf's Promontory) in the Eastern Settlement (See map above). At that time, the climate in Greenland was relatively mild on account of the 'medieval climate optimum,' a medieval warm period in the North Atlantic from ca. 950 to 1250.

The Norse settlers were members of a herding culture, and Greenland's southwestern coastline was appealing with its sheltered fjords and good grazing lands. Eirik's followers established the Eastern Settlement (Eystribyggð) on the southwestern tip of Greenland, and soon there was a Western Settlement (vestribyggð) on the coast 300 miles to the north. Native inhabitants had earlier lived along the coastline but at the time when the Norse settlers arrived the areas were uninhabited . The ancestors of the modern Inuit Greenlanders were living in what is today Northern Canada. A century or so later, they began migrating to Greenland and came into contact with the Norse settlements.

Between the Eastern and Western settlements lay a small middle Norse region of approximately twenty farms. Of the three areas of Norse habitation, the Eastern Settlement was the most populated with approximately 190 farms, 12 parish churches, a cathedral, and Augustinian and Benedictine monasteries. The Western Settlement had approximately ninety farms and four churches. The count of sites increases as archaeologists undertake more excavations.

2.2 READING – 'LAND-TAKING' IN GREENLAND (*LANDNÁMABÓK*)

The Book of Settlements (*Landnámabók*) provides additional information about Herjolf Bardarson. Unlike the reading passage in the previous lesson from *Grœnlendinga saga*, the passage below from *Landnámabók* does not mention Herjolf's wife or his son Bjarni. Instead it tells of Herjolf's second *landnám*, or 'landtaking,' this time in northwest Greenland. Herjolf arrived with Eirik the Red, who was Norwegian-born. Eirik lived in Iceland for many years. After killing a neighbor in a feud, he served out a sentence of three years' banishment from Iceland by exploring unknown lands to the west.

Eirik´s Saga tells that Eirik chose the name 'Greenland' for these new lands in order to entice people to follow him there, knowing that the name 'Iceland' sounded inhospitable. Returning to Iceland, Eirik announced his intention to settle Greenland. According to Ari Fróði in *Íslendingabók*, Eirik led fourteen ships of settlers from Iceland to Greenland 'fourteen or fifteen winters before Christianity came here to Iceland.'

This reading selection from *Landnámabók* is found in entries 79 and 92 from the *Hauksbók* and *Sturlubók* versions of *Landnámabók*. As in this reading selection, *Landnámabók* is a compilation of often short accounts about Iceland's first settlers. There were several versions of *Landnámabók*. The first was written in the early twelfth century but is lost, and we know little about it. Another version called *Melabók* (*M*, the book of Mel [a placename]) exists chiefly as parts incorporated into the two principle versions, *Hauksbók* (*H, named for its author Haukr* Erlendsson, a lawspeaker in the early 1300s) and *Sturlubók* (*S, named for its author a famous 13th century chieftain, Sturla Þórðarson*).

Landnámabók (H79, S92)	*The Book of Settlements* (H79, S92)
Herjólfr hét maðr	[A] man was called Herjolf
Bárðarson Herjólfssonar;	the son of Bard, the son of Herjolf;
hann fór til Grœnlands með Eiríki.	he went to Greenland with Eirik [the Red].
Herjólfr nam Herjólfsfjörð	Herjolf took [claimed] Herjolf's Fjord
ok bjó á Herjólfsnesi. (*H79*)	and lived at Herjolfsnes.
Eiríkr nam Eiríksfjörð ok bjó í	Eirik took Eirik's Fjord and lived at
Brattahlíð,	Brattahlid,
en Leifr sonr hans eptir hann. (*S92*)	and Leif, his son, after him.

VOCABULARY

❖**á** *prep* [*w dat*] on; upon; at; in

Bárðr <-ar> *m* Bard (*personal name*)

Barðarson *m* Bard's son (*personal name*)

bjó *1/3 sg past of* **búa** lived

Brattahlíð *f* Brattahlid (*place name*), Steep-Slope

❖**búa** <býr, bjó, bjuggu, búinn> *vb* live in a place, dwell, inhabit, live

Eiríkr <-s> *m* Eirik (*personal name*)

Eiriksfjörðr *m* Eiriksfjord (*place name*), Eirik's Fjord

❖**en** *conj* but; (*less frequently*) and

❖**eptir** *prep* [*w acc*] after (*in time*)

❖**fara** <ferr, fór, fóru, farinn> *vb* go, travel; move

fór *1/3 sg past of* **fara** went

Grœnland *n* Greenland

❖**hann** <*acc* hann, *dat* honum, *gen* hans> *pron* he

hans *pron* (*gen of* **hann**) his

❖**heita** <heitr, hét, hétu, heitinn> *vb* call, give a name to; call, call on;

(*intrans w pres* heitir) be called, be named; [*w dat*] promise

Herjólfr <-s> *m* Herjolf (*personal name*)

Herjólfsfjörðr *m* Herjolfsfjord (*place name*), 'Herjolf's Fjord'

Herjólfsnes *n* Herjolfsnes (*place name*), Herjolf's Headland

hét *1/3 sg past of* **heita** was named

❖**í** *prep* [*w dat*] in, within; at

❖**maðr** <*acc* mann *dat* manni, *gen* manns, *nom & acc pl* menn, *dat* mönnum, *gen* manna> *m* man; person, human being

❖**með** *prep* [*w acc/dat*] with

nam *1/3 sg past of* **nema** took

nema <nemr, nam, námu, numinn> *vb* take; claim (land)

❖**ok** *conj* and

❖**sonr** <*dat* syni, *gen* sonar, *pl* synir, *acc* sonu> *m* son

❖**til** *prep* [*w gen*] to

In the vocabularies, the notations **<-s>** or **<-ar>** appear immediately following masculine nouns. These notations indicate whether that noun takes its genitive with **-s** (for example, *Eirikr,* genitive *Eiriks*) or with **-ar** (for example, Barðr genitive Barðar). The -s is the more common of the two masculine genitive endings.

2.3 EXERCISE – THE READING SELECTION FROM *LANDNÁMABÓK*
Match the Old Icelandic on the left with the correct English translation on the right.

1. Herjólfr hét maðr
2. Bárðarson Herjólfssonar;
3. hann fór til Grœnlands með Eiríki.
4. Herjólfr nam Herjólfsfjörð
5. ok bjó á Herjólfsnesi.

a. Herjolf took (claimed) Herjolf's Fjord
b. Eirik took Eirik's Fjord and lived at Brattahlid,
c. and Leif his son after him.
d. [A] man was called Herjolf
e. the son of Bard, [who was] the son of

6. Eiríkr nam Eiríksfjörð ok   Herjolf;
   bjó í Brattahlíð,   f. he went to Greenland with Eirik [the
7. en Leifr sonr hans eptir   Red].
   hann.   g. and lived at Herjolfsnes.

2.4 CULTURE – VINLAND (VÍNLAND)

Shortly after Herjolf Bardarson settled in Greenland, his son Bjarni Herjolfsson set out from Iceland to join his father in Greenland, but Bjarni became lost in fog. He sailed off course, and sighted a new land of forests to the west and south of Greenland. *Grœnlendinga saga* tells that Bjarni refused to land and explore his discovery. For his lack of initiative, he was much criticized when he finally reached Greenland and settled there.

We know for certain that Norse seafarers reached the North American continent because Norse archaeological remains dating to about A.D. 1000 have been found at L'Anse aux Meadows in Newfoundland. But exactly who these settlers were is not clear. The sagas tell that in Greenland, Leif Eiriksson bought Bjarni's ship and then set out as the leader of an expedition intent on settling the new land. Leif the Lucky (*inn heppni*), as he was called, visited several places on the North American coast. These included *Helluland* ('Slab-Land,' Baffin Island), *Markland* ('Forest-Land,' Labrador), and *Vínland* ('Vine-Land').

Leif's attempt to settle in Vinland failed, and he and his party returned to Greenland. Others, such as Leif's brother and sister, Thorvald and Freydis, and later Thorfinn Karlsefni and his wife Gudrid, are said to have led further parties west. Ultimately, they were outnumbered and driven off by the *skrælingjar* (sg *skrælingr*), the unflattering Norse term for both North American Indians and Greenlandic Inuits.

Although the Norse Greenlanders had neither the resources nor the population to colonize the North American continent, they continued to sail there for wood and perhaps other provisions. An entry in the Icelandic Annals for the year 1347 states, 'In this year a Greenlandic ship arrived in Iceland loaded with wood. It had been blown off course in returning from Vinland.' The Norse colony in Greenland began to decline after 1300. The climate grew colder and sailing became more dangerous due to increased drift-ice. The Greenland settlement became isolated from the outside world for years at a time, and by the 1500s the Norse colony ceased to exist. The exact end of the colony is unknown. Possibly the last of the nearly forgotten Norse of Greenland abandoned the colony. They may also have died out or been carried off by European slavers or pirates.

2.5 GRAMMAR TOOLBOX. DEFINITE AND INDEFINITE ARTICLE

The definite article is the word 'the.' As noted below, the Old Norse definite article declines for case, number, and gender. There is no indefinite article (*a, an*) in Old Icelandic, although sometimes the numeral 'one,' (*einn*) or its variations is used for emphasis.

In translation into English, the indefinite article usually has to be added.

Hann var frændi Herjólfs.	He was *a* kinsman of Herjolf.
Hann var efniligr maðr.	He was *a* promising man.
Hon var dóttir Þorgerðar.	She was *a* daughter of Thorgerð.

The ON definite article.

	M	F	N		M	F	N
Sg *nom*	inn	in	it	**Pl**	inir	inar	in
acc	inn	ina	it		ina	inar	in
dat	inum	inni	inu		inum	inum	inum
gen	ins	innar	ins		inna	inna	inna

When the definite article is used with an adjective, as in ***inn** fyrsti fugl* 'the first bird,' ***it** fyrsta korn* 'the first grain,' and *Eiríkr **inn** rauði* 'Eirik the Red,' the article precedes the adjective.

When used without an adjective, the definite article is added as a suffix to the noun after its case ending. For example, the nouns *maðr* 'man,' *bók* 'book,' and *land* become *maðr**inn*** (*m*) 'the man,' *bók**in*** (*f*) 'the book,' and *land**it*** (*n*) 'the land.' When the case ending of a noun ends in a vowel, the initial *-i-* of the article is dropped. For example, *kona* 'woman' plus the feminine article *in* becomes *konan* (*kona* + *in* > *konan*). So also *frændi* 'kinsman' or 'friend' becomes *frændinn* (*frændi* + *inn* > *frændinn*). The definite article is discussed in more detail later.

When the definite article stands alone, it is sometimes spelled with an initial *h-* (for example, ***h**inn,* ***h**in,* ***h**it*). Modern Icelandic always uses the *h-*.

2.6 PROPER NOUNS

Below are examples of names encountered in the readings of the first lessons. With a few exceptions, proper nouns decline like regular nouns. For instance, *Eiríkr* and *Herjólfr* take the same set of endings as the masculine nouns *konungr* and *víkingr*. Each proper noun, like all nouns, is either strong or weak. They do not change. The names below are divided into strong and weak. As we'll see in the next lesson, weak nouns take a simpler set of endings than strong nouns.

	STRONG MASCULINE					WEAK MASCULINE	
nom	Eiríkr	Herjólfr	Þorsteinn	Bárðr	Björn	Bjarni	Hjalti
acc	Eirík	Herjólf	Þorstein	Bárð	Björn	Bjarna	Hjalta
dat	Eiríki	Herjólfi	Þorsteini	Bárði	Birni	Bjarna	Hjalta
gen	Eiríks	Herjólfs	Þorsteins	Bárðar	Bjarnar	Bjarna	Hjalta

Nouns have their peculiarities. For example, the name *Þorsteinn* ends with an *-n* rather than the more usual nominative masculine ending *-r*. Rather than being absent, the nominative *-r* has changed to *-n* in order to match the preceding *-n-*. This change is a regular process discussed later, but probably because it is simply easier to pronounce the sound of double -n than -nr. Other masculine names, such as *Björn* and *Bjarni* (see above), decline with different sets of endings. These too are explained in later lessons.

The first reading passage of this lesson contains only one feminine name, *Þorgerðr*. An example of a common type of feminine noun, *Þorgerðr*, like many masculine nouns, ends in *-r* in the nominative singular. Feminine names in *-r* follow the pattern of *Þorgerðr*: *-r*, *-i*, *-i*, *-ar*. Other feminine names take different sets of endings.

	STRONG FEMININE				*WEAK FEMININE*	
nom	Þorgerðr	Sigríðr	Freydís	Ólöf	Gyða	Þyri
acc	Þorgerði	Sigríði	Freydísi	Ólöfu	Gyðu	Þyri
dat	Þorgerði	Sigríði	Freydísi	Ólöfu	Gyðu	Þyri
gen	Þorgerðar	Sigríðar	Freydísar	Ólafar	Gyðu	Þyri

2.7 GRAMMAR TOOLBOX. VERBS

Verbs express action, existence, or happenings. Verb usage in Old Norse largely corresponds to Modern English. Verbs are at the core of language, and this section provides an overview of the different aspects of Old Norse verbs. It is not to be memorized, but used as a resource as verbs are presented in the coming lessons.

- A verb agrees with the subject of the sentence in **person** (1st, 2nd, 3rd) and **number** (*sing*ular and plural) Person and number are indicated by endings, called personal endings.
- Old Norse has two verb **tenses**: present and past. Reference to future events is expressed in several ways: use of the present tense; use of auxiliary verbs such as *munu* ('shall', 'will') and *skulu* ('shall'); and use of time expressions, such as *á morgun* ('tomorrow').
- Verbs have three **moods**: indicative, subjunctive, and imperative. Mood reflects a speaker's attitude toward the reality of a statement. The indicative is the most common and is used when an utterance is believed to be true. The subjunctive expresses doubt or uncertainty. The imperative is used in commands.
- Old Norse verbs have three types of **voice**: active, middle, and passive. The active and middle have their own sets of endings, while the passive is formed using an auxiliary verb and past participle (a verb form which indicates certain tenses and can function as an adjective). For example, the heart is beating or the enemy is/was beaten, carrying the meaning of a beating heart and a beaten enemy.
    - In the **active voice** the subject performs the action (for example, he kicks, he kicked).
    - In the **passive voice**, the subject undergoes the action (for example, he is kicked, he was kicked).
    - Verbs with **middle** endings have a range of functions, but fundamentally they are used in a reflexive manner. That is, they express action which

reflects back onto the subject (for example, he kicked himself). Hence the subject both performs and undergoes the action. The middle occasionally has passive meaning.

Verbs in Old Norse are either **strong** or **weak**, depending on the formation of their past tense. A small third type of verb, called **preterite-present** verbs, shows features of both strong and weak verbs.

- **Strong verbs** distinguish present and past tense by changing their root vowel. English is similar. For example, the present tense of the verb 'take' is 'takes,' but changes its root vowel in past tense 'took.'
- **Weak verbs** form their past by adding a **dental suffix** (*d*, *t*, or *ð*). For example, the past tense of *kalla* 'call' is *kallaði* with dental suffix *ð*. English also employs a dental suffix 'd' (sometimes 't'). For example, the past of 'call' is 'called.'
- **Preterite-present** verbs show features of both strong and weak verbs. There are only ten of these verbs in Old Norse. Despite being few in number, they are frequent because they are often employed as **modal auxiliaries**, helping verbs that denote a sense of obligation, intention, need, or probability. Modals are also frequent in English, which employs modals in a manner similar to Old Norse. For example, 'I sail to Iceland' can be modified by adding an auxiliary to express obligation, 'I **ought** to sail to Iceland' (*Ek **skal** sigla til Íslands*) and or 'I **have** to sail to Iceland (*Ek **á** at sigla til Íslands*').

Old Norse makes frequent use of **infinitives** and **participles**.
- **Infinitives** are fixed, unchanging verb forms. For example, *taka* meaning 'to take' and *kalla* meaning 'to call' are infinitives. Infinitives do not take endings in order to indicate person, number, or tense. Whereas English employs the word 'to' to denote an infinitive, Old Norse on occasion employs *at* ('to') but mostly does not. Instead the infinitive in Old Norse is the core verb form by itself. Dictionaries of Old Norse, as those of English, refer to verbs by their infinitives.
- **Participles** are adjectives derived from verbs. There are present and past participles, each having its own set of endings. For example, *takandi* 'taking' is a present participle (adjective, ON *-andi* = English '-ing') and *tekinn* 'taken' is a past participle (adjective).

In summary, verbs are **strong** or **weak** (with a few preterite-presents) and have:
-**person**: 1st, 2nd, or 3rd
-**number**: singular or plural
-**tense**: present, past and future
-**mood**: indicative, subjunctive, or imperative
-**voice**: active or middle or passive (usually with an auxiliary verb)

2.8 VERBS, INFINITIVES

Almost all Old Norse verbs form the infinitive by adding -*a* to the verb stem (the basic verb minus any endings), for example, *at gefa* 'to give' and *at fara* 'to go.' The infinitive is commonly used with auxiliary verbs as, for example, in English 'I want **to give**.' When the infinitive is used in this way, it is called a complementary infinitive.

Ek vil **nema** land.	*I want **to take** land.*
Ek vil **fara**.	*I want **to go**.*
Hon vill **búa** á Drepstokki.	*She wants **to live** at Drepstokk.*
Ingólfr vill **gefa** Herjólfi land.	*Ingolf wants **to give** land to Herjolf.*

The following list gives the infinitive and the past tense of verbs in this lesson. In order to help distinguish infinitives in Old Norse, such words will be frequently preceded by the particle *at*, which corresponds to English 'to.'

INFINITIVE	TRANSLATION	PAST TENSE (3ʳᵈ PERSON SINGULAR)	
at búa	*to live*	bjó	*lived*
at fara	*to go*	fór	*went*
at sjá	*to see*	sá	*saw*
at gefa	*to give*	gaf	*gave*
at heita	*to be named*	hét	*was named*
at nema	*to take*	nam	*took*
at vera	*to be*	var	*was*
at verða	*to become*	varð	*became*

2.9 LINKING VERBS – *VERA, VERÐA,* AND *HEITA*

In the sentence *Herjólfr nam land* 'Herjolf took land,' the subject (*Herjólfr*) performs an action (*nam* 'took') on an object (*land*). Many verbs, such as *nema, gera,* and *gefa* describe actions. Some verbs, however, such as *vera* 'to be,' *verða* 'to become,' and *heita* 'to be called' do not convey action; rather, they link the subject to a noun, adjective, or pronoun usually following the verb (thus linking the two words). Given its function, one could substitute an equals sign for a linking verb and lose little of the meaning. Hence one might consider the sentence *Leifr hét maðr* as *Leifr = maðr* and the same sentence could be *maðr hét Leifr* (a man was called Leif).

A word connected to the subject by a linking verb is known as a subject complement, because it is equal to or describes the subject. For example, 'The land was Greenland' (noun = noun) or 'The land was fertile' (Noun described by adjective). A subject complement, like the subject of the sentence, is in the nominative case. Adjectives or nouns used as subject complements are commonly known as predicate adjectives and predicate nouns.

Below are examples of sentences in which linking verbs connect the subject with a subject complement. Both subject and subject complement are in the nominative case.

PREDICATE NOUNS

Leifr er **sonr** Eiríks.	*Leif* is the *son* of Eirik.
Hon var **dóttir** Ingólfs.	*She* was a *daughter* of Ingolf.
Haraldr varð **konungr** Nóregs.	*Harald* became *king* of Norway.
Maðrinn hét **Ingólfr**.	*The man* was called *Ingolf*.
Þorgerðr hét **kona** hans.	*Thorgerd* was the name of his *wife*.
	[His *wife* was called *Thorgerd*.]

PREDICATE ADJECTIVES

Bjarni var **efniligr**.	*Bjarni* was *promising.*
Freydís er **fögr**.	*Freydis* is *beautiful.*
Barnit er **lítit**.	*The child* is *little.*
Óðinn er **vitr**.	*Odin* is *wise.*
Frigg varð **reið**.	*Frigg* became *angry.*
Þórr er **sterkr**.	*Thor* is *strong.*

In contrast to the examples above, the sentences below contain action verbs with direct objects in the accusative case. For example in English, 'She kicked the ball.'

Ingólfr gaf Herjólfi land.	Ingolf gave Herjolf land.
Herjólfr nam Herjólfsfjörð.	Herjolf took Herjolfsfjord.

2.10 CULTURE – THE FAMILY AND STURLUNGA SAGAS

The word *saga* is connected with the Norse verb 'to say' (*segja*) and means both 'history' and 'story.'

The family sagas are one of the world's great literatures. Called in Icelandic *Íslendingasögur* (*Sagas of the Icelanders*), they are prose stories written in Old Norse/Icelandic about people and events during the years 860 to 1030. Based on oral stories and genealogies from the Viking Age, saga writing on parchment began in Iceland in the twelfth century and reached its height in what is called the classical period in the thirteenth century.

The family sagas are a literature of conflict. Region by region and often family by family, they lavish attention on intimate details of private life that other medieval literatures largely ignore. Many issues can stir the action. Disputes begin over insults, property claims, honor, status, power, seductions, inheritance, love, bodily injury, and missing livestock. There are accusations of witchcraft, fights over beached whales, cheating, stealing, harboring of outlaws, and vengeance sought for scurrilous or erotic verse. Repeatedly in the stories, individuals and families contend for prestige and survival in a rural society that accepted open feuding as the means for regulating wealth, power, and honor.

The family sagas vary in length from slim, tightly woven tales with several key players to sprawling epics spanning generations. Additionally there are *þættir*, episodic short tales which tend to concentrate on a particular anecdote, event, or conflict in the life of a notable individual or travels abroad.

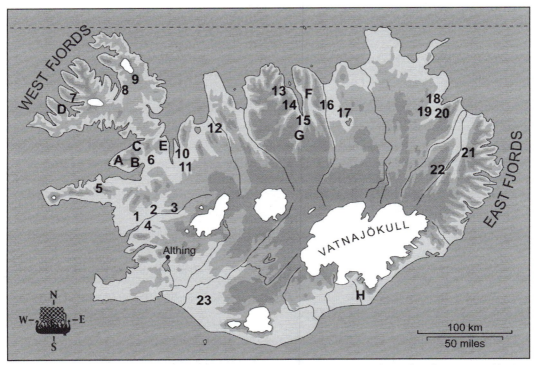

Figure 15. Locations of Major Family and Sturlunga Sagas. Numbers refer to family sagas and letters to Sturlunga sagas. English and Old Norse titles are given in the list below. When a saga takes place in several regions, the map shows where the main character was raised.

Sturlunga Saga is a compilation of sagas named after the Sturlungs, an influential Icelandic family of chieftains who became especially powerful in the thirteenth century. The sagas in the Sturlung compilation (*Sturlunga saga*), along with the bishops' sagas (*biskupa sögur*) are often called contemporary sagas (*samtíðarsögur*). The twelfth- and thirteenth-century events that the contemporary sagas describe transpired about the same time that the narratives were written.

Like the family sagas, the sagas that make up the Sturlung compilation often concentrate on conflict and feud. The two groups of sagas differ from each other in social emphasis. The family sagas are regional in nature. *Sturlunga Saga* focuses on quarrels among powerful chieftains with aspirations for large-scale control. In particular, *Sturlunga Saga* details events of the last decades of the Old Icelandic Free State, recounting the power struggles that led to the Norwegian takeover of Iceland in 1262-64.

MAJOR FAMILY SAGAS (*ÍSLENDINGASÖGUR*)

1. *Egil's Saga* (*Egils saga Skalla-Grímssonar*)
2. *Hen-Thorir's Saga* (*Hænsa-Þóris saga*)
3. *The Saga of Gunnlaug Serpent-Tongue* (*Gunnlaugs saga ormstungu*)
4. *The Saga of the Slayings on the Heath* (*Heiðarvíga saga*)
5. *The Saga of the People of Eyri* (*Eyrbyggja saga*)
6. *The Saga of the People of the Laxardal* (*Laxdæla saga*)
7. *Gisli Sursson's Saga* (*Gísla saga Súrssonar*)
8. *The Saga of the Sworn Brothers* (*Fóstbræðra saga*)
9. *The Saga of Havard of Isafjord* (*Hávarðar saga Ísfirðings*)
10. *The Saga of the Confederates* (*Bandamanna saga*)
11. *Grettir's Saga* (*Grettis saga Ásmundarsonar*)
12. *The Saga of the People of Vatnsdal* (*Vatnsdæla saga*)
13. *The Saga of the People of Svarfadardal* (*Svarfdæla saga*)
14. *Field-Ljot's Saga* (*Valla-Ljóts saga*)
15. *Killer-Glum's Saga* (*Víga-Glúms saga*)
16. *The Saga of the People of Ljosavatn* (*Ljósvetninga saga*)
17. *The Saga of Reykjadal and of Killer-Skuta* (*Reykdæla saga ok Víga-Skútu*)
18. *The Saga of the People of Weapon's Fjord* (*Vápnfirðinga saga*)
19. *The Tale of Thorstein Staff-Struck* (*Þorsteins þáttr stangarhöggs*)
20. *The Tale of Ale-Hood* (*Ölkofra þáttr*)
21. *The Saga of Droplaug's Sons* (*Droplaugarsona saga*)
22. *The Saga of Hrafnkel Frey's Priest* (*Hrafnkels saga Freysgoða*)
23. *Njal's Saga* (*Njáls saga,* also known as *Brennu-Njáls saga, The Saga of Burnt Njal*)

STURLUNGA SAGA (*STURLUNGA SAGA*)

A. *The Saga of the Icelanders* (*Íslendinga saga*)
B. *The Saga of Sturla* (*Sturlu saga*)
C. *The Tale of Geirmund Helskin* (*Geirmundar þáttr heljarskinns*)
D. *The Saga of Hrafn Sveinbjarnarson* (*Hrafns saga Sveinbjarnarsonar*)
E. *The Saga of Thorgils and Haflidi* (*Þorgils saga ok Hafliða*)
G. *The Saga of the Priest Gudmund the Good* (*Prestssaga Guðmundar góða*)
F. *The Saga of Gudmund the Worthy* (*Guðmundar saga dýra*)
H. *The Saga of the Men of Svinfell* (*Svínfellinga saga*)

2.11 CULTURE – SAGA GENRES

In addition to the family and Sturlunga Sagas, medieval Icelanders wrote several other kinds of sagas. These include the bishops' sagas, concentrating on the lives of distinguished Icelandic churchmen; the kings' sagas (*konungasögur*), which relate the history of Scandinavian kings with a focus on the kings of Norway; sagas of antiquity (*fornaldarsögur*), consisting of mythic-legendary tales recounting fabulous and sometimes mythic stories of epic heroes such as the dragon slayer Sigurd, the slayer of Fafnir (*Sigurðr Fáfnisbani*), and the bear warrior, Bodvar Bjarki (*Böðvarr Bjarki*). In addition, there are the saints' lives (*heilagramanna sögur*) mostly about foreign saints; the knights' sagas (*riddarasögur*) which are translations or adaptations of continental medieval romances; and tall tales called lying sagas (*lygisögur*).

2.12 GRAMMAR TOOLBOX. ADJECTIVES

Adjectives are words that describe and modify nouns and pronouns. In the reading passage *mikill* ('big') and *sterkr* ('strong') are adjectives. They describe the noun *maðr*, hence *mikill maðr og sterkr* ('a big man and strong').

- In Old Norse, adjectives agree in gender, case, and number with the nouns they modify
- Old Norse adjectives have both strong and weak forms with different endings.
- Adjectives take strong endings unless preceded by a definite article, demonstrative pronoun, or other determining word, in which case they take weak endings.
- Adjectives decline similar to nouns and are discussed in coming lessons following the presentation of nouns.

2.13 OLD NORSE WORD PARADIGMS

'Paradigm' is an English word derived from Latin *paradigma* and Greek *paradeigma* meaning 'model.' In descriptions of Old Norse grammar, paradigms are models or patterns of verbs, nouns, and adjectives. They show endings according to the different cases (nom, acc, dat, gen) and sound changes within words. See *Appendix A: Quick Guide to Old Norse Grammar* which contains the most useful basic paradigms. This study tool will help with mastering the basic paradigms of verb conjugations and noun and adjective declensions.

2.14 VOCABULARY – LIST 2. THE MOST FREQUENT WORDS IN THE SAGAS

NOUNS	ADJECTIVES	PRONOUNS	NUMERALS
mál – speech; case, matter	**lítill** – little	**ek** – I	**tveir** – two
	illr – bad, ill	**þú** – you	
	sannr – true		
sonr – son			
hönd – hand			

VERBS	PREPOSITIONS AND ADVERBS	CONJUNCTIONS
koma – to come	**þá** – then	**en** – but
fara – to go, travel	**þar** – there	
munu – will	**um** – about	

EXERCISES

2.15 Vocabulary. Match the verbs in each column with their English meanings by drawing a line between the two. If needed, use the Vocabulary at the rear of the book.

Ex:	vilja	to live
	búa	to want
1	sjá	to become
2	nema	to go
3	heita	to give
4	fara	to be named
5	vera	to take, claim
6	gefa	to see
7	verða	to be

2.16 Cases. The genitive case usually denotes possession. Give the genitive form for each name below to complete the saga title. Then use the list of Family Sagas in this lesson to translate the title.

	PERSONAL NAME	OLD ICELANDIC TITLE	ENGLISH TITLE
Ex:	Glúmr	*Víga- Glúms saga*	*Killer-Glum's Saga*
1	Ljótr	*Valla-*	
2	Gísli	*saga Súrssonar*	
3	Gunnlaugr	*saga ormstungu*	

2.17 Verb Forms. Complete the chart below.

	VERB (PAST TENSE)	ENGLISH MEANING	INFINITIVE
Ex: gaf		*gave, granted*	*at gefa*
1			at búa
2.	fór		
3.	sá		
4			at heita
5.	nam		
6			at vera
7			at verða

2.18 Translation Review. Translate the following passage from *Landnámabók* back into Old Norse. Refer to the previous reading sections.

[A] man was called Herjolf	*Herjólfr hét maðr*
the son of Bard, the son of Herjolf;	_____
he went to Greenland with Eirik.	_____
Herjolf took Herjolf's Fjord	_____
and lived at Herjolfsnes.	_____
Eirik took Eirik's Fjord	_____
and lived at Brattahlid,	_____
and Leif, his son, after him.	_____

2.19 Gender and Meaning of Nouns. Complete the chart below. Refer to the previous reading sections.

NOUN	GENDER	ENGLISH MEANING
The words are found in the reading passages.		
Ex: hlíð	*feminine*	*mountain-side, slope*
1. _____	_____	son
2. nes	_____	_____
3. fjörðr	_____	_____
4. hönd	_____	_____
5. fé	_____	_____
6. bróðir	_____	_____
7. land	_____	_____
8. dagr	_____	_____

2.20 Word Frequency. Referring to the list of *The Most Frequent Words* given in this lesson, write the words from the different grammatical categories and translate.

OLD NORSE	ENGLISH	OLD NORSE	ENGLISH
NOUNS		*ADJECTIVES*	
1 _____	_____	4 _____	_____
2 _____	_____	5 _____	_____
3 _____	_____	6 _____	_____
VERBS		*PREPOSITIONS AND ADVERBS*	
7 _____	_____	10 _____	_____
8 _____	_____	11 _____	_____
9 _____	_____	12 _____	_____

2.21 The Definite Article. Decline the definite article.

	M	F	N		M	F	N
Sg *nom*	_____	in _____	_____	Pl	inir _____	_____	_____
acc	_____	_____	it _____		_____	inar _____	_____
dat	_____	_____	_____		_____	_____	inum _____
gen	ins _____	innar _____	_____		inna _____	_____	_____

Add the suffixed definite article to the nouns below. (The following nouns are in the nominative case.) Check the gender of each word in order to use the correct article.

Ex: maðr   *maðrinn* _____

1. fjörðr _____
2. hönd _____
3. land _____
4. sonr _____
5. nes _____

6. hlíð _____
7. konungr _____
8. skip _____
9. frændi _____
10. kona _____

2.22 Proper Nouns. Give the correct form of the proper noun in parentheses and translate. Refer to the section on proper nouns in the lesson.

1. _____ bjó fyrst á Drepstokki. (Herjólfr)

   _____

2. Þorgerðr sá _____. (Eiríkr)

   _____

3. Ingólfr gaf _____ land. (Þorgerðr)

   _____

4. Hann var frændi _____. (Bárðr)

   _____

5. _____ bjó fyrst á Drepstokki. (Þorsteinn)

   _____

6. Þorgerðr sá _____. (Bjarni)

   _____

7. Ingólfr gaf _____ land. (Björn)

   _____

8. Hann var frændi _____. (Þyri)

   _____

LESSON 3
DENMARK: RUNESTONES
AND THE FIRST VIKING STATE

Skalat maðr rúnar rísta, nema vel ráða kunni
(A man should not carve runes, unless he well knows how to control them)

Figure 16. The Runestone, front and back, of King Gorm the Old (Gormr inn gamli) at Jelling, Denmark. Gorm was the last pagan king of Denmark. He founded the Jelling Dynasty.

3.1 CULTURE – RUNES

Runes were the writing of the ancient Scandinavians, and surviving runic inscriptions are a main source of social, historical, and linguistic information. Runes are an alphabet, not a pictographic or a syllabic script. Much as we might call our alphabet the ABCs, the runic alphabet was composed of letters and called the futhark after the first six runes or runic letters, ᚠᚢᚦᚨᚱᚲ. Runes were carved on wood, stone, bone, antler, and metal. They were and used for identification, commemoration, messages, and magic. Runic inscriptions are the closest of all written sources to the speech of the Viking Age.

The earliest runes date to the first century A.D. Almost surely, the runes were adapted from writing systems in use in the Roman Empire. At that time there was considerable contact between the Roman world and Germanic peoples. Speakers of Proto

Old Norse and other Germanic languages probably adapted the letters of either Latin or Northern Italic alphabets to fit the sounds of their own languages. They modified the letters in order to make them more suitable for carving.

Those who designed the individual runes used straight strokes, a feature which worked well with wood grain. Messages were usually short due to the limitations imposed by pieces of wood, strips of bark, bones, or tablets of wax. The use of pen and ink and the art of preparing pages of vellum for manuscripts were unknown in Scandinavia before the conversion to Christianity, beginning in the tenth century.

In Viking times the use of runes was common, and the Norse of the period left traces of their runic writing in most places where they traveled. Spelling was not standardized and letters were often left out of words. For example, -m- is missing from the word *kubl* (= *kumbl*) and -n- from *kunukR* (= *konungr*) in King Gorm's stone pictured above and translated in the Reading selection below. Rune carvers sounded out words and missing letters such as the -m- in *kumbl* were sometimes barely pronounced and easily dropped. Words were abbreviated, punctuation erratic, and word divisions often missing. Modern runologists sometimes are at odds on how to translate a passage.

Runes were carved by members of all social classes, but runestones were especially raised or paid for by property owners. Many runestones honor the dead, and they often indicate the wealth and authority of those who erected the monuments. Inscriptions proclaim family relationships, inheritance rights, authority, and property claims. Runestones, such as those at Jelling, announce the claims of aristocrats and royalty. Runes were sometimes written in poetic meter (see the runic verses in *Viking Language 2: The Old Norse Reader.*)

3.2 READING – THE SMALL RUNESTONE AT JELLING, DENMARK

RUNES	*TRANSLITERATION*
(*front*) ᛁ ᚠᚢᚱᛘᛦ ᛁ ᚠᚢᚾᚢᚴᛦ ᛁ	(*front*) : kurmR : kunukR :
ᛁᚴᛆᚱᚦᛁᛁᚠᚢᛒᛚᛁᚦᚢᛋᛁᛁ	: karþi : kubl : þusi :
ᛁᛆᚠᛏᛁᚦᚢᚱᚢᛁᛁᚠᚢᚾᚢ	: aft : þurui : kunu
(*back*) ᛁᛋᛁᚾᛆᛁᛏᛆᚾᛘᛆᚱᚴᛆᛦᛁᛒᚢᛏ	(*back*) : sina : tanmarkaR : but

STANDARDIZED OLD NORSE	*TRANSLATION*
Gormr konungr gerði kumbl þessi ept Þurvi (Þyri) konu sína, Danmarkar bót.	King Gorm made these monuments in memory of Thyri, his wife, Denmark's adornment.

VOCABULARY

bót <*acc* bót, *pl* bœtr> *f* cure, remedy; adornment

Danmörk <*gen* Danmarkar> *f* Denmark

❖**eptir** (*also* **ept**) *prep* [*w acc*] after (*in time*); in memory of; [*w dat*] after, along

❖**gera** (*also* **gøra**) <-ði, -ðr~gerr> *vb* make;

do, act

gerði *3sg past of* **gera**

Gormr <-s> *m* Gorm (*personal name*); first king of the Jelling dynasty in Denmark

❖**kona** <*acc* konu, *gen pl* kvenna> *f* wife; woman

❖**konungr** <-s, -ar> *m* king

kumbl <*pl* kumbl> *n* burial monument, mound or cairn (frequently used on Danish and Swedish rune stones in the

plural)

❖**sinn** <*f acc sg* sína> *refl poss pron* his, her, its own

❖**þessi** <*n acc pl* þessi> *dem pron* this, these

Þurvi *f* Thurvi (*personal name corresponding to Old Icelandic* **Þyri**)

Þyri <*acc* Þyri> *f* Thyri (*personal name*)

3.3 CULTURE – THE ELDER AND YOUNGER RUNIC ALPHABETS

The futhark had several regional variations, and after its appearance in the first centuries A.D., it changed over time. Different Germanic peoples, including Goths, Anglo-Saxons, Frisians, and early Scandinavians, used somewhat different runic alphabets. Until into the eighth-century, the basic runic alphabet consisted of 24 letters and is known as the elder futhark. We know the full elder futhark from carvings on the Gotlandic Kylver runestone from ca. 400 A.D. and the Vadstena bracteate from ca. 600. The elder futhark divides into three groups or families called *ættir*, as below:

The Elder Futhark (24 Letters)

ᚠᚢᚦᚨᚱᚲᚷᚹ　ᚺᚾᛁᛃᛈᛇᛉᛊ　ᛏᛒᛖᛗᛚᛜᛟᛞ

f u þ a r k g w　h n i j E p R s　t b e m l ng o d

Roughly 260 of the approximately 350 known elder futhark inscriptions are found in Scandinavia. The remainder are from continental Europe, with some from as far east as the Black Sea. Surviving inscriptions in the elder futhark are usually short and appear on artifacts such as jewelry, tools, and weapons. Typically they are found in graves and bogs and on materials that have the best chance of preservation, such as bone and metal. Presumably, there were longer inscriptions on wood, leather, and other organic materials, which have been lost. The 65 or so early inscriptions found on runestones appear late in the elder futhark period and only in Scandinavia.

The Younger Futhark (16 Letters)

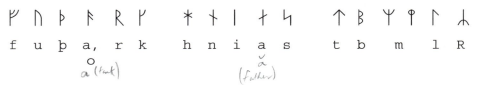

f u þ a, r k　h n i a s　t b m l R

Around the start of the Viking Age, the futhark was shortened to 16 letters. This shortened runic alphabet is known as the younger futhark and is the futhark taught in this book. The

Gørlev runestone from Sjælland in Denmark preserves the earliest complete example of the younger futhark. It dates from ca. 900.

The runic letters of the younger futhark are simpler than those of the elder futhark. Each letter of the Viking Age futhark has only one vertical mark or 'stave' and can be carved easily and quickly. The individual runes of the younger futhark are called 'long-branch runes,' because they are carved with full or long strokes. With local variations and differences among carvers, the younger futhark, with its sixteen long branch runes, was the common form of writing throughout the Viking Age. Like the elder futhark, the younger futhark is divided into three *ættir,* but the 'families' are shorter in the younger futhark.

Inscriptions in the younger futhark have been found in many overseas regions of Norse activity. For example, they existed in the north of Greenland, where an inscription from the fourteenth century has been found. A runic inscription has been found in Iceland from around the year 900. Carved on a stone spindle whorl, the runes name a woman called Vilbjörg as the owner. Writing runes is also mentioned repeatedly in the sagas. Inscriptions have also been found in southern regions as far away as Greece. Especially in the tenth and eleventh centuries, the Byzantine Empire was a frequent destination for Norse traders and warriors.

Short-twig runes are a variant of the younger futhark. They are usually found in Sweden and Norway.

Short-twig Runes

Short-twig runes were easier to carve than long-branch runes, and they were often used as a cursive script among traders. Some inscriptions mix the two systems, such as those found on the Isle of Man, where Viking Age settlers came from different regions of Scandinavia.

Notes on Runes:

- As letters in an alphabet, individual runes reflect sounds. The following discussion of these sounds relies on the International Phonetic Alphabet which provides a uniform system of letters and symbols for writing speech sounds.
- One quickly noticeable feature of the futhark is that there are two *r*-runes. In the elder futhark, R represents the sound /r/, while ⅄ represents the sound /z/. In West Scandinavia (Norway and Iceland), the two sounds merged in the early Viking Age into a trilled *r*, while in East Scandinavia (Denmark and Sweden), the two sounds remained different until the end of the Viking Age. Nevertheless rune carvers in the late Viking Age sometimes used the two runes interchangeably. The modern convention is to transliterate the R rune as lower case *r* and the ⅄ rune as upper

case ***R***.

- There are also two runes for variants of the sound *-a-*: ᛅ and ᚬ. The ᛅ rune represents /a/ as in modern English 'father,' while ᚬ is nasalized as the /a/ in 'tank.'
- The younger futhark did not distinguish between a number of vowel and consonant sounds in use during the Viking Age. For example, the runes ᛁ, ᛅ, and ᚢ are letters for the vowels /i/, /a/, and /u/, but there are no specific runes for the common sounds /e/ and /o/ (although ᚬ later came to be used for /o/). Similarly there are letters for the consonants /b/, /t/ and /k/, but not for /p/, /d/and /g/. It is not certain whether rune carvers saw the lack of separate letters as much of a problem. As explained below, they often employed one letter for several similar sounds, a solution which simplified spelling but not reading.
- The runes ᚾ and ᛙ (/n/ and /m/) were often dropped before certain consonants. Hence on the runestone at Jelling, the word *konungr* is spelled ᚴᚢᚾᚢᚴᛦ (*kunukR*), dropping the second /n/.
- The long-branch *m*-rune is carved in two variants: ᛘ and ᛙ.

3.4 Runic Letters Which Spell More Than One Sound

Figure 17. Runic and Latin Equivalents.

RUNE	LATIN LETTER EQUIVALENTS
ᛒ	b / p
ᛏ	d / t
ᚴ	g / k
ᚠ	v / f
ᚦ	ð / þ
ᛁ	i / e/ æ/ j
ᚢ	u / o / y/ ø/ w
ᛅ	a / æ
ᚬ	a / o/ ö

The reduction in the number of characters from 24 letters of the elder futhark to 16 of the younger resulted in a single letter representing several similar sounds. For example, in the younger futhark the runic symbol ᛒ represents both sounds /b/ and /p/, and ᛏ represents /d/ and /t/.

In the same way, a single rune could represent several distinct vowel sounds with some overlap. For instance, the rune ᚢ represented the vowels /u/, /o/, /y/, /ø/, and /w/. The two *a*-runes show considerable overlap with ᚬ and ᛅ representing the sounds /a/, /æ/, /o/ and /ö/.

3.5 Runic Spelling Variations and Standardized Old Norse

Spelling often varies among runic inscriptions because of differences in pronunciation, regional dialects, and the lack of a recognized spelling standard. For example, *gerði*, the past tense of *gera*, is spelled ᚴᛅᚱᚦᛁ (*karþi/gærði*) on the Jelling stone in this lesson and ᚴᛁᛅᚱᚦᛁ (*kiarþi/gjærði*) in the Swedish Ramsund inscription given in a later lesson.

Similar spelling variations exist in manuscripts. For example, the verb *gera* 'do, make' is spelled *gøra*, *göra*, *görva*, *görwa*, *giörva*, *giora*, and *gjöra* in different manuscripts. To overcome the problem of variation, scholars adopted a standardized Old Norse spelling, which is often used in saga editions, dictionaries, and transcriptions of runic inscriptions. Standardized Old Norse is based principally on Old Icelandic, the most conservative of the dialects and the one that we know most about because Iceland has the largest number of written sources.

Later Runic Variations Toward the end of the Viking Age additional variants of the younger futhark were developed. For example, in the eleventh century, dotted runes appeared, adding sounds such as /e/, /g/, and /y/.

ᛂ	ᚵ	ᚤ
e	g	y

In the mid-eleventh century toward the end of the Viking Age, an expanded medieval futhark came into use in Norway and a few other areas. Sometimes called 'futhork,' it incorporated short-twig runes. This alphabet, like other revised, later runic alphabets, continued in active use for several centuries after the Viking Age.

Following the conversion to Christianity, runic writing was increasingly influenced by medieval Latin. In some instances, runes were used to carve Latin inscriptions. One such inscription is found on a leather shoe from Bergen dating to the end of the twelfth century. It bears a variation of the phrase known from Virgil, *Amor vincit omnia* (Love conquers all). Runes with varying alterations remained in usage until early modern times especially in rural parts of Scandinavia.

3.6 Exercise – Runic Script

Follow the pattern below for changing or transliterating runes into standardized Old Norse.

Runic Script	*Transliteration*	*Standardized Old Norse*
Ex: ᛏᛅᚾᛘᛅᚱᚴᛅᛦ	tanmarkaʀ	Danmarkar
1. ᚴᚢᚱᛘᛦ	______	______
2. ᚦᚢᚱᚢᛁ	______	______
3. ᛋᛁᚾᛅ	______	______
4. ᛒᚢᛏ	______	______

RUNIC SCRIPT	TRANSLITERATION	STANDARDIZED OLD NORSE
5. ᚼᛈᛏ	_____	_____

Reverse the process above and write the following words in runes.

STANDARDIZED OLD NORSE	TRANSLITERATION	YOUNGER FUTHARK LONG-BRANCH RUNES
6. konungr	kunukR	_____
7. konu	kunu	_____
8. kumbl	kubl	_____
9. þessi	þusi	_____
10. bót	but	_____

3.7 READING – GORM AND THYRI (ÓLÁFS SAGA TRYGGVASONAR IN MESTA)

King Gorm and his wife Thyri are also know from Icelandic writings. *The Greatest Saga of King Olaf Tryggvason* (*Óláfs saga Tryggvasonar in mesta*) contains the reading passage below. Both the thirteenth-century Icelandic saga and the tenth-century Danish runestone agree in their reference to Queen Thyri as *Danmarkarbót* (Denmark's Adornment').

Óláfs saga Tryggvasonar in mesta (63. kap)

Gormr, sonr Hörða-Knúts, var mikill maðr ok sterkr. Hann var atgervimaðr. En ekki[5] var hann kallaðr vitr maðr.

Gormr fekk konu, er Þyri hét. Hon var dóttir Haralds jarls af Jótlandi. Hann var kallaðr Klakk-Haraldr. Þyri var fríð kona. Hon var mestr skörungr af konum á Norðrlöndum. Hon hét Þyri Danmarkarbót.

The Greatest Saga of King Olaf Tryggvason (Ch 63)

Gorm, son of Horda-Knut, was a big and strong man. He was an accomplished man. But he was not called a wise man.

Gorm married a woman, who was called Thyri. She was the daughter of Earl Harald of Jutland, who was called Klakk-Harald. Thyri was a beautiful woman. She was the most notable of women in Scandinavia. She was called Thyri, Denmark's Adornment.

VOCABULARY

❖**af** *prep* [*w dat*] of, by; off (of), out of, from

atgervimaðr *m* a man of accomplishments

❖**á** *prep* [*w dat*] on; upon; at; in

❖**dóttir** <*acc, dat, & gen* dóttur, *pl* dœtr, *dat* dœtrum, *gen* dœtra> *f* daughter

❖**ekki** *adv* not

❖**en** *conj* but; (*less frequently*) and

❖**er** *rel particle* who, which, that

❖**fá** <fær, fekk, fengu, fenginn> *vb* get, take, procure; grasp; marry; **fekk konu** got married, *lit*. got a wife

fekk *1/3sg past of* **fá**

❖**fríðr** <*f* fríð, *n* frítt> *adj* beautiful,

---

[5]   **ekki:** OI had two words for 'not': *ekki* and *eigi*. (Modern Icelandic employs *ekki*.)

handsome, fine

❖**hann** <*acc* hann, *dat* honum, *gen* hans> *pron* he

❖**heita** <heitr, hét, hétu, heitinn> *vb* be called, be named

hét *1/3sg past of* **heita**

❖**hon** <*acc* hana, *dat* henni, *gen* hennar> *pron* she

Hörða-Knútr <-s> *m* Horda-Knut (*personal name*)

❖**jarl** <-s, -ar> *m* earl

Jótlandi (*dat*) *n* Jutland

❖**kalla** <-að-> *vb* call

kallaðr *ppart of* **kalla** called

Klakk-Haraldr <-s> *m* Klakk-Harald (*personal name*)

❖**kona** <*gen pl* kvenna> *f* wife; woman

❖**maðr** <*acc* mann *dat* manni, *gen* manns, *nom & acc pl* menn, *dat* mönnum,

gen manna> *m* man; person, human being

mestr *superl adj* greatest

❖**mikill** <*f* mikil, *n* mikit, *comp* meiri, *superl* mestr> *adj* big, tall, great; much

Norðrlönd <*dat* Norðrlöndum> *n pl* the Northern countries or region, Scandinavia

❖**ok** *conj* and

skörungr <-s, -ar> *m* a notable man or woman, leader

❖**sonr** <*dat* syni, *gen* sonar, *pl* synir, *acc* sonu> *m* son

❖**sterkr** *adj* strong

var *1/3sg past of* **vera**

❖**vera** <er; var, váru; verit> *vb* be

❖**vitr** <*acc* vitran> *adj* wise

3.8 CULTURE – GORM THE OLD AND THE DANISH JELLING DYNASTY

Danish history begins in the fifth or sixth century with the legendary Skjöldung Dynasty. This famous family had its royal seat at Hleiðr, modern-day Lejre, on the Danish island of Sjælland (in Old Norse, Sjáland). The Skjöldungs figure prominently in the Icelandic *Hrólfs saga kraka* and the Old English *Beowulf*. Both epics are set in Denmark during the Migration Period, and many of the same people appear in both stories.

Although Frankish writings hint at events in Denmark and mention Danish kings such as Godfred, who opposed Charlemagne and the Frankish Empire, there are relatively few historical sources for Danish history until about 930. At that time a new family of overlords emerges in Demanrk in central Jutland (Jótland) with a power base at Jelling (Jalangrsheiðr). Members of the Jelling dynasty immortalized themselves through ambitious building programs and monuments. These latter include the runestones read in this and the next lesson.

The founder of the Jelling dynasty, King Gorm the Old, was the last pagan king of Denmark. King Gorm's runestone, mentioning his wife Thurvi or Þyri, is the first native documentary source to use the term 'Denmark.' During Gorm's lifetime, Hedeby (Heiðabýr/Heiðarbýr or Heiðarbær, 'town' or 'dwelling' [*bær*] on the heath [*heiðr*]), became a major Viking trading center for goods moving between the Baltic region and Western Europe. Merchants arrived in Hedeby transporting exotic wares and large quantities of silver coinage. Some of the trade goods had come up the great rivers of Russia from places as far away as the territory of the Volga Bulgars, the Khaganate of the Khazars, regions of Central Asia, the Greek Byzantine Empire, and the Caliphate of Baghdad. Once in Hedeby, trade goods from the Baltic and further east were transported on roads across southern Jutland. This valuable traffic was protected by the Danevirke (Old Norse, Danavirki, the fortified 'wall of the Danes') before arriving at the Danish port town of Ribe (Ripar) on the North Sea. There the freight was again loaded onto ships for distribution to Frisia, Britain, and Western Europe. This overland route from Hedeby on the Baltic to Ribe on the North Sea avoided sailing north of Jutland through the Eyrarsund and the Jótlandshaf ('The Jutland Sea') waters where Vikings lay in wait.

Figure 18. Viking Age Denmark (Danmörk) included parts of what is today southern Sweden. Although the smallest of the Scandinavian countries, Denmark had the highest percentage of arable land and was the wealthiest and most densely populated of the Viking states. Exposed to attacks from the Frankish Empire to the south, Vikings to the north, and Slavic pirates on the Baltic (*Eystrasalt*), Denmark developed early into a cohesive monarchy capable of resisting foreign threats.

About the year 930, Gorm's kingdom probably included all of northern and central Jutland. The southern part of the Jutland peninsula, including Hedeby, seems to have come under his power a few years later, giving him control of the valuable trade route protected by the Danavirki. Gorm's authority to the east of Jutland is more difficult to determine. It probably extended at times to the islands of Fyn (Fjón) and Sjælland (Sjáland), areas which outsiders, such as the Franks and peoples of England, considered Danish. At times Gorm's power may have also extended across the straits to Skåne (Skáney), Halland, and Blekinge

(Bleking), which today are in Sweden.

Gorm sired a long-lived line of powerful Viking Age kings. His son, Harald Bluetooth (Haraldr blátönn, ca. 958–987) solidified the authority of the dynasty and expanded the Danish kingdom. Harald christianized the Danes and probably built the Viking Age ring fortresses in Denmark. His son Svein (Sweyn) Forkbeard (Sveinn tjúguskegg, 987–1014) revolted against Harald, and Svein may have killed his father.

Soon after ascending the throne, Svein began a series of Viking raids against England. In the years 1013 and 1014 the raids turned into a full scale invasion, and Svein succeeded in conquering England. In 1014, Svein was recognized as king of England, only to die five weeks later. Svein was succeeded by his son, Knut. Known as Canute the Great (Knútr inn ríki), he became the king of England in 1016. A few years later, after the death of his brother in Denmark, Canute also became king of Denmark.

Canute the Great died in 1035, and Danish control of England ended with the early deaths of Canute's sons. The Danish claim to English kingship resurfaced in 1066. At that time, Harald Hardradi (Harðraði, 'Hard Counsel') of Norway asserted that, because he had a claim to the throne of Denmark, he was holder of the Danish claim to England. Harald Hardradi's defeat in 1066 at Stamford Bridge outside of York ended his claim.

Many written sources about the medieval history of Denmark as well as extensive archaeological evidence have survived. The written sources include the Old English poem *Beowulf*, Alcuin's biography of St. Willibrord (the 'Apostle of the Frisians'), Rimbert's *Life of St. Ansgar*, the *Anglo-Saxon Chronicle*, the *Annales Regni Francorum* (*The Royal Frankish Annals*), the *Orosius* of Alfred the Great, the eleventh century *Gesta Hammaburgensis Ecclesiae Pontificum* (*History of the Archbishops of Bremen*) by Adam of Bremen, the *Gesta Danorum* (*History of the Danes*) by Saxo Grammaticus (ca. 1200), the thirteenth- or fourteenth-century Icelandic *Knýtlinga saga* (*The Saga of Canute's Descendants*), scraps of *Skjöldunga saga* (*The Saga of the Skjoldungs*) and *Hrólfs saga kraka* (*The Saga of King Hrolf Kraki*). So also there are numerous runic inscriptions.

3.9 PERSONAL PRONOUNS – 1ST AND 2ND PERSONS

Leaving runes aside and returning to Old Norse Grammar. The 1st and 2nd person pronouns ('I' and 'you') have singular, plural (more than two), and dual (only two) forms. They show many parallels with English (*mín* 'mine,' *þú* 'thou,' *þín* 'thine,' *oss* 'us'). The distinction between possessive pronouns and 1st and 2nd person pronouns in the genitive is explained later.

	1ST		*2ND*	
Sg *nom*	ek	I	þú	you
acc	mik	me	þik	you
dat	mér	me	þér	you
gen	mín	my	þín	your

		1ST		2ND				1ST		2ND	
Pl	*nom*	vér	we	þér	you	**Dual**	vit	we	þit	you
	acc	oss	us	yðr	you		okkr	us	ykkr	you
	dat	oss	us	yðr	you		okkr	us	ykkr	you
	gen	vár	our	yðar	your		okkar	our	ykkar	your

Old Norse has two ways to say 'we' (*vér* and *vit*) and likewise two ways to say 'you' plural (*þér* and *þit*). One is plural and the other is dual. The dual pronouns *vit* and *þit* refer to only two people, while the plural pronouns *vér* and *þér* refer to three or more. The 2nd person plural (*þér*) and dual pronouns (*þit*) also have older forms *ér* and *it*. The 2nd person plural possessive pronoun *yðar* also has an older form, *yðvar*.

Vér förum heim.	**We** [more than two] are going home.
Vit förum heim.	**We** [the two of us] are going home.
Þér gerðuð þessi kumbl.	**You** [more than two] made these monuments.
Þit gerðuð þessi kumbl.	**You** [the two of you] made these monuments.

Speakers could be more specific with pronouns by adding a name. For instance, *vit Þorsteinn'* means 'we, Þorsteinn and I.'

3.10 EXERCISE – PERSONAL PRONOUNS – 1ST AND 2ND PERSONS
Fill in the correct personal pronoun in each of the following sentences.

Ex: *Vér*_____ (we) höfum bók.   We have a book.
1. _____ (I) geri kumbl.   I make a monument.
2. Þú spyrr _____ (me).   You ask me.
3. _____ (you, *sg*) kallar.   You call.
4. Ek gaf _____ (you, *sg*) land.   I gave you land.
5. _____ (we, the two of us) höfum land. We have land.
6. _____ (I) fór heim.   I went home.
7. _____ (you, *pl*) gerið kumbl.   You are making monuments.

3.11 PERSONAL PRONOUNS – 3RD PERSON

The 3rd person pronouns (*he*, *she*, *it*, *they*) decline in the following way.

		M		**F**		**N**	
Sg	*nom*	hann	he/it	hon	she/it	þat	it
	acc	hann	him/it	hana	her/it	þat	it
	dat	honum	him/it	henni	her/it	því	it

gen	hans	his/its	hennar	her(s)/its	þess	its

	M		F		N	
Pl nom	þeir	they	þær	they	þau	they
acc	þá	them	þær	them	þau	them
dat	þeim	them	þeim	them	þeim	them
gen	þeira	their(s)	þeira	their(s)	þeira	their(s)

Because gender in Old Norse is largely arbitrary, many words considered neuter in English have masculine or feminine gender in Old Norse, for example *fjörðr* (*m*) 'fjord' and *bók* (*f*) 'book.' When pronuons refer to such masculine and feminine nouns, the pronouns *hann* and *hon* are employed and translated as 'it.' For example, *Herjólfsfjörðr er á Grœnlandi* becomes **Hann** *er á Grœnlandi* '**It** is in Greenland.'

Old Norse distinguishes gender in the plural: *þeir* (*m*), *þær* (*f*), and *þau* (*n*). When referring to a mixed group of males and females, the neuter form *þau* is used, as in the following example from *Völsunga saga*:

Rerir fekk sér konu ok eru **þau**   Rerir got himself a wife, and **they** were
mjök lengi ásamt.   together (*ásamt*) a very (*mjök*) long [time].

A plural pronoun followed by one or more names can have more than one meaning. For example, *þeir Þórólfr ok Björn* could mean 'Thorolf and Bjorn,' or it could signify 'Thorolf and Bjorn and their companions or followers.' One relies on the context in the sentence to decide which of the two meanings fits best.

3.12 EXERCISE – PERSONAL PRONOUNS – 3rd Person

A.   Identify the personal pronouns below. State the gender, case, and number of each and translate.

Ex: henni   *henni : f dat sg*   *her*

1. hann   _____   _____

2. hennar   _____   _____

3. þat   _____   _____

4. þær   _____   _____

5. þeim   _____   _____

B.   Fill in the correct missing pronoun below and translate.

Ex: *hann*   (*m nom sg*)   *he* _____

1. _____ (*m dat sg*)   _____

2.	_____ (*fem gen sg*)	_____
3.	_____ (*m gen pl*)	_____
4.	_____ (*n dat sg*)	_____
5.	_____ (*f nom pl*)	_____
6.	_____ (*f dat sg*)	_____

3.13 NOUNS – STRONG AND WEAK

All nouns in Old Norse fall into one of two broad declension types: *strong* or *weak*. Weak nouns have a simpler set of endings than strong nouns. A particular noun's declension type never changes. For example, the noun *konungr* is always strong while *goði* (chieftain) is always weak. Likewise the proper noun *Herjólfr* is strong and *Bjarni* is weak.

In the nominative, most strong masculine nouns end in *-r*, and many weak masculine nouns end in *-i*. Many weak feminine nouns end in *-a*, and many weak neuter nouns end in *-t* or *-d*. This simple guideline works in many instances but there are numerous exceptions.

Below are examples of the most important types of strong and weak nouns. Using these words as models the student will be able to identify the majority of Old Norse nouns.

Most nouns that end in *-a* are feminine and decline like *tunga*. But note, a few weak neuter nouns also end in *-a*. The most common of these are the body parts *auga* 'eye,' *eyra* 'ear,' *hjarta* 'heart,' *lunga* 'lung,' *ökkla* 'ankle,' and *nýra* 'kidney.' All decline like *auga*.

STRONG	M KONUNGR	F RÚN	N KUMBL	WEAK	M GOÐI	F TUNGA	N AUGA
Sg *nom*	konungr	rún	kumbl	**Sg** *nom*	goði	tunga	auga
acc	konung	rún	kumbl	*acc*	goða	tungu	auga
dat	konungi	rún	kumbli	*dat*	goða	tungu	auga
gen	konungs	rúnar	kumbls	*gen*	goða	tungu	auga
Pl *nom*	konungar	rúnar	kumbl	**Pl** *nom*	goðar	tungur	augu
acc	konunga	rúnar	kumbl	*acc*	goða	tungur	augu
dat	konungum	rúnum	kumblum	*dat*	goðum	tungum	augum
gen	konunga	rúna	kumbla	*gen*	goða	tungna	augna

Transl: *konungr* 'king,' *rún* 'rune,' *kumbl* 'monument,' *goði* 'chieftain,' *tunga* 'tongue,' *auga* 'eye'

3.14 THE VERB *VERA* 'TO BE' – PRESENT AND PAST

Vera, one of the most frequently used verbs, is, as in English, irregular.

	PRESENT TENSE						
Sg *1st*	ek	**em**	(*I am*)	**Pl**	vér (vit)	**erum**	(*we are*)
2nd	þú	**ert**	(*you are*)		þér (þit)	**eruð**	(*you are*)
3rd	hann	**er**	(*he, she, it is*)		þeir	**eru**	(*they are*)

PAST TENSE

Sg 1st	ek	**var**	(*I was*)	**Pl**	vér (vit)	**várum**	(*we were*)
2nd	þú	**vart**	(*you were*)		þér (þit)	**váruð**	(*you were*)
3rd	hann hon þat	**var**	(*he, she, it was*)		þeir þær þau	**váru**	(*they were*)

Poems and runestones often employ archaic forms of *vera*, with *-s-* instead of *-r-* (*es* 'is' for *er*, *vas* 'was' for *var*).

3.15 EXERCISE – THE VERB *VERA*

A.   Fill in the spaces next to the pronouns with the appropriate verb forms from the list below and translate.

em   var   váruð   ert   várum   eru   vart   er   váru   eruð   var   erum

PRESENT TENSE

Ex: vér *erum; we are*

1. þú _____
2. ek _____
3. þér_____
4. hon _____
5. þær _____

PAST TENSE

Ex: þau *váru; they were*

6. vér _____
7. þú _____
8. þér _____
9. ek _____
10. þat _____

B.   Fill in the spaces below with the correct form of *vera* 'to be' and translate.

PRESENT TENSE

Ex: Þau *eru* frá Íslandi.   *They are from Iceland*

1.   Sigríðr _____ kona.   _____

2.   Þeir _____ konungar.   _____

3.   Vér _____ frá Grœnlandi.   _____

4.   Hann _____ góðr maðr.   _____

5.   Þit _____ frá Nóregi.   _____

6.   Ek _____ konungr.   _____

PAST TENSE

Ex: Þau *váru* frá Íslandi.   *They were from Iceland*

7.   Sigríðr _____ kona.   _____

8.   Þau _____ frá Norðrlöndum.   _____

9.   Hon _____ Danmarkar bót.   _____

10.   Hann _____ góðr maðr.   _____

11.   Þér _____ frá Nóregi.   _____

12.   Ek _____ konungr.   _____

3.16 CULTURE – *SON* AND *DÓTTIR* IN NAMES

Scandinavians during the Viking period and Icelanders today have patronyms, a Greek word meaning a name received from the father rather than a family last name. Eirik Thorvaldsson (the Red) is a good example of the way people were named. According to Icelandic written tradition, he was born in Rogaland, Norway, the son of Thorvald Asvaldsson. Hence Eirik carried the patronym Thorvaldsson (*Eiríkr Þorvaldsson*). His nickname, 'the Red' (*inn rauði*), probably refers to the red color of his hair.

Patronyms are formed according to the rules of ON grammar. Þorvaldr, the name of Eirik's father, is a proper noun. It ends in *-r*, is in the nominative case. Note the double *-ss-* in *Þorvaldsson*. The first *-s-* (Þorvalds-) is the genitive marker, the second *-s-* starts the word *son*. In English the name would be *Thorvald's son*. Some names, such as *Bárðr*, have a genitive in *-ar*, hence *Bárðarson*. Other names such as *Atli* have a genitive in *-a*, hence *Atlason*.

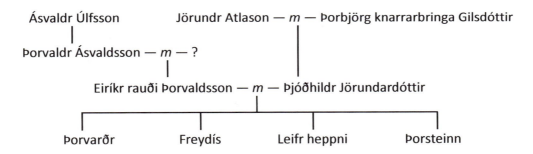

Figure 19. The Family Tree of Eirik the Red (Eirikr rauði). *'m'* = 'married'

On occasion, men were known by their mother's name, especially if they were raised without a father. For example, the *Hildiríðarsynir* ('sons of Hildiríðr') in *Egil's Saga* were named after their mother *Hildiríðr*. Men could also be known by their mother's name if she was viewed as more prominent or capable than the father. For example, the *Droplaugarsynir* in *Droplaugarsona saga* took their name from their mother *Droplaug*.

Women were also known by their father's name to which they added *dóttir*, hence *Freydís Eiríksdóttir*. Women did not change their names when they married, which followed from the lack of family surnames. For example, when *Þjóðhildr Jörundardóttir* married *Eiríkr inn rauði Þorvaldsson*, she continued to be *Þjóðhildr Jörundardóttir*. She and her husband had two different last names, just as did her parents *Jörundr Atlason* and *Þorbjörg*

Gilsdóttir. When *Þjóðhildr* and *Eiríkr* had a son named *Leifr*, he was called *Leifr Eiríksson* and his sister *Freydís* was called *Freydís Eiríksdóttir*.

People were known not only by their first names and patronyms (father's name) but also by nicknames. Hence *Leifr Eiríksson* was known as *inn heppni* ('the lucky') or *Leifr inn heppni Eiríksson* (often the *inn* is dropped), while his maternal grandmother was called *Þorbjörg knarrarbringa* ('boat-breasted'). *The Saga of Thorstein the White* (*Þorsteins saga hvíta*, Ch 8) offers insight into how nicknames were viewed. Discussing the young man *Brodd-Helgi* and his nickname *Brodd*, 'Spike', the saga explains that when *Brodd-Helgi* was alive in the tenth century, 'people thought that it was much more auspicious to have two names. It was a common belief then that people who had two names lived longer.'

3.17 EXERCISE – *SON* AND *DÓTTIR*.

Genealogies are a crucial aspect of Old Icelandic texts. They date events and providing a means for people to understand their relationships to others within the small society. In contrast to the modern nuclear family, medieval families were large, extended groups. Icelanders were keenly aware of genealogical and marital relationships. Saga narratives often cannot be fully understood unless the reader is able to work out the relevant family connections.

Review the information about family trees and Icelandic names in this and the previous chapter and fill in the information below. Create your family tree in the Old Norse style! Give both first and last names for each individual and remember that each person is someone's *son* or *dóttir*. If you are uncertain about the name of an ancestor, invent a name.

Ex: John has two siblings, Pete and Kate. Their parents are Phil and Jennifer. Phil's parents are Mike and Helen, while Jennifer's parents are Jack and Ann. In Icelandic terms, John would be known as John Philsson, Pete as Pete Philsson, Kate as Kate Philsdóttir, Phil as Phil Mikesson, and Jennifer as Jennifer Jacksdóttir.

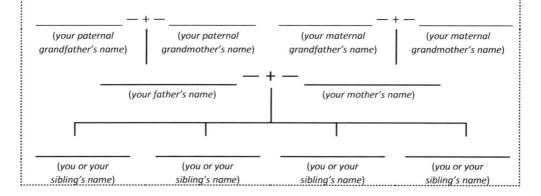

3.18 VOCABULARY – LIST 3. THE MOST FREQUENT WORDS IN THE SAGAS

NOUNS	ADJECTIVES	PRONOUNS	NUMERALS
fé – wealth, livestock	**fár** – few	**sinn** – his/her/their (own)	**þrír** – three
bróðir – brother	**dauðr** – dead		
M **vetr** – winter	**stórr** – big		
land – land			

VERBS	PREPOSITIONS AND ADVERBS	CONJUNCTIONS
mæla – to speak	**nú** – now	**er** – who, which, that; when; where
vilja – to want	**við** – with; against	
taka – to take	**með** – with	
skulu – shall	**svá** – so; such	

EXERCISES

3.19 Timetable of Early Danish History. Put the following important events from the Early History of the Danish Kingdom in the correct chronological sequence.

_1___ First construction of the Danevirke and Hedeby.
_____ The Icelandic saga *Hrólfs saga kraka* is written.
_____ King Godfred opposes Charlemagne's northerly expansion.
_____ Harald Bluetooth builds the great ring fortresses of Denmark.
_____ King Gorm the Old reigns at Jelling as the last pagan king of Denmark.

3.20 Personal Pronouns. Decline the 3rd person pronouns in the singular and plural. Remember, 3rd person pronouns have three genders: masculine, feminine and neuter — *hann, hon, þat* 'he, she, it' — and are the most common pronouns in Old Norse.

	M	F	N
Sg *nom*	hann	hon	þat
acc			
dat			
gen			
Pl *nom*	þeir	þær	þau
acc			
dat			
gen			

3.21 Verb Conjugation: Present Tense of *Vera*. Fill in the correct form of *vera* 'to be' in the present tense and translate the sentences.

1. Ek _____ konungr.

    _____

2. Vit _____ konungar.

    _____

3. Þú _____ sterkr.

    _____

4. Þér _____ í Brattahlíð.

    _____

5. Hann _____
    landnámsmaðr.

    _____

6. Þeir _____
    landnámsmenn.

    _____

3.22 Strong and Weak Nouns. On the model of strong and weak nouns presented in this lesson, decline the following six nouns: *haugr, nál, mál, tími, tunga,* and *eyra*.

STRONG	HAUGR *(M)*	NÁL *(F)*	MÁL *(N)*
Sg *nom*	_____	_____	_____
acc	_____	_____	_____
dat	_____	_____	_____
gen	_____	_____	_____
Pl *nom*	_____	_____	_____
acc	_____	_____	_____
dat	_____	_____	_____
gen	_____	_____	_____

Transl: *haugr* 'mound,' *nál* 'needle,' *mál* 'speech'

WEAK	TÍMI *(M)*	VIKA *(F)*	EYRA *(N)*
Sg *nom*	_____	_____	_____
acc	_____	_____	_____
dat	_____	_____	_____
gen	_____	_____	_____
Pl *nom*	_____	_____	_____
acc	_____	_____	_____
dat	_____	_____	_____
gen	_____	_____	_____

Transl: *tími* 'time,' *vika* 'week,' and *eyra* 'ear'

3.23 Review: Gender and Meaning of Nouns. Complete the chart below.

	NOUN	GENDER	ENGLISH MEANING
Ex:	maðr	*masculine*	*man, person*
1	_____	_____	woman

2.	skörungr	_____	_____
3	_____	_____	daughter
4.	atgervimaðr	_____	_____
5.	land	_____	_____
6	_____	_____	earl
7.	konungr	_____	_____
8.	kumbl	_____	_____
9	_____	_____	son
10.	bót	_____	_____

3.24 Verbs. Complete the chart below by giving the English translation and the infinitive of the verb.

VERB (PAST TENSE)	ENGLISH MEANING	INFINITIVE
Ex: vildi	_wished_	_vilja_
1. hét	_____	_____
2. gerði	_____	_____
3. var	_____	_____
4. nam	_____	_____
5. fekk (konu)	_____	_____

3.25 Linking Verbs. As discussed earlier, a noun connected to the subject by a linking verb is called a predicate noun, and an adjective, a predicate adjective. In Old Norse, predicate nouns and adjectives are in the same case as the subject, that is, the nominative case. In the passages below, circle the linking verbs, underline the predicate nouns and adjectives, and translate. Use the Vocabulary as needed.

1.   Herjólfr hét maðr Bárðarson Herjólfssonar; hann fór til Grœnlands með Eiríki. Herjólfr nam Herjólfsfjörð ok bjó á Herjólfsnesi. Eiríkr nam Eiríksfjörð ok bjó í Brattahlíð, en Leifr sonr hans eptir hann.

_____
_____
_____
_____

2.   Gormr konungr gerði kumbl þessi ept (eptir) Þyri konu sína, Danmarkar bót.

_____
_____
_____

3.   Gormr, sonr Hörða-Knúts, var mikill maðr ok sterkr. Hann var atgervimaðr. En ekki var hann kallaðr vitr maðr.

_____

4. Gormr fekk konu, er Þyri hét. Hon var dóttir Haralds jarls af Jótlandi. Hann var kallaðr Klakk-Haraldr. Þyri var fríð kona. Hon var mestr skörungr af konum á Norðrlöndum. Hon hét Þyri Danmarkarbót.

_____

_____

_____

_____

3.26 Word Frequency. Using _List 3. The Most Frequent Words_ given in this lesson, write the second group of the most frequently used words from the different grammatical categories and translate.

OLD NORSE	ENGLISH	OLD NORSE	ENGLISH
NOUNS		**ADJECTIVES**	
1 _____ _____		4 _____ _____	
2 _____ _____		5 _____ _____	
3 _____ _____		6 _____ _____	
VERBS		**PREPOSITIONS AND ADVERBS**	
7 _____ _____		11 _____ _____	
8 _____ _____		12 _____ _____	
9 _____ _____		13 _____ _____	
10 _____ _____		14 _____ _____	

LESSON 4
KINGS AND HEROES

Opt kemr sólskin eptir skúr
(Often sunshine comes after a shower)

Figure 20. The Large Jelling Runestone, Denmark, was commissioned by King Harald Bluetooth (*Haraldr blátönn*) Gormsson. Side A is shown here.

4.1 READING – THE LARGE RUNESTONE AT JELLING

Harald Bluetooth (ca. 958-987) centered his power at Jelling in Jutland. He is the first Danish king of the Viking Age who is more historical than legendary, and Harald's reign was a time when the monarchy in Denmark consolidated its power. One of Harald's most enduring legacies was the conversion of the Danes to Christianity around 965. It is unclear whether Harald's own baptism, supposedly by the missionary Poppo, was a political move or an action motivated by religious belief. However, Harald's handling of his parents' memorials, two large burial mounds at Jelling, shows that he adjusted the authority of his dynasty to the new religion.

The Jelling mounds were placed on top of an earlier monument, a huge outline of a ship constructed from large erected stones. One of the mounds contained a chamber grave, while the other was a cenotaph, an empty monument commemorating an event or someone's life or death. Harald's monuments were integrated into the new Christian religious culture by the construction of a church between the mounds and the carving of the large Jelling runestone. This runestone has three sides. Side A is shown above and sides B and C are pictured below. Side C is carved with one of the earliest images of Christ known in Scandinavia. Harald's massive Jelling stone is found near the smaller runestone of Gorm the Old, Harald's father. Parts of the Jelling stone, particularly on Side C, are weathered.

RUNES

Side A

᛬ᚼᛆᚱᛆᛚᛏᚱ᛬ᚴᚢᚾᚢᚴᛦ᛬ᛒᛆᚦ᛬ᚠᛆᚢᚱᚢᛆ

ᚴᚢᛒᛚ᛬ᚦᛆᚢᛋᛁᚠᛏ᛬ᚴᚢᚱᚠᚠᛆᚦᚢᚱᛋᛁᚾ

ᛆᚢᚴᛆᚠᛏ᛬ᚦᛆᚢᚱᚢᛁ᛬ᚠᚢᚦᚢᚱ᛬ᛋᛁᚾᛆ᛬ᛋᛆ

ᚼᛆᚱᛆᛏᚱᛁᛆᛋ᛬ᛋᚾᛦᛆ᛬ᚢᛆᚾ᛬ᛏᛆᚾᛘᛆᚢᚱᚴ᛬

Side B

ᛆᛚᛆ᛬ᛆᚢᚴ᛬ᚾᚢᚱᚢᛁᛆᚴ

Side C

ᛆᚢᚴᛏᛆᚾᛁᚴᛆᚱᚦᛁᚴᚱᛁᛋᛏᚾᛆ

TRANSLITERATION

:haraltr : kunukR : baþ : kaurua

kubl : þausi aft : kurm faþur sin

auk aft : þãurui : muþur : sina : sa

haraltr ias : sãR : uan : tanmaurk

ala : auk : nuruiak

auk tani karþi kristnã

STANDARDIZED OLD NORSE

Haraldr konungr bað gera kumbl þessi[6] ept Gorm föður sinn ok ept Þyri móður sína--sá Haraldr es[7] sér vann Danmörk alla ok Norveg ok Dani gerði kristna.

TRANSLATION

King Harald commanded these monuments to be made in memory of Gorm his father and Thyri his mother--that Harald who won all Denmark for himself and Norway and made the Danes Christian.

VOCABULARY

alla *f acc sg of* **allr**

❖**allr** <*f* öll, *n* allt> *adj pron* all, entire, whole

bað *1/3sg past of* **biðja**

❖**biðja** <biðr, bað, báðu, beðinn> *vb* ask, beg; command, tell; **biðja gera**

command to be made

Dani *acc pl of* **Danir**

Danir *m pl* (the) Danes

❖**eptir** (*also* **ept**) *prep* [*w acc*] after (*in time*); in memory of; [*w dat*] after, along

---

[6] **bað gera kumbl þessi:** 'commanded these monuments to be made.'

[7] **es** = *er*, the relative particle 'who.' The runestone has the spelling ᛁᛏᚼ. However, the initial rune of this word is somewhat obscured and not depicted in the illustration at the beginning of the lesson.

❖**er** (*also* **es**) *rel particle* who, which, that

❖**faðir** <*acc* föður, *dat* föður~feðr, *gen* föður, *pl* feðr, *dat* feðrum, *gen* feðra> *m* father

❖**gera** (*also* **gøra**) <-ði, -ðr~gerr> *vb* make; do, act

gerði *3sg past* of **gera**

kristinn *adj* Christian

kristna *m acc pl of* **kristinn**

kumbl <*pl* kumbl> *n* burial monument, mound or cairn

❖**móðir** <*acc, dat, & gen* móður, *pl* mœðr, *dat* mœðrum, *gen* mœðra> *f* mother

Noregr (*also* **Norvegr** *or* **Nóregr**) <-s> *m* Norway

❖**sá** <*f* sú, *n* þat> *dem pron* that (one)

❖**sik** <*dat* sér, *gen* sín> *refl pron* him-/her-/it-/oneself, themselves

❖**sinn** <*m acc sg* sinn, *f acc sg* sína> *refl poss pron* his, her, its own

vann *1/3sg past of* **vinna**

vinna <vinnr, vann, unnu, unninn> *vb* gain, win; work; perform, accomplish

❖**þessi** <*n acc pl* þessi> *dem pron* this, these

Figure 21. Sides B and C of the Jelling Runestone.

4.2 EXERCISE – READING THE LARGE RUNESTONE AT JELLING

Review the reading above and decide whether the following statements are true (*rétt*) or false (*rangt*).

RÉTT eða RANGT?

1. Haraldr konungr bað gera kumbl þessi eptir föður sinn.   _____
2. Þyri var móðir Haralds.   _____
3. Haraldr var faðir Gorms.   _____
4. Gormr var faðir Haralds.   _____
5. Haraldr vann sér Ísland.   _____

4.3 GRAMMAR TOOLBOX. VOWELS AND CONSONANTS

Vowels and consonants are the phonetic building blocks of word sounds.

VOWELS are sounds made by the free passage of air through the mouth, without closing the mouth or narrowing it to the point where the sound is obstructed. Vowels in Old Icelandic had no glide immediately following as is often the case in English and Modern Icelandic. A glide is a sound that begins with one vowel and changes to another vowel within the same syllable, as (-oi-) in boil or (-i-) in fine).

Consonants are sounds made by narrowing or closing the vocal tract, resulting in an obstruction of the free flow of air. Most Old Icelandic consonants are similar to corresponding sounds in modern English.

4.4 *U*-UMLAUT

Umlaut, also called vowel mutation or vowel shift, is a linguistic term borrowed from German referring to the change in pronunciation that some vowels undergo when followed by certain other vowels. Old Icelandic has two systems of umlaut: *u*-umlaut and *i*-umlaut. This section presents *u*-umlaut; *i*-umlaut comes in a later lesson.

U-umlaut is the change of the vowel -*a*- to -*ö*- (sometimes -*u*-) in specific grammatical contexts. For example, the root vowel -*a*- in the word *saga* (nom sg) becomes -*ö*- in the accusative, dative, and genitive, hence *sögu*. *U*-umlaut has its origins in a pre-Viking Age sound assimilation, in which the vowel -*a*- changed because of a -*u* in a following syllable or ending and became more like the following *u*. In many instances, the change simplified pronunciation.

U-Umlaut in Initial (Stressed) Syllables. In Old Norse, -*a*- in an initial (stressed) syllable changes to -*ö*- when a -*u*- follows in the next syllable (*saga*, pl *sögur*).

NOUNS				VERBS		
	ARMR	**STAÐR**	**SAGA**		**KALLA**	**VAKA**
Sg *nom*	armr	staðr	saga	*1sg*	kalla	vaki
acc	arm	stað	sögu	*2*	kallar	vakir
dat	armi	stað	sögu	*3*	kallar	vakir
gen	arms	staðar	sögu			
Pl *nom*	armar	staðir	sögur	*1pl*	köllum	vökum
acc	arma	staði	sögur	*2*	kallið	vakið
dat	örmum	stöðum	sögum	*3*	kalla	vaka
gen	arma	staða	sagna			

Transl: armr (*m*) 'arm,' *staðr* (*m*) 'place, stead,' *saga* (*f*) 'what is said, story'

U-umlaut can also occur when no vowel at all follows in the next syllable. An example is the nominative plural of strong neuter nouns like *land* (pl *lönd*). In such instances, the *-u* in the ending which originally caused the change was lost. Words like *lönd* are discussed in later lessons.

U-Umlaut in Non-Initial (Unstressed) Syllables. In non-initial syllables (that is, in unstressed second or third syllables) *-a-* shifts to *-u-*. For example, *herjaði* (he raided) becomes *herjuðu* ('they raided'). This change is less frequent. It mostly occurs in the past plural of weak verbs. For example *leita* 'look for' and *elska* 'love':

3sg past	leitaði	'he/she/it searched'	*3pl past*	leit**u**ðu	'they searched'
3sg past	elskaði	'he/she/it loved'	*3pl past*	elsk**u**ðu	'they loved'

Notes on *U*-Umlaut
- *U*-umlaut does not occur if a vowel other than *-u-* follows in the next syllable. For example, *landinu* 'the land (*dat*)' does not show *u*-umlaut because an *-i-* intervenes between *-a-* of the stem and *-u* of the article.
- *U*-umlaut applies to words containing *-a-* in both stressed and unstressed syllables followed by *-u-*. For instance *kallaði* 'he called' and *kölluðu* 'they called.' In this example, the *-u* of the ending shifted the *-a-* of the unstressed syllable to *-u-* (stem *kallað-* became *kalluð-*), in turn triggering the change of *-a-* to *-ö-* in the initial syllable (*kölluðu*).
- In some compound words *a* shifts to *ö* (*viðtaka*, gen *viðtöku*; *atganga*, gen *atgöngu*).
- Some Old Norse grammars and texts use the letter *ǫ* for *ö* (for example, *dǫlum* and *kǫlluðum*). This book always employs *ö*, hence *dölum* and *kölluðum*.

4.5 EXERCISE – *U*-UMLAUT

Decline the nouns *garpr*, *garðr*, and *gata* below. *Garpr* and *garðr* decline like *armr*, and *gata* like *saga*.

GARPR	GARÐR	GATA

Sg			
nom	_____	_____	_____
acc	_____	_____	_____
dat	_____	_____	_____
gen	_____	_____	_____
Pl			
nom	_____	_____	_____
acc	_____	_____	_____
dat	_____	_____	_____
gen	_____	_____	_____

Transl: *garpr* (*m*) 'bold man,' *garðr* (*m*) 'enclosed space,' *gata* (*f*) 'path'

4.6 STRONG AND WEAK VERBS

Verbs in Old Norse are either strong or weak. The difference between strong and weak verbs cannot be determined by the infinitive alone but in how verbs form their past tense.

A strong verb forms its past tense by changing its root vowel. For example, the 3sg past of *taka* is *tók*, *gefa–gaf*, and *vinna–vann*. English strong verbs form their past tense in the same way: *take, give, win* become *took, gave, won*.

Weak verbs form their past tense by adding to the stem a suffix containing *-ð-*, *-d-*, or *-t-*. For example, the 3sg past of *kalla* is *kallaði*, *telja–taldi*, and *mæla–mælti*. Because the tip of the tongue comes into contact with the teeth during pronunciation of *-ð-*, *-d-*, and *-t-*, this suffix is called a dental suffix. English similarly adds a dental suffix in the past tense of weak verbs (*call, count, tell,* and *have* become *called, counted, told,* and *had*).

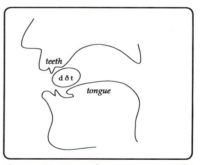

Figure 22. Dental Consonants. Old Norse *d, t,* and *ð* are called dental consonants because these sounds are pronounced where shown in the mouth when the tongue advances to touch the front teeth.

4.7 EXERCISE – STRONG AND WEAK VERBS

Identify the following verbs as weak or strong and translate.

1. nam (*inf* nema)_____
2. kallaði (*inf* kalla)_____
3. mælti (*inf* mæla)_____
4. bjó (*inf* búa)   _____
5. fór (*inf* fara)   _____
6. tók (*inf* taka)   _____
7. herjaði (*inf* herja)_____
8. gerði (*inf* gera)   _____

4.8 WEAK VERBS IN THE PRESENT TENSE

Verbs agree with the subject of the sentence in person (1st, 2nd, 3rd) and number (*sg* or *pl*). Person and number fuse into *one set* of endings, given in the box to the right.

Weak verbs fall into four conjugations. They all take the same endings in the present tense, but they show small differences which help to distinguish them. A verb stays in its particular conjugation,

Present Tense Endings

	SINGULAR	PLURAL
1st	–	-um
2nd	-r	-ið
3rd	-r	-a

- 1st, 2nd, and 4th conjugation verbs insert a linking vowel before the endings in the singular. In the 1st conjugation the linking vowel is -a- (*kallar*), in the 2nd and 4th -i- (*mælir, vakir*), and the 3rd has no linking vowel (*telr*).
- The 2nd and 4th conjugations have the same endings in both present and past, but they show several small differences including variations of stem vowels and past participles.

The verbs below demonstrate the four conjugations. (Note there are three ways to translate the Old Norse present tense into English. For example, *ek kalla* can be translated 'I call,' 'I am calling,' or 'I do call') since they all denote present tense in English.

Verbs – Prsent Tense

	PRONOUN	1ST CONJUG *KALLA*	2ND CONJUG *MÆLA*	3RD CONJUG *TELJA*	4TH CONJUG *VAKA*
Sg 1st	ek	kalla	mæli	tel	vaki
2nd	þú	kallar	mælir	telr	vakir
3rd	hann, hon, þat	kallar	mælir	telr	vakir
Pl 1st	vér	köllum	mælum	teljum	vökum
2nd	þér	kallið	mælið	telið	vakið
3rd	þeir, þær, þau	kalla	mæla	telja	vaka

The 1st plural ending -um triggers u-umlaut (*kalla, köllum; vaka, vökum*).

Verbs in Old Norse consist of stems and endings (the stem is the basic part of the word to which the linking vowel and endings are added). For example, *kalla, mæla, telja,* and *vaka* have in the present tense the stems *kall-, mæl-, telj-,* and *vak-*.

Verbs with stems endings in -j- (such as *telja*) only retain -j- when followed by an ending beginning with -a- (*selja*) or -u- (*teljum*), otherwise -j- is dropped (*telr, telið*). *Vilja* is irregular in 2nd and 3rd persons (*vill*). All verbs of the 3rd conjugation have stems ending in -*j*- (called 'stem final -j'). The other conjugations have only a few such verbs, for example *herja* (1st conjug), *fylgja* (2nd conjug), and *segja* (4th conjug).

A few weak verbs have stems ending in -*v*- (*søkkva, byggva*). These verbs only retain -*v* before an ending beginning with -*a*- or -*i*- (*søkkvir, søkkvið*), otherwise -*v*- is dropped (*søkkum*).

4.9 WORD FREQUENCY – WEAK VERBS

Below, arranged by conjugation, are the most common weak verbs found in the sagas.

1ST CONJUG	2ND CONJUG	3RD CONJUG	4TH CONJUG
kalla 'call'	*gera* 'do; make'	*leggja* 'lay'	*segja* 'say'
leita 'search'	*mæla* 'speak'	*setja* 'set'	*hafa* 'have'
svara 'answer'	*senda* 'send'	*skilja* 'part'	*trúa* 'believe'
tala 'talk'	*veita* 'grant'	*spyrja* 'ask'	*þola* 'tolerate'
ætla 'intend'	*sœkja* 'seek'	*vilja* 'want'	
	þykkja 'seem'		

Many of the weak verbs below appear in the reading passages and exercises.

1ST CONJUG	2ND CONJUG	3RD CONJUG	4TH CONJUG
blóta 'sacrifice'	*dœma* 'judge'	*berja* 'strike'	*vaka* 'be awake'
eggja 'incite'	*fella* 'fell'	*flytja* 'move, carry'	*þegja* 'be silent'
elska 'love'	*flýja* 'flee'	*hyggja* 'think'	
herja 'raid'	*fœra* 'bring'	*krefja* 'demand'	
gnaga 'gnaw'	*leiða* 'lead'	*selja* 'give'	
lofa 'praise'	*nefna* 'name'	*telja* 'count'	
skipa 'arrange'	*sigla* 'sail'	*temja* 'tame'	

4.10 EXERCISE – WEAK VERBS IN THE PRESENT TENSE

Fill in the correct form of the verbs in the present tense. Give conjugation and number and translate in the spaces below.

Ex: (kalla) Vér ___*köllum; 1st conjugation; we (pl) call*___.

1.   (mæla) Þú _____.
2.   (kalla) Þér _____
_____.
3.   (vaka) Vit _____
_____.
4.   (telja) Ek _____
_____.
5.   (eggja) Hon _____

```
        _____.
    6.  (gera) Þær _____

        _____.
    7.  (veita) Þú _____

        _____.
    8.  (þegja) Vér _____.
    9.  (spyrja) Vit _____.
   10.  (vilja) Ek _____.
   11.  (elska) Þeir _____.
   12.  (leggja) Hann _____.
   13.  (senda) Þit _____.
   14.  (setja) Hon _____.
   15.  (fœra) Þér _____.
   16.  (lofa) Ek_____.
   17.  (tala) Vér _____.
   18.  (segja) Þú _____.

        _____.
   19.  (hyggja) Hann _____

        _____.
   20.  (skilja) Þau _____.
```

4.11 THE REFLEXIVE POSSESSIVE PRONOUN *SINN*

In English there is ambiguity in the possessive pronouns *his*, *her*, *its*, and *their*. For example, in the statement *Hrolf killed his king*, a wider context is needed to determine whether Hrolf killed his own king or somebody else's king.

Old Icelandic is more precise. When a possessive pronoun ('his,' 'her,' 'its,' 'their') refers back to a subject in the 3rd person (*Þórólfr, Island*, etc.), a special pronoun *sinn* 'his [own], her [own], its [own], their [own]' is used. Compare the sentences below.

> Þórólfr drap konung **sinn**.   *Thorolf killed **his** [own] king.*
> Þórólfr drap konung **hans**.   *Thorolf killed **his** [somebody else's] king.*

The difference in meaning is also evident in the following sentences adapted from *The Prose Edda*, the thirteenth-century treatise on mythology and poetry:

> Tók Óðinn þá við konu **sinni**. *Then Odin lived with **his** [own] wife.*
> Tók Óðinn þá við konu **hans**.   *Then Odin lived with [received] **his** [another's] wife.*

Sinn behaves much like an adjective. It agrees with the noun it modifies in gender, case, and number. In the example above, *sinni* is feminine dative singular because the feminine noun it modifies, *konu*, is in the dative singular. The full declension of *sinn* is given in the table below. It is the same as the definite article *inn* given earlier.

	M	F	N		M	F	N
Sg *nom*	sinn	sín	sitt	**Pl**	sínir	sínar	sín
acc	sinn	sína	sitt		sína	sínar	sín
dat	sínum	sinni	sínu		sínum	sínum	sínum
gen	síns	sinnar	síns		sinna	sinna	sinna

Note that the *-i-* in *sinn* is short when it precedes a double consonant (*-nn-* and *-tt-*), while it is long elsewhere. (The possessive pronouns *minn* 'my' and *þinn* 'your' decline the same way as *sinn*.)

Unlike the possessive pronoun *sinn*, *hans* is the genitive of the personal pronoun *hann* given earlier and only changes to reflect the gender of the **subject**.

	M	F	N		ALL GENDERS
Pl *gen*	hans (*his*)	hennar (*her*)	þess (*its*)	**Pl**	þeira (*their*)

Sinn is used only when it refers back to the subject in the same sentence. In the following examples from the readings, *sinn* and *sína* refer back to the subject *Haraldr*.

Haraldr konungr bað gera kumbl þessi ept Gorm föður **sinn** ok ept Þyri móður **sína**.

Hans, hennar, þess, þeira are used when the possessive pronoun refers back to the subject of a different sentence.

Skútaðar-Skeggi hét maðr ágætr í Nóregi. **Hans** sonr var Björn.

4.12 Exercise – The Pronoun *Sinn* and Personal Pronouns

Complete the following sentences with the correct pronoun.

1. Hann sá konuna _____ (He saw his [own] wife)
2. Hann sá konuna _____ (He saw his [someone else's] wife)

3. Hon hjálpaði dóttur _____ (She helped her [own] daughter)
4. Hon hjálpaði dóttur _____ (She helped her [someone else's] daughter)

Note: hjálpa takes a dative object.

5. Hann ok konan _____ hittu Gunnar (He and his wife met Gunnar)

> Remember: reflexive pronouns only refer *back* to the subject.

4.13 READING – MIDFJORD-SKEGGI (*LANDNÁMABÓK*) AND HROLF KRAKI'S SWORD

Medieval Icelanders had a good understanding of the northern world. Some traveled widely during the Viking Age, and many were well versed in the legends, history, and myths of their northern culture. In the twelfth century, when writing in Old Icelandic with ink on parchment became common, many oral traditions were written down.

Midfjord-Skeggi was a famous tenth-century Icelander who appears in a number of sagas, including *Laxdœla Saga*, *Kormak's Saga* (*Kormáks saga*), and *The Saga of Thord Menace* (*Þórðar saga hreðu*). The passage below from the *Book of the Settlements* tells of Skeggi's father and grandfather, and the settling of the family in Midfjord (Miðfjörðr) in northern Iceland. Skeggi travelled widely and was know as a *Hólmsgarðsfari*, a merchant who voyaged to Novgorod (Hólmsgarðr), deep in northern Russia, fortrade in furs, slaves, Arabic silver coins, and valuable glass beads.

The passage recounts that Skeggi, while on a Viking voyage in the Baltic, broke into the grave mound of Hrolf Kraki and carried away that king's famous sword Skofnung. In the *Saga of King Hrolf Kraki* (*Hrólf saga kraka*), Hrolf uses Skofnung to slice off the buttocks of Adils, the sorcerer king of Sweden.

Weapons frequently had names and special magical power. Some were said to be forged by dwarves (*dvergar*, sg *dvergr*) or dark-elves (*dökkálfar*, sg *dökkálfr*). Special weapons, such as Hrolf Kraki's sword, had histories and were well known. Hrolf's sword *Sköfnungr* means 'Shin-Bone' and is known from several tales. It is briefly mentioned in the reading passage below, but the Old Norse audience would have understood its value. Likewise, Sigurd the dragon slayer had a famous sword called Gram (*Gramr*). A renowned treasure, its origin is carefully recounted in *The Saga of the Volsungs*. Other swords of legend are *Hneitir* ('Wounder'), *Dragvendill* ('Draw-Wand'), and the cursed sword *Tyrfingr* ('Tarry'). Axes were often named after giantesses and troll-wives (*trollkonur*, sg *trollkona*) and had names such as *Gnepia* ('Towering'), *Fála* ('Frightener'), and *Vígglóð* ('Battle-Bright'). The gods' most famous weapons were Odin's spear, *Gungnir,* and Thor's hammer, *Mjöllnir*.

Landnámabók (S 174)

Skútaðar-Skeggi hét maðr ágætr í Nóregi. Hans sonr var Björn. Hann var kallaðr Skinna-Björn, því at hann var Hólmgarðsfari ok farmaðr mikill. Hann fór til Íslands ok nam Miðfjörð ok Línakradal.

Book of the Settlements (S 174)

Hans sonr var Miðfjarðar-Skeggi; hann var garpr mikill ok farmaðr. Hann herjaði í austrveg í Danmörk við Sjáland ok fór at brjóta haug[8] Hrólfs konungs kraka ok tók hann þar ór haugi[9] Sköfnung, sverð Hrólfs, ok øxi Hjalta,[10] ok mikit fé annat

VOCABULARY

at *inf marker* to

❖**annarr** <*f* önnur, *n* annat> *adj pron* one of two, other, another

austrvegr <-s, -ir> *m* the east, i.e., the Baltic (*lit* the 'eastern way'); **fara í austrveg** trading or raiding in the Baltic or journeying east and south down the rivers of Russia

❖**ágætr** *adj* excellent, noble, distinguished

brjóta <brýtr, braut, brutu, brotinn> *vb* break, break up, break open

❖**fara** <ferr, fór, fóru, farinn> *vb* go, travel; move

farmaðr *m* sea-farer, merchant, trader

❖**fé** <*gen* fjár, *gen pl* fjá> *n* cattle, sheep; wealth, money

fór *1/3sg past of* **fara**

garpr <-s, -ar> *m* a bold, daring, courageous, or warlike man or woman

haugr <-s, -ar> *m* burial mound

herja <-að-> *vb* raid, harry; make war

herjaði *3sg past of* **herja** 'raided'

Hjalti *m* Hjalti (*personal name*) (*hjalt* = 'sword hilt')

Hólmgarðr <-s> *m* Holmgard (*place name, modern* Novgorod in northern Russia)

Hólmgarðsfari *m* voyager to **Hólmgarðr**

Hrólfr kraki <*gen* Hrólfs kraka> *m* Hrolf Kraki (*personal name*)

❖**í** *prep* [*w acc*] into (*motion*); [*w dat*] in, within, at (*position*)

Ísland *n* Iceland

❖**kalla** <-að-> *vb* call

kallaðr *ppart of* **kalla** 'called'

❖**konungr** <-s, -ar> *m* king

Línakradalr <-s> *m* Linakradale (*place name*), 'Valley of Linen Fields'

Miðfjardar-Skeggi *m* Skeggi of Midfjord (*personal name*)

Miðfjörðr *m* Midfjord (*place name*)

❖**mikill** <*f* mikil, *n* mikit, *comp* meiri, *superl* mestr> *adj* big, tall, great; much, very

mikit fé annat *n* other great treasure

nam *1/3sg past of* **nema**

nema <nemr, nam, námu, numinn> *vb* take; claim land

Nóregr <-s> *m* Norway

❖**ór** (*also* **úr**) *prep* [*w dat*] out of, from

Sjáland *n* Zealand (*place name,* Sjælland in Modern Danish)

skinn *n* skin

Skinna-Björn *m* Bjorn Fur-Skins (*personal name*)

Sköfnungr *m* Skofnung, possibly 'Shin Bone,' name of King Hrolf's sword

---

[8] **fór at brjóta haug:** 'he went to break open the burial mound.'

[9] **tók hann þar ór haugi:** 'there he took from the mound.'

[10] Hjalti was one of King Hrolf Kraki's legendary champions.

❖**sverð** *n* sword
❖**taka** <tekr, tók, tóku, tekinn> *vb* take
❖**til** *prep* [*w gen*] to
tók *1/3sg past of* **taka** 'took'
❖**við** *prep* [*w acc*] at, by, close to

❖**þar** *adv* there
því at *conj* for, because
øx <*acc/dat* øxi, *gen* øxar, *pl* øxar> *f* axe

Skutad Skeggi was the name of an excellent man in Norway. His son was Bjorn. He was called Bjorn Fur-Skins, because he was a voyager to Holmgard [Novgorod, in northern Russia] and a great merchant. He went to Iceland and took Midfjord and Linakradale.

His son was Skeggi of Midfjord; he was a very bold man and a seafarer. He raided in the East [the Baltic region] in Denmark near Zealand and went to break open the burial mound of King Hrolf Kraki, and there he took from the mound Skofnung, the sword of Hrolf, and the axe of Hjalti, and other great treasure

---

4.14 EXERCISE – READING *LANDNÁMABÓK*

Based on the reading above, are the following statements true (*rétt*) or false (*rangt*)?

RÉTT eða RANGT?

1.   Skútaðar-Skeggi bjó í Nóregi.   _____
2.   Skinna-Björn var sonr Hrólfs konungs.   _____
3.   Björn fór til Íslands.   _____
4.   Miðfjarðar-Skeggi var farmaðr.   _____
5.   Miðfjarðar-Skeggi herjaði í Nóregi.   _____
6.   Konungr hét Skinna-Björn.   _____
7.   Miðfjarðar-Skeggi var garpr mikill.   _____

4.15 CULTURE – HARALD BLUETOOTH FORGES A VIKING AGE STATE

Harald Bluetooth expanded the power, which he inherited from his father Gorm, and forged Denmark into Viking Age Scandinavia's first enduring royal state. As part of his state building, Harald undertook a series of large-scale building projects throughout the Danish kingdom. In particular he augmented the border defenses. On the southern border he strengthened the Danevirke fortification and the rampart around Hedeby in response to military and economic pressure from the Frankish Empire. A series of German invasions began in 974, and it was nine years before Harald's son, Svein Forkbeard, defeated the Germans. Around 980 powerful circular forts were constructed in the major subdivisions of the Danish kingdom at Trelleborg on Sjælland, Nonnebakken on Fyn, Fyrkat and Aggersborg in Jutland. A simpler fort at Trelleborg in Skåne (Old Norse *Skáney*) was also constructed.

The forts were mostly close to the sea. They provided training grounds for royal warriors and housing for their families. The forts may have also served as centers of royal administration and tax collection. Probably they were royal strongholds designed to control the local populations. At about the time the forts were constructed. Jelling received a massive wooden palisade, and an enormous one kilometer-long, two-lane wooden bridge leading to Jelling was built nearby at Ravninge Enge. This bridge consumed huge quantities of lumber. It must have been a highly impressive construction, a monument to the dynasty.

While Harald seems to have increased his authority over parts of what is today southern Sweden, he also suffered defeat on several occasions. Runestones in Skåne refer to a defeat at Uppsala, probably in the 980s, where Harald's son Toki is said to have died. Harald's Jelling runestone also claims that he ruled Norway. This claim is probably exaggerated. More likely Harald exercised control over southeast Norway for a time. After a long life, Harald was deposed and perhaps killed during a revolt by his son Svein Forkbeard.

4.16 VOCABULARY – LIST 4. THE MOST FREQUENT WORDS IN THE SAGAS

NOUNS	ADJECTIVES	PRONOUNS	NUMERALS
kona – woman *f*	**gamall** – old	**sjá** – this	**tólf** – twelve
ráð – advice; plan *h*	**kyrr** – quiet		
dagr – day *m*	**fyrri** – former		
frændi – kinsman *m*	**varr** – aware		

VERBS	PREPOSITIONS AND ADVERBS	CONJUNCTIONS
ganga – to walk	**eigi** – not	**sem** – who,
gera – to do; make	**fyrir** – before; for	which,
verða – to become	**af** – of; from	that; as
kveða – to speak	**ekki** – not	

EXERCISES

4.17 U-Umlaut. Decline and then translate *gata*, *kona*, and *saga* in the spaces provided below, applying *u*-umlaut where necessary. (Note, *kona* has an irregular genitive plural, *kvenna*.) Use the resources of the lesson and the Vocabulary.

	SAGA	GATA	KONA
Sg *nom*	*saga*		*kona*
acc			
dat			
gen		*götu*	

Pl *nom*	_____	*götur* _____	_____
acc	_____	_____	_____
dat	*sögum* _____	_____	_____
gen	_____	_____	*kvenna* _____

Translate: saga_____, gata_____, kona_____.

4.18 Vocabulary Review. Match the Norse word with its meaning in English.

1.	*mikill*	A.	for, because
2.	*garpr*	B.	won
3.	*sverð*	C.	man
4.	*maðr*	D.	excellent
5.	*øx*	E.	his (own)
6.	*ágætr*	F.	bade, commanded
7.	*því at*	G.	sword
8.	*at kalla*	H.	woman; wife
9.	*at gera*	I.	earl
10.	*at spyrja*	J.	to ask
11.	*bað*	K.	to call
12.	*ept*	L.	father
13.	*sá*	M.	that (one)
14.	*sinn*	N.	was called
15.	*vann*	O.	a bold man
16.	*kona*	P.	to do; to make
17.	*faðir*	Q.	axe
18.	*var kallaðr*	R.	time
19.	*jarl*	S.	after, in memory of
20.	*tími*	T.	great

4.19 *U*-Umlaut. For each of the words below, give the form indicated in parentheses and mark its gender. Note that some words do not show *u*-umlaut.

Ex: saga (*acc pl*): *sögur*   *f*_____

1.	dalr (*dat pl*): _____	5.	kalla (*1pl pres.*): _____
2.	vargr (*acc sg*): _____	6.	saga (*acc sg*): _____
3.	kambr (*dat pl*): _____	7.	gata (*nom pl*): _____
4.	armr (*dat sg*): _____	8.	tala (*1sg pres.*): _____

Transl: *vargr* (m) 'wolf', *kambr* (m) 'comb.' **Note:** Words in the exercises that do not appear in the lesson can be found in the vocabulary at the end of the book if no definition is given in the Exercise.

4.20 Present Tense of Common Weak Verbs. Conjugate the following verbs and translate. Assume the neuter objects are singular.

gera

1. Ek _____ kumbl.

2. Þú _____ sverð.

3. Hann _____ øxi.

spyrja

7. Ek _____ konung.

8. Þú _____ Ingólf.

9. Hon _____ farmann.

kalla

13. Ek _____.

14. Þú _____.

15. Hann _____.

4. Vér _____ skip.

5. Þér _____ haug.

6. Þeir _____ hús.

10. Vit _____ landnámsmann.

11. Þit _____ hana.

12. Þau _____ konu.

16. Vér _____.

17. Þér _____.

18. Þær _____.

4.21 Translation and Parsing.

A.   Translate the following passage from the reading . Some words are underlined for use in exercise B.

Skútaðar-Skeggi <u>hét</u> maðr ágætr í <u>Nóregi</u>. <u>Hans</u> sonr var Björn. Hann var kallaðr Skinna-Björn, því at hann <u>var</u> Hólmgarðsfari ok farmaðr mikill. Hann fór til Íslands ok <u>nam</u> Miðfjörð ok Línakradal. Hans sonr var Miðfjarðar-Skeggi; hann var garpr mikill ok farmaðr. Hann herjaði í austrveg í Danmörk við Sjáland ok fór at brjóta <u>haug</u> Hrólfs <u>konungs</u> kraka ok tók hann þar ór haugi Sköfnung, <u>sverð</u> Hrólfs, ok øxi Hjalta, ok mikit fé annat.

_____

_____

_____

_____

_____

_____

_____

_____

_____

_____

_____

B.   Identify grammatically the <u>underlined</u> words in the text above. If you need help, see the vocabulary under the reading passage in the lesson.

Examples:

maðr   *m nom sg of the noun maðr 'man'*

hann   *m nom sg of the 3ʳᵈ person pronoun*

tók   *3ʳᵈ person sg past tense of the verb taka 'take'*

til   *prep with gen, 'to'*

1. hét   _____

2. Nóregi   _____

3. Hans   _____

4. var   _____

5. nam   _____

6. haug   _____

7. konungs _____

8. sverð   _____

4.22 Reading Comprehension. Based on the reading passage in the lesson, decide which of the following statements are *rétt* or *rangt*.

RÉTT EÐA RANGT?

1.   Skútaðar-Skeggi hét maðr.   _____

2.   Björn var farmaðr.   _____

3.   Skútaðar-Skeggi var Danmarkarbót.   _____

4.   Sonr Skútaðar-Skeggja nam Línakradal.   _____

5.   Skútaðar-Skeggi fór at brjóta haug Hrólfs konungs
     kraka.   _____

6.   Sköfnungr var sverð Hjalta.   _____

7.   Björn herjaði í austrveg.   _____

8.   Miðfjarðar-Skeggi tók øxi Hjalta ok mikit fé annat. _____

4.23 Weak Verbs. Translate the following phrases into Old Norse using the verbs: *svara* 'answer,' *leita* 'search,' *leggja* 'lay,' *sœkja* 'seek,' *sigla* 'sail,' *segja* 'say,' *tala* 'talk,' *veita* 'grant,' *hyggja* 'think,' and *þykkja* 'seem.' Identify the conjugations of these weak verbs.

Ex: I speak.   _Ek mæli._   _2nd conjug_
1. You (*sg*) answer.   _____   _____
2. We (*dual*) search.   _____   _____
3. You (*pl*) lay.   _____   _____
4. They (*f*) seek.   _____   _____
5. She sails.   _____   _____
6. He says.   _____   _____
7. They (*n*) talk.   _____   _____
8. I grant.   _____   _____
9. They (*m*) think.   _____   _____
10. It seems.   _____   _____

4.24 Weak Verbs. Give the present tense of the following verbs and translate.

senda

1. Vér _sendum_____.
   We (pl) send.
2. Þær _____.

3. Ek _____.

4. Þau _____.

5. Þat _____.

6. Hon _____.

7. Þú _____.

8. Þit _____.

setja

9. Ek _set_____.
   I set.
10. Þeir _____.

11. Þér _____.

12. Hann _____.

13. Þú _____.

14. Þau _____.

15. Hon _____.

16. Vér _____.

svara

17. Hann _svarar_____.
    He answers.
18. Vér _____.

19. Þú _____.

20. Ek _____.

21. Þér _____.

22. Þær _____.

23. Hon _____.

24. Vit _____.

4.25 The Reflexive Possessive Pronoun *Sinn*.

A.   Fill in the correct form of *sinn* for the noun it modifies and translate.

> **Ex:**   Eiríkr gaf Herjólfi spjót (*sg*) *sitt*_____.
>
> *Eirik gave Herjolf his spear.*

1.   Eiríkr gaf syni _____ land.

   _____

2.   Þeir gera kumbl (*pl*) _____.

   _____

3.   Hon gaf móður _____ land.

   _____

4.   Hrólfr tók ór haugi sverð (*sg*) _____.

   _____

5.   Hjalti tók ór haugi øxi _____.

   _____

B.   Fill in the correct form of *sinn* or the 3rd person pronoun (*hans* or *hennar*) as appropriate and translate.

> **Ex:**   Skútaðar-Skeggi hét maðr ágætr í Nóregi. _Hans_____ (his) sonr var Björn.
>
> *Skeggi of Skutad was the name of an excellent man in Norway. His son was Bjorn.*

1.   Gormr konungr gerði kumbl þessi ept Þyri konu _____ (his own).

   _____

2.   Ásgerðr bjó á Drepstokki með syni _____ (his: that is, Herjolf's)

   _____

3.   Haraldr konungr spyrr frænda _____ (his own).

   _____

4.   Haraldr jarl af Jótlandi var faðir _____ (her).

   _____

5.   Kona Herjólfs hét Ásgerðr. Björn var sonr _____ (their).

   _____

6.   Óláfr ok Bjarni fara til lands _____ (their own).

   _____

C. Possessive pronouns *minn* 'my' and *þinn* 'your' decline like *sinn*. Fill in and translate.

Ex: Eiríkr sá son _minn_____ (my).   Eiríkr sá son _þinn_____ (your).

   _Eirik saw my son._____   _Eirik saw your son._____

1. Ek mæli við (*with*) son _____ (my).

   _____

2. Þorsteinn reist (*carved*) rúnar _____ (your).

   _____

3. Þyri fór til Nóregs með syni _____ (my).

   _____

4. Gormr konungr var frændi _____ (your).

   _____

4.26 Verbs in Past Tense. Complete the chart below, giving the infinitive and translation.

VERB (PAST TENSE)	ENGLISH MEANING	INFINITIVE
Ex: *vildi*	_want_	_vilja_
1. *tók*	_____	_____
2. *gaf*	_____	_____
3. *fór*	_____	_____
4. *herjaði*	_____	_____
5. *bað*	_____	_____
6. *vann*	_____	_____
7. *gerði*	_____	_____

4.27 Word Frequency Review. Write out *List 4. The Most Frequent Words* and translate.

OLD NORSE	ENGLISH	OLD NORSE	ENGLISH
NOUNS		**ADJECTIVES**	
1 _____ _____		5 _____ _____	
2 _____ _____		6 _____ _____	
3 _____ _____		7 _____ _____	
4 _____ _____		8 _____ _____	
VERBS		**PREPOSITIONS AND ADVERBS**	
9 _____ _____		13 _____ _____	
10 _____ _____		14 _____ _____	
11 _____ _____		15 _____ _____	
12 _____ _____		16 _____ _____	

LESSON 5

SWEDEN: A FAMILY RUNESTONE

Eigi er allt gull sem glóar
(All that glows is not gold)

Figure 23. The Ramsund Runestone, Sweden depicts the tale of Sigurd, the slayer of the serpentine dragon-monster Fafnir. The carving shows Sigurd roasting Fafnir's heart, sucking the dragon's blood from his thumb, and listening to the forest birds. Sigurd follows the advice of the birds and kills the smith Regin, who lies decapitated alongside his tools and bellows. Grani, Sigurd's horse which was chosen for young Sigurd by Odin, is tethered to the tree. On Grani's back is the treasure taken from Fafnir. This treasure, which contains the magical ring, becomes the 'Rhine Gold.'

5.1 CULTURE – LANDS OF THE SWEDES (SVÍAR) AND GOTHS (GAUTAR)

The Ramsund Runestone is in Uppland Sweden, and runestones are among our major sources for the Viking Age history of the people of this region. Otherwise, there is little documentary evidence from the region regarding early political history and state development. A single national identity does not emerge until the late twelfth century. Forests and bogs separate the populated regions of Central Sweden, making communication between areas difficult for much of the year. Long standing clan and tribal rivalries were also a factor. The two major regional divisions were the lands of the Goths (Gautar) in modern south central Sweden around lakes Vättern (Vatnsbú) and Vänern (Vænir) and the territory of the Swedes (Svíar) further north in central Sweden around Lake Mälaren (Lögr). These two regions, known as Gautland and Svíaland, were economically and politically independent for much of their earliest history.

The Svíar developed elements of statehood as early as the Late Germanic Iron Age (ca. 600–800). This historical period in central Sweden is known as the Vendel Period because of rich boat graves and other archaeological finds from burial mounds at Vendel and Valsgärde north of Lake Mälaren. The kingdom of the Svíar was centered at Uppsala

(Uppsalir, often called Old Uppsala), which remained a pagan cult center throughout the Viking Age. The wealth of the Svíar and their kings lay in controlling trade over the Baltic

Figure 24. Viking Age Sweden (Svíaland or Svíþjóð) faced east and dominated the Baltic Sea (Eystrasalt) and its trade. Shaded regions show areas of Swedish settlement and trade in the Baltic. The Gautar lived around the lakes Vænir and Vatnsbú. Skáney (modern Skåne) is today in Sweden. During the Viking Age, Skáney was part of Denmark, and the Danes controlled both sides of the straits leading in and out of the Baltic.

Sea in such goods as amber, silver, silk, iron, fur, and slaves.

Around 800, a permanently occupied trade and administrative center was established at Birka on Björkö Island in the middle of Lake Mälaren. It was connected through trade across the Baltic and down the rivers of Russia to the Byzantine Empire, central Asia, and the Caliphate of Baghdad. The burials on Björkö, many of which are high-status chamber graves, attest to a wealth of imported items in the form of glassware, jewelry, bronze vessels, coins, and pottery. Excavations also point to a sizeable population of resident merchants and craftsmen. Birka remained important until the 900s, when changes in water levels, religion, and politics resulted in the rise of Sigtuna as a royal Christian center on the northern shore of the lake.

The Gautar (the Geatas or Geats of the Old English poem *Beowulf*) from Gautland did not attain the prominence or wealth of the Svíar. For several centuries the Gautar maintained a separate kingdom in the face of competition from the Svíar as well as from neighboring Danes and Norwegians. Svíar and Gautar may have had at times an uneasy alliance. Óláfr Skautkonungr (Olaf Eiriksson), king of the Svíar (ca. 980–1022) was the first in king in Viking times to rule both regions. Olaf's reign was troubled. He was a Christian but, because of the strength of the pagan majority, he did not force conversion. The union of the two peoples under Olaf did not survive his reign. Lasting unification occurred only after Christianity took hold throughout the regions at the end of the twelfth century, a period relatively late in the conversion of Scandinavia.

5.2 READING – SIGURD THE DRAGON-SLAYER ON THE RAMSUND RUNESTONE

The Jelling runestones in the previous lessons were carved at the order of King Gorm the Old and his son, King Harald Bluetooth. However, most of the approximately 3,000 runestones known from Scandinavia were carved for non-royal people. Most often, runestones were commissioned by local elites, who used the stones to commemorate their dead, note events, record the deeds of the living, proclaim inheritance rights, property ownership, and group identity to passers-by.

The eleventh-century memorial stone from Ramsund in Södermanland, Sweden, is a non-royal runestone. Members of a family of local landowners had the stone carved to commemorate the construction of a causeway, a raised earthen path or bridge (*brú*) across swampy ground. The carving is on a large flat rock outcropping near the causeway. The runes tell that Sigríðr, a prominent local woman, commissioned the carving. Sigríðr publically makes known her relationships to the men in her family. These include her father, Ormr, her recently deceased father-in-law, Hólmgeirr, and her husband, Sigrøðr Hólmgeirsson, as well as her son Alrekr, from a previous marriage. The nearby Kjula runestone adds that the father of Alrekr was Spjútr, a known Viking.

This information had a purpose. If, as seems likely, one or both of the sons of Sigríðr were dead at the time this stone was carved, she or her surviving son stood to inherit from three lines of descent: from Ormr, Spjútr, and Hólmgeirr. The stone announces the considerable inheritance of Sigríðr to all who wish to use the public causeway and keep their feet dry.

The runic inscription implies that Sigríðr and/or Hólmgeirr was Christian. The choice of the pagan hero, Sigurd the Dragon Slayer, as the decorative motif accompanying a

Christian inscription is indicative of the contemporaneous mixing of religious cultures.

RUNES	**TRANSLITERATION**

ᛋᛁᚱᛁᚦᛦ᛬ᚠᛁᛏᚱᚦᛁ᛬ᛒᚢᚱ᛬ᚦᛆᛋᛁ᛬

ᛏᚱᛁᛙᛋ᛬ᛏᚢᛏᛁᛆ᛬ᚢᚱᛘᛋ᛬ᚠᚢᚱ᛬

ᛋᛆᛚᚢ᛬ ᚼᚢᛚᛘᚴᛁᚱᛋ᛬ᚠᛆᚦᚢᚱ᛬

ᛋᚢᚠᚱᚢᚦᛆᚱ᛬ ᛒᚢᛏᛆᛏᛆ᛬ᛋᛁᛋ

siriþr : kiarþi : bur : þosi

: muþiR : alriks : tutiR : urms :

fur : salu : hulmkirs : faþur :

sukruþar : buata : sis

STANDARDIZED OLD NORSE	**TRANSLATION**

Sigríðr gerði brú þessa móðir Alreks[11] dóttir Orms fyr sálu Hólmgeirs föður Sigrøðar búanda síns.

Sigrid, Alrek's mother, Orm's daughter, made this bridge for the soul of Holmgeir, the father of Sigrod, her husband.

VOCABULARY

Alrekr <-s> *m* Alrek (*personal name*)

❖**bóndi** (*also* **búandi**) <*gen* bónda, *pl* bœndr> *m* husband; farmer

brú <*gen* brúar, *pl* brúar~brúr~brýr> *f* bridge; causeway built over swampy ground

búandi <*pl* búendr> *see* **bóndi**

❖**dóttir** <*acc, dat, & gen* dóttur, *pl* dœtr, *dat* dœtrum, *gen* dœtra> *f* daughter

❖**faðir** <*acc* föður, *dat* föður~feðr, *gen* föður, *pl* feðr, *dat* feðrum, *gen* feðra> *m* father

❖**fyrir** (*also* **fyr**) *prep* [*w acc*] for, on behalf of

❖**gera** (*also* **gøra**) <-ði, -ðr~gerr> *vb* make; do, act

gerði *see* **gera**

Hólmgeirr <-s> *m* Holmgeir (*personal name*)

❖**móðir** <*acc, dat, & gen* móður, *pl* mœðr, *dat* mœðrum, *gen* mœðra> *f* mother

Ormr <-s> *m* Orm (*personal name*)

sála *f* soul

Sigríðr <*acc & dat* Sigríði, *gen* Sigríðar> *f* Sigrid (*personal name*)

Sigrøðr <-ar> *m* Sigrod (*personal name*)

❖**þessi** <*f acc sg* þessa> *dem pron* this

5.3 CULTURE – SIGURD THE DRAGON SLAYER

The Ramsund stone depicts part of a longer tale whose origins lie deep within the protohistoric Iron Age. The complete story is told in *The Saga of the Volsungs* (*Völsunga saga*), one of the great tales of western storytelling. The unknown Icelandic author who wrote the saga in the thirteenth century based his prose epic on stories found in older heroic poetry. *Völsunga saga* recounts the mythic deeds of the dragon slayer, Sigurd the

---

[11] The noun phrases *móðir Alreks* and *dóttir Orms* are in apposition with *Sigríðr*. Similarly, *föður Sigrøðar* is in apposition with *Hólmgeirs* and *búanda síns* is in apposition with *Sigrøðar*.

Volsung. It is a story of love, betrayal, the vengeance of a barbarian queen, and schemes of Attila the Hun.

The saga describes events from the ancient wars among the kings of the Burgundians, the Huns, and the Goths. It treats some of the same legends as the Middle High German epic poem, the *Nibelungenlied*. In both accounts, though in different ways, Sigurd (Siegfried in the German tradition) acquires the Rhine Gold and then becomes tragically entangled in a love triangle involving a supernatural woman. In the saga, this woman is a Valkyrie, one of Odin's warrior-maidens who choose the slain for Valhalla following a battle. In a section of the saga, the Valkyrie recounts runic lore.

The pictorial scenes on the Ramsund stone witness that this legendary/mythological story told in Icelandic saga and poetry was also known in Viking Age Sweden. The carving contains considerable detail about a tale filled with magic and shape-changing. On the bottom right of the carving, Sigurðr Fáfnisbani (the slayer, or bane, of the dragon Fáfnir) thrusts his sword up into the monster. In the center Sigurd's horse Grani is loaded with Fafnir's treasure. Forest birds perch in the tree branches. To the left, Sigurd roasts Fafnir's heart. According to *The Saga of the Volsungs*, Sigurd tests if the heart is fully roasted by touching the meat with his thumb. The boiling blood burns the young hero's finger, and Sigurd sucks his burned thumb. When the blood enters his mouth, he understands the speech of the birds. They warn him that the smith Regin, his companion, foster-father, and the brother of Fafnir, intends to kill him. Alerted to Regin's treachery, Sigurd kills the smith, whose smithing tools and decapitated head are shown on the stone.

In the nineteenth century, the Volsung story with the schemes of one-eyed Odin, a magical ring, and the sword that was reforged was rediscovered and became widely known throughout Europe. Translated into many languages, *The Saga of the Volsungs* became a primary source for writers of fantasy and for those interested in myths, legends, and the ancient past of Northern Europe.

The saga deeply influenced William Morris in the nineteenth century and J. R. R. Tolkien in the twentieth. Tolkien, in particular found inspiration in *The Saga of the Volsungs* and the account of the Sigurd story in *The Prose Edda*. He adapted the sword that was reforged, ring of power, the dragon lying on the hoard, and the creature who lived a shadow life in the earth and early possessed the ring. So too, Richard Wagner drew heavily upon the Norse Volsung material in composing his operatic Ring Cycle. Wagner especially focused on Odin's single-minded obsession with regaining the ring by means of the hero, Siegfried/Sigurd.

5.4 SHORT AND LONG VOWELS – STRESSED AND UNSTRESSED

Vowels in Old Norse are short or long. A quick distinction is that short vowels are those in the alphabet without accents. Short vowels are pronounced in a more lax (unstressed) manner and often more rapidly than long vowels, which tend to be stressed. Long vowels are:

- those with an acute mark (*á, é, í, ó, ú, ý*)

- digraphs (a combination of two letters spelling one sound), for example æ and œ
- diphthongs (vowels of two parts) such as *ei, au, ey, jö, and ja*.

Stress in ON words is usually on the first syllable. This means vowels occurring in initial syllables are usually stressed. For example, the short *-i-* in the word *vinr* 'friend' or the short -e- in *selr* 'seal' is stressed. The concepts of stress and long vowel length are of importance for the following discussion of the Special Stem Rules.

5.5 SPECIAL STEM RULES

Much can be gained by learning two rules which we call the Special Stem Rules. These rules explain changes at the end of many words that would otherwise seem irregular, and they account for some of the more puzzling aspects of Old Norse and Modern Icelandic. Learning these two rules makes it possible to avoid otherwise endless memorization of individual words.

The two rules concern changes at the boundary between a word's stem (a word minus its ending) and the ending. They apply specifically when an ending *-r* is added to words whose stem ends in *-l-, -n-, -r-,* or *-s-*. Adding the ending *-r* potentially forms the combinations *-lr, -nr,* or *-sr* at the end of words, but this is not always what happens.

Special Stem Rule 1, The *-r* Change Rule. Rule 1 concerns doubling of the stem final consonant instead of adding the ending *-r*. The result is *-ll* instead of *-lr*, *-nn* instead of *-nr*, and *-ss* instead of *-sr*. Specifically, **when a vowel precedes a stem-final *-l-, -n-,* or *-s-*,** the ending *-r* changes to match the preceding *-l-, -n-,* or *-s-* (hence *-ll, -nn,* or *-ss*). Examples are the nouns *stóll* (stem *stól-*), *steinn, áss, jökull,* and the adjectives *sæll, mikill, litill, vænn,* and *lauss*. A few exceptions occur when *-l-, -n-,* or *-s-* follows a stressed short vowel, as in the nouns *vinr* and *selr.*

Special Stem Rule 2, The *-r* Drop Rule. Rule 2 concerns no replacement for the dropped *-r* ending. **When a consonant precedes a stem-final *-l-, -n-, -r-,* or *-s-* is,** the ending *-r* drops. For example, the nouns *vagn* (gen *vagns,* stem *vagn-*), *karl, hrafn, sigr, vetr, Björn, þurs,* and the adjectives *fagr, vitr*.

- In a few words, such as *sigr* and *fagr,* the *-r-* at the end is not an ending *-r* but the final consonant of the stem. These words do not add the nominative masculine ending *-r* to the stem. The genitive singular (for example, *sigrs* with the stem *sigr* + the genitive *-s* ending) shows that the *-r-* at the end of the word in the nominative case is not a nominative ending. Other words in this group include *akr* (gen *akrs*), *aldr* (gen *aldrs*), *hafr* (gen *hafrs*), *otr* (gen *otrs*), and *vetr* (gen *vetrar*).
- Words with stems ending in *-s-* drop genitive singular *-s* as well as the ending *-r,* for example, *þurs* (gen *þurs*) and *Þorgils* (gen *Þorgils*). The word *lax* (where *-x* is pronounced *ks*) behaves in the same way.

•

In light of the two Special Stem Rules, consider the list of the 246 most frequent words given in Appendix A.

5.6 VERBS AND THE SPECIAL STEM RULES

With a few exceptions, verbs also follow the special stem rules. For instance, 3sg present *skínn* (*skín + r*) 'it shines' and *kýss* (*kýs + r*) 'he chooses' come from the infinitives *skína* and *kjósa*.

5.7 EXERCISE – SPECIAL STEM RULES

Give the stem of the following strong masculine nouns and state the applicable rule. If no Special Stem Rule applies, write 'n/a' (not applicable).

Ex: steinn (*gen* steins)   *stein-*   *Rule 1 (r-Change)*

      vetr (*gen* vetrs)   *vetr-*   *Rule 2 (r-Drop)*

1.   stóll (*gen* stóls) _____
2.   selr (*gen* sels) _____
3.   hrafn (*gen* hrafns) _____
4.   akr (*gen* akrs) _____
5.   karl (*gen* karls) _____

5.8 WORDS WITH STEM ENDINGS -*J*- AND -*V*-

As noted earlier, the stem is the part of the word to which one adds endings. For example, the nouns *haugr*, *konungr*, and *saga* have the stems *haug-*, *konung-*, and *sag-*.

Some words, such as the noun *söngr* 'song,' the adjective *ríkr* 'powerful,' and the verb *telja* 'count' have stem-final -*j*- or -*v*- in certain forms: *söngva* (gen pl), *ríkjum* (dat pl), and the verb *teljum* (2nd pl). Two basic rules govern the presence of -*j*- or -*v*- in these words.

•   Stem-final -*j*- precedes endings which begin with -*a* and -*u*, (vowels that disappear), for example *segið* 'you (pl) say,' from *segja*.

•   Stem-final -*v*- precedes endings which begin with -*a* and -*i*; -*v*- also occurs before -*u*- when between two vowels (*hávum*, dat pl of *hár* 'high'). Stem-final -*v*- between vowels is also sometimes spelled -*f*- (*háfum*).

5.9 STRONG NOUNS – INTRODUCTION

All nouns in Old Norse fall into one of two broad declension types: strong or weak. The terms strong and weak have little significance but are mostly useful for classification. Strong nouns have a wider range of endings than weak nouns and are grouped into four major types. By looking at the nominative singular form alone, it is not possible to determine a strong noun's type. Instead, the types are based on common characteristics of the endings the nouns take and the root vowel changes that take place in the stems.

The following chart shows common examples of the different types of strong noun across the three genders.

	MASCULINE	FEMININE	NEUTER
Type 1	konungr, hersir	rún, för	skip, kvæði
Type 2	staðr, vinr	höfn, borg	
Type 3	fjörðr, skjöldr		
Type 4	maðr, vetr	vík, tönn	

Masculine strong nouns are found in all four types. Type 1 masculines are by far the largest group. Feminine strong nouns are found in all types, but rarely in Type 3. Neuter strong nouns are always Type 1. There are also nouns which do not easily fit into these categories, such as nouns whose stems end in a long vowel, and these are discussed in later lessons.

5.10 STRONG NOUNS – TYPE 1 MASCULINE

The majority of strong masculine nouns belong to Type 1, including names such as *Haraldr*, *Ragnarr*, *Þorgeirr*, *Óláfr*, *Eiríkr*, and *Herjólfr*.

	KONUNGR	ARMR	SKÓGR	HERSIR	SÖNGR	ENDINGS
Sg *nom*	konung**r**	arm**r**	skóg**r**	hersir	söng**r**	**-r**
acc	konung	arm	skóg	hersi	söng	–
dat	konung**i**	arm**i**	skóg**i**	hersi	söng**vi**	**-i**
gen	konung**s**	arm**s**	skóg**ar**	hersi**s**	söng**s**	**-s, ar**
Pl *nom*	konung**ar**	arm**ar**	skóg**ar**	hers**ar**	söng**var**	**-ar**
acc	konung**a**	arm**a**	skóg**a**	hers**a**	söng**va**	**-a**
dat	konung**um**	**ör**m**um**	skóg**um**	hers**um**	söng**um**	**-um**
gen	konung**a**	arm**a**	skóg**a**	hers**a**	söng**va**	**-a**

Transl: *konungr* 'king,' *armr* 'arm,' *skógr* 'forest,' *hersir* 'lord,' *söngr* 'song.'

- The great majority of Type 1 masculines follow the declension of *konungr* and *armr*.
- Some Type 1 masculines have gen sg *-ar*, for example, *skógr* (gen *skógar*).
- About 20 Type 1 nouns, such as *hersir*, *hirðir*, and *læknir*, insert *-i-* in the singular, as do proper names such as Grettir, Skírnir, Rerir, and Ymir.
- A few Type 1 masculines, such as *söngr*, show stem final *-v-*. Others are *hörr*, *már*, *sær*, *spörr*, as well as the names Sigtryggr, Nörr, and Niðhöggr.

Masculine with Special Stem Rules (See Special Stem Rules above). *Sveinn*, 'boy,' (also the man's name, Sveinn) shows Rule 1 (-r Change) and *otr*, 'otter,' and *karl*, 'old man,' exemplify Rule 2 (-r Drop).

	SVEINN	OTR	KARL	ENDINGS
Sg *nom*	sveinn	otr	karl	-l, n, s, –
acc	svein	otr	karl	–
dat	sveini	otri	karli	-i
gen	sveins	otrs	karls	-s, ar
Pl *nom*	sveinar	otrar	karlar	-ar
acc	sveina	otra	karla	-a
dat	sveinum	otrum	körlum	-um
gen	sveina	otra	karla	-a

5.11 EXERCISE – STRONG NOUNS – TYPE 1 MASCULINE

The strong masculine nouns *víkingr* and *hestr* follow the pattern of *konungr*. *Jarl* follows *karl*. Decline these nouns below.

	VÍKINGR	HESTR	JARL
Sg			
nom	_____	_____	_____
acc	_____	_____	_____
dat	_____	_____	_____
gen	_____	_____	_____
Pl			
nom	_____	_____	_____
acc	_____	_____	_____
dat	_____	_____	_____
gen	_____	_____	_____

Transl: *víkingr* 'Viking,' *hestr* 'stallion,' and *jarl* 'earl'

5.12 THE NOUNS *MAÐR* AND *SONR*

Two of the most commonly used nouns in the sagas are somewhat irregular. These are *maðr* and *sonr*, words which are cognate with English *man* and *son*.

Maðr means 'man' as well as 'person,' whether male or female, and in the plural 'men' or 'people.' It is frequently used in compounds, such as *landnámsmaðr* 'settler,' *farmaðr* 'trader,' and *þingmaðr* 'thingman, the follower of an Icelandic *goði*.'

The -ð- in *maðr* is the result of a sound change in which -nn- changed to -ð- when followed by -r-. Hence, *mannr* from an earlier stage of the language became *maðr* in the nominative singular while -nn- was retained in other cases. Another example of this change occurs in the adverb *suðr* 'to the south,' based on the stem *sunn-* (compare the adverb *sunnan* 'from the south').

		MAÐR	**SONR**	**EGILSSON**
Sg *nom*		maðr	sonr	Egilsson
	acc	mann	son	Egilsson
	dat	manni	syni	Egilssyni
	gen	manns	sonar	Egilssonar
Pl *nom*		menn	synir	Egilssynir
	acc	menn	sonu	Egilsonu
	dat	mönnum	sonum	Egilssonum
	gen	manna	sona	Egilssona

Sonr declines with a *-y-* in the dat sg (*syni*) and nom pl (*synir*). It also drops the nom *-r* ending when used in compounds (Egils**son**, Bárðar**son**).

5.13 EXERCISE – *MAÐR* AND *SONR*
Decline *maðr* and *sonr* in the following sentences and translate. The case is provided for you in the column on the left.

Ex: Þorsteinn hét _*maðr*_____.   _*Menn*_____ fara til Grœnlands.
    There was a man named Þorstein.   *Men travel to Greenland.*

CASE	SINGULAR	PLURAL
nom	1. Herjólfr hét _____.	5. _____ gera brú þessa.
acc	2. Þorgerðr sá _____.	6. Þyri sá _____.
dat	3. Hon bjó á Drepstokki með _____.	7. Hon var með _____.
gen	4. Hon gerði brú þessa fyr sálu _____.	8. Þeir fara til _____.

Ex: Bjarni hét _*sonr*_____ Herjólfs.   _*Synir*_____ hans búa á Drepstokki.
    The son of Herjolf was named Bjarni.   *His sons live at Drepstokki.*

CASE	SINGULAR	PLURAL
nom	9. _____ hans fór til Grœnlands.	13. _____ hans fóru til Grœnlands.
acc	10. Óláfr mælir við _____ sinn.	14. Ingólfr mælir við _____ sína.

11. Hann bjó á Drepstokki með ___   15. Hann bjó á Drepstokki með _____
dat   ___sínum.   sínum.

_____   _____

gen 12. Hon var móðir _____ **hans**.   16. Móðir   hans hét Ásgerðr.

_____   _____

5.14 THE WEAK VERB *HAFA* IN THE PRESENT TENSE

The weak verb *hafa* 'have' is one of the most frequently used verbs in Old Norse. It belongs to the 4th conjugation and is irregular in the present singular.

Present Tense

Sg 1st	ek	hef	(I have)	Pl	vér (vit)	hö**fum**	(we have)
2nd	þú	hef**r**	(you have)		þér (þit)	haf**ið**	(you have)
3rd	hann	hef**r**	(he, she, it has)		þeir	haf**a**	(they have)

Hafa also frequently occurs with the vocalic link *-i-* between verb stem and ending in the present singular: *ek hefi; þú hefir; hann hefir.*

5.15 EXERCISE – *HAFA*

Complete the sentences with the correct forms of *hafa* in the present tense.

Ex: ek *hef* _____   6. hann _____

_____   _____

1. þér _____   7. vit _____

                                         _____

2. vér _____   8. þau _____

3. þeir _____   _____

_____   9. þit _____

4. hon _____   _____

_____   10. þær _____

5. þú _____   _____

_____   11. Haraldr _____

                                         _____

5.16 GRAMMAR TOOLBOX. PREPOSITIONS

Prepositions are words that introduce phrases specifying time, place, direction, and manner. In prepositional phrases, nouns and pronouns become objects. Prepositions affect nouns by governing or determining their case.

There are relatively few prepositions, and it is best to learn them according to the case(s) they govern. Some prepositions require their nouns to be in the accusative, some in the dative, and some in the genitive. Another important group takes either the accusative or the dative, depending on the intended meaning.

Prepositions Taking the Accusative. A few prepositions principally take the accusative.

> *umfram* beyond, more than
> *gegnum* through (also *í gegnum*)

gegnum vegginn (*acc*)	*through* the wall
í gegnum eyjarnar (*acc*)	*through* the islands

Prepositions Taking the Dative.

> | | |
> |---|---|
> | *af* of, out of, from | *nær* near |
> | *at* towards, against, at, to | *ór* or *úr* from |
> | *frá* from, about | *undan* (from) under, (from) |
> | *hjá* by, near, with | beneath, near (to) |
> | *móti* against, contrary to, toward | |
> | (usually *á móti* or *í móti*) | |

af skipi (*dat*)	*from* a ship
hjá Haraldi (*dat*)	*with* Harald
móti honum (*dat*)	*against* him
ór Noregi (*dat*)	*from* Norway
undan ströndum (*dat*)	*near* to shore

Prepositions Taking the Genitive.

> *meðal* among, between
> *milli* between
>   (also *á milli*, *í milli*)
> *til* to

á milli Vágs ok Reykjaness (*gen*)	*between* Vag and Reykjanes
til skipsins (*gen*)	*to* the ship

Prepositions Taking Either the Accusative or the Dative.

á on, onto	*of* over, for
eptir (*ept*) after	*um* around, about; across
fyrir (*fyr*) before, in front of	*undir* (*und*) under
í in, into	*við* against, toward, with
með with	*yfir* over

Hann gekk **á** skip (*acc*).	*He went* **onto** *a ship.*
Hann gekk **á** skip**i** (*dat*).	*He walked about* **on** *a ship.*
Hann stóð **á** skip**i** (*dat*).	He stood **on** a ship.

These prepositions usually take the accusative when they express motion (for example, moving into, onto, or towards something). In contrast, they usually take the *dative* when expressing static position (that is, lack of motion, for example 'walking on a ship' or 'standing on the deck').

In the first example, *á* indicates motion toward the ship, requiring the noun to take the accusative. In the second and third examples, *á* indicates a stationary position with respect to the ship, thus requiring the dative.

The preposition *um* normally takes the accusative, for example, *um skipit* (*acc*) 'around the ship,' *bera öl um eld* (*acc*) 'carry ale across the fire.' On occasion, as for example in time expressions, *um* takes the dative, *bæði um haustum* (*dat*) *ok várum* (*dat*) 'around both the fall and spring,'

Með ('with') is somewhat special. The object of this preposition usually takes the accusative case if it is a thing or person being brought, carried, or forced.

Þeir hljópu á brott **með** kon**ur** (*acc*) þeirra, lausafé (*acc*), ok bátinn (*acc*).
They ran off with their women, chattels, and the boat.

If the object of *með* is a person or thing and expresses accompaniment (being 'with' someone or something), then the dative is mostly used.

Þórólfr var **með** konung**i** (*dat*).	*Thorolf was* **with** *the king.*

Prepositions Taking Either the Accusative or the Genitive. Prepositions ending in -*an* take accusative when expressing motion and genitive when expressing static position.

> **handan** 'on the other side of'
> **innan** 'from the inside'
> **neðan** 'from below'
> **ofan** 'above the surface of'
> **útan** 'from the outside'

Hann kom **útan** fjörð**inn** (*acc*).	*He came* (*from the outside*) **into** *the fjord.*
Hann stóð **útan** dyra (*gen*).	*He stood* **outside** *the door.*

When preceded by *fyrir*, prepositions ending with -*an* answer the question 'place where' and take the accusative case, for example

fyrir ofan sjó	*above the water*
fyrir útan hús	*outside the house*
fyrir ofan garð	*above the farm*
fyrir neðan brú	*below the bridge*
fyrir útan fjall	*beyond the mountain*

5.17 READING – A MAN OF MODERATION (*GUNNLAUGS SAGA ORMSTUNGU*)

Icelandic chieftains (*goðar*, sg *goði*, or *höfðingjar*, sg *höfðingi*) played the role of advocate and upheld a standard of moderation, termed *hóf*. An individual who observed this standard was called a *hófsmaðr*, a person of justice and temperance. The opposite of a *hófsmaðr* was an *ójafnaðarmaðr*, an unequal, overbearing, and aggressive person. *The Saga of Gunnlaug Serpent-Tongue* (*Gunnlaugs saga ormstungu*) describes the chieftain Thorstein Egilsson, whose penchant for restraint was in marked contrast with the temperament of his father, the Viking warrior-poet Egil Skalla-Grimsson.

Gunnlaugs saga ormstungu (ch 1)

Þorsteinn hét maðr; hann var Egilsson, Skalla-Grímssonar, Kveld-Úlfssonar hersis ór Nóregi; en Ásgerðr hét móðir Þorsteins ok var Bjarnardóttir. Þorsteinn bjó at Borg í Borgarfirði; hann var auðigr at fé ok höfðingi mikill, vitr maðr ok hógværr ok hófsmaðr um alla hluti. Engi var hann afreksmaðr um vöxt eða afl sem Egill,[12] faðir hans, en þó var hann it mesta afarmenni[13] ok vinsæll af allri alþýðu.

VOCABULARY

❖**af** *prep* [*w dat*] of, by; off (of), out of, from

afarmenni *n* a big or strong man

afl *n* physical strength

afreksmaðr *m* outstanding or exceptional man

❖**allr** <*m acc pl* alla, *f dat sg* allri, *f* öll, *n* allt> *adj pron* all, entire, whole

alþýða *f* all the people, the majority of the people, the public, the common people

at *prep* [*w dat*] at, in; as to, as, with respect to; on account of, by reason of; close up to, around, by

❖**auðigr** <*acc* auðgan> *adj* rich, wealthy; **auðigr at fé** very wealthy

Ásgerðr <*acc & dat* Ásgerði, *gen* Ásgerðar> *f* Asgerd (*personal name*)

Bjarnardóttir *f* daughter of Bjorn (*personal name*)

Borg *f* Borg (*place name*)

Borgarfjörðr <*dat* Borgafirði> *m* Borg's Fjord (*place name*)

búa *vb* live in a place, dwell; **bjó** (*3sg past*)

❖**eða** *conj* or

Egill <*dat* Agli, *gen* Egils> *m* Egil (*personal name*)

en þó *adv* nevertheless

❖**engi** <*f* engi, *n* ekki> *indef pron* no one, none, no

❖**fé** <*gen* fjár, *gen pl* fjá> *n* cattle, sheep; wealth, money

hersir <-is, -ar> *m* regional military leader in Norway; chieftain; lord

❖**hlutr** <-ar, -ir, *acc pl* hluti> *m* lot; thing

hófsmaðr *m* man of moderation

hógværr *adj* gentle

höfðingi <*gen* -ja, *pl* -jar> *m* leader; chieftain; captain

inn, in, it *art* the

Kveld-Úlfsson *m* son of Kveld-Ulf (*personal name*), kveld-Ulfr, Night-Wolf

---

[12] **Engi var hann ... sem Egill:** 'He was not an outstanding man in size or strength like Egil.'
[13] **it mesta afarmenni:** 'a most powerful or strong man.'

mesta *wk n nom sg superl adj from* **mikill** most

❖**mikill** <*f* mikil, *n* mikit, *comp* meiri, *superl* mestr> *adj* big, tall, great; much, very

Nóregr <-s> *m* Norway

❖**ór** (*also* **úr**) *prep* [*w dat*] out of, from

❖**sem** *conj* as

Skalla-Grímsson *m* the son of Skalla-Grim (*personal name*), Bald-Grim

um alla hluti in every way

❖**vinsæll** *adj* beloved, popular

❖**vitr** <*acc* vitran> *adj* wise

vöxtr <*acc* vöxt, *dat* vexti, *gen* vaxtar, *pl* vextir, *acc* vöxtu> *m* size, stature, growth; shape

Þorsteinn <-s> *m* Thorstein (*personal name*)

TRANSLATION

There was a man named Thorstein. He was the son of Egil, the son of Skalla-Grim, the son of Kveld-Ulf, a chieftain from Norway; and Thorstein's mother was named Asgerd and was the daughter of Bjarni. Thorstein lived at Borg in Borg's Fjord; he was very wealthy and a great leader, a wise man and gentle and a man of moderation in all respects. He was not an outstanding man in size or strength as Egil, his father. Nevertheless he was an extremely strong man and popular among the people.

5.18 WORD FREQUENCY VOCABULARY – LIST 5. THE MOST FREQUENT WORDS IN THE SAGAS

NOUNS	ADJECTIVES	PRONOUNS	NUMERALS
jarl – earl	**sterkr** – strong	**hon** – she, it	**fjórir** – four
faðir – father	**ungr** – young	**allr** – all	
ferð – journey	**víss** – certain; wise		
sumar – summer	**vándr** – bad		

VERBS	PREPOSITIONS AND ADVERBS	CONJUNCTIONS
þykkja – to seem	**eptir** – after	**ef** – if
eiga – to own	**vel** – well	**eða** – or
láta – to let	**upp** – up	
heita – to call; be named	**síðan** – then	

EXERCISES

5.19 Readings. Give the gender, case, number and English meaning of the underlined nouns from the Ramsund runestone.

Sigríðr gerði <u>brú</u> þessa <u>móðir</u> <u>Alreks</u> <u>dóttir</u> <u>Orms</u> fyr <u>sálu</u> <u>Hólmgeirs</u> <u>föður</u> <u>Sigrøðar</u> <u>búanda</u> síns.

NOUN	GENDER	CASE	NUMBER	ENGLISH
1. Sigríðr				
2. brú				
3. móðir				
4. Alreks				
5. dóttir				
6. Orms				
7. sálu				
8. Hólmgeirs				
9. föður				
10. Sigrøðar				
11. búanda				

5.20 Readings. The following sentences come from the readings. Put the words into proper order.

Ex: þessi / Haraldr / eptir / kumbl / gera / Gorm / bað / konungr

Haraldr konungr bað gera kumbl þessi eptir Gorm.

1. gerði / Hólmgeirs / brú / Sigríðr / fyrir / þessa / sálu

2. móðir / Ásgerðr / en / Þorsteins / hét / Bjarnardóttir / var / ok

3. höfðingi / hann / mikill / fé / ok / auðigr / var / at

4. afreksmaðr / eða / Egill / afl / engi / vöxt / var / sem / um / hann

5.21 Readings. Translate the following passage from the *Saga of Gunnlaug Serpent Tongue*.

Þorsteinn hét maðr; hann var
Egilsson, Skalla-Grímssonar,
Kveld-Úlfssonar hersis ór Nóregi;
en Ásgerðr hét móðir Þorsteins
ok var Bjarnardóttir.

5.22 Special Stem Rules. Give the stem of the following strong masculine nouns and state the applicable rule. If no Special Stem Rule applies, write 'n/a' (not applicable).

Ex: steinn (*gen* steins)   *stein-*   *Rule 1 (r-Change)*

        vetr (*gen* vetrs)   *vetr-*   *Rule 2 (r-Drop)*

1. hafr (*gen* hafrs)

2. hamr (*gen* hams)

3. morginn (*gen* morgins) _____   _____

4. hungr (*gen* hungrs) _____   _____
5. vagn (*gen* vagns) _____   _____
6. sveinn (*gen* sveins) _____   _____
7. sigr (*gen* sigrs) _____   _____
8. jötunn (*gen* jötuns) _____   _____
9. þegn (*gen* þegns) _____   _____
10. hagr (*gen* hags) _____   _____
11. angr (*gen* angrs) _____   _____

5.23 Nouns. Decline the following Type 1 strong masculine nouns. *Hundr* and *fiskr* decline like *konungr*, *læknir* like *hersir*, and *hörr* like *söngr*.

	HUNDR	FISKR	LÆKNIR	HÖRR
Sg *nom*	_____	_____	_____	_____
acc	_____	_____	_____	_____
dat	_____	_____	_____	_____
gen	_____	_____	_____	_____
Pl *nom*	_____	_____	_____	_____
acc	_____	_____	_____	_____
dat	_____	_____	_____	_____
gen	_____	_____	_____	_____

Transl: hundr 'dog,' *fiskr* 'fish,' *læknir* 'physician,' *hörr* 'flax, linen'

5.24 *Sonr* and *Maðr*. Identify the case and number of the nouns *maðr* and *sonr* in the passage below from *Gunnlaugs saga ormstungu*.

Þorsteinn hét <u>maðr</u>; hann var Egils<u>son</u>, Skalla-Gríms<u>sonar</u>, Kveld-Úlfs<u>sonar</u> hersis ór Nóregi.

1. maðr _____   3. Egilsson _____

2. Skalla-Grímssonar _____   4. Kveld-Úlfssonar _____

5.25 Prepositions.

A.   Translate the following sentences.

1. Bjarni gekk á skip.   _____
2. Ásgerðr gekk á skipi.   _____

B.   Fill in the blanks with the appropriate preposition.

í   til   eptir   á   á milli

1.   Haraldr konungr bað gera kumbl þessi _____ Gorm föður sinn ok
     eptir Þyri móður sína.

2.   Skútaðar-Skeggi hét maðr ágætr _____ Nóregi.

3.   Hann fór _____ Íslands ok nam Miðfjörð ok Línakradal.

4.   Hann var _____ skipi.

5.   Ingólfr gaf Herjólfi land _____ Vágs ok Reykjaness.

5.26 Verb Review. Conjugate the verbs *vera* and *hafa* in the present tense.

   vera

1.   Ek _____ kona Herjólfs.   4.   Vér _____ víkingar.

2.   Þú _____ kona Herjólfs.   5.   Þér _____ víkingar.

3.   Hon _____ kona Herjólfs.   6.   Þeir _____ víkingar.

   hafa

7.   Ek _____ skip.   10.   Vér _____ skip.

8.   Þú _____ skip.   11.   Þér _____ skip.

9.   Hann _____ skip.   12.   Þeir _____ skip.

5.27 Pronoun Review. Fill in the blanks with the correct pronouns.

   Ex: Ingólfr gaf Herjólfi land.

   ___*Hann*___ gaf Herjólfi land. Ingólfr gaf ___*honum*___ land.

1.   Herjólfr var frændi Alreks.

     _____ var frændi Alreks. Herjólfr var frændi _____.

2.   Herjólfr fór til Grœnlands með Eiríki.

     _____ fór til Grœnlands með Eiríki. Herjólfr fór til Grœnlands með
     _____.

3.   Móðir Bjarna hét Þorgerðr. (Remember that Bjarni is a man's name)

     _____ hét Þorgerðr. Móðir _____ hét Þorgerðr.

4.   Haraldr gerði kumbl eptir Gorm.

     _____ gerði kumbl eptir Gorm. Haraldr gerði kumbl eptir _____.

5.28 Genealogy. Beginning with *Kveld-Úlfr*, chart the genealogy in the reading passage from *Gunnlaugs Saga* by filling in the family tree below. The wife of *Þorsteinn* was *Jófríðr* and one of their children was *Helga in fagra* (Helga the Fair).

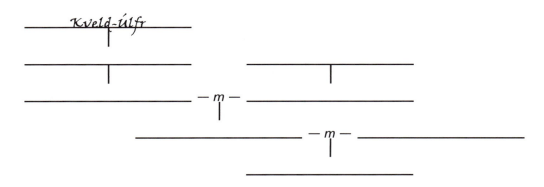

5.29 Runic Script. Fill in the blanks below. The first line has been done as an example.

RUNIC SCRIPT	TRANSLITERATION	STANDARDIZED OLD NORSE
Ex: ᛋᛁᚱᛁᚦᛦ	*siriþr*	*Sigríðr*
1. ᛘᚢᚦᛁᛆ	_____	_____
2. ᚠᛆᚦᚢᚱ	_____	_____
3. ᛋᛆᚢᚢ	_____	_____
4. _____	hulmkirs	_____
5. ᛒᚢᛏᛏᛏ	_____	_____
6. _____	fur	_____
7. _____	tutiR	_____

5.30 Runic Script. Write your name and the names of three other people.

_____   _____   _____   _____

Note on Runic spelling: Represent the pronunciation of the word as closely possible. See the preceding lesson for a list of runic equivalents for some letters in the English alphabet not found in the younger futhark. If you don't know which rune to use, experiment by pronouncing the rune and word aloud. Viking Age rune masters followed the same process. They depended on their ear.

LESSON 6
SACRAL KINGSHIP IN ANCIENT SCANDINAVIA

Er mér úlfsins ván, er ek eyrun sé
(I expect a wolf when I see its ears)

Figure 25. The Swedes Kill Their King, Domaldi.

6.1 CULTURE – THE YNGLINGS IN SWEDEN AND NORWAY

The passages in this lesson recount legendary history from Icelandic written sources. The first reading is from *The Saga of The Ynglings* (*Ynglinga saga*), the opening section of Snorri Sturluson's *Heimskringla*, a history of the kings of Norway. *Ynglinga saga* is a mixture of mythic and legendary stories about the Ynglingar, a line of Swedish rulers who claimed descent from the fertility god Yngvi-Freyr, and the family took its name from this god. Although the Ynglings were from Sweden (Svíþjóð or Svíaland), its members formed alliances with families in other Scandinavian regions.

One branch of the Ynglings rose to prominence in the Vík region of southern Norway. The second reading of this lesson tells of Halfdan the Black (Hálfdan svarti) an early member of the Norwegian Ynglingar. Halfdan started as a petty king ruling the small kingdom of Agder. Through war and negotiation, he greatly increased the size of his kingdom until he became a powerful chieftain in Vestfold. Halfdan was the ancestor of Norway's Viking Age kings, who called themselves Ynglingar.

6.2 READING – DOMALDI SACRIFICED FOR BETTER HARVESTS (*YNGLINGA SAGA*, FROM *HEIMSKRINGLA*)

The following passage is about Domaldi, a Swedish Ynglingr King. It takes place during a severe famine in Sweden, which lasted over three autumns. The story is told according to a chronology involving *it fyrsta haust* 'the first autumn,' *annat haust* 'the second autumn,' and *it þriðja haust* 'the third autumn.'

Ynglinga saga (ch 15)

Dómaldi tók arf eptir föður sinn, Vísbur, ok réð löndum. Á hans dögum gerðisk sultr ok seyra[14] í Svíþjóð. Þá hófu Svíar blót stór at Uppsölum. It fyrsta haust[15] blótuðu þeir yxnum, en batnaði ekki árferð. En annat haust hófu þeir mannblót, en árferð var söm eða verri. En it þriðja haust kómu Svíar fjölmennt til Uppsala at hefja blót. Þá áttu höfðingjar ráðagørð sína, ok kom þat ásamt með þeim,[16] at hallærit stóð af Dómalda, konungi þeira, ok þat með,[17] at þeir skyldu blóta honum ok veita honum atgöngu ok drepa hann ok rjóða stalla með blóði hans, ok svá gerðu þeir.

VOCABULARY

af *prep* [*w dat*] from, by

❖**annarr** <*f* önnur, *n nom & acc sg* annat> *adj pron* one of two, other, another; second

arfr <-s> *m* inheritance

at *prep* [*w dat*] at, in

❖**at** *conj* that

at *inf marker* to

atganga *f* attack

❖**á** *prep* [*w acc*] onto, on, towards (*motion*); with respect to; [*w dat*] on; upon; at; in (*position*)

árferð *f* season, harvest

ásamt *adv* together

áttu *3pl past of* **eiga**

batna <-að-> *vb* improve; *impers* [*e-m*] **batnar** one recovers

batnaði *3sg past of* **batna**

blóð *n* blood

blót *n* sacrifice

blóta <-að> *vb* [*w acc*] worship; worship with sacrifice; [*w dat*] sacrifice, sacrifice in worship

blótuðu *3pl past of* **blóta** (*wk vb*)

❖**dagr** <*dat* degi, *gen* dags, *pl* dagar, *dat* dögum> *m* day

Dómaldi *m* Domaldi (*personal name*)

❖**drepa** <drepr, drap, drápu, drepinn> *vb* slay, kill, smite

❖**eða** *conj* or

❖**eiga** <á, átti, áttr> *pret-pres vb* own, have, possess; **eiga ráðagørð** take council

❖**ekki** *adv* not

fjölmennt *adv* in crowds, in large numbers

❖**fyrstr** <*wk n acc sg* fyrsta> *superl adj of* **fyrri** first

❖**gera** (*also* **gøra**) <-ði, -ðr~gerr> *vb* make;

---

[14] **gerðisk sultr ok seyra:** 'there was hunger and starvation.'

[15] **it fyrsta haust, annat haust, it þriðja haust:** In Old Norse, the accusative case is used without a preposition to express the time when something happens.

[16] **kom þat ásamt með þeim:** 'it was agreed among them.'

[17] **ok þat með:** 'accordingly,' 'and along with that.'

do, act; **gerask** *mid* become, come to pass, occur, happen

gerðisk *3sg past mid of* **gera**

gerðu *3pl past of* **gera**

hallæri *n* famine; **hallæri-t** the famine

haust *n* autumn

hefja <hefr, hóf, hófu, hafinn> *vb* lift, raise, heave; begin

hófu *3pl past of* **hefja**

höfðingi <*gen* -ja, *pl* -jar> *m* leader; chieftain

❖**í** *prep* [*w acc*] into (*motion*); [*w dat*] in, within, at (*position*)

kom *1/3sg past of* **koma**

❖**koma** <kemr~kømr, kom, kómu~kvámu, kominn> *vb* come

kómu *3pl past of* **koma**

mannblót *n* human sacrifice

❖**með** *prep* [*w acc*] with (*in the sense of bringing, carrying, or forcing*); [*w dat*] with (*in the sense of accompanying or togetherness*); **með** *adv* as well, with it

❖**ráða** <ræðr, réð, réðu, ráðinn> *vb* [*w dat*] advise, counsel; rule, govern, manage; **réð löndum** ruled over (his) lands

ráðagørð *f* council

réð *1/3sg past of* **ráða**

rjóða <rýðr, rauð, ruðu, roðinn> *vb* redden

❖**samr** <*f* söm, *n* samt> *adj pron* same

seyra *f* starvation

❖**sinn** *refl poss pron* his, her, its own

sína *f acc sg of* **sinn**

❖**skulu** <skal, skyldi, *past inf* skyldu> *pret-pres vb* shall (*obligation, purpose, necessity, fate*); should

skyldu *3pl past of* **skulu**

stalli *m* altar (heathen)

❖**standa** <stendr, stóð, stóðu, staðinn> *vb* stand; **standa af [e-u]** be caused by [sth]

stóð *1/3sg past of* **standa**

❖**stórr** <*n acc pl* stór> *adj* big

sultr <-ar> *m* hunger

❖**svá** *adv* so, thus; so

Svíar *m pl* the Swedes

Svíþjóð *f* Sweden (*place name*)

söm *see* **samr**

❖**taka** <tekr, tók, tóku, tekinn> *vb* take; **taka arf** inherit

tók *1/3sg past of* **taka**

Uppsalir <*dat pl* Uppsölum, *gen pl* Uppsala> *m pl* Uppsala (*place name*)

uxi (*also* **oxi**) <*acc, dat, & gen* uxa, *pl* yxn~øxn, *dat* yxnum~øxnum, *gen* yxna~øxna> *m* ox

❖**veita** <-tti, -ttr> *vb* grant, give, offer; assist; **veita [e-m] atgöngu** attack [sb]

verri *comp adj of* **illr** worse

Vísburr <-s> *m* Visbur (*personal name*)

yxnum *see* **uxi**

❖**þá** *adv* then, at that time

þeir <*acc* þá, *dat* þeim, *gen* þeira~þeirra> *pron* they (*m pl*)

þriði <*n acc sg* þriðja> *ord num* third

TRANSLATION

Domaldi took the inheritance after [the death of] his father Visbur and ruled over his lands. In his days there was famine and starvation in Sweden. Then the Swedes began large sacrifices in Uppsala. The first autumn they sacrificed oxen, but the season did not improve. A second autumn they sacrificed humans, but the harvest was the same or worse. In the third autumn, the Swedes came in great numbers to Uppsala to make sacrifices. Then the chieftains held a council. They agreed that the famine was due to Domaldi, their king, and because of that, they should sacrifice him and attack him and kill him and redden the altars with his blood. And so they did.

6.3 CULTURE – THE TEMPLE AT UPPSALA AND HUMAN SACRIFICE

Accounts of pagan religious practice survive in medieval Christian writings. A famous example comes from the German cleric Adam of Bremen. Writing ca. 1070, Adam described what he had heard of the temple at Uppsala in Sweden. This building, he reports, contained cult statues of gods similar to Thor, Odin, and Frey. Adam, who wrote in Latin, gives an account of a pagan festival which a traveler described to him:

> It is customary also to solemnize in Uppsala, at nine-year intervals, a general feast of all the provinces of Sweden. From attendance at this festival no one is exempted. Kings and people all and singly send their gifts to Uppsala and, what is more distressing than any kind of punishment, those who have already adopted Christianity redeem themselves through these ceremonies. The sacrifice is of this nature: of every living thing that is male, they offer nine heads, with the blood of which it is customary to placate gods of this sort. The bodies they hang in the sacred grove that adjoins the temple. Now this grove is so sacred in the eyes of the heathen that each and every tree in it is believed to be divine because of the death or putrefaction of the victims. Even dogs and horses hang there with men. A Christian seventy-two years old told me that he had seen their bodies suspended promiscuously.
>
> (Trans. Francis J. Tschan. *History of the Archbishops of Hamburg-Bremen*)

Adam's Christian viewpoint, education, and perhaps his imagination may have influenced his description. Nevertheless, from this and other sources, it seems clear that open-air, blood sacrifice was a part of pagan Norse religious practice.

6.4 STRONG NOUNS – TYPE 1 FEMININES AND NEUTERS

Feminine. Most strong feminine nouns belong to Type 1. An important feature is *u*-umlaut in the nominative, accusative, and dative singular. *U*-umlaut in these nouns recalls a time in the language when -*u* existed as an ending. This ending was dropped before the time of the Viking Age, but its effect remained on stems containing the vowel -*a*-, as in the words *mön* (stem *man*-, gen *manar*) and *för* (stem *far*-, gen *farar*).

	RÚN	FÖR	KERLING	SKEL	ÖR	HEIÐR	ENDINGS
Sg *nom*	rún	för	kerling	skel	ör	heiðr	–, -r
acc	rún	för	kerling	skel	ör	heiði	–, -i
dat	rún	för	kerlingu	skel	ör	heiði	–, -u, -i
gen	rúnar	farar	kerlingar	skeljar	örvar	heiðar	-ar
Pl *nom*	rúnar	farar	kerlingar	skeljar	örvar	heiðar	-ar
acc	rúnar	farar	kerlingar	skeljar	örvar	heiðar	-ar
dat	rúnum	förum	kerlingum	skeljum	örum	heiðum	-um
gen	rúna	fara	kerlinga	skelja	örva	heiða	-a

Transl: *rún* 'rune,' *för* 'journey,' *kerling* 'old woman,' *skel* 'shell,' *ör* 'arrow,' *heiðr* 'heath'

- The large majority of Type 1 feminines follows the declension of *rún* and *för*.
- Some Type 1 feminines, such as *skel* and *ey*, have a stem final *-j-* which appears only before *-a-* and *-u-*. So do many feminine names, such as *Signý* (acc *Signýju*).
- Some, such as *ör* (see above), have stem final *-v-* which appears only before *-a-* and *-i-*.
- Some, such as *laug, ull, ey, hel,* and those ending in *-ing* (*kerling*) and *-ung* (*lausung*) have the ending *-u* in the dative singular.
- Some, such as *heiðr* and *hildr*, have *-r* in the nominative and *-i* in the accusative and dative singular. Feminine names ending in *-r* decline like *heiðr* (*Ásgerðr, Þorgerðr, Brynhildr, Gunnhildr,* and *Sigríðr*). Names ending in *-dís*, such as *Freydís* and *Ásdís*, have no *-r* in the nominative singular, but otherwise decline like *Ásgerðr*. Nouns like *heiðr*, but whose stems end in *-k-* or *-g-*, show stem-final *-j-* before *-a-* and *-u-*: *ylgr* (pl *ylgjar*), *gýgr* (pl *gýgjar*) and *rygr* (pl *rýgjar*).

Neuter. All strong neuter nouns belong to Type 1 and decline much like the masculines. These nouns show *u*-umlaut in the nominative and accusative plural, as in the word *land* (pl *lönd*). In words of more than one syllable, *u*-umlaut shifts *-a-* to *-ö-* in the first syllable (stressed) and to *-u-* in following (unstressed) syllables, for example *herað*, pl *heruð*.

	SKIP	LAND	HERAÐ	KYN	HÖGG	KVÆÐI	ENDINGS
Sg *nom*	skip	land	herað	kyn	högg	kvæði	–, -i
acc	skip	land	herað	kyn	högg	kvæði	–, -i
dat	skipi	landi	heraði	kyni	höggvi	kvæði	-i
gen	skips	lands	heraðs	kyns	höggs	kvæðis	-s, -is
Pl *nom*	skip	lönd	heruð	kyn	högg	kvæði	–, -i
acc	skip	lönd	heruð	kyn	högg	kvæði	–, -i
dat	skipum	löndum	heruðum	kynjum	höggum	kvæðum	-um
gen	skipa	landa	heraða	kynja	höggva	kvæða	-a

Transl: *skip* 'ship,' *land* 'land,' *herað* 'district,' *kyn* 'kin,' *högg* 'blow,' *kvæði* 'poem'

- The majority of Type 1 neuters follow the declension of *skip*, *land*, and *herað*.
- Some Type 1 neuters, such as *kyn*, have stem-final *-j-*. So also *egg*, *men*, *nef*, and *ský*.
- Some, such as *högg* (see above), have stem-final *-v-* (which appears before *-a-* and *-i-*). So also, *böl*, *mjöl*, and *smjör*.
- Others, like *kvæði*, insert *-i-* before the endings except in the dative and genitive plural. So also *leyfi, ørendi, enni* and *fylki*. Nouns of this group with roots ending in *-k-* or *-g-*, such as *fylki* and *ríki,* have stem-final *-j-*, for example, *fylkjum, fylkja* and *ríkjum, ríkja*.

6.5 Exercise – Strong Nouns, Type 1 Feminines and Neuters

Decline *mön* (feminine), *nál* (feminine), and *bak* (neuter).

	MÖN	NÁL	BAK
Sg nom	_____	_____	_____
acc	_____	_____	_____
dat	_____	_____	_____
gen	_____	_____	_____
Pl nom	_____	_____	_____
acc	_____	_____	_____
dat	_____	_____	_____
gen	_____	_____	_____

Transl: *mön* 'mane,' *nál* 'needle,' *bak* 'back'

6.6 Past Tense of Weak Verbs

All weak verbs form their past tense by adding a suffix containing a dental consonant (*-ð-*, *-d-*, or *-t-*) plus the past tense ending. For example: *kall-að-a* 'I called,' *mæl-t-a* 'I spoke,' *tal-d-a* 'I counted,' and *vak-t-a* 'I woke.' All weak verbs share the same past tense endings but differ somewhat in the dental suffix.

Past Tense Endings of Weak Verbs		
	Singular	**Plural**
1st	-a	-um
2nd	-ir	-uð
3rd	-i	-u

1st conjugation weak verbs insert the past tense dental suffix *-að-* before the endings (*kall-**að**-i*). The past endings *-um*, *-uð*, and *-u* trigger *u*-umlaut in the plural, changing *-að-* to *-uð-* (*köll-**uð**-u*). All other weak verbs add a dental suffix without a linking vowel (*mæl-**t**-i, tal-**d**-i, vak-**t**-i*).

| | | 1ˢᵀ CONJUG | 2ᴺᴰ CONJUG | 3ᴿᴰ CONJUG | 4ᵀᴴ CONJUG |
		KALLA	*MÆLA*	*TELJA*	*VAKA*
Sg *1ˢᵗ*	ek	kalla**ð**a	mæl**t**a	tal**d**a	vak**t**a
2ⁿᵈ	þú	kalla**ð**ir	mæl**t**ir	tal**d**ir	vak**t**ir
3ʳᵈ	hann	kalla**ð**i	mæl**t**i	tal**d**i	vak**t**i
Pl *1ˢᵗ*	vér	köll**uð**um	mæl**t**um	töl**d**um	vök**t**um
2ⁿᵈ	þér	köll**uð**uð	mæl**t**uð	töl**d**uð	vök**t**uð
3ʳᵈ	þeir	köll**uð**u	mæl**t**u	töl**d**u	vök**t**u

- A few important 2ⁿᵈ conjugation weak verbs have irregular past tense stems. These are *sœkja* (3sg past *sótt-i*), *þykkja* (*þótt-i*) and *yrkja* (*ort-i*). Note that in English the same verbs, such as *seek* (past *sought*) and *think* (past *thought*), show similar irregularity. The same pattern can be seen in *work* and the archaic past tense form *wrought* (*worked*).

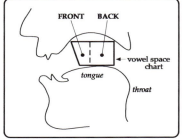

Figure 26. The Vowel Space Chart and the Vocal Tract, showing the portion of the vocal tract used for the production of vowels.

- 3ʳᵈ conjugation weak verbs often show vowel alternation between present and past. The two most common patterns are *e-a* (*telja*, *ta*ldi*) and *y˜-u* (*spyrja*, *spurði*).

- The past tense of the important 4ᵗʰ conjugation weak verb *hafa* is regular: *ek hafða, þú hafðir, hann hafði, vér höfðum, þér höfðuð, þeir höfðu.*

6.7 VOWEL SOUNDS AND ASSIMILATION

Assimilation is a process in which one sound becomes more like a neighboring sound in its pronunciation, acquiring one or more of its attributes. Factors differentiating one vowel from another are positions of the tongue and lips. For example, when pronouncing the vowel in the English word 's**ee**' (the phonetic symbol **i** in the Figure), the lips are spread and the tongue is forward and up toward the roof of the mouth. When pronouncing the vowel in the English word 's**ue**,' however, the lips assume a more rounded shape and the tongue is farther back.

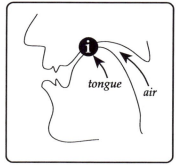

Figure 27. Pronunciation of the Vowel *i*, as in English 'see.'

Vowels can be charted according to whether they are high, mid, or low and front or back. The terms describe the position of the tongue. Additionally each vowel is rounded or unrounded, depending upon the shape of the lips while the vowel is being pronounced. The vowel in the word 's**ee**' is

Figure 28. The Vowel *i*.

high, front, and unrounded, while the vowel in 'sue' is high, back, and rounded.

Vowels can be plotted on a vowel space chart which is an effective tool for visualizing the relative position of vowels in the mouth. Because the sound *i* (as in 'see)' is produced high in the mouth with the tongue raised toward the front of the mouth, it is found high and front on the vowel space chart.

The two charts below, one for short vowels and one for long vowels, plot the positions in the mouth of thirteenth-century Old Icelandic vowels.

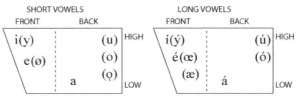

Figure 29. Old Icelandic Vowel System. Vowels within parentheses are rounded.

6.8 *I*-UMLAUT

Old Icelandic exhibits a series of regular vowel alternations known as *i*-umlaut. Unlike *u*-umlaut, which applies only to the vowel -*a*- (*saga*, gen *sögu*), *i*-umlaut operates on a range of vowels. The following chart gives the full set of *i*-umlaut vowel alternations.

VOWEL		WITH *I*-UMLAUT	VOWEL		WITH *I*-UMLAUT
a	>	**e**	**u**	>	**y**
á	>	**æ**	**(j)ú/jó**	>	**ý**
o	>	**ø** (later **e**)	**ö(ǫ)**	>	**ø**
ó	>	**œ**	**au**	>	**ey**

These alternations occur throughout Old Icelandic grammar.

- The plurals of certain types of nouns; for example, *faðir*, pl *feðr*; *maðr*, pl *menn*; *bróðir*, pl *brœðr*; *áss* 'god,' pl *æsir*.

SHORT VOWELS   LONG VOWELS

Figure 30. I-Umlaut of Old Icelandic Vowels. Vowels within parentheses are rounded.

- The dative singular of some nouns; for example, *völlr* 'field, plain' (stem *vall-*), dat *velli*; *hönd* 'hand' (stem *hand-*), dat *hendi*.

- The comparative and superlative forms of adjectives; for example, *fagr*, *fegri*, *fegrstr* 'fair, fairer, fairest'; *hár*, *hær(r)i*, *hæstr* 'high, higher, highest'; *stórr*, *stœrri*, *stœrstr* 'big, bigger, biggest.'

- The present singular of strong verbs; for example, *fara, hon ferr* 'she travels'; *standa, hon stendr* 'she stands'; *ráða, hon ræðr* 'she rules'; *róa* 'row,' *hon rœr* 'she rows.'

Like *u*-umlaut, *i*-umlaut in Old Icelandic goes back to a process of sound assimilation in pre-Viking times. Back vowels were fronted when followed by a suffix containing *-i-* (or *-j-*). For example, *á* (back and low) in *áss* becomes *æ* (front and high) in *æsir* as noted in the accompanying vowel charts.

By the Viking Age, the conditioning environment for *i*-umlaut was lost in many words, but the fronted vowels remained. These fronted vowels became part of the grammar of the language. For instance, a shifted vowel marks the difference between singular and plural in many nouns, such as *maðr* (pl *menn*), *gás* (pl *gæss*), *fótr* (pl *fœtr*), and *mús* (pl *mýss*). English also went through a period of *i*-umlaut and employs a shifted vowel in the plural of the same words: *man* (pl *men*), *goose* (pl *geese*), *foot* (pl *feet*), and *mouse* (pl *mice*). *I*-umlaut plays a similar role in strong verbs, distinguishing present singular from plural.

INFINITIVE		*3SG PRES WITH I-UMLAUT*
fara	>	ferr
ráða	>	ræðr
koma	>	kømr
fljúga	>	flýgr
hlaupa	>	hleypr

In Old Icelandic, a suffix containing an *-i-* cannot be used to predict the application of *i*-umlaut. Some examples which do not show shifted vowels are *landi* (dat sg of *land*), *staði* (dat sg of *staðr*), *farinn* (ppart of *fara*), *standinn* (ppart of *standa*), *farið* (2pl pres of *fara*), and *standið* (2pl pres of *standa*). Some examples which do show shifted vowels are *degi* (dat sg of *dagr*) and *tekinn* (ppart of *taka*).

6.9 IDENTIFYING THE FOUR WEAK VERB CONJUGATIONS

This section introduces a series of steps enabling the identification of a weak verb's conjugation, provided one knows its infinitive and past tense stem (the 3sg past minus its ending).

Step 1. Does the weak verb have a past tense stem ending in *-að-* (for example *kalla*, *kallaði*)? If yes, it is 1st conjugation. If no, proceed to step 2.

Step 2. Does the root vowel of the infinitive show *i*-umlaut (is the vowel *-e-*, *-æ-*, *-ø-*, *-œ-*, *-y-*, *-ý-*, or *-ey-*)? If no, the verb is 4th conjugation. If yes, proceed to step 3. **Exceptions:** *segja* and *þegja* are 4th conjugation, *vilja* is 3rd conjugation, and a small number of single-syllable verbs ending in *-á* or *-já*, such as *spá*, are 2nd conjugation.

Step 3. Is the stem long or short (see explanation in the box below)? If long, the verb is 2nd conjugation. If short the verb is 3rd conjugation. **Exception:** *gera* belongs to the 2nd conjugation.

To determine a weak verb's stem length, one counts the number of vowels and consonants in the stem, starting with the vowel.

Long stems consist of a short vowel followed by two consonants (**send**-a, **erf**-a, **fylg**-ja, **yrk**-ja, **þykk**-ja) or a long vowel followed by a single consonant (**mæl**-a, **þýð**-a, **sœk**-ja, **heyr**-a). These are 2nd conjugation.

Short stems consist of a short vowel followed by a single consonant (**tel**-ja, **ber**-ja, **spyr**-ja, **vil**-ja) or a long vowel followed by no consonant at all (**kný**-ja). These are 3rd conjugation. (Note that -gg- counts as a single consonant when determining stem length, hence leggja (past lagði) and hyggja (hugði) are 3rd conjugation verbs.)

6.10 EXERCISE – IDENTIFYING WEAK VERB CONJUGATIONS

Identify the conjugations of each weak verb below and translate.

Ex: kalla, kallaði _____1st, call_____

1. ætla, ætlaði _____
2. veita, veitti _____
3. tala, talaði _____
4. hafa, hafði _____
5. skilja, skildi _____
6. vaka, vakti _____
7. setja, setti _____
8. mæla, mælti _____
9. svara, svaraði _____
10. segja, sagði _____
11. þora, þorði _____
12. leita, leitaði _____
13. senda, sendi _____
14. una, unði _____

6.11 VERBS – VOICE, AN INTRODUCTION

There are three **voices**: active, middle, and passive. In Old Norse, verbs have active and middle endings, while the passive voice is usually expressed with a helping verb and past participle. Voice answers the following important question: what is the role of the subject in the sentence?

Verbs with **active** endings indicate that the subject *performs* the action expressed by the verb. All the verb endings and formations discussed to this point in the book are active, and the readings contain many examples.

Dómaldi **réð** löndum.	*Domaldi ruled the lands.*
Blótuðu þeir yxnum.	*They sacrificed oxen.*
Hófu þeir mannblót.	*They began human sacrifices.*

A verb generally takes **middle** endings when the subject performs an action on or for him- or herself. This use of the middle is called reflexive because the action reflects back on the subject. Although usage of the middle voice centers around the reflexive, it has been extended to encompass a range of related functions, such as the expression of reciprocal actions (actions performed by subjects on 'each other'). These will be discussed in more detail later in this book.

The middle voice is easily recognized by its distinctive endings. In the 1sg the ending is *-umk* and in the 1pl *-umk* or *-umsk*. The 2nd and 3rd persons add *-sk* to the active endings. The following examples come from the readings.

> Á hans dögum **gerðisk** sultr ok seyra í Svíþjóð.
> *In his days there was famine and starvation in Sweden.*

> **Beiddusk** allir at hafa líkit með sér.
> *All asked to take the body for themselves.*

> En þeir **sættusk** svá, at líkinu var skipt í fjóra staði.
> *And they agreed among themselves that the*
> *body would be divided between four places.*

	ACTIVE GERA		MIDDLE GERASK	
	PRES	PAST	PRES	PAST
Sg *1st*	geri	gerða	gerumk	gerðumk
2nd	gerir	gerðir	gerisk	gerðisk
3rd	gerir	gerði	gerisk	gerðisk
Pl *1st*	gerum	gerðum	gerum(s)k	gerðum(s)k
2nd	gerið	gerðuð	gerizk	gerðuzk
3rd	gera	gerðu	gerask	gerðusk

In the middle voice *-r-* drops before *-sk* (for example, *gerir* becomes *gerisk*). When a dental (*-ð-, -d-, -t-*) precedes *-sk*, the dental drops and *-sk* changes to *-zk* (for example, *gerið* becomes *gerizk*).

The **passive** voice is used when the subject undergoes an action rather than performing it. The passive does not have a distinct set of endings but employs the auxiliary verb *vera* (also *verða* or *hafa*) with a past participle. The reading contains several examples.

Lík hans **var flutt** á Hringaríki.	*His body was moved to Hringariki.*
Var höfuðit **lagit** í haug at Steini.	*The head was placed in a mound at Stein.*
ok **eru kallaðir** Hálfdanarhaugar.	*and [they] are called Halfdan's mounds.*

6.12 CULTURE – SNORRI STURLUSON AND *HEIMSKRINGLA*

Both readings in this lesson come from *Heimskringla*, attributed to the Icelandic chieftain

Snorri Sturluson (1179–1241). *Heimskringa* is a major source for the medieval history, myth, and legend of the Scandinavian countries as well as a work of great literary merit.

Figure 31. Snorri Sturluson

The oldest, complete extant manuscript of *Heimskringla* dates from the seventeenth century. It was probably about this time that *Heimskringla* acquired its name, which means 'Orb of the World.'

Heimskringla begins with *Ynglinga saga* whose opening words are '*Kringla heimsins*,' a phrase that may originally be a translation of Latin *Orbis Terrarum* ('The Orb of the World'). *Ynglinga saga* uses these words because it provides a description of world geography before tracing the lineage of the Yngling kings back to their mythical origins.

Although we know a good deal about Snorri as one of the most powerful Icelandic chieftains of his time, the medieval sources tell little about him as a writer. For this reason, it is not certain how much, if any, Snorri himself wrote of *Heimskringla* or the other texts which are often attributed to him. Perhaps Snorri, who was a rich man, supplied the vision for the work and commissioned writers, whom he oversaw. It seems likely that the majority of *Heimskringla* was written in the 1220s and 1230s.

Heimskringla consists of a short prologue and 16 individual sagas. The first, *Ynglinga saga*, begins in mythic times and traces the descent of the Norwegian kings from the gods down to Halfdan the Black (*Hálfdan svarti*), who is the focus of the second saga. The rest of the sagas are dedicated to individual kings, arranged chronologically according to their reigns. *Heimskringla* reveals the characters of the individual kings through their actions. The work tells history as collections of stories motivated by the personalities of the different kings.

Heimskringla relies on three main sources: oral tradition, skaldic verse, and written Icelandic and Norwegian prose. Snorri had the opportunity to collect local oral traditions when he visited Norway in 1218–1220, and he would have known stories of the kings told in Iceland. Of the probable written prose sources, several have survived. These include the manuscripts *Morkinskinna* and *Fagrskinna*, the Norwegian *Ágrip af Nóregs konunga sögum*, as well as several Icelandic sagas. Snorri also incorporated some 600 verses from over 70 skalds into his work. Some of these poems, often a stanza or two, were used for dramatic effect in well-known stories. Others seem to have been the sole source for the episodes in which they appear. Even today, Heimskringla remains a major source for early Scandinavian myth, legend, and history. Without it, our knowledge of Viking Age, especially in Norway, would be much diminished.

Figure 32. King Halfdan's Sleigh Falls Through the Ice

6.13 READING – HALFDAN THE BLACK'S BODY IN FOUR PARTS (*HÁLFDANAR SAGA SVARTA*, FROM *HEIMSKRINGLA*)

The Saga of King Halfdan the Black (*Hálfdanar saga svarta*) is found in *Heimskringla* and *Fagrskinna*. Halfdan was a petty king in the *Víkin* region of Southern Norway. He carved out a small kingdom on the Vestfold side of the Oslo Fjord in the mid-ninth century.

Halfdan was the son of Queen Asa, who may be one of the two women, whose skeletons were found buried in the Oseberg ship. This extensively carved royal coastal barge was excavated in 1904 and is one of the two most complete ship burial sites unearthed in Norway. The other major ship burial is the Gokstad ship as in the Oslo Fjord area.

From Halfdan came a great dynasty. His son was Harald Fairhair (*Haraldr hárfagri*), the king who is said to have conquered most of Norway in the late ninth century. The saga reports that Halfdan died unexpectedly at the age of 40 at the height of his power while returning from a feast. He and his entourage drowned when his sleigh fell through the ice of Lake Rand during a spring thaw.

The reading passage below reclates that, upon Halfdan's death, people from each of the four *fylki* ('counties' or 'districts') of his kingdom sought to have the king buried in their own region in order to secure the continued prosperity and fertility of future harvests. The account may be an echo of sacred kingship in Old Scandinavia. The solution was to divide the king's body into four parts and build burial mounds for the parts in different regions of the kingdom.

Hálfdanar saga svarta (ch 9)
Hann hafði verit allra konunga ársælstr. Svá mikit gerðu menn sér um hann, at þá er[18] þat

---

[18] **þá er:** 'then when,' but better translated as simply 'when.'

spurðusk, at hann var dauðr ok lík hans var flutt á Hringaríki ok var þar til graptar ætlat,[19] þá fóru ríkismenn af Raumaríki ok af Vestfold ok Heiðmörk ok beiddusk allir at hafa líkit með sér ok heygja í sínu fylki, ok þótti þat vera árvænt þeim,[20] er næði. En þeir sættusk svá, at líkinu var skipt í fjóra staði,[21] ok var höfuðit lagit í haug at Steini á Hringaríki, en hverir fluttu heim sinn hluta ok heygðu, ok eru þat allt kallaðir Hálfdanarhaugar.

VOCABULARY

❖**allr** <*m nom pl* allir, *gen pl* allra, *f* öll, *n* allt> *adj pron* all, entire, whole

allt *adv* completely; everywhere

❖**á** *prep* [*w acc*] onto, on, towards (*motion*); with respect to; [*w dat*] on; upon; at; in (*position*)

ársæll *adj* fortunate as to the seasonal harvest; **allra konunga ársælstr** of all kings the most harvest-fortunate

ársælstr *superl of* **ársæll**

árvænn <*f* árvæn, *n* árvænt> *adj* promising a good seasonal harvest

beiða <beiddi, beiddr> *vb* ask, beg; **beiðask** *mid* ask for, request on one's own behalf

beiddusk *3pl past mid of* **beiða**

❖**dauðr** <*f* dauð, *n* dautt> *adj* dead

❖**er** *rel particle* who, which, that

❖**fara** <ferr, fór, fóru, farinn> *vb* go, travel

❖**fjórir** <*m acc pl* fjóra> *num* four

flutt moved, carried (*ppart of* **flytja**)

flytja <flutti, fluttr> *vb* convey, move, carry

fóru *3pl past of* **fara**

fylki *n* province

❖**gera** (*also* **gøra**) <-ði, -ðr~gerr> *vb* make; do, act; **gera sér mikit um [e-n]** make much of or admire [sb]

graptar *see* **gröptr**

gröptr <*dat* grepti, *gen* graptar> *m* digging, burial

❖**hafa** <hef(i)r, hafði, haft> *vb* have; hold, keep; take

haugr <-s, -ar> *m* burial mound

Hálfdanarhaugar *m pl* Halfdan's Mounds

Heiðmörk *f* Heidmork (*place name*)

❖**heim** *adv* (to) home, homeward

heygja <-ði, -ðr> *vb* bury in a mound

hluti *m* part

Hringaríki *n* Hringariki (*place name*)

hverir *m nom pl of* **hverr**

❖**hverr** <*m nom pl* hverir> *indef pron* each, every, all

❖**höfuð** <*dat* höfði, *pl dat* höfðum, *gen* höfða> *n* head; **höfuð-it** the head

kallaðir called (*ppart of* **kalla**)

lagit placed (*ppart of* **leggja**)

❖**leggja** <lagði, lagiðr~lagðr~laginn> *vb* lay, place, put

lík *n* body; corpse; **lík-it** (*acc*), **lík-inu** (*dat*) the body

❖**með** *prep* [*w acc*] with (*in the sense of bringing, carrying, or forcing*); [*w dat*] with (*in the sense of accompanying or togetherness*)

❖**mikit** *adv* greatly

ná <náir, -ði, nát> *vb* [*w dat*] get, obtain

næði would get (*3sg/pl past subjunct of* **ná**)

Raumaríki *n* Raumariki (*place name*)

---

[19] **til graptar ætlat:** 'intended for burial'

[20] **þótti þat...þeim:** 'that seemed to them'

[21] **at líkinu var skipt í fjóra staði:** Note that *líkinu* is dative singular and there is no nominative subject in this clause to agree with the verb *var*. Impersonal constructions such as these are discussed later in the book.

ríkismaðr *m* great man, prominent man, wealthy man, man of power

skipt divided (*ppart of* **skipta**)

skipta <-ti, -tr> *vb* [*w dat*] divide; share

spurðusk was learned (*3pl past mid of* **spyrja**)

❖**spyrja** <spurði, spurðr> *vb* ask; hear, hear of, learn, be informed of, find out

❖**staðr** <*dat* stað~staði, *gen* staðar, *pl* staðir, *acc pl* staði> *m* place

Steinn <-s> *m* Stein (*place name*), 'Stone'

sætta <-tti, -ttr> *vb* reconcile; make peace among; **sættask** *mid* come to terms, agree, be reconciled

sættusk *3pl past mid of* **sætta**

❖**vera** <er; var, váru; verit> *vb* be

verit been (*ppart of* **vera**)

Vestfold *f* Vestfold (*place name*)

þótti *3sg past of* **þykkja**

❖**þykkja** <þykkir, þótti, þótt> *impers vb* seem to be; [*w dat subj*] think, seem (to one)

❖**ætla** <-að-> *vb* intend

ætlat intended (*ppart of* **ætla**)

TRANSLATION

Of all kings he had been the most fortunate with good harvests. Men admired him so much that when it was learned he was dead, that his body had been carried to Hringariki and was intended for burial there, prominent men traveled from Raumariki and from Vestfold and Heidmork [to Hringariki]. All asked to take the body for themselves to bury it in their own districts. It was thought to ensure good harvests for whoever obtained it. And they agreed among themselves that the body would be divided among four places. The head was placed in a mound at Stein in Hringariki, and each of them took home his part and buried it in a mound, and [these mounds] are all called Halfdan's Mounds.

6.14 WORD FREQUENCY VOCABULARY – LIST 6. THE MOST FREQUENT WORDS IN THE SAGAS

NOUNS	ADJECTIVES	PRONOUNS	NUMERALS
dóttir – daughter	**langr** – long	**sik** – him/herself/ themselves	**sex** – six
þing – assembly	**sárr** – wounded	**annarr** – other; second	
orð – word	**hálfr** – half		
hestr – horse	**vænn** – beautiful		

VERBS	PREPOSITIONS AND ADVERBS	CONJUNCTIONS
búa – to live, dwell; prepare	**þó** – nevertheless	**hvárt** – whether
sjá – to see	**heim** – (to) home	
ríða – to ride	**út** – out	
svara – to answer	**frá** – from	

EXERCISES

6.15 Readings. Are the following statements true or false?

RÉTT eða RANGT?

1. Dómaldi tók arf eptir sonr sinn.   _____
2. Vísburr var faðir Dómalda.   _____
3. Var í Svíþjóð sultr ok seyra.   _____
4. Svíar blótuðu yxnum.   _____
5. Svíar blótuðu mönnum.   _____
6. Svíar áttu ráðagørð.   _____
7. Svíar blótuðu konungi.   _____

6.16 Readings. Use the following words below to complete the sentences.

réð   haust   sultr   yxnum   seyra   blót   þriðja

1. Dómaldi _____ löndum.
2. Þá hófu Svíar _____ stór at Uppsölum.
3. It fyrsta _____ blótuðu þeir _____.
4. En it _____ haust kómu Svíar fjölmennt til Uppsala.
5. Var í Svíþjóð _____ ok _____.

6.17 Vocabulary. Match each of these verbs with its English meaning by drawing a line between the two.

Ex:

vilja   to live
búa   to want

VERBS			*NOUNS*	
		lík	attack
		haust	famine
		fylki	mound
hefja	take	hallæri	altar
flytja	sacrifice	sultr	province
taka	hold; begin; raise	haugr	harvest
blóta	bury in a mound	atganga	hunger
ráða	carry, move	árferð	body
heygja	advise	stalli	autumn

6.18 Nouns. Decline the following Type 1 strong nouns:

Feminine. *Skör* and *nál* decline like *för*, *dögg* like *ör*, and *elfr* like *heiðr*.

Sg nom	SKÖR	NÁL	DÖGG	ELFR
acc	_____	_____	_____	_____
dat	_____	_____	_____	_____
gen	_____	_____	_____	_____
Pl nom	_____	_____	_____	_____
acc	_____	_____	_____	_____

dat	_____	_____	_____	_____
gen	_____	_____	_____	_____

Transl: *skör*, 'edge,' *nál* 'needle,' *dögg* 'dew,' *elfr* 'river'

Neuter. *Barn* and *þing* decline like *land*, *egg* like *kyn*, and *fylki* like *kvæði*.

	BARN	ÞING	EGG	FYLKI
Sg nom	_____	_____	_____	_____
acc	_____	_____	_____	_____
dat	_____	_____	_____	_____
gen	_____	_____	_____	_____
Pl nom	_____	_____	_____	_____
acc	_____	_____	_____	_____
dat	_____	_____	_____	_____
gen	_____	_____	_____	_____

Transl: *barn* 'child,' *þing* 'assembly,' *egg* 'egg,' *fylkt* 'province'

6.19 Weak Verbs. Conjugate the weak verbs *kalla*, *mæla*, *telja*, and *vaka* in the past tense.

	1ST CONJUGATION KALLA	2ND CONJUGATION MÆLA	3RD CONJUGATION TELJA	4TH CONJUGATION VAKA
ek	_____	_____	_____	_____
þú	_____	_____	_____	_____
hann	_____	_____	_____	_____
vér	_____	_____	_____	_____
þér	_____	_____	_____	_____
þeir	_____	_____	_____	_____

6.20 Vowels and *I*-umlaut. Fill in the blanks in the chart below.

VOWEL		WITH I-UMLAUT	VOWEL		WITH I-UMLAUT
1. **a**	>	_____	5. **u**	>	_____
2. **á**	>	_____	6. **(j)ú/jó**	>	_____
3. **o**	>	_____	7. **ö**	>	_____
4. **ó**	>	_____	8. **au**	>	_____

6.21 Identifying Weak Verb Conjugations. The infinitive and 3sg past are given below for ten weak verbs. Identify the conjugation of each, using the three-step method discussed earlier in the lesson. Pay special attention to the -*gg*- in *hyggja* and *leggja*. Are these long or short stems?

Ex: svara, svaraði _____1st_____
1. gera, gerði _____   6. hyggja, hugði _____

2. sœkja, sótti   _____   7. horfa, horfði   _____
3. kaupa, keypti   _____   8. spyrja, spurði   _____
4. vilja, vildi   _____   9. skipa, skipaði   _____
5. þykkja, þótti   _____   10. leggja, lagði   _____

6.22 Weak Verbs. Translate the following phrases into Old Norse and identify the weak verb's conjugation.

	OLD NORSE	CONJUGATION
Ex: I called (*kalla*).	*ek kallaða*	*1st*
1. They (*f*) said (*segja*).		
2. You (*pl*) raided (*herja*).		
3. We (*dual*) made (*gera*).		
4. He sacrificed (*blóta*).		
5. She answered (*svara*).		
6. They (*m*) carried (*flytja*).		
7. You (*sg*) intend (*ætla*).		
8. They (*f*) say(*mæla*).		

6.23 Weak Verb Conjugations. Identify each weak verb below and indicate its conjugation.

	PERSON, NUMBER, TENSE	CONJUGATION
Ex: köllum	*1pl pres*	*1st*
gerði	*3sg past*	*2nd*
1. geri		
2. herjaði		
3. veittir		
4. blótuðu		
5. þegi		
6. leiðið		
7. setti		
8. töluðuð		
9. mælta		
10. spurðu		

6.24 Weak Verb *Hafa*. Conjugate *hafa*.

	PRESENT	PAST
Sg *ek*	_____	_____
þú	_____	_____
hann	_____	_____
Pl *vér*	_____	_____

þér | _____   _____
þeir | _____   _____

6.25 Voice. Identify the underlined verbs and verb phrases as active, middle, or passive.

Ex: It fyrsta haust <u>blótuðu</u> þeir yxnum.   __active__

1.   Á hans dögum <u>gerðisk</u> sultr ok seyra í Svíþjóð.   _____

2.   En it þriðja haust <u>kómu</u> Svíar fjölmennt til Uppsala at hefja blót.   _____

3.   Hann <u>hafði verit</u> allra konunga ársælstr.   _____

4.   <u>Beiddusk</u> allir at hafa líkit með sér ok heygja í sínu fylki.   _____

5.   Hann <u>herjaði</u> í austrveg í Danmörk við Sjáland.   _____

6.   En þeir sættusk svá, at líkinu <u>var skipt</u> í fjóra staði.   _____

7.   En þeir <u>sættusk</u> svá, at líkinu var skipt í fjóra staði.   _____

8.   Ok <u>eru</u> þat allt <u>kallaðir</u> Hálfdanarhaugar.   _____

LESSON 7
NORWAY'S HARALD FAIRHAIR
AND HIS SON EIRIK BLOODAXE

Illt er at fljúga fjaðralauss
(It is bad to fly without feathers)

7.1 CULTURE – HARALD FAIRHAIR

Harald (*Haraldr hárfagri*) was the son of Halfdan the Black and a member of the Norwegian Yngling Dynasty. Harald began his career as a chieftain. He ruled a series of small, separated kingdoms which his father had acquired in Vestfold in the *Víkin* region (see the accompanying map in this lesson). In the 860s, Harald began the conquest of all Norway (*Nóregr*).

Figure 33. The Sea Battle at Hafrsfjord. Sea battles were often fought as floating land battles. Ships of allies were tied together, and men moved from one ship to another. Here, King Harald meets his opponents in the battle at Hafrsfjord in Western Norway.

According to the sagas, Harald had vowed not to cut his hair until he attained his goal, and Icelandic sources often refer to him as Harald Shaggyhair (*Haraldr lúfa*). After his conquest, in which he seems to have brought a large part of the southern coastal region of Norway under his control, he had his hair cut and was called 'Fairhair.'

7.2 READING – HARALD FIGHTS HIS WAY TO THE THRONE (*GRETTIS SAGA ÁSMUNDARSONAR*)

At the time of Harald's conquest, Norway was divided into chieftaincies and petty kingdoms. Harald conquered many of them. His final victory came at Hafrsfjord (ca. 885-990) in southwestern Norway, where Harald and his allies defeated the combined fleet of his remaining opponents. Many Icelandic sagas begin with stories about Harald, and according to *Grettir's Saga* (*Grettis saga Ásmundarsonar*) in the passage below, Harald's enemies were led by Kjotvi the Wealthy (Kjötvi inn auðgi), Thorir Long Chin (Þórir haklangr), and King Sulki.

Grettis saga Ásmundarsonar (ch 2)

Þenna tíma var ófriðr mikill í Nóregi; brauzk þar til ríkis Haraldr lúfa, sonr Hálfdanar svarta; hann var áðr konungr á Upplöndum. Síðan fór hann norðr í land ok átti þar margar orrostur, ok hafði hann jafnan sigr. Herjaði hann svá suðr eptir landinu ok lagði undir sik, hvar sem hann fór; en er[22] hann kom upp á Hörðaland,[23] kom í móti honum múgr ok margmenni. Váru þar formenn: Kjötvi inn auðgi ok Þórir haklangr ok þeir Suðr-Rygirnir ok Súlki konungr.[24] Fundr þeira Haralds konungs varð á Rogalandi, í firði þeim, er heitir í Hafrsfirði.

VOCABULARY

❖**áðr** *adv* before; already

átti *3sg past of* **eiga**

brauzk *3sg past mid of* **brjóta**

brjóta <brýtr, braut, brutu, brotinn> *vb* break, break up, break open; **brjótask til ríkis** fight for the kingdom

❖**eiga** <á, átti, áttr> *pret-pres vb* own, have, possess

en er *conj* but when

❖**eptir** *prep* [*w dat*] after, for; along; **eptir landinu** along the coast

❖**er** *rel particle* who, which, that; *conj* when; where

❖**fara** <ferr, fór, fóru, farinn> *vb* go, travel; move

firði *see* **fjörðr**

fjörðr *m* fjord; **firði** (*dat*)

formaðr *m* leader, chieftain

fór *1/3sg past of* **fara**

❖**fundr** <-ar, -ir> *m* meeting; finding, discovery

❖**hafa** <hef(i)r, hafði, haft> *vb* have; hold, keep

Haraldr lúfa *m* Harald Shaggyhair (*personal name*)

Hafrsfjörðr *m* Hafrsfjord (*place name*); **í Hafrsfirði** in Hafrsfjord

Hálfdan svarti *m* Halfdan the Black (*personal name*)

herja <-að-> *vb* raid, harry; make war

❖**hvar** *interrog adv* where; **hvar sem** wherever

Hörðaland *n* Hordaland (place name)

jafnan *adv* always; constantly; equally

Kjötvi inn auðgi *m* Kjotvi the Wealthy (*personal name*)

kom *1/3sg past of* **koma**

❖**koma** <kemr~kømr, kom, kómu~kvámu, kominn> *vb* come

❖**leggja** <lagði, lagiðr~lagðr~laginn> *vb* lay, place, put; **leggja undir sik** conquer

margmenni *n* multitude, many men

❖**margr** <*f* mörg, *f acc pl* margar, *n* margt~mart> *adj* (*w sg*) many a; (*w pl*) many

❖**móti** (*also* **á móti** *and* **í móti**) *prep* [*w dat*] towards; against, contrary to

múgr <-s, -ar> *m* crowd

norðr *adv* north, northward

orrosta *f* battle

---

[22] **en er:** 'but when'

[23] **Rogaland** and **Hörðaland**: Rogaland and Hordaland are regions in Western Norway. In early times, before King Harald Fairhair unified Norway, many such small regions in Norway were independent chiefdoms ruled by warlords or petty kings.

[24] **þeir Suðr-Rygirnir ok Súlki konungr:** 'King Sulki and his South Rogalanders'

ófriðr <-ar> *m* war, strife; *lit* un-peace, unrest

ríki <*dat pl* ríkjum, *gen pl* ríkja> *n* power; realm; kingdom

Rogaland *n* Rogaland (*place name*)

❖**sá** <*f* sú, *n* þat> *dem pron* that (one)

sigr <-rs> *m* victory

❖**síðan** *adv* then

suðr *adv* south, southward

Suðr-Rygirnir *m pl* South Rogalanders

Súlki konungr *m* King Sulki (*personal name*)

❖**svá** *adv* so, thus; such; then; so (*denoting degree*)

tími *m* time

❖**undir** *prep* [*w acc/dat*] under, underneath

❖**upp** *adv* up

Upplönd *n pl* uplands, highlands (*place name*)

varð *1/3sg past of* **verða**

❖**verða** <verðr, varð, urðu, orðinn> *vb* become; happen, take place

þeim *dat sg of* **sá**

þenna *see* **þessi**

❖**þessi** <*m acc sg* þenna> *dem pron* this, these

Þórir haklangr *m* Thorir Longchin (*personal name*)

TRANSLATION

At this time there was great strife in Norway. Harald Shaggyhair, the son of Halfdan the Black, was fighting his way to power. He was previously a king in the Uplands. Then he went north into the country, and there he had many battles and always had victory. He then raided south along the coast and he conquered wherever he went. But when he came up into Hordaland, a large number of men opposed him. The chieftains there were Kjotvi the Wealthy, Thorir Longchin, and King Sulki and his South Rogalanders. Their encounter with King Harald took place in Rogaland, in that fjord which is called Hafrsfjord.

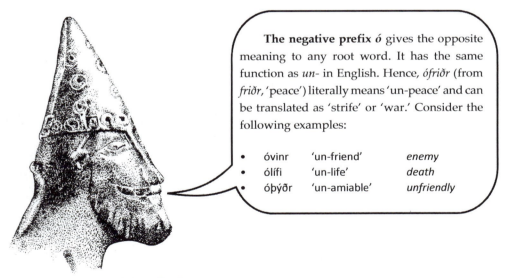

The **negative prefix** *ó* gives the opposite meaning to any root word. It has the same function as *un-* in English. Hence, *ófriðr* (from *friðr*, 'peace') literally means 'un-peace' and can be translated as 'strife' or 'war.' Consider the following examples:

- óvinr   'un-friend'   *enemy*
- ólífi   'un-life'   *death*
- óþýðr   'un-amiable'   *unfriendly*

Figure 34. The Negative Prefix *ó*.

7.3 CULTURE – HARALD FAIRHAIR

Sources about Harald, all of which were written centuries after his death, suggest that he pursued his goals with intelligence and ruthlessness. He obtained an alliance with Hakon, the Earl of Lade (Hákon Hlaðajarl), the powerful ruler of the Trondelag region (Þrœndalǫg,

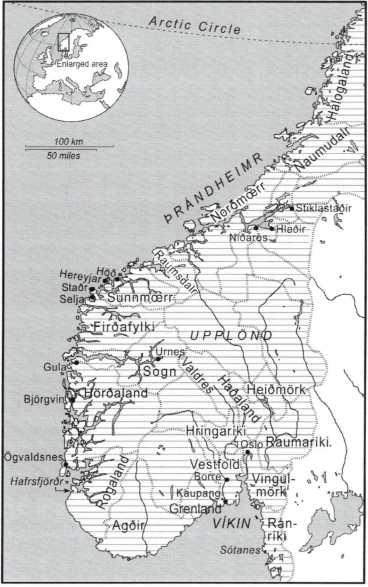

Figure 35. Viking Age Norway (*Noregr*).

Modern Norwegian Trøndelag) further north up the coast. The alliance secured both ends of a lucrative trade route between Vestfold and Trondelag. Together the allies subdued West Norway, the fjord region whose Vikings had preyed upon the rich trade moving north and south along the coast.

Harald and his northern allies relied on substantial sea power. Their efforts culminated in the decisive victory at Hafrsfjord. Although Icelandic sagas refer to Harald as ruler of all Norway, his control over Norway's inland and northern regions was weak.

The cohesiveness of Harald's mostly coastal realm did not last long after his death in the 930s. In becoming Norway's recognized king, Harald Fairhair set a pattern for later Norwegian kings.

After Harald's death, dynastic struggles among his many heirs and conflicts with the rival dynasty of the northern earls of Lade, launched Norway into violent power struggles that lasted into the thirteenth century.

7.4 REFLEXIVE PRONOUNS

Old Norse employs the 3rd person reflexive pronoun *sik* when referring back to the subject. This pronoun, in both singular and plural, has only three forms: *sik, sér, sín* (acc, dat, gen). These are used for all three genders and mean 'himself,' 'herself,' 'itself,' and 'themselves.' Compare the following:

Reflexive Pronoun *Sik*	
nom	—
acc	**sik**
dat	**sér**
gen	**sín**

	H e l g i
	*took **him***
Helgi hafði **hann** í brott.	*[someone else] away.*
Helgi hafði **sik** í brott.	*Helgi took **himself** away.*
Mennirnir fengu **þeim** skip.	*The men procured a ship **for them** [for others].*
Mennirnir fengu **sér** skip.	*The men procured a ship **for themselves**.*
Ásgerðr fór heim til **hennar**.	*Asgerd went home [to someone else's home].*
Ásgerðr fór heim til **sín**.	*Asgerd went home [to her own home].*

There is no distinction between personal and reflexive pronouns in the 1st and 2nd persons. Hence *mik, mér, mín* means either 'me' or 'myself,' and *þik, þér, þín* 'you (sg)' or 'yourself.' Likewise *oss, oss, vár* means either 'us' or 'ourselves,' and *yðr, yðr, yðar* 'you (pl)' or 'yourselves.'

Hann sér **mik**.	*He sees **me**.*
Ek sé **mik**.	*I see **myself**.*
Hon sér **þik**.	*She sees **you**.*
Þú sér **þik**.	*You see **yourself**.*

7.5 Exercise – Reflexive Pronouns

Choose the Old Norse equivalent, a or b, of each English sentence below.

1. *I have given myself a name.*

   a) Þeir hafa gefit mér nafn.

   b) Ek hefi gefit mér nafn.

2. *King Gormr made a monument for himself.*

   a) Gormr konungr gerði sér kumbl.

   b) Gormr konungr gerði oss kumbl.

3. *Hrafnkell had a great temple built for himself.*

   a) Hrafnkell lét gera þér hof mikit.

   b) Hrafnkell lét gera sér hof mikit.

7.6 STRONG NOUNS – TYPE 2

Type 2 strong nouns include masculines and feminines but no neuters.

Masculine. The principal difference between Type 1 and Type 2 masculines is that Type 1 has -*a*- in the nominative and accusative plural (*konungar, konunga*) and Type 2 has -*i*- (*staðir, staði*). Also, Type 2 masculines usually lack dative singular -*i*.

		STAÐR	VINR	GESTR	ELGR	BŒR	ENDING
Sg	nom	staðr	vinr	gestr	elgr	bœr	-r
	acc	stað	vin	gest	elg	bœ	–
	dat	stað	vin	gesti	elg	bœ	–, -i
	gen	staðar	vinar	gests	elgs~elgjar	bœjar	-ar, -s
Pl	nom	staðir	vinir	gestir	elgir	bœir	-ir
	acc	staði	vini	gesti	elgi	bœi	-i
	dat	stöðum	vinum	gestum	elgjum	bœjum	-um
	gen	staða	vina	gesta	elgja	bœja	-a

Transl: *staðr* 'place,' *vinr* 'friend,' *gestr* 'guest,' *elgr* 'elk,' *bœr* 'farmstead'

- Some Type 2 masculines have genitive singular ending -*ar*, some -*s*; a few employ both.
- Some have stem-final -*j*- (*bœr, bœjum*).

Feminine. Type 2 has -*ir* in the plural where Type 1 has -*ar*. These nouns show *u*-umlaut in the nominative, accusative, and dative singular when the stem contains -*a*-. Some Type 2 feminines, such as *jörð* and *borg*, have the ending -*u* in the dative singular. Nevertheless, most follow the declension of *öxl*, *höfn*, and *norn*, shown below.

		ÖXL	HÖFN	NORN	JÖRÐ	BORG	ENDING
Sg	nom	öxl	höfn	norn	jörð	borg	–
	acc	öxl	höfn	norn	jörð	borg	–
	dat	öxl	höfn	norn	jörðu	borgu	–, -u
	gen	axlar	hafnar	nornar	jarðar	borgar	-ar
Pl	nom	axlir	hafnir	nornir	jarðir	borgir	-ir
	acc	axlir	hafnir	nornir	jarðir	borgir	-ir
	dat	öxlum	höfnum	nornum	jörðum	borgum	-um
	gen	axla	hafna	norna	jarða	borga	-a

Transl: *öxl* 'shoulder,' *höfn* 'harbor,' *norn* 'Norn,' *jörð* 'earth,' *borg* 'town'

7.7 EXERCISE – TYPE 2 STRONG NOUNS

Decline the masculines *hugr* (like *staðr*), *svanr* (like *gestr*) as well as the feminines *þökk* (like *öxl*), *höll* (like *jörð*).

	HUGR M	SVANR M	ÞÖKK F	HÖLL F
Sg *nom*	*hugr*	*svanr*	*þökk*	*höll*
acc				
dat				
gen				
Pl *nom*				
acc				
dat				
gen				

Transl: *hugr* 'mind,' *svanr* 'swan,' *þökk* 'thanks,' *höll* 'hall'

Manuscripts show some nouns declining as both Type 1 and 2, and for these nouns both forms probably existed in the spoken language. For instance, the dative of *staðr* in some texts is *stað* and in others *staði*. Similarly, *gestr* shows alternate dative forms *gest* and *gesti*, *skógr*, 'forest' has *skógi* and *skóg*, and *vegr* 'wall' has *vegi* and *veg*. In the plural, the word for whale, *hvalr*, has either *hvalar* or *hvalir*, and the word for a prosecution or accusation, *sök*, either *sakar* or *sakir*. In some instances there is a chronological sequence. For example, the word for dale or valley, *dalr*, has *dal* (with *dali* attested in the oldest texts), and in the plural *dalar* or *dalir* (with *dalir* winning out in Modern Icelandic).

7.8 WEAK NOUNS

Weak nouns come in all three genders. In general they are quite regular and have a simpler set of endings than strong nouns.

Masculine. Weak masculine nouns, such as *goði*, *hluti*, and *arfi* always end in *-i* in the nominative singular. The plural endings are identical to Type 1 masculine strong nouns such as *konungr*. Some weak masculine nouns, such as *bryti*, *höfðingi*, and *vöðvi*, have stems ending in *-j-* or *-v-*.

	GOÐI	HLUTI	ARFI	BRYTI	VÖÐVI	ENDINGS
Sg *nom*	goð**i**	hlut**i**	arf**i**	bryt**i**	vöð**vi**	**-i**
acc	goð**a**	hlut**a**	arf**a**	bryt**ja**	vöð**va**	**-a**
dat	goð**a**	hlut**a**	arf**a**	bryt**ja**	vöð**va**	**-a**
gen	goð**a**	hlut**a**	arf**a**	bryt**ja**	vöð**va**	**-a**

Pl nom	goðar	hlutar	arfar	brytjar	vöðvar	-ar
acc	goða	hluta	arfa	brytja	vöðva	-a
dat	goðum	hlutum	örfum	brytjum	vöðum	-um
gen	goða	hluta	arfa	brytja	vöðva	-a

Transl: *goði* 'chieftain,' *hluti* 'part,' *arfi* 'heir,' *bryti* 'bailiff,' *vöðvi* 'muscle'

The noun *uxi* ('ox' sg, 'oxen' pl) is irregular in the plural: *yxn, yxn, yxnum, yxna*.

Feminine. Weak feminine nouns are characterized by *-u* in most endings and show *u*-umlaut, for example *saga~sögu*. The genitive plural ending is *-na*. Genitive plural *kvenna* (from *kona* 'woman') is irregular.

	SAGA	*KONA*	*KIRKJA*	*VÖLVA*	*ENDINGS*
Sg nom	saga	kona	kirkja	völva	-a
acc	sögu	konu	kirkju	völu	-u
dat	sögu	konu	kirkju	völu	-u
gen	sögu	konu	kirkju	völu	-u

Pl nom	sögur	konur	kirkjur	völur	-ur
acc	sögur	konur	kirkjur	völur	-ur
dat	sögum	konum	kirkjum	völum	-um
gen	sagna	kvenna	kirkna	[unattested]	-na

Transl: *saga* 'story,' *kona* 'woman,' *kirkja* 'church,' *völva* 'seeress'

- The stems of some weak feminine nouns, such as *kirkja* and *gyðja*, end in *-j-* . Of these, only those with roots ending in *-k-* or *-g-* take *-na* in the genitive plural (*kirkna*). The genitive plural of all others with stem-final *-j-* is *-a* (*gyðja*).
- The stems of a few weak feminine nouns end in *-v-* (*völva, slöngva*). The genitive plural of these nouns is unattested (i.e. no examples known from manuscripts or runic inscriptions).
- A small group of weak feminine nouns ends in *-i* in all cases of the singular. Most denote abstract notions and have no plurals.

	SPEKI	*REIÐI*	*ELLI*	*FRŒÐI*
	speki	reiði	elli	frœði
	speki	reiði	elli	frœði
	speki	reiði	elli	frœði
	speki	reiði	elli	frœði

Transl: *speki* 'wisdom,' *reiði* 'anger,' *elli* 'age,' *frœði* 'knowledge'

Neuter. There are only a few weak nouns, and all take the ending *-a* in the singular. Most refer to parts of the body (*auga, hjarta, lunga, eyra, nýra* and *eista*).

		AUGA	*HJARTA*	*LUNGA*	*EYRA*	*ENDINGS*
Sg	*nom*	auga	hjarta	lunga	eyra	-a
	acc	auga	hjarta	lunga	eyra	-a
	dat	auga	hjarta	lunga	eyra	-a
	gen	auga	hjarta	lunga	eyra	-a
Pl	*nom*	augu	hjörtu	lungu	eyru	-u
	acc	augu	hjörtu	lungu	eyru	-u
	dat	augum	hjörtum	lungum	eyrum	-um
	gen	augna	hjartna	lungna	eyrna	-na

Transl: *auga* 'eye,' *hjarta* 'heart,' *lunga* 'lung,' *eyra* 'ear'

7.9 EXERCISE – WEAK NOUNS

Decline *bardagi* (m), *gata* (f), and *eyra* (n).

		BARDAGI M	*GATA* F	*EISTA* N
Sg	*nom*	_____	_____	_____
	acc	_____	_____	_____
	dat	_____	_____	_____
	gen	_____	_____	_____
Pl	*nom*	_____	_____	_____
	acc	_____	_____	_____
	dat	_____	_____	_____
	gen	_____	_____	_____

Transl: *bardagi* 'battle,' *gata* 'path,' *eista* 'testicle'

7.10 NOUNS WHOSE STEMS END IN A LONG VOWEL

A few common nouns, such as *mór, skór, á, brú,* and *bú,* have stems ending in a long vowel. These nouns often drop the vowel of the case ending; for example, *á + ar* becomes *ár* 'rivers.'

		MÓR M	*SKÓR* M	*Á* F	*BRÚ* F	*BÚ* N	*TRÉ* N
Sg	*nom*	mór	skór	á	brú	bú	tré
	acc	mó	skó	á	brú	bú	tré
	dat	mó	skó	á	brú	búi	tré
	gen	mós	skós	ár	brúar	bús	trés

	M	M	F	F	N	N
Pl *nom*	móar	skúar	ár	brúar~brúr~brýr	bú	tré
acc	móa	skúa	ár	brúar~brúr~brýr	bú	tré
dat	móm	skóm	ám	brúm	búm	trjám
gen	móa	skúa	á	brúa	búa	trjá

Transl: *mór* 'moor,' *skór* 'shoe,' *á* 'river,' *brú* 'bridge,' *bú* 'farm,' *tré* 'tree'

Figure 36. Ships Riding at Anchor in a Fjord. The sails of the two ships on the right have been taken down and used as tents for the crew in harbor.

7.11 READING – EIRIK BLOODAXE, THE KING'S SON, RECEIVES A SHIP (*EGILS SAGA SKALLA-GRÍMSSONAR*)

In the following passage from Egil's Saga, Prince Eirik Bloodaxe (Eiríkr blóðøx), the favorite son of King Harald Fairhair, admires a ship owned jointly by two companions, the Icelander Thorolf Skalla-Grimsson and the well-born Norwegian Bjorn Brynjolfsson. The companions see an opportunity to gain favor with the future king of Norway.

Egils saga Skalla-Grímssonar (ch 36)

Þórólfr ok Björn höfðu karfa,[25] er reru á borð tólf menn eða þrettán,[26] ok höfðu nær þrjá tigu manna;[27] skip þat höfðu þeir fengit um sumarit í víking; þat var steint mjök fyrir ofan

---

[25] **Karfi** was a fast, coastal rowing ship often used in raiding. It was long and narrow with 6, 12 or 16 rowers on each side. Such boats were also used on large lakes.

[26] **er reru á borð tólf menn eða þrettán:** 'which 12 or 13 men rowed on a side.'

[27] **höfðu nær þrjá tigu manna:** 'they had (a crew) of nearly 30 men.'

sjó ok var it fegrsta. En er þeir kómu til Þóris,[28] fengu þeir þar góðar viðtökur, ok skipit flaut tjaldat fyrir bœnum.

    Þat var einn dag, er þeir Þórólfr ok Björn gengu ofan til skipsins. Þeir sáu, at Eiríkr konungsson var þar, hann gekk stundum á skipit út, en stundum á land upp, hann stóð þá ok horfði á skipit.

    Þá mælti Þórólfr: "Vandliga hyggr þú at skipinu, konungsson; hversu lízk þér á?"

    "Vel," segir hann, "skipit er it fegrsta," segir hann.[29]

    "Þá vil ek gefa þér skipit," sagði Þórólfr, "ef þú vill þiggja."[30]

    "Þiggja vil ek," segir Eiríkr.

VOCABULARY

at *conj* that

á *prep* [*w acc*] onto; with respect to

borð *f* side of a ship; **á borð** on each side

bœr (*also* bær) <*gen* bœjar~býjar, *pl* bœir, *dat* bœjum, *gen* bœja> *m* farm, farmhouse, farmstead; landed estate; **bœ-num**) the farmstead

❖**dagr** <*dat* degi, *gen* dags, *pl* dagar> *m* day

❖**einn** <*f* ein, *n* eitt, *ord* fyrstr 'first'> *num* one; *indef pron* a, an, a certain one

en *conj* and, but

❖**er** *rel particle* who, which, that; *conj* when; where

❖**fagr** <*f* fögr, *n* fagrt, *comp* fegri, *superl* fegrstr> *adj* beautiful, fair, attractive

❖**fá** <fær, fekk, fengu, fenginn> *vb* get, take, procure; **fá góðar viðtökur** be welcomed well

fegrstr *superl adj of* **fagr**; **it fegrsta** the most beautiful

fengit *ppart of* **fá**

fengu *3pl past of* **fá**

flaut *1/3sg past of* **fljóta**

fljóta <flýtr, flaut, flutu, flotinn> *vb* float; **skipit flaut** the ship floated (at anchor)

fyrir ofan *prep* [*w acc*] above

❖**ganga** <gengr, gekk, gengu, genginn> *vb* walk; go; **ganga til** go up to, go toward

❖**gefa** <gefr, gaf, gáfu, gefinn> *vb* give, grant

gekk *1/3sg past of* **ganga**

gengu *3pl past of* **ganga**

❖**góðr** <*f* góð, *f acc pl* góðar, *n* gott; *comp* betri, *superl* beztr> *adj* good

hersir <-is, -ar> *m* regional military leader in Norway; chieftain

horfa <-ði, horft> *vb* turn, look (in a particular direction); **horfði á skipit** he looked at the ship

❖**hversu** *adv* how

hyggja <hugði, hugðr~hugaðr> *vb* think, believe; **vandliga hyggr þú at skipinu** you carefully consider the ship

karfi *m* a fast, coastal rowing ship

---

[28] **En er þeir kómu til Þóris:** 'And when they arrived at Thórir's home.' Earl Thorir Hroaldsson (*Jarl Þórir Hróaldsson*) was a *hersir* in Firðafylki in Western Norway. A *hersir* was a Norwegian regional military leader. King Harald Fairhair abolished the regional small kings of Norway but kept the title of *hersir*, giving it to some of his own followers such as *Þórir hersir*. Although not royal, a *hersir* had noble status and functioned much as a local chieftain. The office was hereditary.

[29] Present tense *segir* contrasts with past tense *mælti* in the previous sentence. The abrupt change from past to present within a narrative is common in Old Norse texts and is sometimes called the 'historic present.'

[30] **ef þú vill þiggja:** 'if you are willing to accept [it].'

❖**koma** <kemr~kømr, kom, kómu~kvámu, kominn> *vb* come

kómu *3pl past of* **koma**

konungsson *m* prince

líta <lítr, leit, litu, litinn> *vb* look; *mid* **lítask [e-m]** appear (seem) to [sb]; **hversu lízk þér á?** How do you like [it]?

lízk *3sg pres mid of* **líta**

❖**mjök** *adv* much, very

❖**mæla** <-ti, -tr> *vb* say, speak

❖**nær** *adv* almost, nearly

❖**ofan** *adv* from above, down; downwards

reru *3pl past of* **róa**

róa <rœr, røri~reri, røru~reru, róinn> *vb* row

❖**segja** <sagði, sagt> *vb* say

sáu *3pl past of* **sjá**

❖**sjá** <sér, sá, sá(u), sénn> *vb* see, look

sjór <*gen* sjóvar~sjófar> *m* the sea; **fyrir ofan sjó** above the waterline

❖**skip** *n* ship; **skip-it** (*nom & acc*), **skipi-nu** (*dat*), **skips-ins** (*gen*) the ship

❖**standa** <stendr, stóð, stóðu, staðinn> *vb* stand

steina <-di, -dr> *vb* paint

steint *ppart of* **steina**; **steint mjök** fully painted

stóð *1/3sg past of* **standa**

stundum ... stundum *conj* sometimes ... sometimes, at times ... at times

❖**sumar** <*pl* sumur> *n* summer; **um sumarit** in the summer

tjalda <-að-> *vb* pitch a tent

tjaldat *ppart of* **tjalda** tented with its awning up

❖**tólf** <*ord* tólfti 'twelfth'> *num* twelve

❖**upp** *adv* up; **á land upp** up onto land

❖**út** *adv* out; **á skipit út** out onto the ship

vandliga *adv* carefully

❖**vel** *adv* well

viðtaka *f* reception

❖**vilja** <2/3sg pres vill, vildi, viljat> *vb* wish, want

vill *2/3sg pres of* **vilja**

víking *f* raid; **í víking** on a raid

þiggja <þiggr, þá, þágu, þeginn> *vb* accept

Þórólfr <-s> *m* Thorolf (*personal name*)

þrettán *num* thirteen

þrír tigir <*m acc pl* þrjá tigu> *num* thirty

TRANSLATION

Thorolf and Bjorn had a fast ship, which twelve or thirteen men rowed on a side, and they had a crew of nearly thirty men. They had gotten the ship in the summer on a raid. It was fully painted down to the waterline and was extremely handsome. And when they came to Hersir Thorir's home, they received there a good reception, and the ship floated (at anchor) with its sail tented as an awning just off the farmstead.

One day when Thorolf and Bjorn went down to the ship, they saw that Prince Eirik was there. He went first out onto the ship and then up onto land. Then he stood and looked at the ship.

Then Thorolf spoke, "You are carefully considering the ship, prince; what do you think of her?"

"I like it," he said. "The ship is extremely beautiful."

"Then I want to give you the ship," said Thorolf, "if you are willing to accept it."

"I will accept it," says Eirik.

7.12 Culture – Eirik Bloodaxe – A Viking King in England

Harald Fairhair was succeeded by his favorite son, Eirik Bloodaxe. Eirik began his reign by sharing the throne with two of his brothers, but he killed them both. Despite his renown as a warrior, Eirik's cruelty made him unpopular, earning him many enemies. Around the year 936, Eirik's half-brother, Hakon the Good (Hákon góði), drove him from the country. Eirik sailed to England. In 948 the English Archbishop Wulfstan and Vikings in Northumbria invited Eirik to assume the kingship of York (Jórvík) which was in Viking hands. The English King Eadred drove Eirik out within the year. York was a great prize, and next Olaf Sigtryggsson, the Hiberno-Norse king of Dublin, took control of the town. But Olaf was expelled and Eirik regained York in 952.

Viking success in England often relied on local support, and Eirik's fortunes faded when Eadred arrested Archbishop Wulfstan. In 954 Eirik was again toppled from his shaky throne. That same year, he was ambushed while crossing the Pennines and fell at the battle of Stainmore. Norse power in the north of England now waned, and king Eadred assumed control of York and Northumbria.

7.13 Reading – A Cruel King, A Cunning Wife, and Their Promising Children (*Haralds saga ins hárfagra*, from *Heimskringla*)

This passage from the *Saga of King Harald Fairhair* (*Haralds saga ins hárfagra*) gives a memorable description of the royal pair, Eirik and his wife Gunnhild.

Haralds saga ins hárfagra (ch 43)

Eiríkr var mikill maðr ok fríðr, sterkr ok hreystimaðr mikill, hermaðr mikill ok sigrsæll, ákafamaðr í skapi, grimmr, óþýðr ok fálátr. Gunnhildr, kona hans, var kvenna fegrst,[31] vitr ok margkunnig, glaðmælt ok undirhyggjumaðr mikill ok in grimmasta. Þau váru börn þeira Eiríks ok Gunnhildar:[32] Gamli var ellstr, Guthormr, Haraldr, Ragnfrøðr, Ragnhildr, Erlingr, Guðrøðr, Sigurðr slefa. Öll váru börn Eiríks fríð ok mannvæn.

Vocabulary

❖**allr** *<f* öll, *n* allt, *n nom & acc pl* öll> *adj pron* all, entire, whole

ákafamaðr *m* an aggressive man

barn *<pl* börn> *n* child

Eiríkr *m* Eirik (*personal name*)

ellstr *superl of* **gamall**

Erlingr <-s> *m* Erling (*personal name*)

❖**fagr** *<f* fögr, *n* fagrt, *comp* fegri, *superl* fegrstr> *adj* beautiful, fair, attractive

fálátr *adj* silent, reserved, taciturn

fegrstr *<f* fegrst, *n* fegrst> *superl of* **fagr**

❖**fríðr** *<f* fríð, *n* frítt, *n nom pl* fríð> *adj* beautiful, handsome, fine

❖**gamall** *<acc* gamlan, *f* gömul, *n* gamalt, *comp* ellri, *superl* ellstr> old; **ellstr** oldest

Gamli *m* Gamli (*personal name*), the Old One

---

[31] **kvenna fegrst**: 'fairest of women.'

[32] **Þau váru börn þeira Eiríks ok Gunnhildar**: 'These were the children of Eirik and Gunnhild.'

glaðmæltr *adj* cheerful in speech

grimmastr *superl of* **grimmr**

grimmr *adj* cruel, savage; severe, stern; (*f nom sg wk superl*) **in grimmasta** the severest

Guðrøðr <-s> *m* Gudrod (*personal name*)

Gunnhildr *f* Gunnhild (*personal name*)

Guthormr <-s> *m* Guthorm (*personal name*)

hermaðr *m* a warrior

hreystimaðr *m* a valiant man, champion

❖**kona** <*gen pl* kvenna> *f* wife; woman

kvenna *gen pl of* **kona**

mannvænn <*n nom pl* mannvæn> *adj* promising

margkunnigr *adj* skilled in magic

óþýðr *adj* unfriendly; intimidating

Ragnfrøðr <-s> *m* Ragnfrod (*personal name*)

Ragnhildr <*acc & dat* Ragnhildi, *gen* Ragnhildar> *f* Ragnhild (*personal name*)

sigrsæll *adj* victorious, lucky in battle

Sigurðr slefa *m* Sigurd the Slobberer (*personal name*)

skap *n* state, condition; temper, mood

slefa *f* slobber, slobberer (as nickname)

❖**sterkr** *adj* strong

undirhyggjumaðr *m* a guileful or deceitful person

❖**vitr** <*f* vitr, *n* vitrt> *adj* wise

öll *see* **allr**

TRANSLATION

Eirik was a big and handsome man, strong and valiant, a great and victorious warrior, impetuous by nature, cruel, unfriendly and taciturn. Gunnhild, his wife, was the most beautiful of women, wise and skilled in magic, cheerful in speech, a person full of guile, and extremely severe. These were the children of Eirik and Gunnhild: Gamli was the oldest, Guthorm, Harald, Ragnfrod, Ragnhild, Erling, Gudrod, and Sigurd the Slobberer. All of Eirik's children were handsome and promising.

NOTE: At this point in the book, the English translations and vocabularies for the Old Norse reading passages end. The comprehensive Vocabulary at the rear of the book will aid your translations.

7.14 WORD FREQUENCY VOCABULARY – LIST 7. THE MOST FREQUENT WORDS IN THE SAGAS

NOUNS	*ADJECTIVES*	*PRONOUNS*	*NUMERALS*
nótt – night	**verðr** – worthy	**hinn** – the other	**fimm** – five
tíðindi – news, tidings	**líkr** – alike	**hverr** – each, every; who?	
fundr – meeting	**vitr** – wise		
lið – following, troops	**harðr** – hard		

VERBS	PREPOSITIONS AND ADVERBS	CONJUNCTIONS
spyrja – to ask; learn	**hér** – here	**bæði** – both
biðja – to ask; tell	**mjök** – very	
mega – may	**þegar** – at once	
fá – to get, obtain	**ór** – out of, from	

EXERCISES

7.15 Reading Comprehension. Based on the second reading decide whether the following statements are true or false.

RÉTT eða RANGT?

1. Þórólfr kom á skipi. _____
2. Eiríkr er konungr. _____
3. Þórólfr ok Björn váru víkingar. _____
4. Þórólfr gaf Eiríki skip. _____
5. Eiríkr vill (wants) þiggja skipit. _____
6. Björn er konungsson. _____
7. Konungsson hyggr vandliga at skipinu. _____
8. Björn horfði á skipit. _____
9. Þórólfr ok Björn gengu eigi ofan til skipsins. _____
10. "Skipit er it fegrsta," sagði Björn. _____

7.16 Reading Comprehension. Read the short passage below and give the case, number, and gender for each of the underlined nouns.

Þórólfr ok Björn höfðu karfa, er reru á <u>borð</u> tólf <u>menn</u> eða þrettán, ok höfðu nær þrjá tigu manna; skip þat höfðu þeir fengit um sumarit í víking; þat var steint mjök fyrir ofan <u>sjó</u> ok var it fegrsta. En er þeir kómu til Þóris, fengu þeir þar góðar <u>viðtökur</u>, ok skipit flaut tjaldat fyrir bœnum.

Þat var einn dag, er þeir Þórólfr ok Björn gengu ofan til skipsins. Þeir sáu, at Eiríkr <u>konungsson</u> var þar, hann gekk stundum á skipit út, en stundum á <u>land</u> upp, hann stóð þá ok horfði á skipit.

NOUN	GENDER	CASE	NUMBER
Ex: skipi	*neuter*	*dative*	*singular*
1. borð	_____	_____	_____
2. menn	_____	_____	_____
3. sjó	_____	_____	_____
4. viðtökur	_____	_____	_____

5. konungsson   _____   _____   _____
6. land   _____   _____   _____

7.17 Reflexive Pronouns. Complete the following sentences with the correct pronoun.

1. Hann hafði _____ í brott (He got himself away)
2. Hann hafði _____ í brott (He got him [someone else] away)

3. Hann fekk _____skip (He got himself a ship)
4. Hann fekk _____skip (He got him [someone else] a ship)

Note: hjálpa takes a dative object

7.18 Infinitives. Give the infinitives of the following verbs.

Ex: váru   _vera_____

1. sagði   _____   5. gerði   _____   9. hyggr   _____
2. höfum   _____   6. fór   _____   10. vill   _____
3. fluttu _____   7. nam   _____   11. kómu   _____
4. var   _____   8. hét   _____   12. reru   _____

7.19 Strong Nouns Type 1. Decline *heimr* (*m*) 'world,' *för* (*f*) 'journey,' and *land* (*n*) 'land'

	HEIMR (M)	FÖR (F)	LAND (N)
Sg *nom*	_____	_____	_____
acc	_____	_____	_____
dat	_____	_____	_____
gen	_____	_____	_____
Pl *nom*	_____	_____	_____
acc	_____	_____	_____
dat	_____	_____	_____
gen	_____	_____	_____

7.20 Strong Nouns Type 2. Decline *fundr* (*m*) 'meeting' and *ferð* (*f*) 'journey.'

	FUNDR (M)	FERÐ (F)
Sg *nom*	_____	_____
acc	_____	_____
dat	_____	_____
gen	_____	_____
Pl *nom*	_____	_____
acc	_____	_____
dat	_____	_____
gen	_____	_____

7.21 Weak Nouns. Decline *goði* (*m*) 'chieftain,' *saga* (*f*) 'story,' and *hjarta* (*n*) 'heart.'

	GOÐI (M)	SAGA (F)	HJARTA (N)
Sg nom	_____	_____	_____
acc	_____	_____	_____
dat	_____	_____	_____
gen	_____	_____	_____
Pl nom	_____	_____	_____
acc	_____	_____	_____
dat	_____	_____	_____
gen	_____	_____	_____

7.22 Verbs. Change the underlined words from singular to plural and rewrite the sentences. Remember verbs must agree with their subjects, singular or plural.

SINGULAR	PLURAL
Ex: <u>Hann</u> hyggr at skipi.	*Þeir hyggja at skipi.*

1. <u>Ek</u> horfi á <u>skip</u>.   _____
2. <u>Þú</u> gerðir <u>brú</u>.   _____
3. <u>Hon</u> kallar at <u>manni</u>.   _____
4. <u>Víkingr</u> herjaði <u>land</u>.   _____
5. <u>Ek</u> mælta við <u>hana</u>.   _____
6. <u>Maðr</u> hugði at <u>konungi</u>.   _____

7.23 Sentence Completion. Complete the sentences with the correct forms of the words given below.

     sála   fara   með   segja   hafa   til   vera   höfðingi   vilja   gera   brú

1. "Skipit er it fegrsta," _____ hann. (present tense)
2. Vér _____ gefa þér skipit. (present tense)
3. Þeir _____ fengit skip í víking. (past tense)
4. Þorsteinn _____ _____ mikill ok auðigr at fé. (past tense)
5. Hon _____ _____ fyr _____ Hólmgeirs. (past tense)
6. Ek _____ _____ Íslands _____ Eiríki. (past tense)

7.24 Review: Special Stem Rules. Give the stem for each of the following strong masculine nouns, and state the applicable Special Stem Rule (see earlier lesson). Remove the ending of the genitive singular to find the stem for each noun. If no Special Stem Rule applies, write "N/A."

Ex: steinn (*gen* steins)   *stein-*_____   *Rule 1, r-Change*_____

1. vinr (*gen* vinar)   _____   _____
2. otr (*gen* otrs)   _____   _____
3. jökull (*gen* jökuls)   _____   _____
4. fugl (*gen* fugls)   _____   _____
5. hváll (*gen* hváls)   _____   _____
6. ofn (*gen* ofns)   _____   _____
7. íss (*gen* íss)   _____   _____
8. hafr (*gen* hafrs)   _____   _____
9. fundr (*gen* funds)   _____   _____
10. kjóll (*gen* kjóls)   _____   _____
11. fleinn (*gen* fleins)   _____   _____
12. gísl (*gen* gísls)   _____   _____

7.25 Review: Prepositions. Give correct forms of the nouns in parentheses and translate.

1. Hann gekk á _____ (skip) út.
    _____

2. Sigríðr bjó hjá _____ (jarl).
    _____

3. Haraldr konungr fór til _____ (Nóregr).
    _____

4. Ingólfr bjó á milli _____ (Vágr) ok _____ (Reykjanes).
    _____

5. Elfráðr inn ríki (Alfred the Great) var konungr í _____ (England).
    _____

6. Böðvarr gekk móti _____ (dýr).
    [The neuter noun *dýr* 'beast' declines like *land*_____

LESSON 8
HARALD HARDRADI IN CONSTANTINOPLE

Frændr eru frændum verstir
(Kinsmen are worst to kinsmen)

8.1 CULTURE – HARALD AND THE VARANGIANS

The Norse name for Constantinople was Mikligarðr, meaning 'the great city.' The name is formed from *mikill* 'great, large' and *garðr* (cognate with English 'yard') meaning 'enclosure,' and suggesting a fenced-in area such as around a farm. In this instance it is a walled city. The word *garðr* is also found in Old Norse mythological place names such as Ásgarðr (home of the *Æsir* gods), Miðgarðr ('Middle Enclosure,' often called Middle Earth), and Útgarðr ('Outer Enclosure' or home of the giants).

The most famous Norse visitor to Constantinople was Harald Hard-Counsel (Haraldr harðráði), a descendent of Harald Fairhair. He ruled as king of Norway from 1045 to 1066, but his ascent to the throne was not easy. *Heimskringla*, other Icelandic writings, and a Greek chronicle recount his exploits and rise to kingship.

Harald's half-brother was Saint Olaf Haraldsson, king of Norway from 1015 to 1028. Olaf's reign came to an end when the Danish King Canute claimed the throne of Norway.

Figure 37. The Route Probably Taken by Haraldr Harðráði after St. Olaf's defeat at Stiklastad (Stiklastaðir) in 1030, as well as his later journey to Sicily. Many Norse merchants and warriors traveled to Constantinople (Mikligarðr) from the Baltic Sea, following this route.

Attempting to regain his kingdom, Olaf was killed in 1030 at the battle of Stiklastad (Old Norse Stiklastaðir, Modern Norwegian Stiklestad). Harald Hardradi, fifteen years of age, fought alongside his half-brother, and after Olaf was killed, a wounded Harald escaped across the mountains into Sweden.

For the next fifteen years Harald lived in exile. He went first to Sweden and then descended the rivers of what is today Russia and the Ukraine. There he served in the army of Jaroslav the Wise, the Prince of Kiev (Kænugarðr) from the Norse-Slavic Rurikid dynasty. Harald quickly rose to prominence in the service of the Kievan ruler and was promised Elizabeth, Jaroslav's daughter. Before the marriage, Harald set off with 500 warriors for Constantinople, the capital of the Greek-speaking Byzantine or eastern Roman Empire. There he offered his service to Emperor Michael IV. Norsemen called the Greek emperor *stólkonungr* 'throne king.' Michael reigned with his powerful wife, Empress Zoe, and they accepted Harald and his men into their service.

Scandinavians in the Byzantine Empire were called Varangians. In the Byzantine army, they formed the emperor's personal bodyguard and were known as the Varangian Guard. The name 'Varangian' comes from ON *várar*, meaning 'pledges' or 'oaths.' The Varangians (*Væringjar*, sg *Væringi*) were 'men of the pledge,' referring to the customary pledge of fellowship taken by the groups of Scandinavians who traded along the Russian rivers.

Harald came to Constantinople with 500 men and was not immediately a member of the Varangian Guard. First, he and his mercenaries were incorporated into the Byzantine army and sent to fight corsairs (pirates) in the Aegean Sea. As the campaigns continued, the Varangians turned to him as their leader in battle. The Byzantine Greek source *Logos nuthetikos* (*Oration of Admonition to an Emperor*), written in the 1070s, confirms Harald's participation in military campaigns and his ascent to leadership of the Varangian Guard.

Harald campaigned widely in the Mediterranean from roughly 1035 until 1044. He fought against Bulgars, Saracens, and Lombards. Harald probably came into contact with Normans from Normandy, the descendants of Vikings who at that time were installing themselves in Southern Italy and Sicily.

Ostensibly, the Varangian Guard was subordinate to the leader of the Byzantine army. In Harald's time, the leader was the Greek general George (ON Gyrgir) Maniakes, a relative of the empress. Harald frequently clashed with him for control of the Guard and undermined Maniakes by holding back the Varangians from fighting when the full army assembled for battle. When Harald chose to fight, the Varangians fought successfully and distinguished themselves. Finally, a frustrated Maniakes gave Harald independent command. The Varangians then fought separately from the rest of the army and won victories. Harald became famous.

Harald spent over ten years in the Varangian Guard and amassed a huge amount of wealth as its commander. Icelandic and Byzantine sources agree that Empress Zoe forbade Harald to return to his native country. She imprisoned him, but Harald escaped from Constantinople. After stopping in Kiev to fulfill his wedding vow, he returned home to Norway in 1045. There he demanded a share of the throne of Norway and Denmark, which at the time were claimed jointly by his nephew Magnus the Good. Magnus agreed reluctantly, and the two ruled uneasily together until Magnus died in 1047. After Magnus' death, Harald became sole ruler of Norway, though his grip on Denmark was tenuous.

8.2 Reading – Harald Hardradi Leads the Varangian Guard (*Haralds saga Sigurðarsonar*, from *Heimskringla*)

Harald was the most famous Scandinavian to enter into the service of the Byzantine Emperor. The following passage from *Haralds saga Sigurðarsonar* (*The Saga of Harald Sigurdsson*) in *Heimskringla* describes his arrival in Mikligarðr and his rise to leadership.

Haralds saga Sigurðarsonar (ch 3)

Þá réð fyrir Griklandi Zóe dróttning in ríka ok með henni Michael kátalaktús.[33] En er Haraldr kom til Miklagarðs ok á fund dróttningar,[34] þá gekk hann þar á mála[35] ok fór þegar um haustit á galeiðr með hermönnum þeim.[36] Þeir fóru út í Griklandshaf. Hélt Haraldr sveit af sínum mönnum. Höfðingi yfir herinum hét Gyrgir. Hann var frændi dróttningar. Haraldr var lítla híð[37] í herinum, ok allir Væringjar fóru saman,[38] þegar er bardagar váru. Kom þá svá, at[39] Haraldr varð höfðingi yfir öllum Væringjum. Fóru þeir Gyrgir[40] víða um Griklandseyjar, unnu þar herskap mikinn á kussurum.

> ### 8.3 Exercise – Translating from *Haralds saga Sigurðarsonar*
> When translating an Old Norse sentence, first identify the verb and then find its subject. Match the verb to a noun which stands in the **nominative case** AND **agrees** with it in person (1st, 2nd, or 3rd) and number (singular or plural). For each sentence below, circle the verb, underline the subject, and translate.
>
> 1. Þá réð fyrir Griklandi Zóe dróttning in ríka.
>
>   _____
>
>   In Old Norse when a word other than the subject appears before the verb (in

---

[33] **Michael kátalaktús:** Old Norse sources refer to Michael by his nickname *kátalaktús* (Greek for 'money-changer,' his profession before his marriage to Empress Zoe). He is more generally known as Michael the Paphlagonian, after his home country.

[34] **ok á fund dróttningar:** 'and to a meeting with the empress.'

[35] **þá gekk hann þar á mála:** 'there [at that meeting] he then entered into the service [of the empress].'

[36] **fór þegar um haustit á galeiðr með hermönnum:** 'he went that very autumn onto the galleys with his warriors.'

[37] **lítla hríð:** 'for a short time'; the accusative can be used without a preposition to express a duration of time.

[38] **allir Væringjar fóru saman:** 'all the Varangians assembled as a group'; that is, they abandoned their original units and formed a special troop.

[39] **Kom þá svá, at...:** 'It so happened that...'

[40] **þeir Gyrgir:** 'Gyrgir and his men.'

this instance the adverb *þá* 'then'), the subject follows the verb later in the main clause.

What is the infinitive of *réð*?_____

2. ok með henni Michael kátalaktús.

    _____

    This clause relies on an understood verb. What is this verb? _____

3. En er Haraldr kom til Miklagarðs ok á fund dróttningar,

    _____

    En er is composed of two conjunctions meaning 'but when.'

4. þá gekk hann þar á mála

    _____

    What type of word is *þar*? _____

5. ok fór [hann] þegar um haustit á galeiðr með hermönnum þeim.

    _____

    A prepositional phrase consists of a preposition and its object (*í Brattahlíð, á Íslandi*, etc). How many prepositional phrases occur in this clause? _____

With the information above, translate the full passage:_____

_____

_____

_____

_____

_____

_____

_____

_____

8.4 CULTURE – THE RUS ACROSS RUSSIA AND FURTHER

Norse ventures down the rivers of Russia began in the mid-seventh century and were dominated by Swedes. Traders were initially drawn to the region by the availability of furs and slaves (see the discussion of Ibn Fadlan and the Rus in the Introduction). Slavic peoples, inhabitants of Russia, and eventually Greeks, Arabs, and Western Europeans came to call these Norse traders the Rus. The name Rus was adopted by the traders themselves. It may have originated from *routsi*, a Finnish term for Sweden, which seems to have derived from ON *róðr* (gen *róðs*), referring to rowing or men who rowed such as 'a crew of rowers.' The name Rus is also the origin of the modern name Russia.

The Rus themselves called the region of the Eastern Baltic austrvegr ('the way east'). Further inland, they gave it the name, Garðaríki 'land of the towns,' which extended from Lake Ladoga in the north to the lands of the Greeks and the people down the Volga leading to Persia and Arab lands in the south. The fortified river towns of Novgorod and Kiev became important centers of Norse trade and influence. Both towns were near portages, areas where boats and trade goods were transported overland between rivers. Novgorod was especially well-placed for a trading center. It lay between the Volga, Dnieper, Dvina, and Lovat Rivers and could control movements between the Baltic and the Black Sea or the Caspian Sea.

The two towns Novogrod and Kiev were rivals until Prince Oleg of Novgorod captured Kiev ca. 882 and made Kiev his capital. Strong leadership along the rivers was necessary to protect trading fleets, which were open to attack on the Dnieper from neighboring Slavic tribes and steppe nomads, such as the Pechenegs and Bulgars. From Kiev, trade contacts stretched south to the Byzantine Empire and from there into the Mediterranean.

Those Rus traders and warriors, who took a more easterly route in Russia, sailed down the Volga River. Some left the Volga and went east overland along what became known as the silk road. Others reached the lands of the Khazars, a semi-nomadic group of Turkic peoples whose rulers in the seventh and eighth centuries adopted Judaism. At the time of the Rus in the ninth and tenth centuries, the Khazars guarded and taxed the river trade routes. They ruled a huge territory north, east, and west of the Black and Caspian Seas as well as lands between these two great bodies of water. Reaching the Caspian, some Norse traders and warriors continued further south to the lands of the Caliphate of Baghdad.

Especially in the late ninth and tenth centuries, Norse merchants and warriors returned from Russia to the Baltic with large quantities of Arabic silver coins called dirhams. In the Baltic area, as well as in parts of Eastern Europe, dirhams brought north by Rus traders were for a time, the major currency. Despite the huge coins hoards found buried in Baltic Scandinavia, the majority of imported Arabic silver was melted down. It was used in trade with continental Western Europe, which relied on the Rus trade links as a major source of silver and acces to goods coming from the east.

In the tenth century, Norse leaders such as Saint Olaf of Norway and his half brother Harald Hardradi had many connections with the Kievan Rus. As the tenth century passed, the Rus in Russia integrated with the local Slavic population. Influenced by Byzantium, the Kievan Rus converted to Orthodox Christianity in 988. The last ruler of the Kievan Rus to have a Scandinavian name was Igor (a form of Ingvar), who died in 945, but Rus rulers recognized their origins and maintained dynastic ties with Scandinavian rulers well into the eleventh century.

8.5 NOUNS – KINSHIP TERMS IN -IR

Five words for family members, *bróðir*, *dóttir*, *faðir*, *móðir*, and *systir*, form a small class of nouns. All have *i*-umlaut in the plural. Along with dative *föður* and *bróður*, some manuscripts show the more archaic datives *feðr* and *brœðr*.

	M			**F**		
	FAÐIR	**BRÓÐIR**	**SYSTIR**	**DÓTTIR**	**MÓÐIR**	**ENDINGS**
Sg *nom*	faðir	bróðir	systir	dóttir	móðir	-ir
acc	föður	bróður	systur	dóttur	móður	-ur
dat	föður, feðr	bróður, brœðr	systur	dóttur	móður	-ur, [(i)]-r
gen	föður	bróður	systur	dóttur	móður	-ur
Pl *nom*	feðr	brœðr	systr	dœtr	mœðr	[(i)]-r
acc	feðr	brœðr	systr	dœtr	mœðr	[(i)]-r
dat	feðrum	brœðrum	systrum	dœtrum	mœðrum	[(i)]-um
gen	feðra	brœðra	systra	dœtra	mœðra	[(i)]-a

Transl: *faðir* 'father,' *bróðir* 'brother,' *systir* 'sister' *dóttir* 'daughter,' *móðir* 'mother'

More distant relations are expressed by compounds such as *móðurbróðir* 'uncle (mother's brother),' *föðurmóðir* '(paternal) grandmother (father's mother),' *föðursystir* 'aunt (father's sister),' and *bróðurdóttir* 'niece (brother's daughter).'

8.6 NOUNS WHOSE STEMS END IN -ND-

Nouns such as *bóndi* and *frændi* belong to a small group of masculine nouns known as *nd*-nouns. These end in *i* in the nominative singular and decline like weak masculines, but in the nominative and accusative plural have the ending -*r* with *i*-umlaut. *Nd*-nouns derive from present participles; for example, *gefandi* 'the giving one' from *gefa* and *bóndi* (a shortening of *búandi*) 'the one living (there)' from *búa*.

	BÓNDI	**FRÆNDI**	**GEFANDI**	**ENDINGS**
Sg *nom*	bóndi	frændi	gefandi	-i
acc	bónda	frænda	gefanda	-a
dat	bónda	frænda	gefanda	-a
gen	bónda	frænda	gefanda	-a
Pl *nom*	bœndr	frændr	gefendr	[(i)]-r
acc	bœndr	frændr	gefendr	[(i)]-r
dat	bóndum	frændum	geföndum	-um
gen	bónda	frænda	gefanda	-a

Transl: *bóndi* 'farmer,' *frændi* 'kinsman,' *gefandi* 'giver'

8.7 PRESENT TENSE OF STRONG VERBS

Strong verbs, of which there are about two hundred, are among the most frequently used verbs in Old Norse. They take the same basic set of endings in the present tense as weak verbs. The endings are added to the present stem (found by removing the -*a* of the infinitive). Additionally, in the present singular the root vowel shows *i*-umlaut where possible. For instance, strong verbs with root vowel -*á*- in the infinitive (*ráða*,

Present Tense Endings of Strong Verbs		
	SINGULAR	PLURAL
1st	–	-um
2nd	-r	-ið
3rd	-r	-a

láta, and *fá*) have -*æ*- in the present singular (*hann ræðr* 'he advises,' *hann lætr* 'he allows,' and *hann fær* 'he gets').

The vowels -*i*-, -*í*-, -*e*-, and -*y*- never undergo *i*-umlaut and hence remain unchanged in the present singular. For example, strong verbs with -*e*- in the infinitive (*bera, verða*) show no change of vowel in the present singular (*hann berr, hann verðr*).

		LÍTA	*BJÓÐA*	*VERÐA*	*BERA*	*GEFA*	*FARA*	*RÁÐA*
Sg 1st	ek	lít	býð	verð	ber	gef	fer	ræð
2nd	þú	lítr	býðr	verðr	berr	gefr	ferr	ræðr
3rd	hann	lítr	býðr	verðr	berr	gefr	ferr	ræðr
Pl 1st	vér	lítum	bjóðum	verðum	berum	gefum	förum	ráðum
2nd	þér	lítið	bjóðið	verðið	berið	gefið	farið	ráðið
3rd	þeir	líta	bjóða	verða	bera	gefa	fara	ráða

Transl: *bera* 'carry,' *bjóða* 'offer; invite,' *fara* 'go,' *líta* 'look,' *ráða* 'advise, counsel,' *verða* 'become'

There are two other important points to bear in mind when forming the present tense of strong verbs.

1. Verbs with root vowel -*a*-, such as *fara, standa*, and *ganga*, undergo *u*-umlaut in the 1pl, where the ending is -*um*. Hence *förum* 'we travel,' *stöndum* 'we stand,' and *göngum* 'we go.'

2. Some strong verbs, such as *hefja, sitja, deyja*, and *liggja*, have present tense stems ending in -*j*-, while others, such as *höggva* and *syngva* have stem-final -*v*-. These verbs drop -*j*- and -*v*- according to the rules discussed earlier.

It is worth mentioning that *heita* is irregular in the present singular, inserting an -*i*- when it means 'to be called': *heiti, heitir, heitir*. When used with an accusative object, it conjugates in a regular manner, that is, without an -*i*-: *heit, heitr, heitr*. For example, *Hann heitir Gísli* 'He is called Gisli', but *Gisli heitr á menn sína* 'Gisli calls to his men.'

8.8 PAST TENSE OF STRONG VERBS

Strong verbs form their past tense by changing their root vowel, for example, *koma* (past sg *kóm*, past pl *kómu*, past participle *kominn*), *gefa* (past sg *gaf*, past pl *gáfu*, past participle *gefinn*). Compare English *come, came, has/is come* and *give, gave, has/is given*.

Past Tense Endings of Strong Verbs		
	SINGULAR	PLURAL
1st	–	-um
2nd	-t	-uð
3rd	–	-u

Strong verbs in Old Norse have five principal parts. Using *gefa* as an example, these are:

1) infinitive   *gefa* 'give'
2) 3sg present   *hann gefr* 'he gives'
3) 3sg past   *hann gaf* 'he gave'
4) 3pl past   *þeir gáfu* 'they gave'
5) past participle (m nom sg)   *var gefinn* 'was given'

Learning the principal parts of strong verbs is a short cut for mastering Old Norse, because they provide the stems to which one adds the endings. Using *gefa* as an example, the past singular adds endings to the stem *gaf-* (*gaf, gaft, gaf*) and the past plural to the stem *gáf-* (*gáfum, gáfuð, gáfu*).

Strong verbs fall into seven major classes according to the pattern of vowel alternations exhibited by their principal parts.

CLASS	EXAMPLE
I:	**líta** <lítr, leit, litu, litinn> *vb* look
II:	**bjóða** <býðr, bauð, buðu, boðinn> *vb* offer; invite
III:	**verða** <verðr, varð, urðu, orðinn> *vb* become
IV:	**bera** <berr, bar, báru, borinn> *vb* carry
V:	**gefa** <gefr, gaf, gáfu, gefinn> *vb* give
VI:	**fara** <ferr, fór, fóru, farinn> *vb* go, travel
VII:	**ráða** <ræðr, réð, réðu, ráðinn> *vb* advise, counsel; rule, govern; decide

Each of the strong verb classes will be examined in more detail in upcoming lessons. These strong verbs conjugate in the past as follows:

		LÍTA	BJÓÐA	VERÐA	BERA	GEFA	FARA	RÁÐA
Sg 1st	ek	leit	bauð	varð	bar	gaf	fór	réð
2nd	þú	leizt	bautt	vart	bart	gaft	fórt	rétt
3rd	hann	leit	bauð	varð	bar	gaf	fór	réð

Pl 1st	vér	litum	buðum	urðum	bárum	gáfum	fórum	réðum
2nd	þér	lituð	buðuð	urðuð	báruð	gáfuð	fóruð	réðuð
3rd	þeir	litu	buðu	urðu	báru	gáfu	fóru	réðu

Two rules help explain the change in consonants found in the principal parts of a few strong verbs. For instance, *verða*, *varð*, **urðu**, **orðinn** and *binda*, **batt**, *bundu*, *bundinn*.

- *v*- drops before *-o-* or *-u-*. Hence the 4th and 5th principal parts of *verða* (above) and those of *vinna*: *vinnr*, *vann*, **unnu**, **unninn**.
- Strong verbs whose stems end in *-nd-*, *-ng-*, and *-ld-* have *-tt*, *-kk*, and *-lt* in the past singular (and the imperative, discussed below). Hence *binda*, *ganga*, and *halda* become in the past singular *batt*, *gekk*, and *hélt*.

8.9 EXERCISE – PRINCIPAL PARTS OF STRONG VERBS

Give the requested form of each of the following verbs by referring to the principal parts (see Vocabulary at end of book).

Ex: fara (*3sg pres*)   _ferr_____

1. gefa (*3pl past*)   _____
2. koma (*past part*)   _____
3. ganga (*3sg past*)   _____
4. heita (*2pl past*)   _____
5. hefja (*1sg pres*)   _____
6. draga (*1pl pres.*)   _____
7. ráða (*2sg pres*)   _____
8. verða (*3pl past*)   _____
9. nema (*1sg pres*)   _____
10. halda (*2pl pres*)   _____

8.10 PAST TENSE ENDING -*T* OF STRONG VERBS

When the 2sg past ending *-t* is added to strong verbs whose third principal part ends in a dental consonant (*-t-*, *-ð-*, or *-d-*) or a long vowel (such as *-é-*, *-á-*, or *-ó-*), the following rules apply.

- *-t-* or *-tt-* preceded by a vowel changes to *-z-*. For example, the third principal part of *geta* is *gat*; hence *gat + t > gazt*. Another example is *binda*: *batt + t > bazt*.
- *-ð-* changes to *-t-*. For example, the third principal part of *ráða* is *réð*; hence *réð + t > rétt*.
- A dental consonant preceded by *-r-*, *-l-*, or *-s-* changes to *-t* and no ending is added. For example, for the verbs *verða*, *halda*, and *ljósta*: *varð + t > vart*, *hélt + t > hélt*, and *laust + t > laust*.
- After a long vowel the ending *-t* doubles. For example, *sjá* has 2sg past *sátt*.

8.11 EXERCISE – PAST TENSE ENDING -*T* OF STRONG VERBS

Give the principal parts and 2sg past tense for each of the following strong verbs.

	PRINCIPAL PARTS	2SG PAST
Ex: geta	*getr, gat, gátu, getinn*	*gazt*
1. binda		
2. ráða		
3. verða		
4. halda		
5. ljósta		
6. sjá		

8.12 READING – HARALD HARDRADI SENDS FAMINE RELIEF TO ICELAND (*HARALDS SAGA SIGURÐARSONAR*, FROM *HEIMSKRINGLA*)

After Norway's King Magnus the Good (Magnús góði, 1024-1047) died without leaving an heir, Harald Hardradi set about brutally consolidating his power as sole king of Norway, and he gained a reputation among Norwegians as a harsh and uncompromising tyrant. Icelandic literature, however, generally paints a favorable picture of Harald, not least because of the aid he granted to Iceland during a famine by permitting the export of grain to Iceland. The following passage from *Haralds saga Sigurðarsonar* in *Heimskringla* claims that no chieftain seen in the northern lands was as *djúpvitr* ('deep-witted' or 'resourceful') as Harald.

Haralds saga Sigurðarsonar (ch 36, from *Heimskringla*)

Haraldr konungr var maðr ríkr ok stjórnsamr innan lands, spekingr mikill at viti, svá at þat er alþýðu mál,[41] at engi höfðingi hefir sá verit[42] á Norðrlöndum, er jafndjúpvitr hefir verit sem Haraldr eða ráðsnjallr. Hann var orrustumaðr mikill ok inn vápndjarfasti. Hann var sterkr ok vápnfœrr betr en hverr maðr annarra,[43] svá sem fyrr er ritat.

Hann var ok inn mesti vinr hegat til allra landsmanna. Ok þá er var mikit hallæri á Íslandi, þá leyfði Haraldr konungr fjórum skipum mjölleyfi til Íslands.

Translate: _____

_____

_____

_____

_____

_____

_____

_____

_____

---

[41] **alþýðu mál:** 'common report,' 'talk or consensus of the general public.'
[42] **at engi höfðingi hefir sá verit:** 'that no one had been such a chieftain.'
[43] **en hverr maðr annarra:** 'than any other man.'

8.13 Grammar Toolbox. Verb Mood

Mood is the expression of a speaker's attitude concerning the likelihood that a statement is true. It is also connected with commands and requests. There are three moods in Old Norse: indicative, imperative, and subjunctive.

The **indicative** is sometime called the mood of truth-telling. It is used when the speaker believes his or her utterance to be factual. For example, *gerði* is 3sg past indicative of *gera*, and *köllum* is 1pl present indicative of *kalla*. The indicative is generally the most frequently encountered mood in Old Norse texts, and the verb endings and formations learned to this point in the book have been indicative.

The **imperative** expresses commands and requests. Old Norse has only one imperative form: the 2sg imperative, used when addressing a single person. See the next section for the details on its formation.

The **subjunctive** is used when the speaker wishes to express uncertainty about the truth of a statement. Typically this occurs when describing an action which is potential, doubtful, or contrary to fact (something that *might be*) rather than concrete or factual (something that *is*). For example, in *Vápnfirðinga saga*, Brodd-Helgi makes a proposal for something he would like to see happen in the future, using the subjunctive of *vera*, "en ek mun koma til þings, ok **sém** vit þá báðir saman." (And I will come to the assembly, and we would then be both together [in pursuing a legal case].)

The subjunctive is also frequently used in indirect speech; that is, speech which recounts what someone has said without necessarily using his or her exact words. In the following example from *Vápnfirðinga saga*, the saga writer reports Bjarni's question to the shepherd without quoting him and uses *segi*, present subjunctive of *segja. Í þetta mund kom smalamaðr inn at Hofi, ok spurði Bjarni, hvat hann **segi** tíðenda.* (At that moment a shepherd came indoors at Hof and Bjarni asked what news he had.)

8.14 Commands and the Imperative Mood of Verbs

When addressing a command or request to a single person, Old Norse uses the imperative mood. When addressing more than one person, it employs the indicative.

Commands to one person. The imperative of 1st conjugation weak verbs looks just like the infinitive, for example, *tala* 'talk!' and *svara* 'answer!' Most other verbs form the imperative by dropping the -*a* of the infinitive. For example, the imperatives of the weak verbs *mæla* and *gera* are *mæl* 'talk!' and *ger* 'do!,' and the imperatives of the strong verbs *gefa* and *koma* are *gef* 'give!' and *kom* 'come!' Verbs such as *spyrja* and *höggva* drop stem final -*j*- or -*v*- along with the -*a* of the infinitive, giving *spyr* 'ask!'and *högg* 'strike!' *Vápnfirðinga saga* contains the following examples.

"**Mæl** við mik slíkt, er þér líkar," segir Þorsteinn, "en **tala** ekki slíkt við Brodd-Helga," segir hann.

"**Far** þú heim sem tíðast ok **lát** eigi verða við vart."

"**Tell** me such things as you like," says Thorstein, "but do not **tell** such to Brodd-Helgi," he says.

"**Travel** home as quickly as possible and **let** no one become aware of your journey."

- Most 4th conjugation weak verbs drop the -a of the infinitive but add -i. for example, *þegja* and *duga* have imperatives *þegi* 'be silent!' and *dugi* 'be useful!'

- Commands are often followed by a pronoun, as in *högg þú* 'strike!' In many of these instances, the pronoun loses its status as a separate word, with the initial *þ*- of *þú* assimilating to the preceding consonant, and the vowel becoming short: *kallaðu* (*kalla* + *þú*), *skjóttu* (*skjót* + *þú*), *þegiðu* (*þegi* + *þú*). Pronouns attached to the end of a verb are called enclitic pronouns.

- As mentioned above in discussing the past tense of strong verbs, the imperative provides the environment for the change of -*nd*-, -*ng*-, and -*ld*- to -*tt*, -*kk*, and -*lt*, for example, the imperatives of *bind*a, *gang*a, and *hald*a are *bitt*, *gakk*, and *halt*.

- The 3sg indicative is also sometimes used to express a command, as in the example from *Sturlunga saga* below, *Eigi skal [hann] höggva*, meaning 'He shall not strike,' or 'Don't let him strike.'

Commands to more than one person. Examples of commands given to more than one person using the indicative are *mælið* 'speak!,' *takið* 'take!', *skjótið* 'shoot!' When the speaker is part of a group, there is an additional way to issue a command. In these instances, the 1pl present indicative can be used, for example, *tökum* 'let's take,' *skjótum* 'let's shoot.' This usage is sometimes called the hortative, a term from Latin meaning 'encourage.'

Snorri Sturluson's Death

Símon knútr bað Árna höggva hann.

"Eigi skal höggva," sagði Snorri.

"**Högg** þú," sagði Símon.

"Eigi skal höggva," sagði Snorri.

Eptir þat veitti Árni honum banasár, ok þeir Þorsteinn unnu á honum.

An imperative is used in a famous passage from the *Sturlunga saga* compilation describing the violent death of Snorri Sturluson in *Íslendinga saga* (Ch. 152). In order to create alliances with other chieftains Snorri had married his daughters to important leaders, but the marriages ended and the alliances soured. In the year 1241, two of his former sons-in-law surprised Snorri at his estate at Reykholt in western Iceland. They found Snorri hiding in his secret cellar under the house, and Símon knútr ordered Árni beiskr to strike (*höggva*) Snorri, who responds back to Árni 'he shall not strike.' In the end Símon, Árni, and Þorsteinn work over (*vinna á*) Snorri, killing him.

8.15 THE PRESENT SUBJUNCTIVE OF VERBS

All verbs form the present subjunctive by adding the subjunctive endings to the verb stem (found by dropping the final -*a* of the infinitive). For example, the stem of *hlaupa* is *hlaup*- and the stem of *spyrja* is *spyrj*-. Verbs with stem final -*j*- such as *spyrja*, drop -*j*- before subjunctive endings beginning with -*i*-. Below are examples of verbs conjugated in the present subjunctive.

Subjunctive Endings		
	SINGULAR	PLURAL
1st	-a	-im
2nd	-ir	-ið
3rd	-i	-i

INFINITIVE	KALLA	GERA	SPYRJA	HAFA	RÁÐA	EIGA
PRES STEM	KALL-	GER-	SPYRJ-	HAF-	RÁÐ-	EIG-
Sg *ek*	kalla	gera	spyrja	hafa	ráða	eiga
þú	kallir	gerir	spyrir	hafir	ráðir	eigir
hann	kalli	geri	spyri	hafi	ráði	eigi
Pl *vér*	kallim	gerim	spyrim	hafim	ráðim	eigim
þér	kallið	gerið	spyrið	hafið	ráðið	eigið
þeir	kalli	geri	spyri	hafi	ráði	eigi

- Verbs *vera* and *sjá* are irregular in the present subjunctive. They resemble each other, although they are not cognate forms: *vera* (*sé, sér, sé, sém, séð, sé*) and *sjá* (*sjá, sér, sé, sém, séð, sé*).

8.16 CULTURE – HARALD HARDRADI, A VIOLENT END

Harald's reign in Norway was turbulent. Although he centralized power and founded the town of Oslo, he faced constant threats of rebellion from the prosperous Trondelag region in north-central Norway. A complex and forceful character, Harald ruthlessly suppressed any opposition to his power. He carried on a long and unsuccessful war to conquer Denmark and burned to the ground the Danish trading town of Hedeby. He and King Sveinn Ástríðarson (in English known as Sven Estridsson) of Denmark eventually signed a peace treaty in 1064. This truce freed Harald for his next adventure, his attempted conquest of England.

With the death of the Anglo-Saxon King Edward the Confessor in 1066, Harald saw a chance to claim England. He based his claim to the English throne on a treaty between his predecessor Magnus the Good (died 1047) and the earlier Danish King Horda-Knut (Hörða-Knútr, died 1042), who for a short period also ruled England. Harald gathered an invasion force of 300 ships and perhaps as many as 9,000 men. He landed on the coast near York and quickly defeated the northern English army. Before Harald could enjoy his victory, the English king Harold Godwinsson of Wessex surprised Harald at Stamford bridge near York. The Norwegians were caught without their heavy armor and Harald was killed. The English defeated the Norwegians decisively and only a small portion of the invading army made it back to Norway. With Harald's death, the twilight of the Viking Age arrived.

8.17 WORD FREQUENCY VOCABULARY – LIST 8. THE MOST FREQUENT WORDS IN THE SAGAS

NOUNS	ADJECTIVES	PRONOUNS	NUMERALS
bœr – farm	**vanr** – accustomed	**minn** – my	**tíu** – ten
bóndi – farmer	**heill** – whole	**engi** – no (one)	
sverð – sword	**lauss** – loose, free	**nökkurr** – some,	
hlutr – thing;	**sekr** – guilty	a certain	
part		**þinn** – your	

VERBS	PREPOSITIONS AND ADVERBS	CONJUNCTIONS
ætla – to intend	**fram** – forward	**þótt** – although
vita – to know	**yfir** – over	
leggja – to lay, place	**fyrr** – before	
bera – to carry, bear	**áðr** – before	

Exercises

8.18 Reading Old Norse. Circle the verb, underline the subject, and translate.

1. Þeir fóru út í Griklandshaf.

   _____

2. Hélt Haraldr sveit af sínum mönnum.

   _____

3. Höfðingi yfir herinum hét Gyrgir.

   _____

4. Hann var frændi dróttningar.

   _____

5. Haraldr var lítla hríð í herinum,

   _____

6. ...ok allir Væringjar fóru saman,...

   _____

7. ...þegar er bardagar váru.

   _____

8. Kom [þat] þá svá,...

   _____

9. at Haraldr varð höfðingi yfir öllum Væringjum.

   _____

8.19 *I*-Umlaut. Strong verbs show *i*-umlaut in the present singular. Fill in the blanks below.

INFINITIVE	3SG PRESENT	MEANING
Ex: fara	*ferr*	*go, travel*
1. draga		
2. halda		
3 standa		
4. koma		
5. láta		
6. fá		
7. fljúga		
8. búa		

8.20 The Present Tense of Strong Verbs and *I*-Umlaut.

A. Below are strong verbs in the 3sg present, all showing *i*-umlaut. Give the infinitive for each.

Ex: stendr   *standa*

1. ræðr		5.	heldr	
2. tekr		6.	flýgr	
3. fær		7.	býr	
4. kømr		8.	dregr	

B. Give the 3sg present for the following strong verbs. This exercise is the reverse of the previous exercise.

Ex: kala 'freeze'   *kelr*

1. hlaupa 'leap'		6.	slá 'strike'	
2. krjúpa 'creep'		7.	grafa 'dig'	
3. róa 'row'		8.	gróa 'grow'	
4. snúa 'turn'		9.	aka 'drive'	
5. súpa 'sip'		10.	auka 'increase'	

C. Verbs with front vowels such as -*e*-, -*i*-, and -*í*- in their infinitives do not undergo *i*-umlaut. Give the 3sg present tense for the following strong verbs.

Ex: hefja   *hefr*

1. gefa		4.	verða	
2. liggja		5.	ríða	
3. nema		6.	sitja	

8.21 Past Tense of Strong Verbs. Rewrite the following sentences so that the verb appears in the past tense, then translate.

Ex: Ek bý í Reyðarfirði.   *Ek bjó í Reyðarfirði.*

I lived in Reydarfjord.

1. Þú gengr á skip. _____

   _____

2. Heitir hann eigi Haraldr konungr? _____

   _____

3. Vér komum þangat. _____

   _____

4. Þér sjáið son hans. _____

   _____

5. Þau ganga til hans. _____

   _____

8.22 Strong Verbs. Conjugate the following strong verbs using the principal parts provided below.

A. verða <verðr, varð, urðu, orðinn> *vb* become

	PRESENT		**PAST**
Sg *ek*	_____	**Sg** *ek*	_____
þú	_____	*þú*	_____
hann	_____	*hann*	_____
Pl *vér*	_____	**Pl** *vér*	_____
þér	_____	*þér*	_____
þeir	_____	*þeir*	_____

PAST PARTICIPLE

Hann er _____ konungr. 'He has become king.'

B. taka <tekr, tók, tóku, tekinn> *vb* take

	PRESENT		**PAST**
Sg *ek*	_____	**Sg** *ek*	_____
þú	_____	*þú*	_____
hann	_____	*hann*	_____
Pl *vér*	_____	**Pl** *vér*	_____
þér	_____	*þér*	_____
þeir	_____	*þeir*	_____

PAST PARTICIPLE

Hestrinn var _____ af Ólafi. 'The horse was taken from Olaf.'

C. fara <ferr, fór, fóru, farinn> *vb* go, travel

	PRESENT		PAST
Sg *ek*	_____	**Sg** *ek*	_____
þú	_____	*þú*	_____
hann	_____	*hann*	_____
Pl *vér*	_____	**Pl** *vér*	_____
þér	_____	*þér*	_____
þeir	_____	*þeir*	_____

PAST PARTICIPLE

Hann var _____ út til Íslands. 'He had gone out to Iceland.'

8.23 Present Tense of Strong Verbs. Give the infinitive for each of the underlined verbs in the passage below and convert to 3sg or plural present, as appropriate.

Þá <u>réð</u> fyrir Griklandi Zóe dróttning in ríka ok með henni Michael kátalaktús. En er Haraldr <u>kom</u> til Miklagarðs ok á fund dróttningar, þá <u>gekk</u> hann þar á mála ok <u>fór</u> þegar um haustit á galeiðr með hermönnum þeim. Þeir <u>fóru</u> út í Griklandshaf. <u>Hélt</u> Haraldr sveit af sínum mönnum. Höfðingi yfir herinum <u>hét</u> Gyrgir. Hann var frændi dróttningar. Haraldr var lítla hríð í herinum, ok allir Væringjar fóru saman, þegar er bardagar váru. Kom þá svá, at Haraldr <u>varð</u> höfðingi yfir öllum Væringjum. Fóru þeir Gyrgir víða um Griklandseyjar, <u>unnu</u> þar herskap mikinn á kussurum.

		INFINITIVE	PRESENT				INFINITIVE	PRESENT
Ex: réð		*ráða*	*ræðr*					
1.	kom	_____	_____		5.	hélt	_____	_____
2.	gekk	_____	_____		6.	hét	_____	_____
3.	fór	_____	_____		7.	varð	_____	_____
4.	fóru	_____	_____		8.	unnu	_____	_____

8.24 Strong Verbs. Fill in the blanks below with the correct form of the strong verbs in the past tense.

1. Hann _____ á Dreppstokki. (búa)
2. Vér _____ stundum á skipit út. (ganga)
3. Þau _____ skipit. (sjá)
4. Björn ok Þórólfr _____ til Grœnlands. (koma)
5. Hon _____ Sigríðr. (heita)
6. Þú _____ með landnámsmönnum. (koma)
7. Þér _____ í Reykjavík. (búa)
8. Hon _____ hesta. (sjá)
9. Ek _____ Njáll. (heita)
10. Hann _____ til Nóregs. (fara)

8.25 Weak and Strong Verbs. Give the infinitives for the verbs in the sentences below and identify them as weak or strong.

	INFINITIVE	WEAK OR STRONG?
1. Eiríkr nam Eiríksfjörð.		
2. Haraldr vann sér Danmörk.		
3. Dómaldi réð löndum.		
4. Hann herjaði í austrveg.		
5. It fyrsta haust blótuðu þeir yxnum.		
6. En at skilnaði mælti Óláfr.		
7. Reið Gunnarr þá vestr.		
8. Árferð batnaði ekki.		
9. Hann stóð þá.		
10. Þá svaraði Þórólfr.		

8.26 Strong Verbs. Give the principal parts and 2sg past tense for each of the following strong verbs.

	PRINCIPAL PARTS	2SG PAST
Ex: geta	*getr, gat, gátu, getinn*	*gazt*
1. láta		
2. ráða		
3. draga		
4. binda		
5. bjóða		
6. búa		
7. heita		

Figure 38. The Ed (Boulder) Inscription from Uppland, Sweden.

8.27 Reading Exercise. The Ed (Boulder) Inscription from Uppland, Sweden speaks of Rognvald, who served as a officer in the Byzantine army.

ᚱᚢᚾᛏ · ᚱᛁᛋᛏᛏ · ᛚᛁᛏ · ᚱᛏᚼᚾᚢᛏᛚᛏᚱ · ᚼᚢ
ᛏᚱ ᛏ · ᚠᚱᛁᚴᛚᛏᛏᛏᛁ · ᚢᛏᛋ · ᛚᛁᛋ · ᚠᛏᚱᚢᚾᚴᛁ ·

TRANSLITERATION

runa · rista · lit · rahnualtr · huar a griklanti · uas · lis · forunki·

STANDARDIZED OLD NORSE

Rúna[r] rísta lét Ragnvaldr, hverr á Griklandi vas li[ð]s foringi.

VOCABULARY

foringi *m* captain, commander, leader
Grikland *n* Greece, Byzantine Empire (*place name*)
hverr *rel pron* who
láta <lætr, lét, létu, látinn> *vb* allow, permit; have something done
lið *n* band of men, troop
Ragnvaldr <-s> *m* Ragnvald (*personal name*)

rísta <rístr, reist, ristu, ristinn> *vb* carve, engrave; **láta rísta rúnar** have runes carved
rún <*pl* -ar> *f* rune, a letter in the runic 'futhark'
vas (*older form of* **var**) *3sg past of* **vera**

Translate:_____

_____

_____

_____

8.28 Imperative Mood: Strong Verbs. Give the imperative form for each of the strong verbs below. (Hint: the consonant clusters -*nd* and -*ng* require a change at the end of a word.)

Ex: koma   *kom*_____

1. draga _____   4. gefa   _____
2. fara _____   5. höggva_____
3. standa _____   6. ganga   _____

8.29 Imperative Mood: Weak Verbs. Identify the conjugation of each weak verb and provide its imperative form.

Ex: mæla, mælti   *2ⁿᵈ conjug*   *mæl*_____

1. gera, gerði   _____   _____
2. spyrja, spurði   _____   _____
3. svara, svaraði   _____   _____
4. veita, veitti   _____   _____
5. tala, talaði   _____   _____
6. þegja, þagði   _____   _____

8.30 Subjunctive Mood: Present Tense. Conjugate these verbs in the present subjunctive. Keep in mind that verbs with stem-final -*j*- drop -*j*- before endings beginning in -*i*-.

	LEITA	DRAGA	KOMA	HORFA	SKILJA	HÖGGVA
Sg *ek*	_____	_____	_____	_____	_____	_____
þú	_____	_____	_____	_____	_____	_____
hann	_____	_____	_____	_____	_____	_____
Pl *vér*	_____	_____	_____	_____	_____	_____
þér	_____	_____	_____	_____	_____	_____
þeir	_____	_____	_____	_____	_____	_____

LESSON 9
RAIDING IN THE WEST

Af hreinu bergi kemr hreint vatn
(From a clean mountain comes clean water)

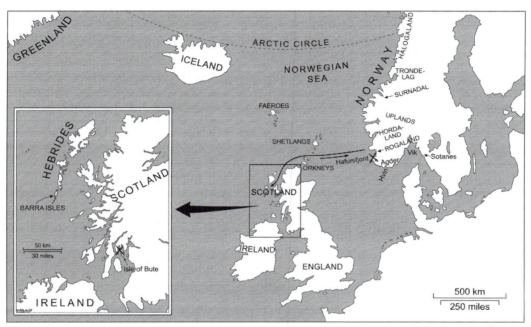

Figure 39. Raids and Battles of the 9th-Century Norwegian Viking Onund Tree-Foot (Önundr tréfótr). Onund, who is from Rogaland in West Norway, raids in Scotland, the Hebride Islands, and Ireland. Returning to Norway, he fights against Harald Fairhair at the Battle of Hafrsfjord ca. 870. Fleeing Norway after Harald's victory, Onund sails to Iceland where he settles down.

9.1 READING – ONUND TREE-FOOT RAIDS IN THE WEST (*GRETTIS SAGA ÁSMUNDARSONAR*)

Grettir's Saga opens with the story of Grettir's ancestor Onund Tree-Foot (*tréfótr*, meaning peg-leg), a Norwegian Viking. Onund raided for years in the Hebrides, Scotland, and Ireland. Before he settled in Iceland late in the *landnám* period, Onund had opposed Harald Fairhair's rise to power. In the sea battle of Hafrsfjord, Onund attacked King Harald's ship. In the fight, he lost a leg and earned his nickname. The saga says: 'Onund's wound was healed, but for the rest of his life he walked with a wooden leg.' The following passage introduces Onund's lineage and describes his Viking raids *vestr um haf* ('west across the sea' in the British Isles).

Grettis saga Ásmundarsonar (ch 1) Önundr hét maðr; hann var Ófeigs sonr burlufótar,[44] Ívars sonar beytils.[45] Önundr var bróðir Guðbjargar, móður Guðbrands kúlu, föður Ástu, móður Óláfs konungs ins helga.[46] Önundr var upplenzkr at móðurætt, en föðurkyn hans var mest um Rogaland ok um Hörðaland. Önundr var víkingr mikill ok herjaði vestr um haf. Með honum var í hernaði Bálki Blæingsson af Sótanesi ok Ormr inn auðgi; Hallvarðr hét inn þriði félagi þeira;[47] þeir höfðu fimm skip.

Þeir herjuðu um Suðreyjar, ok er þeir kómu í Barreyjar, var þar fyrir konungr sá,[48] er Kjarvalr hét; hann hafði ok fimm skip. Þeir lögðu til bardaga við hann[49] ok varð þar hörð hríð;[50] váru Önundar menn ákafir. Féll mart af hvárumtveggjum, en svá lauk,[51] at konungr flýði einskipa; tóku þeir Önundr þar bæði skip ok fé mikit ok sátu þar um vetrinn. Þrjú sumur herjuðu þeir um Írland ok Skotland; síðan fóru þeir til Nóregs.

Translate: _____

_____

_____

_____

_____

_____

_____

_____

_____

_____

_____

_____

_____

_____

_____

9.2 EXERCISE – READING *GRETTIR'S SAGA*

---

[44] **Ófeigs sonr burlufótar:** 'the son of Ofeig Clumsy-Foot.' Note the word order in which *sonr* intervenes between name and nickname.

[45] **Ívars sonar beytils:** this phrase takes the genitive to agree with *Ófeigs*.

[46] **móður Óláfs konungs ins helga:** 'the mother of King Olaf the Saint.' Nicknames are frequently preceded by a form of the definite article. The article agrees with its noun (here, a name) in case, number, and gender.

[47] **Hallvarðr hét inn þriði félagi þeira:** 'Hallvard was the name of their third companion'; *lit.*, 'the third companion of theirs was called Hallvard.'

[48] **var þar fyrir konungr sá:** 'that king was there.'

[49] **Þeir lögðu til bardaga við hann:** 'They engaged him in battle.'

[50] **hörð hríð:** 'a hard fight.'

[51] **en svá lauk:** 'and so it ended.'

Based on the reading above, are the following statements *rétt* or *rangt*?

	RÉTT EÐA RANGT?
1. Önundr var Ófeigsson.	
2. Önundr var bróðir Ívars.	_____
3. Föðurkyn Önundar var mest um Miðfjörð.	_____
4. Bróðir Guðbjargar var Önundr.	_____
5. Bálki Blæingsson drap Önund.	_____
6. Inn þriði félagi þeira var Hallvarðr.	_____
7. Konungr hét Herjólfr.	_____
8. Konungr hafði fimm skip.	_____
9. Önundr ok menn hans herjuðu um Írland ok Skotland.	_____

9.3 Culture – Western Norway

Grettir's Saga, a text whose author was well versed in Norwegian geography,[52] tells that Onund Tree-Foot's paternal line was from Rogaland and Hörðaland. These districts of Western Norway, along with Sogn, Firðafylki, Sunnmœrr, and Raumsdal just to the north, bordered the Atlantic coastline with deep fjords, sometimes reaching far inland. The climate was temperate, due to a northern arm of the Gulf Stream, but arable land for tilling was in short supply. Western Norwegians exploited maritime resources to supplement their diet, and seafaring was a way of life.

The West Norwegians also watched the trading wealth of their neighbors to the north and south sail past the mouths of their fjords, and they were not averse to seizing trading ships when they could. Stamping out piracy in Western Norway was one of the goals of Harald Fairhair's conquest. He was from the Vík region to the south, a center of trade. Harald's goals were shared by leaders of Norway's more northerly Trondelag region, and the Tronders allied with Harald. Faced with the rise of a centralized kingship in Norway aimed at ending their piracy, many West Norwegians sought land in newly discovered Iceland and other Atlantic islands.

9.4 More on the Definite Article

A distinguishing feature of the Scandinavian languages is that they normally affix the definite article to the end of a noun, for example *hestrinn* 'the horse,' *konan* 'the woman,'

---

[52] For a discussion of *Grettir's Saga* and a series of maps showing Onund's and Grettir's travels and adventures see Davide Zori and Jesse Byock, 'Introduction' to *Grettir's Saga*. Trans. J. Byock. Oxford: Oxford World Classics, Oxford University Press, 2009. The edition includes a full rendering of Grettir's verses translated by Russell Poole.

and *barnit* 'the child.' The declension of the definite article was introduced earlier.

The basic rule is that the definite article follows the noun's case ending, for example *hestrinn* (*hestr* + *inn*). When the noun ends in a vowel, the initial *i-* of the suffixed article is lost, for example *hestinum* (*hesti* + *inum*).

		HESTR + INN M	KONA + IN F	BARN + IT N
Sg *nom*		hestrinn	konan	barnit
	acc	hestinn	konuna	barnit
	dat	hestinum	konunni	barninu
	gen	hestsins	konunnar	barnsins
Pl *nom*		hestarnir	konurnar	börnin
	acc	hestana	konurnar	börnin
	dat	hestunum	konunum	börnunum
	gen	hestanna	kvennanna	barnanna

Concerning the suffixed definite article:

- The initial *i-* of the suffixed article is always lost in the masculine nominative plural and the feminine nominative/accusative plural, for example *hestarnir* (*hestar* + *inir*), *hallirnar* (*hallir* + *inar*), *konurnar* (*konur* + *inar*).
- In the dative plural, the noun loses the final *-m* of the ending, and the article loses its initial *i-*, for example, *konungunum* (*konungum* + *inum*), *mönnunum* (*mönnum* + *inum*), *höllunum* (*höllum* + *inum*), *börnunum* (*börnum* + *inum*).
- Nouns of one syllable that end in a vowel, such as *á* 'river,' *brú* 'bridge,'and *bú* 'farmstead' do not drop the *-i-* when the article consists of one syllable, hence feminine nominative singular *áin* (*á* + *in*). Otherwise the *-i-* is dropped as expected, for example, dative singular *ánni* (*á* + *inni*).
- The noun *maðr* has special forms, nominative plural *mennirnir* and accusative plural *mennina*.

9.5 STRONG NOUNS – TYPE 3

Type 3 contains only masculine nouns, with most following the patterns of *völlr* and *skjöldr*. These nouns show vowel alternations as the result of *u-* and *i-*umlaut as shown in the chart below. The exception is the feminine noun *hönd* (hand), singular: *hönd, hönd, hendi, handar*, plural: *hendr, hendr, höndum, handa*.

	VÖLLR	ÖRN	SKJÖLDR	BJÖRN	FJÖRÐR	ÞÁTTR	
Sg *nom*	völlr	örn	skjöldr	björn	fjörðr	þáttr	} *u*-umlaut
acc	völl	örn	skjöld	björn	fjörð	þátt	
dat	velli	erni	skildi	birni	firði	þætti	*i*-umlaut

gen	vallar	arnar	skjaldar	bjarnar	fjarðar	þáttar	

Pl *nom*	vellir	ernir	skildir	birnir	firðir	þættir	*i*-umlaut	
acc	völlu	örnu	skjöldu	björnu	fjörðu	þáttu	} *u*-umlaut	
dat	völlum	örnum	skjöldum	björnum	fjörðum	þáttum		
gen	valla	arna	skjalda	bjarna	fjörða	þátta		

Transl: *völlr* 'field,' *örn* 'eagle,' *skjöldr* 'shield,' *björn* 'bear,' *fjörðr* 'fjord,' *þáttr* 'tale'

- Some Type 3 nouns, such as *örn* and *björn*, drop nominative singular *-r*, in accordance with the Special Stem Rules.
- A few, such as *viðr*, *litr*, and *tigr*, have root vowel *-i-* with no alternation; for example, *tigr* 'ten' declines in the singular *tigr, tig, tigi, tigar.*
- *Áss* 'god' has variants in several of its case forms: *áss, ás, æsi~ás, áss~ásar,* (pl) *æsir, ásu~æsi, ásum, ása.*

9.6 STRONG NOUNS – TYPE 4

Type 4 is a small class containing only masculine and feminine nouns and is characterized by *i*-umlaut and the ending *-r* in the nominative and accusative plural.

Masculine. There are only five Type 4 masculine nouns:

	FÓTR	*MAÐR*	*NAGL*	*VETR*	*FINGR*
Sg *nom*	fótr	maðr	nagl	vetr	fingr
acc	fót	mann	nagl	vetr	fingr
dat	fœti	manni	nagli	vetri	fingri
gen	fótar	manns	nagls	vetrar	fingrar~fingrs

	FÓTR	*MAÐR*	*NAGL*	*VETR*	*FINGR*	
Pl *nom*	fœtr	menn	negl	vetr	fingr	} *i*-umlaut
acc	fœtr	menn	negl	vetr	fingr	
dat	fótum	mönnum	nöglum	vetrum	fingrum	
gen	fóta	manna	nagla	vetra	fingra	

Transl: *fótr* 'foot,' *maðr* 'man,' *nagl* 'fingernail,' *vetr* 'winter,' *fingr* 'finger'

- *Nagl* drops the plural ending *-r*, as do *vetr* and *fingr*, whose stems end in *-r*, in accordance with the Special Stems Rules.
- Note *fótr* shows *i*-umlaut in the dative singular.

Feminine. There are fewer than 30 Type 4 feminine nouns.

	RÓT	*MÚS*	*VÍK*	*TÖNN*	*KÝR*
Sg *nom*	rót	mús	vík	tönn	kýr
acc	rót	mús	vík	tönn	kú
dat	rót	mús	vík	tönn	kú

gen	rótar	músar	víkr	tannar	kýr

Pl *nom*	rœtr	mýss	víkr	tennr~teðr	kýr	} *i*-umlaut
acc	rœtr	mýss	víkr	tennr~teðr	kýr	
dat	rótum	músum	víkum	tönnum	kúm	
gen	róta	músa	víka	tanna	kúa	

Transl: *rót* 'root,' *mús* 'mouse,' *vík* 'bay,' *tönn* 'tooth,' *hönd* 'hand,' *kýr* 'cow'

- Some Type 4 nouns are irregular; for example, *vík* has genitive singular *víkr*, and *kýr* has nominative and genitive singular *kýr*.

9.7 DEMONSTRATIVE PRONOUNS *ÞESSI* AND *SÁ*

The pronouns *þessi* and *sá* mean 'this (one)' and 'that (one).'

	M	**F**	**N**
Sg *nom*	þessi ~ sjá	þessi ~ sjá	þetta
acc	þenna	þessa	þetta
dat	þessum	þessar(r)i ~ þessi	þessu
gen	þessa	þessar(r)ar ~ þessar	þessa
Pl *nom*	þessir	þessar	þessi
acc	þessa	þessar	þessi
dat	þessum	þessum	þessum
gen	þessa ~ þessar(r)a	þessa ~ þessar(r)a	þessa ~ þessar(r)a

	M	**F**	**N**
Sg *nom*	sá	sú	þat
acc	þann	þá	þat
dat	þeim	þeir(r)i	því
gen	þess	þeir(r)ar	þess
Pl *nom*	þeir	þær	þau
acc	þá	þær	þau
dat	þeim	þeim	þeim
gen	þeira	þeira	þeira

- The neuter singular and plural of all genders of *sá* are identical to the 3rd person pronoun.
- *Sá* also often occurs with the suffixed article, for example, ***sá** konungr**inn***.

Gormr konungr gerði kumbl **þessi**.   *King Gorm made **these** monuments.*

Sigríðr gerði brú **þessa** fyr sálu Hólmgeirs. *Sigrid made **this** bridge for Holmgeir's soul.*

Þá vil ek gefa þér skip **þetta**.	*Then I wish to give you **this** ship.*
Þessi var ekki konungsmaðr.	***This one** was not a follower of the king.*
Haraldr er faðir manns **þessa**.	*Harald is **this** man's father.*
Af **því** var hann kallaðr Eiríkr blóðøx.	*For **that** reason he was called Eirik Bloodaxe.*
Þeim manni gaf Ingólfr land.	*Ingolf gave land to **that** man.*
Sú kona var dóttir hennar.	***That** woman was her daughter.*
Þeir menn fóru til Englands.	***Those** men went to England.*
Í **þá** tíð var hallæri mikit.	*At **that** time there was a great famine.*

9.8 Clauses – Independent, Dependent, and Relative

Clauses are units of speech consisting of at least a subject and a verb. Being able to distinguish independent, dependent, and relative clauses helps in translating Old Norse.

> **Independent clauses** stand by themselves as grammatically complete sentences.

Þorsteinn hét maðr.	*A man was called Thorstein.*
Þá vil ek gefa þér skipit.	*Then I wish to give you the ship.*
Hann fór til Grœnlands með Eiríki.	*He went to Greenland with Eirik.*

Many sentences consist of two or more independent clauses joined by a coordinating conjunction, such as *ok* or *en*, or a two-part conjunction (correlative) such as *bæði ... ok* or *hvárki ... né*. The latter are called correlative clauses, which can be thought of as a subtype of independent clause.

Herjólfr nam land **en** Ingólfr var frændi hans.	*Herjolf took land **and** Ingolf was his kinsman.*
Önundr var upplenzkr at móðurætt, **en** föðurkyn hans var mest um Rogaland ok um Hörðaland.	*Onund was an Uplander (highlander) on his mother's side, **while** his father's family was mostly from Rogaland and Hörðaland.*
Tóku þeir Önundr **bæði** skip **ok** fé mikit ok sátu þar um vetrinn.	*Onund and his men took **both** ships **and** much treasure and stayed there for the winter.*
Hvárki Eiríkr **né** Björn gekk á skipit.	***Neither** Eirik **nor** Bjorn went onto the ship.*

In the first of the two correlative sentences above, there is one subject, Onund, who took two objects: ships in one clause, and treasure in the other. In the second correlative sentence, there are two independent subjects: Eirik and Bjorn with verb in the singular. Hence, each subject is performing an individual act and has its own clause.

When two or more independent clauses share the same subject or verb, the subject or verb is not repeated after the first clause.

Eiríkr stóð þá **ok** horfði á skipit.	Eirik stood then **and** looked at the ship.
Þorgerðr hét kona hans, **en** Bjarni sonr þeira, **ok** var efniligr maðr.	His wife was called Thorgerd, **and** their son (was called) Bjarni, **and** (he) was a promising man.

Dependent clauses cannot stand alone as complete sentences but are linked to a main clause by a subordinating conjunction such as *er, ef, því at, at*. The dependent clauses are underlined in the following sentences.

Þat var einn dag, **er** <u>þeir Þórólfr ok Björn gengu ofan til skipsins.</u>	That was one day, **when** <u>Thorolf and Bjorn went down to the ship.</u>
Þá vil ek gefa þér skipit, **ef** <u>þú vill þiggja.</u>	Then I wish to give to you the ship, **if** <u>you wish to accept [it].</u>
Herjólfr gaf Ingólfi land, **því at** <u>hann var frændi hans.</u>	Herjolf gave land to Ingolf, **because** <u>he was his kinsman.</u>
Hann segir, **at** <u>hann sé konungr Nóregs.</u>	He says **that** <u>he is king of Norway.</u>

Þá er 'then when' is frequently employed in place of *er*. Both are translated as 'when.'

Þá er <u>Högni kom í Noreg</u>, spurði hann at Héðinn hafði siglt vestr um haf.	**When** <u>Hogni arrived in Norway</u>, he learned that Hedin had sailed west over the sea.

Relative clauses are a type of dependent clause which refers back to a noun in the main clause. In Old Norse, the relative particles *er* or *sem* ('who,' 'which,' or 'that') introduce relative clauses. *Er* and *sem* are indeclinable; that is, they never change form. In the following sentences, the relative particle is in bold and the word it refers to is underlined.

Eigi er allt <u>gull</u> **sem** glóar.	Not all is <u>gold</u> **that** glows. (All that glows is not gold.)
<u>Konungr sá</u> **er** Högni er nefndr átti <u>dóttur</u>, **er** Hildr hét.	<u>That king</u> **who** is named Hogni had a <u>daughter</u> **who** was called Hild.
Hann er <u>maðrinn</u> **sem** kom.	He is the <u>man</u> **who** came.
Þá mælti Eiríkr jarl við þann <u>mann</u>, **er** sumir nefna Finn.	Then Earl Eirik spoke to that <u>man</u> **whom** some call Finn.

Often a form of the demonstrative *sá* precedes the relative particle *er* or *sem* and agrees with the noun of the *main* clause in gender, number, and case.

Kringla heimsins, **sú er** mannfólkit byggvir, er mjök vágskorin. (**sú** = f nom sg)	The circle of the world, (that one) **which** mankind inhabits, is much cut by bays.
Hann sá konu, **þá er** hann fekk. (**þá** = f acc sg)	He saw a woman, (that one) **whom** he got [in marriage].

9.9 EXERCISE – MAIN AND DEPENDENT CLAUSES.

Identify the underlined clauses as either independent or dependent.

Ex: <u>Þat kom ásamt með þeim</u>, at hallærit stóð at Dómaldi. _main clause_

1. <u>Er þeir kómu í Barreyjar</u>, var þar fyrir konungr sá, er Kjarvalr hét.
   _____

2. Þeir lögðu til bardaga við hann, ok <u>varð þar hörð hríð</u>. _____

3. Féll mart af hvárumtveggjum, en svá lauk, <u>at konungr flýði einskipa</u>; tóku þeir Önundr þar bæði skip ok fé mikit ok sátu þar um vetrinn. _____

4. <u>Þrjú sumur herjuðu þeir</u> um Írland ok Skotland. _____

9.10 VERBS – THE PAST SUBJUNCTIVE

A. Weak verbs form their past subjunctive by adding the subjunctive endings to the past tense stem, for example, *þeir kallaði, ek svaraða, þú talaðir*. In the past subjunctive, 3rd and 4th conjugation weak verbs show *i*-umlaut, hence 3sg past indicatives *spurði, taldi, krafði, vakti, hafði, sagði, þótti* become subjunctives *spyrði, teldi, krefði, vekti, hefði, segði, þœtti*.

Subjunctive Endings		
	SINGULAR	**PLURAL**
1st	-a	-im
2nd	-ir	-ið
3rd	-i	-i

INFINITIVE	**SVARA**	**MÆLA**	**LEGGJA**	**VAKA**	**HAFA**
PAST STEM	**SVARAÐ-**	**MÆLT-**	**LAGÐ-**	**VAKT-**	**HAFÐ-**
Sg *ek*	svaraða	mælta	legða	vekta	hefða
þú	svaraðir	mæltir	legðir	vektir	hefðir
hann	svaraði	mælti	legði	vekti	hefði
Pl *vér*	svaraðim	mæltim	legðim	vektim	hefðim
þér	svaraðið	mæltið	legðið	vektið	hefðið
þeir	svaraði	mælti	legði	vekti	hefði

B. Strong verbs add the subjunctive endings to the past subjunctive stem found by dropping the ending *-u* from the past plural and applying *i*-umlaut. (To find the past plural of strong verbs look to the fourth principal part, for example *gefa, gefr, gaf, **gáfu**, gefinn*.) Take the past plural (*gáfu*), drop the ending *-u* (*gáf-*), then apply *i*-umlaut (*gæf-*).

INFINITIVE	**BJÓÐA**	**VERÐA**	**BERA**	**FARA**	**RÁÐA**
3PL PAST	**BUÐU**	**URÐU**	**BÁRU**	**FÓRU**	**RÉÐU**
Sg *ek*	byða	yrða	bæra	fœra	réða

þú	byðir	yrðir	bærir	fœrir	réðir
hann	byði	yrði	bæri	fœri	réði

Pl *vér*	byðim	yrðim	bærim	fœrim	réðim
þér	byðið	yrðið	bærið	fœrið	réðið
þeir	byði	yrði	bæri	fœri	réði

- The past subjunctive of *vera* is regular (past plural *váru*, past subjunctive stem *vær-*): *væra, værir, væri, værim, værið, væri.*
- Verbs with past subjunctive stems ending in *-k-* and *-g-*, along with the verb *sá*, insert *-j-* in the 1sg, for example, *fengja* (*fá*), *tœkja* (*taka*), *drœgja* (*draga*), *sæja* (*sá*).
- Class VII verbs such as *hlaupa, auka,* and *ausa,* with *-au-* in the infinitive and *-jó-* in the past, have alternate past subjunctive stems. For example, *hlaupa* sometimes forms its past subjunctive from the stem *hlyp-*, and sometimes from the stem *hlœp-*.

9.11 EXERCISE – THE PAST SUBJUNCTIVE OF VERBS

Conjugate the verbs *tala, hafa, gjalda,* and *koma* in the past subjunctive.

	TALA	*HAFA*	*GJALDA*	*KOMA*
Sg *ek*	_____	_____	_____	_____
þú	_____	_____	_____	_____
hann	_____	_____	_____	_____
Pl *vér*	_____	_____	_____	_____
þér	_____	_____	_____	_____
þeir	_____	_____	_____	_____

9.12 READING – MURDER, FOSTERAGE, AND A WIDOW'S RESOURCEFULNESS (*GRETTIS SAGA ÁSMUNDARSONAR*)

During the Viking Age, women of the property-holding, free-farmer class had significant legal rights. By custom they ran the household and many of the farm industries. A woman was by law subordinate to her husband (*húsbóndi*) when he was home, but when her husband was away, the *húsfreyja*, or mistress of the house, often assumed full charge. In times of feud and conflict, many women acted independently, as in the following passage from *Grettir's Saga*.

Ondott Crow, a prominent Norwegian *bóndi*, landed in a dispute with Grim, the king's *hersir* (local military commander). The dispute over payments to the king resulted in Ondott's death. Anticipating an attack by the king's men on the family farm, Ondott's widow Signy gathers her husband's wealth under cover of darkness and escapes with their two sons by boat to her father's farm. She then sends her sons into fosterage with another family, a common custom that was intended to seal political ties between families.

Grettis saga Ásmundarsonar (ch 7) Þetta haust drap Grímr hersir Öndótt kráku fyrir þat, er hann náði eigi fénu[53] til handa konungi;[54] en Signý, kona Öndótts, bar á skip allt lausafé þeira þegar ina sömu nótt[55] ok fór með sonu sína, Ásmund ok Ásgrím, til Sighvats, föður síns. Litlu síðar[56] sendi hon sonu sína í Sóknadal til Heðins, fóstra síns, ok unðu þeir þar lítla hríð[57] ok vildu fara aptr til móður sinnar. Fóru þeir síðan ok kómu til Ingjalds tryggva í Hvini at jólum; hann tók við þeim fyrir áeggjun Gyðu, konu sinnar; váru þeir þar um vetrinn.

Translate: _____

_____

_____

_____

_____

_____

_____

_____

_____

_____

_____

_____

_____

_____

_____

_____

_____

9.13 CULTURE – VIKING IN THE BRITISH ISLES AND WESTERN EUROPE

In the last years of the eighth century, a wave of seaborne raids in the British Isles and Western Europe announced the arrival of the Viking Age. Scandinavian navigational techniques and ship technology had developed to the point where Norse mariners were freed from the older sailing technique of following the coast. Now they were able to cross the open waters of the North Sea and the Atlantic. The speed and shallow draft of the Scandinavian clinker-built ships were ideal for launching surprise attacks inland along rivers where most wealthy trading sites were located.

Viking raiders took advantage of the political disunity and conflicts among the Picts, Scots, Anglo-Saxons, and Irish, and the leaders of Viking armies turned to their advantage dynastic problems within the Carolingian Empire. Employing the mobility afforded them

---

[53] **fyrir þat, er hann náði eigi fénu** (*fé* + *inu*): 'for the [reason] that, he did not get the payment.'
[54] **til handa konungi:** 'for the king.'
[55] **þegar ina sömu nótt:** 'at once on that same night.'
[56] **litlu síðar:** 'a little later.'
[57] **unðu þeir þar lítla hríð:** 'they didn't like staying there but for a little while'

by their ships, Vikings moved opportunistically between different regions, preying upon the weakest opponent. By the end of the Viking Age, the raiders had left their mark on the political and social landscape of northern Europe.

In the Frankish domains Viking attacks undermined the power of the Carolingian rulers, and Vikings quickened the splintering of the Carolingian empire. In Ireland Vikings caused long periods of warfare and unrest, but also stimulated trade and the growth of towns. In England the northmen with their threat of conquest, were catalysts for the unification of the country under the Wessex kings who rose as the single power capable of resisting the Vikings. North of Scotland, the Earldom of Orkney became a Viking state, which developed into a regional maritime power. Its Earls (*jarlar*) continued to launch raids into the twelfth century. The coastal regions of Scotland were often harried and settled by Norse seafarers, while spme of the inland regions were partly spared.

The Viking Age in Western Europe falls into essentially four phases. The raids began on a small scale in the late eighth century and were led by warrior chiefs, sometimes called sea kings, because they ruled from ships. The leadership of the Viking raiders reflects the splintered social organizations in Scandinavia, which at the time was divided into small-scale, petty kingdoms and local chieftaincies. During the middle of the ninth century, Viking armies began to spend the winter in foreign lands. They built camps and occupied fortified sites, which allowed them to continue raiding throughout much of the year. This change resulted in the conquest of certain regions. The third phase, from roughly the late ninth to mid-tenth century, was a period of response by the indigenous peoples of northern Europe and the British Isles to the conquests of the Vikings. With varying degrees of success, the local populations re-conquered areas from the raiders, who had become colonists and settled down in their midst.

The fourth phase of the Viking Age began in the late tenth century. By that time, the Scandinavian homelands were solidifying into larger kingdoms. Scandinavian princes had become powerful enough to attempt royal conquests. England was the great prize, and two future kings of Norway, Olaf Tryggvason (995-1000) and Olaf Haraldsson (St. Olaf, 1015-1028), rose to prominence as Viking commanders in England. The Danish kings Svein Forkbeard and Canute the Great and the Norwegian Harald Harddradi led invasions of England in the eleventh century. Finally in 1066 William of Normandy conquered England. He and many of his Normans were descended from Viking invaders, who had settled in northern France a century and a half earlier.

9.14 Word Frequency Vocabulary – List 9. The Most Frequent Words in the Sagas

Nouns	Adjectives	Pronouns	Numerals
sök – cause, reason	**vinsæll** – popular	**slíkr** – such	**sjau** – seven
bú– farm	**skyldr** – related; necessary, obliged	**báðir** – both	
höfuð – head		**várr** – our	

móðir – mother   **miðr** – middle

víg – slaying   **fullr** – full

VERBS	PREPOSITIONS AND ADVERBS	CONJUNCTIONS
gefa – to give	**saman** – together	**nema** – except
finna – to find	**inn** – inside	
ráða – to advise; rule	**undir** – under	
sitja – to sit	**heldr** – rather	
standa – to stand	**brott** – away	

EXERCISES

9.15 Definite Article. Decline masculine *dvergrinn* 'the dwarf,' feminine *konan* 'the woman,' and neuter *landit* 'the land.'

		DVERGR + INN	KONA + IN	LAND + IT
Sg	*nom*	dvergrinn	konan	landit
	acc			
	dat			
	gen			
Pl	*nom*			
	acc			
	dat			
	gen			

9.16 Demonstrative Pronouns. Complete the charts of *þessi* 'this' and *sá* 'that.'

		M	F	N	M	F	N
Sg	*nom*	þessi			sá		
	acc						
	dat						
	gen						
Pl	*nom*						
	acc						
	dat						
	gen						

9.17 Demonstrative Pronouns. Fill in the correct demonstrative pronoun for the following sentences.

   Ex: Gormr konungr gerði *þessi*____ (these) kumbl.

1. Haraldr gaf mér _____ (this) sverð.
2. Hann tók _____ (that) sverð.
3. Vér fórum til _____ (that) manns.
4. Óláfr tók við _____ (this) konu.
5. Sigríðr gerði _____ (that) brú.
6. Hon nam _____ (this) land.
7. Þær sáu _____ (that) konung.
8. _____ (that) kona hét Sigríðr.

9.18 Strong Verbs. Below is a list of common strong verbs and their principal parts.

   bera <berr, bar, báru, borinn> *vb* bear, carry

   bjóða <býðr, bauð, buðu, boðinn> *vb* offer; invite

   draga <dregr, dró, drógu, dreginn> *vb* pull, draw, drag

   fara <ferr, fór, fóru, farinn> *vb* go, travel

   fá <fær, fekk, fengu, fenginn> *vb* fetch, get; give, deliver

   ganga <gengr, gekk, gengu, genginn> *vb* go, walk

   gefa <gefr, gaf, gáfu, gefinn> *vb* give

   halda <heldr, hélt, héldu, haldinn> *vb* hold, keep

   hefja <hefr, hóf, hófu, hafinn> *vb* lift, raise; begin

   heita <heitir, hét, hétu, heitinn> *vb* be called

   koma <kemr~kømr, kom, kómu~kvómu~kvámu, kominn> *vb* come

   nema <nemr, nam, námu, numinn> *vb* take, learn

   ráða <ræðr, réð, réðu, ráðinn> *vb* advise, counsel; rule, govern

   verða <verðr, varð, urðu, orðinn> *vb* become

   vinna <vinnr, vann, unnu, unninn> *vb* gain, win; work

A. Conjugate *bera* in the present and past tense.

	PRESENT	PAST
Sg *ek*	_____	_____
þú	_____	_____
hann	_____	_____
Pl *vér*	_____	_____
þér	_____	_____
þeir	_____	_____

B. Identify each of the verbs below as in the example.

   Ex: berr   *3sg pres of bera 'carry'*

1. hélduð _____
2. gekk _____
3. verð _____
4. heitið _____
5. bar _____
6. réðum _____
7. hafinn _____
8. drögum _____

C. Provide the correct form for each of the verbs below.

Ex: gefa (*2sg pres*)   *gefr*_____

1. koma (*2sg pres*)_____
2. vinna (*2pl past*) _____
3. hefja (*2sg past*) _____
4. ráða (*3sg past*) _____

5. nema (*1pl past*) _____
6. fá (*1sg pres*)   _____
7. draga (*3pl pres*)_____
8. fara (*1pl pres*)   _____

9.19 Verbs. Give the principal parts for the underlined strong verbs in the passage below.

Þeir herjuðu um Suðreyjar, ok er þeir <u>kómu</u> í Barreyjar, var þar fyrir konungr sá, er Kjarvalr <u>hét</u>; hann hafði ok fimm skip. Þeir lögðu til bardaga við hann, ok <u>varð</u> þar hörð hríð; váru Önundar menn ákafir. <u>Féll</u> mart af hvárumtveggjum, en svá <u>lauk</u>, at konungr flýði einskipa; <u>tóku</u> þeir Önundr þar bæði skip ok fé mikit ok <u>sátu</u> þar um vetrinn. Þrjú sumur herjuðu þeir um Írland ok Skotland; síðan <u>fóru</u> þeir til Nóregs.

INFINITIVE	PRES SG	PAST SG	PAST PL	PAST PARTICIPLE
_____	_____	_____	kómu	_____
_____	_____	hét	_____	_____
_____	_____	varð	_____	_____
_____	_____	féll	_____	_____
_____	_____	lauk	_____	_____
_____	_____	_____	tóku	_____
_____	_____	_____	sátu	_____
_____	_____	_____	fóru	_____

9.20 Strong Nouns – Type 3. Decline the nouns *völlr*, *köttr*, and *fjörðr* below.

	VÖLLR	KÖTTR	FJÖRÐR
Sg *nom*	_____	_____	_____
acc	_____	_____	_____
dat	_____	_____	_____
gen	_____	_____	_____
Pl *nom*	_____	_____	_____
acc	_____	_____	_____
dat	_____	_____	_____
gen	_____	_____	_____

9.21 Strong Nouns – Type 4. Decline the nouns *fótr*, *vetr*, and *bók* below.

	FÓTR (M)	VETR (M)	BÓK (F)
Sg *nom*	_____	_____	_____
acc	_____	_____	_____
dat	_____	_____	_____

gen	_____	_____	_____
Pl nom	_____	_____	_____
acc	_____	_____	_____
dat	_____	_____	_____
gen	_____	_____	_____

9.22 The Conjunction, Relative Particle and Verb er. Translate. Remember that *er* has several meanings: 'when,' 'who,' 'which,' 'that,' and 'is.'

Ex: Haraldr konungr bað gera kumbl þessi, sá Haraldr **er** sér vann Danmörk.

King Harald commanded these burial mounds to be made, that Harald <u>who</u> won for himself Denmark.

1. Skútaðar-Skeggi hét maðr ágætr í Nóregi. Hans sonr var Björn; **er** kallaðr var Skinna-Björn.

   _____

   _____

2. Þeir herjuðu um Suðreyjar, ok **er** þeir kómu í Barreyjar, var þar fyrir konungr sá, **er** Kjarvalr hét.

   _____

   _____

3. Þat var einn dag, **er** þeir Þórólfr ok Björn gengu ofan til skipsins.

   _____

   _____

4. En **er** Haraldr kom til Miklagarðs ok á fund dróttningar, þá gekk hann þar á mála.

   _____

   _____

5. Haraldr var lítla hríð í herinum, ok allir Væringjar fóru saman, þegar **er** bardagar váru.

   _____

   _____

9.23 Subjunctive Mood: Past Tense of Weak Verbs. Fill in the chart below.

	MEANING	**CONJUGATION**	**PAST STEM**
Ex: kalla	*'call'*	*1ˢᵗ conjugation*	*kallað*
1. senda	_____	_____	_____
2. telja	_____	_____	_____
3. veita	_____	_____	_____
4. hafa	_____	_____	_____
5. tala	_____	_____	_____

Weak verbs add the subjunctive endings to the past tense stem to form the past subjunctive. 3rd and 4th conjugation verbs also show *i*-umlaut of the root vowel.

Give the past tense stems and past subjunctive stems for the following verbs.

	PAST TENSE STEM	PAST SUBJUNCTIVE STEM
Ex: kalla	*kallað-*	*kallað-*
6. tala		
7. senda		
8. telja		
9. hafa		

9.24 Subjunctive Mood: Past Tense of Strong Verbs. Fill in the chart below.

	MEANING	PRINCIPAL PARTS	PAST PLURAL STEM
Ex: draga	*'pull'*	*dregr, dró, drógu, dreginn*	*dróg-*
1. brjóta			
2. verða			
3. líta			
4. koma			
5. taka			

Strong verbs add subjunctive endings to the past plural stem with *i*-umlaut of the stem vowel. Give the past tense stems and past subjunctive stems for the following verbs.

	PAST PLURAL STEM	PAST SUBJUNCTIVE STEM
Ex: draga	*dróg-*	*drœg-*
6. brjóta		
7. verða		
8. líta		
9. koma		
10. taka		

Conjugate the five strong verbs below in the past subjunctive.

	BRJÓTA	VERÐA	LÍTA	KOMA	TAKA
Sg *ek*					
þú					
hann					
Pl *vér*					
þér					
þeir					

9.25 Reading Runes. The Fläckebo (Hassmyra) Runestone commemorates a Swedish *húsfreyja* (lady of the house).

RUNES

ᛒᚢᚨᛏ ᛏᛁ·ᚠᚢᚦᚱ·ᚼᚢᛚᚴᚤᚠᛁᛏᚱ·
ᛚᛁᛏ·ᚱᛁᛋᚨ·ᚢᚠᛏᛁᚨ·ᚠᚦᛁᛏᛁᛋᚢ·
ᚠᚢᛏᚢ·ᛋᛁᚾᚨ·ᚠᚢᚤᛒᚱ·ᚼᛁᚠᚱᚨᛏ·
ᛏᛁᛚ·ᚼᛅᛋᚢᛁᛘᚢᚱᚨ·ᛁᚠᛁ·ᛒᛁᛏᚱ·ᚦᚨᚾ·
ᛒᚨᛁ·ᚱ ᛏᚦᚱ·ᚱᛅᚦᚨᛚᛁᚱ·
ᚱᛁᛋᛏᛁ·ᚱᚢᚾᛁ·ᚦᛁᛋᚨ·ᛋᛁᚠᛘᚢᚾᛏᚨᚱ·
ᚢᚨᚱ·ᚠᚦᛁᛏᛁᛋᚨ·ᛋᛁᛋᛏᚱ·ᚠᚢᚦ

TRANSLITERATION

buonti kuþr hulmkoetr lit resa ufteʀ oþintisu kunu seno kumbr hifrya til hasuimura iki betr þon byi raþr roþbalir risti runi þisa sikmuntaʀ uaʀ oþintisa sestʀ kuþ

STANDARDIZED OLD NORSE

Bóndi góðr Hólmgautr lét reisa eptir Óðindísu konu sína. Kømr hýsfreyja til Hasvimýra ekki betr, sú er býi ræðr. Rauð-Balli risti rúnar þessar. Sigmundar var Óðindísa systir góð.

Figure 40. The Fläckebo (a) Runestone from Västmanland, Sweden.

VOCABULARY

bý (*var of* **bú**) <*dat pl* býum> *n* home, house, household; farm; estate

Hólmgautr <-s> *m* Holmgaut (*personal name*)

Hasvimýrar *m pl* Hasvimyrar (*place name*)

hýsfreyja (*var of* **húsfreyja**) *f* housewife

kømr (*var of* **kemr**) *2/3sg pres of* **koma**

láta <lætr, lét, létu, látinn> *vb* allow, permit; have something done

mýrr <*acc* & *dat* mýri, *gen* mýrar, *pl* mýrar>

f moor, bog, swamp

Óðindísa *f* Odindisa (*personal name*)

Rauð-Balli *m* Red-Balli (*personal name*)

ráða <ræðr, réð, réðu, ráðinn> *vb* advise, counsel; rule, govern

reisa <-ti, -tr> *vb* raise; **láta reisa [stein]** have a stone raised

rista <-ti, -tr> *vb* cut, carve, engrave

Sigmundr <-ar> *m* Sigmund (*personal name*)

Translate:_____

_____

_____

_____

LESSON 10
BEACHED WHALES IN ICELAND

Betri er ein kráka í hendi en tvær í skógi
(Better one crow in the hand than two in the wood)

10.1 CULTURE – COMPETITION FOR RESOURCES

Although descended from Norse peoples with sea-going traditions, Icelanders lacked the forest resources of Scandinavia to ensure a cost-effective supply of ocean-going ships. This factor restricted their fishing and limited their subsistence strategies. They became a largely land-locked livestock farming society in the midst of a fertile ocean teeming with whales and other sea life.

Without seaworthy ships to circumvent the island most travel was done on horseback and transport with pack horses. An extensive system of horse paths developed that led to almost every part of the country and formed a highly serviceable communications web. There were no roads for wheeled carts in the highlands, and few if any such roads in the valleys.

Icelanders relied on relatively small boats. These were built from mostly driftwood and were only suitable for close coastal fishing. Such fishing often yielded large quantities of catch. Lacking a good supply of salt, they wind-dried several types of fish, especially cod, for the winter. Given the limitations of their boats, Icelanders rarely hunted whales on the open sea. It is also unlikely that

Figure 41. The Strands in Iceland's West Fjords (*Grettir's Saga*). Trouble brews when a dispute over a beached whale at Rifsker escalates into a fight, involving people up and down the coast. The map traces their sailing routes to the battle.

they herded whales into bays, forcing them aground, as did their Norwegian counterparts with better ship-building timbers at their disposal. Icelanders searched the coastline looking for beached whales esteemed for their enormous quantities of meat, fat, and bone.

In the years following Iceland's settlement, social and economic development was dictated by competition for the land's limited resources. Common lands were called *almenningar*. Especially along the coast these public lands offered opportunities for enterprising individuals to find driftage (wood, whales, etc.) to increase their store of provisions and saleable merchandise. Leaving the protection of one's farmstead and neighborhood to hunt and gather foodstuffs in the often desolate *almenningar* could be dangerous. Competition was fierce and disputes often arose over finds. Seal-hunting was important for skins, meat, and oil, but beached whales were the real prizes along the coast.

Grettir's Saga offers some of the most detailed information in the medieval sources about the value of beached whales. Bloated and raised to the surface by the gases of decay in their stomachs and bowels, these dead creatures were huge treasures. Individuals and allies were prepared to fight for possession when whale carcasses washed ashore following storms.

10.2 READING – A WHALE WASHES ASHORE (*GRETTIS SAGA ÁSMUNDARSONAR*)

The readings for this lesson concern a famine in the West Fjords recounted in *Grettir's Saga*. Conflict over resources begins a feud which involves Onund Tree-Foot's sons, Thorgrim Gray-Streak (Hærukollr) and Thorgeir Flask-Back (flöskubakr). The sons have taken over their father's farm at Kaldbak ('Cold-Back Mountain') in the Strands (Strandir). Onund was given the farm by the original *landnámsmaðr* Eirik Snare. Eirik, whose farm was at Arness (Árnes) on the bay Trekyllisvik (called Vík or Víkin in the reading), originally owned all rights to driftage on the Strands. Flosi, Eirik's son and heir, resents that his father gave away these valuable driftage rights, particularly in this time of shortage.

After a storm, local inhabitants check the beaches for driftage. A man named Thorstein discovers a beached whale at Rifsker on Reykjanes, a headland midway on the coast between Kaldbak and Arness. The whale is a large rorqual (*reyðr*), and Thorstein sends a messenger to notify his leader Flosi of the need for assistance. Thorgrim Gray-Streak also learns of the whale. Thorgrim and Flosi are heads of households. They are local leaders among the second generation Icelanders, and each claims the whale. As the news of the whale spreads, men in small boats row from all corners of the Strands to share in the find. They offer support to their allies, either to Thorgrim and the men of Kaldbak (*Kaldbeklingar*) or Flosi's people (*Víkrmenn*).

Flosi and his men reach the whale first. They immediately begin cutting and flensing (slicing the blubber from the bones). When Thorgrim and the men of Kaldbak arrive, the sides dispute who has the proper claim to the whale. The dispute centers around whether Flosi's father Eirik Snare, the first settler in the region, had legally given driftage rights to Thorgrim's father, Onund Tree-Foot. Thorgrim asserts his ownership. Using legal language, he forbids Flosi and Flosi's allies to take away any part of the whale.

Grettis saga Ásmundarsonar (ch 12)

Í þann tíma kom hallæri svá mikit á Ísland, at ekki hefir jafnmikit komit. Þá tók af náliga allan sjávarafla ok reka. Þat stóð yfir mörg ár.

Á einu hausti urðu þangat sæhafa kaupmenn á hafskipi ok brutu þar í Víkinni. Flosi tók við þeim fjórum eða fimm. Steinn hét sá er fyrir þeim var.[58]...Um várit kom veðr mikit af norðri; þat helzk nær viku. Eptir veðrit könnuðu menn reka sína.[59] Þorsteinn hét maðr, er bjó á Reykjanesi. Hann fann hval rekinn innan fram á nesinu,[60] þar sem hét at Rifskerjum[61]: þat var reyðr mikil. Hann sendi þegar mann til Flosa í Vík ok svá til næstu bœja....Flosi kom fyrst ok þeir Víkrmenn; þeir tóku þegar til skurðar ok var dreginn á land upp sá [hvalr], er skorinn var...

Í því kómu Kaldbeklingar[62] með fjögur skip. Þorgrímr veitti tilkall til hvalsins ok fyrirbauð Víkrmönnum skurð ok skipti ok brautflutning[63] á hvalnum.

Translate: _____

_____

_____

_____

_____

_____

_____

_____

_____

_____

_____

_____

The saga goes on to tell how Flosi, having the larger force, demands that Thorgrim prove his rights to the driftage. Thorgrim initially decides not to attack, but at that moment a ship with reinforcements arrives from the south. The ship is captained by Svan, one of Thorgrim's allies. Svan quickly offers his support to Thorgrim. Returning to the Icelandic text:

---

[58] **er fyrir þeim var:** 'who was their leader.'

[59] **reka sína:** The men referred to here are the Icelandic owners of the shoreline checking their driftage.

[60] **hval rekinn innan fram á nesinu:** 'a whale washed onto Rifsker (the shallow rocky reef) out on the headland.' *Fram á nesinu* denotes the outermost point of the headland.

[61] **þar sem hét at Rifskerjum:** 'at that place which was called *at Rifskerjum* (beside Rifsker).' Place names in Old Norse frequently include prepositions. English has some examples of this as well, for instance, Stratford-on-Avon. The preposition is best omitted in translation.

[62] **Kaldbeklingar:** 'the men of Kaldbak.' The suffixes *-ingr* (pl *-ingar*), *-lingr* (pl *-lingar*), and *-ungr* (pl *-ungar*) are frequently used to denote members of a family or group.

[63] The phrase *skurð ok skipti* 'cutting and dividing' and the word *brutflutning* 'carrying away' were legal terms used in connection with driftage rights.

Þá reri skip innan yfir fjörðu, ok sóttu knáliga róðrinn; þeir kómu at brátt. Þat var Svanr af Hóli ór Bjarnarfirði ok húskarlar hans; ok þegar hann kom, bað hann Þorgrím eigi láta ræna sik;[64] en þeir váru áðr vinir miklir, ok bauð Svanr honum lið sitt.

Translate: _____

_____

_____

_____

_____

Thorgrim accepts Svan's offer and the two prepare to fight. The story of the battle continues later in this lesson.

10.3 EXERCISE – *GRETTIR'S SAGA*

Review Reading I and decide whether the following statements are true or false.

RÉTT EÐA RANGT?

1. Hallæri stóð yfir mörg ár.   _____
2. Kaupmenn urðu sæhafa.   _____
3. Þorsteinn fann hval.   _____
4. Þorsteinn bjó í Danmörk.   _____
5. Kaldbeklingar kómu með fimm skip.   _____
6. Þorgrímr veitti tilkall til hvalsins.   _____

10.4 STRONG ADJECTIVES

As noted earlier adjectives modify nouns and agree in gender, case, and number with the nouns they modify. Old Norse adjectives have both strong and weak forms and decline in many instances similar to nouns. Adjectives take strong endings unless preceded by a definite article, demonstrative pronoun or other determining word, in which case they take weak endings. This section presents the rules for strong adjectives. The next lesson discusses weak adjectives.

The strong adjective *spakr* 'wise' is declined below as an example.

	M	F	N		M	F	N
Sg *nom*	spak**r**	sp**ö**k	spak**t**	**Pl**	spak**ir**	spak**ar**	sp**ö**k
acc	spak**an**	spak**a**	spak**t**		spak**a**	spak**ar**	sp**ö**k

---

[64] **bað hann Þorgrím eigi láta ræna sik:** 'he told Thorgrim not to let himself be robbed.'

dat	spö**kum**	spa**kri**	spö**ku**		spö**kum**	spö**kum**	spö**kum**
gen	spaks	spak**rar**	spaks		spak**ra**	spak**ra**	spak**ra**

- Adjectives containing -*a*- undergo *u*-umlaut (*spakr*, dat *spökum*).
- Some adjectives, such as *ríkr* and *døkkr*, have stem-final -*j*- or -*v*-, for example, *ríkr* <-j-> 'powerful,' (m *ríkr, ríkjan, ríkjum, ríks, ríkir, ríkja, ríkjum, ríkra*) and *døkkr* <-v-> 'dark' (*døkkr, døkkvan, dökkum, døkks, døkkvir, døkkva, døkkum, døkkra*).
- The neuter singular ending -*t* is doubled when added to an adjective whose stem ends in a long vowel (for example, *fár, hár,* and *blár* become *fátt, hátt,* and *blátt*).
- When neuter singular -*t* is added to an adjective whose stem ends in a dental (-*ð*-, -*d*-, or -*t*-), the final dental of the stem changes to -*t*-. For example, *fríðr* and *óðr* become *frítt* and *ótt*. When a consonant precedes the stem final dental (*harðr, kaldr*), the dental assimilates to the ending -*t* (*hart-t, kalt-t*), and then the ending -*t* is dropped (*hart, kalt*).

10.5 EXERCISE – NOUNS AND STRONG ADJECTIVES

Decline *ungr maðr* 'young man,' *ung kona* 'young woman,' and *ungt barn* 'young child.'

	UNGR MAÐR	**UNG KONA**	**UNGT BARN**
Sg *nom*	_____	_____	_____
acc	_____	_____	_____
dat	_____	_____	_____
gen	_____	_____	_____
Pl *nom*	_____	_____	_____
acc	_____	_____	_____
dat	_____	_____	_____
gen	_____	_____	_____

10.6 STRONG ADJECTIVES OF TWO SYLLABLES

Like two-syllable nouns, adjectives whose second syllable consists of a short vowel and a single consonant, lose the vowel of the second syllable if the ending begins in a vowel. For example, the adjective *auðigr* (stem *auðig*-) in the accusative loses the -*i*- of the second syllable and becomes *auðgan* (*auðig*- + -*an*). Other common adjectives which shorten the stem are *mikill, lítill, gamall, göfugr,* and *heilagr*.

auðigr 'wealthy'

	M	**F**	**N**		**M**	**F**	**N**
Sg *nom*	auðigr	auðig	auðigt	**Pl**	auðgir	auðgar	auðig
acc	auðgan	auðga	auðigt		auðga	auðgar	auðig

| dat | auðgum | auðigri | auðgu | | auðgum | auðgum | auðgum |
| gen | auðigs | auðigrar | auðigs | | auðigra | auðigra | auðigra |

When the second syllable is dropped, long vowels in the first syllable tend to shorten before two consonants. For instance, the long -í- in *lítill* becomes short in dative *litlum* and the diphthong -ei- in *heilagr* shortens to -e-, giving dative *helgum*. In the fourteenth- or fifteenth-century, adjectives like these began to keep the second-syllable vowel in all cases (for example, *auðigan* rather than *auðgan*). The retention of this vowel in such adjectives is one of the distinctions between Old and Modern Icelandic.

10.7 Strong Adjective Endings

Strong adjectives take endings similar to strong nouns. Deviations are explained by a few rules. We suggest reviewing the earlier section on the Special Stem Rules. This section explains the patterns resulting when an -r ending is added to a noun or adjective whose stem ends in -l-, -n-, -r-, or -s- (stem-final -l-, -n-, -r-, or -s-). It also explains the apparent lack of the nominative -r ending in masculine words such as *Þorsteinn* and *fugl*.

- Adjectives whose stems end in -l, -n, -r, -s follow the Special Stem Rules, either changing -r (*vænn*, *lauss*, and *gamall*) or dropping -r (*fagr*). These rules apply to all endings beginning in -r (-r, -ri, -rar, -ra), for example, *vænn, vænni, vænnar, vænna*; *fagr, fagri, fagrar, fagra*.
- The adjectives *mikill* and *lítill* have a few slightly irregular forms: *mikinn* (m acc sg), *lítinn* (m acc sg), *mikit* (n nom/acc sg), and *lítit* (n nom/acc sg).

		LAUSS 'LOOSE, FREE'			VÆNN 'BEAUTIFUL, FINE'	
	M	**F**	**N**	**M**	**F**	**N**
Sg *nom*	lauss	laus	laust	vænn	væn	vænt
acc	lausan	lausa	laust	vænan	væna	vænt
dat	lausum	laussi	lausu	vænum	vænni	vænu
gen	lauss	laussar	lauss	væns	vænnar	væns
Pl *nom*	lausir	lausar	laus	vænir	vænar	væn
acc	lausa	lausar	laus	væna	vænar	væn
dat	lausum	lausum	lausum	vænum	vænum	vænum
gen	laussa	laussa	laussa	vænna	vænna	vænna

		FAGR 'BEAUTIFUL, FAIR'			GAMALL 'OLD'	
	M	**F**	**N**	**M**	**F**	**N**
Sg *nom*	fagr	fögr	fagrt	gamall	gömul	gamalt
acc	fagran	fagra	fagrt	gamlan	gamla	gamalt
dat	fögrum	fagri	fagru	gömlum	gamalli	gömlu

gen	fagrs	fagrar	fagrs	gamals	gamalla r	gamals
Pl nom	fagrir	fagrar	fögr	gamlir	gamlar	gömul
acc	fagra	fagrar	fögr	gamla	gamlar	gömul
dat	fögrum	fögrum	fögrum	gömlum	gömlum	gömlum
gen	fagra	fagra	fagra	gamla	gamla	gamla

	MIKILL 'GREAT'			**LÍTILL 'LITTLE'**		
	M	**F**	**N**	**M**	**F**	**N**
Sg nom	mikill	mikil	mikit	lítill	lítil	lítit
acc	mikinn	mikla	mikit	lítinn	litla	lítit
dat	miklum	mikilli	miklu	litlum	lítilli	litlu
gen	mikils	mikillar	mikils	lítils	lítillar	lítils
Pl nom	miklir	miklar	mikil	litlir	litlar	lítil
acc	mikla	miklar	mikil	litla	litlar	lítil
dat	miklum	miklum	miklum	litlum	litlum	litlum
gen	mikilla	mikilla	mikilla	lítilla	lítilla	lítilla

An adjective agrees with its noun, even when the two are not next to each other in a sentence. The word order of *vitr maðr ok hógværr* (adjective-noun-conjunction-adjective) is a common pattern in Old Norse. Notice in the example below that *göfugs manns ok ágæts* is in the genitive case and matches *Gríms*, and that *mikill maðr ok sterkr* is in the nominative case and matches *Egill*. The word order in the translation has been changed to make these relationships clearer.

Hann var auðigr at fé ok höfðingi mikill, vitr maðr ok hógværr.	*He was wealthy and a great leader, a wise and gentle man.*
Egill var sonr Gríms, göfugs manns ok ágæts, mikill maðr ok sterkr.	*Egil, a big and strong man, was the son of Grim, a noble and excellent man.*

10.8 EXERCISE – STRONG ADJECTIVES

Decline the adjectives *spakr* and *mikill* below.

	SPAKR MAÐR	**MIKILL MAÐR**
Sg nom	_____ maðr	_____ maðr
acc	_____ mann	_____ mann
dat	_____ manni	_____ manni
gen	_____ manns	_____ manns
Pl nom	_____ menn	_____ menn
acc	_____ menn	_____ menn

	SPAKR MAÐR		MIKILL MAÐR	
dat	_____	mönnum	_____	mönnum
gen	_____	manna	_____	manna

Transl: *spakr maðr* 'wise man,' *mikill maðr* 'large man'

10.9 VERBS – PAST PARTICIPLES

Past participles are adjectives derived from verbs, and their endings are almost the same as the strong adjectives endings. Past participles, like adjectives, agree in gender, case, and number with the nouns they modify. For instance, in the sentence *Skipit flaut **tjaldat** fyrir bœnum* 'The ship floated **tented** [with a cloth over the mast serving as a tent] in front of the farmstead,' the participle *tjaldat* agrees with the subject *skipit* (both neuter). In the sentence, *Hann var **kallaðr** Skinna-Björn*, the participle *kallaðr* agrees with the subject *hann*. Weak and strong verbs form their past participle stems differently. There is a fixed set of endings shared by all weak verbs and another fixed set of endings shared by all strong verbs.

Weak Verbs. Weak verbs add endings to the past-tense stem (for example, *kallað-*), found by removing the past-tense ending *-i* of the 3rd sg (for example, past-tense stem *kallað-* from *kallaði*, and *nefnd-* from *nefndi*). The past participles of *kalla* and *nefna* are declined below as examples.

		KALLAÐR (KALLA)			NEFNDR (NEFNA)		
		M	F	N	M	F	N
Sg *nom*		kallaðr	kölluð	kallat	nefndr	nefnd	nefnt
acc		kallaðan	kallaða	kallat	nefndan	nefnda	nefnt
dat		kölluðum	kallaðri	kölluðu	nefndum	nefndri	nefndu
gen		kallaðs	kallaðrar	kallaðs	nefnds	nefndrar	nefnds
Pl *nom*		kallaðir	kallaðar	kölluð	nefndir	nefndar	nefnd
acc		kallaða	kallaðar	kölluð	nefnda	nefndar	nefnd
dat		kölluðum	kölluðum	kölluðum	nefndum	nefndum	nefndum
gen		kallaðra	kallaðra	kallaðra	nefndra	nefndra	nefndra

Some weak verbs show peculiarities in forming their past participles.

- The verb *gera* (also *gøra*) has past participle *gerr* (*m*), *ger* (*f*), *gert* (*n*).
- Some 3rd conjugation weak verbs insert *-i-* before the dental suffix in the past participle. For example, the past participles of *berja* and *glymja* are *bariðr* and *glumiðr*. The verbs that follow this pattern end in *-ja* in the infinitive. However, not all verbs ending in *-ja* belong to the 3rd conjugation. For example, the past participle of the 1st conjugation verb *herja* follows the same pattern as *kallaðr*.
- 4th conjugation weak verbs typically have past participles with *-að-* (*-at*) like the 1st conjugation. These usually only occur in the neuter, *vakat*, *lifat*, *unat*, and *trúat*.
- A few employ the suffix *-in-* rather than a dental when the adjective ending begins with

a consonant. For example, the past participle of *erja* 'plow' is *arinn* and declines in the masculine singular *arinn* (nom), *arðan* (acc), *arðum* (dat), *arins* (gen).

- Some verbs derive past participles from related but somewhat different stems. For example, *leggja* has the past participle *lagðr* or *lagiðr* or *laginn*.

10.10 Past Participles of Strong Verbs

The past participle of strong verbs is the fifth principal part (for example *taka, tekr, tók, tóku, **tekinn***). Past participles are formed according to the Special Stem Rules (for example, *tekinn* from *tekin + r*), and two-syllable stem shortening (for example, *teknum*). The final -*n*- of the past participle stem drops before the neuter singular ending -*t* (for example, *tekit, farit, numit*). Note that the masculine accusative singular has the ending -*n* rather than -*an* (*tekinn* vs *kallaðan*). In other words, the past participle endings of strong verbs look very much like the declension of the definite article.

Past Participle of *Taka* 'Take'

	M	F	N		M	F	N
Sg *nom*	tekinn	tekin	tekit	**Pl**	teknir	teknar	tekin
acc	tekinn	tekna	tekit		tekna	teknar	tekin
dat	teknum	tekinni	teknu		teknum	teknum	teknum
gen	tekins	tekinnar	tekins		tekinna	tekinna	tekinna

A few adjectives decline like the past participles of strong verbs, for example, *feginn* 'glad, joyful,' *heiðinn* 'heathen,' and *kristinn* 'Christian.'

10.11 Verbs – Present and Past Perfect of Verbs

The verb *hafa* is used with a past participle to form either the present or past perfect (from the Latin *perfectum* 'completed'), constructions which have exact parallels in English (*has seen, had seen*). In Old Norse the perfect is formed by conjugating *hafa* in the present or past and adding the neuter singular past participle.

Eiríkr **hefir numit** Eiríksfjörð ok býr í Brattahlíð. (*present perfect*)	Eirik **has taken** Eirik's Fjord and lives at Brattahlíð.
Ingólfr **hefir gefit** Herjólfi land á milli Vágs ok Reykjaness. (*present perfect*)	Ingolf **has given** Herjolf land between Vag and Reykjanes.
Skip þat **höfðu** þeir **fengit** um sumarit í víking. (*past perfect*)	They **had gotten** that ship during the summer while raiding.

Verbs of motion such as *fara, koma, ganga*, and others which do not take direct objects are called intransitive verbs. They typically use *vera* rather than *hafa* in forming the perfect. Because *vera* is a linking verb, the past participle agrees with the subject in gender, case, and number.

| Haraldr **er farinn**. (*present perfect*) | Harald **has gone**. |
| Þá **var** Högni konungr **farinn** í konunga-stefnu. (*past perfect*) | At that time King Hogni **had gone** to a meeting of kings. |

Occasionally the perfects of intransitive verbs are formed with *hafa* rather than *vera*. As a general rule, perfects of intransitive verbs formed with *vera* focus on the result of the action, while those with *hafa* focus on the action itself.

| Aldri **hefir** dúfa **komit** ór hrafns eggi. | Never **has** a dove **come** out of a raven's egg. |

The verb *vera* always forms its perfect with *hafa*, while *verða* employs *vera*.

| Þessi orrosta **hefir** einhver **verit** mest í Nóregi. | This battle **was (has been)** the greatest ever in Norway. |
| Haraldr **var orðinn** konungr Nóregs. | Harald **had become** king of Norway. |

10.12 VERBS – PASSIVE VOICE

The past participle is also employed in passive constructions, where the subject does not perform an action but rather undergoes one. As in English, the passive voice is formed with an auxiliary verb and a past participle; for example, *þat er sagt* 'it **is said**'. In Old Norse, the auxiliary verb is either *vera* or *verða*, and the past participle agrees in gender, case, and number with the subject.

Hann **var kallaðr** Klakk-Haraldr.	He **was called** Klakk-Harald.
Skipit **var steint** mjök fyrir ofan sjó.	The ship **was** fully **painted** above the waterline.
Konungr sá er Högni **er nefndr** átti dóttur.	That king who **is named** Hogni had a daughter.
Dóttir hans **var** í braut **tekin**.	His daughter **was taken** away.
Héðinn **var búinn** at berjask.	Hedin **was prepared** to fight.

Passive sentences formed with *verða* introduce a sense of possibility.

| **Verða** þeir ekki **fundnir**. | They **cannot be found**. |
| Blóð **varð** eigi **stöðvat**. | The **blood could** not **be stopped**. |

10.13 READING – THE WHALE DISPUTE TURNS DEADLY (*GRETTIS SAGA*)

The story from *Grettir's Saga* of the fight over the whale at Rifsker continues. Men throughout the area are drawn into the conflict, including a group of Norwegian merchants called *austmenn* 'Eastmen' (as Norway is east of Iceland). The Norwegians' vessel was earlier shipwrecked in Trekyllisvik near Flosi's farm at Arness. Several of the shipwrecked foreigners accepted lodgings at Flosi's farm, a decision which put them under obligation to their host.

Thorgrim cannot prove his rights to the beached whale, and his brother Thorgeir now attacks Flosi's men, who are on the whale flensing. The shipwrecked Norwegian merchants are also on the whale with Flosi's men. They are dangerous opponents because as Viking Age merchants they have better weapons than the Icelanders who are poorly equipped farmers.

The following passage also features a colorful meeting between two enemies: Thorfinn, one of Flosi's men, and Thorgeir, Thorgrim's brother. In an earlier incident Thorfinn had ambushed Thorgeir in the dark and sunk his axe into Thorgeir's back. Hearing the squishy sound of the impact, Thorfinn assumed he had dealt Thorgeir a mortal wound, and he fled, leaving behind his axe. In fact, Thorfinn had buried his axe into a water flask slung over Thorgeir's back. Saved by the flask, Thorgeir gained the nickname Flask-Back. In the passage below, Thorgeir 'returns' the axe to Thorfinn, an example of Icelandic humor.

Following the battle, both sides bring lawsuits for the numerous killings. These suits ultimately end in a division of the disputed shoreline. Later, Onund's son Thorgrim, the grandfather of Grettir the Strong, leaves the area. He moves south to Midfjord, where he buys land at Bjarg, the farm where Grettir is born.

Grettis saga Ásmundarsonar (ch 12)

Þorgeirr flöskubakr réð fyrst upp á hvalinn at húskörlum Flosa.[65] Þorfinnr var fram við höfuðit hvalsins[66] ok stóð í spori, er hann hafði gört sér.[67] Þorgeirr mælti: "Þar fœri ek þér øxi þína." Síðan hjó hann á hálsinn, svá at af tók höfuðit.[68] Flosi var uppi á mölinni, er hann sá þetta; hann eggjaði þá sína menn til móttöku. Nú berjask þeir lengi,[69] ok veitti Kaldbeklingum betr;[70] fáir menn höfðu þar vápn, nema øxar þær, er þeir skáru með hvalinn, ok skálmir.[71] Hrukku Víkrmenn af hvalnum í fjöruna.[72] Austmenn[73] höfðu vápn ok urðu skeinuhættir; Steinn stýrimaðr hjó fót undan Ívari Kolbeinssyni, en Leifr, bróðir Ívars, laust

---

[65] **Þorgeirr flöskubakr réð fyrst upp á hvalinn at húskörlum Flosa:** 'Thorgeir Flask-Back was the first to attack Flosi's men up on the whale.'

[66] **fram við höfuðit hvalsins:** 'forward on the head of the whale.'

[67] **stóð í spori, er hann hafði gört sér:** '(he) stood in the cuts [of the fatty hide], which he had made for himself [in order to secure his footing as he mounted the whale].'

[68] **svá at af tók höfuðit:** 'so that the head came off.'

[69] **Nú berjask þeir lengi:** 'Then they fought for a long time.'

[70] **veitti Kaldbeklingum betr:** 'the Kaldbak men had the better [of it].'

[71] **skálmir:** 'flensing knives' [long knives or short swords used for cutting up whales]; later *skálm* became the name of a blade affixed to a long wooden shaft.

[72] **af hvalnum í fjöruna:** 'from the whale (*hvali* + *inum*) onto the beach (*fjöru* + *ina*).'

[73] **Austmenn:** Norwegians, 'Eastmen.' Norwegians and Viking Age merchants were usually well armed.

félaga Steins í hel[74] með hvalrifi. Fellu þar menn af hvárumtveggjum.

Translate: _____

_____

_____

_____

_____

_____

_____

_____

_____

_____

_____

_____

_____

10.14 EXERCISE – FROM *GRETTIR'S SAGA*

Complete the following sentences from the Reading section above.

1. Þorfinnr var _____, ok stóð í spori.
2. Þorgeirr mælti: '_____ øxi þína.'
3. Síðan hjó hann _____ höfuðit.

Are the following statements true or false?   *RÉTT EÐA RANGT?*

4. Þorgeirr réð at húskörlum Flosa.   _____
5. Austmenn höfðu eigi vápn.   _____
6. Menn fellu af hvárumtveggjum.   _____

10.15 CULTURE – RESOURCES AND SUBSISTENCE IN ICELAND

From the tenth century on, Iceland suffered periodically from famine and sickness. This island country is a classic example of 'bad year economics,' where matters went well only if nothing went wrong.[75] The country was relatively prosperous in the early centuries, but bad times hit hard. The sagas often speak of these periods, giving a glimpse of the ways in which Icelanders dealt with their difficulties. Most Icelanders who survived to old age experienced several rough periods. By the late tenth century the population had begun to

---

[74] **ljósta í hel:** 'to strike dead.'

[75] See Chapter 3, 'Curdled Milk and Calamities: An Inward Looking Farming Society.' Byock, *Viking Age Iceland*. Pp 43-62.

strain the natural resources. In the thirteenth century, when the climate began to seriously cool, the pressure on resources became even greater.

The variability of the weather and the short, often cool growing seasons at Iceland's northern latitude influenced the way Icelanders farmed and lived. The original settlers immediately saw that the grasses and shrubs were suitable for the cattle and sheep farming they knew in their homelands. The original birch forests, which stretched in many places from the shoreline to the base of the mountains, did not hinder these herdsmen. Since ownership of livestock was a measure of status and wealth, many settlers cleared their properties of trees to increase pasturage.

The native birch offered the settlers a supply of hardwood suitable for hearths and charcoal-making. The land clearings of the settlers, the staggering fuel requirements for making iron from bog ore, and erosion from the uncontrolled grazing of livestock soon reduced the original forests to small stands of trees. After the relatively small number of big trees had been cut down, the remaining birch was of limited use in shipbuilding and house construction. From early on, good timber suitable for building ocean-going ships had to be imported. This expense raised the cost of maintaining such ships, a factor that over time severely limited the Icelanders' ability to compete with Norwegian merchants. It also confined the Icelanders to building houses with driftwood and turf.

10.16 WORD FREQUENCY VOCABULARY – LIST 10. THE MOST FREQUENT WORDS IN THE SAGAS

NOUNS	ADJECTIVES	PRONOUNS	NUMERALS
vinr – friend	fagr – beautiful	hvárr – who,	fimmtán –
vísa – verse	auðigr – wealthy	which (of	fifteen
leið – path	fríðr – beautiful	two)?	
sinn – time	réttr – right,	sjálfr – self	
kveld – evening	correct	samr – same	

VERBS	PREPOSITIONS AND ADVERBS	CONJUNCTIONS
bjóða – to offer; invite	enn – yet, still	né – nor
hlaupa – to leap; run	niðr – down	
kalla – to call	ofan – from above	
halda – to hold	aptr – back	
falla – to fall	móti – against	

EXERCISES

10.17 The Väsby Runestone from Uppland, Sweden. A Viking in England. Translate the runes.

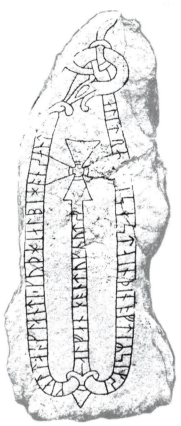

Figure 42. The Väsby Runestone from Uppland, Sweden.

RUNES

ᛅᛚᛁᛏ ᚱᛅᛁᛋᛅ ᛋᛏᛅᛁᚾ ᚦᛁᚾ ᛅᚠᛏᛁᛦ ᛋᛁᚴ
ᚾᛁᛅᛚᚠᛅᚾ·ᚼᚾ ᛏᚢᚴᚾᚢᛏᛋ ᚴᛁᛅᛚᛏ
ᛅᚾᚴᛚᛅᚾᛏᛁ·ᚴᚢᚦ ᚼᛁᛅᛚᛒᛁ ᚼᛅᚾᛋ ᛅᚾᛏ

TRANSLITERATION

alit raisa stain þin oftiR sik sialfan · hon tuknuts kialt anklanti · kuþ hialbi hons ant

STANDARDIZED OLD NORSE

Áli [lé]t reisa stein þenna [e]ptir sik sjálfan. Hann tók [K]núts gjald á [E]nglandi. Guð hjálpi hans önd.

VOCABULARY

Áli *m* Ali (*personal name*)

England *n* England

önd <*dat* önd ~ öndu, *gen* andar, *pl* andir > *f* breath; life; spirit, soul

Knútr *m* King Canute the Great (inn ríki)

gjald *n* payment; tribute; reward

Translate:_____

_____

_____

_____

_____

10.18 Strong Verbs List and Review. In addition to the verbs in the lesson, here is a list of fifteen common strong verbs with their principal parts. Test yourself. These verbs are among the most frequent words in the sagas.

biðja <biðr, bað, báðu, beðinn> *vb* ask; command

binda <bindr, batt, bundu, bundinn> *vb* bind

bíða <bíðr, beið, biðu, biðinn> *vb* await

búa <býr, bjó, bjuggu, búinn> *vb* live (at a place); prepare

drepa <drepr, drap, drápu, drepinn> *vb* smite, kill

falla <fellr, féll, féllu, fallinn> *vb* fall

finna <finnr, fann, fundu, fundinn> *vb* find

kveða <kveðr, kvað, kváðu, kveðinn> *vb* say, to recite (verse)

láta <lætr, lét, létu, látinn> *vb* let
liggja <liggr, lá, lágu, leginn> *vb* lie
ríða <ríðr, reið, riðu, riðinn> *vb* ride
sitja <sitr, sat, sátu, setinn> *vb* sit
sjá <sér, sá, sá, sénn> *vb* see
standa <stendr, stóð, stóðu, staðinn> *vb* stand
taka <tekr, tók, tóku, tekinn> *vb* take

A. Conjugate *taka* in the present and past tense.

	PRESENT		PAST
Sg *ek*	_____	**Sg** *ek*	_____
þú	_____	*þú*	_____
hann	_____	*hann*	_____
Pl *vér*	_____	**Pl** *vér*	_____
þér	_____	*þér*	_____
þeir	_____	*þeir*	_____

B. Identify each of the verbs below and translate the infinitive form.

Ex: bindr   *3sg pres. of binda 'bind'*

1. lét   _____
2. láguð   _____
3. riðu   _____
4. sjáið   _____
5. finn   _____
6. beið   _____
7. sitjum   _____
8. drapt   _____

C. Provide the requested form for each of the verbs below and translate the infinitive.

Ex gefa (*2sg pres*)   *gefr 'give'*

1. falla (*3sg pres*)   _____
2. liggja (*2pl past*)   _____
3. bíða (*2sg pres*)   _____
4. kveða (*1pl past*)   _____
5. búa (*3pl past*)   _____
6. binda (*1sg past*)   _____
7. standa (*3sg past*)   _____
8. biðja (*1pl pres*)   _____

10.19 Strong Adjectives. Decline the adjective *langr* 'long.'

	M	F	N
Sg *nom*	*langr*	*löng*	*langt*
acc	_____	_____	_____
dat	_____	_____	_____
gen	_____	_____	_____

Pl nom	_____	_____	_____
acc	_____	_____	_____
dat	_____	_____	_____
gen	_____	_____	_____

10.20 Strong Adjectives. Decline the two-syllable adjective *auðigr*.

	M	F	N
Sg nom	*auðigr*	*auðig*	*auðigt*
acc	_____	_____	_____
dat	_____	_____	_____
gen	_____	_____	_____

Pl nom	_____	_____	_____
acc	_____	_____	_____
dat	_____	_____	_____
gen	_____	_____	_____

10.21 Past Participles. Give the infinitives for the underlined past participles.

INFINITIVE(S)

1. Þann tíma kom hallæri svá mikit á Ísland, at ekki hefir
   jafnmikit <u>komit</u>.   _____
2. Hann fann hval <u>rekinn</u> innan fram á nesinu.   _____
3. Hvalrinn var <u>dreginn</u> á land upp sá, er <u>skorinn</u> var.   _____
4. Þorfinnr var fram við höfuðit hvalsins ok stóð í spori,
   er hann hafði <u>gört</u> sér.   _____

10.22 Verbs. Give the 3sg present tense and infinitive for the underlined verbs.

Þorgeirr flöskubakr <u>réð</u> fyrst upp á hvalinn at húskörlum Flosa. Þorfinnr var fram við höfuðit hvalsins ok <u>stóð</u> í spori, er hann hafði gört sér. Þorgeirr <u>mælti</u>: "Þar fœri ek þér øxi þína." Síðan <u>hjó</u> hann á hálsinn, svá at af <u>tók</u> höfuðit. Flosi var uppi á mölinni, er hann <u>sá</u> þetta; hann <u>eggjaði</u> þá sína menn til móttöku.

	3SG PRESENT	INFINITIVE			3SG PRESENT	INFINITIVE
Ex: réð	*ræðr*	*ráða*				
1. stóð	_____	_____	4.	tók	_____	_____
2. mælti	_____	_____	5.	sá	_____	_____
3. hjó	_____	_____	6.	eggjaði	_____	_____

10.23 Verbs – Passive and Past Perfect Constructions. Translate the following sentences and identify the underlined constructions as present or past passive/perfect.

1. Konungr sá er Högni <u>er nefndr</u> átti dóttur.

   _____

   _____

2. Skipit <u>var steint</u> mjök fyrir ofan sjó.

   _____

   _____

   _____

3. Héðinn <u>var búinn</u> at berjask.

   _____

   _____

10.24 Strong Forms of the Adjectives *mikill* and *lítill*. These important adjectives appear everywhere in Old Norse texts. In declining, keep in mind the following:

- The Special Stem Rules apply, and endings beginning in *-r* change to match the stem-final *-l-*, for example *mikill* (*mikil + r*), *lítilli* (*lítil + ri*).
- The loss of the vowel in two-syllable stems before endings beginning in a vowel. Compare strong *mikill* with weak *mikli* (*mikil + i*), hence *mikill maðr* and *inn mikli maðr*.
- Stem-final *-l* drops before the neuter singular ending *-t*, hence *mikit*, *lítit*.
- The ending of the strong masculine accusative singular is *-n* rather than *-an*, hence *mikinn*, *lítinn*.
- The long *í* in *lítill* becomes short when followed by two consonants (compare *lítill barn* with *it litla barn*).

	MIKILL MAÐR	MIKIL KONA	MIKIT BARN
Sg nom	_____	_____	_____
acc	_____	_____	_____
dat	_____	_____	_____
gen	_____	_____	_____
Pl nom	_____	_____	_____
acc	_____	_____	_____
dat	_____	_____	_____
gen	_____	_____	_____

	LÍTILL MAÐR	LÍTIL KONA	LÍTIT BARN
Sg nom	_____	_____	_____
acc	_____	_____	_____
dat	_____	_____	_____
gen	_____	_____	_____
Pl nom	_____	_____	_____
acc	_____	_____	_____

dat | _____   _____   _____

gen | _____   _____   _____

10.25 Runes. Translate the following runestone from Tingsflisan in Köpings Parish on the Swedish island, Öland.

RUNES

ᚦᚢᚱᛁᛉ:ᚭᚢᚴ ᚦᚢᚱᛋᛏ ᛏᛁᚾ:
ᛅᚢᚴ:ᚦᚢᚱᚠᛅᛋᛏᚱ:ᚦ ᛏᛁᛉ:
ᛒᚱᛆᚦᚱ:ᚱᛆᛁᛋᛏᚢ:ᛋᛏ ᛏᛁᚾ:ᛅᛏ:
ᚠᚢᛏᚠᚢᛋ:ᚠᛆᚦᚢᚱ:ᛋᛁᚾ:ᚠᚢᚦ:
ᚼᛁᛆᛚᛒᛁ:ᛋᛁᚢᛚ:ᚼᛆᚾᛋ:

TRANSLITERATION

þuriR : auk þurstain : auk : þurfastr : þaiR : bryþr : raistu : stain : at : kunfus : faþur : sin : kuþ : hialbi : siul : hans :

STANDARDIZED OLD NORSE

Þórir ok Þorsteinn ok Þorfastr þeir brœðr reistu stein at Gunnfús fóður sinn. Guð hjálpi sál hans.

Figure 43. The Tingsflisan Runestone from Öland, Sweden.

VOCABULARY

Gunnfúss<-ar> *m* Gunnfus (*personal name*)

hjálpa <helpr, halp, hulpu, hólpinn> *vb* save; help; **Guð hjálpi sál hans** may God save his soul

reisa <-ti, -tr> *vb* raise

sál <-ar, -ar> *f* soul

Þorfastr <-s> *m* Thorfast (*personal name*)

Translate:_____

_____

_____

_____

LESSON 11

THE ENDLESS BATTLE

Aldri hefir dúfa komit ór hrafns eggi
(Never has a dove come from a raven's egg)

Figure 44. A Gotland Picture Stone shows a woman standing between two armies ready for battle, one on the land and the other arriving by sea. She appears to be welcoming or negotiating between the two sides much as Hild does in the reading passages below.

11.1 READING – THE BATTLE OF THE HJADNINGS (*SKÁLDSKAPARMÁL*, FROM *THE PROSE EDDA*)

Skáldskaparmál in *The Prose Edda* tells the tale of an endless contest. Called *Hjaðningavíg* this battle (*víg*) was known throughout the northern lands. In addition to the *Prose Edda*, versions of the story are preserved in Saxo Grammaticus's *History of the Danes* and several sagas. In *The Prose Edda*, the story begins in the world of men when King Hedin steals a woman named Hild. Her aged father, King Hogni, sets out to find her. Hogni follows Hedin's ships along the coast of Norway. After sailing westwards, he catches Hedin in the Orkneys at High Island (*Háey*). Before the battle begins, it is clear that the father, Hogni, has little chance of victory, but he refuses all offers of reconciliation.

Skáldskaparmál: Konungr sá er Högni er nefndr[76] átti dóttur, er Hildr hét. Hana[77] tók at herfangi konungr sá er Héðinn hét, Hjarrandason. Þá var Högni konungr farinn[78] í konungastefnu; en er hann spurði at herjat var í ríki hans,[79] ok dóttir hans var í braut tekin, þá fór hann með sínu liði at leita Héðins, ok spurði til hans at Héðinn hafði siglt norðr með

---

[76]   **er Högni er nefndr:** 'who is named Hogni.' The first *er* is the relative particle ('who' or 'which') and introduces a relative clause. The second *er* is the 3sg present of *vera* 'to be.'

[77]   **Hana:** *acc sg of the fem. pronoun* **hon** – this is a good reminder of the governance of case rather than word order in ON.

[78]   **Þá var Högni konungr farinn:** 'At that time Hogni had gone.'

[79]   **en er hann spurði at herjat var í ríki hans:** 'and when he heard that there had been raiding in his kingdom.' *En* is a conjunction meaning 'and' or 'but,' and *er* is a conjunction meaning 'when.'

landi.[80]

Þá er Högni konungr kom í Noreg, spurði hann at Héðinn hafði siglt vestr um haf. Þá siglir[81] Högni eptir honum allt til Orkneyja; ok er hann kom þar sem heitir Háey,[82] þá var þar fyrir Héðinn með lið sitt. Þá fór Hildr á fund föður síns, ok bauð honum men at sætt af hendi Héðins,[83] en í öðru orði[84] sagði hon at Héðinn væri búinn at berjask, ok ætti Högni[85] af honum engrar vægðar ván.[86] Högni svarar stirt dóttur sinni; en er hon hitti Héðin, sagði hon honum, at Högni vildi enga sætt, ok bað hann búask til orrostu, ok svá gøra þeir hvárirtveggju, ganga upp á eyna,[87] ok fylkja liðinu.

Translate: _____

_____

_____

_____

_____

_____

_____

_____

_____

_____

_____

_____

_____

_____

_____

_____

_____

_____

11.2 EXERCISE – CLOSE READING OF THE BATTLE OF THE HJADNINGS

    Ex: *Konungr sá [er Högni er nefndr] átti dóttur [er Hildr hét].*

---

[80] **með landi:** 'along the coast.'

[81] It is common in Old Icelandic narrative for the author to switch from the past to the present tense for the sake of vividness, sometimes within the same sentence. This is usually rendered in the past tense in English translations.

[82] **ok er hann kom þar sem heitir Háey:** 'And when he came there [to the place] which is called Hoy.'

[83] **ok bauð honum men at sætt af hendi Héðins:** 'and she offered him a necklace as reconciliation on behalf of Hedin.'

[84] **í öðru orði:** 'at the same time, likewise'

[85] **sagði hon at Héðinn væri...ok ætti Högni:** 'she said that Hedin was...and Hogni had.' *Væri* from *vera* and *ætti* from *eiga* are examples of the subjunctive mood when used in indirect speech.

[86] **af honum engrar vægðar ván:** 'no hope of mercy from him' (*lit.* 'from him hope of no mercy').

[87] **ganga upp á eyna** ('go up onto the islands'), a phrase in Old Norse texts. Islands were often the designated arenas for duels or battles.

The main clause of this sentence is *Konungr sá átti dóttur*. Note that a relative clause (*er Högni er nefndr*) intervenes between the subject and verb. A second relative clause (*er Hildr hét*) describes the noun *dóttur*. Leaving the relative clauses aside for a moment, the verb and subject of the main clause are *átti* (3sg past of *eiga* 'have') and *konungr sá* (m nom sg).

Each relative clause contains its own subject and verb. The subject of the first is understood to be *konungr sá* while the subject of the second is understood to be *dóttur*. The verbs of the two relative clauses are *er* (*nefndr*) 'is (named)' and *hét* 'was called.'

Verb: *er (3sg pres of vera 'be')*   Verb: *hét (3sg past of heita 'be called')*

A. *Hana tók at herfangi konungr sá [er Héðinn hét, Hjarrandason].*
1. Identify *hana*: _____ (**Hint:** *Hana* cannot be the subject. Is it an object?)

Identify the verb and subject of the main clause.
2. Verb: _____   3. Subject: _____

There is one relative clause in this sentence. Identify its verb and subject.
4. Verb: _____   5. Subject: _____

B. *Þá var Högni konungr farinn í konungastefnu,*
1. What part of speech is *þá*? _____

Identify the verb and subject.
2. Verb: _____   3. Subject: _____

The word *farinn* is a past participle meaning 'gone' or 'traveled.'
Verbs of motion like *fara* and others which do not take direct objects (intransitive verbs) use *vera* rather than *hafa* in forming the perfect (*var farinn* 'had gone'). The use of *vera* requires that the participle agree with the subject in case, number, and gender (here, m nom sg to agree with the subject).

4. A prepositional phrase includes a preposition, its object, and, if present, any modifiers of the object. What is the prepositional phrase in this sentence? _____

C. *en er hann spurði*
This sentence begins with the conjunction *en* 'and, but' linking it with the previous sentence. The next word, *er*, is the conjunction meaning 'when.' Identify the subject and verb of this clause.
1. Verb: _____   2. Subject: _____

The dependent clause *er hann spurði* sets up two more dependent clauses which tell the reader what Hogni learned.

D. *at herjat var í ríki hans ok dóttir hans var í braut tekin*
In the clause *at herjat var í ríki hans* the subject is not expressed. The sentence *þat var herjat* has the meaning 'there was raiding.'

1. What kind of phrase is *í ríki hans*? _____ (**Hint:** Noun phrase, verb phrase, or prepositional phrase?)

Identify the subject and verb of the clause *dóttir hans var í braut tekin*.
2. Verb: _____   3. Subject: _____
Í braut 'away' is a two-part adverb modifying the verb. In this clause, the auxiliary verb (*var*) and past participle form a verb phrase. The auxiliary verb takes the endings for person, number, and tense, while the main verb (here in the form of a past participle) supplies the meaning.

4. What is the meaning of the verb phrase *var tekin*? _____

E. *þá fór hann með sínu liði at leita Héðins*
The main clause of the sentence begins with the adverb *þá*. Identify the subject and verb.
1. Verb: _____   2. Subject: _____
The verb *fór* is used here in connection with the infinitive *leita*, indicating purpose. Together the verb *fór* and the infinitive *leita* form a verb phrase (*fór at leita* 'went to seek').

3. What is the case of *Héðins* and why? **Hint:** Check the vocabulary entries for the verbs if you are unsure.
_____

F. *ok spurði til hans*
1. Verbs are often used in connection with a preposition to render other meanings. What is the meaning of *spyrja til*? _____

2. Who or what is the subject of *spurði til*? _____ (You may have to go back to the Reading passage.)

G. *at Héðinn hafði siglt norðr með landi.*
What is the subject and verb of this clause?
1. Subject: _____   2. Verb: _____

3. What kind of construction is *hafði siglt*? _____

11.3 WEAK ADJECTIVES

Adjectives take weak endings when preceded by a definite article (*inn, in, it*) or certain other preceding words, such as a demonstrative pronoun (*sá, þessi*) or a possessive pronoun (*minn, þinn*).

In the singular, weak adjectives take the same endings as weak nouns. In the plural the endings are the same for all genders: *-u, -u, -um, -u*.

ENDINGS OF WEAK ADJECTIVES

	M	F	N		M	F	N
Sg nom	-i	-a	-a	Pl	-u	-u	-u
acc	-a	-u	-a		-u	-u	-u
dat	-a	-u	-a		-um	-um	-um
gen	-a	-u	-a		-u	-u	-u

SPAKR 'WISE'

	M	F	N		M	F	N
Sg nom	spaki	spaka	spaka	Pl	spöku	spöku	spöku
acc	spaka	spöku	spaka		spöku	spöku	spöku
dat	spaka	spöku	spaka		spökum	spökum	spökum
gen	spaka	spöku	spaka		spöku	spöku	spöku

- Some adjectives have stem-final *-j-* or *-v-*. For example, *ríkr* and *døkkr* decline in the masculine singular as *ríki, ríkja, ríkja, ríkja*, and in the plural as *ríkju, ríkju, ríkjum, ríkju*. So also masculine singular *døkkvi, døkkva, døkkva, døkkva*, and plural *døkku, døkku, døkkum, døkku*.
- When used with adjectives, a demonstrative pronoun usually is accompanied by the definite article, for example, *sá inn góði konungr* 'that good king,' or *sú in spaka kona* 'that wise woman.'

Example of a Weak Adjective Declined with Definite Article and Noun.

	INN DJARFI KONUNGR	*IN DJARFA DRÓTTNING*	*IT DJARFA BARN*
Sg nom	inn djarfi konungr	in djarfa dróttning	it djarfa barn
acc	inn djarfa konung	ina djörfu dróttning	it djarfa barn
dat	inum djarfa konungi	inni djörfu dróttningu	inu djarfa barni
gen	ins djarfa konungs	innar djörfu dróttningar	ins djarfa barns
Pl nom	inir djörfu konungar	inar djörfu dróttningar	in djörfu börn
acc	ina djörfu konunga	inar djörfu dróttningar	in djörfu börn

| dat | inum djörfum konungum | inum djörfum dróttningum | inum djörfum börnum |
| gen | inna djörfu konunga | inna djörfu dróttninga | inna djörfu barna |

Examples of Adjectives in Strong and Weak Usage.

STRONG		WEAK	
ágætr konungr	*an excellent king*	**inn** ágæti konungr	*the excellent king*
góð kona	*a good woman*	**in** góða kona	*the good woman*
stórt skip	*a large ship*	**it** stóra skip	*the large ship*
fyrstr fugla	*early birds*	**inn** fyrsti fugl	*the early bird*

11.4 EXERCISE – NOUNS WITH THE DEFINITE ARTICLE AND WEAK ADJECTIVES

Decline the following noun phrases.

	M– INN UNGI MAÐR	*F–* IN UNGA KONA	*N–* IT UNGA BARN
Sg *nom*	_____	_____	_____
acc	_____	_____	_____
dat	_____	_____	_____
gen	_____	_____	_____
Pl *nom*	_____	_____	_____
acc	_____	_____	_____
dat	_____	_____	_____
gen	_____	_____	_____

11.5 STRONG VERBS – GUIDELINES FOR DISTINGUISHING STRONG VERB CLASSES

Strong verbs fall into seven classes. Each class is differentiated by a particular series of root vowels. Class I has the following distinctive vowel series: long -*í*- in the infinitive and present tense; -*ei*- in the past singular; and short -*i*- in the past plural and past participle. Linguists refer to the system of root vowel change in strong verbs as 'ablaut.'

Guideline Chart for Distinguishing Strong Verb Classes. A strong verb's class can often be determined from the infinitive. For instance, Class I strong verbs have *í* in the infinitive while Class II have *jú, jó*, or *ú*. The following chart is a guide to identify strong verb classes from the infinitive. 'C' refers to a consonant following the root vowel. 'R' refers to the four consonants *r, l, m, n*, known as resonants. On occasion there are exceptions to these rules. For example, Class V *fregna* and Class VI *standa* have two consonants after the vowel.

	INFINITIVE	EXAMPLES
Class I:	í	líta, rísa
Class II:	jú, jó, ú	kr**jú**pa, b**jó**ða, l**ú**ka
Class III:	eCC, jaCC, jáCC, iNC	ver**ð**a, g**j**al**d**a, h**já**l**p**a, **bind**a
	(*also* øCCv, yNCv)	s**økk**va, **syng**va

Class IV:	eR	skera, stela, nema
Class V:	eC, iCj	gefa, vega, biðja
Class VI:	aC, eCj	fara, aka, draga, hefja
Class VII:	aCC, au, á, ei (also ö, ó, á, ú)	halda, falla, hlaupa, gráta, heita

C = *any consonant*   R (*resonant*) = r, l, n, *or* m   N (*nasal*) = n *or* m

11.6 STRONG VERBS – CLASS I

Class I strong verbs, as mentioned above, have a characteristic *í* in the infinitive. Verbs of this first class do not show *i*-umlaut in the present singular since -*í*- is already a front vowel (3sg *lítr, ríðr, skínn, svíkr*).

í	*í*	*ei*	*i*	*i*
INFINITIVE	3SG PRES	3SG PAST	3PL PAST	PPART
bíða 'wait'	bíðr	beið	biðu	biðinn
bíta 'bite'	bítr	beit	bitu	bitinn
drífa 'drive'	drífr	dreif	drifu	drifinn
líta 'look'	lítr	leit	litu	litinn
ríða 'ride'	ríðr	reið	riðu	riðinn
skína 'shine'	skínn	skein	skinu	skininn
svíkja 'betray'	svíkr	sveik	sviku	svikinn

DRÍFA IN PRESENT AND PAST						
PRESENT				PAST			
Sg *ek*	dríf	**Pl** *vér*	drífum	**Sg** *ek*	dreif	**Pl** *vér*	drifum
þú	drífr	*þér*	drífið	*þú*	dreift	*þér*	drifuð
hann	drífr	*þeir*	drífa	*hann*	dreif	*þeir*	drifu

- Class I strong verbs such as *hníga*, *síga*, and *stíga* have in the past singular either *hné*, *sé*, and *sté* or *hneig*, *seig*, and *steig*.

11.7 STRONG VERBS – CLASS II

Class II strong verbs have the vowel -*jú*-, -*jó*-, or -*ú*- in the infinitive with past singular -*au*-. Verbs of this second class show *i*-umlaut in the present singular: *hann krýpr, lýkr, brýtr*, etc.

jú (jó, ú)	ý	au	u	o
INFINITIVE	3SG PRES	3SG PAST	3PL PAST	PPART
krjúpa 'creep'	krýpr	kraup	krupu	kropinn
lúka 'close'	lýkr	lauk	luku	lokinn
brjóta 'break'	brýtr	braut	brutu	brotinn
ljósta 'strike'	lýstr	laust	lustu	lostinn
skjóta 'shoot'	skýtr	skaut	skutu	skotinn
bjóða 'offer'	býðr	bauð	buðu	boðinn

- Verbs with stems ending in -g- such as *fljúga*, *ljúga*, and *smjúga* have -au- or -ó- in the past singular, for example, *flaug~fló*, *laug~ló*, and *smaug~smó*.
- Class II strong verbs have -jó- rather than -jú- in the infinitive when followed by m, n, t, ð, s, r, and l.

KRJÚPA IN PRESENT AND PAST

	PRESENT				PAST			
Sg *ek*	krýp	**Pl** *vér*	krjúpum	**Sg** *ek*	kraup	**Pl** *vér*	krupum
þú	krýpr	*þér*	krjúpið	*þú*	kraupt	*þér*	krupuð
hann	krýpr	*þeir*	krjúpa	*hann*	kraup	*þeir*	krupu

11.8 EXERCISE – STRONG VERBS, CLASS I AND II

Identify the class of the following strong verbs and define.

Ex: skjóta   *Class II, 'shoot'*

1. líða _____
2. skína _____
3. ljúga _____
4. njóta _____
5. stíga _____
6. lúta _____

11.9 VERBS TAKING DATIVE AND GENITIVE OBJECTS

Some verbs take their objects in the dative rather than the accusative case. Examples are *þjóna, banna, spilla* and *þakka*. In the following examples, the verbs are underlined and their subjects are bolded.

Hann <u>bannar</u> **mönnum** at fara.   *He forbids men to go.*
Hann <u>þakkar</u> **þeim**.   *He thanks them.*
Hann <u>þjónaði ekki</u> **konungi**.   *He did not serve a king.*
Hon <u>vill eigi spilla</u> **meydómi** sínum.   *She does not want to spoil her maidenhood.*

Some verbs take objects in either the accusative or dative case depending on the intended meaning. For example, when the object appears in the dative, *bjóða* means 'invite,' but when the object appears in the accusative, it means 'offer.'

Hann **býðr þeim** at koma.   *He **invites them** to come. (dat)*
Hann **býðr skjöld** sinn konungnum.   *He **offers** his **shield** to the king. (acc)*

The objects of a number of verbs can be understood as 'instruments.' For instance, in the sentence *hann leggr **sverði*** 'he thrusts with a sword,' the sword is the instrument of the action. This usage of the dative case is called the instrumental dative.

Hann heldr **sverði**.   *He grasps a sword.*
Hann kastar **steini**.   *He throws a stone.*
Hann leggr **spjóti**.   *He thrusts with a spear.*
Hann skýtr **ör**.   *He shoots an arrow.*

Verbs taking their objects in the genitive often involve needing or lacking. Examples are *biðja* 'ask (for a woman in marriage),' *sakna* 'miss someone or something,' *hefna* 'avenge,' *gjalda* 'pay for,' and *þurfa* 'need.'

Egill biðr **Ásgerðar**.   *Egill asks for [proposes marriage to] Ásgerðr.*
Hann saknar **Englands**   *He misses England.*
Munu margir **þess** gjalda.   *Many will pay for this.*
Þeir þurfa **hersis**.   *They need a chieftain.*

11.10 EXERCISE – VERBS TAKING DATIVE OR GENITIVE OBJECTS
Complete the following sentences and translate.

Ex: Hann heldr _sverðinu_____. (sverðit)
 _He holds the sword._____

1. Óðinn leggr _____. (spjótit)

   _____

2. Haraldr bannar _____ at fara. (menn)

   _____

3. Þórólfr biðr _____. (hon)

   _____

4. Hon býðr _____ at koma. (þeir)

   _____

5. Hann saknar _____ (kona) sinnar.

   _____

6. Höfðingi þakkar _____. (menn þeir)

   _____

7. Loki kastar _____. (steinn)

   _____

11.11 READING – THE BATTLE OF THE HJADNINGS CONTINUES (*SKÁLDSKAPARMÁL*, FROM *THE PROSE EDDA*)

The earlier reading ended with the kings Hedin and Hogni ready for battle on Háey. In a last effort to avoid slaying his new father-in-law, Hedin offers Hogni reconciliation. Fate, however, is now running its course.

Figure 45. A Swedish Picture Stone from Lärbrö Hammars. Again the woman may be intervening between the two armies.

Hogni has already drawn 'Dain's Inheritance' (*Dáinsleif*), a sword forged by the dwarves that must kill each time it is unsheathed. The battle begins, but it takes an otherworldly turn. It never concludes. Hild, who bears a valkyrie name meaning 'battle,' intercedes. Each night she raises the fallen warriors so that the fight begins anew and continues until Ragnarok, the final battle at the end of the world.

Hjaðningavíg from *Skáldskaparmál*

Þá kallar Héðinn á Högna, mág sinn, ok bauð honum sætt ok mikit gull at bótum. Þá svarar Högni: 'of síð bauztu þetta,[88] ef þú vill sættask, því at nú hefi dregit Dáinsleif, er dvergarnir gørðu, er manns bani skal verða, hvert sinn er bert er,[89] ok aldri bilar í höggvi, ok ekki sár grœr.'

Þá svarar Héðinn: 'sverði hœlir þú þar, en eigi sigri.' Þá hófu þeir orrostu þá er Hjaðningavíg er kallat, ok börðusk þann dag allan, ok at kveldi fóru konungar til skipa. En Hildr gekk of nóttina til valsins, ok vakði upp með fjölkyngi alla þá er dauðir váru;[90] ok annan dag gengu konungarnir á vígvöllinn ok börðusk, ok svá allir þeir er fellu hinn fyrra daginn.[91] Fór svá sú orrosta hvern dag eptir annan, at allir þeir er fellu, ok öll vápn þau er lágu á vígvelli, ok svá hlífar, urðu at grjóti. En er dagaði, stóðu upp allir dauðir menn, ok börðusk, ok öll vápn váru þá ný. Svá er sagt í kvæðum, at Hjaðningar skulu svá bíða ragnarøkrs.

Translate: _____
_____
_____
_____

---

[88] **of síð bauztu þetta:** 'Too late you offered this.' The pronoun *þú* is often added in a reduced form to the end of the verb (here, *bauztu < bauzt þú*).

[89] **hvert sinn er bert er:** 'each time when it (*sverð*) is unsheathed.'

[90] **alla þá er dauðir váru:** 'all those who were dead.'

[91] **hinn** = *inn*.

_____

_____

_____

_____

_____

_____

_____

_____

_____

_____

_____

_____

_____

_____

_____

_____

_____

11.12 POSSESSIVE PRONOUNS

Possessive pronouns function much like adjectives, agreeing with the nouns they modify in case, number, and gender. The 1st and 2nd person possessive pronouns are as follows:

	SINGULAR	DUAL	PLURAL
1st	minn 'my'	okkarr 'our'	várr 'our'
2nd	þinn 'your'	ykkarr 'your'	yð(v)arr 'your'

- Possessive pronouns decline like strong adjectives (except in the masculine accusative singular, where the ending is -n).
- *Minn* and *þinn* decline like *sinn*, with short -i- before double -nn- and double -tt-, and long -í- elsewhere (nom *minn*, dat *mínum*).
- The double -nn- is an assimilation of -n- and the -r- of the ending. For instance, feminine dative singular *minni* is composed of the stem *min-* and the strong ending -ri.
- The remaining possessives decline as expected, with *okkarr, ykkarr,* and *yð(v)arr* (dat. *yðrum*) obeying the two-syllable shortening rule. *Yð(v)arr* is declined below as an example.

	M	F	N		M	F	N
Sg *nom*	yð(v)arr	yður	yð(v)art	**Pl**	yðrir	yðrar	yður
acc	yð(v)arn	yðra	yð(v)art		yðra	yðrar	yður
dat	yðrum	yð(v)arri	yðru		yðrum	yðrum	yðrum
gen	yð(v)ars	yð(v)arrar	yð(v)ars		yð(v)arra	yð(v)arra	yð(v)arra

To express possession in the 3rd person, Old Norse uses **personal** pronouns in the genitive: *hans*, *hennar*, *þess*, and *þeira* or the reflexive possessive pronoun *sinn*.

11.13 VERBS – IMPERSONAL CONSTRUCTIONS

An impersonal construction refers to the use of a verb without a subject. Impersonal constructions are very common in Old Norse. They fall into four categories.

1. Verbs which refer to natural events such as the weather, the passage of time, the changing of seasons, the coming of dawn and dusk, and so forth are impersonal. In English it is usually necessary to translate such sentences with a subject 'it.'

En er **dagaði**, stóðu upp allir dauðir menn.	*And when [it] **dawned**, all the dead men rose.*
Nú **líðr** svá fram til jóla.	*Now [it] **wears on** to Yule.*
Líðr fram haustinu ok **tekr** at vetra.	*The autumn passes and [it] begins **to draw near winter**.*

Other such verbs are *nátta <-að->* 'become night, grow dark,' *regna <-di>* 'to rain,' *snjófa <-að->* 'snow,' *hausta <-að->* 'draw near autumn,' *sumra <-að->* 'draw near summer,' and *vára <-að->* 'draw near spring.'

2. A verb is sometimes used impersonally when the focus is on the action or the object, and the subject is of little importance. In sentences such as these, one must supply the omitted subject in translation.

Svá **er sagt** í kvæðum, at Hjaðningar skulu svá bíða ragnarøkrs.	*Thus [it] **is said** in the poems, that the Hjadnings shall remain [abide] in this way until Ragnarok.*
Hér **hefr upp** ok segir frá þeim manni, er Sigi er nefndr.	*Here [the tale] **begins** and tells about that man, who is named Sigi.*

3. With some verbs, such as *dreyma* 'dream,' *minna* 'remember,' *skilja* 'differ,' *líka* 'like,' and *batna* 'recover,' the subject plays the role of an experiencer of an emotional or physical state. Such verbs often place the subject in the accusative or dative case. The verb is impersonal, because there is no nominative subject with which it can agree in person and number. Such verbs are in the 3rd singular.

Mik dreymdi draum. (*accusative subject*)	*I dreamed a dream.*
Ávalt er ek sé fagrar konur, þá minnir **mik** þeirar konu. (*accusative subject*)	*Whenever I see beautiful women, I remember that woman.*
Þetta líkaði **Eiríki** stórilla. (*dative subject*)	*Eirik liked this very little.*

Herjólfi batnaði síns meins. (*dative subject*)
> ***Herjólf*** *recovered from his injury.*

Þykkir **mér** ráð at þú farir at finna Gizur hvíta.
> *I think it is (it seems **to me**) a good plan that you go find Gizur the White.*

4. In the passive voice of verbs which do not take direct objects (intransitive verbs).
    En er Högni spurði at **herjat var** í ríki hans, fór hann með sínu liði at leita Héðins.
    > *And when Hogni learned that **there had been raiding** in his kingdom, he went with his troops to seek out Hedin.*

11.14 THE INDEFINITE PRONOUN *ENGI*

Engi (or *eingi*) 'no one, none, no' is a compound of *einn* 'one' and the negative particle *-gi*, with masculine singular *engi* deriving from *einn+gi*, feminine *engi* from *ein+gi*, and neuter *ekki* from *eitt+gi*. Most other case forms add endings to the stem *eng-*.

	M	F	N		M	F	N
Sg nom	engi	engi	ekki	Pl	engir	engar	engi
acc	engi~engan	enga	ekki		enga	engar	engi
dat	engum	engri	engu~einugi		engum	engum	engum
gen	einskis~engis	engrar	einskis~engis		engra	engra	engra

Engi heilsaði Þorvarði.
> ***No one*** *greeted Þorvarðr.*

Högni átti af honum **engrar** vægðar ván.
> *Hogni had hope of **no** mercy from him.*

Högni vildi **enga** sætt.
> *Hogni wanted **no** settlement.*

Aldri bilar Dáinsleif í höggvi, ok **ekki** sár grœr.
> *Dainsleif never misses when it strikes, and **no** wound [ever] heals.*

Neuter singular *ekki* frequently serves as an adverb in place of *eigi* 'not.'

11.15 THE INDEFINITE PRONOUN *ANNARR*

Annarr (stem *annar-*) 'one of two, other, another' is a common word whose declension makes sense in light of three sound changes.

1. *U*-umlaut applies, resulting in the change of *-a-* to *-ö-* or *-u-*.
2. The vowel of the second syllable drops when adding an ending beginning with a vowel in accordance with the two-syllable shortening rule.
3. The loss of the vowel of the second syllable brings the stem-final *-r-* directly into contact with the preceding *-nn-*, triggering a change of *-nn-* to *-ð-*. (This is the same change seen in the word *maðr*, stem *mann-* plus nominative ending *-r*.)

		M	F	N			M	F	N
Sg	*nom*	annarr	önnur	annat	**Pl**	aðrir	aðrar	önnur
	acc	annan	aðra	annat		aðra	aðrar	önnur
	dat	öðrum	annarri	öðru		öðrum	öðrum	öðrum
	gen	annars	annarrar	annars		annarra	annarra	annarra

Annarr is also used in the meaning 'second,' as in *annan dag* 'on the second day.'

11.16 DIRECT AND INDIRECT SPEECH

The readings in this lesson about the endless battle offer several examples of direct and indirect speech. Direct speech reports a speaker's exact words and is enclosed by quotation marks (*Þá svarar Högni*: 'Of síð bauztu þetta'). Indirect speech recounts what someone has said without necessarily using his or her exact words and is usually introduced by a verb of saying, knowing, or thinking. Old Icelandic renders indirect speech in several ways.

The indirect statement can be expressed in a dependent clause (introduced by the conjunction *at*), where the verb of the indirect statement stands in the indicative mood. In the following sentences, the verbs of the indirect statement are bolded.

Svá er sagt í kvæðum, at Hjaðningar **skulu** (*3pl pres indic*) svá bíða ragnarøkrs.	*Thus it is said in poetry that the Hjadnings **will** in this way remain [abide] until Ragnarok.*

The indirect statement can also be expressed in a dependent clause (introduced by the conjunction *at*), where the verb of the indirect statement is in the subjunctive mood.

Hon sagði, at Héðinn **væri** (*3sg past subj*) búinn at berjask.	*She said that Hedin **was** prepared to fight.*

The subject of the indirect statement is put into the accusative case, and the verb appears as an infinitive. This usage is discussed in more detail further on in the book.

Direct Speech:	
Konungrinn sagði lögin.	*The king recited the law.*
Indirect Speech:	*She **heard the king recite** the*
Hon **heyrði konunginn segja** lögin.	*law.*

11.17 GRAMMAR TOOLBOX. ADVERBS

Adverbs are words which describe verbs, adjectives, or other adverbs. They answer the questions *when? where?* and *how?*

- Abverbs add information about time, manner, or place. Examples are *nú* 'now,' *hér* 'here,' *vandliga* 'carefully', and *skjótliga* 'quickly.'

- Adverbs are indeclinable; they never change form to agree in gender, case or number with other words. Adverbs typically derive from adjectives or nouns, for example in English by adding '-ly' hence brave / bravely and man / manly. In ON adverbs are usually formed by adding -a, -liga, -um, or -t to the stem of an adjective. The ending -liga corresponds to the English -ly.

ADVERB	ADJECTIVE/NOUN	STEM
illa 'badly'	illr 'bad'	ill-
víða 'widely'	víðr 'wide'	víð-
skjótliga 'swiftly'	skjótligr 'swift'	skjótlig-
vandliga 'carefully'	vandr 'difficult'	vand-
tómliga 'slowly'	tómr 'slow'	tóm-
bráðum 'soon'	bráðr 'sudden'	bráð-
tíðum 'often'	tíðr 'frequent'	tíð-
stundum 'sometimes'	stund 'a while'	stund-
skjótt 'suddenly'	skjótr 'quick'	skjót-
hátt 'loudly'	hár 'high'	há-
þykkt 'thickly'	þykkr 'thick'	þykk-

- One adjective may engender multiple adverbs with different meanings, for example, the adjective langr 'long' underlies the adverbs

PLACE FROM	PLACE WHERE	PLACE TO
héðan 'from here'	hér 'here'	hingat 'to here'
þaðan 'from there'	þar 'there'	þangat 'to there'
hvaðan 'from where'	hvar 'where'	hvert 'to where'

lengi 'for a long time,' and löngum 'a long time, constantly.'

- Adverbs ending in -(a)t denote motion towards a place; for example, hingat 'to here.'
- Adverbs in -an denote motion away from a place; for example, norðan 'from the north,'
- When fyrir precedes an adverb ending in -an, it forms a two-word adverb answering the question 'place where,' for example fyrir útan 'outside' and fyrir ofan 'above.' This method is also used to express points of the compass (fyrir

Points of the Compass

PLACE FROM	PLACE WHERE	PLACE TO
norðan	fyrir norðan	norðr
sunnan	fyrir sunnan	suðr
austan	fyrir austan	austr
vestan	fyrir vestan	vestr

norðan). 'Place where' employs fyrir (fyrir norðan), 'place to' uses the suffix -r (norðr), and 'place from' -an (norðan).

11.18 WORD FREQUENCY VOCABULARY – LIST 11. THE MOST FREQUENT WORDS IN THE SAGAS

NOUNS	ADJECTIVES	PRONOUNS
vápn – weapon	**næstr** – next	**sumr** – some
morginn –	**kunnigr** – known;	**hvárrtveggi** – each of the

morning   cunning, skilled in   two, both

hús – house   magic

fótr – foot   **líkligr** – likely

spjót – spear   **reiðr** – angry

VERBS	*PREPOSITIONS AND ADVERBS*	*CONJUNCTIONS*

skilja – to part, separate; understand   **hjá** – by, near   **enda** – and yet

illa – badly

lengi – for a long time

drepa – to kill   **hversu** – how

setja – to set   **þangat** – to there

liggja – to lie

leita – to search

EXERCISES

11.19 Definite Article Review. Decline masculine *sveinninn* 'the lad,' feminine *leiðin* 'the path,' and neuter *bakit* 'the back.'

	SVEINN + INN	LEIÐ + IN	BAK + IT
Sg *nom*	_____	_____	*bakit*
acc	*sveininn*	_____	_____
dat	_____	_____	_____
gen	_____	_____	_____
Pl *nom*	_____	*leiðirnar*	_____
acc	_____	_____	_____
dat	_____	_____	_____
gen	_____	_____	_____

11.20 Definite Article. Fill in the blanks below with the correct form of the noun and the definite article.

konungrinn

1. _____(*nom*) gerði kumbl.

2. Ek sá _____(*acc*).

3. Ek bjó hjá _____(*dat*).

4. Ek vil gefa þér hest _____(*gen*).

hersirinn

5. Eiríkr hét _____ (nom).
6. Ek sá _____ (acc).
7. Eiríkr fór til Grœnlands með _____ (dat).
8. Hann horfði á skipit _____ (gen).

11.21 Weak Adjectives. Decline *langr* below as a weak adjective.

	M	F	N
Sg nom	*langi*		
acc			
dat			
gen			
Pl nom			
acc			
dat			
gen			

11.22 Weak Adjectives. Fill in the correct forms of the adjectives below.

	M	F	N
Sg nom	inn *hagi* dvergr	in *væna* kona	it *fagra* land
acc	inn _____ dverg	ina _____ konu	it _____ land
dat	inum _____ dvergi	inni _____ konu	inu _____ landi
gen	ins _____ dvergs	innar _____ konur	ins _____ lands
Pl nom	inir _____ dvergar	inar _____ konur	in _____ lönd
acc	ina _____ dverga	inar _____ konur	in _____ lönd
dat	inum _____ dvergum	inum _____ konum	inum _____ löndum
gen	inna _____ dverga	inna _____ kvenna	inna _____ landa

11.23 Weak Adjectives. Fill in the correct form of the adjective and translate.

1. Alrekr inn _____ (ríkr) var vænn.

    _____

2. Þessi _____ (góðr) dóttir Hólmgeirs gerði brú.

    _____

3. Þorsteinn var it _____ (stórr) barn.

    _____

4. Sá maðr er skrifaði Íslendingabók hét Ari inn _____ (fróðr) Þorgilsson.

    _____

5. Helgi bjó í inum _____ (grœnn) dal, sem kallaðr er Helgadalr.

    _____

6. Óláfr sendi menn eptir inni _____ (ungr) konu.

11.24 Proper Nouns. Decline the names Eirik the Red and Helga the Fair below.

	EIRÍKR INN RAUÐI	*HELGA IN FAGRA*
Sg *nom*	_____	_____
acc	_____	_____
dat	_____	_____
gen	_____	_____

11.25 Adverbs. Fill in the correct adverb in the sentences below.

1. Þeir vildu eigi vera _____ (here) við heiðna menn.
2. Hann hleypr _____ (to there).
3. _____ (from where) kemr vindr? (From *The Prose Edda*)
4. Gunnarr sagði þeim _____ (to where) hann ætlaði [at ganga].
5. Hús stendr _____ (there) út við garðinn.
6. Haraldr kom _____ (to here) til Miklagarðs.
7. Vándir menn fara til Heljar ok _____ (from there) í Niflhel. (From *The Prose Edda*)
8. _____ (where) er Grikklandshaf?
9. Þórolfr kom _____ (from here).

11.26 Strong Verbs – Class I. *Klífa* 'climb' is a typical Class I strong verb with principal parts *klífr, kleif, klifu, klifinn.* Conjugate *klífa* in present and past.

	PRESENT		PAST
Sg *ek*	_____	**Sg** *ek*	_____
þú	_____	*þú*	_____
hann	_____	*hann*	_____
Pl *vér*	_____	**Pl** *vér*	_____
þér	_____	*þér*	_____
þeir	_____	*þeir*	_____

Other Class I strong verbs follow the pattern of *klífa*. Give the principal parts for each of the verbs below.

Ex: bíta   *bítr, beit, bitu, bitinn* _____

1. drífa   _____
2. þrífa   _____
3. skríða   _____
4. líta   _____
5. grípa   _____
6. rísta   _____

Give the infinitives for each of the verbs below.

Ex: bitum   *bíta*

7.	gínum	9.	leið	11.	skein
8.	bíðið	10.	risinn	12.	sveið

Fill in the correct form of the Class I strong verbs below using *klífa* as a model.

Ex: ríða (*1sg pres*)   *ríð*

13. bíta (*2pl past*) _____   16. þrífa (*2sg past*) _____
14. rísa (*1pl past*) _____   17. drífa (*1pl pres*) _____
15. klífa (*1sg past*) _____   18. grípa (*3sg past*) _____

11.27 Strong Verbs – Class II. *Strjúka* 'stroke' is a typical Class II strong verb with principal parts *strýkr, strauk, struku, strokinn*. Conjugate *strjúka* in present and past.

	PRESENT		PAST
Sg *ek*	_____	**Sg** *ek*	_____
þú	_____	*þú*	_____
hann	_____	*hann*	_____
Pl *vér*	_____	**Pl** *vér*	_____
þér	_____	*þér*	_____
þeir	_____	*þeir*	_____

A small number of Class II strong verbs have *-ú-*, for example *lúka, lúta*. Verbs have *-jó-* rather than *-jú-* when followed by *-m-, -n-, -t-, -ð-, -s-, -r-,* or *-l-*, for example, *fl**jó**ta, b**jó**ða, k**jó**sa, l**jó**sta*. Apart from the infinitive, most Class II strong verbs have principal parts following the pattern of *strjúka*. Give the principal parts for each of the verbs below.

Ex: ljúga   *lýgr, laug, lugu, loginn*
1. drjúpa _____
2. skjóta _____
3. krjúpa _____
4. bjóða _____
5. ljósta _____
6. kljúfa _____

Give the infinitives for each of the verbs below.

Ex: skutu   *skjóta*

7.	bauð	9.	kaus	11.	njótið
8.	krýpr	10.	lostinn	12.	brýtr

Fill in the correct form of the Class II strong verbs below following the model of *strjúka*.

Ex: skjóta (*1sg pres*)   *skýt*
13. krjúpa (*2pl past*) _____   16. gjósa (*1sg past*) _____
14. rjóða (*3sg pres*) _____   17. drjúpa (*1pl pres*) _____

15. kljúfa (*2sg past*) _____   18. ljósta (*3sg past*) _____

11.28 Weak Forms of the Adjectives *mikill* and *lítill*. Decline, keeping in mind the following:

- Loss of vowel in two syllable stems before endings beginning in a vowel. Compare strong *mikill* with weak *mikli* (*mikil + i*), hence *mikill maðr* and *inn mikli maðr*.
- The long *í* in *lítill* becomes short when followed by two consonants (compare *lítill barn* with *it litla barn*).

	INN MIKLI MAÐR	*IN MIKLA KONA*	*IT MIKLA BARN*
Sg *nom*	_____	_____	_____
acc	_____	_____	_____
dat	_____	_____	_____
gen	_____	_____	_____
Pl *nom*	_____	_____	_____
acc	_____	_____	_____
dat	_____	_____	_____
gen	_____	_____	_____

	INN LITLI MAÐR	*IN LITLA KONA*	*IT LITLA BARN*
Sg *nom*	_____	_____	_____
acc	_____	_____	_____
dat	_____	_____	_____
gen	_____	_____	_____
Pl *nom*	_____	_____	_____
acc	_____	_____	_____
dat	_____	_____	_____
gen	_____	_____	_____

LESSON 12
FEUD IN ICELAND'S EAST FJORDS

Engi er allheimskr, ef þegja má
(No one is a complete fool, if he is able to keep his mouth shut.)

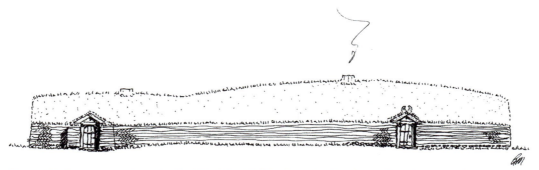

Figure 46. Reconstruction of a Turf Hall (*Skáli*) Worthy of a Chieftain. This drawing of an Icelandic long house is based on an archaeological understanding of such buildings.

12.1 READING – HELGI EARNS HIS NICKNAME (*VÁPNFIRÐINGA SAGA*)

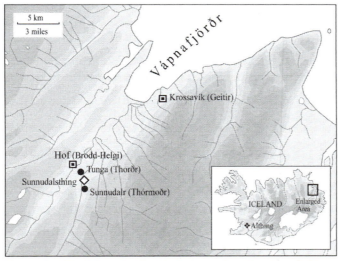

Figure 47. The Sites of a Tenth-Century Feud in *Vápnfirðinga saga*. In addition to personal animosities, the feud was a contest over resources between two chieftains: Geitir, living on the coast at Krossavík, and Brodd-Helgi inland at Hóf.

This and the next lesson take their readings from the opening chapters of *Vápnfirðinga saga* (*The Saga of the People of Weapon's Fjord*). This saga, a tale of feud and vengeance, sweeps through two generations of closely related chieftain families in Iceland's East Fjords (*Austfirðir*). The narrative is steeped in local politics, and the reader is taken deep into the lives of medieval Icelanders – some honorable, some less so.

Vápnfirðinga saga is a model of saga narration. The opening passage below presents the status of the story's main characters: contentious chieftains and farmers.

In particular, the passage introduces one of the story's main protagonists, Helgi, the son of Thorgils. The history of the family begins with Helgi's grandfather, the *landnámsmaðr* Thorstein the White. In his old age, Thorstein raised Helgi after Helgi's father Thorgils was killed. The passage also relates how Thorstein's family came to possess the farmstead Hof, the best land in Weapon's Fjord, after its first owner, the *landnámsmaðr* Steinbjorn, squandered his wealth.

Following a description of Helgi's character and competitive nature, the saga tells a short story in which he uses trickery to ensure that his bull will win a fight. The episode, which exposes a feature of Helgi's bullying nature, explains how he got his nickname Brodd-Helgi (Spike-Helgi).

Vápnfirðinga saga is a typical family saga. Its narrative is built around a series of quarrels, feuds, and resolutions. Almost nothing is superfluous in the dense information given at the beginning. The sagas delineate familial, marriage, and fosterage relationships, and these bring with them obligations. Often the narratives trace lineages back to *landnámsmenn* and sometimes back to Norway. Genealogies take into account both major and seemingly minor figures who will later enter the tale.

Below are two columns. The column on the left contains the opening chapter of *Vápnfirðinga saga*. The one on the right identifies key elements in the order that they appear. Opening details in a saga often provide the background necessary to make sense of coming action, including long-simmering disputes and feuds. As with many sagas, *Vápnfirðinga saga* opens with Iceland's colonization or *landnám*. In this instance, it is 'landtaking' in Weapon's Fjord, and the first chapters explain kinship relations, land ownership rights, and hint at animosities.

Vápnfirðinga saga (ch 1)

Þar hefjum vér þenna þátt, er sá maðr bjó at Hofi í Vápnafirði, er Helgi hét. Hann var sonr Þorgils Þorsteinssonar, Ölvis sonar, Ásvalds sonar, Øxna-Þóris sonar. Ölvir var lendr maðr í Nóregi um daga Hákonar jarls Grjótgarðssonar.

Þorsteinn hvíti kom fyrst út til Íslands þeira langfeðga[92] ok bjó at Toptavelli fyrir útan Síreksstaði. En Steinbjörn bjó at Hofi, sonr Refs ins rauða.[93] Ok er honum

Protagonist: Helgi.
Setting: Hof in Vapnafjord.
Helgi's lineage: father (Thorgils), grandfather (Thorstein), great-grandfather (Olvir), etc.
Aristocratic lineage: Olvir, a landed man in Norway.
Dating: Earl Hakon (ca. 900), contemporary of King Harald Fairhair.

The founder of Helgi's family in Iceland: The *landnámsmaðr* Thorstein the White.
Thorstein's first land-claim: the not-so-valuable farm at Toptavöllr.
How Thorstein acquired the farmstead Hof: the *landnámsmaðr* Steinbjorn mismanages his valuable land-claim at Hof and sells it to Thorstein. Steinbjorn's family.

---

[92] **kom fyrst út til Íslands þeira langfeðga:** 'was the first of that lineage to come out to Iceland.'
[93] **sonr Refs ins rauða:** 'the son of Ref the Red,' with *sonr* in apposition with *Steinbjörn*.

eyddisk fé fyrir þegnskapar sakar,[94] þá keypti Þorsteinn Hofsland ok bjó þar sex tigu vetra. Hann átti[95] Ingibjörgu Hróðgeirsdóttur ins hvíta.

Þorgils var faðir Brodd-Helga. Hann tók við búi Þorsteins. Þorkell ok Heðinn vágu Þorgils, föður Brodd-Helga, en Þorsteinn hvíti tók þá enn við búi ok fœddi upp Helga, sonarson sinn.

Helgi grows up without a father: Old Thorstein raises his grandson Helgi.

Helgi var mikill maðr ok sterkr ok bráðgörr, vænn ok stórmannligr, ekki málugr í barnœsku, ódæll ok óvægr þegar á unga aldri.[96] Hann var hugkvæmr ok margbreytinn.

Helgi described: big and strong, difficult and taciturn, fickle.

Frá því er sagt[97] einnhvern dag at Hofi, er naut váru á stöðli, at graðungr var á stöðlinum, er þeir frændr áttu,[98] en annarr graðungr kom á stöðulinn, ok stönguðusk graðungarnir. En sveinninn Helgi var úti ok sér, at þeira graðungr dugir verr ok ferr frá.[99] Hann tekr mannbrodd einn ok bindr í enni graðunginum,[100] ok gengr þaðan frá þeira graðungi betr. Af þessum atburði var hann kallaðr Brodd-Helgi.

Helgi's character illustrated: a boy who likes to win.

Helgi earns his nickname.

Var hann afbragð þeira manna allra, er þar fœddusk upp í heraðinu, at atgørvi.[101]

Translate:_____

_____

---

[94] **honum eyddisk fé fyrir þegnskapar sakar:** 'he squandered his wealth on account of his generosity (by his open-handedness).'

[95] **átti:** 'was married to'; *átti*, past tense of *eiga*, literally means 'to have' or 'to possess,' but here it connotes 'to be married to.' This verb was used almost exclusively for the male partner in a marriage, as a woman was seldom said to 'possess' her husband.

[96] **þegar á unga aldri:** 'already at a young age.'

[97] **frá því er sagt:** 'it is said,' or, literally, 'about this it is told.'

[98] **er þeir frændr áttu:** 'which those kinsmen owned.'

[99] **þeira graðungr dugir verr ok ferr frá:** 'their bull gets the worst of it and backs off.'

[100] **í enni graðunginum:** 'on the bull's forehead.' Old Icelandic employs the dative case to denote possession of body parts, hence *graðunginum*.

[101] **afbragð ... at atgørvi:** 'the most outstanding ... in abilities,' 'the most talented.' Two of the major manuscripts use the word *afbragð*, 'outstanding example, paragon,' whereas one uses *afbrigði*, 'deviation, transgression, offense.'

_____
_____
_____
_____
_____
_____
_____
_____
_____
_____
_____
_____
_____
_____
_____
_____
_____
_____
_____

12.2 CULTURE – NORSE FARMSTEADS

The basic element of a Scandinavian farmstead (*húsabœr*) is the long house. The reconstructed long house at Stöng in southern Iceland is an example of an eleventh-century farmstead in Iceland. While the farm at Stöng contains some specifically Icelandic characteristics, it shares much in common with farms all over the Viking world.

The Stöng farmstead was abandoned in 1104 due to the eruption of the volcano Hekla. The foundations lay buried under thick layers of volcanic ash and pumice until they were excavated in 1939 by a Scandinavian archaeological team led by Aage Rousell. This excavation and more recent ones provide an unusually clear picture of farm life in the late Viking Age. The large farmhouse faced southwest with turf walls between 1.3 and 2 meters thick (4.3 to 6.6 feet). Around the farmhouse was a cluster of outbuildings, including a smithy, a small church with a surrounding graveyard, and a cowshed with ten stalls.

Stöng was a costly buildingapproximately 25 meters (82 feet) in length and was average-sized for a prosperous Icelandic farm. The main parts of the building were a central hall called a fire hall (*eldskáli*) with wood-lined walls and a longfire down the center of the floor. Attached to the fire hall and accessed by an interior passage way was a secondary large room called a *stofa* or 'stove room.' People slept in the fire hall on wide benches set against the long walls. A locking timber bed-closet (*lokrekkjugólf, lokrekkja* or *lokhvíla*) would have provided the master and mistress of the farm with some privacy (and protection in case of intruders). The house had one outside door at the front end of the main hall. Two smaller rooms were attached to the back of the main hall. One was the pantry or food-storage room; the other was a large latrine.

The floor of the building was dirt. The floor surface became compact and hard because of the oils and lipids of everyday life. The entrance was paved with flat stones.

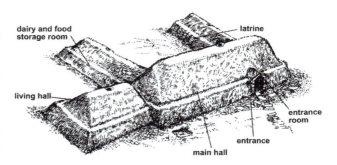

The room at the far left was probably a *stofa*, a room which had several uses. The name *stofa* is related to the English word 'stove' (Scandinavian *stue* / *stuga*), and originally it meant a heated room. At times the *stofa* may have been used for cooking and eating as well as for a family sitting room in the evenings. The fireplace was a partly sunken stone hearth box, in contrast to the long-fires (*langeldar*) that ran down the middle of the *skáli*. The wall benches in the *stofa* were much narrower than those in the main hall. They were used for sitting, and the room was likely used as a feasting hall. At the far

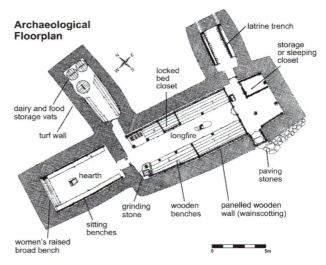

Figure 48. The Long House (*Skáli*) at *Stöng*, Iceland.

end was a raised wooden platform called a *pallr*. Written sources mention women working on such platforms. Loom weights, spindle whorls and other evidence of wool-working were found in the *stofa*.

Of the two backrooms at Stöng, the one for food-storage was the larger. Impressions in its floor reveal the placement of three large wooden vats. The vats were sunk into the earth to keep them cool. They stored protein-rich curdled milk (*skyr*) and possibly meat pickled in sour whey.

The second backroom appears to have been a latrine. It had deep, stone-lined gutters along both side walls. Openings at floor level in the rear turf wall seem suitable for waste removal. The size of the latrine and the length of the trenches indicate that a substantial number of people could be accommodated at one time. Throughout Scandinavia, visiting the latrine was often a communal undertaking. One saga reveals that the latrine of a Viking Age farmhouse in Norway had room for 'eleven people to sit on either side.' Because the wooden fixtures have not survived, it is unclear whether the people at Stöng sat over holes on long wooden benches, as in the example from Norway, or whether they rested on a horizontal wooden pole running just above and parallel to the trench as was also a custom in Norway into modern times.

12.3 THE INDEFINITE PRONOUN *NÖKKURR*

Indefinite pronouns, such as *nökkurr* 'a certain,' 'any' or 'some,' are pronouns which, even in context, have no specific identifiable referent. *Nökkurr* declines much like a strong adjective but does not follow the two-syllable shortening rule and drops the final *-r-* of the stem before neuter singular *-t.*

	M	F	N		M	F	N
Sg *nom*	nökkurr	nökkur	nökkut	**Pl**	nökkurir	nökkurar	nökkur
acc	nökkurn	nökkura	nökkut		nökkura	nökkurar	nökkur
dat	nökkurum	nökkurri	nökkuru		nökkurum	nökkurum	nökkurum
gen	nökkurs	nökkurrar	nökkurs		nökkurra	nökkurra	nökkurra

Hann spyrr, ef **nökkur** er fróðr maðr inni.	He asks if **anybody** inside is a wise man.
Þeir fengu **nökkura** njósn af ferð Ásgerðar.	They received **some** news about Asgerd's journey.
Þeir kómu at á **nökkuri** ok gengu með ánni til fors **nökkurs**.	They came to **a certain** river and followed the river to **a certain** waterfall.

Nökkurr has several variants, including *nakkvarr, nakkverr, nøkkvarr,* and *nekkvarr.*

12.4 PRONOUNS – *HVERR* AND *HVÁRR*

The pronouns *hverr* and *hvárr* function as both interrogative pronouns (used to introduce questions) and indefinite pronouns. *Hverr* is the more common of the two. As an interrogative, it means 'who? what? which (one)?' As an indefinite pronoun, *hverr* means 'each, every (one).' *Hvárr* has the same basic meaning as *hverr*, but is used when referring to two persons (*hvárr maðr*, 'each' or 'one [man] of the two') or groups (*hvárir þeira* 'both'). In the neuter singular, *hverr* employs *hvat* as an interrogative, and *hvert* as an indefinite pronoun.

	M	F	N		M	F	N
Sg *nom*	hverr	hver	hvat~hvert	**Pl**	hverir	hverjar	hver
acc	hvern	hverja	hvat~hvert		hverja	hverjar	hver
dat	hverjum	hverri	hverju		hverjum	hverjum	hverjum
gen	hvers	hverrar	hvers		hverra	hverra	hverra

Hverr sagði þetta?	**Who** said that?
Hvat er at segja frá þeim stað?	**What** is there to say about that place?
Sá baugr er **hverjum** höfuðsbani, er á.	That ring is death to **everyone**, who owns it.

Hvern dag ríða Æsir upp um Bifröst.	*Every day the Æsir ride up across Bifrost.*
Hvárr við annan.	*Each to (or with) the other.*

12.5 The Indefinite Pronoun *Einnhverr*

Einnhverr 'some, somebody, a certain one' is a compound of *einn* 'one' and the pronoun *hverr*. Endings are added to the stem *einhver(j)-*, except in the nom and acc of masculine and neuter singular (These forms, where *ein-* declines, are in italics in the chart below).

	M	F	N		M	F	N
Sg nom	*einnhverr*	einhver	*eitthvert*	**Pl**	einhverir	einhverjar	einhver
acc	*einnhvern*	einhverja	*eitthvert*		einhverja	einhverjar	einhver
dat	einhverjum	einhverri	einhverju		einhverjum	einhverjum	einhverjum
gen	einhvers	einhverrar	einhvers		einhverra	einhverra	einhverra

12.6 The Pronoun *Hvárrtveggi*

Hvárrtveggi means 'each of the two, either' in the singular, and 'both' in the plural. *Hvárrtveggi* is a compound word (*hvárr + tveggi*) in which **both** elements decline.

	M	F	N
Sg nom	hvárrtveggi	hvártveggja	hvárttveggja
acc	hvárntveggja	hváratveggju	hvárttveggja
dat	hvárumtveggja	hvárritveggju	hvárutveggja
gen	hvárstveggja	hvárrartveggju	hvárstveggja
Pl nom	hvárirtveggju	hvárartveggju	hvártveggju
acc	hváratveggju	hvárartveggju	hvártveggju
dat	hvárumtveggjum	hvárumtveggjum	hvárumtveggjum
gen	hvárratveggju	hvárratveggju	hvárratveggju

Fellu þar menn af **hvárumtveggjum**.	*Men fell [died] there on both sides.*
Höfðu þeir **hvárirtveggju** mikit lið.	*Both sides had a large force.*

12.7 Strong Verbs – Class III

Class III is characterized by two, sometimes three consonants following the root vowel (*verð-a*, *dett-a*, *bjarg-a*, *vinn-a*, *finn-a* and *søkkv-a*). Below is the basic vowel pattern for this class, followed by a common variant. As noted earlier, in several verbs of this class, *-nd*, *-ng*, *-ld* changes to *-tt*, *-kk*, *-lt* in the second principal part, for example *gjalda*, past singular *galt*.

Basic Pattern of Class III

e (ja, já)	*e*	*a*	*u*	*o*
INFINITIVE	3SG PRES	3SG PAST	3PL PAST	PPART
bresta 'break'	brestr	brast	brustu	brostinn
sleppa 'slip'	sleppr	slapp	sluppu	sloppinn
verða 'become'	verðr	varð	urðu	orðinn
gjalla 'yell'	gellr	gall	gullu	gollinn
gjalda 'pay'	geldr	galt[*]	guldu	goldinn
skjálfa 'shake'	skelfr	skalf	skulfu	skolfinn
hjálpa 'help'	helpr	halp	hulpu	holpinn

[*] Strong verbs whose stems end in -nd-, -ng-, and -ld- have -tt, -kk, and -lt in the past singular.

A few verbs of this class, such as *gjalla* 'to yell,' *gjalda* 'to pay,' and *bjarga* 'to save' have -ja- in the infinitive, while others such as *hjálpa~hjalpa* 'to help' and *skjálfa~skjalfa* 'to shake' have both -já- and -ja-. These verbs all have -e- in the present singular: *hann gellr, geldr, bergr, helpr, skelfr.*

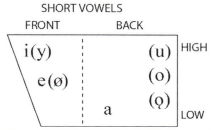

SHORT VOWELS

Figure 49. Short Vowel Placement in the Mouth

A number of Class III verbs have -i- in the infinitive when followed by -n- or -m- (*spinna, vinna, binda, finna,* and *svimma*) and follow a slightly different pattern. In these verbs, the vowels -e- and -o- in the infinitive and past participle are raised to -i- and -u-.

Common Variant of Class III

i	*i*	*a*	*u*	*u*
INFINITIVE	3SG PRES	3SG PAST	3PL PAST	PPART
finna 'find'	finnr	fann	fundu	fundinn
binda 'bind'	bindr	batt[†]	bundu	bundinn
springa 'jump'	springr	sprakk[†]	sprungu	sprunginn
vinna 'win'	vinnr	vann	unnu[✿]	unninn[✿]
brenna[*] 'burn'	brennr[*]	brann	brunnu	brunninn
renna[*] 'run'	rennr[*]	rann	runnu	runninn

[*] *brenna* and *renna* have older infinitive forms *brinna* and *rinna* with 3sg pres forms *brinnr* and *rinnr*.
[†] Strong verbs whose stems end in -nd-, -ng-, and -ld- have -tt, -kk, and -lt in the past singular.
[✿] A -v- drops before -o- or -u-.

A few Class III verbs have stem-final -v-, resulting in two other vowel patterns, illustrated by *søkkva* 'to sink' and *syngva* 'to sing.'

søkkva <søkkr, sökk, sukku, sokkinn> to sink
syngva <syngr, söng, sungu, sunginn> to sing

These verbs sometimes appear with -*j*- rather than -*v*-, as for instance *syngja*.

Two common Class III verbs show minor irregularities: *bregða* <*bregðr*, **brá**, *brugðu*, **brugðinn**> and *drekka* <*drekkr, drakk, drukku,* **drukkinn**>.

12.8 VERBS – PRESENT PARTICIPLES

Present participles describe ongoing actions and are formed by adding the suffix -*and*- to the present stem plus an ending (*sitjandi* 'sitting,' *gefandi* 'giving'). They function as adjectives, agreeing in gender, case, and number with the nouns they modify and take a special set of weak endings, with -*i* in the feminine singular and in all genders of the plural.

THE PRESENT PARTICIPLE *GEFANDI* 'GIVING'

	M	F	N		M	F	N
Sg *nom*	gefandi	gefandi	gefanda	**Pl**	gefandi	gefandi	gefandi
acc	gefanda	gefandi	gefanda		gefandi	gefandi	gefandi
dat	gefanda	gefandi	gefanda		geföndum	geföndum	geföndum
gen	gefanda	gefandi	gefanda		gefandi	gefandi	gefandi

Verbs such as *sjá* and *fá*, which end in a long vowel, have contracted forms *sjándi* and *fándi*.

The following examples are taken from the *Saga of the Volsungs* (*Völsunga saga*).

Þeir finna eitt hús ok tvá menn **sofandi** í húsinu með digrum gullhringum.	*They found a house and two men **sleeping** in the house with thick gold rings.*
Á skildi váru [rúnar] ristnar, þeim er stendr fyr **skínanda** guði.	*On the shield, runes were cut, that one which stands in front of [protects] the **shining** god.*
Guðrún gekk **hlæjandi** ok gaf þeim at drekka af stórum kerum.	*Gudrun went **laughing** and gave them [something] to drink from large vessels.*

When used with *vera*, the present participle adds a sense of possibility or necessity.

Hjördís gekk í valinn eptir orrostuna um nóttina ok kom at þar, sem Sigmundr konungr lá, ok spyrr, ef hann **væri græðandi**.	*Hjordis went among the slain during the night after the battle and came to where King Sigmund lay, and asked [him] if he **could be healed**.*

12.9 READING – THE OUTLAW SVART STEALS OLD THORSTEIN'S SHEEP (*VÁPNFIRÐINGA SAGA*)

In the second chapter of *Vápnfirðinga saga* the precocious twelve-year-old Spike-Helgi successfully prosecutes a man called Svart for killing his neighbor Skidi. Declared an outlaw, Svart lives in the mountains and steals livestock from the local people. When he takes sheep from Helgi's grandfather, Thorstein, their shepherd tells Thorstein the news. The old man tells the shepherd to keep the news from Helgi.

Vápnfirðinga saga (ch 2)

Maðr hét Svartr, er kom út hingat[102] ok gerði bú í Vápnafirði. It næsta honum bjó sá maðr, er Skíði hét. Hann var félítill. Svartr var mikill maðr ok rammr at afli ok vel vígr ok óeirðarmaðr inn mesti. Þá Svart ok Skíða skilði á um beitingar,[103] ok lauk því svá, at Svartr vá Skíða. En Brodd-Helgi mælti eptir vígit ok gerði Svart sekan. Þá var Brodd-Helgi tólf vetra gamall.

Eptir þat lagðisk Svartr út á heiði þá, er vér köllum Smjörvatnsheiði, skammt frá Sunnudal, ok leggsk á fé Hofsverja[104] ok gerði miklu meira at en honum var nauðsyn til.[105]

Sauðamaðr at Hofi kom inn einn aptan ok gekk inn í lokrekkjugólf Þorsteins karls, þar sem[106] hann lá sjónlauss. Ok mælti Þorsteinn: "Hversu hefir at farit í dag, félagi?"[107] segir hann.

"Sem verst," segir hinn;[108] "horfinn er geldingrinn þinn inn bezti," segir sauðamaðr, "ok þrír aðrir."

"Komnir munu til sauða annarra manna,"[109] segir hann, "ok munu aptr koma."

"Nei, nei," segir sauðamaðr, "þeir munu aldri aptr koma."

"Mæl við mik slíkt, er þér líkar,"[110] segir Þorsteinn, "en tala ekki slíkt við Brodd-Helga."

Translate: _____

_____

_____

_____

_____

_____

_____

_____

_____

_____

_____

_____

_____

_____

_____

---

[102] **er kom út hingat:** 'who came out here [to Iceland].'

[103] **þá Svart ok Skíða skilði á um beitingar:** 'Svart and Skidi disagreed over grazing rights.'

[104] **leggsk á fé Hofsverja:** 'began to prey upon the livestock of the people of Hof.'

[105] **en honum var nauðsyn til:** 'than was necessary for him.'

[106] **þar sem:** 'there where.'

[107] **hversu hefir at farit í dag, félagi?:** 'how have things gone today, friend?'

[108] **hinn:** *dem pron* 'the other one.'

[109] **komnir munu til sauða annarra manna:** 'they must have joined with some other people's sheep.'

[110] **slíkt er þér líkar:** 'such as it pleases you.'

_____

_____

_____

_____

_____

_____

12.10 CULTURE – ICELANDIC CHIEFTAINS, *GOÐAR*

Vápnfirðinga saga is set in a distinct social environment. The unknown medieval saga teller/author who committed to parchment this story of feud between the families at Hof and Krossavik understood the operation of power and politics in Icelandic society and concentrates on conflict between leaders. Icelandic chieftains were more political leaders than the warrior chiefs of many contemporary Scandinavian cultures. They possessed only slight formal authority to police, and until well into the thirteenth century had means to control the surrounding population. The *goðar*, unlike chieftains in more complex Viking Age societies did not oversee community works such as extensive irrigation systems, waterways or fortifications, whose upkeep and defense would offer a lucrative leadership niche. They were unable to limit access of local farmers to natural resources and had only limited privileged, control over a region's surplus production.

Not a commanding nobility, the *goðar* in *Vápnfirðinga saga* functioned as leaders of interest groups composed of free land-holding farmers (*bændr*, sg *bóndi*). *Bændr* chose their chieftain as the right to enter into alliances with leaders was not limited by the territorial location of their farms. Free farmers were called thingmen (*þingmenn*, sg *þingmaðr*) and were the chieftain's legally recognized followers. *Goðar* represented the interests of their *þingmenn* at assemblies and acted as their advocates in disputes.

Icelandic chieftains were legal specialists. They offered their service to farmers in need, often for payment although they were not formally obligated to as chieftains to help. A *bóndi* who had become a *þingmaðr* ('thingman', 'follower,' or 'retainer') of a *goði* was referred to as being *í þingi* ('in thing') with the chieftain.

Like other prominent farmers, chieftains were wealthy enough to weather bad times, but as individuals and as a group, they had only limited ability to compel farmers to do their bidding. As described in *Vápnfirðinga saga*, a chieftain's thingmen possessed the leeway both to resist their chieftain's demands and to make demands on the chieftain.

The office of a *goði* was called a *goðorð*, a term that means the "word" (*orð*) of a *goði*. A chieftaincy or *goðorð* was treated as a private possession that normally passed to a family member, though not necessarily to a first son. In addition to being inherited, a *goðorð* could be purchased, shared or received as a gift. The actual number of chieftains at any particular time in early Iceland was more than the number of chieftaincies, because each of those who shared part of a *goðorð* could call himself a *goði*.

Whether in pagan or Christian times, the *goðar* were a small-scale elite. The term *goði* is sometimes translated as priest-chieftain because it is derived from the Old Norse word *goð*, meaning 'god.' Probably the term stems from the responsibilities that early Icelandic chieftains had as priests of the old religion. When Iceland peacefully converted to Christianity in the year 999-1000, many *goðar* exchanged their previous religious functions for that of Christian priests. In some instances, chieftains themselves became priests, in other instances they made their sons, relatives, or slaves priests. Embracing the new beliefs, many chieftains were able to profit through the management of church property in the eleventh and twelfth centuries.

12.11 WORD FREQUENCY VOCABULARY – LIST 12. THE MOST FREQUENT WORDS IN THE SAGAS

NOUNS	*ADJECTIVES*	*PRONOUNS*
sveinn – boy, lad	**ríkr** – powerful	**yðr** – you (*pl*)
vár – spring	**fjölmennr** – well	**okkarr** – us (*dual*)
kostr – choice	attended; numerous	**einhverr** – someone
skjöldr – shield	**skammr** – short; brief	
bak – back	**göfugr** – noble	

VERBS	*PREPOSITIONS AND ADVERBS*	*CONJUNCTIONS*
veita – to grant	**aldri** – never	**hvárgi** – neither
sœkja – to seek	**nær** – nearly	
höggva – to strike	**mikit** – greatly	
senda – to send	**milli** – between	
geta – to get	**útan** – from out	

EXERCISES

12.12 Reading. For each of the underlined words in this passage from *Vápnfirðinga saga*, provide the relevant grammatical information, dictionary (infinitive) form, and translation.

Helgi var mikill maðr ok <u>sterkr</u> ok bráðgörr, vænn ok stórmannligr, ekki málugr í barnœsku, ódæll ok óvægr <u>þegar</u> á unga aldri. Hann var hugkvæmr ok margbreytinn.
    Frá <u>því</u> er sagt einnhvern dag at <u>Hofi</u>, er <u>naut</u> váru á <u>stöðli</u>, at graðungr var á <u>stöðlinum</u>, er þeir frændr áttu, en annarr graðungr kom <u>á</u> stöðulinn, ok stönguðusk graðungarnir. En sveinninn Helgi var úti ok sér, at <u>þeira</u> graðungr <u>dugir</u> verr ok <u>ferr</u> frá. Hann tekr mannbrodd einn ok bindr í enni graðunginum, ok gengr þaðan frá þeira graðungi <u>betr</u>. Af þessum atburði var hann kallaðr Brodd-Helgi.

Ex: sterkr _____*adj. m nom sg of sterkr 'strong'*_____
1. þegar _____
2. því _____
3. Hofi _____

4. naut _____

5. stöðli _____

6. stöðlinum _____

7. á _____

8. þeira _____

9. dugir _____

10. ferr _____

11. betr _____

12.13 Strong Verbs Review: Present and Past Tense. Fill in the correct form of each verb in the present or past tense as directed.

1. Hann _____ honum gripi (bjóða, *pres*).

   Hann _____ honum gripi (bjóða, *past*).

2. Gunnarr _____ hundinum (strjúka, *pres*).

   Gunnarr _____ hundinum (strjúka, *past*).

3. Konungrinn _____ um haustit (koma, *pres*).

   Konungrinn _____ um haustit (koma, *past*).

4. Maðr _____ í skóga (ganga, *pres*).

   Maðr _____ í skóga (ganga, *past*).

5. Hundr _____ eigi (bíta, *pres*).

   Hundr _____ eigi (bíta, *past*).

6. Vér _____ í hús (ganga, *pres*).

   Vér _____ í hús (ganga, *past*).

7. Þér _____ á eldaskálana (líta, *pres*).

   Þér _____ á eldaskálana (líta, *past*).

12.14 Strong Verbs – Classes I-III. Class I strong verbs have *í* in the infinitive while Class II have *jú*, *jó*, or *ú*. Class III infinitives contain *-e-*, *-ja-*, *-já-* or *-i-* followed by two consonants (not counting a stem-final *-j-* or *-v-*).

	INFINITIVE	*EXAMPLES*
Class I:	í	líta, rísa
Class II:	jú, jó, ú	str**jú**ka, b**jó**ða, l**ú**ka
Class III:	eCC, jaCC, jáCC, iNC	ver**ð**a, b**jarg**a, sk**jálf**a, vi**nn**a
	C = *any consonant*	N (*nasal*) = n *or* m

Identify the classes of the following strong verbs.

Ex: skjóta   *Class II*

1.	snerta	_____	5.	bjarga	_____
2.	drjúpa	_____	6.	bíta	_____
3.	klífa	_____	7.	hverfa	_____
4.	lúka	_____	8.	vinna	_____

12.15 Strong Verbs – Classes I–III. Give the strong verb classes for each of the following infinitives and then provide the requested grammatical form.

	STRONG VERB CLASS	REQUESTED FORM
Ex: bíða (*1sg pres*)	*Class I*	*bíð*
1. finna (*2pl past*)	_____	_____
2. verða (*1pl pres*)	_____	_____
3. líta (*3pl pres*)	_____	_____
4. lúta (*2sg past*)	_____	_____
5. svíkja (*1sg past*)	_____	_____
6. ljósta (*1pl past*)	_____	_____
7. gjalla (*3sg past*)	_____	_____
8. ríða (*3sg pres*)	_____	_____
9. springa (*2pl pres*)	_____	_____
10. fljúga (*3pl past*)	_____	_____
11. søkkva (*2pl pres*)	_____	_____
12. syngva (*1pl past*)	_____	_____

12.16 Pronouns *Hverr* and *Einnhverr*. Decline the noun phrases below.

	HVERR PENNINGR	EITTHVERT SKIP
Sg *nom*	_____	_____
acc	_____	_____
dat	_____	_____
gen	_____	_____
Pl *nom*	_____	_____
acc	_____	_____
dat	_____	_____
gen	_____	_____

12.17 Strong and Weak Verbs. Give the correct form of each verb below.

Ex: gefa <gefr, gaf, gáfu, gefit>   (*3sg pres*) *gefr*

1. fara <ferr, fór, fóru, farit>   (*3pl past*) _____
2. gera <-ði, -ðr~gerr>   (*2sg pres*) _____
3. koma <kemr, kom, kómu, kominn>   (*1sg past*) _____

4. herja <-að->   (*2pl past*) _____
5. ganga <gengr, gekk, gengu, genginn> (*3sg past*) _____
6. verða <verðr, varð, urðu, orðinn>   (*2pl pres*) _____

12.18 Strong Verbs – Class III. *Sleppa* 'slip, slide, escape,' a typical Class III strong verb with principal parts *sleppr, slapp, sluppu, sloppinn*. Conjugate *sleppa* in the present and past.

	PRESENT		PAST
Sg *ek*	_____	**Sg** *ek*	_____
þú	_____	*þú*	_____
hann	_____	*hann*	_____
Pl *vér*	_____	**Pl** *vér*	_____
þér	_____	*þér*	_____
þeir	_____	*þeir*	_____

A number of Class III strong verbs have infinitives with *-ja-* or *-já-* rather than *-e-* (*bjarga, hjálpa*). Apart from the infinitive, these verbs have the same principal parts as *sleppa*. Infinitives with *-i-* have *-u-* (rather than *-o-*) in the past participle. Remember that *brenna* comes from an older form *brinna*, which governs the vowel (*-u-*) in the past participle. Give the principal parts for each of the verbs below.

Ex: spretta *sprettr, spratt, spruttu, sprotinn*
1. snerta _____
2. bjarga _____
3. spinna _____
4. hjálpa _____
5. bresta _____
6. brenna _____

Keeping in mind that *-v-* drops before *-o-* or *-u-* give the principal parts for the verbs below.

Ex: hverfa *hverfr, hvarf, hurfu, horfinn*
7. verða _____
8. vinna _____
9. verpa _____
10. þverra _____

Strong verbs change *-nd-* to *-tt-*, *-ng-* to *-kk-*, and *-ld-* to *-lt-* in the third principal part. Give the 3sg past for the verbs below.

Ex: binda *batt*
11. springa _____   12. gjalda _____   13. vinda _____

Give the infinitives for each of the verbs below.

Ex: vinnr   *vinna*

14. varð _____   16. dottinn _____   18. drukku _____

15. spunnu _____   17. fann _____   19. urðu _____

Fill in the correct forms of the Class III strong verbs below.

Ex: finna (*1sg past*)   *fann*

20. bjarga (*2pl past*) _____   24. bresta (*1sg past*) _____

21. spinna (*1pl pres*) _____   25. snerta (*1pl past*) _____

22. svimma (*3pl pres*) _____   26. verða (*3sg past*) _____

23. gjalla (*2sg past*) _____   27. hjálpa (*3sg pres*) _____

12.19 The Bro Church Runestone from Uppland, Sweden speaks of Ginnlaug, the daughter of Holmgeir and sister of Sigrod (Sigröðr). These people are from the same extended family as those mentioned on the Ramsund Runestone.

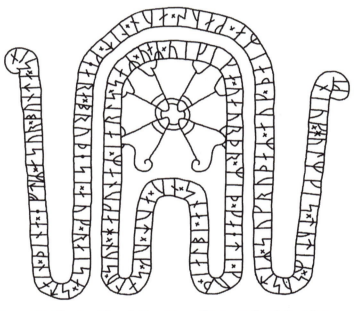

Like the Ramsund Stone, the Bro Stone commemorates a wife, Ginnlaug's construction of a causeway over swampy ground and the raising of a memorial stone in memory of her husband Assur (Össur).

Figure 50. The Bro Church Runestone from Uppland, Sweden

The Bro stone is also about Ginnlaug. It announces Ginnlaug's status to travelers who accept her gift of dry passage over the swamp. About the husband, Assur, the runestone tells that he held the military rank 'Viking-guard,' a warden (*vörðr*) or leader of the regional coastal defense force keeping watch against Viking raids from the sea. This information reveals the threat of Vikings to the Swedish coast.

Assur's father, Earl Hakon, was possibly the Norwegian Hákon hlaða-jarl ('Earl of Lade') Sigurðarson from Trondelag. Hákon, mentioned earlier, was the *de facto* ruler of most of Norway from ca. 970–995. The title *jarl* identifies him as a nobleman second only to a king.

Both this inscription and the one at Ramsund record Christian sentiments at a time when Sweden was still nominally pagan. These stones witness that elements of the two religions were current at the time of the conversion and perhaps afterward.

RUNES

ᛒᛁᚾᛚᚢᚴ×ᚼᚢᛚᛘᚴᛁᛌ×ᛏᚢᛏᛁᛦ×ᛌᛦᛌᛏᛁᛦ×ᛌᚢᚴᚱᚢᚦᛅᛦ×ᛏᚢᚴ×ᚦᛅᛁᛦᛅ×
ᚠᛅᚢᛌ×ᛅᚢᚾ×ᛚᛁᛏ×ᚠᛁᛅᚱᛅ×ᛒᚱᚢ×ᚦᛁᛌᛁ×ᛅᚢᚴ×ᚱᛅᛁᛌᛅ×ᛌᛏᛅᛁᚾ×ᚦᛁᚾᛅ×
ᛁᚠᛏᛁᛦ×ᛅᛌᚢᚱ×ᛒᚢᛅᛏᛅ×ᛌᛁᚾ×ᛌᚢᚾ×ᚼᛅᚴᚢᚾᛅᛦ×ᛁᛅᚱᛚᛌ×ᛌᛅᛦ×
ᚢᛅᛦ×ᚢᛁᚴᛁᚴᛅ×ᚢᛅᚢᚱᚦᚱ×ᛘᛁᚦ×ᚴᛅᛁᛏᛁ×ᚴᚢᚦ×ᛁᛅᛚᛒᛁ×ᛅᚾᛌ×ᚾᚢ×ᛅᚢᛏ×
ᚢᚴ×ᛌᛅᛚᚢ×

TRANSLITERATION

kinluk × hulmkis × tutiR × systiR × sukruþaR × auk × þaiRa × kaus × aun × lit × keara × bru
× þesi × auk × raisa × stain × þina × eftiR × asur × bunta × sin × sun × hakunaR × iarls × saR
× uaR × uikika × uaurþr × miþ × kaeti × kuþ × ialbi × ans × nu × aut × uk × salu ×

STANDARDIZED OLD NORSE

Ginnlaug, Hólmgeirs dóttir, systir Sigrøðar ok þeira Gauts,[111] hon lét gera brú þessi[112] ok
reisa stein þenna eptir Assur, búanda sinn, son Hákonar jarls. Sá var víkingavörðr með
gæti.[113] Guð hjálpi hans nú önd ok sálu.

VOCABULARY

Assurr (*also* **Özurr**) <-s> *m* Assur (*personal name*)

Gautr <-s> *m* Gaut (*personal name*)

Ginnlaug <-ar> *f* Ginnlaug (*personal name*)

gæta <gætti, gætt> *vb* [*w gen*] watch, tend, take care of

gætir <-is, -ar> *m* keeper, guard

Gætir <-is> *m* Gaetir (*personal name*)

vörðr <*dat* verði, *gen* varðar, *pl* verðir, *acc* vörðu, *gen* varða> *m* warden; guard, watch

Translate:_____

_____

_____

_____

_____

_____

---

[111] **ok þeira Gauts:** 'and of Gaut and his brothers.'

[112] **þessi:** The correct form in Standardized Old Norse would be accusative *þessa* to match *bru*.

[113] **gæti:** The meaning of *gæti* is unclear. If in the singular (*gæti*), it could be a man's name (*Gætir*), but this is a very unusual name. Possibly the word could be plural (*gæta*), making Assur the commander of a troop of guards. It might also be part of a formulaic expression and read *...með. Gæti [vor] Guð [ok]...* meaning, '...also. May God watch over us and...'

LESSON 13
SPIKE-HELGI KILLS A THIEF
IN WEAPON'S FJORD

Þá er hart þegar einn hrafninn kroppar augun ór öðrum
(Times are bad when one raven picks out the eyes of another)

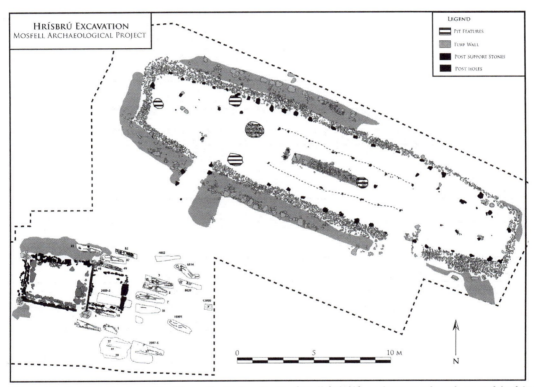

Figure 51. Archaeological Site Plan of a Icelandic Turf Hall (*Skáli*) and Stave Church at Hrísbrú in the Mosfell Valley, Iceland. The plan shows the excavation of a high-status Viking Age long house, church, and graveyard. This large longhouse was built early in the settlement period around the year 900. The smaller stave church (front bottom left) was built of drift wood timbers around the time Iceland converted to Christianity. The site, described in *Egil's Saga* and *Gunnlaug's Saga*, was the home of the Mosfell chieftains, including Grímr Svertingsson, Iceland's Law -Speaker from 1002-1004. The concluding chapters of *Egil's Saga* take place at this farmstead. Egil Skalla-Grimsson died and was buried there. The site was excavated as part of the Mosfell Archaeological Project.

13.1 READING – SPIKE-HELGI HUNTS DOWN SVART (*VÁPNFIRÐINGA SAGA*)

This lesson continues the reading of the opening chapters of *Vápnfirðinga saga*.

On the farmstead of Hof, Thorstein instructs the shepherd not inform his young grandson Brodd-Helgi about the theft of sheep. The shepherd disobeys Thorstein and tells

Helgi about the theft. Helgi arms himself for a fight. He shrewdly wedges the lower end of a thin, flat stone into his pants to shield his belly and chest. After sneaking out of the longhouse at night, Helgi follows the thief's tracks through the snow up onto Smjörvatnsheiðr (Butter Lake Heath). When they meet, the thief Svart curses Brodd-Helgi and his family. In the sagas, curses serve as a literary device of anticipation. They indicate that tragedy will follow. In this case, Helgi's family suffers two generations of blood feud.[114] In the passage below, a man of importance comes of age.

Vápnfirðinga saga (ch 2)

Brodd-Helgi spurði sauðamanninn, hversu flakkat hefði,[115] um daginn eptir. En hann hafði öll in sömu svör[116] við hann sem við Þorstein. Brodd-Helgi lét sem hann heyrði eigi ok fór í rekkju um kveldit. Ok er aðrir menn váru sofnaðir, reis hann upp ok tók skjöld sinn, ok gekk hann síðan út.

Þess er getit, at hann tók upp einn hellustein, mikinn ok þunnan, ok lét annan enda í brœkr sínar, en annan fyrir brjóst. Hann hafði í hendi boløxi mikla á hávu skapti. Hann ferr, unz hann kemr í sauðahús, ok rekr þaðan spor, því at snjór var á jörðu.

Hann kemr á Smjörvatnsheiði upp frá Sunnudal. Svartr gekk út ok sá mann knáligan kominn ok spurði, hverr þar væri.[117] Brodd-Helgi sagði til sín. "Þú munt ætla at fara á fund minn[118] ok eigi ørendislaust," segir hann.

Svartr hljóp at honum ok leggr til hans með höggspjóti miklu, en Brodd-Helgi brá við skildinum, ok kom á útanverðan skjöldinn ok kemr í helluna,[119] ok sneiddi af hellunni svá hart, at hann féll eptir laginu.[120] En Brodd-Helgi høggr á fótinn, svá at af tók.[121]

Þá mælti Svartr: "Nú gerði gæfumun okkar,"[122] segir hann, "ok muntu verða banamaðr minn, en sá ættangr mun verða í kyni yðru héðan af,[123] at alla ævi mun uppi vera,[124] meðan

---

[114] For feud in *Vápnfirðinga saga* see Chapter 13, 'Friendship, Blood Feud, and Power: *The Saga of the People of Weapon's Fjord'* in Byock, *Viking Age Iceland*. London: Penguin Books, 2001, pp. 233-251. For more on feud, see Chapters 10, 'Systems of Power: Advocates, Friendship, and Family Networks,' 11, 'Aspects of Blood Feud,' and 12, 'Feud and Vendetta in a 'Great Village' Community,' pp. 184-232.

[115] **hversu flakkat hefði**: 'how things went wandering about [with the sheep]'; *hefði* is 3sg past subj of *hafa*. In indirect questions, the verb is often in the subjunctive.

[116] **öll in sömu svör**: 'all the same replies.'

[117] **ok spurði, hverr þar væri**: 'and he asked who might be there.' Another indirect question with the subjunctive (*væri*: 3sg. past subj. of *vera*).

[118] **Þú munt ætla at fara á fund minn** : 'You probably intend to come find me.' The verb *munu* is used when a speaker believes that a future event is likely to happen. *Munu* is a preterite-present verb (see section later in this lesson).

[119] **ok [högg] kom á útanverðan skjöldinn ok kemr í helluna**: 'and [the blow] landed on the outer part of the shield and struck against the stone.' The blow glances off the edge of the shield and strikes the stone covering Helgi's chest.

[120] **hann fell eptir laginu**: 'he [Svart] fell along with the blow.' Svart lost his balance.

[121] **svá at af tók**: 'so that [the foot] was cut off.'

[122] **Nú gerði gæfumun okkar**: *impersonal construction*, 'now the difference in luck between us has been revealed.'

[123] **mun verða í kyni yðru heðan af**: 'will come to pass on your kin henceforth.' Svart puts a curse on Spike-Helgi's family.

[124] **at alla ævi mun uppi vera**: 'that will last for all time.'

landit er byggt." Eptir þetta hjó Helgi hann banahögg.

Nú vaknar Þorsteinn karl heima á Hofi ok gengr af rekkju sinni ok tekr í rúm Brodd-Helga.[125] Var þat kalt orðit. Hann vekr upp húskarla sína ok biðr þá fara at leita Brodd-Helga. Ok er þeir kómu út, rökðu þeir spor hans alla leið ok fundu hann þar sem Svartr lá dauðr.

Síðan huldu þeir hræ Svarts ok höfðu með sér allt þat, sem fémætt var.[126] Varð Brodd-Helgi víðfrægr ok lofaðr mjök af alþýðu fyrir þetta þrekvirki, er hann hafði unnit, jafnungr sem hann var enn at aldri.[127]

Translate: _____

_____
_____
_____
_____
_____
_____
_____
_____
_____
_____
_____
_____
_____
_____
_____
_____
_____
_____
_____
_____

13.2 CULTURE – ASSEMBLIES AND COURTS IN ICELAND, BACKGROUND TO THE SAGAS

Með lögum skal land várt byggja en með ólögum eyða
(With law must our land be built or with lawlessness laid waste)

Njal's Saga

The core of the Icelandic legislative and judicial system was the Althing (*Alþingi*), the yearly

---

[125] **ok tekr í rúm Brodd-Helga:** 'and he touches Spike-Helgi's bed.'
[126] **ok höfðu með sér allt þat, sem fémætt var:** 'and recovered everything which was valuable.'
[127] **jafnungr sem hann var enn at aldri:** 'as young as he still was at that age.'

national assembly. This thing (*þing*) or assembly was founded around the year 930 to

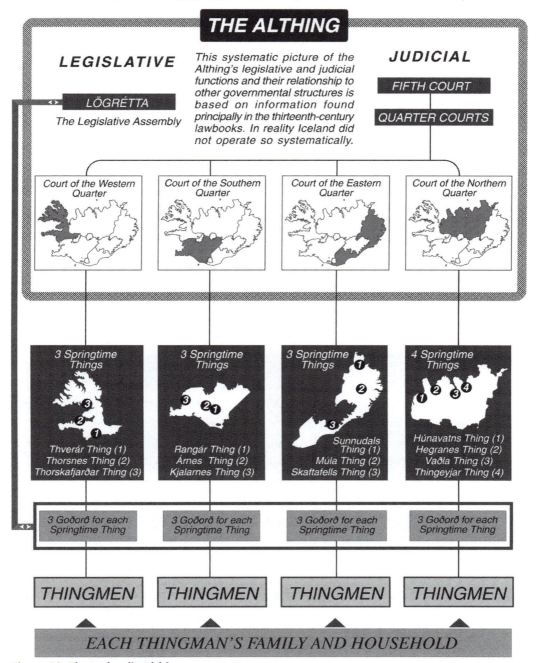

Figure 52. The Icelandic Althing.

provide a basis for country-wide governance, hence the name Althing. The Althing met in June at *Þingvöllr* (the Thing Plain) in the southwestern part of the island and lasted for two weeks. This was the time when travel was easiest, the days longest, and the weather mildest. Hundreds of people from all over Iceland, including pedlars, ale-brewers, tradesmen, and young adults seeking spouses converged on *Þingvöllr*. With its large lake and the mountains in the distance, the site is one of great natural beauty. For two weeks the Althing became a national capital. Friendships and political alliances were initiated, continued, or broken. Marriages and divorces were arranged, information passed, promises given, business transacted, and sagas recounted. *Vápnfirðinga saga,* like many sagas, includes scenes of legal actions and negotiations at the Althing and at local assemblies. These smaller regional assemblies were called spring time assemblies (*várþing*).

The *goðar* managed the proceedings of the assemblies. At the Althing they made and amended laws at the *lögrétta,* the legislative council of the Althing. There is little information about the operation of the earliest Althing, but sagas, histories, and lawbooks give detailed accounts of the assembly's composition after it underwent a constitutional reform in the mid-960s.

The reform of ca. 965 divided the island into quarters. It established four quarter courts at the Althing for resolving serious conflicts at the national level. Now, as long as the matter was of consequence, individuals could begin an action at the Althing rather than at a local spring assembly. The quarter courts at the Althing also served as appellate courts for decisions taken at the spring time assemblies. Cases that were deadlocked at a *várþing* could also be referred to that region's quarter court at the Althing.

The only significant national office in the Icelandic governmental system was that of law-speaker (*lögsögumaðr*). He was elected chairman of the *lögrétta* for a three-year term. Annually at the Althing's law rock (*lögberg*), the law-speaker recited a third of the law from memory. Attendance at this ceremony was required of each *goði,* accompanied by two advisers. They and other interested people sat on the surrounding grassy slope, probably offering emendations or corrections and taking part in discussions of legal issues. Among other duties, the law-speaker had to announce publicly any laws passed by the *lögrétta.* The *lögrétta* could also call on the law-speaker to furnish any part of the law its members needed in considering legislation. If faced with a difficult point of law or a lapse of memory, the law-speaker was required to consult five or more legal experts (*lögmenn*).

13.3 STRONG VERBS – CLASSES IV AND V

Class IV and V strong verbs share a number of features. Both classes in their basic patterns have -*e*- in the infinitive (*bera, gefa*), -*a*- in the past singular (*bar, gaf*), and -*á*- in the past plural (*báru, gáfu*). Class IV typically has -*o*- in the past participle while class V has -*e*- (*borinn, gefinn*).

Class IV verbs generally have a single -*l*-, -*r*-, -*m*-, or -*n*- following the root vowel of the infinitive; for example, *bera, stela, nema* (exceptions: *vefa, sofa, troða*).

Class V verbs generally have a single consonant other than -*l*-, -*r*-, -*m*-, or -*n*- following the root vowel; for example, *drepa, gefa, geta* (exceptions: *vera, fregna*, and verbs with stem-final -*j*-).

Class IV

e INFINITIVE	*e* 3SG PRES	*a* 3SG PAST	*á* 3PL PAST	*o* PPART
bera 'carry'	berr	bar	báru	borinn
stela 'steal'	stelr	stal	stálu	stolinn
skera 'cut'	skerr	skar	skáru	skorinn
nema 'take'	nemr	nam	námu	numinn
fela 'hide'	felr	fal	fálu	fólginn
koma 'come'	kemr	kom	kómu~kvámu	kominn

BERA IN PRESENT AND PAST

	PRESENT					PAST		
Sg *ek*	ber	**Pl** *vér*	berum		**Sg** *ek*	bar	**Pl** *vér*	bárum
þú	berr	*þér*	berið		*þú*	bart	*þér*	báruð
hann	berr	*þeir*	bera		*hann*	bar	*þeir*	báru

Nema and *fela* have slightly irregular past participles (*numinn* and *fólginn*). *Koma* is irregular.

The verbs *troða*, *sofa*, and *vefa* are somewhat irregular.

INFINITIVE	3SG PRES	3SG PAST	3PL PAST	PPART
troða 'tread'	treðr~trøðr	trað	tráðu	troðinn
sofa 'sleep'	sefr~søfr	svaf	sváfu ~ sófu	sofinn
vefa 'weave'	vefr	óf ~ vaf	ófu ~ váfu	ofinn

Class V

e INFINITIVE	*e* 3SG PRES	*a* 3SG PAST	*á* 3PL PAST	*e* PPART
drepa	drepr	drap	drápu	drepinn
gefa	gefr	gaf	gáfu	gefinn
geta	getr	gat	gátu	getinn
kveða	kveðr	kvað	kváðu	kveðinn
vera	er	var	váru	verit (*n sg* only)
biðja	biðr	bað	báðu	beðinn
sitja	sitr	sat	sátu	setinn
liggja	liggr	lá	lágu	leginn
vega	vegr	vá	vágu	veginn
fregna	fregn	frá	frágu	freginn

DREPA IN PRESENT AND PAST										

	PRESENT					**PAST**				
Sg *ek*	drep	**Pl** *vér*	drepum		**Sg** *ek*	drap	**Pl** *vér*	drápum	
þú	drepr	*þér*	drepið		*þú*	drapt	*þér*	drápuð	
hann	drepr	*þeir*	drepa		*hann*	drap	*þeir*	drápu	

Class V verbs with stem-final *-j-* have *-i-* in the infinitive (*biðja, sitja*). When a *-g-* precedes stem-final *-j-*, the *-g-* doubles (*liggja, þiggja*). Verbs which end in *-g(g)-* (*vega, liggja*) drop the *-g(g)-* and lengthen *-a-* to *-á-* in the past singular (*vá* 'he killed,' *lá* 'he lay'). The *-g-* is retained in the past plural (*vágu, lágu*). *Fregna* 'learn' follows this pattern but is unusual in having an *-n-* in the infinitive and present tense.

The verb *sjá* is irregular.

INFINITIVE	3SG PRES	3SG PAST	3PL PAST	PPART
sjá 'see'	sér	sá	sá(u)	sénn

13.4 PRETERITE-PRESENT VERBS

The preterite-presents are a group of ten important verbs, whose present tense looks like the past tense of strong verbs. For example, the present singular of the preterite-present verb *þurfa* 'need' is *ek þarf, þú þarft, hann þarf*. This corresponds to the past singular of a strong verb like *finna* 'find': *ek fann, þú fannt, hann fann*. This peculiar feature of the class, with the present looking like the past, gives rise to its name. Preterite is an old grammatical term referring to the past tense, hence 'preterite-present' means 'past-present.'

Preterite-presents are often used as modal auxiliaries, helping verbs which modify the meaning of main verbs. They often correspond in meaning and form to English verbs: *kann* ('can'), *má* ('may'), *skal* ('shall'). Modals inject a sense of obligation, intention, need, or probability to main verbs. For example, a sense of obligation can be added to the sentence 'I sail to Iceland' by adding a modal auxiliary: 'I **ought** to sail to Iceland' or 'I **have** to sail to Iceland' (*Ek **skal** sigla til Íslands* and *Ek **á** at sigla til Íslands*).

THE TEN PRETERITE-PRESENTS

eiga 'own, possess; be married or related to;' (*w* at) 'have to'

kná 'be able to'

kunna 'know, understand;' [with *at*] 'be able, can; know how to; happen, chance'

mega 'may, be permitted to, can'

muna 'remember'

munu 'will (probability), would'

skulu 'will (obligation), should'

unna 'love'

þurfa 'need, want;' (with *at*) 'need (to do something)'

vita 'know'

Two general rules describe the formation of preterite-present verbs.

- In the present tense, preterite-presents behave like the past tense of strong verbs. All preterite-presents apart from *munu* show a change of root vowel between singular and plural; for example, (*þarf* ~ *þurfum*).
- In the past tense, preterite-presents behave like the past tense of weak verbs. They add the past tense endings of weak verbs to an invariant past tense stem containing a dental suffix (*þurf-t-*).

Þurfa Conjugated in Present and Past

	PRESENT					PAST			
Sg *ek*	þarf	**Pl** *vér*	þurfum		**Sg** *ek*	þurfta	**Pl** *vér*	þurftum
þú	þarft	*þér*	þurfuð		*þú*	þurftir	*þér*	þurftuð
hann	þarf	*þeir*	þurfu		*hann*	þurfti	*þeir*	þurftu

The Remaining Preterite-Presents

PRESENT	EIGA	MEGA	KUNNA	MUNA	MUNU	SKULU	VITA
Sg *ek*	á	má	kann	man	mun	skal	veit
þú	átt	mátt	kannt	mant	munt	skalt	veizt
hann	á	má	kann	man	mun	skal	veit
Pl *vér*	eigum	megum	kunnum	munum	munum	skulum	vitum
þér	eiguð	meguð	kunnuð	munuð	munuð	skuluð	vituð
þeir	eigu	megu	kunnu	munu	munu	skulu	vitu
PAST							
Sg *ek*	átta	mátta	kunna	munda	munda	skylda	vissa

Like weak verbs: (*þú áttir, hann átti, vér áttum, þér áttuð, þeir áttu*, etc).

Two preterite-presents, *unna* and *kná*, do not appear above. *Unna* conjugates like *kunna*, and *kná* like *mega*. The verb *kná* is rare and does not possess a full set of forms.

Regarding *munu* and *skulu*

- Two preterite-presents, *munu* and *skulu*, have infinitives ending in -*u*. Although both are often translated as 'will,' *munu* expresses probability and *skulu* expresses obligation or intention. *Munu* and *skulu* have special forms *mundu* and *skyldu* (called past-tense infinitives) used in indirect speech; for example, *Hann kvazk mundu fara til Nóregs*, 'He said he would travel to Norway.'
- *Munu* and *skulu* frequently occur as subjunctive *myndi* and *skyldi*. The subjunctive adds a sense of doubt or uncertainty and can be translated as 'would' and 'should.'
- Variants of *munu* and *skulu* sometimes occur in the present subjunctive with *i*-umlaut; for instance, *hann myni* and *hann skyli* rather than *hann muni* and *hann skuli*.

13.5 PRETERITE-PRESENT VERBS – MODALS WITH AND WITHOUT *AT*

When employed as modal auxiliaries, three of the preterite-presents (*eiga*, *kunna*, and *þurfa*) require the infinitive marker *at* to be used with the infinitive of the main verb.

Hann á **at** gera brú.	*He must make a bridge.*
Hann kann **at** gera brú.	*He knows how to make a bridge.*
Hann þarf **at** gera brú.	*He needs to make a bridge.*

Four others (*mega*, *kná*, *munu*, and *skulu*) generally omit *at*.

Hann má gera brú.	*He may [is permitted to] make a bridge.*
Hann kná gera brú.	*He can [is able to] make a bridge.*
Hann mun gera brú.	*He will [is likely to] make a bridge.*
Hann skal gera brú.	*He shall make a bridge.*

The remaining three preterite-presents (*vita*, *muna*, *unna*) are chiefly used as main verbs.

13.6 EXERCISE – PRETERITE-PRESENT VERBS

Complete the following sentences with the correct form of the verb in the present tense.

1. Eiríkr _____ (*eiga*) at gera kumbl.
2. Ek _____ (*mega*) gefa þér land.
3. Þú _____ (*þurfa*) at koma.
4. Otrinn _____ (*munu*) eta laxinn.
5. Þú _____ (*skulu*) fara til Danmarkar.
6. Ormr _____ (*kunna*) at sigla skip.
7. Sigríðr _____ (*skulu*) spyrja konuna.
8. Konan _____ (*mega*) fara at Dreppstokki.

13.7 COMPARATIVE AND SUPERLATIVE ADJECTIVES

In addition to their simple forms, adjectives have comparative and superlative degrees. An example is English 'wise,' whose comparative is 'wis**er**' and superlative, 'wis**est**.' ON comparative and superlative adjectives are similar to English, with most adding to the adjective stem the suffix *-ar-* in the comparative and *-ast-* in the superlative, followed by a case ending. For example, the adjective *spak-r* 'wise' has the stem *spak-*; its comparative is *spak-**ar**-i* and superlative is *spak-**ast**-r*.

POSITIVE	COMPARATIVE	SUPERLATIVE
spakr 'wise'	spakari 'wiser'	spakastr 'wisest'
sterkr	sterkari	sterkastr
hvítr	hvítari	hvítastr

A smaller number of adjectives add the comparative suffix -r- and superlative suffix -st- and show i-umlaut. For example, lang-r becomes leng-r-i and leng-st-r.

Positive	Comparative	Superlative
langr	lengri	lengstr
ungr	yngri	yngstr
hár	hæri ~ hærri	hæstr

Comparatives with -r- follow the Special Stem Rules. For example, sæll 'blessed' has comparative sælli 'more blessed' (sæl- + -ri).

Positive	Comparative	Superlative
sæll	sælli (sæl + ri)	sælstr
vænn	vænni (væn + ri)	vænstr
fagr	fegri (fagr + ri)	fegrstr

Two-syllable adjectives with a short second syllable drop the vowel preceding the suffixes -ari and -astr. For instance, the comparative of auðigr is auðgari and the superlative is auðgastr.

Positive	Comparative	Superlative
auðigr	auðgari	auðgastr
göfugr	göfgari	göfgastr

Just like English 'good, better, and best,' a few common adjectives have different roots in the comparative and superlative.

Positive	Comparative	Superlative
gamall 'old'	ellri 'older, elder'	ellztr 'oldest, eldest'
góðr	betri	beztr
illr	verri	verstr
vándr	verri	verstr
lítill	minni	minnstr
margr	fleiri	flestr
mikill	meiri	mestr

13.8 Comparative Adjective Endings

Comparatives take the same set of weak endings as found in the present participle, bolded in the chart below.

	-AR- PLUS ENDING			*-R-* PLUS ENDING		
	M	**F**	**N**	**M**	**F**	**N**
Sg *nom*	spakari	spakari	spakara	lengri	lengri	lengra
acc	spakara	spakari	spakara	lengra	lengri	lengra
dat	spakara	spakari	spakara	lengra	lengri	lengra
gen	spakara	spakari	spakara	lengra	lengri	lengra
Pl *nom*	spakari	spakari	spakari	lengri	lengri	lengri
acc	spakari	spakari	spakari	lengri	lengri	lengri
dat	spökur**um**	spökur**um**	spökur**um**	lengr**um**	lengr**um**	lengr**um**
gen	spakari	spakari	spakari	lengri	lengri	lengri

13.9 SUPERLATIVE ADJECTIVE ENDINGS

Superlatives decline as regular adjectives, taking strong or weak endings according to whether they are preceded by a definite article, demonstrative pronoun, or other determining word.

	-AST- PLUS ENDING		*-ST-* PLUS ENDING	
	STRONG	**WEAK**	**STRONG**	**WEAK**
m	spakastr maðr	inn spakasti maðr	hæstr maðr	inn hæsti maðr
f	spökust kona	in spakasta kona	hæst kona	in hæsta kona
n	spakast barn	it spakasta barn	hæst barn	it hæsta barn

Adjectives whose stems end in a dental consonant (*-t-*, *-d-*, *-ð-*) drop the dental when adding the superlative suffix *-st-*, which becomes *-zt-*, for example, *beztr* from *bet-* + *-st-*.

13.10 USAGE OF COMPARATIVE AND SUPERLATIVE ADJECTIVES

Comparison is often expressed with the conjunction *en*, corresponding to English 'than.' The persons, places, or things which are compared are in the same case.

Þetta skip er lengra en **þat**.	***This ship** is longer than **that one**.*
Sól er bjartari en **máni**.	***The sun** is brighter than **the moon**.*
Hann á fleiri **óvini** en **vini**.	*He has more **enemies** than **friends**.*
Skipit var skjótara en **fugl**.	***The ship** was swifter than **a bird**.*

Comparison can also be expressed when the subject is in the nominative case and the noun compared is in the dative without *en*.

Skipit var **fugli** skjótara.	*The ship was swifter **than a bird**.*
Haki ok Hekja váru **dýrum** skjótari.	*Haki and Hekja were swifter **than animals**.*
Sól er **mána** bjartari.	*The sun is brighter **than the moon**.*

The dative case is also used by the adjective when answering questions such as 'by how much' or 'by how little.'

Hafði Sigmundr lið **miklu** minna.	*Sigmund had a **much** smaller ('smaller **by much**') force.*
En **litlu** síðar kom Óðinn heim.	*And a **little** later ('later **by a little**') Odin came home.*

Below are a few more examples of the comparative from the readings.

En annat haust hófu þeir mannblót, en árferð var söm eða **verri**.	*And the second autumn they sacrificed humans, but the harvest was the same or **worse**.*
Hvat er **fleira** at segja?	*What **more** is there to say?*
Bjarni hét son þeira inn **yngri**, en Lýtingr inn **ellri**.	*Bjarni was the name of their **younger** son and Lyting, the **elder**.*

Below are examples of the superlative from *The Prose Edda* and sagas.

Þat er allra grasa **hvítast**.	*It is the **whitest** of all herbs.*
Hann er **vitrastr** ásanna.	*He is the **wisest** of all the Æsir.*
"Skipit er it **fegrsta**," segir hann.	*"The ship is **very fair**," he says.*
Sigurðr var inn **ágætasti** allra herkonunga.	*Sigurd was the **most excellent** of all warlords.*

13.11 EXERCISE – COMPARATIVE AND SUPERLATIVE ADJECTIVES

Fill in the spaces below.

	MEANING	COMPARATIVE	MEANING	SUPERLATIVE	MEANING
Ex: spakr	wise	spakari	wiser	spakastr	wisest
1. svartr					
2. bjartr					
3. langr					
4. ungr					
5. hár					
6. góðr					
7. illr					
8. lítill					
9. margr					
10. mikill					

13.12 COMPARATIVE AND SUPERLATIVE ADVERBS

Comparative and superlative adverbs are indeclinable words formed with the suffixes *-ar* or *-r* in the comparative and *-ast* or *-st* in the superlative. Those taking *-r* and *-st* show *i*-umlaut.

POSITIVE	COMPARATIVE	SUPERLATIVE
opt 'often'	opt**ar** 'more often'	opt**ast** 'most often'
síð 'late'	síð**ar** 'later'	síð**ast** 'latest'
víð**a** 'widely'	víð**ar** 'more widely'	víð**ast** 'most widely'
skjót**t** 'speedily'	skjót**ar** 'more speedily'	skjót**ast** 'most speedily'
fag**rt** 'fairly, finely'	fe**gr** 'more fairly'	fe**grst** 'most fairly'
leng**i** 'for a long time'	leng**r** 'for a longer time'	leng**st** 'for the longest time'
tómlig**a** 'slowly'	tómlig**ar** 'more slowly'	tómlig**ast** 'most slowly'

- Adverbs formed with suffix -*a*, -*t*, or -*i* drop this suffix before adding comparative -*ar*/-*r* or superlative -*ast*/-*st*.
- The comparative suffixes -*ar* and -*r* often appear in early texts as -*arr* and -*rr*; for example, *optarr* and *síðarr*.
- Some adverbs form their comparatives with the suffix -*ara* or -*ra*; for example, *tíðara* 'more frequently,' *breiðara* 'more broadly,' *spakara* 'more wisely.' Those taking -*ra*, such as *lengra* 'longer (of space or distance),' show *i*-umlaut.

Some common adverbs form their positive and comparative/superlative degrees from different roots.

POSITIVE	COMPARATIVE	SUPERLATIVE
vel 'well'	betr	bezt~bazt
illa 'badly'	verr	verst
mikit 'much'	meir(a)	mest
mjök 'much'	meir(a)	mest
lítit 'little'	minnr~miðr	minnst
snemma 'early'	fyrr	fyrst
gjarna 'willingly'	heldr	helzt

Examples of comparative and superlative adverbs from the readings.

Böðvarr mælti: 'Ekki muntu fá skjaldborgina gerða **lengr**.'	Bodvar said, "You will not be able to make your shield wall any **longer**."
Herjólfr bjó **fyrst** á Drepstokki.	Herjolf lived **first** at Drepstokkr.
Önundr var upplenzkr at móðurætt, en föðurkyn hans var **mest** um Rogaland ok um Hörðaland.	Önund was an uplander (highlander) on his mother's side, but his father's family was **mostly** from Rogaland and Hordaland.

13.13 READING – BRODD-HELGI'S RELATIONSHIP TO GEITIR (*VÁPNFIRÐINGA SAGA*)

Family connections over several generations play a particularly important role in *Vápnfirðinga saga*, which focuses on two families: the *Hofsverjar* (the people of Hof) and the *Krossvíkingar* (the people of Krossavík). The early part of the saga describes the friendship between the youths Brodd-Helgi of Hof and Geitir of Krossavik. This friendship is not destined to last after they become brothers-in-law and prominent local chieftains.

The passage below defines the kinship and political relationships between the groups.

Vápnfirðinga saga (ch 3)

Í þann tíma, er Þorsteinn [hvíti] bjó at Hofi ok Brodd-Helgi óx upp með honum, þá bjó sá maðr í Krossavík inni ýtri,[128] er Lýtingr hét ok var Ásbjarnarson, Óláfs sonar langháls. Hann var vitr maðr ok vel auðugr at fé.

Hann átti konu, er Þórdís hét, dóttur Herlu-Bjarna Arnfinnssonar. Þau áttu tvá sonu,[129] þá er við þessa sögu koma.[130] Hét annarr Geitir, en annarr Blængr. Halla hét dóttir Lýtings, en önnur Rannveig, ok var hon gipt í Klifshaga í Øxarfjörð þeim manni, er Óláfr hét.

Þeir váru mjök jafngamlir, brœðr ok Brodd-Helgi, ok var með þeim vinfengi mikit. Brodd-Helgi fekk Höllu Lýtingsdóttur, systur þeira brœðra. Þeira dóttir var Þórdís todda, er átti Helgi Ásbjarnarson. Bjarni hét son þeira inn yngri, en Lýtingr inn ellri. Bjarni var at fóstri í Krossavík með Geiti. Blængr var rammr at afli ok hallr nökkut í göngu. Geitir átti Hallkötlu Þiðrandadóttur, föðursystur Droplaugarsona.[131]

Svá var vingott með þeim Brodd-Helga ok Geiti, at þeir áttu hvern leik saman ok öll ráð ok hittusk nær hvern dag, ok fannsk mönnum orð um, hversu[132] mikil vinátta með þeim var.

Í þann tíma bjó sá maðr í Sunnudal, er Þormóðr hét ok var kallaðr stikublígr. Hann var sonr Steinbjarnar körts ok bróðir Refs ins rauða á Refsstöðum ok Egils á Egilsstöðum. Börn Egils váru Þórarinn, Hallbjörn, Þröstr ok Hallfríðr, er átti Þorkell Geitisson. Synir Þormóðar váru þeir Þorsteinn ok Eyvindr, en þeir synir Refs Steinn ok Hreiðarr. Allir váru þeir þingmenn Geitis. Hann var spekingr mikill.

Samfarar þeira Höllu ok Brodd-Helga váru góðar. Lýtingr var at fóstri í Øxarfirði með Þorgilsi skinna. Brodd-Helgi var vel auðigr at fé.

Translate the reading above: _____

_____

_____

_____

_____

_____

_____

_____

_____

_____

_____

_____

---

[128] **Krossavík inni ýtri:** 'Krossavik the outer,' distinguishing its position on the bay. The phrase is in the dative case.

[129] **Hann átti konu...Þau áttu tvo sonu:** 'He was married to a woman...They had two sons.' The verb *eiga*, ('own') here denotes familial relationships through marriage or kinship.

[130] **þá er við þessa sögu koma:** 'those who come forward in this saga.'

[131] **föðursystur Droplaugarsona:** 'the aunt [father's sister] of the sons of Droplaug,' for whom *Droplaugarsona saga* is named.

[132] **ok fannsk mönnum orð um, hversu** 'and people commented on how....'

_____
_____
_____
_____
_____
_____
_____
_____
_____
_____
_____
_____

EXERCISES

13.14 Strong Verbs. Classes IV and V are very similar, differing principally in the vowel of the past participle (IV has -o-, V has -e-). For example, *bera* (IV) has principal parts *berr, bar, báru, borinn*, while *gefa* (V) has *gefr, gaf, gáfu, gefinn*. Conjugate *gefa* in present and past below.

	PRESENT		PAST
Sg *ek*	_____	**Sg** *ek*	_____
þú	_____	*þú*	_____
hann	_____	*hann*	_____
Pl *vér*	_____	**Pl** *vér*	_____
þér	_____	*þér*	_____
þeir	_____	*þeir*	_____

When the vowel of the infinitive (-*e*-) is followed by a single -*l*-, -*m*-, -*n*-, or -*r* the verb is Class IV. When followed by any other consonant, the verb is Class V. A few Class V strong verbs have stem-final -*j*- and have -*i*- in the infinitive and present tense, but otherwise follow the pattern of *gefa*.

Give the principal parts of the verbs below.

Ex: bera   *berr, bar, báru, borinn* _____
     reka   *rekr, rak, ráku, rekinn* _____
     biðja   *biðr, bað, báðu, beðinn* _____
  1. skera   _____
  2. leka   _____
  3. geta   _____
  4. meta   _____

    5. drepa   _____

    6. stela   _____

    7. sitja   _____

    8. kveða   _____

Class V strong verbs having -*g(g)*- in the infinitive (*vega*) drop -*g(g)*- in the third principal part and lengthen -*a*- to -*á*- (*vá*). The -*g*- doubles in the infinitive and present tense for verbs with stem-final -*j*- (*lig**g**ja, þig**g**ja*). Give the principal parts for the following verbs.

    Ex: vega   *vegr, vá, vágu, veginn* _____

    9. liggja   _____

    10. þiggja   _____

Fill in the correct forms of the verbs below.

    Ex: reka (*1sg pres*)   *rek* _____

11. kveða (*2pl past*) _____	14. nema (*1pl past*) _____
12. leka (*3sg past*) _____	15. skera (*2sg past*) _____
13. geta (*1pl pres*) _____	16. liggja (*1sg past*) _____

13.15 Strong Verbs. The class of most strong verbs can be identified from the infinitive alone. Below are rules that help distinguish among the five classes introduced so far.

    Class I: infinitive contains -*í*-

    Class II: infinitive contains -*jú*-, -*jó*-, or -*ú*-

    Class III: infinitive contains -*e*-, -*ja*-, -*já*- or -*i*- (also -*ø*- or -*y*-) followed by two consonants (not counting stem-final -*j*- or -*v*-)

    Class IV: infinitive contains -*e*- followed by a resonant (either -*l*-, -*m*-, -*n*-, or -*r*-)

    Class V: infinitive contains -*e*- or -*i*- followed by a single consonant other than -*l*-, -*m*-, -*n*-, or -*r*- (not counting stem-final -*j*-)

There are a few exceptions to these rules; for example, *búa* is a Class VII strong verb (not Class II) and *fregna* is Class V (not Class III).

	INFINITIVE	*EXAMPLES*
Class I:	í	líta, rísa
Class II:	jú, jó, ú	strjúka, bjóða, lúka
Class III:	eCC, jaCC, jáCC, iNC	verða, bjarga, skjálfa, vinna
	(*also* øCCv, yNCv)	hrøkkva, syngva
Class IV:	eR	stela, skera
Class V:	eC, iCj	gefa, eta, sitja

C = *any consonant*   R (*resonant*) = r, l, n, *or* m   N (*nasal*) = n *or* m

Based on the table given above, identify the class of the following strong verbs.

Ex: binda   *Class I*

1. leka _____
2. bera _____
3. njóta _____
4. spinna _____
5. lesa _____
6. hjálpa _____
7. súpa _____
8. hverfa _____
9. reka _____
10. bjóða _____
11. nema _____
12. líða _____

13.16 Preterite-Present Verbs. Translate the sentences and give the infinitive for each of the underlined preterite-present verbs.

Meanings

eiga 'own, possess; have to'

kná 'be able to'

kunna 'be able'; (*w* at) 'happen, chance'

mega 'may, be permitted to'

muna 'remember'

munu 'will (probability), would'

skulu 'will (obligation), should'

unna 'love'

þurfa 'need'

vita 'know'

Ex: Hon <u>mun</u> koma hingat it sama haust.

*She will come here the same autumn.*   *munu*

1. Þú <u>átt</u> at fara til Noregs.

   _____   _____

2. Vér <u>skulum</u> gera öl.

   _____   _____

3. Þér <u>kunnuð</u> at ríða hesta.

   _____   _____

4. Þær <u>þurftu</u> at spyrja goðann.

   _____   _____

5. Ek <u>má</u> mæla við konunginn.

   _____   _____

6. Þú <u>munt</u> verða frændi.

    _____   _____

The following sentences come from *Hrólfs saga kráka*.

VOCABULARY

ey *f* island

hátt *adv* loudly

haukr *m* hawk

lundr *m* grove

nærri *comp adv* very near

❖**sjálfr** *adj pron* self, oneself, himself, herself, itself, themselves

❖**þegar** *adv* at once, immediately; **þegar á morgin** first thing in the morning

7. Lundr einn stóð nærri höllinni, er konungr <u>átti</u>.

    _____   _____

8. <u>Skal</u> ek fara sjálfr til eyjarinnar þegar á morgin.

    _____   _____

9. Svipdagr mælti svá hátt, at allir <u>máttu</u> heyra.

    _____   _____

10. En Hrólfr konungr <u>átti</u> þann hauk, er Hábrók hét.

    _____   _____

13.17 Preterite-Present Verbs. Give the infinitives and meanings of the following verbs.

	INFINITIVE	*FORM*	*TRANSLATION*
Ex: skalt	*skulu*	*2sg. pres.*	*you will*
1. þurfum	_____	_____	_____
2. munt	_____	_____	_____
3. mátt	_____	_____	_____
4. skal	_____	_____	_____
5. meguð	_____	_____	_____
6. kann	_____	_____	_____
7. skuluð	_____	_____	_____
8. veizt	_____	_____	_____

13.18 Comparative Adjectives. Comparative adjectives always take the special set of weak endings given in this lesson. Decline *sterkari* below.

	M	F	N
Sg *nom*	sterkari	_____	_____
acc	_____	_____	_____
dat	_____	_____	_____
gen	_____	_____	_____
Pl *nom*	_____	_____	_____
acc	_____	_____	_____
dat	_____	_____	_____
gen	_____	_____	_____

13.19 Superlative Adjectives. Superlative adjectives take the same set of strong and weak endings as regular adjectives. Decline strong and weak *ríkastr*.

STRONG	M	F	N
Sg *nom*	ríkastr	_____	_____
acc	_____	_____	_____
dat	_____	_____	_____
gen	_____	_____	_____
Pl *nom*	_____	_____	_____
acc	_____	_____	_____
dat	_____	_____	_____
gen	_____	_____	_____

WEAK	M	F	N
Sg *nom*	ríkasti	_____	_____
acc	_____	_____	_____
dat	_____	_____	_____
gen	_____	_____	_____
Pl *nom*	_____	_____	_____
acc	_____	_____	_____
dat	_____	_____	_____
gen	_____	_____	_____

13.20 Reading Exercise. Translate the following stanza from the Eddic poem *Hávamál* (*The Sayings of the High One*). The High One refers to Odin, and the stanza is in *ljóðaháttr*, meaning 'chant-meter.' For ON poetry see *Viking Language 2: The Old Norse Reader*.

Deyr fé,   _____

deyja frændr,   _____

deyr sjálfr it sama;   _____

Ek veit einn,   _____

at aldri deyr: _____

dómr um dauðan hvern.   _____

VOCABULARY

❖**aldri** *adv* never

❖**dauðr** *<f* dauð, *n* dautt> *adj* dead

deyja <deyr, dó, dó, dáinn> *vb* die

dómr <-s, -ar> *m* court; judgement

❖**einn** *<f* ein, *n* eitt, *ord* fyrstr 'first'> *num* one; *indef pro* a, an, a certain one

❖**fé** *<gen* fjár, *gen pl* fjá> *n* cattle, sheep; wealth, money

❖**frændi** *<pl* frændr> *m* kinsman

❖**hverr** *<f* hver, *n* hvert> *indef pron* each, every, all

❖**samr** *<f* söm, *n* samt> *adj pron* same; **it sama** the same, likewise

❖**sjálfr** *adj pron* self, oneself, himself, herself, itself, themselves

❖**vita** <veit, vissi, vitaðr> *pret-pres vb* know

LESSON 14
NORSE MYTHOLOGY AND THE WORLD TREE YGGDRASIL

Fróðr er hverr fregnvíss
(Wise is he who is curious)

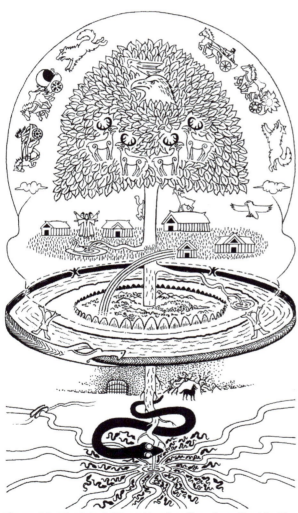

Figure 53. The World Tree Yggdrasil as described in *The Prose Edda* and the reading sections of this lesson.

14.1 CULTURE – THE WORLD TREE

In Old Norse mythology, the World Tree Yggdrasil (Yggdrasill) was the *axis mundi* or cosmic pillar at the center of the universe. The Tree united the nine mythological worlds, binding them into a dynamic cosmos. Rising into the highest reaches of space, Yggdrasil is a giant, holy ash tree whose branches spread over all realms.

The concept of a world tree exists in many mythologies. In the case of the Scandinavian world tree, the idea may have an Indo-European origin. A world tree is also a feature of circumpolar peoples as far back as the Stone Age.

Although Viking Age Scandinavians likely interpreted the tree in different ways, the name 'Yggdrasill' offers some clues. A possible interpretation is that *Ygg-* comes from one of Odin's many names. *Yggr* means the 'terrible one' and is perhaps connected to Odin's role as god of the hanged. *Drasill* is an ancient term for 'horse.' Hence Yggdrasill may mean 'Ygg's horse' and is a metaphor for a gallows tree.

This view assumes that ancient Scandinavians saw a similarity between how people ride horses and how a hanged person bobs as he 'rides' the gallows. The gallows tree is a fitting symbol for the causeway connecting the heavens and the underworld. It is a significant site for the passage between life and death.

The Prose Edda and several Eddic poems, such as *Grímnismál* (*The Lay of Grimnir*) and *Vafþrúðnismál (The Lay of Vafthrudnir)*, describe the different worlds and their dwellers. Heaven (*himinn*) rises above the Tree's foliage. It was formed early in the history of the world by the gods and is contained within the vault of the skull (see the accompanying Illustration) of the primordial giant *Ymir* ('Roarer'). Four dwarves, each standing at one of the four geographical directions, hold the skull in place. Daily the sun and the moon ride across the heavens in their chariots chased by two cosmic wolves. At the end of the world, at Ragnarok, the wolves will finally catch the two celestial bodies and swallow them.

Below the branches of the World Tree lies Asgard (Ásgarðr), the home of the gods. Odin lives there in his hall Valhalla, which he shares with his army of slain warriors, the Einherjar. In Asgard, one of the roots of the Tree takes sustenance from Urd's Well (Urðarbrunnr, 'the Well of Fate') where three prophetic women called Norns (Nornir) live.

The Rainbow Bridge (Bifröst) leads down from Asgard to the home of men in Midgard (Miðgarðr, 'Middle Enclosure' or 'Middle Earth'). A wall encloses Midgard, separating it from the outer region called Utgard (Útgarðr, 'Outer Enclosure'). In this outer region lies Jotunheim (Jötunheimr, 'home of the giants' or *jötnar*, sg *jötunn*).

Beyond Utgard is the outer sea. In it lies the fearsome Miðgarðsormr ('Midgard worm' or 'serpent'). This malevolent creature lies at the far edge of the sea, biting his tail as he encircles Middle Earth.

The Underworld called Niflheim (*Niflheimr*) lies below. Monsters and serpents live in this dark region of ice rivers. They gnaw on the roots of the Tree. Hel lies in the underworld. The realm of the dead, Hel is also the name of the goddess who oversees this place of the dead. Her unlucky charges enter the underworld by passing through the Gates of Hel before crossing the bridge Gjallarbrú. Old Scandinavian Hel was a pre-Christian concept that was understood to be a shadowy region much like the Greek Hades. As the bleak realm, Hel stood in contrast to Valhalla (Valhöll), where Odin's fallen warriors fight and feast each day.

The Prose Edda often provides mythological information through an exchange of questions and responses. For example, in reply to the question, 'How shall we name the sky?' *The Skáldskaparmál* section of *The Prose Edda* lists several kennings (poetic descriptions), revealing a vision of the Norse cosmos.

By calling it Ymir's head and hence the giant's skull, the burden or heavy load on the dwarves, and the helmet of the dwarves Vestri, Austri, Suðri or Norðri (West, East, South, or North), the land of the sun, moon and heavenly bodies, constellations and winds, or the helmet or house of the air, of the earth and of the sun. So said Arnór the Jarls' Poet.

Hvernig skal kenna himin? Svá at kalla hann Ymis haus ok þar af jötuns haus ok erfiði eða byrði dverganna eða hjálm Vestra ok Austra, Suðra, Norðra land sólar ok tungls ok himintungla, vagna ok veðra, hjálma eða hús lofts ok jarðar ok sólar. Svá kvað Arnórr jarlaskáld.

Skaldskaparmál specifies that these lines were said by the Icelandic poet Arnórr Þórðarson jarlaskáld. Although he lived a thousand years ago, we know something about Arnor. In some ways, he is a good example of the depth of information that we have about people who were not especially important. A good poet, Arnór was a seafaring merchant, who lived from ca. 1012-1070s. He often sailed between Norway and the Orkney Islands where it is said that he composed for the Orkney Earls and was remembered in Icelandic sources as jarlaskáld, 'the Jarls' Poet'.

14.2 READING – GANGLERI ASKS ABOUT YGGDRASIL (*GYLFAGINNING*, FROM *THE PROSE EDDA*)

Gylfaginning, the main narrative section of *The Prose Edda*, tells the story of the creation, the struggles and doom of the gods. *Gylfaginning* means the 'deluding (*ginning*) of Gylfi,' and Gylfi, we are told, is a Swedish king who purposefully wanders into the hall of the Æsir in order to learn about them. Gylfi's deluding refers to his being a victim of an elaborate optical illusion (*sjónhverfing*) practiced by three formidable god-like figures whom he meets in the hall.

Gylfaginning is written as a dialogue between Gylfi and the three figures, all manifestations of Odin. Before meeting the Æsir, Gylfi disguises himself as a traveler named Gangleri, a name meaning 'strider,' 'walker,' or 'wanderer.' In the Æsir's majestic but illusory hall, the three figures are seated upon three thrones, one above the other. They name themselves Hár, Jafnhár, and Þriði ('High,' 'Just-As-High,' and 'Third').

Gangleri's dialogue with Hár, Jafnhár, and Þriði quickly becomes a contest of wisdom. Gangleri is told at the start of the contest that he will not escape unharmed unless he grows wiser, a threat which raises the stakes of the mythological exchange. In the following passages, Gangleri learns about the three roots of the World Tree and more.

Gylfaginning (ch 15)

Þá mælti Gangleri: 'Hvar er höfuðstaðrinn eða helgistaðrinn goðanna?'

Hár svarar: 'Þat er at aski Yggdrasils; þar skulu goðin eiga dóma sína hvern dag."

Þá mælti Gangleri: "Hvat er at segja frá þeim stað?"[133]

Þá segir Jafnhár: "Askrinn er allra trjá mestr ok beztr; limar hans[134] dreifask yfir heim allan, ok standa yfir himni. Þrjár rœtr trésins halda því [tré] upp, ok standa afar breitt.

Ein er með Ásum, enn önnur[135] með Hrímþursum, þar sem forðum var Ginnungagap; hin þriðja [rót] stendr yfir Niflheimi, ok undir þeirri rót er Hvergelmir, en Níðhöggr gnagar neðan rótina. En undir þeirri rót, er til Hrímþursa horfir, þar er Mímisbrunnr, er spekt ok

---

[133] **Hvat er at segja frá þeim stað?:** 'What is there to say about that place?'
[134] **limar hans:** 'its limbs' (referring to *askr*, a masculine noun).
[135] **enn önnur:** 'yet another.'

mannvit er í fólgit;[136] ok heitir sá Mímir, er á brunninn.[137] Hann er fullr af vísindum, fyrir því at hann drekkr ór brunninum af horninu Gjallarhorni. Þar kom Alföðr, ok beiddisk eins drykkjar af brunninum, en hann fekk eigi fyrr en hann lagði auga sitt at veði.[138]

Þriðja rót asksins stendr á himni; ok undir þeirri rót er brunnr sá, er mjök er heilagr, er heitir Urðarbrunnr; þar eigu goðin dómstað sinn. Hvern dag ríða Æsir þangat upp um Bifröst; hon[139] heitir ok Ásbrú.

Translate: _____

_____

_____

_____

_____

_____

_____

_____

_____

_____

_____

_____

_____

_____

_____

_____

_____

14.3 READING – NORNS, WELL OF FATE, AND BALDR (*GYLFAGINNING*, FROM *THE PROSE EDDA*)

Gangleri learns that the World Tree is home to many creatures and gods. In the top branches sits a wise eagle with a hawk on its beak. Below among the roots of the Tree lives the monstrous serpent Niðhöggr ('Hateful Striker'). The squirrel Ratatoskr runs up and down between the two carrying insults.

The tree suffers greatly and the Norns who live beside Urðarbrunnr help to sustain it. They decide people's fate at birth. Their names are Urðr 'Fate' or 'That Which Has Become', Verðandi 'Becoming,' and Skuld 'Debt' or 'That Which Should Become.'

Gylfaginning (ch 16)

Þá mælti Gangleri: "Hvat er fleira at segja stórmerkja frá askinum?"[140]

Hár segir: "Mart er þar af at segja.[141] Örn einn sitr í limum asksins, ok er hann margs

---

[136] **er spekt ok mannvit er í fólgit:** 'wherein wisdom and intelligence are hidden.'

[137] **er á brunninn:** 'who possesses the well.' In this case *á* is the 3sg pres form of the verb *eiga*.

[138] **fyrr en hann lagði auga sitt at veði:** 'until he placed his eye as a pledge.'

[139] **hon:** 'it' (referring to *Bifröst*, a feminine noun).

[140] **Hvat er fleira at segja stórmerkja frá askinum?:** 'What more concerning great wonders is there to say about the ash?'

[141] **Mart er þar af at segja:** 'There is much to say of [it].'

vitandi;[142] en í milli augna honum sitr haukr sá, er heitir Veðrfölnir. Íkorni sá, er heitir Ratatoskr, rennr upp ok niðr eptir askinum, ok berr öfundarorð milli arnarins ok Níðhöggs. En fjórir hirtir renna í limum asksins ok bíta barr. Enn svá margir ormar eru í Hvergelmi með Níðhögg, at engi tunga má telja."

"Enn er þat sagt, at nornir þær, er byggja Urðarbrunn, taka hvern dag vatn í brunninum, ok með aurinn þann er liggr um brunninn, ok ausa upp yfir askinn,[143] til þess at eigi skyli limar hans tréna eða fúna.[144] En þat vatn er svá heilagt, at allir hlutir, þeir sem þar koma í brunninn, verða svá hvítir sem[145] hinna sú, er skjall heitir, er innan liggr við eggskurn.[146] Sú dögg, er þaðan af fellr á jörðina, þat kalla menn hunangsfall, ok þar af fœðask býflugur.[147] Fuglar tveir fœðask í Urðarbrunni; þeir heita svanir, ok af þeim fuglum hefir komit þat fuglakyn, er svá heitir."

Translate: _____

_____

_____

_____

_____

_____

_____

_____

_____

_____

_____

_____

Gangleri also asks about the gods. In the passage below, he learns about Baldr, Odin's enigmatic son. (Note the five superlatives.)

Snorra Edda (ch 22)

Þá mælir Gangleri: 'Spyrja vil ek tíðinda af fleiri Ásunum.'

Hár segir: 'Annarr sonr Óðins er Baldr, ok er frá honum gott at segja. Hann er beztr, ok hann lofa allir. Hann er svá fagr álitum ok bjartr, svá at lýsir af honum,[148] ok eitt gras er

---

[142] **ok er hann margs vitandi:** 'and it knows much,' lit 'is knowing of much,' that is, the eagle sees much of the world from the limb of the ash.

[143] If the Norns are themselves pouring their mixture over the ash tree, perhaps this locates Asgard (and, oddly, one of its roots) above, or nearly above, the tree. On the other hand, perhaps it is the root that draws the Norns' mixture up over the tree from the well in Asgard. It is also possible that the Norns are either quite large or quite mobile.

[144] **til þess at eigi skyli limar hans tréna eða fúna:** 'so that its limbs should not dry up or rot.' The verb *skyli* is 3pl present subjunctive of *skulu*.

[145] **svá hvítir sem:** 'as white as.'

[146] **er innan liggr við eggskurn:** 'which lies within against the eggshell.'

[147] **ok þar af fœðask býflugur:** 'and bees nourish themselves on this.'

[148] **svá at lýsir af honum:** 'that light shines from him.'

svá hvítt, at jafnat er til Baldrs brár.[149] Þat er allra grasa hvítast, ok þar eptir mátt þú marka fegrð hans,[150] bæði á hár ok á líki.[151] Hann er vitrastr ásanna ok fegrst talaðr ok líknsamastr. En sú náttúra fylgir honum at engi má haldask dómr hans. Hann býr þar, sem heitir Breiðablik. Þat er á himni.

_____

14.4 Strong Verbs – Class VI

Long -ó- in the past tense is the distinguishing feature of Class VI strong verbs, whose basic pattern is -a- in the infinitive, -ó- in past singular and plural, and -a- in the past participle (*fara, fór, fóru, farinn*). In the present singular, Class VI strong verbs show *i*-umlaut (*ekr, dregr, tekr, ferr, stendr*). Similarly, *flá* and *slá*, with long -á-, have present singular *flær* and *slær*.

a (e, á, æ, ey) INFINITIVE	e 3SG PRES	ó 3SG PAST	ó 3PL PAST	a PPART
fara 'go, travel'	ferr	fór	fóru	farinn
standa 'stand'	stendr	stóð	stóðu	staðinn
aka 'drive'	ekr	ók	óku	ekinn
draga 'drag'	dregr	dró	drógu	dreginn
taka 'take'	tekr	tók	tóku	tekinn
flá 'flay'	flær	fló	flógu	fleginn
slá 'strike'	slær	sló	slógu	sleginn
hefja 'begin'	hefr	hóf	hófu	hafinn
sverja 'swear'	sverr	sór	sóru	svarinn
hlæja 'laugh'	hlær	hló	hlógu	hleginn
deyja 'die'	deyr	dó	dó(u)	dáinn

[149] **eitt gras er svá hvítt, at jafnat er til Baldrs brár:** 'one herb is so white that it is likened to Baldr's eyelash.'
[150] **ok þar eptir mátt þú marka fegrð hans:** 'and accordingly, you can judge his beauty.'
[151] **bæði á hár ok á líki:** 'both of his hair and of his body.'

FARA IN PRESENT AND PAST

	PRESENT				**PAST**		
Sg *ek*	fer	**Pl** *vér*	förum	**Sg** *ek*	fór	**Pl** *vér*	fórum
þú	ferr	*þér*	farið	*þú*	fórt	*þér*	fóruð
hann	ferr	*þeir*	fara	*hann*	fór	*þeir*	fóru

- When the stem ends in -*g*- or -*k*- (*draga, aka*), the past participle has -*e*- instead of -*a*- (*dreginn, ekinn*).
- A few have -*á*- in the infinitive (*flá, slá*) and -*g*- in the past plural (*flógu, slógu*).
- Those with stems ending in -*j*- show *i*-umlaut in the infinitive (*hefja, hlæja*).

14.5 VERB MIDDLE VOICE – INTRODUCTION AND FORMATION

The middle voice in Old Norse primarily describes reflexive actions, actions which the subject performs on him-, her-, or itself. The endings derive from the reflexive pronouns *mik* and *sik*. The sentences below illustrate the difference in meaning between the active and middle voice.

> Hon klæddi barnit. (*3sg past active*)   *She dressed the child.*
> Hon klæddisk. (*3sg past middle*)   *She dressed (herself).*

The middle voice also has reciprocal, passive, and other specialized meanings, which are explained in more detail below.

Formation of the Middle Voice

The middle voice is formed according to the following rules.
- The 1sg ending is -*umk* (*gerumk* 'I become,' *gerðumk* 'I became'). In strong verbs the root vowel of the 1sg matches the root vowel of the 1pl (see the past tense of *gefask* in the chart below).
- Apart from 1sg -*umk*, the middle ending is -*sk*, added directly to the active endings (*nefndi* + *sk* > *nefndisk* 'he named himself,' *börðu* + *sk* > *börðusk* 'they fought [among themselves]'). Two important sub-rules apply here.
    1) -*r*- drops before -*sk* (*gerir* + *sk* > *gerisk*, *eignar* + *sk* > *eignask*).
    2) A dental (-*ð*-, -*d*-, -*t*) plus -*sk* changes to -*zk*, for example, *eignizk* (*eignið* + *sk*) and *kvazk* (*kvað* + *sk*). This change also applies when a loss of -*r* before -*sk* exposes a dental (*kveðr* + *sk* > *kveð* + *sk* > *kvezk*).
- The 1pl sometimes has the ending -*umk* rather than -*umsk* (*brjótumk* or *brjótumsk*).

Below are four examples of weak verbs, *gerask* 'become,' *eignask* 'claim for oneself, get to own,' *berjask* 'fight,' and one strong verb *gefask* 'show oneself, prove good (bad).'

Present	*GERASK*	*EIGNASK*	*BERJASK*	*GEFASK*
Sg *ek*	gerumk	eignumk	berjumk	gefumk
þú	gerisk	eignask	bersk	gefsk
hann	gerisk	eignask	bersk	gefsk
Pl *vér*	gerum(s)k	eignum(s)k	berjum(s)k	gefum(s)k
þér	gerizk	eignizk	berizk	gefizk
þeir	gerask	eignask	berjask	gefask
Past				
Sg *ek*	gerðumk	eignuðumk	börðumk	göfumk
þú	gerðisk	eignaðisk	barðisk	gafzk
hann	gerðisk	eignaðisk	barðisk	gafsk
Pl *vér*	gerðum(s)k	eignuðum(s)k	börðum(s)k	gáfum(s)k
þér	gerðuzk	eignuðuzk	börðuzk	gáfuzk
þeir	gerðusk	eignuðusk	börðusk	gáfusk

Other Forms of the Middle Voice
* Participles add *-sk* to their corresponding active forms.
* Middle past participles are confined to perfect constructions (neuter singular only). For instance, *eignazk* derives from *eignat + sk*, and similarly *farizk* (*farit + sk*), and *litizk* (*litit + sk*). For example, from *Heimskringla* about King Harald Fairhair of Norway: *Hafði hann þá* **eignazk** *land allt* 'He had then **taken for himself** the entire country.'
* Middle present participles are rare. Examples are *brjótandisk* (broken) and *farandisk* (traveled).
* Middle imperatives are also rare. They add *-sk* to their corresponding active forms; for example, the 2sg command *bersk* 'fight!' < *berj + sk*, 2pl *berizk* 'fight among yourselves!,' and 1pl *berjumsk* 'let's fight!'.

14.6 Verb Middle Voice – Meaning and Use

Middle verbs have reflexive, reciprocal, passive, as well as idiomatic meanings.

Reflexive meaning: *Verja* 'defend' becomes *verjask* 'defend oneself.' In the sentence below from *Völsunga saga*, the verbs *bregðask* and *leggjask* have reflexive meanings.

Fáfnir **brásk** í ormslíki	*Fáfnir* **changed himself** *into the likeness of a*
ok **lagðisk** á gullit.	*dragon and* **laid himself** *(lay) on the gold.*

Reciprocal meanings convey actions that two or more parties do *to one another*. Note the reciprocal meanings in the verbs *skilja* 'part' and *berja* 'strike' in the following sentences.

Nú **skiljask** þeir.	*Now they **part** (from each other).*
Brœðr **börðusk**.	*The brothers **fought** (struck each other).*
Nú **berjask** þeir lengi, ok veitti Kaldbeklingum betr.	*They **fight** (struck each other) for a long time and the Kaldbak men had the better of it.*

Middle verbs can have either reflexive or reciprocal meaning; for example, *þeir sjásk* means either 'they see **themselves'** (reflexive) or 'they see **one another'** (reciprocal).

Passive meanings are seen in the following sentences where the verbs *byggva* 'settle' and *draga* 'pull, drag' express actions performed on their subjects.

Ísland **byggðisk**.	*Iceland **was settled**. (Íslendingabók)*
Stafirnir **drógusk** með grunni, allt til þess er þeir váru lausir undir bryggjunum.	*The pilings **were dragged** along the bottom, until finally they were loose under the bridge. (Heimskringla, describing the Vikings pulling down London Bridge.)*

Idiomatic meanings frequently occur, particularly when used in combination with a preposition; for example, *lagðisk út.* Idiomatic meanings can usually be traced back to one of the functions above, although in some instances the connection is obscure. For example:

Eptir þat **lagðisk** Svartr **út*** á heiði þá, er vér köllum Smjörvatnsheiði.	*After that Svartr **set** (literally, 'lay or set himself') out onto that heath, which we call Smjorvatnsheidi. (Vápnfirðinga saga, ch 2)*

   *__leggja__ 'lay, set,' **leggjask** 'set oneself (*reflexive*),' **leggjask út** 'set out (into the wilderness to live as an outlaw)'

[Þorleifr] talði veðrit ótrúligt **gerask***.	*[Thorleifr] said the weather **was becoming** unpredictable. (Vápnfirðinga saga, ch 5)*
Á hans dögum **gerðisk*** í Svíþjóð sultr ok seyra.	*In his days **there was** a famine and starvation in Sweden. (Ynglingasaga)*

   *__gera__ 'make, do,' **gerask** 'make itself (*reflexive*); to become, occur, happen'

Some middle verbs are used in **impersonal** constructions; that is, they are used without an expressed or overt subject in the nominative case. These are often verbs of *perception* (seeing, hearing, etc) where the subject is placed in the dative case.

Hversu **lízk þér á*** mey þessa?	*How **do you like** this maiden?*

   *__líta__ 'look,' **lítask** 'appear, seem,' **lítask [e-m] á** 'seem (good) [to somebody], to be pleasing [to somebody]'

| En er hann sá bauginn, þá **sýndisk*** honum fagr. | *And when he saw the ring, then it **seemed** beautiful to him.* ("Otter's Ransom," from *The Prose Edda*) |

*sýna 'show,' **sýnask** 'seem,' **mér sýnisk** 'it seems to me'

14.7 CARDINAL NUMBERS 1 TO 20

The cardinal numbers one through four decline, agreeing in case, number, and gender with the nouns they modify. When used in the plural, *einn* means 'some.' The first four numbers decline in a manner similar to the definite article and to strong adjectives.

		M	F	N		M	F	N
Sg	nom	einn	ein	eitt	**Pl**	einir	einar	ein
	acc	einn	eina	eitt		eina	einar	ein
	dat	einum	einni	einu		< einum >		
	gen	eins	einnar	eins		< einna >		

	M	F	N	M	F	N	M	F	N
nom	tveir	tvær	tvau	þrír	þrjár	þrjú	fjórir	fjórar	fjögur
acc	tvá	tvær	tvau	þrjá	þrjár	þrjú	fjóra	fjórar	fjögur
dat	< tveim(r) >			< þrim(r) >			< fjórum >		
gen	< tveggja >			< þriggja >			< fjögurra >		

The cardinal numbers *fimm* through *tuttugu* do not decline.

1	einn	6	sex	11	ellifu	16	sextán
2	tveir	7	sjau	12	tólf	17	sjautján
3	þrír	8	átta	13	þrettán	18	átján
4	fjórir	9	níu	14	fjórtán	19	nítján
5	fimm	10	tíu	15	fimmtán	20	tuttugu

For cardinal numbers above 20 and ordinals, see the next Lesson.

14.8 THE PAST SUBJUNCTIVE OF PRETERITE-PRESENT VERBS

These verbs form their past subjunctive stems by applying *i*-umlaut to the past tense stem. Below are five of the most common.

INFINITIVE	*EIGA*	*ÞURFA*	*SKULU*	*MUNU*	*MEGA*
PAST STEM	ÁTT-	ÞURFT-	SKYLD-	MUND-	MÁTT-
Sg ek	ætta	þyrfta	skylda	mynda	mætta
þú	ættir	þyrftir	skyldir	myndir	mættir
hann	ætti	þyrfti	skyldi	myndi	mætti

Past Stem	*Átt-*	*Þurft-*	*Skyld-*	*Mund-*	*Mátt-*
Pl *vér*	ættim	þyrftim	skyldim	myndim	mættim
þér	ættið	þyrftið	skyldið	myndið	mættið
þeir	ætti	þyrfti	skyldi	myndi	mætti

- Variants of past subjunctive preterite-presents without *i*-umlaut sometimes occur: *mynda ~ munda, þyrfta ~ þurfta, skylda ~ skulda, kynna ~ kunna.*

14.9 Two-Syllable Nouns – Syncopated Stems

Syncope refers to the loss of a vowel or consonant in a word. In Old Norse, syncopated nouns are nouns that lose the vowel of their second syllable in certain case forms. In nouns where this occurs, the second syllable is part of the stem and consists of a short vowel and a single consonant. Some examples are the strong masculine nouns *hamarr* (stem *hamar-*), *jökull* (stem *jökul-*), *himinn* (stem *himin-*), *jötunn* (stem *jötun-*) as well as the strong neuter noun *sumar* (stem *sumar-*). These nouns drop the vowel of their second syllable before endings that begin with a vowel, hence syncope occurs in dative *hamri* (*hamar + -i*) but not genitive *hamars* (*hamar + -s*).

Note that names often do not follow this rule, for example, *Gunnarr* (dative *Gunnari*), *Einarr*, and *Reginn*.

	Hamarr (M)	*Jökull (M)*	*Sumar (N)*
Sg *nom*	hamarr	jökull	sumar
acc	hamar	jökul	sumar
dat	hamri	jökli	sumri
gen	hamars	jökuls	sumars
Pl *nom*	hamrar	jöklar	sumur
acc	hamra	jökla	sumur
dat	hömrum	jöklum	sumrum
gen	hamra	jökla	sumra

Transl: *hamarr* 'hammer; crag' *jökull* 'glacier,' *sumar* 'summer'

14.10 Exercise – Vowel Loss in Two-Syllable Nouns

Masculines *aptann* and *þumall* follow the pattern of *hamarr*, and neuter *höfuð* follows the pattern of *sumar*. Decline these below.

	Aptann	*Þumall*	*Höfuð*
Sg *nom*	_____	_____	_____
acc	_____	_____	_____
dat	_____	_____	_____
gen	_____	_____	_____

Pl *nom*	_____	_____	_____
acc	_____	_____	_____
dat	_____	_____	_____
gen	_____	_____	_____

Transl: *aptann* 'evening,' *þumall* 'thumb,' *höfuð* 'head'

EXERCISES

14.11 *Reading Passage Review, Askr Yggdrasils.* [152] Referring to the reading passage, use the words below to fill in the blanks.

rót	hvern	dag	þar	goðin	himni	drykkjar	heilagr
brunninn	auga	þriðja	forðum	gnagar	horninu	vísindum	
svarar	himni	afar	breitt	dóma	beztr	heim	helgistaðrinn

Þá mælti Gangleri: "Hvar er höfuðstaðrinn eða _____ (holy place) goðanna?" Hár _____ (answers): "Þat er at aski Yggdrasils; þar skulu goðin eiga _____ (judgments / court) sína hvern dag." Þá mælti Gangleri: "Hvat er at segja frá þeim stað?" Þá segir Jafnhár: "Askrinn er allra trjá mestr ok _____ (best); limar hans dreifask yfir _____ (earth) allan, ok standa yfir _____ (heaven). Þrjár rœtr trésins halda því upp, ok standa _____ _____ (extremely broad).

Ein er með Ásum, enn önnur með hrímþursum, þar sem _____ (once; of old) var Ginnunga-gap; hin _____ (third) stendr yfir Niflheimi, ok undir þeirri _____ (root) er Hvergelmir, en Niðhöggr _____ (gnaws) neðan rótina.

En undir þeirri rót, er til hrímþursa horfir, _____ (there) er Mímisbrunnr, er spekt ok mannvit er í fólgit; ok heitir sá Mímir, er á _____ (the well). Hann er fullr af _____ (wisdom), fyrir því at hann drekkr ór brunninum af _____ (horn) Gjallarhorni. Þar kom Alföðr, ok beiddisk eins _____ (drink) af brunninum, en hann fekk eigi fyrr en hann lagði _____ (eye) sitt at veði.

Þriðja rót asksins stendr á _____ (heaven); ok undir þeirri rót er brunnr sá, er mjök er _____ (holy), er heitir Urðarbrunnr; þar eigu _____ (the gods) dómstað sinn. _____ _____ (each day) ríða Æsir þangat upp um Bifröst; hon heitir ok Ásbrú."

---

[152] **Askr Yggdrasils:** The name of the World Tree also appears as *Askr Yggdrasill* (two nominatives).

14.12 Reading Passage and Demonstrative Pronoun Review. Fill in the correct form of the demonstrative *sá* in the spaces below.

1. En í milli augna honum sitr haukr _____, er heitir Veðrfölnir.
2. Íkorni _____, er heitir Ratatoskr, rennr upp ok niðr eptir askinum.
3. Enn er þat sagt, at nornir _____, er byggja Urðarbrunn, taka hvern dag vatn í brunninum, ok með aurinn _____ er liggr um brunninn, ok ausa upp yfir askinn.
4. En _____ vatn er svá heilagt, at allir hlutir, _____ sem þar koma í brunninn, verða svá hvítir sem hinna _____, er skjall heitir, er innan liggr við eggskurn.
5. _____ dögg, er þaðan af fellr á jörðina, þat kalla menn hunangsfall, ok þar af fœðask býflugur.
6. Þeir heita svanir, ok af _____ fuglum hefir komit þat fuglakyn, er svá heitir.

14.13 Strong Verbs Class VI. *Fara* is a typical Class VI strong verb with principal parts *ferr, fór, fóru, farinn*. Conjugate *fara* in present and past.

	PRESENT		PAST
Sg *ek*	_____	**Sg** *ek*	_____
þú	_____	*þú*	_____
hann	_____	*hann*	_____
Pl *vér*	_____	**Pl** *vér*	_____
þér	_____	*þér*	_____
þeir	_____	*þeir*	_____

Give the principal parts of the verbs below. Keep in mind that a few Class VI verbs deviate slightly from the pattern of *fara*.

- When the vowel of the infinitive (-*a*-) is followed by a -*k*- or -*g*-, the vowel of the past participle is -*e*-, for example, *taka*, ppart *tekinn*.
- Class VI strong verbs with stem-final -*j*- have shifted vowels in the infinitive rather than -*a*-, for example, *sverja*, ppart *svarinn*.

Ex: ala	*elr, ól, ólu, alinn*	
taka	*tekr, tók, tóku, tekinn*	
1. skapa	_____	
2. aka	_____	
3. mala	_____	
4. grafa	_____	
5. hefja	_____	
6. skaka	_____	

Give the principal parts for the following verbs. Remember -v- drops before past tense -ó-

    Ex: vaxa   *vex, óx, óxu, vaxinn*

    7. vaða _____

    8. sverja _____

Fill in the correct forms of the verbs below.

    Ex: aka (*1sg pres*)   *ek*

    9. ala (*2pl past*) _____   12. hefja (*3sg past*) _____

    10. standa (*1pl pres*)_____   13. grafa (*1pl past*) _____

    11. skapa (*2sg past*) _____   14. sverja (*1sg pres*) _____

14.14 Verbs: Active and Middle Voice. Conjugate the weak verb *gera* and the strong verb *gefa* in the present and past tense.

	GERA			**GEFA**	
PRESENT	*ACTIVE*	*MIDDLE*		*ACTIVE*	*MIDDLE*
Sg *ek*	_____	_____	**Sg** *ek*	_____	_____
þú	_____	_____	*þú*	_____	_____
hann	_____	_____	*hann*	_____	_____
Pl *vér*	_____	_____	**Pl** *vér*	_____	_____
þér	_____	_____	*þér*	_____	_____
þeir	_____	_____	*þeir*	_____	_____
PAST					
Sg *ek*	_____	_____	**Sg** *ek*	_____	_____
þú	_____	_____	*þú*	_____	_____
hann	_____	_____	*hann*	_____	_____
Pl *vér*	_____	_____	**Pl** *vér*	_____	_____
þér	_____	_____	*þér*	_____	_____
þeir	_____	_____	*þeir*	_____	_____

14.15 Review: I-Umlaut. Most verbs show *i*-umlaut in the past subjunctive.

A. Give the shifted outcomes for each of the following vowels and diphthongs.

	VOWEL	**WITH I-UMLAUT**		**VOWEL**	**WITH I-UMLAUT**		**VOWEL**	**WITH I-UMLAUT**
1	u >	_____	5	a >	_____	9	au >	_____
2	ú >	_____	6	á >	_____	10	ö >	_____
3	o >	_____	7	jú >	_____			
4	ó >	_____	8	jó >	_____			

B. Give the 3sg present indicative for each of the following strong verbs.

   Ex: láta   _lætr_____

   1. gróa   _____   5. ljósta _____
   2. standa   _____   6. sitja   _____
   3. nema   _____   7. höggva _____
   4. auka   _____   8. lúka   _____

14.16 The Altuna Church Runestone, Sweden, has runes and a mythic illustrations. The runes on two sides of the stone tell us among other things that it was carved by Balli and Fröysteinn, followers of Hlífsteinn. The stone seems to commemorate two men who burned to death in a fire.

Depicting the god Thor and his adventures was popular in Viking Age Scandinavia, particularly the tale of Thor's battle with the Miðgarðsormr (the Midgard serpent). On the lower part of the third panel one sees a man with a hammer in his hand standing in a boat. From his other hand, a thick line runs into the water with a large object hanging at the end. A serpentine sea monster lurks coiled below the boat.

These elements fit well with the tale of Thor fishing for the Midgard Serpent from *The Prose* and *Poetic Eddas* and several other West Norse literary sources. The giant Hymir invites Thor to go fishing, and the two row far out to sea. Thor baits a strong hook with the head of Hymir's ox and casts

Figure 54. The Altuna Church Runestone, Sweden.

his line into the ocean. He is fishing for the world-encircling serpent.

But hooking the catch is easier than landing it. Thor pushes his feet through the bottom of the boat (note what looks like a foot underneath the boat). Using the sea floor to brace himself, Thor hauls the serpent up. Thor raises his hammer Mjöllnir, but before he can strike the serpent, the terrified giant Hymir cuts the line. The serpent sinks back into the sea. Thor and the serpent will meet again at Ragnarok, where they kill each other.

The stone is an example of the lack of standard spelling with the sound /e/ spelled with R, and /t/ spelled *þ* or *þt*. Rune carvers and writers (the two were not necessarily the same person) appear to have been of varying skills in sounding out spellings. In some instances, it seems that a person knowledgeable in runes gave a drawing of a runic inscription to an illiterate carver who changed, rearranged, or dropped letters.

RUNES

ᚢᛁᚠᛆᛋᛒᛏᚱ᛭ᚠᚢᛚᚴᛆᚼᛒᚱ᛭ᚴᚢᛒᛆᚱ᛭ᛚᛁᛏᚢ᛭ᚱᛁᛋᛆ᛭ᛋᛒᛏᛁᚿ᛭ᛌᛒᛏᛁ᛭
ᛌᛁᚿ᛭ᚠᛆᛒᚢᚱ᛭ᚢᛚᚠᛆᛋᛒ᛭ᛆᚱᚠᛆᛋᛏ᛭ᛒᚢᛁ᛭ᚠᛁᛒᚱᚴᛆᚵ᛭ᛒᚢᚱᚿᚢ᛭ᛁᚿ᛭ᛒᛁᚱ᛭
ᛒᛆᛚᛁ᛭ᚠᚱᛁᛋᛒᛁᚿ᛭ᛚᛁᛒ᛭ᛚᛁᚠᛌᛒᛁᚿᛌ᛭ᚱᛁᛋᛒᚢ

TRANSLITERATION

uifasþtr fulkahþr kuþar litu resa sþten Rþti sen faþur ulfasþ arfast
beþi feþrkag burnu en þir bali fresþen liþ lifsþens risþu

STANDARDIZED OLD NORSE

Véfastr, Fólkaðr, [ok] Guðmarr létu reisa stein eptir sinn föður Hólmfast [ok] Arnfast. Bæði feðgar brunnu. En þeir Balli [ok] Fröysteinn lið Hlífsteins[153] ristu.

VOCABULARY

Arnfastr <-s> *m* Arnfast (*personal name*)

Balli (*also* **Baldi**) *m* Balli (*personal name*)

❖**báðir** <*f* báðar, *n* bæði, *gen* beggja > *adj pron dual* both

brenna <brann, brunnu, brunninn> *vb intrans* burn, be consumed by flame

feðgar *m pl* father (feðr) and son(s)

Fólkaðr (*also* **Fólkvarðr**) <-ar> *m* Folkad (*personal name*)

Fröysteinn (*also* **Freysteinn**) <-s> *m* Froystein (*personal name*)

Guðmarr <-s> *m* Gudmar (*personal name*)

Hlífsteinn <-s> *m* Hlifstein (*personal name*)

Hólmfastr <-s> *m* Holmfast (*personal name*)

❖**láta** <lætr, lét, létu, látinn> *vb* let, allow, permit; have something done

❖**lið** *n* band of men, following, troops

reisa <-ti, -tr> *vb* raise; **láta reisa [stein]** have a stone raised

rísta <rístr, reist, ristu, ristinn> *vb* cut; carve, engrave

Véfastr <-s> *m* Vefast (*personal name*)

Translate:_____
_____
_____

---

[153] **...þeir Balli ok Fröysteinn lið Hlífsteins...:** '...those followers of Hlifstein, Balli and Froystein...'

LESSON 15
THE SAGA OF KING HROLF KRAKI

Hálfsögð er saga, ef einn segir
(A story is only half-told, if only one [person] tells it)

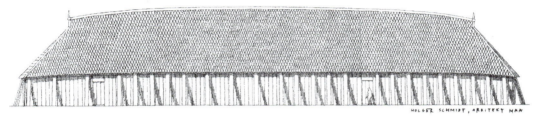

Figure 55. Reconstruction of the Ninth-Century Great Hall at Lejre, Denmark (48.3 meters/52.8 yards in length). A massive wooden building, this princely Viking Age dwelling covered approximately 500 sq. meters (598 sq. yards). Its size can be judged by the man entering the door toward the middle right. The gables at either end of the curved roof ridge are shown as ported to let smoke escape.

15.1 READING – BODVAR RESCUES HOTT FROM THE BONE PILE (*HRÓLFS SAGA KRAKA*)

The Saga of King Hrolf (*Hrólfs saga kraka*) is one of the major *fornaldarsögur*. It recounts the fortunes of King Hrolf, a warrior chieftain who ruled in Denmark in the sixth century long before the Viking Age. Hrolf was widely remembered in the medieval North during the Viking period and afterward as one of the most magnificent kings of 'ancient times.' His saga, which draws on a long oral tradition, narrates the history of Hrolf's treacherous family and the exploits of his twelve champions. Hrolf is mentioned in numerous Icelandic texts, including *The Prose Edda*, *Ynglinga saga*, and *Landnámabók*, and *Hrolf's Saga* shares many affinities with the Old English verse epic *Beowulf*.

Hrolf's greatest champion was Bodvar Bjarki (*Böðvarr Bjarki*). Bodvar's father, Bjorn, was turned into a bear by his scheming stepmother, and Bodvar himself possesses the power of shape-shifting. While journeying to King Hrolf's hall at Lejre (Hleiðargarðr), Bodvar meets an old woman. She tells him the tale of her cowardly son Hott (Höttr), who lives in a pile of bones in the king's stronghold. The king's men make sport of throwing their gnawed meat bones at Hott in the bone pile. The old woman implores Bodvar that when he reaches the king's court, he throw only small bones at her son.

Figure 56. End-View of the Ninth-Century Great Hall at Lejre (11.5 meters/12.6 yards in width) showing the covered walkway under the roof eaves.

The passage below relates how Bodvar rescues Hott, who eventually becomes one of King Hrolf's champions.

Hrólfs saga kraka (ch 23)

Síðan fór Böðvarr leið sína til Hleiðargarðs. Hann kømr til konungs atsetu. Böðvarr leiðir síðan hest sinn á stall hjá konungs hestum hinum beztu[m] ok spyrr engan at;[154] gekk síðan inn í höllina, ok var þar fátt manna.

Hann sezk útarliga,[155] ok sem hann hefir verit þar lítla hríð, heyrir hann þrausk nökkut útar í hornit í einhverjum stað. Böðvarr lítr þangat ok sér at mannshönd kømr upp ór mikilli beinahrúgu, er þar lá; höndin var svört mjök. Böðvarr gengr þangat til ok spyrr hverr þar væri í beinahrúgunni. Þá var honum svarat[156] ok heldr óframliga: 'Höttr heiti ek, bokki sæll.'

'Hví ertu hér,' segir Böðvarr, 'eða hvat gørir þú?'

Höttr segir, 'Ek gøri mér skjaldborg, bokki sæll.'

Böðvarr sagði, 'Vesall ertu þinnar skjaldborgar!'[157] Böðvarr þrífr til hans ok hnykkir honum upp ór beinahrúgunni.

Höttr kvað þá hátt við ok mælti, 'Nú viltu mér bana! Gør eigi þetta, svá sem ek hefi nú vel um búizk áðr, en þú hefir nú rótat í sundr skjaldborg minni, ok hafða ek nú svá gört hana háva útan at mér,[158] at hon hefir hlíft mér við öllum höggum ykkar,[159] svá at ekkert[160] högg hafa komit á mik lengi, en ekki var hon enn svá búin sem ek ætlaða hon skyldi verða.'[161]

Böðvarr mælti: 'Ekki muntu fá skjaldborgina gerða lengr.'[162]

Höttr mælti ok grét: 'Skaltu nú bana mér, bokki sæll?'

Böðvarr bað hann ekki hafa hátt, tók hann upp síðan ok bar hann út ór höllinni ok til vatns nökkurs sem þar var í nánd, ok gáfu fáir at þessu gaum,[163] ok þó[164] hann upp allan. Síðan gekk Böðvarr til þess rúms sem hann hafði áðr tekit,[165] ok leiddi eptir sér Hött ok þar setr hann Hött hjá sér. En hann er svá hræddr at skelfr á honum leggr ok liðr,[166] en þó

---

[154] **ok spyrr engan at:** 'but he asks no one about it.' Bodvar does not seek permission to stable his horse among the king's best.

[155] **Hann sezk útarliga:** 'He seats himself far out (from the center of the hall).'

[156] **Þá var honum svarat:** 'Then an answer was given to him,' *lit* 'then it was answered to him.'

[157] **Vesall ertu þinnar skjaldborgar:** 'You and your shield-wall are pathetic.'

[158] **hafða ek nú svá gört hana háva útan at mér:** 'I had built it (the shield-wall) so high around me'

[159] **ykkar:** although Hott uses the genitive of the dual pronoun *þit* here, the sense is the same as the genitive of the plural pronoun *þér*. Though an old saga, *Hrolf's Saga* survives in rather late manuscript copies, and in later Icelandic usage *ykkar* becomes indeclinable and is used instead of the plural, as is the case here. Evidently Hott takes Bodvar to be in league with Hrolf's champions.

[160] **ekkert:** a later form of *ekki*, the nom n sg form of the pronoun *engi*. Ekkert agrees with *högg*.

[161] **en ekki var hon enn svá búin sem ek ætlaða hon skyldi verða:** 'but it was not yet as complete as I had intended it should be' (*skyldi*: 3sg past subj).

[162] **fá skjaldborgina gerða lengr:** 'be able to build the shield-wall any longer.' *Gerða* agrees with *skjaldborgina* and is the feminine accusative singular form of the past participle *gerðr*. When used with a following past participle, *fá* takes the metaphorical sense 'to be able to.'

[163] **gáfu fáir at þessu gaum:** 'few paid attention to this.'

[164] **þó:** 3sg past of *þvá* 'to wash.'

[165] That is, the sitting and sleeping bench that Bodvar had taken earlier.

[166] **leggr ok liðr:** 'leg and joint,' a stock expression that gives the sense, 'all over his body.'

þykkisk hann skilja, at[167] þessi maðr vill hjálpa sér. Eptir þat kveldar ok drífa menn í höllina ok sjá Hrólfs kappar at Höttr er settr á bekk upp, ok þykkir þeim sá maðr hafa gört sik œrit djarfan, er þetta hefir til tekit.[168] Illt tillit hefir Höttr, þá er hann sér kunningja sína, því at hann hefir illt eitt af þeim reynt;[169] hann vill lifa gjarnan ok fara aptr í beinahrúgu sína, en Böðvarr heldr honum, svá at hann náir ekki í brottu at fara,[170] því at hann þóttisk ekki jafnberr fyrir höggum þeira, ef hann næði þangat at komask,[171] sem hann er nú.

Hirðmenn hafa nú sama vanda, ok kasta fyrst beinum smám um þvert gólfit til Böðvars ok Hattar. Böðvarr lætr sem hann sjái eigi þetta.[172] Höttr er svá hræddr at hann tekr eigi mat

né drykk, ok þykkir honum þá ok þá[173] sem hann muni vera lostinn.[174]

Ok nú mælti Höttr til Böðvars: 'Bokki sæll, nú ferr at þér stór knúta, ok mun þetta ætlat okkr til nauða.'[175] Böðvarr bað hann þegja. Hann setr við holan lófann[176] ok tekr svá við knútunni; þar fylgir leggrinn með.[177] Böðvarr sendi aptr knútuna ok setr á þann sem kastaði, ok rétt framan í hann[178] með svá harðri svipan at hann fekk bana. Sló þá miklum ótta yfir hirðmennina.[179]

15.2 CULTURE – *THE SAGA OF KING HROLF KRAKI* AND *BEOWULF*

The story of *Hrolf's Saga* was well known before the saga was written as a comprehensive prose rendering in thirteenth or fourteenth-century Iceland. Hrolf's story has close similarities with *Beowulf*, written from the eighth to the early eleventh centuries. Both compositions draw on a common legendary tradition of events concerning the actions of the fifth- and/or sixth-century Danish kingdom of the Skjoldungs (OE Scyldinga). Although separated by time and place, the later Icelandic and the earlier Danish narratives agree on many of the characters and the settings. This affinity is based on shared oral traditions.

Hrolf's Saga and *Beowulf* tell of a powerful champion whose bear-like characteristics may echo distant cultic practices. The similarities are striking. Both heroes, Beowulf and Bodvar Bjarki, begin their journeys to Denmark from the land of the Goths (ON Gautar, OE Geatas, Modern Swedish Götar). Each is related to the Danish king and both have names that connect to the word 'bear.' Bjarki means 'little bear,' and Beowulf is a compound

---

[167] **en þó þykkisk hann skilja, at...:** 'although he seemed to understand that...'

[168] **er þetta hefir til tekit:** 'who has undertaken this.'

[169] **hann hefir illt eitt af þeim reynt:** 'he has experienced only evil from them.'

[170] **svá at hann náir ekki í brottu at fara:** 'so that he is not able to get away.'

[171] **ef hann næði þangat at komask:** 'if he should be able to get to there' (*næði*: 3sg past subj of *ná*).

[172] **Böðvarr lætr sem hann sjái eigi þetta:** 'Bodvar lets on as if he does not see it' (*sjái*: 3sg pres subj of *sjá*).

[173] **þá ok þá:** 'nearly every moment.'

[174] **sem hann muni vera lostinn:** 'as if he would be struck' (*muni*: 3sg pres of *munu*).

[175] **mun þetta ætlat okkr til nauða:** 'that will be intended to do us harm.'

[176] **Hann setr við holan lófann:** 'He readies his open palm.'

[177] **með:** 'along with it (i.e., the knucklebone).'

[178] **rétt framan í hann:** 'right in his face.' *Framan*, 'from the front,' indicates that Bodvar and the assailant face each other across the floor.

[179] **Sló þá miklum ótta yfir hirðmennina:** 'Great fear fell upon the king's men.'

meaning 'bee-wolf,' a plausible description for a bear. In each instance, a monster is threatening the Danish king's hall and attacks the hapless retainers of the king at night. The creatures are described differently in the two texts. In *Hrolf's Saga* the attacking monster is called a 'great troll' but then described as a fire-breathing, winged dragon. *Beowulf's* monsters, Grendel and his mother, are more chthonic. They are human-haters who live in a watery underground in the dangerous outlands. Years after Beowulf kills Grendel, when Beowulf is an old king, he is killed by a fiery dragon.

In addition to the characters Beowulf and Bodvar Bjarki, *Hrolf's Saga* and *Beowulf* share other similarities. In *Hrolf's Saga*, King Hroar is a notable figure ruling over the northern English kingdom of Northumberland, while his counterpart in *Beowulf*, King Hrothgar (Hrōðgār), is king of the Danes. Hrothgar is the builder of the magnificent hall Heorot, the object of the monster Grendel's depredations. Although somewhat different, a theme of a treacherous uncle-nephew relationship exists in both the Anglo-Saxon and Scandinavian stories. Halga, the OE counterpart to Helgi in *Hrolf's Saga*, appears in *Beowulf* as a son of Healfdene and brother of Hrothgar. These relationships agree with the saga, where King Halfdan is Helgi's father and Hroar is his brother. In Old English Hrólfr is Hrōðulf.

Old Norse *Hrólfs Saga*, Old English *Bēowulf*, Saxo Grammaticus' Latin *Gesta Danorum (History of the Danes)*, and the Latin paraphrase of the Old Norse *Skjöldunga Saga* often speak of the same or similar characters. Below is a table giving the comparable names and characters in the different stories.

EQUIVALENT CHARACTERS IN OLD NORSE, OLD ENGLISH AND LATIN ACCOUNTS OF KING HROLF KRAKI

Hrólfs Saga	Skjöldunga Saga	Gesta Danorum	Bēowulf
Aðils	Adillus	Athislus	Ēadgils
Böðvarr Bjarki	Bodvarus	Biarco	Bēowulf
Fróði	Frodo	Frotho	Frōda
Hálfdan	Halfdanus	Haldanus	Healfdene
Helgi	Helgo	Helgo	Hālga
Hróarr	Roas	Roe	Hrōðgār
Hrólfr Kraki	Rolfo Krake	Roluo Krake	Hrōðulf
Skjöldr	Skioldus	Skioldus	Scyld Scēfing
Yrsa	Yrsa	Vrsa	Yrse

15.3 ENCLITIC PRONOUNS

Pronouns tacked onto the ends of verbs are known as enclitic pronouns (a Greek term meaning 'leaning on'). Some examples in Old Norse are *ertu, muntu, veiztu* for *ert þú, munt þú,* and *veizt þú,* with *þú* becoming (t)*u*. In *heyrðu* (*heyr þú*) and *segðu* (*seg þú*), the intial *þ-* of *þú* changes to *-ð-*. With the pronoun *ek*, the initial vowel is usually lost, hence *mættak* from *mætta ek,* and *heyrðak* from *heyrða ek*. The vowel loss is sometimes indicated in texts by an apostrophe (*mætta'k* and *heyrða'k*). The readings in this lesson from *Hrolf's Saga* contain several examples of enclitic pronouns.

'Hví **ertu** hér,' segir Böðvarr, 'eða hvat gørir þú?'	*'Why are you here,' said Bodvar, 'and what are you doing?'*
Höttr kvað þá hátt við ok mælti, 'Nú **viltu** mér bana!'	*Hott then replied loudly and said, 'Now you want to kill me!'*
Böðvarr mælti: 'Ekki **muntu** fá skjaldborgina gerða lengr.'	*Bodvar said, 'You will not get your shield wall made any longer.'*
Höttr mælti ok grét: '**Skaltu** nú bana mér, bokki sæll?'	*Hott spoke and cried, 'Are you going to kill me now, good sir?'*

15.4 Strong Verbs – Class VII

Class VII strong verbs fall into five subgroups. In most instances, the vowels of the infinitive and past participle are the same (*heita, heitinn*). The vowels of the past singular and plural are also the same (*hét, hétu*). Like all strong verbs, Class VII verbs show *i*-umlaut in the present singular (**ey**kr, **bý**r, **fæ**r, **ge**ngr, **læ**tr, **blœ**tr).

	Infinitive	*3sg Pres*	*3sg Past*	*3pl Past*	*Ppart*
(i)	heita 'to be named'	heitr	hét	hétu	heitinn
	leika 'to play'	leikr	lék	léku	leikinn
(ii)	auka 'to increase'	eykr	jók	jóku	aukinn
	búa 'to live, dwell'	býr	bjó	bjoggu	búinn
	hlaupa 'to leap'	hleypr	hljóp	hljópu	hlaupinn
	höggva 'to strike'	høggr	hjó	hjoggu	höggvinn
(iii)	fá 'to get'	fær	fekk	fengu	fenginn
	falla 'to fall'	fellr	féll	féllu	fallinn
	ganga 'to walk, go'	gengr	gekk	gengu	genginn
	halda 'to hold'	heldr	hélt	héldu	haldinn
(iv)	blása 'to blow'	blæsr	blés	blésu	blásinn
	gráta 'to weep'	grætr	grét	grétu	grátinn
	láta 'to let'	lætr	lét	létu	látinn
	ráða 'to rule'	ræðr	réð	réðu	ráðinn
	blóta 'to worship, sacrifice'	blœtr	blét	blétu	blótinn
(v)	snúa 'to turn'	snýr	sneri~snøri	sneru~snøru	snúinn
	sá 'to sow'	sær	seri~søri	seru~søru	sáinn
	róa 'to row'	rœr	reri~røri	reru~røru	róinn

The past tense of a handful of Class VII strong verbs (subgroup v), including *sá* 'sow,' *róa* 'row,' *snúa* 'turn,' *gnúa* 'rub,' and *gróa* 'grow,' is unusual in two ways. First, their stems in the past tense end in *-er-* or *-ør-*. For example, *sá* has past tense stem *ser-~sør-*, and *róa* has past tense stem *rer-~rør-*. Second, these strong verbs use the past tense endings of weak verbs. For example, the past tense of *sá* conjugates *sera, serir, seri, serum, seruð,* *seru*. There are also variants with stems ending in *-ør-* (3sg past *seri~søri*).

Handbooks of Old Norse often refer to Class VII as the 'reduplicating class,' so-called because at an earlier stage of the language these verbs formed their past tense stems by adding a partial copy of the verb stem as a prefix. Remnants of this process can be seen in the past tense of the Old Icelandic verbs *róa* (3sg past *reri*) and *sá* (3sg past *seri*).

15.5 VERBS – SUBJUNCTIVE MIDDLE

The middle voice uses the same set of subjunctive endings for both present and past tense. Apart from 1sg *-umk*, these are formed by adding *-sk* to the active subjunctive endings, for example, *hann gerisk* (*gerir + sk > gerisk*), *þér gerizk* (*gerið + sk > gerizk*), and *þeir gerisk* (*geri + sk > gerisk*). *Gerask* and *brjótask* are conjugated below in the middle subjunctive.

SUBJUNCTIVE MIDDLE ENDINGS		
	SINGULAR	PLURAL
1ˢᵗ	-umk	-im(s)k
2ⁿᵈ	-isk	-izk
3ʳᵈ	-isk	-isk

PRESENT	*GERASK*	*BRJÓTASK*		PAST	*GERASK*	*BRJÓTASK*
Sg *ek*	gerumk	brjótumk		**Sg** *ek*	gerðumk	brytumk
þú	gerisk	brjótisk		*þú*	gerðisk	brytisk
hann	gerisk	brjótisk		*hann*	gerðisk	brytisk
Pl *vér*	gerimsk	brjótim(s)k		**Pl** *vér*	gerðimsk	brytim(s)k
þér	gerizk	brjótizk		*þér*	gerðizk	brytizk
þeir	gerisk	brjótisk		*þeir*	gerðisk	brytisk

The 1pl subjunctive sometimes has the ending *-imk* (*brjótimk*) instead of *-imsk* (*brjótimsk*).

15.6 VERBS – SUBJUNCTIVE AND INDIRECT SPEECH IN MAIN AND DEPENDENT CLAUSES

In main clauses the subjunctive is used to express a wish, sometimes with the force of a command, or to describe events which are hypothetical, unlikely, or otherwise unreal.

Friðr **sé** með yðr.	*Peace **be** with you.*
En er Hœnir var staddr á þingum eða stefnum svá at Mímir var eigi nær ok **kœmi** nökkur vandamál fyrir hann, þá svaraði hann æ inu sama. '**Ráði** aðrir,' sagði hann.	*And when Hoenir was present at the asssemblies or meetings such that Mimir was not nearby and a difficult matter **would come** before him, then he answered always the same. **Let others decide**,' he said. (The Prose Edda)*

In dependent clauses the subjunctive is most frequently encountered in conditional sentences expressing possibility (Consider a sentence in English such as: If I were to go to Iceland, I would have to eat hákarl [cured shark]) or speculation about a contrary-to-fact state of affairs (If I had lived in medieval Norway, I would have gone raiding in England).

The subjunctive is also frequently used in indirect speech (speech that is reported rather than quoted) and indirect questions. Below are some examples from *Hrólfs saga kraka*.

Höttr er svá hræddr at hann tekr eigi mat né drykk, ok þykkir honum þá ok þá sem hann **muni** vera lostinn. (possibility)	*Hott was so afraid that he took neither food nor drink, and it seemed to him again and again that he **would** be struck.*
Konungr sagði, at henni **væri** þat makligt fyrir draumblæti sitt ok stórlæti. (indirect speech)	*The king said that it **was** fitting, because of her pride and arrogance.*

Indirect speech recounts what someone has said without using his or her exact words. Old Norse often renders indirect speech in a construction known as the **accusative subject plus infinitive**. In this construction the subject of the indirect statement stands in the *accusative* case and the verb appears as an *infinitive*. (Consider a sentence in English such as: *He knew him to be a man of honor.*) In the examples below the indirect statements are in bold.

Direct Speech:

Hann hœldi Úlfari mjök ok kvað, 'Þú ert göfugr maðr.'	*He praised Ulfar greatly and said, 'You are a noble man.'*

Indirect Speech:

Hann hœldi Úlfari mjök ok **kvað hann vera** göfgan mann.	*He praised Ulfar greatly and **said he was** a noble man.*

When the subject of the main clause refers to the same person as the subject of the indirect statement (**Harald** said **he** [*himself*] *was the rightful heir*), the reflexive pronoun *sik* is used. However, *sik* (the accusative subject) does not stand as an independent word but is attached in the reduced form -*sk* to the end of the verb of the main clause.

Direct Speech:

Úlfarr kvað, 'Ek á arf eptir bróður minn at taka.'	*Ulfar said, 'I ought to take the inheritance after my brother.'*

Indirect Speech:

Úlfarr **kvazk** arf **eiga** eptir bróður sinn at taka. (kvazk = kvað + sk)	*Ulfar **said he ought** to take the inheritance after his brother.*

When the subject of an impersonal construction starts off in the dative or genitive case, it stays in that case when moving into indirect speech.

Direct Speech:

Geitir kvað, 'Henni tóksk óvitrliga til.'	*Geitir said, 'She behaved foolishly.'*

Indirect Speech:

Geitir **kvað henni hafa** óvitrliga til tekisk.   *Geitir **said she had** behaved foolishly.*

15.7 PAST INFINITIVES OF THE VERBS *MUNDU, SKYLDU,* AND *VILDU*

The verbs *munu* and *skulu* have special forms *mundu* and *skyldu,* known as past infinitives. These are only used in indirect speech with the accusative subject and infinitive construction and typically occur when the verb of the main clause is in the past tense. *Mundu* and *skyldu* are usually translated into English as 'would' or 'should.' *Mundu* and *skyldu* are commonly used in prose; another past infinitive *vildu* (for *vilja*) occurs but is rare.

Ok því næst œpir Höttr slíkt sem hann má ok kvað **dýrit mundu gleypa** hann. (*Hrólfs saga*)	*And then Hott cried out as loud as he could and said the **beast would swallow** him.*
Þorbrandssynir kváðu **hann** eigi **mundu** meira **stjórna**, ef hann hirði eigi um slíkt. (*Eyrbyggja saga*)	*The sons of Thorbrand said that **he would command** no more, if he did not care for such [matters].*
Hrafn kvazk enga gripi **vildu** á frest **selja**. (*Vápnfirðinga saga*)	*Hrafn said **he** didn't **want to sell** any [of his] goods on credit.*

In poetry, past infinitives such as *mæltu* 'have spoken' and *fóru* 'have gone' are used more freely.

Þær **hykk** (hygg ek) **mæltu** þvígit fleira. (*Oddrúnargrátr 7*)	*I believe them to have spoken not much more. (I do not believe they said much more.)*
Nú **frák** (frá ek) Þórólf und lok **fóru**. (*Egil's saga, verse 1*)	*Now I heard Þórolfr to have passed away.*

15.8 CARDINAL NUMBERS ABOVE 20

Cardinal numbers up to 20 were covered in the preceding lesson. Numbers above 20 are counted as follows: *tuttugu ok einn* (or *einn ok tuttugu*), *tuttugu ok tveir,* etc.

Multiples of ten from 30 to 110 are expressed with the plural of the masculine noun *tigr* 'ten.' *Tigr* declines as a Type 3 strong noun: *tigr, tig, tigi, tigar; tigir, tigu, tigum, tiga* (variants include *tegr, togr, tugr,* and *tøgr*). In the numbers 30 (*þrír tigir*) and 40 (*fjórir tigir*), *þrír* and *fjórir* decline.

30	þrír tigir	60	sex tigir	90	níu tigir
40	fjórir tigir	70	sjau tigir	100	tíu tigir
50	fimm tigir	80	átta tigir	110	ellifu tigir

When one is counting in multiples of ten with *tigr*, the noun is in the **genitive** case.

Hann sá þrjá tigu mann**a**.	*He saw thirty men.*
Fjórir tigir skip**a** sigldu til Íslands.	*Forty ships sailed to Iceland.*
Hann átti fimm tigu yxn**a**.	*He owned fifty oxen.*

All numbers above 20 which end in 1, 2 ,3, or 4 decline like 1, 2, 3, or 4.

Hann drap tuttugu ok tvá (*m acc*) menn.	*He killed twenty-two men.*
Fjórir tigir ok þrjú (*n nom*) skip sigldu til Íslands.	*Forty-three ships sailed to Iceland.*
Hann átti sex tigu ok átta (*indecl*) sauði.	*He owned sixty-eight sheep.*

When the number modifying the subject ends in 1 (for example 1, 21, 51, 101), the verb is in the singular. For all other numbers, the verb is conjugated in the plural.

Einn maðr ok tuttugu **bjó** í Vápnafirði.	*Twenty-one men lived in Weapons Fjord.*
Tveir menn ok tuttugu **bjuggu** í Vápnafirði.	*Twenty-two men lived in Weapons Fjord.*

The neuter noun *hundrað* and feminine *þúsund* were based on the number 12. In most cases in Old Norse texts, *hundrað* referred to the 'long hundred' 120 and *þúsund* to the 'long thousand' 1200.

	HUNDRAÐ				**ÞÚSAND**		
Sg *nom*	hundrað	**Pl**	hundruð	**Sg** *nom*	þúsund	**Pl**	þúsundir
acc	hundrað		hundruð	*acc*	þúsund		þúsundir
dat	hundraði		hundruðum	*dat*	þúsund		þúsundum
gen	hundraðs		hundraða	*gen*	þúsundar		þúsunda

- *Hundrað* is a neuter noun and has *u*-umlaut in the nominative and accusative plural.
- Large numbers were generally counted by tens and duodecimal hundreds: *tíu hundruð* '1200,' *ellefu hundruð* '1320,' *tólf hundruð* '1440,' etc.
- As with *tigr*, nouns counted with *hundrað* and *þúsund* stand in the genitive case, for example *tíu hundruð manna* '1200 men,' *þúsund skipa* '1200 ships.'

15.9 ORDINAL NUMBERS

Ordinal numbers denote ordering or ranking, that is, 'first, second, third.' With the exception of *fyrstr* and *annarr*, ordinal numbers always take weak adjective endings. Note that *þriði* has a stem-final *-j-* (*it þriðja haust*).

Fyrstr is a superlative adjective and takes both strong and weak endings, for example *fyrstr maðr, inn fyrsti fugl*. *Annarr* is a pronoun and hence has no weak declension.

1st	fyrstr	6th	sétti	11th	ellifti	16th	sextándi
2nd	annarr	7th	sjaundi	12th	tólfti	17th	sjautándi
3rd	þriði <-j->	8th	átti, áttundi	13th	þrettándi	18th	átjándi
4th	fjórði	9th	níundi	14th	fjórtándi	19th	nítjándi
5th	fimmti	10th	tíundi	15th	fimmtándi	20th	tuttugandi

Ordinal numbers above twenty are counted *tuttugandi ok fyrsti* (or *fyrsti ok tuttugandi*), *tuttugandi ok annarr*, *tuttugandi ok þriði*, etc. Counting by tens the ordinals from thirty to ninety are as follows.

30th	þrítugandi	70th	sjautugandi
40th	fertugandi	80th	áttugandi
50th	fimmtugandi	90th	nítugandi
60th	sextugandi		

There are no corresponding ordinals for *hundrað* and *þúsund*. Ordinal numbers are sometimes used in the expression of cardinal numbers. For instance, the number 25, a cardinal number, can be expressed in several ways: *tuttugu ok fimm*, *fimm ins **þriðja** tigar* ('five of the third ten'), or *hálfr **þriði** tigr* ('half the third ten').

15.10 EXERCISE – ORDINAL NUMBERS
The names of the horses of the gods are given in *Gylfaginning*. Fill in the correct form of the ordinal numbers in the spaces below.

Hestar ásanna heita svá: Sleipnir er beztr, hann á Óðinn, hann hefr átta fœtr.

_____ (2nd) er Glaðr, _____ (3rd) Gyllir,

_____ (4th) Glenr, _____ (5th) Skeiðbrimir,

_____ (6th) Silfrintoppr, _____ (7th) Sinir,

_____ (8th) Gils, _____ (9th) Falhófnir,

_____ (10th) Gulltoppr, _____ (11th) Léttfeti.

15.11 READING – BODVAR KILLS THE MONSTER (*HRÓLFS SAGA KRAKA*)

In the passage below from *Hrolf's Saga,* Bodvar sets out against the monster terrorizing Denmark. Having been forbidden by the king to engage the beast, Bodvar steals away in the night with Hott in tow.

Hrólfs saga kraka (ch 23)

Ok sem leið at jólum, gerðusk menn ókátir. Böðvarr spyrr Hött hverju þat sætti.[180] Hann

---

[180] **Böðvarr spyrr Hött hverju þat sætti:** 'Bodvar asked Hott what caused that.'

segir honum, at dýr eitt hafi þar komit tvá vetr í samt,[181] mikit ok ógurligt, 'ok hefir vængi á bakinu, ok flýgr þat jafnan. Tvau haust hefir þat nú hingat vitjat ok gert mikinn skaða. Á þat bíta ekki vápn, en kappar konungs koma ekki heim, þeir sem at eru einna mestir.'[182] Böðvarr mælti: 'Ekki er höllin svá vel skipuð sem ek ætlaða ef eitt dýr skal hér eyða ríki ok fé konungsins.' Höttr segir, 'Þat er ekki dýr, heldr er þat mesta tröll.'...

Böðvarr leyndisk í burt um nóttina. Hann lætr Hött fara með sér, ok gerir hann þat nauðugr, ok kallaði hann sér stýrt í bana. Böðvarr segir, at betr mundi takask.[183] Þeir ganga í burt frá höllinni, ok verðr Böðvarr at bera hann, svá er hann hræddr. Nú sjá þeir dýrit. Ok því næst œpir Höttr slíkt sem hann má ok kvað dýrit mundu gleypa hann.[184] Böðvarr bað bikkjuna hans þegja ok kastar honum niðr í mosann, ok þar liggr hann ok eigi með öllu óhræddr.[185] Eigi þorir hann heim at fara heldr. Nú gengr Böðvarr móti dýrinu...Sverðit gengr ór slíðrum, ok leggr þegar undir bœgi dýrsins ok svá fast, at stóð í hjartanu, ok datt þá dýrit til jarðar dautt niðr.

Bodvar then picks Hott up. He carries Hott to the dead beast and forces him to drink two mouthfuls of its blood and to eat some of the heart. Hott grows strong and courageous. He no longer fears Hrolf's retainers, and he is given a new name. Hott becomes Hjalti, meaning 'sword hilt.' King Hrolf later mentions that Bodvar's greatest achievement was making Hott into one of the king's champions.

15.12 CULTURE – LEGENDARY LEJRE (HLEIÐARGARÐR)

According to *Hrolf's Saga*, the seat of the Skjoldung dynasty was Lejre (*Hleiðargarðr*). There is little doubt that in the early Middle Ages Lejre was a center of power, and several medieval texts preserve the memory of Lejre's social and political prominence. The German chronicler Thietmar of Merseburg knew Lejre as an important capital and pagan cult site. In 1015 he wrote the following description of Lejre based on information learned earlier in 934, when the German Emperor Henry I had invaded Denmark:

> Because I have heard marvellous things about their ancient sacrifices, I will not allow these to pass by unmentioned. In those parts, the centre of the kingdom is a placed called Leire, in the region of Seeland. Every nine years, in the month of January, after the day on which we celebrate the appearance of the Lord [6 January], they all convene here and offer their gods a burnt offering of ninety-nine

---

[181] **dýr eitt hafi þar komit tvá vetr í samt:** 'a beast has come there the past two winters.' (*hafi* 3sg pres subj of *hafa*, used in indirect speech)

[182] **sem at eru einna mestir:** 'who are the greatest of all men' (*einna* signifies an evaluation one-by-one as opposed to an evaluation of all together as a group).

[183] **Böðvarr segir, at betr mundi takask:** 'Bodvar says that things would go better than that.' (*mundi* 3sg past subj of *munu*)

[184] **ok kvað dýrit mundu gleypa hann:** 'and said the beast would swallow him' (*mundu* pst infin of *munu*).

[185] **ok eigi með öllu óhræddr:** 'and not [being] totally unafraid.'

human beings and as many horses, along with dogs and cocks – the latter being used in place of hawks. (Trans. David A. Warner *The Chronicon of Thietmar of Merseburg*)

15.13 READING – HROLF GETS THE NICKNAME KRAKI (*SKÁLDSKAPARMÁL*, FROM *THE PROSE EDDA*)

Skáldskaparmál from *The Prose Edda* recounts how a servant named Vogg (*Vöggr*) gives Hrolf his nickname *kraki* 'pole ladder.' Vogg, who is only a boy, swears an oath to avenge the king if he should be killed. After Hrolf's death, the servant proves his faithfulness when he leads an army and defeats the king's enemies.

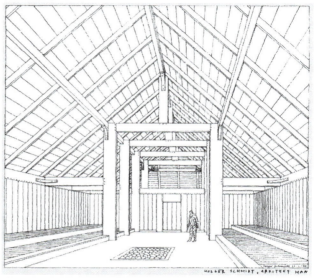

***Skáldskaparmál* (ch 53)** Konungr einn í Danmörk er nefndr Hrólfr kraki. Lítill sveinn ok fátœkr er nefndr Vöggr; hann kom í höll Hrólfs konungs. Þá var konungrinn ungr at aldri ok grannligr á vöxt. Þá gekk Vöggr fyrir hann, ok sá upp á hann. Þá mælti konungrinn: 'Hvat viltu mæla, sveinn, er þú sér á mik?' Vöggr segir: 'Þá er ek var heima, heyrða'k[186] sagt, at Hrólfr konungr at Hleiðru var mestr maðr á Norðrlöndum, en nú sitr hér í

Figure 57. Interior of the Reconstructed Ninth-Century Great Hall at Lejre, excavated by the Danish archaeologist Tom Christensen. On both sides of the great hall are tiered side benches against the walls where people sat and slept. In the center of the floor are stones for the long fire. The steeply pitched roof was supported by two interior rows of massive timbers or posts, whose size may be judged by comparison with the man at center right and the door at the far end.

hásæti kraki einn lítill, ok kallið þér hann konung.' Þá svarar konungr: 'Þú, sveinn, hefir gefit mér nafn, at ek skal heita Hrólfr kraki.'

15.14 CULTURE – BERSERKERS

Berserkers are especially prominent in *Hrolf's Saga*. In the medieval perceptions of pre-Christian Scandinavia, berserkers (*berserkir*, sg *berserkr*) may have been members of cults connected with Odin in his capacity as god of war. *Ynglinga Saga* describes Odin's warriors:

---

[186] **heyrða'k** = *heyrða ek* 'I heard.'

His men went to battle without armor and acted like dogs or wolves. They bit into their shields and were as strong as bears or bulls. They killed men, but neither fire nor iron harmed them. This is called going berserk.

En hans men fóru brynjulausir ok váru galnir sem hundir eða vargar, bitu í skjöldu sína, váru sterkir sem birnir eða griðungar. Þeir drápu mannfólkið en hvártki eldr né járn orti á þá. Þat er kallaðr berserksgangr.

The berserkers of the sagas often appear as the king's elite warriors. At times, they are reminiscent of Odin's own warriors and may be connected to ancient bear cults. The term berserker could mean 'bare shirt,' that is, naked. Berserkers, as a mark of their ferocity and invincibility, are said to have fought without armor. Berserker may also mean 'bear-shirt,' suggesting they fought in bear skins. When the 'berserker-fury' (*berserksgangr*) was upon him, a berserker was thought of as a sort of 'were-bear' (or werewolf) – part man, part beast – who was neither fully human nor fully animal. Although never called a berserker, Bodvar Bjarki shares an affinity with this tradition. During Hrolf's final battle, Bodvar sits quietly in a room and projects his spirit in the form of a huge bear that fights for King Hrolf and is invulnerable to weapons. In his ability to project himself in spirit form, Bodvar displays a supernatural characteristic attributed to Odin.

Berserkers, who were once the coercive arm of kings and Viking chieftains, appear as stock characters in a number of family sagas. They are mostly presented as troublemakers and sources of menace, who are demystified and reduced to bullies and public nuisances.

EXERCISES

15.15 Grammar Review. For the underlined words in this passage from *Hrolf's Saga*, give the relevant grammatical information, dictionary (or infinitive) form, and translation.

Síðan fór Böðvarr <u>leið</u> sína til Hleiðargarðs. Hann kømr til konungs atsetu. Böðvarr leiðir síðan hest sinn á stall hjá konungs <u>hestum</u> hinum beztu[m] ok spyrr engan at; gekk síðan inn í höllina, ok var þar fátt manna.

Hann <u>sezk</u> útarliga, ok sem hann hefir verit þar lítla hríð, heyrir hann þrausk nökkut útar í hornit í einhverjum stað. Böðvarr lítr þangat ok <u>sér</u> at mannshönd kømr upp ór <u>mikilli</u> beinahrúgu, er þar lá; höndin var svört mjök. Böðvarr gengr þangat til ok spyrr hverr þar væri í beinahrúgunni. Þá var honum svarat ok <u>heldr</u> óframliga: 'Höttr heiti ek, bokki sæll.'

'Hví <u>ertu</u> hér,' segir Böðvarr, 'eða hvat gørir þú?'

Höttr segir, 'Ek gøri mér skjaldborg, bokki sæll.'

Böðvarr sagði, 'Vesall ertu þinnar skjaldborgar!' Böðvarr þrífr til hans ok hnykkir honum upp ór beinahrúgunni.

Höttr kvað þá hátt við ok mælti, 'Nú viltu mér bana! <u>Gør</u> eigi þetta, svá sem ek hefi nú vel um <u>búizk</u> áðr, en þú hefir nú rótat í sundr skjaldborg minni, ok hafða ek nú svá gört hana háva útan at mér, at hon hefir hlíft mér við öllum höggum ykkar, svá at engi högg hafa komit á mik lengi, en ekki var hon enn svá búin sem ek ætlaða hon skyldi verða.'

    Böðvarr mælti: 'Ekki muntu fá skjaldborgina gerða lengr.'

Ex: leið   _noun f acc sg 'leið' way_ _____

1. hestum   _____
2. sezk   _____
3. sér   _____
4. mikilli   _____
5. heldr   _____
6. ertu   _____
7. gør   _____
8. búizk   _____
9. skyldi   _____
10. skjaldborgina _____

15.16 Enclitic Pronouns. Rewrite the underlined verbs with full pronouns.

    Ex: 'Hví ertu hér,' segir Böðvarr, 'eða hvat gørir þú?'   _ert þú_

1. Böðvarr sagði, 'Vesall ertu þinnar skjaldborgar!' _____
2. Höttr kvað þá hátt við ok mælti, 'Nú viltu mér bana!' _____
3. Böðvarr mælti: 'Ekki muntu fá skjaldborgina gerða lengr.' _____
4. Höttr mælti ok grét: 'Skaltu nú bana mér, bokki sæll?' _____
5. 'Hvat viltu mæla, sveinn, er þú sér á mik?' _____
6. Vöggr segir: 'Þá er ek var heima, heyrða'k sagt...' _____

15.17 Strong Verbs – Class VII. _Ráða_ is an example of a Class VII strong verb with principal parts _ræðr, réð, réðu, ráðinn._ Conjugate _ráða_ in present and past.

	PRESENT			_PAST_
Sg _ek_	_____		**Sg** _ek_	_____
_þú_	_____		_þú_	_____
hann	_____		_hann_	_____
Pl _vér_	_____		**Pl** _vér_	_____
þér	_____		_þér_	_____
þeir	_____		_þeir_	_____

Class VII verbs usually have the same vowel in the infinitive and past participle, for example, *halda*, ppart *haldinn*, and *láta*, ppart *látinn.* Give the past participles for the Class VII verbs below.

Ex: halda *haldinn*

      lata   *látinn*

1.	auka	_____	4.	blóta	_____
2.	gráta	_____	5.	falla	_____
3.	leika	_____	6.	hlaupa	_____

Most Class VII strong verbs have the same vowel in the past singular and plural. Give the past plural based on the past singular. Then find the infinitive for these Class VII verbs.

	Pst Pl	**Inf**		**Pst Pl**	**Inf**
Ex: lét	*létu*	*láta*			
7. jók	_____	_____	10. blét	_____	_____
8. grét	_____	_____	11. féll	_____	_____
9. lék	_____	_____	12. hljóp	_____	_____

When *-ng* and *-ld* come at the end of a word, these sounds change to *-kk* and *-lt*. Give the 3sg past for the verbs below.

13. ganga _____ 14. halda _____

This change also occurs in a few Class III strong verbs such as *springa* (past sg *sprakk)* and *gjalda* (past sg *galt*).

15.18 Strong Verb Review – Classes I–VII. Give the strong verb class for each of the following infinitives and provide the requested grammatical form. For help, review the Guideline Chart for Distinguishing Strong Verb Classes in Lesson 11.

Ex: halda	*Class VII*		*1sg pres*	*held*
1.	gefa	_____	*3pl pres*	_____
2.	heita	_____	*3pl past*	_____
3.	verða	_____	*1pl pres*	_____
4.	líta	_____	*3pl pres*	_____
5.	draga	_____	*1sg past*	_____
6.	bjóða	_____	*2sg past*	_____
7.	halda	_____	*2pl pres*	_____
8.	svíkja	_____	*1sg past*	_____

15.19 Subjunctive Mood – Active and Middle Voice. Conjugate the following verbs in the present subjunctive.

	GERA			BRJÓTA	
Present	ACTIVE	MIDDLE		ACTIVE	MIDDLE
Sg *ek*	_____	_____	**Sg** *ek*	_____	_____

PRESENT	ACTIVE	MIDDLE			ACTIVE	MIDDLE
þú	_____	_____		*þú*	_____	_____
hann	_____	_____		*hann*	_____	_____
Pl *vér*	_____	_____		**Pl** *vér*	_____	_____
þér	_____	_____		*þér*	_____	_____
þeir	_____	_____		*þeir*	_____	_____

Conjugate the following verbs in the past subjunctive.

PAST	*GERA* ACTIVE	MIDDLE			*BRJÓTA* ACTIVE	MIDDLE
Sg *ek*	_____	_____		**Sg** *ek*	_____	_____
þú	_____	_____		*þú*	_____	_____
hann	_____	_____		*hann*	_____	_____
Pl *vér*	_____	_____		**Pl** *vér*	_____	_____
þér	_____	_____		*þér*	_____	_____
þeir	_____	_____		*þeir*	_____	_____

15.20 Subjunctive of Weak Verbs. Identify each of the following subjunctives.

Ex: leiddim   *1pl past subj*

1. talaðið   _____
2. skipa   _____
3. legði   _____
4. þegir   _____
5. gerðizk   _____
6. hefða   _____

15.21 Subjunctive of Strong Verbs. Identify each of the following subjunctives.

Ex: næma   *1sg past subj*

1. komim   _____
2. stœðið   _____
3. yrða   _____
4. fengi   _____
5. gefumk   _____
6. væri   _____

15.22 Review: Prepositions, Pronouns, and Case Endings. Fill in the blanks.

Konungr einn _____ Danmörk er nefndr Hrólf_____ krak_____. Lítill sveinn ok fátæk_____ er nefndr Vögg_____; hann kom _____ höll Hrólfs konung_____. Þá var konungrin_____ ung_____ at aldri ok grannlig_____ á vöxt. Þá gekk Vögg_____ fyrir _____, ok sá upp á _____. Þá mælti konungrin_____: 'Hvat viltu mæla, svein_____, er þú sér _____ mik?' Vöggr segir: 'Þá er ek var heima, heyrða'k sagt, at Hrólfr konung_____ _____ Hleiðru var mest_____ maðr _____ Norðrlöndum, en nú sitr hér _____ hásæti kraki einn lítil_____, ok kallið þér hann konung.' Þá svarar konung_____: 'Þú, sveinn, hefir gefit mér nafn, at ek skal heita Hrólf_____ krak_____.'

APPENDIX A
QUICK GUIDE TO
OLD NORSE GRAMMAR

A short overview of the most important tables of nouns, pronouns, adjectives, and verbs. For a full Old Norse Reference Grammar see *Viking Language 2: The Old Norse Reader*.

	STRONG MASCULINE NOUNS				**STRONG NEUTER NOUNS**
	Type 1	Type 2	Type 3	Type 4	Type 1
Sg *nom*	hestr (-inn)	staðr	fjörðr	maðr	land (-it)
acc	hest (-inn)	stað	fjörð	mann	land (-it)
dat	hesti (-num)	stað	firði	manni	landi (-nu)
gen	hests (-ins)	staðar	fjarðar	manns	lands (-ins)
Pl *nom*	hestar (-nir)	staðir	firðir	menn	lönd (-in)
acc	hesta (-na)	staði	fjörðu	menn	lönd (-in)
dat	hestum (hestunum)	stöðum	fjörðum	mönnum	löndum (löndunum)
gen	hesta (-nna)	staða	fjarða	manna	landa (-nna)

	STRONG FEMININE NOUNS			**WEAK NOUNS**		
	Type 1	Type 2	Type 4	*masc*	*fem*	*neut*
Sg *nom*	för (-in)	höfn	mús	goði	saga	hjarta
acc	för (-ina)	höfn	mús	goða	sögu	hjarta
dat	för (-inni)	höfn	mús	goða	sögu	hjarta
gen	farar (-innar)	hafnar	músar	goða	sögu	hjarta
Pl *nom*	farar (-nar)	hafnir	mýs	goðar	sögur	hjörtu
acc	farar (-nar)	hafnir	mýs	goða	sögur	hjörtu
dat	förum (förunum)	höfnum	músum	goðum	sögum	hjörtum
gen	fara (-nna)	hafna	músa	goða	sagna	hjartna

STUDENTS QUICK GUIDE, p. 2

	STRONG ADJECTIVE DECLENSION			WEAK ADJECTIVE DECLENSION		
	masc	*fem*	*neut*	*masc*	*fem*	*neut*
Sg *nom*	margr	mörg	mar(g)t	margi	marga	marga
acc	margan	marga	mar(g)t	marga	mörgu	marga
dat	mörgum	margri	mörgu	marga	mörgu	marga
gen	margs	margrar	margs	marga	mörgu	marga
Pl *nom*	margir	margar	mörg	mörgu	mörgu	mörgu
acc	marga	margar	mörg	mörgu	mörgu	mörgu
dat	mörgum	mörgum	mörgum	mörgum	mörgum	mörgum
gen	margra	margra	margra	mörgu	mörgu	mörgu

Examples of Strong Adjective endings. Strong adjectives take endings similar to strong nouns. Deviations are explained by a few rules. We suggest reviewing the Special Stem Rules in Lesson 5 which explain the patterns resulting when an *-r* ending is added to a noun or adjective whose stem ends in *-l-*, *-n-*, *-r-*, or *-s-* (stem-final *-l-*, *-n-*, *-r-*, or *-s-*) and the apparent lack of the nominative *-r* ending in masculine words such as *Þorsteinn* and *fugl*.

	LAUSS 'LOOSE, FREE'			*VÆNN* 'BEAUTIFUL, FINE'		
	M	**F**	**N**	**M**	**F**	**N**
	lauss	laus	laust	vænn	væn	vænt
acc	lausan	lausa	laust	vænan	væna	vænt
dat	lausum	laussi	lausu	vænum	vænni	vænu
gen	lauss	laussar	lauss	væns	vænnar	væns
Pl *nom*	lausir	lausar	laus	vænir	vænar	væn
acc	lausa	lausar	laus	væna	vænar	væn
dat	lausum	lausum	lausum	vænum	vænum	vænum
gen	laussa	laussa	laussa	vænna	vænna	vænna

	FAGR 'BEAUTIFUL, FAIR'			*GAMALL* 'OLD'		
	M	**F**	**N**	**M**	**F**	**N**
Sg *nom*	fagr	fögr	fagrt	gamall	gömul	gamalt
acc	fagran	fagra	fagrt	gamlan	gamla	gamalt
dat	fögrum	fagri	fagru	gömlum	gamalli	gömlu
gen	fagrs	fagrar	fagrs	gamals	gamallar	gamals
Pl *nom*	fagrir	fagrar	fögr	gamlir	gamlar	gömul
acc	fagra	fagrar	fögr	gamla	gamlar	gömul
dat	fögrum	fögrum	fögrum	gömlum	gömlum	gömlum
gen	fagra	fagra	fagra	gamla	gamla	gamla

Student's Quick Guide, p. 3

	MIKILL 'GREAT'			LÍTILL 'LITTLE'		
	M	F	N	M	F	N
Sg nom	mikill	mikil	mikit	lítill	lítil	lítit
acc	mikinn	mikla	mikit	lítinn	litla	lítit
dat	miklum	mikilli	miklu	litlum	lítilli	litlu
gen	mikils	mikillar	mikils	lítils	lítillar	lítils
Pl nom	miklir	miklar	mikil	litlir	litlar	lítil
acc	mikla	miklar	mikil	litla	litlar	lítil
dat	miklum	miklum	miklum	litlum	litlum	litlum
gen	mikilla	mikilla	mikilla	lítilla	lítilla	lítilla

PERSONAL PRONOUNS						
	1st	2nd		3rd		refl
			masc	fem	neut	
Sg nom	ek	þú	hann	hon	þat	—
acc	mik	þik	hann	hana	þat	sik
dat	mér	þér	honum	henni	því	sér
gen	mín	þín	hans	hennar	þess	sín
Dual nom	vit	(þ)it				
acc	okkr	ykkr				
dat	okkr	ykkr				
gen	okkar	ykkar				
Pl nom	vér	(þ)ér	þeir	þær	þau	—
acc	oss	yðr	þá	þær	þau	sik
dat	oss	yðr	þeim	þeim	þeim	sér
gen	vár	yð(v)ar	þeir(r)a	þeir(r)a	þeir(r)a	sín

STUDENT'S QUICK GUIDE, p. 4

DEMONSTRATIVE PRONOUNS

		sá			þessi	
	masc	fem	neut	masc	fem	neut
Sg nom	sá	sú	þat	þessi ~ sjá	þessi ~ sjá	þetta
acc	þann	þá	þat	þenna	þessa	þetta
dat	þeim	þei(r)ri	því	þessum ~ þeima	þessi ~ þessa(r)ri	þessu ~ þvísa
gen	þess	þei(r)rar	þess	þessa	þessar ~ þessa(r)rar	þessa
Pl nom	þeir	þær	þau	þessir	þessar	þessi
acc	þá	þær	þau	þessa	þessar	þessi
dat	þeim	þeim	þeim	þessum	þessum	þessum
gen	þei(r)ra	þei(r)ra	þei(r)ra	þessa ~ þessar(r)a	þessa ~ þessar(r)a	þessa ~ þessar(r)a

INDEFINITE PRONOUNS / DEFINITE ARTICLE

	nökkurr			inn		
	masc	fem	neut	masc	fem	neut
Sg nom	nökkurr	nökkur	nökku(r)t	inn	in	it
acc	nökkurn	nökkura	nökku(r)t	inn	ina	it
dat	nökkurum	nökkurri	nökkuru	inum	inni	inu
gen	nökkurs	nökkurrar	nökkurs	ins	innar	ins
Pl nom	nökkurir	nökkurar	nökkur	inir	inar	in
acc	nökkura	nökkurar	nökkur	ina	inar	in
dat	nökkurum	nökkurum	nökkurum	inum	inum	inum
gen	nökkurra	nökkurra	nökkurra	inna	inna	inna

STUDENT'S QUICK GUIDE, p. 5

All weak verbs form their past tense by adding a suffix containing a dental consonant (-ð-, -d-, or -t-) and the past tense ending, for example *kall-að-a* 'I called,' *mæl-t-a* 'I spoke,' *tal-d-a* 'I counted,' and *vak-t-a* 'I woke.' All weak verbs share the same past tense endings but differ somewhat in the dental suffix.

Past Tense Endings of Weak Verbs		
	SINGULAR	*PLURAL*
1st	-a	-um
2nd	-ir	-uð
3rd	-i	-u

1st conjugation weak verbs insert the past tense dental suffix -*að*- before the endings (*kall-**að**-i*). The past endings -*um*, -*uð*, and -*u* trigger *u*-umlaut in the plural, changing -*að*- to -*uð*- (*köll-**uð**-u*). All other weak verbs add a dental suffix without a linking vowel (*mæl-**t**-i*, *tal-**d**-i*, *vak-**t**-i*).

		1ST CONJUG	2ND CONJUG	3RD CONJUG	4TH CONJUG
		KALLA	*MÆLA*	*TELJA*	*VAKA*
Sg 1st	ek	kalla**ð**a	mæl**t**a	tal**d**a	vak**t**a
2nd	þú	kalla**ð**ir	mæl**t**ir	tal**d**ir	vak**t**ir
3rd	hann	kalla**ð**i	mæl**t**i	tal**d**i	vak**t**i
Pl 1st	vér	köll**uð**um	mæl**t**um	töl**d**um	vök**t**um
2nd	þér	köll**uð**uð	mæl**t**uð	töl**d**uð	vök**t**uð
3rd	þeir	köll**uð**u	mæl**t**u	töl**d**u	vök**t**u

PRINCIPAL PARTS OF STRONG VERBS					
	Infinitive	3sg Present	3sg Past	3pl Past	PPart
Class I	ríða	ríðr	reið	riðu	riðinn
Class II	bjóða	býðr	bauð	buðu	boðinn
Class III	bresta	brestr	brast	brustu	brostinn
Class IV	bera	berr	bar	báru	borinn
Class V	gefa	gefr	gaf	gáfu	gefinn
Class VI	fara	ferr	fór	fóru	farinn
Class VII i)	heita	heitr	hét	hétu	heitinn
ii)	búa	býr	bjó	bjoggu~bjuggu	búinn
iii)	ganga	gengr	gekk	gengu	genginn
iv)	ráða	ræðr	réð	réðu	ráðinn
v)	snúa	snýr	sneri~snøri	sneru~snøru	snúinn

STUDENT'S QUICK GUIDE, p. 6

VERB CONJUGATION		Strong 'fara'	Weak I 'kalla'	Weak II 'mæla'	Weak III 'telja'	Weak IV 'vaka'	'vera'
Present Indicative	1sg	fer	kalla	mæli	tel	vaki	em
	2sg	ferr	kallar	mælir	telr	vakir	ert
	3sg	ferr	kallar	mælir	telr	vakir	er
	1pl	förum	köllum	mælum	teljum	vökum	erum
	2pl	farið	kallið	mælið	telið	vakið	eruð
	3pl	fara	kalla	mæla	telja	vaka	eru
Past Indicative	1sg	fór	kallaða	mælti	talða	vakta	sjá, sé
	2sg	fórt	kallaðir	mæltir	talðir	vaktir	sér
	3sg	fór	kallaði	mælti	talði	vakti	sé
	1pl	fórum	kölluðum	mæltum	tölðum	vöktum	sém
	2pl	fóruð	kölluðuð	mæltuð	tölðuð	vöktuð	séð
	3pl	fóru	kölluðu	mæltu	tölðu	vöktu	sé
Present Subjunctive	1sg	fara	kalla	mæla	telja	vaka	var
	2sg	farir	kallir	mælir	telir	vakir	vart
	3sg	fari	kalli	mæli	teli	vaki	var
	1pl	farim	kallim	mælim	telim	vakim	várum
	2pl	farið	kallið	mælið	telið	vakið	váruð
	3pl	fari	kalli	mæli	teli	vaki	váru
Past Subjunctive	1sg	fœra	kallaða	mælta	telða	vekta	væra
	2sg	fœrir	kallaðir	mæltir	telðir	vektir	værir
	3sg	fœri	kallaði	mælti	telði	vekti	væri
	1pl	fœrim	kallaðim	mæltim	telðim	vektim	værim
	2pl	fœrið	kallaðið	mæltið	telðið	vektið	værið
	3pl	fœri	kallaði	mælti	telði	vekti	væri
Present Participle		farand	kallandi	mælandi	teljandi	vakandi	verandi
Past Participle		farinn	kallaðr	mæltr	taliðr	vakit	verit
Imperative		far	kalla	mæl	tel	vaki	ver

Guideline Chart for Distinguishing Strong Verb Classes. A strong verb's class can often be determined from the infinitive. For instance, Class I strong verbs have *í* in the infinitive while Class II have *jú*, *jó*, or *ú*. The following chart is a guide to identify strong verb classes from the infinitive. 'C' refers to a consonant following the root vowel. 'R' refers to the four consonants *r*, *l*, *m*, *n*, known as resonants. On occasion there are exceptions to these rules. For example, Class V *fregna* and Class VI *standa* have two consonants after the vowel.

	INFINITIVE	*EXAMPLES*
Class I:	í	líta, rísa
Class II:	jú, jó, ú	krjúpa, bjóða, lúka
Class III:	eCC, jaCC, jáCC, iNC	verða, gjalda, hjálpa, binda
	(*also* øCCv, yNCv)	søkkva, syngva
Class IV:	eR	skera, stela, nema
Class V:	eC, iCj	gefa, vega, biðja
Class VI:	aC, eCj	fara, aka, draga, hefja
Class VII:	aCC, au, á, ei (*also* ö, ó, á, ú)	halda, falla, hlaupa, gráta, heita

C = *any consonant*   R (*resonant*) = r, l, n, *or* m   N (*nasal*) = n *or* m

APPENDIX B

THE MOST FREQUENT WORDS IN THE SAGAS

GIVEN IN THE FOLLOWING LISTS:

    A. THE 70 MOST FREQUENT WORDS IN THE SAGAS

    B. THE 246 MOST FREQUENT WORDS IN THE SAGAS (by part of speech)

    C. THE 246 MOST FREQUENT WORDS IN THE SAGAS (in alphabetical order)

A. THE 70 MOST FREQUENT WORDS IN THE SAGAS

1. **ok** – and
2. **sá** – that (one)
3. **hann** – he, it
4. **at** – that
5. **vera** – to be
6. **ek** – I
7. **til** – to
8. **í** – in; into
9. **en** – but
10. **er** – who, which, that; when; where
11. **á** – on; onto
12. **þá** – then
13. **þú** – you
14. **hafa** – to have
15. **maðr** – man, person
16. **þar** – there
17. **segja** – to say
18. **um** – about
19. **koma** – to come
20. **fara** – to go, travel
21. **nú** – now
22. **við** – with; against
23. **munu** – will
24. **með** – with
25. **svá** – so; such
26. **eigi** – not
27. **sinn** – his/her/their (own)
28. **fyrir** – before; for
29. **sjá** – this
30. **sem** – who, which, that; as
31. **af** – of; from
32. **mæla** – to speak
33. **vilja** – to want
34. **mikill** – great
35. **hon** – she, it
36. **allr** – all
37. **taka** – to take
38. **skulu** – shall
39. **ganga** – to walk
40. **gera** – to do; make
41. **verða** – to become
42. **kveða** – to speak
43. **sik** – him/herself/ themselves
44. **þykkja** – to seem
45. **ekki** – not
46. **eptir** – after
47. **annarr** – other; second
48. **hinn** – the other
49. **vel** – well
50. **hverr** – each, every; who?
51. **upp** – up
52. **síðan** – then
53. **eiga** – to own
54. **láta** – to let
55. **heita** – to call; be named
56. **búa** – to live, dwell; prepare
57. **sjá** – to see
58. **einn** – one
59. **ef** – if
60. **ríða** – to ride
61. **konungr** – king
62. **svara** – to answer
63. **þó** – nevertheless
64. **margr** – many
65. **skip** – ship
66. **spyrja** – to ask; learn
67. **minn** – my
68. **góðr** – good
69. **biðja** – to ask; tell
70. **heim** – (to) home

B. THE 246 MOST FREQUENT WORDS IN THE SAGAS (by part of speech)

NOUNS

1. **maðr** – man, person
2. **konungr** – king
3. **skip** – ship
4. **mál** – speech; case, matter
5. **sonr** – son
6. **hönd** – hand
7. **fé** – wealth; livestock
8. **bróðir** – brother
9. **vetr** – winter
10. **land** – land
11. **kona** – woman
12. **ráð** – advice; plan
13. **dagr** – day
14. **frændi** – kinsman

15. **jarl** – earl
16. **faðir** – father
17. **ferð** – journey
18. **sumar** – summer
19. **dóttir** – daughter
20. **þing** – assembly
21. **orð** – word
22. **hestr** – horse
23. **nótt** – night
24. **tíðindi** – news, tidings
25. **fundr** – meeting
26. **lið** – following, troops
27. **bœr** – farm
28. **bóndi** – farmer
29. **sverð** – sword
30. **hlutr** – thing; part
31. **sök** – cause, reason
32. **bú** – farm
33. **höfuð** – head
34. **móðir** – mother
35. **víg** – slaying
36. **vinr** – friend
37. **vísa** – verse
38. **leið** – path
39. **sinn** – time
40. **kveld** – evening
41. **vápn** – weapon
42. **morginn** – morning
43. **hús** – house
44. **fótr** – foot
45. **spjót** – spear
46. **sveinn** – boy, lad
47. **vár** – spring
48. **kostr** – choice
49. **skjöldr** – shield
50. **bak** – back

ADJECTIVES

1. **mikill** – great
2. **margr** – many
3. **góðr** – good
4. **lítill** – little
5. **illr** – bad, ill
6. **sannr** – true
7. **fár** – few
8. **dauðr** – dead
9. **stórr** – big
10. **gamall** – old
11. **kyrr** – quiet
12. **fyrri** – former
13. **varr** – aware
14. **sterkr** – strong
15. **ungr** – young
16. **víss** – certain; wise
17. **vándr** – bad
18. **langr** – long
19. **sárr** – wounded
20. **hálfr** – half
21. **vænn** – beautiful
22. **verðr** – worthy
23. **líkr** – alike
24. **vitr** – wise
25. **harðr** – hard
26. **vanr** – accustomed
27. **heill** – whole
28. **lauss** – loose, free
29. **sekr** – guilty
30. **vinsæll** – popular
31. **skyldr** – related; necessary, obliged
32. **miðr** – middle
33. **fullr** – full
34. **fagr** – beautiful
35. **auðigr** – wealthy
36. **fríðr** – beautiful
37. **réttr** – right, correct
38. **næstr** – next
39. **kunnigr** – known; cunning, skilled in magic
40. **líkligr** – likely
41. **reiðr** – angry
42. **ríkr** – powerful
43. **fjölmennr** – well attended; numerous
44. **skammr** – short; brief
45. **göfugr** – noble

PRONOUNS

1. **sá** – that (one)
2. **hann** – he, it
3. **ek** – I
4. **þú** – you
5. **sinn** – his/her/their (own)
6. **sjá** – this
7. **hon** – she, it
8. **allr** – all
9. **sik** – him/herself/ themselves
10. **annarr** – other; second
11. **hinn** – the other
12. **hverr** – each, every; who?
13. **minn** – my
14. **engi** – no (one)
15. **nökkurr** – some, a certain
16. **þinn** – your
17. **slíkr** – such
18. **báðir** – both
19. **várr** – our
20. **hvárr** – who, which (of two)?
21. **sjálfr** – self
22. **samr** – same
23. **sumr** – some
24. **hvárrtveggi** – each of the two
25. **yðr** – you (*pl*)
26. **okkarr** – us (*dual*)
27. **einhverr** – someone

NUMERALS

1. **einn** – one
2. **tveir** – two
3. **þrír** – three
4. **tólf** – twelve
5. **fjórir** – four
6. **sex** – six
7. **fimm** – five
8. **tíu** – ten
9. **sjau** – seven
10. **fimmtán** – fifteen

VERBS

1. **vera** – to be
2. **hafa** – to have
3. **segja** – to say
4. **koma** – to come
5. **fara** – to go, travel
6. **munu** – will
7. **mæla** – to speak
8. **vilja** – to want
9. **taka** – to take
10. **skulu** – shall
11. **ganga** – to walk
12. **gera** – to do; make
13. **verða** – to become
14. **kveða** – to speak
15. **þykkja** – to seem
16. **eiga** – to own
17. **láta** – to let
18. **heita** – to call; be named
19. **búa** – to live, dwell; prepare
20. **sjá** – to see
21. **ríða** – to ride
22. **svara** – to answer
23. **spyrja** – to ask; learn
24. **biðja** – to ask; tell
25. **mega** – may
26. **fá** – to get, obtain
27. **ætla** – to intend
28. **vita** – to know
29. **leggja** – to lay, place
30. **bera** – to carry, bear
31. **gefa** – to give
32. **finna** – to find
33. **ráða** – to advise; rule
34. **sitja** – to sit
35. **standa** – to stand
36. **bjóða** – to offer; invite
37. **hlaupa** – to leap; run
38. **kalla** – to call
39. **halda** – to hold
40. **falla** – to fall
41. **skilja** – to part, separate; understand
42. **drepa** – to kill
43. **setja** – to set
44. **liggja** – to lie
45. **leita** – to search
46. **veita** – to grant
47. **sœkja** – to seek
48. **höggva** – to strike
49. **senda** – to send
50. **geta** – to get, beget

PREPOSITIONS AND ADVERBS

1. **til** – to
2. **í** – in; into
3. **á** – on; onto
4. **þá** – then
5. **þar** – there
6. **um** – about
7. **nú** – now
8. **við** – with; against
9. **með** – with
10. **svá** – so; such
11. **eigi** – not
12. **fyrir** – before; for
13. **af** – of; from
14. **ekki** – not
15. **eptir** – after
16. **vel** – well
17. **upp** – up
18. **síðan** – then
19. **þó** – nevertheless
20. **heim** – (to) home
21. **út** – out
22. **frá** – from
23. **hér** – here
24. **mjök** – very
25. **þegar** – at once
26. **ór** – out of, from
27. **fram** – forward
28. **yfir** – over
29. **fyrr** – before
30. **áðr** – before
31. **saman** – together
32. **inn** – inside
33. **undir** – under
34. **heldr** – rather
35. **brott** – away
36. **enn** – yet, still
37. **niðr** – down
38. **ofan** – from above
39. **aptr** – back
40. **móti** – against
41. **hjá** – by, near
42. **illa** – badly
43. **lengi** – for a long time
44. **hversu** – how
45. **þangat** – to there
46. **aldri** – never
47. **nær** – nearly
48. **mikit** – greatly

49. **milli** – between
50. **útan** – from out

CONJUNCTIONS

1. **ok** – and
2. **at** – that
3. **en** – but
4. **er** – who, which, that; when; where
5. **sem** – who, which, that; as
6. **ef** – if
7. **eða** – or
8. **hvárt** – whether
9. **bæði** – both
10. **þótt** – although
11. **nema** – except
12. **né** – nor
13. **enda** – and yet
14. **hvárgi** – neither

C. THE 246 MOST FREQUENT WORDS IN THE SAGAS (in alphabetical order)

af – of; from
aldri – never
allr – all
annarr – other; second
aptr – back
at – that
auðigr – wealthy
á – on; onto
áðr – before
bak – back
báðir – both
bera – to carry, bear
biðja – to ask; tell
bjóða – to offer; invite
bóndi– farmer
brott – away
bróðir – brother
bú– farm
búa – to live, dwell; prepare
bæði – both
bœr – farm
dagr – day
dauðr – dead
dóttir – daughter
drepa – to kill
eða – or
ef – if
eiga – to own
eigi – not
einhverr – someone
einn – one
ek – I
ekki – not

en – but
enda – and yet
engi – no (one)
enn – yet, still
eptir – after
er – who, which, that; when; where
fá – to get, obtain
faðir – father
fagr – beautiful
falla – to fall
fara – to go, travel
fá – to get, obtain
fár – few
ferð – journey
fé – wealth; livestock
fimm – five
fimmtán – fifteen
finna – to find
fjórir – four
fjölmennr – well attended; numerous
fótr – foot
fram – forward
frá – from
fríðr – beautiful
frændi – kinsman
fullr – full
fundr – meeting
fyrir – before; for
fyrr – before
fyrri – former
gamall – old

ganga – to walk
gefa – to give
gera – to do; make
geta – to get, beget
góðr – good
göfugr – noble
hafa – to have
halda – to hold
hann – he, it
harðr – hard
hálfr – half
heill – whole
heim – (to) home
heita – to call; be named
heldr – rather
hestr – horse
hér – here
hinn – the other
hjá – by, near
hlaupa – to leap; run
hlutr – thing; part
hon – she, it
hús – house
hvárgi – neither
hvárr – who, which (of two)?
hvárrtveggi – each of the two
hvárt – whether
hverr – each, every; who?
hversu – how
höfuð – head
höggva – to strike

hönd – hand
illa – badly
illr – bad, ill
inn – inside
í – in; into
jarl – earl
kalla – to call
koma – to come
kona – woman
konungr – king
kostr – choice
kunnigr – known; cunning,
     skilled in magic
kveða – to speak
kveld – evening
kyrr – quiet
land – land
langr – long
lauss – loose, free
láta – to let
leggja – to lay, place
leið – path
leita – to search
lengi – for a long time
lið – following, troops
liggja – to lie
líkligr – likely
líkr – alike
lítill – little
maðr – man, person
margr – many
mál – speech; case, matter
með – with
mega – may
miðr – middle
mikill – great
mikit – greatly
milli – between
minn – my
mjök – very
morginn – morning
móðir – mother
móti – against
munu – will
mæla – to speak

nema – except
né – nor
niðr – down
nótt – night
nú – now
nær – nearly
næstr – next
nökkurr – some, a certain
ofan – from above
ok – and
okkarr – us (*dual*)
orð – word
ór – out of, from
ráð – advice; plan
ráða – to advise; rule
reiðr – angry
réttr – right, correct
ríða – to ride
ríkr – powerful
saman – together
samr – same
sannr – true
sá – that (one)
sárr – wounded
segja – to say
sekr – guilty
sem – who, which, that; as
senda – to send
setja – to set
sex – six
sik – him/herself/
     themselves
sinn – his/her/their (own)
sinn – time
sitja – to sit
síðan – then
sjau – seven
sjá – this
sjá – to see
sjálfr – self
skammr – short; brief
skilja – to part, separate;
     understand
skip – ship
skjöldr – shield

skulu – shall
skyldr – related; necessary,
     obliged
slíkr – such
sonr – son
spjót – spear
spyrja – to ask; learn
standa – to stand
sterkr – strong
stórr – big
sumar – summer
sumr – some
svara – to answer
svá – so; such
sveinn – boy, lad
sverð – sword
sœkja – to seek
sök – cause, reason
taka – to take
til – to
tíðindi – news, tidings
tíu – ten
tólf – twelve
tveir – two
um – about
undir – under
ungr – young
upp – up
út – out
útan – from out
vanr – accustomed
varr – aware
vándr – bad
vápn – weapon
vár – spring
várr – our
veita – to grant
vel – well
vera – to be
verða – to become
verðr – worthy
vetr – winter
við – with; against
vilja – to want
vinr – friend

vinsæll – popular
vita – to know
vitr – wise
víg – slaying
vísa – verse
víss – certain; wise
vænn – beautiful
yðr – you (*pl*)

yfir – over
þangat – to there
þar – there
þá – then
þegar – at once
þing – assembly
þinn – your

þó – nevertheless
þótt – although
þrír – three
þú – you
þykkja – to seem
ætla – to intend

Appendix C
Pronunciation of Old Icelandic

Reconstruction of Old Icelandic sounds is by nature approximate. In most instances, we estimate the pronunciation from spellings in manuscripts and rhymes in poetry. There was no standard spelling. Writers and poets often employed their personal or regional pronunciation, and sounds sometimes changed over decades and centuries.

Stress in Icelandic typically falls on the first syllable of the word, for example *kona*, *gerði*, and *konungr* are pronounced **ko**-*na*, **ger**-*ði*, and **kon**-*ungr*, with stress on the first syllable Compounds also have a secondary stress on the second element, for example the syllable -*móð*- in **kon**ung*a***móð**ir, 'mother of kings.'

Vowels are sounds made by the free passage of air through the mouth, that is, without closing the mouth or narrowing it to the point where the sound is obstructed. Vowels in Old Icelandic had no immediately following glide as is often the case in Modern Icelandic and English.

Old Norse vowels are classified as long or short. For most vowels, length is indicated by an acute accent, *á, é, í, ó, ú, ý*; however, the vowels *æ* and *œ* are always long.

Long vowels in Old Icelandic were longer versions of the corresponding short vowels. For example, *a* and *á* were pronounced the same, but *á* seems to have been longer in pronunciation duration until about the year 1200. In Modern Icelandic, many of the long vowels differ from the corresponding short vowels in quality as well as length, for example, *a* (pronounced as in English f<u>a</u>ther) and *á* (as in h<u>ou</u>se).

The vowels *au*, *ei*, and *ey* are diphthongs, a sequence of two vowel sounds pronounced together, with the tongue gliding from the first vowel to the position of the second. For example, *ei* begins with *e* and glides towards *i*. As noted below, these diphthongs are pronounced somewhat differently in Old and Modern Icelandic. Below is a pronunciation chart for Old Icelandic vowels.

accent usually on first syllable

Vowel	Old Icelandic Pronunciation	Old Icelandic
a	as **a** in f**a**ther, but shorter	*faðir*
á	as **au** in c**au**ght but with rounded lips and longer than ǫ/ö	*láta*
e	as **e** in b**e**t	*bekkr*
é	as **e** in b**e**t, but longer	*þér*
i	**i** in s**i**n	*sinn*
í	as **ee** in s**ee**n	*líta*

o	as **o** in s**o**le, but shorter	*k**o**na*
ó	as **o** in b**o**at	*bj**ó**ða*
u	as **oo** in t**oo**k	*s**u**mar*
ú	as **oo** in m**oo**n	*b**ú**a*
y	as **ee** in s**ee**n, but pronounced with rounded lips; as in German *f**ü**r*	*s**y**stir*
ý	as **ee** in s**ee**n, but pronounced with rounded lips; as in German *f**ü**r*, but longer	*b**ý**ðr*
æ	as **a** in n**a**p, but longer	*l**æ**tr*
œ	as **e** in b**e**t, but longer and pronounced with rounded lips; as in German *k**ö**nnen*	*fát**œ**kr*
ø	as **e** in b**e**t, but pronounced with rounded lips; as in German *k**ö**nnen*. By early thirteenth century ø merges with **ǫ**.	*s**ø**kkva*
ǫ (ö)	as **au** in c**au**ght, but pronounced with rounded lips and shorter than á	*f**ǫ**r*
au	as **ow** in c**ow**	*na**u**ð*
ei	as **ay** in m**ay**	*b**ei**ta*
ey	Old Icelandic *e* + *y*	*h**ey**ra*

CONSONANTS are sounds made by a narrowing or closure of the vocal tract, which results in obstruction of the free flow of air. Most Icelandic consonants are similar to corresponding sounds in modern English.

Both Old and Modern Icelandic distinguish the pronunciation of single and double consonants. Double letters form long consonants, for instance, the *-mm-* in *stemma* is pronounced twice as long as the *-m-* in *heima*. In words that employ stop consonants (*p, t, k, b, d, g*) like *staddr* and *liggja*, there is a pause before the release of air forming the consonant.

The consonants *b, d, h, k, l, m, n, s,* and *t* were probably pronounced much as in Modern English. In Old Icelandic *f* and *v* were likely pronounced using both the lower and upper lips. Below is a pronunciation chart for the other Old Icelandic consonants.

CONSONANTS	*OLD ICELANDIC PRONUNCIATION*	*OLD ICELANDIC*

f	1) at the beginning of a word: as **f** in **f**ather	*faðir*
		hafa
	2) in the middle or at the end of a word: as **v** in ha**v**e	
g	at the beginning of word or after *n:* as **g** in **g**ood	*góðr, langr*
	before an *s* or *t:* as **ch** in Scots English lo**ch**	*lagt*
j	as **y** in **y**es	*játa, Herjólfr*
p	as **p** in **p**in	*penningr*
	when preceding *s* or *t:* as **f** in a**f**ter	*skipta*
r	trilled as Scots English **r**	*rauðr*
v	as **w** in **w**est or **v** in vest	*vestr*
þ	as **th** in **th**ing	*þing, Þórr*
ð	as **th** in **th**is, ra**th**er	*bróðir, Óðinn*
x	as **chs** in Scots English lo**chs**	*øx*
z	as **ts** in prin**ts**	*brauzk*

OLD ICELANDIC READ WITH MODERN ICELANDIC PRONUNCIATION

A trend in the teaching of Old Norse – Icelandic is to read the texts with Modern Icelandic pronunciation. For those interested in reading the texts with Modern Icelandic pronunciation, the following two charts provide guidance. Much of the grammar and basic vocabulary of Old Icelandic come into Modern Icelandic with few changes, and employing modern pronunciation is a good start to learning Modern Icelandic.

VOWEL	MODERN ICELANDIC PRONUNCIATION	OLD ICELANDIC
a	as **a** in f**a**ther	*faðir*
	before ng and nk as **ow** in c**ow**	*langr*
á	as **ow** in c**ow**	*láta*
e	as **e** in b**e**d	*bekkr*
é	as **ye** in **ye**s	*þér*
i	as **i** in t**i**n	*sinn*
í	as **ee** in s**ee**n	*líta*
o	as **o** in m**o**re	*kona*
ó	as **o** in g**o**	*bjóða*
ö	as **u** in c**u**t, but with rounded lips	*köttr*
u	as **ou** in sh**ou**ld	*sumar*

ú	as **oo** in m**oo**n	*búa*
y	as **i** in t**i**n	*systir*
ý	as **ee** in s**ee**n	*býðr*
æ, œ	as **i** in mile	*lætr, fátœkr*
au	as **ay** in h**ay** but with rounded lips; Modern Icelandic **ö** + **y**	*nauð*
ei, ey	as **ay** in s**ay**	*leiða, leysa*

CONSONANTS IN MODERN ICELANDIC

- *h, k, l, m, n* are pronounced much as in Modern English.
- The consonants *p, t, k* are pronounced voiceless (with no vibration of the vocal cords), as in English.
- Unlike English, the consonants *b, d, g* are also pronounced voiceless.
- The two consonant series *p, t, k* and *b, d, g* are distinguished from each other by the presence of aspiration (a following puff of air); *p, t, k* are generally aspirated, while *b, d* and *g* are not.
- In Modern Icelandic (and English), the letters *f* and *v* are pronounced with the lower lip in contact with the upper teeth.

CONSONANT	MODERN PRONUNCIATION	OLD ICELANDIC
ð	as **th** in **th**at, bro**th**er	*bróðir, Óðinn*
f	at the beginning of a word: as **f** in **f**ather	*faðir*
	before *n* or *l*: as Modern Icelandic **p**	*nafn, kafli*
	elsewhere: as **v** in ha**v**e	*hafa*
g	at the beginning of a word and after *n*: as **g** in **g**ood, but voiceless	*góðr, langr*
	before an *s* or *t*: as **ch** in Scots English lo**ch**	*lagt*
	after vowels and before *a, u, ð, r* : as **ch** in Scots English lo**ch**, but voiced	*fluga*
	between a vowel and a following *i* or *j* as **y** in **y**et	*eigi, segja*
	between *ó, á, ú,* and a following *a, u*: silent	*fljúga*
	in sequences *angt* and *angs*: silent	*langt, langs*
j	as **y** in **y**es	*játa, Herjólfr*
	when preceding *s* or *t*: as **f** in a**f**ter	*eptir*
r	trilled as Scotch English **r**	*rauðr*
s	as **s** in **s**ink, not as English **z**	*sitja*
þ	as **th** in **th**ing	*þing, Þórr*

A few double consonants in Modern Icelandic have special pronunciations.

- *pp, tt,* and *kk* are pronounced with a preceding *h.* For example, *upp, dóttir,* and *ekki* are pronounced *uʰpp, dóʰttir,* and *eʰkki. pp* is pronounced as *f* in *father* when it precedes *t,* for example, *keppti.*

- *nn* is pronounced much like *tn* when it follows a vowel with an accent mark or diphthong at the end of a word, for example, *einn* [eitn]

- *ll* is pronounced much like *tl* when preceding a vowel, *r,* or *n,* for example, *kalla* [katla], *allr* [atlr]. *ll* is also pronounced *tl* at the end of words, for example, *mikill* [mikitl]. Before *t, d,* and *s* double *ll* is pronounced like a single *l,* for example, *alls* [als], *allt* [alt]. In loan words and nicknames *ll* is pronounced as long *l,* for example, *mylla* 'mill' [milla] and *Kalli* [kalli].

- The sequences *rn* and *rl* usually are pronounced [rtn] and [rtl], for example *Bjarni* [bjartni], *karlar* [kartlar].

Sequences of three consonants are often simplified at the end of a syllable. For example, *b* in the word ***kumbl*** is dropped, and pronounced *kuml* similar to the English 'subtle' pronounced *sutl.* When the sequence occurs over a syllable break, all three consonants are pronounced, for example *land**n**ám* (the syllable breaks between *land-* and *-nám*).

Vocabulary

Order of the Alphabet

The alphabetical order is: **a, á, b, d, ð, e, é, f, g, h, i, í, j, k, l, m, n, o, ó, p, r, s, t, u, ú, v, y, ý, x, z, þ, æ, œ, ö/ø**. Long vowels with accent are listed after the corresponding short vowels without accent (a, á). At the end of the alphabet, **æ** and **œ** are listed separately while **ö** and **ø** are listed together.

Word Frequency

The symbol ❖ marks the 246 most common words in the sagas.

Notes on the Vocabulary

Verbs and prepositions take their objects in various cases, depending on sometimes unpredictable usage. This vocabulary adopts the Icelandic convention of using the pronoun *einnhverr* meaning 'somebody' [sb] and *eitthvat* meaning 'something' [sth] to indicate which case is used with particular verbs.

> **[e-n]** (einhvern) = somebody [sb] *acc*
> **[e-t]** (eitthvat) = something [sth] *acc*
> **[e-m]** (einhverjum) = (for) [sb] *dat*
> **[e-u]** (einhverju) = (for) [sth] *dat*
> **[e-s]** (einhvers) = (of) [sb] or [sth] *gen*

Examples:
> **fala [e-t] af [e-m]** offer to buy [sth] from [sb]
> **firra [e-n] [e-u]** deprive [sb] of [sth]
> **mæla [e-t] við [e-n]** say [sth] to [sb]
> **segja [e-m] frá [e-m]** tell, inform [sb] about [sb]
> **segja [e-m] til [e-s]** tell, inform [sb] where [sth/sb] is to be found

The following conventions are employed in this vocabulary.

- STRONG MASCULINE NOUNS: the genitive singular and nominative plural endings are given after the nominative singular. For example, **heimr** <-s, -ar> *m* world; **vinr** <-ar, -ir> *m* friend.

- ADJECTIVES: the strong masculine accusative singular is given to indicate a stem-final -*j*- or -*v*- or syncope (loss of vowel). For example, **ríkr** <*acc* ríkjan> *adj* powerful, **døkkr** <*acc* døkkvan> *adj* dark, **göfugr** <*acc* göfgan> *adj* noble, distinguished.

- STRONG VERBS: the principal parts (3sg pres, 3sg past, 3pl past, and past participle) are given. For example, **fara** <ferr, fór, fóru, farinn> *vb* go, travel.

- WEAK VERBS: the dental suffix -að- indicates when a weak verb is 1st conjugation. For example, **kalla** <-að-> *vb* call. For all other verbs the dental (-*t*-, -*d*-, or -*ð*-) is given with the ending for 3sg past and past participle, for example **mæla** <-*ti*, -*tr*> *vb* speak. When there is a change in the stem from present to past, the Vocabulary provides the forms in full: **spyrja** <spurði, spurðr> *vb* ask. When a past tense dental is added to a verb whose stem already ends in a dental (*leiða, setja* and *senda*), the two dentals often undergo change. In such instances, the Vocabulary indicates the outcome, hence **leiða** <*-ddi, -ddr*>, *setja* <*-tti, -ttr*>, and **senda** <*-di, -dr*> (that is, past tense *leiddi* 'he led,' *setti* 'he set,' *sendi* 'he sent').

- PRETERITE-PRESENT VERBS: are named so because their present tense looks like the past tense of strong verbs.

When looking up a compound word, go to the final element of the compound. Hence for **landnámsmaðr** look under **maðr**; and for **fyrirbjóða** look under **bjóða**.

Some entries are labeled *defective*, meaning these words lack a full set of forms in the extant sources. For example, the verb *kná*, has no infinitive form in any of the manuscripts. The dictionary form, *kná*, is the 1/3 sg (first and third person) present: **kná** <kná, *1pl* knegum, knátti, *past inf* knáttu> *defective pret-pres vb* be able to, can; could.

ABBREVIATIONS

1dual, 2dual	1st person dual, etc.
1pl, 2pl, 3pl	1st person plural, etc.
1sg, 2sg, 3sg	1st person singular, etc.
acc	accusative
adj	adjective
adv	adverb
art	article (definite)
aux	auxiliary (verb)
comp	comparative (adjective or adverb)
conj	conjunction
conjug	conjugation
dat	dative
def	definite (article)
defect	defective
dem	demonstrative (pronoun)
esp	especially
etc	etcetera
ex	example
f	feminine
fig	figurative
gen	genitive
impers	impersonal (verb)
indecl	indeclinable
indef	indefinite (pronoun)
indic	indicative
inf	infinitive

interrog	interrogative (adverb or pronoun)
intrans	intransitive (verb)
leg	legal usage
lit	literally
m	masculine
mid	middle voice
neg	negative
n	neuter
nom	nominative
num	number
obj	object
OE	Old English
OI	Old Icelandic
ON	Old Norse
ord	ordinal (number)
pl	plural
poet	poetical usage
poss	possessive (pronoun)
ppart	past participle
pref	prefix
prep	preposition
pres	present
pres part	present participle
pret-pres	preterite-present (verb)
pron	pronoun
refl	reflexive (verb or pronoun)
rel	relative (pronoun or particle)
sb	somebody
sg	singular
sth	something
str	strong (adjective or verb)
subj	subject
subjunct	subjunctive
superl	superlative (adjective or adverb)
trans	transitive (verb)
transl	translation
usu	usually
var	variant
vb	verb
w	with
wk	weak (adjective or verb)
=	equals

---

e-n (einhvern) = 'somebody,' *acc.*; **e-t** (eitthvat) = 'something,' *acc.*; **e-m** (einhverjum) = '(for) somebody,' *dat.*; **e-u** (einhverju) = '(for) something,' *dat.*; **e-s** (einhvers) = '(of) somebody or something,' *gen.*

~	Alternative or alternating (spelling)

A

Aðalráðr konungr *m* King Æthelred II (the unready) of England

aðra *f acc sg & m acc pl of* **annarr**

aðrir *m nom pl of* **annarr**

❖ **af** *prep* [*w dat*] of, by; off, out of, from

afar *adv* extremely

afarmenni *n* a big or strong man

afbragð *n* outstanding example; **afbragð þeira manna allra** the most outstanding of all those men

afbrigði *n* deviation, transgression, offense

afl *n* physical strength, might, power; **rammr at afli** extremely strong

afreksmaðr *m* outstanding or exceptional man

aka <ekr, ók, óku, ekinn> *vb* drive

akkeri *n* anchor

akr <akrs, akrar> *m* field, crop

ala <elr, ól, ólu, alinn> *vb* give birth to; bring up, raise (children)

alda *gen pl of* **öld**

aldinn *adj* aged, old

aldr <-rs, -rar> *m* age; lifetime; old age; long period of time

aldregi *adv* never

❖ **aldri** *adv* never

Alföðr <-s> *m* All-Father, i.e., Odin

alheimskr *adj* completely foolish

alin <alnar~álnar> *f* Old Icelandic *ell* (about half a yard); unit of value, typically of woolen cloth

alla *f acc sg & m acc pl of* **allr**

allan *m acc sg of* **allr**

allfríðr *adj* very beautiful

allir *m nom pl of* **allr**

allmikill *adj* very great

❖ **allr** <*f* öll, *n* allt> *adj pron* all, entire, whole

allra *gen pl of* **allr**

allri *f dat sg of* **allr**

allt *adv* completely, entirely; everywhere; **allt til Orkneyja** all the way to the Orkney Islands; **allt til þess** right up to that point; **allt upp undir** right up under

Alrekr <-s> *m* Alrek (*personal name*)

alsnotr *adj* sagacious, wise (of a woman)

alsvartr *adj* pure black

alþýða *f* all the people, the majority of the people, the public, the common people

ambátt (*also* **ambótt**) <*pl* -ir> *f* handmaid, maidservant

ambótt *var of* **ambátt**

andi *m* breath, spirit

Andvari *m* Andvari (*personal name*)

angr <*gen* angrs> *m* grief, sorrow

annan *m acc sg of* **annarr**

❖ **annarr** <*f* önnur, *n* annat> *adj pron* one of two, other, another; *ord* second; **annarr ... annarr** *conj* one ... the other

aptann <*dat* aptni, *gen* aptans, *pl* aptnar> *m* evening

❖ **aptr** <*superl* aptastr~epztr> *adv* back, again

arfi *m* heir

arfr <-s> *m* inheritance

argr *adj* cowardly, effeminate, (passively) homosexual

armr *m* arm

armr *adj* poor, unfortunate, unhappy; vile, wretched, wicked

Arnfastr <-s> *m* Arnfast (*personal name*)

askr <-s, -ar> *m* ash, ash tree; ash spear; small ship; the great ash tree, **Yggdrasill**

Assurr (*also* **Özurr**) <-s> *m* Assur (*personal name*)

at *prep* [*w dat*] at, in; as to, as, with respect to; on account of, by reason of; close up to, around, by

❖ **at** *conj* that

at *inf marker* to

atall <*f* ötul, *n* atalt> *adj* fierce, aggressive

Atall <-s> *m* Atal, name of a Viking (*personal name*)

atburðr <-ar, -ir> *m* occurrence, event; **af þessum atburði** because of this incident

atganga *f* attack

atgervimaðr *var of* **atgørvimaðr**

atgørvi *f and n* ability, talent, accomplishment; **at atgørvi** in ability (*esp physical*)

atgørvimaðr (*also* **atgervimaðr**) *m* a man of accomplishments

atkváma *f* arrival

atlaga *f* attack; laying ships alongside for attack

atróðr <*gen* atróðrs> *m* rowing towards, rowing against

atseta *f* a royal residence

auðgi *weak m nom sg* of **auðigr**

❖ **auðigr** (*also* **auðugr**) <*acc* auðgan> *adj* rich, wealthy; **auðigr at fé** very wealthy

auðugr *var* of **auðigr**

auga *n* eye

auk *prep* [*w gen*] aside from

auka <eykr, jók, jóku, aukinn> *vb* increase, augment; [*w dat*] add; exceed, surpass

aurr <-s> *m* mud

ausa <eyss, jós, jósu, ausinn> *vb* pour, sprinkle; **ausa [e-n]/[e-t] [e-m]** sprinkle [sb/sth] with [sth]; **ausa**

bát bail a boat

austan *adv* from the east

Austmaðr *m* person from the east, Norwegian

austr <-rs, *superl* austastr> *n* east; *adv* eastward

austrför <*pl* austfarar> *f* (*usu in pl*) travels to the east

Austrlönd *n pl* the eastern lands; eastern Europe; Russia and the Orient

austrvegr <-s, -ir> *m* the east, i.e., the Baltic, *lit* the eastern way; **fara í austrveg** trading or raiding in the Baltic or journeying east and south down the rivers of Russia

austrœnn *adj* eastern

auvirðismaðr *m* worthless wretch, wretched man

Á

á <*gen* ár, *pl* ár, *dat* ám, *gen* á> *f* river

á *1/3sg pres* of **eiga**

❖ **á** *prep* [*w acc*] onto, on, towards (*motion*); with respect to; [*w dat*] on; upon; at; in (*position*)

á brott *adv* away

á milli *var* of **milli**

❖ **áðr** *adv* before; already

áeggjun <-ar> *f* egging on, urging

❖ **ágætr** *adj* excellent

ái <á, ár> *m* great-grandfather

ákafamaðr *m* an aggressive man

ákafliga *adv* exceedingly, very; vehemently, impetuosly

ákafr <*f* áköf> *adj* fierce

ál <*pl* -ar> *f* leather strap

Álfheimr *m* Alfheim, World of the Elves

álfr <-s, -ar> *m* elf

Áli *m* Ali (*personal name,* an old shortening for Áleifr~Óláfr)

álit *n* appearance

Álof *f* Alof (*personal name*)

álpt <*pl* álptir~elptr> *f* swan

Álptanes *n* Alptanes (*place name*), Swans' Headland

álög *n pl* dues or taxes

án *prep* [*w gen*] without

ár *n* year

árferð <*pl* -ir> *f* season, harvest

Árnes *n* Arness (*place name*)

Árni *m* Arni (*personal name*)

ársæll *adj* fortunate as to the seasonal harvest; **allra konunga ársælstr** of all kings the most harvest-fortunate

ársælstr *superl* of **ársæll**

árvænn *adj* promising a good seasonal harvest

ásamt *adv* together

Ásbjörn <*gen* Ásbjarnar> *m* Asbjorn (*personal name*)

Ásbrú *f* Asbru, another name for **Bifröst**

Ásdís *f* Asdis (*personal name*)

Ásgarðr *m* Asgard, the residence or fortress of the gods

Ásgerðr <*acc/dat* Ásgerði, *gen* Ásgerðar> *f* Asgerd (*personal name*)

Ásgrímr <-s> *m* Asgrim (*personal name*)

ásjá *f* help, aid, protection; inspection; appearance, shape

Ásmundr <s> *m* Asmund (*personal name*)

áss <*dat* æsi~ás, *gen* áss~ásar, *pl* æsir, *acc* ásu~æsi> *m* god; **Æsir** *pl* one of the two major groups of gods

ást *f* love, affection (frequently used in plural with same meaning)

Ásta *f* Asta (*personal name*)

Ásvaldr <-s> *m* Asvald (*personal name*)

ásynja *f* goddess

át *1/3sg past* of **eta**

❖ **átta** <*ord* áttandi~áttundi, átti, eighth > *num* eight

átti *3sg past* of **eiga**

áttján <*ord* áttjándi, eighteenth> *num* eighteen

---

e-n (einhvern) = 'somebody,' *acc.*; **e-t** (eitthvat) = 'something,' *acc.*; **e-m** (einhverjum) = '(for) somebody,' *dat.*; **e-u** (einhverju) = '(for) something,' *dat.*; **e-s** (einhvers) = '(of) somebody or something,' *gen.*

áttu *3pl past* of **eiga**

ávanr <*f* ávön, *n* ávant> *adj* only in *n* and the phrase
 [e-s] er ávant [sth] is wanted, needed

B

---

bað *1/3sg past* of **biðja**

baðmr <-s> *m* tree

❖ **bak** *n* back

Baldr <-rs> *m* Baldr (*personal name*)

Balli (*also* **Baldi**) *m* Balli (*personal name*)

bana <-að-> *vb* [*w dat*] kill

banahögg *n* death-blow

banamaðr *m* killer, executioner, slayer

banasár *n* fatal wound, death

band <*pl* bönd> band, cord; the act of binding; (*pl*)
 bands, fetters; [*poet*] the gods

bani *m* death, bane, slayer

bann *n* prohibition, ban

banna <-að-> *vb* ban, forbid, prohibit

bar *1/3sg past* of **bera**

bardagi *m* fight, battle; beating, thrashing

barð *n* brim of a helmet or hat; verge or edge of a
 hill; prow of a ship

barn <*pl* börn> *n* child

barnœska *f* childhood

barr *n* foliage, often needles (of pine, etc.)

Barreyjar *f pl* the Barra Isles

batna <-að-> *vb* improve; *impers* [e-m] **batnar** one
 recovers

batnaði *3sg past* of **batna**

batt *1/3sg past* of **binda**

bauð *1/3sg past* of **bjóða**

baugr <-s, -ar> *m* ring, bracelet, armlet

bauzt *2sg past mid* of **bjóða**

bazt *superl adv var* of **bezt**

baztr *superl adj var* of **beztr**

❖ **báðir** <*f* báðar, *n* bæði, *gen* beggja > *adj pron dual*
 both

Bálki Blæingsson *m* Balki Blæingsson (*personal
 name*)

Bárðr <-ar> *m* Bard (*personal name*); **Bárðr svarti**
 Bard the Black

bátr <-s, -ar> *m* boat

beðið *ppart* of **biðja**

beggja *all gen pl* of **báðir**

beiða <beiddi, beiddr> *vb* [*w gen*] ask, beg; **beiða
 [e-n] [e-s]** ask [sb] for [sth]; **beiðask** *mid* ask for,
 request on one's own behalf

beiddisk *3sg past mid* of **beiða**

beiddusk *3pl past mid* of **beiða**

bein *n* bone

beinahrúga *f* bone-pile

beiskr *adj* bitter, acrid; angry, exasperated; painful,
 sore

beiting <*pl* -ar> *f* grazing, pasturage

bekkr <*dat* bekk, *gen* -s~-jar, *pl* -ir> *m* bench

belgr <*dat* belg, *gen* -s~-jar, *pl* -ir> *m* pelt, skin of an
 animal (taken off whole); skin-bag; bellows

bella <bellr, ball, –, –> *defective vb* [*w dat*] hit, hurt

bella <-di, -tr> *vb* [*w dat*] venture (into)

belti *n* belt

ben <*gen* -jar> *f* (mortal) wound

❖ **bera** <berr, bar, báru, borinn> *vb* bear, carry; **bera
 saman** collect; compare; **bera um** carry about;
 bera ørendi sín (upp) fyrir [e-n] plead one's case
 before [sb]; tell one's errand [sb]

berja <barði, barðr~bariðr> *vb* strike, beat; **berjask**
 mid fight

berr *adj* naked, bare; unsheathed (of a sword)

berserkr <-s, -ir> *m* berserker

berserksgangr <-s> *m* fury of a berserker, going
 berserk

betr *comp adv* of **vel**, better

betri *comp adj* of **góðr**, better

beysta <beysti, beystr> *vb* bruise, beat

beytill <-s> *m* horse-prick

bezt (*also* **bazt**) *superl adv* of **vel**, best

beztr (*also* **baztr**) *superl adj* of **góðr**, best

❖ **biðja** <biðr, bað, báðu, beðinn> *vb* ask, beg;
 command, tell; **biðja [e-n] [e-s]** ask [sb] for [sth];
 biðja gera command to be made

bifask <-ði, -ðr *also* -að-> *vb mid* shake, tremble,
 quake; be moved

Bifröst *f* Bifrost, the rainbow bridge that connects
 Miðgarðr and **Ásgarðr**

bikkja *f* female dog, bitch

bila <-að-> *vb* fail

binda <bindr, batt, bundu, bundinn> *vb* bind, tie,
 fasten; bind up (a wound); pledge; **binda í [e-u]**
 bind to [sth], bind on [sth]

bíða <bíðr, beið, biðu, beðinn> *vb* [*w gen*] wait for,
 remain, abide; [*w acc*] suffer, undergo

bíta <bítr, beit, bitu, bitinn> *vb* bite, bite through; rip apart

bjalla <*gen* bjöllu, *pl* bjöllur> *f* bell

bjarg <*pl* björg> *n* rock, boulder; cliff

bjarga <bergr, barg, burgu, borginn> *vb* [*w dat*] save, help

Bjarnardóttir *f* Bjorn's daughter (*personal name*)

Bjarnarfjörðr *m* Bjorn's Fjord (*place name*)

Bjarni *m* Bjarni (*personal name*)

bjartr <*f* björt, *n* bjart> *adj* bright

bjó *1/3sg past* of **búa**

❖ **bjóða** <býðr, bauð, buðu, boðinn> *vb* [*w acc*] offer; [*w dat*] invite; order, command; **bjóða [e-m] sætt** offer [sb] reconciliation; **bjóða [e-n] [e-m] at sætt** offer [sth] to [sb] for reconciliation

björn <*dat* birni, *gen* bjarnar, *pl* birnir, *acc* björnu> *m* bear

Björn <*dat* Birni, *gen* Bjarnar> *m* Bjorn (*personal name*); **Björn buna** Bjorn buna

blautr *adj* soft; soaked, wet

blár <*f* blá *n* blátt> *adj* blue; dark, black

blása <blæsr, blés, blésu, blásinn> *vb* blow

Bleking *f* Blekinge, Denmark (*place name*) now part of Sweden)

blindr *adj* blind

blíðr *adj* happy

blóð *n* blood

blót *n* sacrifice

blóta <blœtr, blét, blétu, blótinn> *vb* [*w acc*] worship; worship with sacrifice; [*w dat*] sacrifice, sacrifice in worship

blóta <-að> *vb* [*w acc*] worship; worship with sacrifice; [*w dat*] sacrifice, sacrifice in worship; curse

blótuðu *3pl past* of **blóta** (*wk vb*)

blunda <-að> *vb* shut the eyes, doze

Blængr <-s> *m* Blaeng (*personal name*)

bogi *m* bow

bokki (*also* **bökki**) *m* buck, fellow (used as a manner of address) **bokki sæll** my good fellow, good sir, boss

Bolli *m* Bolli (*personal name*)

boløx *f* broad-axe

borð *f* board, plank; side of a ship; board, table; board, food, upkeep; **á borð** on one side (of a ship)

borg <*pl* -ir> *f* stronghold, fortification; town

Borg *f* Borg (*place name*)

Borgarfjörðr *m* (*place name*)

borgarmaðr *m* garrisoned soldier; townsman

bóandi <*pl* bóendr> *m var* of **bóndi**

bógr <*dat* bœgi, *gen* bógar, *pl* bœgir, *acc* bógu> *m* shoulder of an animal

bók <*gen* bókar~bœkr, *pl* bœkr> *f* book

ból *n* lair

❖ **bóndi** (*also* **bóandi** & **búandi**) <*gen* bónda, *pl* bœndr> *m* husband; farmer; head of a household

bót <*pl* bœtr> *f* bettering, cure, remedy; adornment; *pl* compensation, atonement; **at bótum** as atonement

brann *1/3sg past* of **brenna**

Brattahlíð *f* Brattahlid (*place name*), Steep-Slope

brauð *n* bread

braut *var* of **brott**

braut *1/3sg past* of **brjóta**

brautflutning <*pl* -ar> *f* carrying off

brauzk *1,2,3sg past* of **brjótask**

brauzt *2sg past* of **brjóta**

brá <*gen* brár, *pl* brár> *f* eyelash

brá *1/3sg past* of **bregða**

bráðgörr *adj* matured early in life, precocious

bráðr <*n* brátt> *adj* sudden; hot-tempered, hasty

bráðum *adv* soon, shortly

brásk *1/3sg past mid* of **bregða**

brátt *adv* soon, suddenly; **brátt er** as soon as

bregða <bregðr, brá, brugðu, brugðinn> *vb* [*w dat*] move quickly; draw, brandish (a weapon); break (faith or an oath); turn, alter, change; break off, leave off, give up; **bregða við [e-u]** ward off with, parry with [sth]; **bregðask** *mid* fail, come to nothing; **bregðask [e-m]** deceive, disappoint [sb]; **bregðask í [e-t]** shapechange, turn into [sth]

breiða <-ddi, -ddr> *vb* spread; stretch; display

Breiðablik *n* Breidablik, the hall of the god Baldr (*place name*)

Breiðafjarðardalir *m pl* the Dales of Breidafjord (*place name*)

Breiðafjörðr *m* Breidafjord,) Broad Fjord (*place name*

breiðara *comp adv* of **breiðr**, more broadly

breiðr <*f* breið, *n* breitt> *adj* broad

brekka *f* slope

brenna <brennr, brann, brunnu, brunninn> *vb intrans* burn

brenna <-di, -dr> *vb trans* burn

bresta <brestr; brast, brustu, brostinn> *vb* burst, break, crash; **bresta niðr** crash down

Brísingamen *n* the necklace of **Freyja**

---

e-n (einhvern) = 'somebody,' *acc.*; **e-t** (eitthvat) = 'something,' *acc.*; **e-m** (einhverjum) = '(for) somebody,' *dat.*;
e-u (einhverju) = '(for) something,' *dat.*; **e-s** (einhvers) = '(of) somebody or something,' *gen.*

brjóst *n* chest, breast

brjóta <brýtr, braut, brutu, brotinn> *vb* break, break up, break open; **brjótask til ríkis** fight for the kingdom

Brodd-Helgi <-s> *m* Spike-Helgi (*personal name*)

broddr <-s, -ar> *m* spike

brotna <-að-> *vb* break

❖ **brott** (*also* **burt** & **(í) braut**) *adv* away, off

❖ **bróðir** <acc/dat/gen bróður, pl brœðr, dat brœðrum, gen brœðra> *m* brother

bróðurgjöld *n pl* wergeld, ransom, or compensation for a dead brother

brunnr <-s, -ar> *m* well; spring

brutu *3pl past* of **brjóta**

brú <gen brúar, pl brúar~brúr~brýr> *f* bridge; causeway built over swampy ground

brúðfé *n* bride's fee or gift

brúðkaup *n* wedding feast

brúðlaup *n* wedding feast

brúðr <acc/dat brúði, gen brúðar, pl brúðir> *f* bride; [*poet*] woman

brúnn *adj* brown

bryggja *f* gangway; pier; bridge

Brynhildr *f* Brynhild (*personal name*)

brynja *f* chain-mail shirt

bryti *m* bailiff

brœkr *f pl* breeches

buna *f* buna (nickname of uncertain meaning, perhaps 'one with ungartered stockings,' i.e. hanging down his leg)

burlufótr *m* clumsy-foot (*meaning uncertain*)

burr <-ar, -ir> *m* [*poet*] son

burt *var* of **brott**

❖ **bú** (*also* **bý**) <dat pl búm> *n* home, house, household; farm; estate

❖ **búa** <býr, bjó, bjoggu~bjuggu, búinn> *vb* live (in a place), dwell, inhabit, live; prepare, make ready; **búask** *mid* prepare, get oneself ready; **búask til [e-s]** prepare oneself for [sth]; **búask um** make oneself secure, prepare

búandi <pl búendr> *m var* of **bóndi**

búfé *n* cattle

búi *m* dweller, inhabitant

búinn *ppart* of **búa** ready, prepared

búizk *ppart* of **búask** (búit + sk)

Búseyra *f* Buseyra, a giantess killed by Thor

búss *m* a type of wood

bygð *f* abode

byggja *var* of **byggva**

byggva (*also* **byggja**) <-ði, -ðr> *vb* settle; occupy, inhabit

byrðr *f* burden

byrja <-að-> *vb* begin

byrr <-jar, -ir> *m* fair wind

bý (*var* of **bú**) <dat pl býum> *n* home, house, household; farm; estate

býfluga *f* bee

❖ **bæði** *adv* both; **bæði ... ok** *conj* both ... and

bæði *n* of **báðir**

bær *var* of **bœr**

bœgi *dat sg* of **bógr**

bœn *f* prayer, request

❖ **bœr** (*also* **bær**) <gen bœjar~býjar, pl bœir, dat bœjum, gen bœja> *m* farm, farmhouse, farmstead; landed estate; town

bœta <-tti, -ttr> *vb* better, make compensation

Böðvarr <-s> *m* Bodvar (*personal name*)

bökki *var* of **bokki**

böl <gen pl bölva> *n* misfortune

bölvasmiðr *m* contriver of mischief, misfortune

börðusk *3pl past mid* of **berja**

D/Ð

daga <-að-> *vb* dawn

dagmál *n* nine in the morning

❖ **dagr** <dat degi, gen dags, pl dagar> *m* day; **í dag** today; **um daginn eptir** (on) the day after, the next day

dagsmark *n* day-mark, time of day

Dala-Kollson *m* son of Dala-Koll (*personal name*) Koll of the Dales

Dalir *m pl* Dalir (*place name*) the Dales

dalr <dat dal, gen dals, pl dalar~dalir> *m* valley, dale

Danir *m pl* the Danes·

Danmarkar *gen* of **Danmörk**

Danmörk <gen Danmarkar> *f* Denmark

danskr *adj* Danish

datt *1/3sg past* of **detta**

❖ **dauðr** <f dauð, n dautt> *adj* dead

daufr *adj* deaf

dautt *n nom/acc sg* of **dauðr**

dáð *f* deed

Dáinsleif *f* Dainsleif, the name of Hogni's sword, Dain's Inheritance

detta <dettr, datt, duttu, dottinn> *vb* drop, fall

deyja <deyr, dó, dó, dáinn> *vb* die

djarfr <*f* djöf, *n* djarft> *adj* bold, daring

djúpauðigr *adj* deep-minded

djúpvitr *adj* deep-witted, resourceful

dó *1/3sg & 3pl past of* deyja

Dómaldi *m* Domaldi (*personal name*)

dómr <-s, -ar> *m* court; judgement

dómstaðr *m* place where court is held

❖ dóttir <*acc/dat/gen* dóttur, *pl* dœtr, *dat* dœtrum, *gen* dœtra> *f* daughter

draga <dregr, dró, drógu, dreginn> *vb* pull, draw, drag

drakk *1/3sg past of* drekka

drap *1/3sg past of* drepa

drapt *2sg past of* drepa

drasill *m* horse (*poet*)

draumblæti *n* pride, haughtiness

dráp *n* killing, murder

dreginn *ppart of* draga

dregit *ppart of* draga

dreifa <-ði, -ðr> *vb* spread, scatter; dreifask *mid* be spread out

dreki *m* dragon-ship

drekka <drekkr, drakk, drukku, drukkinn> *vb* drink

drengiligr *adj* brave, valiant

drengr *m* a bold man

❖ drepa <drepr, drap, drápu, drepinn> *vb* slay, kill, smite; strike, beat, knock; drepa [e-u] í [e-t] stick [sth] into [sth]

Drepstokkr <-s> *m* Drepstokk (*place name*)

dreyma <-ði~di, -t> *vb* [*acc subj and obj*] dream; [e-n] dreymr [e-t] *impers* [sb] dreams [sth]

dreyra <-ði, -t> *vb* bleed, ooze (of blood from a slight wound)

drífa <drífr, dreif, drifu, drifinn> *vb* [*trans*] to drive; [*intrans*] to crowd, throng, drift, hurry

drjúpa <drýpr, draup, drupu, dropinn> *vb* drip

Droplaugarsynir *m pl* the sons of Droplaug

dróttinn <*dat* dróttni~drottni, *gen* dróttins, *pl* dróttnar~drottnar> *m* lord

dróttning <*dat* dróttningu, *pl* dróttningar> *f* queen

drykkr <-jar, -ir> *m* drink

duga <-ði, dugat> *vb* do, show prowess; duga verr come off badly, fare worse (in a contest), to be useful

dunði *3sg past of* dynja

dúfa *f* dove, pigeon

dvelja <dvaldi, dvaldr~dvalinn> *vb* slow, stop

dvergr <-s, -ar> *m* dwarf

dynja <dundi~dunði, dunit> *vb* din, thunder, resound, whir, whizz; pour, shower

dys <-jar> *f* cairn

dýja <dúði, dúit> *vb* shake

dýr *n* wild beast; animal; deer

dœma <-di~ði, -dr~ðr> *vb* judge

dœmðir *ppart (m nom pl) of* dœma

dögg <*dat* dögg~döggu, *gen* döggvar, *pl* döggvar> *f* dew

dögum *dat pl of* dagr

Døkkálfar *m pl* the Dark Elves

døkkr <*m acc sg* døkkvan, *m nom pl* døkkvir, *m acc pl* døkkva, *f acc sg* døkkva, *f pl* døkkvar> *adj* dark

E

❖ eða (*also* eðr) *conj* or; (*introducing a question*) but

eðr *var of* eða

❖ ef *conj* if

efniligr *adj* promising

efri (*also* øfri) *comp adj* upper, inner; latter

efstr (*also* øfstr) *superl adj* uppermost, innermost; last

egg <*gen pl* eggja> *n* egg

egg <*pl* eggjar> *f* edge, blade's edge

eggja <-að-> *vb* incite, goad, egg on, urge

eggskurn *f* egg shell

Egill <*dat* Agli, *gen* Egils> *m* Egil (*personal name*)

Egilsstaðir *m pl* Egilsstadir (*place name*) Egil's Farmstead

❖ eiga <á, átti, áttr> *pret-pres vb* own, have, possess; be married or related to; [*aux*] must, owe, be obligated, have to; eiga ráðagørð take council

❖ eigi *adv* not

eigna <-að-> attribute, dedicate; *mid* eignask get, claim, take, become the owner of

eignaðisk *3sg past mid of* eigna

eignazk *ppart mid of* eigna

eik <-ar, -r> *f* oak, tree

Einarr *m* Einar (*personal name*)

---

e-n (einhvern) = 'somebody,' *acc.*; e-t (eitthvat) = 'something,' *acc.*; e-m (einhverjum) = '(for) somebody,' *dat.*;
e-u (einhverju) = '(for) something,' *dat.*; e-s (einhvers) = '(of) somebody or something,' *gen.*

einheri <-ja, -jar> *m* great champion (addressing Thor); **einherjar** *pl* slain warriors who dwell in Valhöll

❖ **einn** <*f* ein, *n* eitt, *ord* fyrstr, first > *num* one; *indef pro* a, an, a certain one; *adj* alone (when placed after the noun it modifies, **einn** can take on the meaning 'only')

❖ **einnhverr** *adj pron* some, someone, a certain one; (*usu as two words,* **einn hverr**) each, each one; **einnhvern dag** one day

einskipa *adv* with one ship

einu *n dat sg* of **einn**

einvaldi *m* sole ruler, monarch, sovereign

einvaldskonungr *m* sole ruler

Eiríkr <-s> *m* Eirik (*personal name*)

Eiríksfjörðr *m* Eiriksfjord (*place name*), Eirik's Fjord

eista *n* testicle

eitthvat *adj pron* some, something, a certain one

❖ **ek** <*acc* mik, *dat* mér, *gen* mín> *pron* I

ek *1sg pres* of **aka**

ekki *n nom/acc sg* of **engi**

❖ **ekki** *adv* not

eldaskáli *m* fire hall, main hall of a long house, where benches used for sitting and sleeping were warmed by a long fire that ran the length of the hall and was used for cooking

elding *f* the last part of the night before dawn

eldr <-s~ellds~ellz, -ar> *m* fire

elfr <*acc/dat* elfi, *gen* elfar, *pl* elfar> *f* great river

Elfráðr inn ríki *m* Alfred the Great (*personal name*)

elgr <*gen* elgs~elgjar, elgir> *m* elk

elli *f* age

❖ **ellifu** <*ord* ellifti, eleventh > *num* eleven

ellri *comp* of **gamall** older, elder

ellstr *var* of **el(l)ztr)**

elska <-að> *vb* love; **elskask** love one another, **elskask at [e-m]** grow fond of [sb]

el(l)ztr (*also* **ellstr**) *superl* of **gamall** oldest, eldest

❖ **en** *conj* but; and (*in a contrastive sense*); *w comp* than

en er *conj* but when

en þó *adv* nevertheless

❖ **enda** *conj* and (*etc.*); and if; even; even if; and also, and so; and yet

endi (*also* **endir**) <-is, -ar> *m* end

endir *var* of **endi**

endlangr *adj* the whole length of

endr *adv* again, once more

❖ **engi** <*f* engi, *n* ekki> *indef pron* no one, none, no

engill <-s, -ar> *m* angel

engis *var* of **enskis**

Englakonungr *m* king of England

England *n* England

Englar *m pl* the English

engrar *f gen sg* of **engi**

enkis *var* of **enskis**

❖ **enn** *adv* yet, still

enni *n* forehead

enskis (*also* **engis~enkis**) *m/n gen sg* of **engi**

enskr *adj* English

ept *var* of **eptir**

❖ **eptir** (*also* **ept**) *prep* [*w acc*] after (*in time*); in memory of; [*w dat*] after, along; **eptir landinu** along the coast; after somebody

eptri *comp* of **aptr** farther back

epztr (*also* **aptastr**) *superl* of **aptr** farthest back

❖ **er** (*older* **es**) *rel particle* who, which, that; *conj* when; where; as

er *3sg pres* of **vera**

erendi (*also* **ørendi** & **erindi**) *n* errand, mission, result of errand

erfa <-ði, -ðr> *vb* throw a funeral feast; inherit

erfiði *n* trouble, effort

erindi *var* of **erendi**

erja <er, arði, arinn> *vb* plough; scratch, scrape

Erlingr <-s> *m* Erling (*personal name*)

eru *3pl pres* of **vera**

es *older form* of **er**

eta <etr, át, átu, etinn> *vb* eat

ey <*dat* ey~eyju, *gen* eyjar, *pl* eyjar> *f* island

eyða <-ddi, -ddr> *vb* waste; spend; do away with, destroy; make empty; **eyðask** *mid* be squandered, come to naught

eyna *acc sg* of **ey+in**, the island

eykt *f* three in the afternoon

eyra *n* ear

eyri *var* of **eyrr**

eyrir <*acc/dat* eyri, *gen* eyris, *pl* aurar, *acc* aura, *dat* aurum, *gen* aura> *m* an ounce of silver or gold

eyrr (*also* **eyri**) <*acc/dat* eyri, *gen* eyrar, *pl* eyrar> *f* gravelly riverbank; small spit of land running into the sea

eystri *comp* of **austr** more eastern

Eyvindr <-ar> *m* Eyvind (*personal name*)

F

❖ **faðir** <*acc* föður, *dat* föður~feðr, *gen* föður, *pl* feðr, *dat* feðrum, *gen* feðra> *m* father

❖ **fagr** <*f* fögr, *n* fagrt, *comp* fegri, *superl* fegrstr> *adj* beautiful, fair, attractive

❖ **falla** <fellr, féll~fell, féllu~fellu, fallinn> *vb* fall; **fallask** *mid* fail

fann *1/3sg past* of **finna**

❖ **fara** <ferr, fór, fóru, farinn> *vb* go, travel; move; **fara at** go, proceed; **fara frá** leave, back off, back away

farmaðr *m* seaman, seafarer, merchant

farmr *m* cargo

farþegi *m* passenger on a voyage

fast *adv* firmly,

❖ **fá** <fær, fekk, fengu, fenginn> *vb* get, take, procure; grasp; marry; give, deliver; **fekk konu** got married, *lit got a wife*; **fá góðar viðtökur** be welcomed well

Fáfnir *m* Fafnir, a son of Hreidmar who turns himself into a dragon, brother of Regin

fálátr *adj* silent, reserved, taciturn

❖ **fár** <*f* fá, *n* fátt, *comp* fær(r)i, *superl* fæstr> *adj pron* few; cold, reserved; **fátt manna** few men, *lit* few of men

fásénn *adj* rare

fátœkr *adj* poor, wretched

feðgar *m pl* father and son(s)

❖ **feginn** *adj* glad, joyful

fegrð *f* beauty

fegrstr <*f* fegrst, *n* fegrst> *superl* of **fagr**

feigr *adj* fated to die

feitr *adj* fat

fekk *1/3sg past* of **fá**

fela <felr, fal, fálu, fólginn> *vb* hide, conceal

fell *n* hill, mountain

fella <-di, -dr> *vb* fell

fellu *3pl past* of **falla**

fengit *ppart* of **fá**

fengu *3pl past* of **fá**

❖ **ferð** <*pl* -ir> *f* journey; conduct, behavior

ferma <-da, -dr> *vb* load **ferma [e-t] með [e-u]** load [sth] with [sth]

ferr *2/3sg pres* of **fara**

feti *m* strider, stepper, pacer (name for a horse)

❖ **fé** <*gen* fjár, *gen pl* fjá> *n* cattle, sheep; wealth, money

félagi *m* partner, comrade, companion, friend

félítill *adj* short of money, poor

féll *1/3sg past* of **falla**

fémætr *adj* valuable

fénu = **fé** + **inu**

❖ **fimm** <*ord* fimmti, fifth > *num* five

fim(m)tán <*ord* fim(m)tándi, fifteenth> *num* fifteen

fingr <*gen* fingrar~fingrs, *pl* fingr> *m* finger

❖ **finna** <finnr, fann, fundu, fundinn> *vb* find; **finnask** *mid* be found, be perceived, noticed; (*impers*) [*w dat subj*] be found, perceived, noticed by [sb]

Finnr *m* Finn (*personal name*)

firði *dat sg* of **fjörðr**

firr *comp adv* of **fjarri**

first *superl adv* of **fjarri**

fiskr *m* fish

fjaðralauss *adj* without feathers, featherless

fjaðrhamr *m* feather skin, coat, shape

fjall <*pl* fjöll> *n* mountain

fjara *f* ebb-tide, ebb; shore, beach

fjarri <*comp* firr, *superl* first> *adv* far off

fjándi <*gen* fjánda; *pl* fjándr> *m* enemy

Fjón *f* Fyn, Denmark (*place name*)

❖ **fjórir** <*f* fjórar, *n* fjögur, *m acc* fjóra, *dat* fjórum, *gen* fjögurra, *ord* fjórði, fourth > *num* four

fjórtán <*ord* fjórtándi, fourteenth> *num* fourteen

fjórum *dat pl* of **fjórir**

fjöðr *f* feather

fjögur *n nom/acc pl* **fjórir**

fjölð *f* a multitude; [*poet, w gen*] plenty of

fjölði *m* abundance

fjölkunnigr *adj* skilled in magic

fjölkyngi *f* magic, the black art, witchcraft, sorcery

❖ **fjölmennr** *adj* in a large group, numerous; with many people, well-attended

fjölmennt *adv* in crowds, in large numbers

fjör <*dat* fjörvi> *n* life

fjörðr <*dat* firði, *gen* fjarðar, *pl* firðir, *acc* fjörðu> *m* fjord

fjörlausn *f* ransom for one's life; release from life

fjörsegi *m* life-morsel, heart

flagð <*pl* flögð> *n* an ogress, giantess

flaki *m* wicker-work shield or barrier

flakka <-að-> *vb* roam, wander about (as a shepherd

---

e-n (einhvern) = 'somebody,' *acc.*;   **e-t** (eitthvat) = 'something,' *acc.*;   **e-m** (einhverjum) = '(for) somebody,' *dat.*; **e-u** (einhverju) = '(for) something,' *dat.*;   **e-s** (einhvers) = '(of) somebody or something,' *gen.*

with his sheep)

flaska *f* a flask; **flösku-skegg** bottle-beard(*nickname*); **flösku-bakr** bottle-back (*nickname*)

flatnefr *adj* flat-nosed (*in nicknames*)

flaut *1/3sg past* of **fljóta**

flá <flær; fló, flógu; fleginn> *vb* flay; strip (of clothes and of money)

fleginn *ppart* of **flá**

fleinn *m* pike, spear; dart, shaft; fluke of an anchor

fleiri *comp* of **margr** more

flestr *superl* of **margr** most

fljóta <flýtr, flaut, flutu, flotinn> *vb* float; **skipit flaut** the ship floated (at anchor)

fljúga <flýgr, fló~flaug, flugu, floginn> *vb* fly

Flosi *m* Flosi (*personal name*)

fló *1/3 sg past* of **fljúga**

flutt *ppart* of **flytja**

flytja <flutti, fluttr> *vb* convey, move, carry; bring, deliver; tell, recite

flýgr *2/3sg pres* of **fljúga**

flýja <-ði, flýðr~flýiðr> *vb* flee

fnasa <-að-> *vb* snort

forðum *adv* formerly, of old

formaðr *m* captain, leader, chieftain, *lit* fore-man

formáli *m* stipulation, condition; preamble, foreword, preface

forráð *n* administration, management; **til forráða** for rulership

fors <pl -ar> *m* waterfall

forstjóri *m* overseer, leader

forstreymis *adv* downstream

foringi *m* captain, commander, leader

fólginn *ppart* of **fela**

fólgit *ppart* of **fela**

fólk *n* folk, people; [*poet*] battle

Fólkaðr (*also* **Fólkvarðr**) <-ar> *m* Folkad (*personal name*)

fór *1/3sg past* of **fara**

fóru *3pl past* of **fara**

fóstr <gen fóstrs> *n* fostering of a child; **taka til fóstrs** take as a foster child; **vera at fóstri** be a foster-child, be in a fostering relationship

fóstri *m* foster-son

❖ **fótr** <dat fœti, gen fótar, pl fœtr, acc fœtr> *m* foot, foot and leg

❖ **fram** <comp fremr~framar, superl fremst~framast> *adv* forward

framan *adv* from the front; **framan í hann** in his face

framar (*also* **fremr**) *comp adv* of **fram** farthest forward

framast (*also* **fremst**) *superl adv* of **fram** farthest

forward

frami *m* fame

frauð *n* froth; juice

❖ **frá** *prep* [*w dat*] from; about; *adv* away

frák, frá ek *from* **fregna**

fránn *adj* gleaming

fregna <fregn, frá, frágu, freginn> *vb* hear of, be informed; ask; **fr'ak (fr'a ek)** I heard

fregnvíss *adj* curious

freista <-að-> *vb* [*w gen*] try, make trial of

fremr *var* of **framar**

fremst *var* of **framast**

frest *n* delay, respite; **lj'a [e-m] fresta** give [sb]; respite

Freydís <acc/dat Freydísi gen Freydísar> *f* Freydis (*personal name*)

Freyja *f* a fertility goddess

frétt <pl -ir> *f* news

friðr <dat friði, gen friðar> *m* peace

Frigg *f* Frigg, a goddess, wife of Odin

frilla *f* mistress, concubine

fríðastr *superl* of **fríðr**

❖ **fríðr** <f fríð, n frítt> *adj* beautiful, handsome, fine

frost *n* frost

Fróði *m* Frodi (*personal name*)

fróðr <n frótt> *adj* wise

frú <frú~frúar, frúr> *f* mistress, lady

frægr *adj* well-known

❖ **frændi** <pl frændr> *m* kinsman, friend

frœði *f* knowledge

Fröysteinn (*also* **Freysteinn**) <-s> *m* Froystein (*personal name*)

fugl <-s, -ar> *m* bird

fuglakyn *f* family or species of bird

fuglsrödd *f* the speech of a bird, a bird's voice

❖ **fullr** *adj* full

fullsteikinn *ppart* fully roasted

fundinn *ppart* of **finna**

❖ **fundr** <-ar, -ir> *m* meeting; finding, discovery; **koma á fund [e-s]** come to a meeting with [sb]

funi *m* flame

fúna <-að-> *vb* rot, decay

fúss *adj* eager **fúss [e-s]** eager for [sth]

fylgð *f* help, support; guidance; party, followers

fylgja <fylgði, fylgt> *vb* [*w dat*] accompany; follow; help, side with

fylki *n* province

fylkja <-ti, -t> *vb* [*w dat*] draw up (in battle array)

fylla <-di, -dr> *vb* fill; complete; fulfill

fyr *var* of **fyrir**

❖ **fyrir** (*also* **fyr**) *prep* [*w acc/dat*] before, in front of;

along, against; before, preceding, ago; above, superior to; for, on behalf of; for, because of; by, by means of; [*w acc only*] in spite of, against; [*w dat only*] at the head of (leading); **fyrir austan / norðan / sunnan / vestan** in the east / north / south / west ; **fyrir innan** [*w acc*] inside; **fyrir neðan** [*w acc*] below; **fyrir ofan** [*w acc*] above; **fyrir útan** [*w acc*] outside; out beyond; **fyrir** *adv* ahead, in front, before; first, before; at hand, present; **fyrir því at** *conj* because

fyrirbjóða <-býðr, -bauð, -buðu, -boðinn> *vb* forbid

fyr(ir)nema *vb* deprive one of speech, make silent

❖ **fyrr** *comp adv* before, previously, sooner; **fyrr en** *conj* before, sooner than, until

❖ **fyrri** *comp adj* former, previous; *comp adv* (=**fyrr**) before, previously, sooner

fyrrum *adv* formerly, before

fyrst *superl adv* of **fyrr** first

❖ **fyrstr** *superl adj* of **fyrri** first

fyrstr *ord* first

fýsa <-ti, -tr> *vb* urge

fær *3sg pres* of **fá**

fær(r)i *comp adj* of **fár**

fœða <-ddi, -ddr> *vb* feed; rear, bring up; **fœða upp** bring up; **fœðask** *mid* grow up, be brought up; be born; feed oneself, be fed; **fœðask upp** grow up, be brought up

fœra <-ði, -ðr> *vb* bring, present, convey, send, give

föður *acc/dat/gen sg* of **faðir**

föðurkyn *n* father's kin

föðursystir *f* aunt, father's sister

fögr *f nom sg* of **fagr**

för *f* fare, journey; expedition

förum *1pl pres* of **fara**

G

gaf *1/3sg past* of **gefa**

galeið <*pl* galeiðr~galeiðir> *f* galley

❖ **gamall** <*acc* gamlan, *f* gömul, *n* gamalt, *comp* ellri~eldri, *superl* ellztr~elztr~ellstr~eldstr> *adj* old

gaman <*dat* gamni> *n* game, sport; pleasure, enjoyment, delight, joy

Gamli *m* Gamli, the Old One (*personal name*)

❖ **ganga** <gengr, gekk, gengu, genginn> *vb* walk; go; **ganga af** leave, go from; **ganga á [e-t]** encroach upon [sth]; **ganga til** go up to, go toward

ganga <*gen* göngu> *f* a walking, course, procession

Gangleri *m* Gangleri (*personal name, mythological*) Wanderer, the false name adopted by the Swedish king Gylfi

garðr <-s, -ar> *m* enclosed space, yard; fence; court; stronghold, castle

garpr <-s, -ar> *m* a bold, daring, courageous, or warlike man or woman

gata <*gen* götu, *pl* götur> *f* way, path, road

gaumr *m* attention, heed; **gefa at [e-u] gaum** pay attention to [sth]

Gautar *m pl* the Goths

Gautr <-s> *m* Gaut (*personal name*)

gáfu *3pl past* of **gefa**

gás <gásar, gæss> *f* goose

❖ **gefa** <gefr, gaf, gáfu, gefinn> *vb* give, grant

gefandi <gefanda, gefendr> *m* giver

gegn (*also* **í gegn**) *prep* [*w dat*] against

gegnum (*also* **í gegnum**, older **gögnum**) *prep* [*w acc*] through

geirr *m* spear

Geitir <-is> *m* Geitir (*personal name*)

gekk *1/3sg past* of **ganga**

geldingr <-s, -ar> *m* wether, gelded sheep

gengu *3pl past* of **ganga**

❖ **gera** (*also* **gøra**) <-ði, -ðr~gerr> *vb* make; do, act; **gera sér mikit um [e-n]** make much of or admire [sb]; **gerask** *mid* become, come to pass, occur, happen

gerði *3sg past* of **gera**

gerðisk *3sg past mid* of **gera**

gerðu *3pl past* of **gera**

gestr <-s, -ir> *m* guest

❖ **geta** <getr, gat, gátu, getinn> *vb* get; beget [*w gen*] speak of, mention; **[hon] man láta getit** [she] will have it told; **þess er getit** *impers* it is told; [*w ppart of another verb*] be able to; **geta veiddan fisk** be able to catch fish; *impers* [*w dat subj*] **getask at [e-m/e-u]** like, love [sb/sth]

geyja <*3pl past* gó> *defect vb* bark; **geyja á [e-n]** abuse [sb]

gildr *adj* worthy, great; of full value; [*w dat*] valued at

---

e-n (einhvern) = 'somebody,' *acc.*; **e-t** (eitthvat) = 'something,' *acc.*; **e-m** (einhverjum) = '(for) somebody,' *dat.*; **e-u** (einhverju) = '(for) something,' *dat.*; **e-s** (einhvers) = '(of) somebody or something,' *gen.*

Gimlé *m* Gimle, hall inhabited by Light Elves

ginning *f* deception, tricking

Ginnlaug <-ar> *f* Ginnlaug (*personal name*)

Ginnungagap *n* Ginnungagap, the yawning or gaping void, the primeval void from which the world is created

gipta <-ti, -tr> *vb* give away in marriage

gína <gínr, gein, ginu, ginit> *vb* gape, yawn

gísl *m* bailiff; warder; hostage

gjald *n* tribute; payment; reward; compensation; wergeld

gjalda <geldr, galt, guldu, goldinn> *vb* pay, repay; give; [*w gen*] pay for, suffer on account of

gjalla <gellr, gall, gullu, gollinn> *vb* yell, scream

Gjallarhorn *n* Gjallarhorn, Yelling Horn, the horn blown by the god Heimdall to announce the beginning of Ragnarok

gjarn *adj* eager, willing

gjarna~gjarnan *adv* eagerly, willingly, very much

gjósa <gýsr, gaus, gusu, gosinn> *vb* gush, burst out; erupt

glaðmæltr *adj* cheerful in speech

glaðr *adj* glad, cheerful

gleypa <-ti, -tr> *vb* to swallow

Glitnir *m* Glitnir, silver hall belonging to the god Forseti

glóa <-að-> *vb* glow, shine, glitter

glymja <glymr, glumdi, glumiðr> *vb* dash noisily, clatter, rattle, clash

gnaga <-að-> *vb* gnaw

gnesta <gnestr, gnast, gnustu, gnostinn> *vb* crack, clash

Gnitaheiðr *f* Gnitaheath, the health where Fafnir, as a dragon, lies upon great wealth

gnúa <gnýr, gneri, gneru, gnúinn> *vb* rub

goð *n* god

goði *m* chieftain; priest

goðorð *n* chieftaincy

Gormr <-s> *m* Gorm, first king of the Jelling dynasty in Denmark (*personal name*)

góðan *m acc sg* of **góðr**

❖ **góðr** <*f* góð, *n* gott; *comp* betri, *superl* beztr> *adj* good

gólf *n* floor

graðungr <-s, -ar> *m* bull

grafa <grefr, gróf, grófu, grafinn> *vb* dig

Gramr *m* the name of a sword

granahár *n* whisker

Grani *m* Grani, the name of Sigurd's horse

grannligr *adj* slender, slim

gras *n* grass; herb

grár *adj* gray; spiteful, malicious

gráta <grætr, grét, grétu, grátinn> *vb* weep, cry

grátr <-s> *m* weeping

greiða <-ddi, ddr> *vb* comb, unravel; prepare; speed, hasten; pay

Grettir *m* Grettir (*personal name*)

grey *n* dog, greyhound

grét *1/3sg past* of **gráta**

grið *n pl* terms of peace

Grikland *n* Greece, the Byzantine Empire

Griklandseyjar *f pl* the Greek Islands

Griklandshaf *n* the Aegean Sea

grimmr *adj* cruel, savage; severe, stern

gripr <-ar, -ir> *m* (costly) thing, treasure

Grímr <-s> *m* Grim (*personal name*)

grípa <grípr, greip, gripu, gripinn> *vb* grasp, seize

grjót *n* stone; hail of stones

gróa <grœr, greri~grøri, greru~grøru, gróinn> *vb* grow; heal

grund *f* a green field; ground; [*poet*] the earth, the green earth; **Atals grund** land of Atal (kenning for 'sea')

grunnr <-s, -ar> *m* bottom (of the sea or other body of water)

græða~grœða <-ddi, -ddr> *vb* make grow; heal; increase

Grœnland *n* Greenland

Grœnlendingr <-s, -ar> *m* Greenlander

grœnn *adj* green

grœr *2/3sg pres* of **gróa**

gröf <*gen* grafar; *pl* grafir~grafar> *f* pit; grave

gröftr *var* of **gröptr**

gröptr (*also* **gröftr**) <*dat* grepti, *gen* graptar> *m* digging, burial

guð *m*, God *cf* **goð**

Guðbjörg <*acc/dat* -björgu, *gen* -bjargar> *f* Gudbjorg (*personal name*)

Guðbrandr <-s> *m* Gudbrand (*personal name*)

Guðmarr <-s> *m* Gudmar (*personal name*)

Guðormr <-s> *m* Gudorm (*personal name*)

Guðrøðr <-s> *m* Gudrod (*personal name*)

gull *n* gold

gullband *n* golden collar

gullbaugr *m* gold ring

gullhring *n* a gold ring

gullhyrndr *adj* golden-horned, with horns of gold

gullrekinn *ppart* inlaid with gold

Gunnarr <-s> *m* Gunnar (*personal name*)

Gunnfúss <-ar> *m* Gunnfus (*personal name*)

Gunnhildr <*acc/dat* Gunnhildi, *gen* Gunnhildar> *f* Gunnhild (*personal name*)

Gunnlaugr <-s> *m* Gunnlaug (*personal name*)

Guthormr <-s> *m* Guthorm (*personal name*)

Gyða *f* Gyda (*personal name*)

gyðja *f* priestess

gyldr *ppart of* **gylla**

Gylfi *m* Gylfi, king in Sweden, name of a Viking (*personal name*)

gylla <-di~ti, -dr~tr > *vb* gild

gyrða <-ði, -ðr> *vb* gird, put on

Gyrgir *m* Gyrgir, the Greek general Georgios Maniakes

gýgr *f* giantess

Gýríðr <*acc/dat* Gýríði, *gen* Gýríðar> *f* Gyrid (*personal name*)

gæfumunr *m* difference in fortune, turn or shift of luck

gæta <gætti, gætt> *vb* [*w gen*] watch, tend, take care of

gætir <-is, -ar> *m* keeper, guard

Gætir <-ir> *m* Gaetir (*personal name*)

❖ **göfugr** <*acc* göfgan> *adj* noble

gögnum *var of* **gegnum**

Göngu-Hrólfr *m* Hrolf the Walker (*personal name*)

gøra <-ði, -ðr~gørr> *vb* (*var of* **gera**)

H

---

haf *n* sea, the high sea; **vestr um haf** westwards over the sea

❖ **hafa** <hef(i)r, hafði, haft> *vb* have; hold, keep; take; **hafa [e-t] í hendi** hold [sth] in one's hand; **hafa [e-t] með sér** take, bring [sth] with one

hafr <*gen* hafrs, *pl* hafrar> *m* goat

Hafrsfjörðr *m* Hafrsfjord (*place name*)

hafskip *n* ocean-going ship

hagi *m* field, meadow

hagliga *adv* neatly, adeptly, skillfully

hagr *adj* skilled, handy

hagr *m* state, condition, affairs; means

Haki *m* Haki (*personal name*)

haklangr *adj* long-chinned

❖ **halda** <heldr, hélt, héldu, haldinn> *vb* [*w dat*] hold; keep, retain; **halda undan** fly, flee; **halda sveit** hold command over a troop; **halda upp** hold up; **halda við [e-m]** stand or hold against [sth]; **haldask** *mid* hold, last

Halla *f* Halla (*personal name*)

Halland *n* Halland, Denmark (*place name*) now part of Sweden

Hallbjörn *m* Hallbjorn (*personal name*)

Hallfríðr *f* Hallfrid (*personal name*)

Hallgerðr <*acc/dat* Hallgerði, *gen* Hallgerðar> *f* Hallgerd (*personal name*)

Hallkatla *f* Hallkatla (*personal name*)

hallr <*f* höll, *n* hallt> *adj* leaning, sloping; **hallr í göngu** stooped, walking with a stoop

Hallvarðr <-s> *m* Hallvard (*personal name*)

hallæri *n* famine

hamarr <*dat* hamri, *gen* hamars, *pl* hamrar, *acc* hamra, *dat* hömrum, *gen* hamra> *m* hammer

hamr <*dat* hami~ham, *gen* hams, *pl* hamir> *m* a skin, shape

hana *acc sg* of **hon**

handa *gen pl* of **hönd**, *see also* **til handa**

handan *prep* on the other side of

❖ **hann** <*acc* hann, *dat* honum, *gen* hans> *pron* he

hans *poss pron* his

hans *gen* of **hann**

hanzki *m* glove

Haraldr <-s> *m* Harald (*personal name*); **Haraldr blátönn** Harald Bluetooth, king of Denmark (958–987); **Haraldr harðráði** Harald the Ruthless, Norwegian King (1045–1066); **Haraldr hárfagri** Harald Fairhair *also* **Halraldr lúfa** Harald Shaggyhair, Norwegian king who reigned from ca. 860–930; **Klakk-Haraldr** Klakk-Harald

harðhugaðr *adj* ruthless, resolute

❖ **harðr** <*f* hörð, *n* hart> *adj* hard, difficult, severe

harðráðr *adj* hard in council, tyrannical, ruthless

Hasvimýrar *m pl* Hasvimyrar (*place name*)

Hati *m* Hati, the wolf that pursues the moon

haugr <-s, -ar> *m* burial mound

haukr <-s, -ar> *m* hawk

haust *n* autumn, harvest season

hausta <-að> *vb* draw near to autumn

Hábrók *f* Habrok (*personal name*)

hádegi *n* midday, noon

Háey *f* the Island of Hoy (*place name*)

Hákon <-ar> *m* Hakon (*personal name*); **Hákon jarl**

---

e-n (einhvern) = 'somebody,' *acc.*; **e-t** (eitthvat) = 'something,' *acc.*; **e-m** (einhverjum) = '(for) somebody,' *dat.*; **e-u** (einhverju) = '(for) something,' *dat.*; **e-s** (einhvers) = '(of) somebody or something,' *gen.*

Grjótgarðsson *m* Earl Hakon, son of Grjotgard, Stone-Fence

Hálfdanarhaugar *m pl* Halfdan's mounds

Hálfdanr <-ar> *m* Halfdan (*personal name*); **Hálfdanr svarti** Halfdan the Black, 9th century Norwegian king and father of Harald Shaggyhair/Fairhair

❖ **hálfr** *adj* half

háls <*gen* háls, *pl* hálsar> *m* neck

hálsagðr *adj* half-told

hánum *var* of **honum**

hár <*f* há, *n* hátt, *dat pl* há(vu~fu)m, *comp* hæri, *superl* hæstr> *adj* high, tall, long; loud

Hár *m* High, one of the three interrogators of King Gylfi

hár *n* hair

hárfagr *adj* fair-haired (*nickname*)

hásæti *n* high-seat, throne, seat of honor

hátt *adv* loudly; **hafa hátt** make an outcry

háttatal *n* list of meters or verse forms

háva *f acc sg strong* of **hár**

hávu *n dat sg* of **hár**

heðan (*also* **héðan**) *adv* from here, hence; **heðan af** from now on, henceforth

Heðinn (*also* **Héðinn**) <*acc* Heðin, *dat* Heðni, *gen* Heðins> *m* Hedin (*personal name*); **Héðinn Hjarrandason** *m* Hedin Hjarrandi's son

hefði *3sg & pl past subjunct* of **hafa**

hefja <hefr, hóf, hófu, hafinn> *vb* lift, raise, heave; begin; hold; **hefja blót** hold sacrifices

hefna <-di, -dr> *vb* [*w gen*] avenge, take revenge

hegat *var* of **hingat**

Heiðmörk *f* Heidmork (*place name*)

heiðr <*acc/dat* heiði, *gen* heiðar, *pl* heiðar> *f* heath, moor

Heiðrún *m* Heidrun, a goat that gives mead in **Valhöll**

heilagr <*f* heilög, *n* heilagt; *contracted stem w vowel in ending: acc m* helgan> *adj* holy; protected

❖ **heill** *adj* hale, sound, healthy, unscathed; healed; blessed, happy; whole, complete

heilsa <-að-> *vb* [*w dat*] greet

❖ **heim** *adv* home, homeward (*motion toward*)

heima *adv* home, at home (*position*)

heiman *adv* from home

Heimdallr <-s> *m* the watchman god, who guards the rainbow-bridge; one of the Æsir

heimr <-s, -ar> *m* world; earth

heimta <-ti, -tr> *vb* recover; claim

heit *n* promise

❖ **heita** <heitr, hét, hétu, heitinn> *vb* call, give a name to; call, call on; (*intrans w pres* heitir) be called, be named; [*w dat*] promise

heiti *n* name; synonym

heitr *adj* hot

Hekja *f* Hekja (*personal name*)

hel <*dat* helju, *gen* heljar> *f* Hel, abode of the dead, separate from Valhalla, and ruled over by a goddess of the same name; death

❖ **heldr** *comp adv* rather; [*after neg*] on the contrary

Helga *f* Helga (*personal name*)

Helgi *m* Helgi (*personal name*)

helgistaðr *m* holy place

hella <*gen pl* hellna> *f* flat stone, slate

hellusteinn *m* flat slab of rock, flagstone

helmingr *m* half; **í helminga** in halves; equally

helzk *1/3sg past* of **haldask**

helzt *superl adv* most willingly

hendi *dat* of **hönd**

Hengjankjapta *f* Hengjankjapta, a giantess killed by Thor

hennar *gen sg* of **hon** her, hers

henni *dat sg* of **hon**

heppinn *adj* lucky

hepta <-ti, -tr> *vb* bind, fetter; hold back, restrain

herað (*also* **hérað**) <*pl* heruð~heröð> *n* district, country

herðar *f pl* shoulders, upper part of back

herfang *n* booty; **at herfangi** as booty

herja <-að-> *vb* raid, harry; make war

Herjólfr <-s> *m* Herjolf (*personal name*)

Herjólfsfjörðr *m* Herjolfsfjord (*place name*), Herjólf's Fjord

Herjólfsnes *n* Herjolfsnes (*place name*), Herjólf's Headland

herkonungr *m* warrior-king

Herlu-Bjarni Arnfinnsson *m* Herlu-Bjarni, son of Arnfinn (*personal name*)

hermaðr *m* warrior

hernaðr <-ar> *m* plundering, raid

herr <-jar, -jar> *m* army, troops

hersir <-is, -ar> *m* regional military leader in Norway; chieftain

herskapr *m* harrying, warfare

hertogi *m* commander; duke

hervápn *n pl* weapons

❖ **hestr** <-s, -ar> *m* horse, stallion

heygja <-ði, -ðr> *vb* bury in a mound

heyra <-ði, -ðr> *vb* hear

héðan *var* of **heðan**

Héðinn *var* of **Heðinn**

❖ **hér** *adv* here (*position*)

hérað *var* of **herað**

hét *1/3sg past* of **heita**

Hildr *f* Hild (*personal name*) battle

Himinbjörg *n pl* Himinbjorg, place where **Bifröst** enters **Ásgarðr**

himinn <*dat* himni, *gen* himins, *pl* himnar> *m* sky; heaven

hingat (*also* **hegat**) *adv* to here, hither; **hingat til** hitherto, up to this time, until now

❖ **hinn** <*f* hin, *n* hitt> *dem pron* the other one; **á hinn fótinn** on the other foot

hinn, hin, hit *art* = **inn, in, it**

hinna *f* membrane

hirð *f* a king's or earl's bodyguard; the king's men, retainers

hirða <-rði, -rðr> *vb* mind, care for, hide, conceal; keep in a box or chest

hirðir <-is, -ar> *m* herdsman

hirðmaðr *m* king's man, retainer

hirtir *n pl* of **hjörtr**

hitta <-tti, -ttr> *vb* meet with, hit upon; hit; **hittask** *mid* meet one another

Hjaðningavíg *n* the Fight of the Hjadnings

Hjaðningr <*pl* Hjaðningar> *m* a Hjadning

hjalt *n* hilt; sword guard; pommel

Hjalti *m* Hjalti (*personal name*)

Hjarðarholt *n* Hjardarholt, Herd's Hill (*place name*)

hjarta <*pl* hjörtu> *n* heart

hjartablóð *n* heart's blood

❖ **hjá** *prep* [*w dat*] by, near; with, at one's place

hjálmr <-s, -ar> *m* helm, helmet

hjálp *f* help

hjálpa <helpr, halp~hjalp, hulpu, hólpinn> *vb* [*w dat*] help, save

Hjálprekr *m* a legendary king

hjó *1/3sg past* of **höggva**

hjörtr <*dat* hirti, *gen* hjartar; *pl* hirtir, *acc* hjörtu> *m* hart, stag

❖ **hlaupa** <hleypr, hljóp, hljópu, hlaupinn> *vb* leap, spring; run; **hlaupa at [e-m]** leap at, assault [sb]

hlaut *1/3sg past* of **hljóta**

Hleiðargarð *m* Hleiðargarð, the court of Hrolf kraki

Hleiðra (Hleiðr) *m* modern Lejre in Denmark; royal seat of king Hrolf Kraki

Hliðskjálf *f* Hlidskjalf, the seat on which Odin sits in his hall **Valaskjálf**

hlíð <*pl* -ir> *f* mountain-side, slope

Hlíðarendi *m* Hlidarendi, Slope's End (*place name*)

hlíf <*pl* hlífar> *f* shield, cover, protection

hlífa <-ði, -t> *vb* [*w dat*] protect, shelter; show mercy

hlífðit = **hlífði** + **t** (*negative suffix*)

Hlífsteinn <-s> *m* Hlifstein (*personal name*)

hljóta <hlýtr, hlaut, hlutu, hlotinn> *vb* be allocated, receive

hljóp *1/3sg past* of **hlaupa**

hló *1/3sg past* of **hlæja**

Hlórriði *m* [*poet*] Thor

hluti *m* part

❖ **hlutr** <-ar, -ir> *m* lot; thing

hlæja <hlær, hló, hlógu, hleginn> *vb* laugh

hníga <hnígr, hné~hneig, hnigu, hniginn> *vb* sink, fall gently

hnúka <-ði~ti, -ðr~tr> *vb* sit cowering

hnykkja <-ti, -tr> *vb* [*w dat*] pull violently, yank

hof *n* temple (frequently a name for a farm)

Hof *n* Hof (*place name*)

Hofsland *n* the Hof estate

Hofsverjar *m pl* the people of Hof

holr *adj* hollow

holt *n* wood, forest; rough stony hill or ridge

❖ **hon** <*acc* hana, *dat* henni, *gen* hennar> *pron* she

honum (*also* **hánum**) *dat sg* of **hann**

horfa <-ði, horft> *vb* turn, look (in a particular direction); **horfa á [e-t]** look at [sth]

horfinn *ppart* of **hverfa**

horn *n* horn, drinking horn; corner

hófsmaðr *m* man of moderation

hófu *3pl past* of **hefja**

hógværr *adj* gentle

hóll (*var* of **hváll**) <-s, -ar> *m* hill, hillock, knoll

Hóll <-s> *m* Hol, hill (*place name*)

Hólmfastr <-s> *m* Holmfast (*personal name*)

Hólmgarðr <-s> *m* Holmgard (*place name, modern* Novgorod)

Hólmgarðsfari *m* voyager to **Hólmgarðr**

Hólmgautr <-s> *m* Holmgaut (*personal name*)

Hólmgeirr <-s> *m* Holmgeir (*personal name*)

hrafn <-s, -ar> *m* raven

hregg *n* storm, storm and rain

Hreiðarr <-s> *m* Hreidar (*personal name*)

Hreiðmarr <-s> *m* Hreidmar (*personal name*); the father of Otr, Fafnir and Regin

hreinn <-s, -ar> *m* reindeer

hreystimaðr *m* a valiant man, champion

Hringaríki *n* Hringariki (*place name*)

hrista <-ti, -tr> *vb* shake

---

e-n (einhvern) = 'somebody,' *acc.*; **e-t** (eitthvat) = 'something,' *acc.*; **e-m** (einhverjum) = '(for) somebody,' *dat.*; **e-u** (einhverju) = '(for) something,' *dat.*; **e-s** (einhvers) = '(of) somebody or something,' *gen.*

hríð <*pl* -ir> *f* time, while; storm; attack, battle

hrím *n* rime

Hrímþursar *m pl* the Frost Giants

Hrotti *m* the name of a sword

Hróðgeirr <-s> *m* Hrodgeir (*personal name*)

Hrólfr <-s> *m* Hrolf (*personal name*); **Hrólfr kraki** Hrolf Kraki, legendary Danish king

hrósa <-að-> *vb* [*w dat*] praise; boast (of)

hrukku *3pl past* of **hrøkkva**

Hrungnir <-s> *m* Hrungnir, a giant killed by Thor with his hammer

hrútr *m* ram

Hrútr <-s> *m* Hrut (*personal name*) Ram

Hrútsstaðir *m* Hrutsstadir (*place name*) Hrut's Farmstead

hrynja <hrundi, hruninn> *vb* fall, collapse; flow, stream; fall loosely (of clothing); **látum und honum hrynja lukla** let keys jingle about him; **hrynja á hæla [e-m]** shut upon one's heels

hræ <*pl gen* hræva> *n* dead body, corpse, carrion

hræddr *adj* afraid, frightened

hræða <-ddi, -ddr> *vb* [*w acc*] frighten; **hræðask** *mid* be frightened; **hræðask [e-t]** be afraid of [sth]

Hrœrekr <-s> *m* Hroerekr (*personal name*)

hrøkkva <hrøkkr~hrekkr, hrökk, hrukku, hrokkinn> *vb* fall back, recoil

hugkvæmr *adj* clever, crafty

hugr <*dat* hug ~ hugi, *gen* hugar, *pl* hugir> *m* mind; mood, heart, temper

hugsjúkr *adj* distressed, anxious, worried

hulðu *3pl past* of **hylja**

hunangsfall *f* honey-dew

hundr <-s, -ar> *m* hound, dog

hundrað <*pl* hundruð> *n* hundred (*usu* followed by noun in *gen*) (**tólfrætt hundrað** = 120, **tírætt hundrað** = 100)

hungr <-rs> *m (n in younger texts)* hunger; **svelta hungri** starve, die of hunger

❖ **hús** *n* house

húsabœr *m* farmstead

húsfreyja (*also* **hýsfreyja**) *f* housewife, *lit* house-lady

❖ **húskarl** *m* farmhand; king's man, retainer

hvaðan *adv* from where, whence

hvalkváma *f* stranding of a whale

hvalnum *dat sg* of **hvalr+inn**, the whale

hvalr <*gen* hvals, *pl* hvalar~hvalir> *m* whale

hvalrif *n* whale-rib

❖ **hvar** *interrog adv* where; **hvar sem** wherever

hvargi *adv* everywhere; **hvargi sem** wherever,

wheresoever

hvass <*f* hvöss, *n* hvasst> *adj* sharp, keen

hvat *interrog pro* what

hváll (*also* **hóll**) <-s, -ar> *m* hill, hillock, knoll

❖ **hvárgi** <*n* hvárki~hvártki> *adj pron* neither (of two); *conj* **hvárki...né** neither...nor

hvárki *n* of **hvárgi**

❖ **hvárr** *interrog pron* who, which (of two)?; *indef pron* each (of two)

❖ **hvárrtveggi** *indef pron* each of the two

❖ **hvárt** *interrog adv* whether; **hvárt sem~hvárt er** *conj* whether

hvárumtveggjum *dat pl* of **hvárrtveggi**

hveim *dat* of a defective *pron* to whom, for whom

hverfa <hverfr, hvarf, hurfu, horfinn> *vb* be lost, be missing; disappear

Hvergelmir *m* Hvergelmir Seething Well, the home of **Niðhöggr** and source of the rivers in **Niflheimr**

hvergi (*also* **hverrgi**) *pron* each, every one

hvergi *adv* nowhere; [*w gen*] nowhere on

hverir *m nom pl* of **hverr**

hvern *m acc sg* of **hverr**

hvernug *adv* how

❖ **hverr** <*f* hver, *n* hvert> *interrog pron* who, which?; *indef pron* each, every, all

hverrgi *var* of **hvergi**

❖ **hversu** *interrog adv* how, just how

hvert *adv* to where, whither; **hvert er** whithersoever

hvetja <hvet, hvatta, hvöttu, hvattr> *vb* whet, sharpen; encourage

hvé *adv* how

Hvinir *m* Hvinir (*place name*)

hví *interrog adv* why?

hvítast *superl* of **hvítr**

hvítr <*f* hvít, *n* hvítt> *adj* white

hyggja <hugði, hugðr~hugaðr> *vb* think, believe; **hyggja at [e-u]** look at, consider [sth]

hykk = **hygg ek**

hylja <hulði~huldi, huliðr~huldr> *vb* bury, cover over, conceal, hide

hylli *f* loyalty, allegiance, favor

Hyrrokkin *f* Hyrrokkin, a giantess killed by Thor

hýsfreyja (*var* of **húsfreyja**) *f* housewife

hætta <-tti, -tt> *vb* [*w dat*] risk, stake

hœgr *adj* easy, convenient; **hœgri** *comp* right; the right hand

hœgri *comp* of **hœgr**

hœla <-di, hœlt> *vb* [*w dat*] praise, flatter, boast of

Hœnir *m* Hoenir, a god

hœta <-tti, -ttr> *vb* threaten

höfðingi <*gen* -ja, *pl* -jar> *m* leader; chieftain; captain

höfn <*gen* hafnar, *pl* hafnir> *f* holding, possession; harbor

❖ **höfuð** <*dat* höfði, *pl dat* höfðum, *gen* höfða> *n* head

höfuðsbani *m* death

höfuðstaðr *m* chief place; capital

högg <*dat* höggvi> *n* blow, stroke, chop; beheading, execution

högg *2sg imper* of **höggva**

höggspjót *n* broad-bladed spear

❖ **höggva** <høggr, hjó, hjoggu, högg(v)inn> *vb* strike (a blow), chop, hack, hew

Högni *m* Hogni (*personal name*)

höll <*dat* höllu, *gen* hallar, *pl* hallir> *f* hall

❖ **hönd** <*acc* hönd, *dat* hendi, *gen* handar, *pl* hendr, *dat* höndum, *gen* handa> *f* hand; **af hendi [e-s]** on behalf of [sb]

hörð *f nom* & *n nom/acc pl* of **harðr**

Hörða-Knútr <-s> *m* Horda-Knut (*personal name*)

Hörðaland *n* Hordaland (*place name*)

hörr <*dat* hörvi~hörr> *m* flax, linen

Höskuldr <-s> *m* Hoskuld (*personal name*)

Höskuldsstaðir *m pl* Hoskuldsstadir Hoskuld's Farmstead (*place name*)

Höttr <*dat* Hetti, *gen* Hattar> *m* Hott (*personal name*) Hood (the Masked One)

I

iðjumaðr *m* hard-working man

igða *f* a nuthatch

❖ **illa** <*comp* verr, *superl* verst> *adv* badly, ill

❖ **illr** <*comp* verri, superl *verstr*> *adj* bad, evil

illska *f* badness

illt *f* evil (treatment)

Ingibjörg <*gen* Ingibjargar> *f* Ingibjorg (*personal name*); **Ingibjörg Hróðgeirsdóttir ins hvíta** Ingibjorg, daughter of Hrodgeir the White

Ingjaldr <-s> *m* Ingjald (*personal name*); **Ingjaldr tryggvi** Ingjald the True

Ingólfr <-s> *m* Ingolf (*personal name*)

❖ **inn** <*comp* innarr, *superl* innst> *adv* in, into

(*motion toward*)

inn, in, it *art* the

inna <-ti, -tr> relate, tell; **inna til [e-s]** make mention of [sb]

innan *prep* [*w gen*] within; **innan** *adv* from within, outward

innanlands *adv* within the land, at home (as opposed to abroad)

inni *adv* within, inside; in-doors

it *n* of **inn**

Í

❖ **í** *prep* [*w acc*] into (motion); during (time); [*w dat*] in, within, at (position)

í braut (*also* **í brott**) *adv* away

í gögnum *var* of **gegnum**

í móti *var* of **móti**

í nánd *adv* nearby

í samt *adv* in a row

í sundr *adv* asunder

í því *adv* at that time

íkorni *m* squirrel

Írakonungr *m* King of the Irish

Írland *n* Ireland

írskr *adj* Irish

Ísland *n* Iceland

Íslendingabók *f* Book of the Icelanders

íslenzkr *adj* Icelandic

íss <*gen* íss, *pl* ísar> *m* ice

Ívarr <-s> *m* Ivar (*personal name*)

---

e-n (einhvern) = 'somebody,' *acc.*;   **e-t** (eitthvat) = 'something,' *acc.*;   **e-m** (einhverjum) = '(for) somebody,' *dat.*; **e-u** (einhverju) = '(for) something,' *dat.*;   **e-s** (einhvers) = '(of) somebody or something,' *gen.*

J

jafn <*f* jöfn, *n* jafnt> *adj* even, equal

jafna <-að-> *vb* smooth, even out, tidy, trim; make equal (*in comparisons*), equate; **jafna [e-u] til [e-s]** liken [sth] to [sth]

jafnan *adv* always; constantly, equally

jafnberr *adj* equally exposed, naked, or unprotected

jafndjúpvitr *adj* as deep-witted, as deep-scheming, as resourceful

jafngamall *adj* as old, of the same age

Jafnhár *m* Just-as-High, one of three interrogators of King Gylfi

jafnmikill *adj* equally great

jafnungr *adj* as young

❖ **jarl** <-s, -ar> *m* earl

jarlsríki *n* an earldom

jartegn *n* token, evidence, proof (of a thing)

Jófríðr <*acc/dat* Jófríði, *gen* Jófríðar> *f* Jofrid (*personal name*)

jól *n pl* Yule, Yuletide, a great midwinter feast in heathen times, later applied to Christmas

Jótland *n* Jutland (*place name*)

jökull <*dat* jökli, *gen* jökuls, *pl* jöklar> *m* glacier; ice; icicle

jörð <*dat* jörðu, *gen* jarðar; *pl* jarðir> *f* earth; land, ground

Jörð *f* Earth, as goddess and mother of Thor

Jörmungandr *m* Jormungand, name of the Midgard Serpent, the world serpent

jötunheimar *m pl* the land of giants

jötunn <*dat* jötni, *gen* jötuns, *pl* jötnar> *m* giant

K

kaðall <*dat* kaðli, *gen* kaðals, *pl* kaðlar> *m* cable, twisted rope

Kaldbak *n* Cold-Back Mountain

Kaldbeklingar *m pl* the men of Kaldbak

kaldr <*f* köld, *n* kalt> *adj* cold

❖ **kalla** <-að-> *vb* call

kallaðir *ppart* of **kalla** (*m nom pl*)

kallaðr *ppart* of **kalla** (*m nom sg*)

kambr <-s, -ar> *m* comb

kanna <-að-> *vb* search, explore, find out about; **kannask við [e-t]** recognize [sth]

kappi *m* champion

karfi *m* a fast coastal rowing ship

karl <-s, -ar> *m* man; old man; **Þorsteinn karl** old Thorstein, old man Thorstein

Karlstefni *m* Karlstefni (*personal name*)

kasta <-að-> *vb* throw, cast

kaupa <keypti, keyptr> *vb* buy

kaupmaðr *m* merchant

Kári Sölmundarson *m* Kari Solmundarson (*personal name*)

kátalaktús *see* **Michael kátalaktús**

kátr *adj* cheerful

Keila *f* Keila, a giantess killed by Thor

kemr *3sg pres* of **koma**

kenna <-di, -dr> *vb* know, recognize; feel; attribute; teach

kenning *f* poetical periphrasis or metaphor

kenningarnafn *n* nickname

kent *ppart* of **kenna**

kerling *f* old woman

Ketill <-s> *m* Ketil (*personal name*)

keypti *3sg past* of **kaupa**

kirkja *f* church

Kjallandi *f* Kjallandi, a giant killed by Thor

Kjartan <-s> *m* Kjartan (*personal name*)

Kjarvalr <-s> *m* Kjarval (*personal name*)

kjóll *m* ship (poet)

kjósa <kýss, kaus~köri, kusu~kuru, körinn~kosinn> *vb* choose

Kjötvi *m* Kjotvi (*personal name*); **Kjötvi inn auðgi** Kjotvi the wealthy

Klakk-Haraldr <-s> *m* Klakk-Harald (*personal name*)

klettr <-s, -ar> *m* rock, crag

Klifshagi *m* Klifshagi (*place name*), Cliff Meadow

klífa <klífr, kleif, klifu, klifinn> *vb* climb

kljúfa <klýfr, klauf, klufu, klofinn> *vb* cleave, split

klyf <*pl* -jar> *f* pack (for a horse)

klæða <-ddi, -ddr> *vb* clothe

klæði *n* cloth, (*pl*) clothes

kná <kná, *1pl pres* knegum, knátti, *past inf* knáttu> *defective pret-pres vb* be able to, can; could

knáliga *adv* hardily, vigorously

knáligr *adj* hardy, vigorous

knerrir *nom pl* of **knörr**

kneyfa <-ði, -ðr> drink in large gulps

kné <*dat pl* knjám, *gen* knjá> *n* knee

knúta *f* knuckle-bone

knútr <-s, -ar> *m* knot

Knútr <-s> *m* Knut (*personal name*); **Knútr inn ríki**, King Canute the Great

knýja <knýr, knýði~knúði, knúinn> *vb* knock (at the door); press, urge on, compel, force; **knýjask** *mid* struggle on

knörr <*dat* knerri, *gen* knarrar, *pl* knerrir, *acc* knörru> *m* ship; merchant vessel

Kolbeinn <-s> *m* Kolbein (*personal name*)

kollr <-s, -ar> *m* top, summit; head

kom *1/3sg past* of **koma**

❖ **koma** <kemr~kømr, kom, kómu~kvámu, kominn> *vb* come; **koma at** come to, arrive; **koma at [e-u]** come across, arrive at [sth]; **koma ásamt með þeim** they agreed; **koma endr at** regain; **komask** *mid* make one's way

kominn *ppart* of **koma**

komnir *m nom pl* of **kominn**

❖ **kona** <*gen pl* kvenna> *f* wife; woman

konu *acc/dat/gen* of **kona**

konungastefna *f* a meeting of kings

konungdómr *m* kingdom

❖ **konungr** <-s, -ar> *m* king

konungsson *m* prince

korn *n* grain, seed

kostnaðr <-ar> *m* cost, expense

❖ **kostr** <*gen* kostar, *pl* kostir, *acc* kosti~kostu> *m* choice; opportunity; match; state, condition; cost, expense; **at öðrum kosti** else, otherwise

kómu *3pl past* of **koma**

kraki *m* pole ladder; stake

kraptr *m* strength

kráka *f* crow

krás <*pl* -ir> *f* delicacy, dainty (of food)

krefja <krafði, krafðr~krefinn> *vb* crave, claim, demand

kringla *f* circle, disk, orb

kristinn *adj* Christian

Kristr <-s> *m* Christ

krjúpa <krýpr, kraup, krupu, kropinn> *vb* creep; crouch

Krossavík *f* Krossavik, Cross Bay or Inlet, presumably an inlet where a cross was erected, a farmstead

kumbl <*pl* kumbl> *n* burial monument, mound or cairn (frequently used on Danish and Swedish rune stones in the plural)

kunna <kann, kunni, kunnat> *pret-pres vb* can, know how to; feel (an emotion)

❖ **kunnigr** *adj* known; wise; versed in magic

kunningi *m* acquaintance

kurteiss *adj* courteous, well-bred

kuru *3pl past* of **kjósa**

kussari *m* corsair (corsairs were pirates who operated along the Barbary Coast of North Africa)

kúla *f* hump, hunchback

kvað *1/3sg past* of **kveða**

kván (*also* **kvæn**) <*pl* -ir> *f* wife

❖ **kveða** <kveðr, kvað, kváðu, kveðinn> *vb* speak, say; recite verse; **kveða á** fix, determine; **kveða við** reply; **kveðask** *mid* say of oneself; declare

❖ **kveld** *n* evening; **at kveldi** at nightfall

kvelda <-að-> *vb* [impers] become evening

Kveld-Úlfr <-s> *m* Kveld-Ulf, Night Wolf (*personal name*)

kvennváðir *f pl* women's clothing

kverk <*pl* kverkr> *f* the angle below the chin

kvikr *adj* alive

kvikvendi *n* a living creature

kvæði <*gen pl* kvæða> *n* poem

kvæn *var* of **kván**

kyn <*dat pl* kynjum, *gen* kynja> *n* kin; kindred

❖ **kyrr** *adj* still, quiet

kyssa <-ti, -tr> *vb* kiss

kýr <*acc/dat* kú, *gen* kýr, *pl* kýr, *dat* kúm, *gen* kúa> *f* cow

kærleikr *m* affection, friendship

kømr (*var* of **kemr**) *2/3sg pres* of **koma**

körtr <*gen* körts~kartar> *m* short, stocky man (*nickname*)

köttr <kattar, kettir> *m* cat

---

e-n (einhvern) = 'somebody,' *acc.*; e-t (eitthvat) = 'something,' *acc.*; e-m (einhverjum) = '(for) somebody,' *dat.*;
e-u (einhverju) = '(for) something,' *dat.*; e-s (einhvers) = '(of) somebody or something,' *gen.*

L

lag <*pl* lög> *n* thrust, stab

lagit *ppart* of **leggja** placed

lagt *ppart* of **leggja** placed

lamði *3sg past* of **lemja**

❖ **land** <*pl* lönd> *n* land; country; estate

landnám *n* settlement, *lit* land-taking

Landnámabók *f* Book of Settlements

landnámsmaðr *m* settler, *lit* land-take-man (the term refers to both women and men)

landráð *n* the government of the land

landskyld *f* land tax, property tax

landsmaðr *m* countryman, inhabitant or native of a country

landsréttr *m* the law of the land, customary rights

langeldar *m pl* long fires (down the middle of a hall)

langfeðgar *m pl* forefathers, ancestors (through the father's line)

langháls *m* long-necked (*nickname*)

❖ **langr** <*f* löng, *n* langt, *comp* lengri, *superl* lengstr> *adj* long (of distance and time)

langt *adv* for a long time

Laufey *f* goddess, known only as mother of Loki

laug <*dat* laugu, *pl* laugar> *f* bath; hot spring

lauk *1/3sg past* of **lúka**

lausafé *n* movable property, as opposed to lands or even to land and cattle

❖ **lauss** *adj* loose; free, unimpeded

laust *1/3sg past* of **ljósta**

lausung <*dat* lausungu, *pl* lausungar> *f* lying, falsehood

laut *1/3sg past* of **lúta**

lax <*gen* lax, *pl* laxar> *m* salmon

Laxárdalr *m* Laxardal, Salmon River Valley

lá *1/3sg pret* of **liggja**

lágu *3pl past* of **liggja**

❖ **láta** <lætr, lét, létu, látinn> *vb* let, allow, permit; put, place, set; behave; **láta fram** let go, yield, hand over; **láta sem** pretend, make or behave as if, *lit* let on as if; [*w infin*] have something done; *ppart* dead, deceased

látinn *ppart* of **láta** dead, deceased

❖ **leggja** <lagði, lagiðr~lagðr~laginn> *vb* lay, place, put; stab, thrust; **leggja á** impose; **leggja frá** withdraw; **leggja í spánu** smash into pieces; **leggja til** attack (by stabbing); **leggja til barðaga** attack; **leggja til [e-s] með [e-u]** attack [sb] with [sth];

leggja undir sik conquer; **lífit á leggja** lay down one's life; **leggjask** *mid* lay, set oneself; **leggjask á [e-t]** prey upon (of robbers, beasts of prey, *etc*), fall upon, attack [sth]; **leggjask niðr** lay oneself down; **leggjask út** set out (into the wilderness to live as an outlaw)

leggr <-jar, -ir> *m* leg; **leggr ok liðr** every limb

❖ **leið** <*pl* -ir> *f* road, path; way

leið *1/3sg past* of **líða**

leiða <-ddi, -ddr> *vb* lead

Leiði *m* Leid, a giant killed by Thor

leifa <-ði, -ðr> *vb* leave, leave as heritage; to leave behind, abandon, relinquish

Leifr <-s> *m* Leif (*personal name*)

leika <leikr, lék, léku, leikit> *vb* play; **leika sér** play

leikr <-s, -ar> *m* game, play, sport

❖ **leita** <-að-> *vb* [*w gen*] seek, search for; proceed on a journey

leka <lekr, lak, lákum, lekit> *vb* drip, dribble, leak

lemja <lamði, lamiðr~lamdr~laminn> *vb* maim

lendr *adj* describes one who has received a grant of land from a king, landed; **lendr maðr** landholder

❖ **lengi** <*comp* lengr (*time*), lengra (*distance*) *superl* lengst> *adv* long, for a long time

lengr *comp adv* longer (*time*), for a longer time

lengra *comp adv* longer (*distance*), farther

lengst *superl adv* longest, for the longest time

lesa <less, las, lásu, lesinn> *vb* gather; read

leyfa <-ði, -ðr> *vb* [*w dat*] permit, allow

leyfi *n* permission, leave

leyna <-di, -dr> *vb* hide, conceal; **leynask** *mid* hide oneself, be concealed; **leynask í burt** steal away, leave

lék *1/3sg past* of **leika**

lét *1/3sg past* of **láta**

lézt *2sg past* of **láta**

❖ **lið** *n* band of men, following, troops

liðr <*gen* liðar, *pl* liðir, *acc* liðu> *m* joint

lifa <-ði, lifaðr> *vb* live

❖ **liggja** <liggr, lá, lágu, leginn> *vb* lie

limar *f pl* limbs, branches

litla *f acc sg* of **lítill**

litlu *n dat sg* of **lítill**

litr <-ar, -ir> *m* color

Livsteinn <-s> *m* Livstein (*personal name*)

líða <líðr, leið, liðu, liðinn> *vb* pass (*usu* of time); **líða**

at draw toward (of time); **sem leið at jólum** as time passed toward Yule

líf (*also* **lífi**) *n* life; **lífit á leggja** lay down one's life

lífi *var* of **líf**

líflát *n* loss of life, death

lík *n* body; corpse

líka <-að-> *vb impers* [*w dat subj*] like, be pleasing (to one)

líki *n* body; form, shape

❖ **líkligr** *adj* likely, probable

líknsamastr *superl* of **líknsamr**

líknsamr *adj* merciful

❖ **líkr** *adj* like, resembling; probable; promising

lín *n* flax; linen, linen garment

lína *f* bowline, rope; line; bridal veil, *(see also* **lín**)

Línakradalr <-s> *m* Linakradale (*place name*), Valley of Linen Fields

líta <lítr, leit, litu, litinn> *vb* look; **líta á [e-t]** look at [sth]; *mid* **lítask [e-m]** appear (seem) to [sb]

❖ **lítill** <*f* lítil, *n* lítit> *adj* little; **lítla hríð** for a little while; **lítlu síðar(r)** a little later

lítt *adv* little

lízk 2/3sg pres mid of **líta**

ljá <lér, léði, léðr> *vb* [*w gen*] lend; **ljá [e-m] [e-s]** lend [sb] [sth]

Ljósálfar *m pl* the Light Elves

ljóss *adj* light, bright

ljósta <lýstr, laust, lustu, lostinn> *vb* strike; **ljósta í hel** strike dead

ljúga <lýgr, laug~ló, lugu, loginn> *vb* lie, tell a lie; fail

loðbrók *f* shaggy-breech(es) (*nickname*)

lofa <-að-> *vb* praise

logi *m* flame, fire

lokhvíla *f* locking bed-closet

Loki *m* Loki, the trickster god

lokrekkja *f* locking bed-closet

lokrekkjugólf *n* locking bed-closet

lopt *n* sky, heavens, air

lostinn *ppart* of **ljósta**

lófi *m* palm of the hand; **holr lófi** open palm

lund <*pl* -ir> *f* manner; mind, temper; **á þessa lund** in this manner

lundr <-ar, -ir> *m* grove

lunga *n* lung

lúfa *f* shaggy-hair (*nickname*)

lúka <lýkr, lauk, luku, lokinn> *vb* [*w dat*] close; end, conclude; shut

lúta <lýtr, laut, lutu, lotinn> *vb* bend down, bow

Lútr *m* Lut, a giant killed by Thor

lygi *f* lie, falsehood

lykill <*dat* lykli, *pl* luklar, *acc* lukla> *m* key

lysta <-ti, -tr> *vb* intend, wish to

lýsa <-ti, -tr> *vb* light up, illuminate; proclaim, announce; *impers* shine, beam; **lýsa [e-u]** proclaim [sth]; **lýsir af honum** light shines from him

Lýtingr <-s> *m* Lyting (*personal name*)

læknir <-is, -ar> *m* physician

lætr 2/3sg pres of **láta**

lög *n pl* law, laws

lögberg *n* law-rock (where the law was recited)

lögðu 3pl past of **leggja**

lögligr *adj* legal, lawful

lögmaðr *m* lawman

lögretta *f* legislature at the Althing

lögsögumaðr *m* law-speaker

löngu *adv* long, far off; long since

löngum *adv* a long time, constantly

M

❖ **maðr** <*acc* mann, *dat* manni, *gen* manns, nom/*acc pl* menn, *dat* mönnum, *gen* manna> *m* man; person, human being

makligr *adj* fitting, proper, becoming; deserving

mala <melr, mól, mólu, malinn> *vb* grind

mangi *var* of **manngi**

mannblót *n* human sacrifice

mannbroddr *m* spike

manndráp *n* murder

mannfólk *n* mankind

manngi (*also* **mangi**) <*gen* mannskis> *pron* no man, nobody

mannshönd *f* a man's hand

mannvit *n* intelligence

mannvænn *adj* promising

margbreytinn *adj* fickle, capricious, unpredictable

margkunnigr *adj* learned (in magic)

margmenni *n* multitude, many

---

e-n (einhvern) = 'somebody,' *acc.*; **e-t** (eitthvat) = 'something,' *acc.*; **e-m** (einhverjum) = '(for) somebody,' *dat.*; **e-u** (einhverju) = '(for) something,' *dat.*; **e-s** (einhvers) = '(of) somebody or something,' *gen.*

❖ **margr** <*f* mörg, *n* margt~mart, *comp* fleiri, *superl* flestr> *adj* (*w sg*) many a; (*w pl*) many

marka <-að-> *vb* mark, draw; fix; mark as one's property; mark with an emblem; heed, mind; signify, mean; infer, observe; **þar eptir mátt þú marka fegrð hans** accordingly, you can judge his beauty

marr <-s, -ar> *m* horse, steed

mart *var* of **margt**, *n nom/acc sg* of **margr**

matr <-ar, -ir> *m* food

mágr <-s, -ar> *m* brother-, father-, or son-in-law; kinsman

❖ **mál** *n* speech, narrative, talk; language; saying; deliberation, discussion; case, matter, affair; [*leg*] suit, action, case

málafylgjumaðr *m* lawyer

máli *m* contract, agreement; **ganga á mála** take service

málfeti *var* of **málmfeti**

máligr *var* of **málugr**

málmfeti (*also* **málfeti**) *m* name for a horse; **málmfeti varrar** horse pulled by an oar (kenning for 'ship')

málmr *m* metal, ore

málstefna *f* meeting, conference

málugr (*also* **máligr**) <*m pl* málgir> *adj* talkative

mánaðr *var* of **mánuðr**

máni *m* moon

mánuðr (*also* **mánaðr**) <*gen* mánuðar, *pl* mánuðr> *m* month

már <*dat* mávi~máfi, *gen* más, *pl* mávar> *m* gull, sea-gull

mástallr *m* stall of the sea-gull (kenning for 'sea')

mátt *2sg past* of **mega**

mátti *3sg past* of **mega**

❖ **með** *prep* [*w acc*] with (in the sense of bringing, carrying, or forcing); [*w dat*] with (in the sense of accompanying or togetherness); **sigla með landi** sail along the coast; **með** *adv* as well, with it

meðal *prep* [*w gen*] among, between

meðan *conj* while, meanwhile, as long

❖ **mega** <má, mátti, mátt> *pret-pres vb* can, may; be able

megin *n* strength

meiða <-ddi, -ddr> *vb* injure, hurt, damage; **meiðask** *mid* become injured, hurt, damaged

meiðmar *f pl* treasures

meiri *comp adj* of **mikill**

meir(r) *comp adv* more greatly, more

mella *f* noose; [*poet*] giantess

men <*dat pl* menjum, *gen* menja> *n* necklace; [*pl*] treasures, jewels

menn *nom/acc pl* of **maðr**

merki <*dat pl* merkjum, *gen* merkja> *n* boundary; banner, standard; token, mark, sign

mest *superl adv* mostly

mestr *superl adj* of **mikill**

meta <metr, mat, mátu, metinn> *vb* evaluate, value; set a price

mey *acc sg* of **mær**

meydómr *m* maidenhood, virginity

meyjar *gen sg* & *nom/acc pl* of **mær**

meyju *dat sg* of **mær**

mér *dat sg* of **ek**

Michael kátalaktús *m* Michael katalaktus (*personal name*)

miðdegi *see* **hádegi**

Miðfjarðar-Skeggi *m* Skeggi of Midfjord (*personal name*)

Miðfjörðr *m* Midfjord (*place name*)

Miðgarðr *m* Midgard, the Middle Enclosure, Middle Earth

Miðgarðsormr *m* Midgard Serpent, the serpent **Jörmungandr** that encircles the earth

miðla <-að-> *vb* share, hand out; **miðla [e-t] við [e-n]** share [sth] with [sb]

miðnótt *f* midnight

❖ **miðr** <*m acc* miðjan, *n nom* mitt> *adj* middle

miðr *comp adv var* of **minnr**

miðr-aptan *m* middle evening, six in the evening

miðrdegi *see* **hádegi**

mik *acc* of **ek**

❖ **mikill** <*f* mikil, *n* mikit, *comp* meiri, *superl* mestr> *adj* big, tall, great; much, very; **mikill fyrir sér** powerful, strong

mikillátr *adj* proud

mikinn *adv* hard, fast (*m acc sg* of *adj* **mikill**)

❖ **mikit** *adv* greatly

Mikligarðr (**Miklagarðr**) *m* Constantinople

miklu *adv* much (*w comp*)

❖ **milli** *prep* [*w gen*] between (*also* **á milli** *and* **í milli**)

❖ **minn** <mín, mitt> *poss pron* my

minna <-ti, -tr> *vb* remind; **minna [e-n] [e-s]** remind [sb] of [sth]; *impers* **minnir mik** I remember; *mid* [*w gen*] **minnask** remember, call to mind

minni *comp adj* of **lítill**

minnr (*also* **miðr**) *comp adv* of **lítit**

minnst *superl adv* of **lítit**

minnstr *superl adj of* **lítill**

mín *gen* of **ek**

Mímir *m* Mimir, one of the Æsir

Mímisbrunnr *m* Mimisbrunn, the Well of Mimir

mjöðr <dat miði, gen mjaðar> m mead

❖ mjök adv much, very

mjöl <gen pl mjölva> n meal, flour

mjölleyfi n a license to export meal

Mjöllnir m the hammer of Thor

❖ morginn (also morgunn) <gen morgins, pl mornar~morgnar> m morning; á morginn tomorrow

mosi m moss; moorland

❖ móðir <acc/dat/gen móður, pl mœðr, dat mœðrum, gen mœðra> f mother

móður acc/dat/gen sg of móðir

móðurbróðir m mother's brother, uncle

móðurætt f kinsfolk on the mother's side of the family

mór <dat mó, gen mós, pl móar> m moor, heath

❖ móti (also á móti and í móti) prep [w dat] towards; against, contrary to

móttaka f resistance, defense, counter-attack; til móttöku to a defense, to counter-attack

muna <man, mundi, munaðr> pret-pres vb remember, call to mind

munat = muna + t (negative suffix)

mundr <-ar> m bride price

munnr m mouth

munr <-ar, -ir> m difference

❖ munu <mun~man, mundi, past inf mundu> pret-pres vb will, shall; to be sure to, must (probability); would, must (in past tense)

múgr <-s, -ar> m crowd

mús <pl mýss> f mouse

Múspellsheimr m Muspellsheim, the Land of Fire

mylla <pl -ur> f mill

mynda 1sg past subjunct of munu or muna

myrkr adj dark

Mýrkjartan <-s> m Myrkjartan (personal name)

mýrr <acc/dat mýri, gen mýrar, pl mýrar> f moor, bog, swamp

❖ mæla <-ti, -tr> vb say, speak; leg mæla eptir [e-t]/[e-n] take up the prosecution for [sth]/[sb] (who was murdered or wronged); ; mæla við [e-n] speak to or with [sb], say to [sb]

mær <acc mey, dat meyju, gen meyjar, pl meyjar, dat meyjum, gen meyja> f maid, girl, virgin

mætta 1sg past subjunct of mega

Mœrr <acc Mœri, dat Mœri, gen Mœrar > f a region in West Norway

mœta <-tti, -ttr> vb meet

mögfellandi m kin-slaying (one)

mögr <dat megi, gen magar, pl magir, acc mögu> m son, boy

möl <gen malar> f pebbles, gravel

mön <gen manar, pl manar> f mane

Mörðr <gen Marðar> m Mord (personal name)

mörg f nom sg & n nom/acc pl of margr

N

nafn n name

nafnfrægr adj famous

nagl <pl negl> m nail

nam 1/3sg past of nema

nauðgjald n forced payment

nauð(r) f need, difficulty, distress; ætla [e-t] til nauða [e-m] intend [sth] as harm to [sb]

nauðsyn <pl nauðsynjar> f necessity

nauðugr adj unwilling, reluctant

naut n cattle, oxen

ná <náir, -ði, nát> vb [w dat] reach, catch, overtake; get, obtain; [w inf] be able to

nágrindr f pl gates of the dead

nál <pl -ar> f needle

náliga adv nearby; nearly, almost

nánd <-ar, -ir> f proximity

nár <nás, náir> m corpse, dead man

nátta <-að> vb become night, grow dark

náttmál n nine in the evening

náttstaðr m night-quarters

náttúra f natural ability

neðan adv from below, from beneath; without motion beneath, underneath

nef <gen pl nefja> n nose

nefna <-di, -dr> vb name, call

nei adv no

nema <nemr, nam, námu, numinn> vb take; claim land; hear; learn

❖ nema conj except, save, but; [w subjunct] unless

nes n headland

---

e-n (einhvern) = 'somebody,' acc.; e-t (eitthvat) = 'something,' acc.; e-m (einhverjum) = '(for) somebody,' dat.;
e-u (einhverju) = '(for) something,' dat.; e-s (einhvers) = '(of) somebody or something,' gen.

nest *n* traveling provisions

❖ **né** *conj* nor; **hvárki...né** neither...nor; **né...né** not...nor

niðr <*dat* nið, *gen* niðjar~niðs, *pl* niðjar> *m* son, kinsman, relative through marriage

❖ **niðr** *adv* down

Niflheimr *m* Niflheim, the Underworld

Niflhel *f* Niflhel, Dark Hel, place for some dead

nið *n* insult

Níðhöggr *m* Nidhogg, the serpent which dwells in the spring **Hvergelmir**

nítján <*ord* nítjándi nineteenth> *num* nineteen

❖ **níu** <*ord* níundi, ninth > *num* nine

njósn <*pl* -ir> *f* news; spying, scouting, looking out

njóta <nýtr, naut, nutu, notinn> *vb* enjoy

Njörðr *m* Njord, god of the sea, one of the Vanir

norðan *adv* from the north

Norðmaðr <*pl* Norðmenn> *m* Northman, Norseman, Norwegian

Norðmannalið *n* a band of Norsemen

Norðmanndí *n* Normandy

norðr <-rs> *n* the north

norðr *adv* north, northwards

Norðrlönd <*dat* Norðrlöndum> *n pl* the Northern countries or region, Scandinavia

Noregr (*also* **Norvegr** *or* **Nóregr**) <-s> *m* Norway, *lit* northern way

norn <*pl* -ir> *f* norn, one of the three fates; one of various supernatural females who shape people's fates

norrœna *f* Norse, *lit* northern

norrœnn *adj* Norwegian, *lit* northern

Nóatún *n* Njord's home, *lit* precinct of ships (*nóa*), i.e. sea, *see* **Njörðr**

❖ **nótt** (*also* **nátt**) <*gen* nætr, *pl* nætr> *f* night; **of nóttina** during the night

numinn *ppart* of **nema**

❖ **nú** *adv* now

nýr <*acc* nýjan, *f* ný, *n* nýtt> *adj* new

nýra *n* kidney

næði *3sg/pl past subjunct* of **ná**

❖ **nær** *prep* [*w dat*] near; **nær** *adv* almost, nearly

nærri *comp adv* nearer, very near

næst *superl adv* nearest, next; **því næst** thereupon

❖ **næstr** *superl adj* next; nearest

❖ **nökkurr** <*f* nökkur, *n* nökkut> *adj pron* any, anybody; some, a certain

nökkut *adv* somewhat

nökkvi <-a, -ar> *m* boat, ship

Nörðrlönd *var* of **Norðrlönd**

Nörr *m* Norr, (*personal name*)

O

---

of *prep* [*w dat/acc*] over, for; *adv* too

❖ **ofan** *adv* from above, down; downwards; on the uppermost part, at the top of; [*w gen*] above the surface of

ofan á *prep* [*w acc*] down (from above) to

ofan til *prep* [*w gen*] down (from above) to

ofn <-s, -ar> *m* oven

❖ **ok** *conj* and; *adv* also

okkar *gen* of **vit**

okkr *acc/dat* of **vit**

❖ **okkarr** *poss dual pron* our

opt <*comp* optar *superl* optast> *adv* often

❖ **orð** *n* word; repute, fame, report; **í öðru orði** at the same time, likewise, *lit* in a second word

orðit *ppart* of **verða**

orðstírr *m* fame, renown

Orkneyjar *f pl* the Orkney Islands (*place name*)

ormr <-s, -ar> *m* snake, serpent, worm

Ormr <-s> *m* Orm (*personal name*); **Ormr inn auðgi** Orm the Wealthy

ormr-í-auga *n* Snake-in-the-Eye (*nickname*)

ormslíki *n* shape, form of a dragon

orrosta *f* battle; **til orrostu** to or for battle

orrostumaðr *m* warrior, man of battle

oss *acc/dat* of **vér**

otr <*gen* otrs, *pl* otrar> *m* otter

otrbelgr *m* otter pelt or skin

otrgjöld *n pl* wergeld, ransom, or compensation for a dead otter, Otter's ransom

oxi *var* of **uxi**

Ó

ó- *neg pref* un-

ódæll *adj* difficult, quarrelsome, stubborn

óðal <*pl* óðöl> *n* ancestral property, patrimony, allodium, property held in allodial tenure

óðfúss *adj* madly keen, eager

Óðindísa *f* Odindisa (*personal name*)

Óðinn *m* Odin, chief god of the Æsir

óðr <*f* óð, *n* ótt> *adj* frantic; furious, vehement

óeirðarmaðr *m* unruly man

Ófeigr <-s> *m* Ofeig (*personal name*)

óframliga *adv* timidly

ófriðr <-ar> *m* war, strife

ógurligr *adj* awful, terrible

óhræddr *adj* unafraid

ójafn *adj* uneven, unequal

ójafnaðarmaðr *m* an overbearing, unjust man

ók *1/3sg past* of aka

ókátr *adj* gloomy

ókembdr <*n* ókembt> *ppart* unkempt

Óláfr <-s> *m* Olaf (*personal name*); Óláfr pái Olaf the Peacock

Ólöf <*gen* Ólafar> *f* Olof (*personal name*)

ólög *n* lawlesness

❖ ór (*also* úr) *prep* [*w dat*] out of, from, from inside of; made of

óráð *n* evil plan

óríkr *adj* weak

óskorinn <*n* óskorit> *ppart* uncut, unshorn

ósætt *f* disagreement

ótta *f* the last part of the night before dawn

óttask <-að-> *vb* be afraid

ótti *m* fear

óvandr *adj* unwary

óvinr *m* enemy

óvitrliga *adv* foolishly

óvægr *adj* harsh, unmerciful

óx *1/3sg past* of vaxa

óþýðr *adj* unfriendly; intimidating

P

pallr *m* step; raised platform along the side(s) of a hall

papi *m* pope; priest. Name for the Irish anchorites said to be in Iceland when the first Norse settlers arrived.

pái (*also* pá) *m* peacock (*nickname*)

penningr *m* coin, penny; piece of property, article

prestr *m* priest

R

Ragnarr <-s> *m* Ragnar (*personal name*); Ragnarr loðbrók Ragnar Shaggy-breeches, a legendary Viking chieftain of the 9th century

ragnarøk(k)r <-rs> *n* Ragnarok, the twilight of the gods, the world's end (*also referred to as* ragna rök *n pl* doom of the gods; *see* rök)

Ragnfrøðr <-s> *m* Ragnfrod (*personal name*)

Ragnhildr <*acc/dat* Ragnhildi, *gen* Ragnhildar> *f* Ragnhild (*personal name*)

Ragnvaldr <-s> *m* Ragnvald (*personal name*)

ragr <*f* rög, *n* ragt> *adj* effeminate, cowardly, (passively) homosexual

rammr <*f* römm, *n* rammt> *adj* strong; mighty, powerful; rammr at afli extremely strong

---

e-n (einhvern) = 'somebody,' *acc.*;   e-t (eitthvat) = 'something,' *acc.*;   e-m (einhverjum) = '(for) somebody,' *dat.*;
e-u (einhverju) = '(for) something,' *dat.*;   e-s (einhvers) = '(of) somebody or something,' *gen.*

Rangárvellir *m pl* Rangarvellir (*place name*) Rang River Plains

rangr <*f* röng, *n* rangt> *adj* crooked, unjust; wrong, false

Rannveig <-ar> *f* Rannveig (*personal name*)

Ratatoskr (*also* **Ratatöskr**) <-s> *m* Ratatosk, the squirrel that carries insults between **Níðhöggr** and the eagle

Rauð-Balli *m* Red-Balli (*personal name*)

rauðr <*f* rauð, *n* rautt> *adj* red (frequently as a descriptor for gold)

Raumaríki *n* Raumariki (*place name*)

❖ **ráð** *n* advice, counsel; plan

❖ **ráða** <ræðr, réð, réðu, ráðinn> *vb* [*w dat*] advise, counsel; rule, govern, manage; **réð löndum** ruled over (his) lands; **ráða at** attack; **ráða fyrir [e-u]** rule over [sth]; **ráða um við [e-t]** deliberate or think about [sth]

ráðagørð <*pl* -ir> *f* council; **eiga ráðagørð** take council

ráðsnjallr *adj* wise in counsel

ráku *3pl past of* **reka**

Refill *m* the name of a sword

Refr <-s> *m* Ref (*personal name*) Fox; **Refr inn rauði** Ref the Red

Refsstaðir *m pl* Refsstadir (*place name*) Ref's Farmstead

regin <*dat pl* rögnum, *gen* ragna> *n pl* (divine) powers, gods

Reginn <-s> *m* Regin; son of Hreidmar, brother of Fáfnir the dragon

regna <-di, -t> *vb* rain

reiddisk *2/3sg past of* **reiðask**

reið *1/3sg past of* **ríða**

reiðask <-ddi, -ddr> *vb* become angry

reiði *f* wrath, anger; **af reiði** in anger, out of anger

reiði *m* ship's equipment

❖ **reiðr** *adj* angry, offended

reis *1/3sg past of* **rísa**

reisa <-ti, -tr> *vb* raise; **láta reisa stein** have a stone raised

reka <rekr, rak, ráku, rekinn> *vb* drive, herd; drive onto shore, wreck; [*w gen*] take vengeance for; **reka spor** follow tracks or footprints

rekaviðr *m* driftwood

reki *m* driftage, a thing drifted ashore, wreck

rekja <rakði~rakti, rakiðr~rakðr~raktr> *vb* track, trace

rekkja *f* bed; **fara í rekkju** go to bed

reknir *ppart of* **reka**

renna <rennr, rann, runnu, runninn> *vb intrans* run

renna <-di, -dr> *vb trans* run; put to flight

reri *3sg past of* **róa**

Rerir <-s> *m* Reri (*personal name*)

reru *3pl past of* **róa**

reyðr <*acc/dat* reyði, *gen* reyðar, *pl* reyðar> *f* rorqual, large baleen whale

Reykjanes *n* Reykjanes, Headland of Smoke (*place name*)

Reykjarvík *f* Reykjavik, Bay of Smoke (modern Reykjavík)

reyna <-di, -dr> *vb* try, prove; experience

réð *1/3sg past of* **ráða**

rétt *adv* directly

❖ **réttr** <*f* rétt, *n* rétt> *adj* straight; correct, right, just

réttr <-ar> *m* law

rif <*dat pl* rifjum> *n* rib; reef (in the sea)

Rifsker <*dat pl* Rifskerjum> *n* Rifsker (*place name*), Rocky or Rib Reef

rista <-ti, -tr> *vb* cut, carve, engrave

rita <-að-> *vb* write *var of* **ríta**

❖ **ríða** <ríðr, reið, riðu, riðinn> *vb* ride

Ríkarðr <-ar> *m* Richard

ríki <*dat pl* ríkjum, *gen pl* ríkja> *n* power; realm; kingdom

ríkismaðr *m* great man, prominent man, wealthy man, man of power

❖ **ríkr** <*acc* ríkjan> *adj* powerful, mighty

rísa <ríss, reis, risu, risinn> *vb* arise, rise, stand up; **rísa upp** rise up, get up

rísmál *n* six in the morning

rísta <rístr, reist, ristu, ristinn> *vb* cut; carve, engrave; carve, form by carving; **láta rísta rúnar** have runes carved

ríta <rítr, reit, ritu, ritinn> *vb* write; scratch, cut

rjóða <rýðr, rauð, ruðu, roðinn> *vb* redden

rjúfa <rýfr, rauf, rufu, rofinn> *vb* break; break a hole in; **rjúfa sáttmál** break an agreement or truce; (*impers*) **rýfr veðrit** the weather clears

Roðbertr löngumspaði <-s> *m* Robert Longsword

Rogaland *n* Rogaland (*place name*)

róa <rœr, røri~reri, røru~reru, róinn> *vb* row

róðr <*gen* róðrar, *pl* róðrar> *m* rowing, pulling

rógmálmr *m* gold, metal of strife

rót <*gen* rótar, *pl* rœtr> *f* root

róta <-að-> *vb* [*w dat*] throw into disorder; **róta [e-u] í sundr** knock [sth] apart

rúm *n* bed; space, seat

rún <*pl* -ar> *f* secret, mystery; rune, a letter in the runic futhark

rygr <-jar> *f* housewife

ræna <-di, -dr ~ -ti, -tr> *vb* rob, steal, plunder; **ræna [e-n] [e-t]** rob [sb] of [sth]

rœða <-ddi, -ddr> *vb* speak; converse, discuss

rœtr *nom/acc pl* of **rót**

rög *f nom sg & n nom/acc pl* of **ragr**

Rögnvaldr <-s~ar> *m* Rognvald (*personal name*)

rök *n pl* judgment, doom

rökðu *3pl past* of **rekja**

røk(k)r <-rs> *n* twilight

røru *3pl past* of **róa**

röskr <*acc* röskvan> *adj* sturdy, vigorous, brave

röst <*gen* rastar, *pl* rastir> *f* unit of distance between two resting places (perhaps equivalent to the Old Scandinavian mile)

S

---

saga <*pl* sögur> *f* what is said, story, saga, tale, legend, history; **saga til [e-s]** a story about [sth]

sakar *gen* of **sök**

sakeyrir *m* fine

sakna <-að> *vb* [*w gen*] miss, feel the loss of

salr <*dat* sal, *gen* salar, *pl* salir> *m* hall

❖ **saman** *adv* together

samför < *pl* samfarar> *f* (*usu in pl*) relationship, marriage

sammœðr *adj* of the same mother

❖ **samr** <*f* söm, *n* samt> *adj pron* same; **ina sömu nótt** on the same night; **it sama** the same, likewise

sannnefni *n* appropriate, truthful name

❖ **sannr** <*f* sönn, *n* satt> *adj* true

sauðahús *n* sheep pen, sheep-fold

sauðamaðr *m* shepherd

sauðr <-ar, -ir> *m* sheep

sautján (*also* **sjautján**) <*ord* sautjándi, seventeenth> *num* seventeen

❖ **sá** <*f* sú, *n* þat> *dem pron* that (one)

sá <sær, søri~seri, søru~seru, sáinn> *vb* sow

sá *1/3sg past* of **sjá**

sál *f var* of **sála**

sála *f* soul

sáld *n* cask, vat

sámr *adj* swarthy, blackish

sár *n* wound

❖ **sárr** *adj* wounded; painful, sore

❖ **sáttr** *adj* reconciled, at peace

sátu *3pl past* of **sitja**

sáu *3pl past* of **sjá**

seggr <*pl* seggir, *gen* seggja> *m* man

❖ **segja** <sagði, sagt> *vb* say; **segja frá [e-u]** reveal, tell about [sth]; **segja [e-m] til [e-s]** tell, inform [sb] of [sth]; **segja til sín** give one's name

❖ **sekr** <*acc* sekan~sekjan> *adj* guilty; convicted, condemned to outlawry; **gera [e-n] sekan** condemn [sb] to outlawry

selja <-di, -dr> *vb* hand over to another; sell; **seljast** *mid* give oneself up

❖ **sem** *rel particle* who, which, that; *conj* as; (*w superl*) as ... as possible; where

❖ **senda** <-di, -dr> *vb* send

sendimaðr *m* messenger

senn *adv* at once, straight away

❖ **setja** <-tti, -ttr> *vb* set, seat, place; **setja til ríkis** put in power; **setja á** hurl at; **setja upp** set, stand up; **setja við** prepare; **setjask** *mid* seat oneself, sit

❖ **sex** <*ord* sétti, sixth > *num* six

sex tigir *num* sixty

sextán <*ord* sextándi, sixteenth> *num* sixteen

seyra *f* starvation

sezk *2/3sg pres* of **setjask** (setr + sk)

sém *1pl pres subjunct* of **vera**

sér *dat* of **sik**

sér *2/3sg* of **sjá**

sétti *ord* sixth

Sif *f* Sif, a goddess, the wife of Thor

Sigfaðir *m* Victory-father, a name for **Óðinn**

Sighvatr <-s> *m* Sighvat (*personal name*)

sigla <-di, -dr> *vb* sail

sigla *f* mast

Sighvatr <-s> *m* Sighvat (*personal name*); **Sighvatr inn rauði** Sighvat the Red

Sigi *m* Sigi (*personal name*)

Sigmundr <-ar> *m* Sigmund (*personal name*)

Signý <-jar> *f* Signy (*personal name*)

sigr <-rs> *m* victory

sigra <-að-> *vb* to defeat

Sigríðr <*acc/dat* Sigríði, *gen* Sigríðar> *f* Sigrid

---

e-n (einhvern) = 'somebody,' *acc.*; e-t (eitthvat) = 'something,' *acc.*; e-m (einhverjum) = '(for) somebody,' *dat.*;
e-u (einhverju) = '(for) something,' *dat.*; e-s (einhvers) = '(of) somebody or something,' *gen.*

(*personal name*)

sigrsæll *adj* victorious

Sigrøðr <-ar> *m* Sigrod (*personal name*)

Sigtryggr <-s> *m* Sigtrygg (*personal name*)

Sigurðr <-ar> *m* Sigurd (*personal name*); **Sigurðr slefa** Sigurd the Slobberer

❖ **sik** <*dat* sér, *gen* sín> *refl acc pron* him-/her-/it-/oneself, themselves

silfr *n* silver

silki *n* silk

silkitreyja *f* silken jacket

❖ **sinn** *n* time (of repetition); **eitt sinn** one time; **einu sinni** once; **hvert sinn** every

❖ **sinn** <*f* sín, *n* sitt> *refl poss pron* his, her, its, their own

❖ **sitja** <sitr, sat, sátu, setinn> *vb* sit; reside

síð <*comp* síðr *superl* sízt> *adv* late

síðar *var* of **síðarr**

síðarr (*also* **síðar**) *comp adv* of **síð**, later

❖ **síðan** *adv* then, later, afterwards

síðr *superl* of **síð**

síga <sígr, sé~seig, sigu, siginn> *vb* sink gently down; glide, move slowly

Símon knútr *m* Simon Knot (*personal name*)

sín *gen* of **sik**

sína *f acc sg* of **sinn**

Síreksstaðir *m pl* Sireksstadir (*place name*) Sirek's Farmstead

sízt *conj* since, for

sízt *superl adv* of **síð**

sjaldan *adv* seldom

sjautján *var* of **sautján**

❖ **sjau** <*ord* sjaundi, seventh > *num* seven

❖ **sjá** *var* of **þessi**

❖ **sjá** <sér, sá, sá(u), sénn> *vb* see, look; understand; **sjá á [e-m]** look upon [sb]

sjái *3sg & pl pres subjunct* of **sjá**

Sjáland *n* Zealand, Sjælland in modern Danish (*place name*)

❖ **sjálfr** *adj pron* self, oneself, himself, herself, itself, themselves

sjávarafli *m* catch of fish, bounty of the sea

sjónhverfing *f* optical illusion (caused by a spell)

sjónlauss *adj* blind, sightless

sjór <*gen* sjóvar~sjófar> *m* the sea; **fyrir ofan sjó** above the waterline

skaði *m* harm, damage; death

skafa <skefr, skóf, skófu, skafinn> *vb* scrape, shave

skaka <skekr, skók, skóku, skekinn> *vb* shake

skal *1/3sg pres* of **skulu**

Skallagrímr <-s> *m* Skalla-Grim, Bald-Grim

(*personal name*)

skalt *2sg pres* of **skulu**

❖ **skammr** *adj* short; brief

skammt *adv* a short distance, not far (*place*)

skap *n* state, condition; temper, mood

skapa <-að- *or* skepr, skóp, skópu, skapinn> *vb* shape, form, make, create

skapt <*pl* sköpt> *n* handle, shaft; **á hávu skapti** on a long shaft

skarpr <*f* skörp, *n* skarpt> *adj* scorched, pinched, chafing

skattr <-s, -ar> *m* tribute, tax

skáld *n* poet, skald

skáldskaparmál *n pl* poetic diction

skáli *m* main hall, sleeping hall

skálm <*pl* -ir> *f* short sword, cleaver

Skáney *f* Skåne, Denmark (*place name*), now part of Sweden

skáru *3pl past* of **skera**

skegg *n* beard

skeinuhættr *adj* likely to wound

skel *f* shell

skelfr *2/3sg pres* of **skjálfa**

skellr <*pl* -ir> *m* blow, stroke

sker <*dat pl* skerjum, *gen pl* skerja> *n* skerry, isolated rock sticking out of the sea

skera <skerr, skar, skáru, skorinn> *vb* cut

skikkja *f* cloak

❖ **skilja** <-di~ði, skiliðr~skildr~skilinn> *vb* part, separate, divide; understand; **þá skilr á um [e-t]** *impers* they fall out over, differ, disagree about [sth]

skillingr <-s, -ar> *m* shilling, i.e. piece of money; *pl* money

skilnaðr <-s> *m* parting

skinn *n* skin, fur

Skinna-Björn *m* Bjorn Fur-Skins (*personal name*)

skinni *m* skinner (*nickname*)

❖ **skip** *n* ship

skipa <-að-> *vb* arrange, array; man, occupy

skipför <*gen* skipfarar, *pl* skipfarar> *f* a voyage, sailing, passage of a ship

skipt *ppart* of **skipta** (*n nom/acc*)

skipta <-ti, -tr> *vb* [*w dat*] divide; share; change

skipti *n* division

skíð *n* ski, piece of wood; **skíð Atals grundar** ski of the land of Atal (kenning for 'ship')

skíð *n* stick

Skíði *m* Skidi (*personal name*)

skína <skínr, skein, skinu, skininn> *vb* shine

Skínir *m* Skinir (*personal name*)

skjaldborg *f* shield-wall, protection

skjall *n* the white membrane of an egg

skjálfa <skelfr, skalf, skulfu, skolfinn> *vb* tremble, shake

skjóta <skýtr, skaut, skutu, skotinn> *vb* shoot

skjótliga *adv* swiftly

skótligr *adj* swift

skjótr *adj* quick

skjótt *adv* suddenly

❖ **skjöldr** <*dat* skildi, *gen* skjaldar,*pl* skildir, *acc* skjöldu> *m* shield

Skoll *m* Skoll, the wolf that pursues the sun

skorinn *ppart of* **skera**

skorta <-ti, -t> *vb* be lacking to one; [e-n] skortir [e-t] [sb] is short of [sth]

skot *n* shooting, shot, missiles

Skotland *n* Scotland

skógr <-ar, -ar> *m* wood, forest

skór <*dat* skó, *gen* skós, *pl* skúar, *acc* skúa, *dat* skóm, *gen* skúa> *m* shoe

skríða <skríðr, skreið, skriðu, skriðinn> *vb* crawl

Skrýmir <-s> *m* Skrymir, name of a giant

Skuld *f* Skuld (*personal name, mythological*) Debt, that which should become, one of the three Norns

❖ **skulu** <skal, skyldi, *past inf* skyldu> *pret-pres vb* shall (*obligation, purpose, necessity, fate*); should

skurðr <-ar, -ir> *m* a cutting, slice; a trench; the flensing of a whale

skúr *f* shower

Skútaðar-Skeggi *m* Skeggi of Skutad (*personal name*)

skyld <*pl* -ir> *f* tax, due; incumbrance (on an estate); reason, sake

❖ **skyldr** *adj* bound, obliged; due; urgent; related by kinship

skyldu *3pl past of* **skulu**

skyli *3sg & pl pres subjunct of* **skulu**

skynda <-di, -dr> *vb* [*w dat*] hurry

skyr *n* curdled milk

ský <*gen pl* skýja> *n* cloud

Sköfnungr (*also* **Sköflungr**) *m* Skofnung, possibly Shin Bone, the name of King Hrolf's sword

skökull <*dat* skökli, *gen* skökuls> *m* harness

skör <*gen* skarar> *f* locks, hair

skörungr <-s, -ar> *m* a notable man or woman, leader

slá <slær, sló, slógu, sleginn> *vb* strike

slefa *f* saliva, slobber, slobberer (as nickname)

Sleipnir *m* Sleipnir, Odin's horse

sleppa <sleppr, slapp, sluppu, sloppinn> *vb* slip; escape, slip away; fail, slip up

slíðrar (*also* **slíðrir**) *f pl* sheath, scabbard

slíðrir *var of* **slíðrar**

❖ **slíkr** *adj* such

slíkt *adv* in such a way

sló *1/3sg past of* **slá**

smalamaðr *m* shepherd

smár <*f* smá, *n* smátt> *adj* small

smiðja <-u, -ur> *f* smithy

smiðr *m* smith

smjúga <smýgr, smaug~smó, smugu, smoginn> *vb* creep through an opening; pierce

smjör <*dat* smjörvi> *n* butter

Smjörvatnsheiðr *f* Smjorvatnsheid (*place name*), Butter-Lake Heath

sneiða <-ddi, -ddr> *vb* slice; glance off

snemma (*also* **snimma**) <*comp* snemr, *superl* snemst> *adv* early

snemr *comp of* **snemma**

snerta <snertr, snart, snurtu, snortinn> *vb* touch; concern

snimma *var of* **snemma**

snjófa <-að> *vb* snow

snjór <*gen* snjóvar~snjófar> *m* snow

snúa <snýr, sneri~snøri, sneru~snøru, snúinn> *vb* turn; twist, plait, braid; **snúask til** turn oneself to

Snækólfr *m* Snaekolf (*personal name*)

sofa <søfr~sefr, svaf, sváfu, sofinn> *vb* sleep

sofna <-að-> *vb* fall asleep; **vera sofnaðr** have fallen asleep

sokkr <-s, -ar> *m* sock, stocking; **einir sokkar** a pair of socks

sonargjöld *n pl* wergeld, ransom, or compensation for a dead son

sonarsonr *m* grandson

❖ **sonr** <*dat* syni, *gen* sonar, *pl* synir, *acc* sonu> *m* son

Sóknadalr *m* Soknadale (*place name*)

sól <*dat* sól~sólu> *f* sun; day

sólskin *n* sunshine

sómi *m* an honor

Sótanes *n* Sotaness (*place name*)

sótti *3sg past of* **sœkja**

sóttu *3pl past of* **sœkja**

---

e-n (einhvern) = 'somebody,' *acc.*; e-t (eitthvat) = 'something,' *acc.*; e-m (einhverjum) = '(for) somebody,' *dat.*;
e-u (einhverju) = '(for) something,' *dat.*; e-s (einhvers) = '(of) somebody or something,' *gen.*

spaði *m* spade, shovel

spakara *comp adv* of *adj* **spakr** more wisely

spakr <*f* spök, *n* spakt> *adj* wise

spápáði,*vb* prophesy, fortell

spánn (*also* **spónn**) <*dat* spæni, *gen* spánar, *pl* spænir, *acc* spænir> *m* chip, shaving; spoon

spekð (*also* **spekt**) *f* peace; wisdom

speki *f* wisdom

spekingr <-s, -ar> *m* wise person, sage

spekt (*also* **spekð**) *f* peace; wisdom

spilla <-ti, -tr> *vb* [*w dat*] spoil, destroy

spillir *m* spoiler; **spillir bauga** spoiler of rings, generous prince

spinna <spinnr, spann, spunnu, spunninn> *vb* spin

❖ **spjót** *n* spear, lance

Spjútr <-s> *m* Spjut (*personal name*)

spor *n* track, trail, footprint; step, foothold

spónn *var* of **spánn**

spretta <sprettr, spratt, spruttu, sprottinn> *vb* spring up, burst forth; start, spring; sprout

springa <springr, sprakk, sprungu, sprunginn> *vb* jump, spring; issue forth; burst; die from overexertion or grief

spurði *3sg past* of **spyrja**

spurðusk *3pl past mid* of **spyrja**

❖ **spyrja** <spurði, spurðr> *vb* ask; hear, hear of, learn, be informed of, find out; **spyrja til [e-s]** have news of [sb], learn of [sb]; **spyrja [e-n] at [e-u]** ask [sb] about [sth]; **spyrjask** *mid*

spörr <*pl* sparvar> *m* sparrow

staddr (*ppart* of **steðja**) placed, present; situated

❖ **staðr** <*dat* stað~staði, *gen* staðar, *pl* staðir> *m* stead, parcel of land; place, spot; abode, dwelling

stafr <*gen* -s, *pl* stafar~stafir> *m* wooden staff, stick; pole, timber

stalli <-a, -ar> *m* altar (heathen)

stallr <-s, -ar> *m* stall; pedestal

❖ **standa** <stendr, stóð, stóðu, staðinn> *vb* stand; stay, remain; stand, stick; rest, stop; befit, become; catch, overtake; **standa af [e-u]** be caused by [sth]; **standa undir [e-u]** be subject to [sth]; **standa undir [e-t]** support, approve of [sth]; **standa við [e-u]** withstand [sth]; **standa yfir** last

stanga <-að-> *vb* ram, (head)butt, gore (of cattle); **stangask** *mid* butt each other

starf *n* work

steði <*gen* steðja> *m* anvil

steðja <-ddi, -ddr> *vb* stop; fix, settle

stefna <-di, -dr> *vb* aim at, go in a certain direction; call, call together, summon

stefna *f* direction, course; meeting; appointment; summons

steikja <-ði~ti, -ðr~tr> *vb* roast

steina <-di, -dr> *vb* paint

Steinbjörn *m* Steinbjorn, Stone-Bear (*personal name*)

steinn <-s, -ar> *m* stone; cave or stone dwelling; [*poet*] precious stone, jewel

Steinn <-s> *m* Stein (*place name*) Stone

steint *ppart* of **steina**

stela <stelr, stal, stálu, stolinn> *vb* steal

sterkastr *superl* of **sterkr**

❖ **sterkr** *adj* strong

stikublígr *m* stick-gazer, miser (*nickname*)

stinnr *adj* stiff, unbending, strong

stirðr <*n* stirt> *adj* stiff, rigid; harsh, severe

stirt *adv* harshly

stíga <stígr, sté~steig, stigu, stiginn> *vb* step, tread; **stíga á hest** mount a horse

stjarna <*gen* stjörnu, *pl* stjörnur> *f* star

stjórna <-að> [*w dat*] rule over, govern, command

stjórnsamr *adj* ambitious, overbearing

stofa *f* stove room, a room in a long house, secondary to the **eldaskáli** and warmed by a stove of flat stones; served as a living room, where women worked the looms, families sat in the evenings, and feasts were held

stokkr <-s, -ar> *m* trunk or log of wood; wooden beam; base under an anvil

stolinn *ppart* of **stela**

stormr *m* storm

stóð *1/3sg past* of **standa**

stóll <-s, -ar> *m* stool, chair; bishop's see; king's throne or residence

stórlátr *adj* proud, haughty, arrogant

stórmannligr *adj* magnificent, grand

stórmennska *f* magnanimity

stórmerki *n pl* great wonders

❖ **stórr** <*comp* stœrri, *superl* stœrstr> *adj* big

strandhögg *n* a shore raid, piracy; **høggva strandhögg** engage in piracy

Strandir *f pl* Strandir (*place name*), the Strands

straumr <*gen* straums, *pl* straumar> *m* stream

strá <-ði, -ðr> *vb* strew, spread

strengja <-da, -dr> swear solemnly; string tight

strjúka <strýkr, strauk, struku, strokinn> *vb* stroke, rub, wipe; caress; smooth, brush

strönd <*dat* ströndu~strönd, *gen* strandar, *pl* strendr~strandir> *f* strand, coast, shore; border, edge

stund *f* a while, a time; hour

stundum ... stundum *conj* sometimes ... sometimes, at times ... at times

stýra <-ði, -t> *vb* [*w dat*] steer, command; rule, govern; manage

stýrimaðr *m* captain, steersman

stöðlinum = **stöðli** + **inum**, *dat sg* of **stöðull**

stöðull <*dat* stöðli> *m* milking pen (for cows)

stöðva <-að-> *vb* stop, halt

stökk *1/3sg past* of **støkkva**

støkkva <støkkr, stökk, stukku, stokkinn> *vb* spring, burst, leap; be sprinkled

stöng <stangar, stangir~stengr> *f* staff, pole

suðr <-rs> *n* south

suðr *adv* south, southwards

Suðreyjar *f pl* the Hebrides (from a Norwegian perspective, *lit* the South Isles)

Suðrlönd *n pl* the Southlands, Germany

Suðrmaðr *m* South-man, southerner; a German, a Saxon

Suðr-Rygirnir *m pl* South Rogalanders

suðrœnn *adj* southern

sultr <-ar> *m* hunger

❖ **sumar** <*pl* sumur> *n* summer; **um sumarit** in the summer; **hvert sumar** every summer

sumir *m nom pl* of **sumr**

❖ **sumr** *adj pron* some

sumra <-að> *vb* draw near summer

sumur *n nom/acc pl* of **sumar**

sundfœrr *adj* able to swim; **sundfœrr of sæ** seaworthy, *lit* able to swim over the sea

sundr *adv* asunder

sunna *f* sun

sunnan *adv* from the south

Sunnudalr *m* Sunnudal (*place name*)

Surtr *m* Surt, the lord of **Múspellsheimr**

sú <*acc* þá, *dat* þeir(r)i, *gen* þeir(r)ar> *f sg dem* of **sá** that (one)

Súðvirki *n* Southwark (*place name*)

Súlki *m* Sulki (*personal name*)

súpa <sýpr, saup, supu, sopinn> *vb* sip, drink; take a sip

svaf *1/3sg past* of **sofa**

svalr *adj* cool

svaltz *variant* of **svalzt**

svalzt *2sg past* of **svelta**

svanr <-s, -ir> *m* swan

Svanr *m* Svan, Swan (*personal name*)

svar <*pl* svör> *n* answer, reply

❖ **svara** <-að-> *vb* [*w dat*] answer

svardagi *m* oath

Svartálfheimr *m* Svartalfheim (*place name, mythological*) world of the dark elves

svartr <*f* svört, *n* svart> *adj* black

Svartr *m* Svart (*personal name*), Black

❖ **svá** *adv* so, thus; such; then; so (*denoting degree*); **svá at** such that, with the result that; **svá sem** so as, as; **svá mikill at** so great

❖ **sveinn** <-s, -ar> *m* boy, lad; servant; page

Sveinn tjúguskegg <*gen* Sveins> *m* Svein Forkbeard, king of Denmark (987–1014)

sveit <*pl* sveitir> *f* group or body of men; troop, band, company; region, district

sveiti *m* sweat, blood

svelgja <svelgr, svalg, sulgu, sólginn> *vb* swallow

svelta <sveltr, svalt, sultu, soltinn> *vb* die (of starvation); starve, suffer hunger; **svelta hungri** starve, die of hunger

❖ **sverð** *n* sword

sverðsegg *f* sword's edge

sverja <svarði, svarðr *or* sverr, sór, sóru, svarinn> *vb* swear (an oath)

svimma <svimmr, svamm, summu, summinn> *vb* swim

svipan *f* swing, blow

Svipdagr <-s> *m* Svipdag (*personal name*)

svipstund *f* moment

svipta <-ti, -tr> *vb* sweep; throw, fling

Svíar *m pl* the Swedes

svíða <svíðr, sveið, sviðu, sviðinn> *vb* singe, burn

svíkja <svíkr, sveik, sviku, svikinn> betray, deceive, cheat, defraud

Svívör *f* Svivor, a giantess killed by Thor

Svíþjóð *f* Sweden

svör *nom/acc pl* of **svar**

syngva <syngr, söng, sungu, sunginn> *vb* sing

syni *dat* of **sonr**

systir <*acc/dat/gen* systur, *pl* systr> *f* sister

sýna <-di, -dr> *vb* show; **sýnask** *mid* seem, appear

sýnum *adv* by sight, apparently

sæhafa *indecl adj* sea-tossed, driven off one's course; **verða sæhafa** be driven off-course

Sæhrímnir *m* Sæhrimnir, the boar who feeds the warriors in **Valhöll**

sæll *adj* fortunate, happy

---

e-n (einhvern) = 'somebody,' *acc.*;　**e-t** (eitthvat) = 'something,' *acc.*;　**e-m** (einhverjum) = '(for) somebody,' *dat.*;　**e-u** (einhverju) = '(for) something,' *dat.*;　**e-s** (einhvers) = '(of) somebody or something,' *gen.*

sær <*acc* sæ, *dat* sævi~sæ, *gen* sævar> *m* the sea

sæta <-tta, -tt> *vb* [*w dat*] wait in ambush, waylay; undergo, suffer; bring about, cause

sætt <*pl* sættir, *dat* sáttum, *gen* sátta> *f* settlement, reconciliation, atonement, agreement; **at sætt** as atonement

sætta <-tti, -ttr> *vb* reconcile; make peace among; **sættask** *mid* come to terms, settle, agree, be reconciled

sættusk *3pl past mid* of **sætta**

❖ **sœkja** <sótti, sóttr> *vb* seek; pursue; **sœkja til [e-s]** seek out [sb]

sœmð *f* honor

sœnskr *adj* Swedish

❖ **sök** <*gen* sakar; *pl* sakar~sakir> *f* cause, reason, sake; **fyrir [e-s] sakar** on account of, because of [sth]

sök *f* thing, case

søkkva <søkkr, sökk, sukku, sokkinn> *vb* sink

söm *f nom sg* & *n nom/acc pl* of **samr**

sömu *str n dat sg*, *wk f acc/dat/gen sg* & *all wk nom/acc/gen pl* of **samr**

söngr <-s, -var> *m* song

T

❖ **taka** <tekr, tók, tóku, tekinn> *vb* take, catch, seize; take hold of, grasp; reach, touch; [*w inf*] begin; *impers* [e-t] **taka af** [sth] comes loose, comes off; [sth] ceases; **taka arf** inherit; **taka [e-t] á [e-u]** touch [sth] with [sth]; **taka [e-m] fegins hendi** receive [sb] gladfully, joyfully; **taka í sundr** cut asunder; **taka [e-n] höndum** seize or capture [sb]; **taka upp [e-t]** pick up [sth]; **taka við [e-m]** take in, receive, or welcome [sb] into one's house; **taka við [e-u]** receive, take possession of, acquire, inherit [sth]; **taka til** begin

tal *n* talk, parley, conversation

❖ **tala** <-að-> *vb* talk, speak; **tala við [e-n]** speak to [sb]

telja <talði~taldi, talið~taldr~talinn> *vb* count; reckon, consider

temja <temr, tamði~tamdi, tamði~tamdr, taminn> *vb* tame; train, exercise

Temps *f* the river Thames

tigr <*gen* tigar; *pl* tigir, *acc* tigu> *m* ten; a decade

❖ **til** *prep* [*w gen*] to; of; on; too

til handa *prep* [*w dat*] for

tilkall <*pl* tilköll> *n* claim

tillagagóðr *adj* well-disposed, reliable

tillit *n* look, glance (*cf* líta)

tíðara *comp adv* of *adj* **tíðr**

tíðendi *var* of **tíðindi**

❖ **tíðindi** (*also* **tíðendi**) *n pl* news, events, tidings

tíðr *adj* frequent

tíðum *adv* often

tími *m* time

tírœðr *adj* counted by tens, ten tens

❖ **tíu** <*ord* tíundi, tenth > *num* ten

tívar *m pl* gods (*plural only, in poetic usage*)

tjalda <-að-> *vb* pitch a tent

tjaldat *ppart* of **tjalda**, tented; with its awning up

toddi *m* bit, piece, morsel (*nickname*)

topt <-ir> *f* homestead; the walls or foundations of a (former) building

Toptavöllr *m* Toptavoll (*place name*)

tók *1/3sg past* of **taka**

tóku *3pl past* of **taka**

❖ **tólf** <*ord* tólfti, twelfth > *num* twelve

tólfræðr *adj* counted by twelves, twelve tens

tómliga *adv* slowly

tómr *adj* slow

tré <*dat* tré, *gen* trés, *pl* tré, *dat* trjám, *gen* trjá> *n* tree; wood

tréna <-að-> *vb* dry up

troða <treðr~trøðr, trað, tráðu, treðinn> *vb* tread; cram, pack; **troðask** (*mid*) crowd upon each other

troll (*also* **tröll**) *n* monstrous inhuman creature; human with troll characteristics

trollkona *f* troll-wife, a giantess

trúa (*also* **trú**) <trú> *f* faith, word of honor, religious faith, belief

trúa <-ði, trúat> *vb* believe

trúr *adj* true

tryggvi *m* the True (*nickname*)

tröll *var* of **troll**

tunga *f* tongue; language, tongue; tongue of land a the meeting of two rivers

tuttugu <*ord* tuttugandi~tuttugundi, twentieth> *num* twenty

tún *n* enclosure, farmstead; hayfield, homefield; [*poet*] dwellings, precincts

❖ **tveir** <*f* tvær, *n* tvau, *acc m* tvá, *dat* tveim(r), *gen* tveggja, *ord* annarr, second > *num* two

typpa <-ti~typði, -tr~typðr> *vb* top, crown

týja <*3sg pres* týr, *3sg past* týði> *vb* do, work; [*w dat*] help, assist; *impers* avail, **týði ekki** it was of no avail

tæla <-di, -dr> *vb* trick, betray

tœki *3sg & pl past subjunct of* **taka**

tönn <*gen* tannar, *pl* tenn~tennr~teðr> *f* tooth

U

Uðr *var of* **Unnr**

ulfr *var of* **úlfr**

ull <*dat* ullu> *f* wool

ullarlagðr *m* tuft of wool

❖ **um** *prep* [*w acc*] about; around; across; for, because of; beyond; during, for, in, by (*time*); [*w dat—in poetic and older texts*] over; by, in (*time*); [*w vb of motion*] over, past, beyond, across

um *adv*, pre-verbal particle (untranslatable, but carrying connotation of completion)

um þvert *adv* (diagonally) across

umhverfis *prep and adv* around

una <-ði, unat> *vb* dwell, stay, abide, live at; [*w dat*] enjoy, be happy in, be content with a thing **unðu þeir þar lítla hríð** they did not like staying there but for a little while

und *prep w acc/dat* under

❖ **undan** *prep* [*w dat*] from under, from beneath; away from; just off, near to

undarligr *adj* strange

❖ **undir** *prep* [*w acc/dat*] under, underneath

undirhyggjumaðr *m* a guileful or deceitul person

unðu *3pl past of* **una**

❖ **ungr** <*comp* yngri, *superl* yngstr> *adj* young

unna <ann, unni, unnt~unnat> *pret-pres vb* grant, allow, bestow; [*w dat*] love; **unna [e-m] [e-s]** let [sb] have [sth]

unnit *ppart of* **vinna**

Unnr (*also* **Uðr**) <*acc* Unni, *dat* Unni, *gen* Unnar> *f* Unn (*personal name*)

unnu *3pl past of* **vinna**

uns *var of* **unz**

unz (*also* **uns**) *conj* until, till

❖ **upp** *adv* up, upward (*motion toward*)

upphiminn *m* heaven (above)

uppi *adv* up (*position*); **vera uppi** to live, last

upplenzkr *adj* of or pertaining to the Uplands (Norwegian highlands)

Upplönd *n pl* Uplands (*place name*) Norwegian highlands

Uppsalir *m pl* Uppsala (*place name*)

Urðarbrunnr *m* Urdarbrunn, the Well of Fate

Urðr *f* Urd, Fate, that which should become, one of the three Norns

urðu *3pl past of* **una**

uxi (*also* **oxi**) <*acc/dat/gen* uxa, *pl* yxn~øxn, *dat* yxnum~øxnum, *gen* yxna~øxna> *m* ox

Ú

Úlfar *m* Ulfar (*personal name*)

úlfr <-s, -ar> *m* wolf

úr *var of* **ór**

❖ **út** *adv* out, outward (*motion toward*), out to Iceland

❖ **útan** *adv* from outside; from abroad, from Iceland, from without; (*without motion*) outside

útanverðr *adj* the outward, outside, outer part of

útar *comp adv* farther out

útarliga *adv* far out

Útgarðr *m* Utgard, the Outer Enclosures, the home of the giants (*place name*)

---

e-n (einhvern) = 'somebody,' *acc.*;   e-t (eitthvat) = 'something,' *acc.*;   e-m (einhverjum) = '(for) somebody,' *dat.*; e-u (einhverju) = '(for) something,' *dat.*;   e-s (einhvers) = '(of) somebody or something,' *gen.*

úti *adv* out (*place*), outside, out-of-doors

útlagi *m* an outlaw

útlendr *adj* foreign

V

---

vaða <veðr, óð, óðu, vaðinn> *vb* wade (through water); rush (at an opponent)

vagn <-s, -ar> *m* wagon, vehicle

vaka <-ti, vakat> *vb* be awake

vakna <-að-> *intrans vb* awake, get up

Valaskjálf *f* Valaskjalf, Odin's silver-roofed hall

vald *n* power

Valdres *n* Valdres, a highland region in Norway

Valhöll *f* Valhalla, the Hall of the Slain

Valir *m pl* the inhabitants (*esp* Celtic) of France

valkyrja *f* a chooser of the slain, valkyrie

Valland *n* France

valr *m* corpses on the battlefield, the slain

valr <-s, -ir> *m* hawk

vandahús *n* wicker house

vandamál *n* complicated case, difficult matter

vandi *m* habit; custom

vandliga *adv* carefully

vandr *adj* difficult

Vanir *m pl* one of the two major groups of gods

vann *1/3sg past* of **vinna**

❖ **vanr** *adj* accustomed, wont; **vanr** **[e-u]** accustomed to [sth]; usual

var *1/3sg past* of **vera**

varð *1/3sg past* of **verða**

varðveita <-tta, -ttr> *vb* keep, preserve, watch, defend

vargr <-s, -ar> *m* wolf

varla *adv* hardly, scarcely

varmr *adj* warm

❖ **varr** <*f* vör, *n* vart> *adj* aware; cautious, wary

vas (older form of **var**) *1/3sg past* of **vera**

vatn <*gen* vatns~vatz~vaz, *pl* vötn> *n* water, fresh water; lake

vaxa <vex, óx, óxu, vaxinn> *vb* grow

vá *1/3sg past* of **vega**

vágr <-s, -ar> *m* bay, inlet; wave, sea

Vágr *m* Vag, Bay (*place name*)

vágskorinn *pp* **vágr** + **skorinn**, bay-cut, cut with bays or inlets

vágu *3pl past* of **vega**

ván <*pl* vánir> *f* hope, expectation, prospect

❖ **vándr** *adj* (qualitatively) bad, wretched; (morally) bad, wicked

❖ **vápn** *n* weapon

vápnaðr *ppart* armed

Vápnafjörðr *m* Vapnafjord, Weapon's Fjord

vápndjarfr *adj* fearless, daring in battle; **inn vápndjarfasti** the most fearless in battle

vápnfœrr *adj* skilled in arms

❖ **vár** *n* spring

vár *gen* of **vér** our (pl)

Vár *f* perhaps a goddess associated with pledges; **Várar hendi** by the hand of Var

vára <-að> *vb* draw near spring

várar *f pl* oath, solemn vow

❖ **várr** *poss pl pron* our

várþing *n* spring assembly

veð <*dat pl* veðjum, *gen* veðja> *n* pledge

veðr *n* weather; wind; storm

Veðrfölnir *m* Vedrfolnir, the hawk which sits between the eyes of the eagle atop **Yggdrasill**

vefa <vefr, óf~vaf, ófu~váfu, ofinn> *vb* weave

vega <vegr, vá, vágu, veginn> *vb* kill, slay; fight

veggr <*dat* vegg, *gen* -jar~-s, -ir> *m* wall

❖ **vegr** <*gen* vegar~vegs, *pl* vegir~vegar, *acc* vegu~vega> *m* way, road; mode, manner; direction; side

veiða <-ddi, -ddr> *vb* catch; hunt

veiðr <*acc/dat* veiði, *gen* veiðar, *pl* veiðar> *f* hunting, fishing, catch

veit *1/3 pres sg* of **vita**

veizla *f* feast

veiztu = **veizt þú** *2sg pres* of **vita**, you know

❖ **veita** <-tti, -ttr> *vb* grant, give, offer; assist; **veita [e-m] atgöngu** attack [sb]; **veita [e-m] atlögu** attack [sb]; **veita atróðr** set out rowing (toward); **[e-m] veita betr** [sb] has the better of it; **veita tilkall** make a claim

veizla *f* feast, banquet

vekja <vakði~vakti, vakiðr~vaktr~vakinn> *trans vb* wake, awake; **vekja [e-n] upp** wake [sb] up

❖ **vel** <*comp* betr, *superl* bezt~bazt> *adv* well; very; **vel at sér** gifted, capable

velli *dat sg* of **völlr**

❖ **vera** <er, var, váru, verit> *vb* be; last; **vera fyrir** lead; **vera þar fyrir** be there present; **vera vel at kominn** be welcome; **vera við** be present, take part in

❖ **verða** <verðr, varð, urðu, orðinn> *vb* become, happen; have to; **verða at [e-u]** become [sth]; **verða at grjóti** turn to stone; **verða at sœtt** reconcile; **verða sæhafa** be driven off-course (*when sailing*)

Verðandi *f* Verdandi (*personal name, mythological*) Becoming or Happening, one of the three norns

❖ **verðr** *adj* [*w gen*] worthy; **verðr [e-s]** worthy of [sth]

ver-gjarn *adj* eager for men, lustful

verit *ppart* of **vera** (*n*)

verja <varði, variðr~varðr> defend, **verja [e-u]** keep [sth] away; **verjask** (*mid*) defend oneself

verk *n* work

verpa <verpr, varp, urpu, orpinn> *vb* throw

verr <-s, -ar> *m* [*poet*] husband; [*pl*] men

verr *comp adv* worse

verri *comp adj* of **illr** and **vándr**, worse

verst *superl adv* of **illa**, worst; **sem verst** as bad as it can be, as bad as possible

verstr *superl adj* of **illr** and **vándr**

veröld *f* world

vesall *adj* pathetic, miserable, wretched

vestan *adv* from the west

Vestfold *f* Vestfold (*place name*)

vestr <*gen* vestrs> *n* west; *adv* westward, **vestr um haf**, west over the ocean (to Britain)

vestri *comp* of **vestr**

Vestrlönd *n pl* the Weslands, the British Isles and France

vestrvegir *m, pl* the west, i.e., toward the British Isles and beyond, *lit* the western ways

vestrœnn *adj* western

❖ **vetr** <*gen* vetrar, *pl* vetr> *m* winter; **um vetrinn** for the winter

vetra <-að> *vb* draw near winter

vexti *dat* of **vöxtr**

Véfastr <-s> *m* Vefast (*personal name*)

vél *f* deceit, trick

vér <*acc/dat* oss, *gen* vár> *pron* we (*pl*)

❖ **við** *prep* [*w acc*] at, by, close to; with; according to, after; [*w dat*] against; toward; with

viðartaug <*pl* -ar> *f* a flexible and tough twig

viðr <*gen* viðar, *pl* viðir, *acc* viðu> *m* tree; forest, wood; timber

viðtaka <*gen* viðtöku, *pl* viðtökur> *f* reception

vika *f* week

Vilhjálmr *m* William (*personal name*); **Vilhjálmr bastarðr** *m* William the Conqueror, illegitimate son of Robert Longsword

vili *m* desire

❖ **vilja** <2/3sg pres vill, vildi, viljat> *vb* wish, want

vill *2/3sg pres* of **vilja**

vinaboð *n* feast for one's friends

vinátta *f* friendship (*esp* a sincere, personal friendship)

vinda <vindr, vatt, undu, undinn> *vb* twist, wring, squeeze; wind, hoist; turn, swing; **vindask** (*mid*) make a sudden movement, turn oneself away

vindr <*gen* -s~-ar> *m* wind, air

vinfengi *n* friendship (*esp* a contractual alliance)

vingóðr <*f* vingóð, *n* vingott> *adj* good towards one's friends, friendly

Ving-Þórr *m* [*poet*] brandishing-Thor

vinna <vinnr, vann, unnu, unninn> *vb* gain, win; work; perform, accomplish; **vinna herskap á [e-m]** win battles against [sb]

❖ **vinr** <-ar, -ir> *m* friend

❖ **vinsæll** *adj* beloved, popular

virða <-ði, -ðr> *vb* evaluate, value, appaise

virðing *f* respect, value

vist *f* food, provisions; stay; abode

vit *n* sense, wit, intelligence, understanding

vit <*acc/dat* okkr, *gen* okkar> *pron* we (*dual*)

❖ **vita** <veit, vissi, vitaðr> *pret-pres vb* know; **vita fram** or **vita fyrir** know the future, foresee

vitandi *pres part* of **vita**, knowing

vitja <-að-> *vb* [*w gen*] go to a place; visit

❖ **vitr** <*acc* vitran> *adj* wise, intelligent

vitrast *superl* of **vitr**

víða *adv* widely, far and wide

víðfrægr *adj* widely-renowned, famous

víðr *adj* wide

❖ **víg** *n* battle; homicide, manslaughter, killing

vígja <-ði, -ðr> *vb* consecrate, hallow

vígr *adj* able to fight; **vígr vel** well-skilled in arms

vígvöllr *m* battlefield

vík <*gen* víkr, *pl* víkr> *f* bay

Vík *f* Vik, Bay (*place name*)

Víkin *f* the Vík region, Oslo fjord

víking <*pl* -ar> *f* raid; **í víking** on a raid

---

e-n (einhvern) = 'somebody,' *acc.*; e-t (eitthvat) = 'something,' *acc.*; e-m (einhverjum) = '(for) somebody,' *dat.*;
e-u (einhverju) = '(for) something,' *dat.*; e-s (einhvers) = '(of) somebody or something,' *gen.*

víkingavörðr <-varðar, -verðir> *m* Viking-Guard (coast guard against Vikings)

víkingr <-s, -ar> *m* Viking

víkja <víkr, veik, viku, vikinn> *vb* [*w dat*] move, turn; *impers* **nú víkr sögunni** now the saga shifts

Víkrmaðr *m* man from Vik

❖ **vísa** *f* verse

Vísburr <-s> *m* Visbur (*personal name*)

vísindi *n pl* knowledge, intelligence

❖ **víss** *adj* certain; wise; known

víst *adv* certainly

vísundr <-s, -ar> *m* bison

vítt *adv* far

vægð *f* mercy, forbearance

vængr <-jar, -ir> *m* wing

❖ **vænn** *adj* beautiful, fine, handsome; likely, to be expected; hopeful, promising

vænta <-ti, vænt> *vb* [*w gen*] expect, hope for

væri *3sg & pl past subjunct* of **vera**

Væringi <*pl* Væringjar> *m* Varangian, the name of the Norse warriors who served as bodyguards to the emperors of Constantinople in the Varangian Guard

vætr *n indecl* nothing

vættr <*dat* vætti, *gen* vættar, *pl* vættir> *f* creature, being; supernatural being, spirit

vöðvi *m* muscle

Vöggr *m* Vogg (*personal name*)

völlr <*dat* velli, *gen* vallar, *pl* vellir, *acc* völlu, *gen* valla> *m* field, plain

Völlr *m* Voll, field (*place name*)

völuspá *f* the sybil's prophecy

völva <*gen* völu, *pl* völur> *f* seeress, sybil

vörðr <*dat* verði, *gen* varðar, *pl* verðir, *acc* vörðu, *gen* varða> *m* warden; coastguard, watchman

vörr <*dat* verri, *gen* varrar, *pl* verrir, *acc* vörru> *m* a pull of an oar

vöxtr <*dat* vexti, *gen* vaxtar, *pl* vextir, *acc* vöxtu> *m* size, stature, growth; shape

Y

yðarr (*also* **yðvarr**) *poss pl pron* your

❖ **yðr** *acc/dat* of *pl pron* **þér**, you

yðru *n dat* of **yðarr**

yð(v)ar *gen* of *pl pron* **þér**

yðvarr *var* of **yðarr**

❖ **yfir** *prep* [*w acc/dat*] over, above, across

Yggdrasill *m* Yggdrasil, name of the World Tree

ykkar *gen* of *dual pron* **þit**

ykkarr *poss dual pron* your

ykkr *acc/dat* of *dual pron* **þit**, you

ylgr <-jar> *f* she-wolf

Ymir *m* Ymir (*personal name*)

yngri *comp* of **ungr**

yrkja <orti, ortr> *vb* work, *esp* cultivate; compose (verses); **yrkja á [e-t]** set about; *mid* attack one another, **yrkisk á um [e-t]** it begins

yxnum *dat pl* of **uxi**

Ý

ýrit (*also* **œrit**) *adv* sufficiently

ýtri *comp adj* outer, outermost

ýztr *superl adj* outermost

Z

Zóe dróttning in ríka *f* Empress Zoe the Great

þ

þaðan *adv* from there, thence; **þaðan frá** from that point onward

þagði *3sg past* of **þegja**

þakka <-að> *vb* [*w dat*] thank

❖ **þangat** *adv* to there, thither (*motion toward*)

Þangbrandr <-s> Thangbrand (*personal name*)

þann *acc sg* of *dem* **sá**

❖ **þar** *adv* there; **þar sem** *conj* where

þat <*acc* þat, *dat* því, *gen* þess>*pron* it; *n nom/acc* of *dem* **sá** that (one)

þau <*acc* þau, *dat* þeim, *gen* þeira~þeirra> *n pl pron* they; those (ones)

❖ **þá** *adv* then, at that time

þá *f acc sg* of **sú**; *m acc pl* of **þeir**

þá er *conj* when

þás = **þá es** (**þá er**)

þáttr <*dat* þætti, *gen* þáttar, *pl* þættir, *acc* þáttu> *m* tale, short

❖ **þegar** *adv* at once, immediately; already; **þegar á morgin** first thing in the morning; **þegar á unga aldri** already by a young age; **þegar um haustit** that very autumn

þegja <þegir, þagði, þagat> *vb* be silent

þegn *m* subject; freeman, a good man

þegnskapr <*gen* -ar> *m* generosity, open-handedness

þeim *m dat sg* of *dem* **sá** that (one) & *all dat pl* of **þeir/þær/þau** they; those (ones)

þeima (*also* **þessum**) *m dat sg* & *all dat pl* of **þessi**

þeir <*acc* þá, *dat* þeim, *gen* þeira~þeirra> *pron* they; those (ones) (*m pl*)

þeira (*also* **þeirra**) *pron gen pl* of **þeir/þær/þau** they; their

þeirra *var* of **þeira**

þekkja <-ti~þekti~þekði~þátti, -tr~þektr~þekðr> *vb* perceive, notice; know, recognize; **þekkjast** *mid* know one another

þenna *m acc sg* of **þessi**

þess *m/n gen sg* of **sá/þat**

❖ **þessi** (*also* **sjá**) <*f* þessi, *n* þetta, *m acc sg* þenna, *m dat sg* & *all dat pl* þessum~þeima, *m/n gen sg* þessa, *m nom pl* þessir, *all gen pl* þessa~þessar(r)a, *f acc sg* þessa, *f dat sg* þessi~þessar(r)i, *f gen sg* þessar~þessar(r)ar, *n dat sg* þessu~þvísa, *n nom/acc pl* þessi> *dem pron* this, these

þetta *n nom/acc sg* of **þessi**

þér *dat* of **þú**

þér <*acc/dat* yðr, *gen* yðarr~yðvarr> *pl pron* you

Þiðrandi *m* Thidrandi (*personal name*)

þiggja <þiggr, þá, þágu, þeginn> *vb* accept; receive; accept lodgings

þik *acc* of **þú**

❖ **þing** *n* assembly, *lit* thing

þingmaðr *m* thingman, the follower of an Icelandic chieftain

Þingvöllr *m* the Thing-Plain (*place name*)

❖ **þinn** <þín, þitt> *poss pron* your (*sg*)

þit <*acc/dat* ykkr, *gen* ykkar> *dual pron* you

þín *gen* of **þú**

þjóð <*dat* þjóðu, *gen* þjóðar, *pl* þjóðir> *f* people, nation

þjófr *m* thief

þjófsaugu *n pl* thief's eyes

þjóna <-að> *vb* [*w dat*] serve

þollr *m* a tree; fir tree

þora <-ði, þorat> *vb* dare

Þorfastr <-s> *m* Thorfast (*persoanl name*)

Þorfinnr <-s> *m* Thorfinn (*personal name*)

Þorgeirr <-s> *m* Thorgeir (*personal name*); **Þorgeirr flöskubakr** Thorgeir Flask-Back

Þorgerðr <*acc/dat* Þorgerði, *gen* Þorgerðar> *f* Thorgerd (*personal name*)

Þorgils <*gen* Þorgils> *m* Thorgils (*personal name*); **Þorgils Þorsteinssonar** Thorgils, son of Thorstein (*personal name*)

---

e-n (einhvern) = 'somebody,' *acc.*;   **e-t** (eitthvat) = 'something,' *acc.*;   **e-m** (einhverjum) = '(for) somebody,' *dat.*;
e-u (einhverju) = '(for) something,' *dat.*;   **e-s** (einhvers) = '(of) somebody or something,' *gen.*

Þorgrímr *m* Thorgrim (*personal name*)

Þorkell <-s> *m* Thorkel (*personal name*); **Þorkell Geitisson** *m* Thorkel, son of Geitir

Þorleikr <-s> *m* Thorleik (*personal name*)

Þormóðr <-ar> *m* Thormod (*personal name*)

Þorsteinn <-s> *m* Thorstein (*personal name*); **Þorsteinn hvíti** *m* Thorstein the White

❖ þó *adv* yet, though, nevertheless

þó *1/3sg past of* þvá

Þóra *f* Thora (*personal name*)

Þórarinn <-s> *m* Thorarin (*personal name*)

Þórdís <-ar> *m* Thordis (*personal name*)

Þórðr <-ar> *m* Thord (*personal name*)

Þórir <*gen* Þóris> *m* Thorir (*personal name*)

Þórólfr <-s> *m* Thorolf (*personal name*)

Þórr <*dat* Þór~Þóri, *gen* Þórs> *m* Thor, god of thunder, husband of Sif, son of Odin and Earth

❖ þótt *conj* although

þótti *3sg past of* þykkja

þóttu [*poet*] = þó at þú

þrasa <*3sg pres* þrasir> *vb* be belligerent

þrausk *n* rummaging

þreifa <-að-> *vb* touch or feel with one's hand; **þreifask** *mid* fumble, grope

þrekvirki *n* courageous deed, feat of strength

þrettán <*ord* þrettándi, thirteenth> *num* thirteen

þriðjungr <-s> *m* a third

þriði <*f* þriðja, *n* þriðja > *ord num* third

Þriði *m* Third, one of the three interrogators of King Gylfi

þrífa <þrífr, þreif, þrifu, þrifinn> *vb* grasp; **þrífa til [e-s]** grab hold of [sb/sth]

❖ þrír <*f* þrjár, *n* þrjú, *acc m* þrjá, *dat* þrim(r), *gen* þriggja, *ord* þriði, third > *num* three

þrír tigir *num* thirty

þrjá *m acc pl of* þrír

þrjár *f nom/acc pl of* þrír

þrjú *n nom/acc pl of* þrír

þrúðugr *adj* strong, powerful

Þrymr <-s> *m* a lord among the giants

þræll <-s, -ar> *m* thrall, slave

Þröstr <-s> *m* Throst (*personal name*)

þumall <*dat* þumli, *gen* þumals, *pl* þumlar> *m* thumb

þumlungr <-s, -ar> *m* thumb (of a glove)

❖ þungr <*comp* þyngri, *superl* þyngstr> *adj* heavy

þunnr *adj* thin

þurfa <þarf, þurfti, þurft> *pret-pres vb* [*aux*] need; [*w gen*] need, have need of

þurs <*dat* þursi, *gen* þurs, *pl* þursar> *m* giant, ogre

Þurvi *f* Thurvi (*personal name corresponding to Old Icelandic* Þyri

❖ þú <*acc* þik, *dat* þér, *gen* þín> *pron* you (*sg*)

þúsund <-ar, -ir> *f* thousand, usually long thousand, twelve hundred

þvá <þvær, þó, þógu, þveginn> *vb* wash

þverr *adj* across; *see also* **um þvert**

þverra <þverr, þvarr, þurru, þorrinn> *vb* wane, grow less, decrease

Þvinnill <-s> *m* Thvinnil, name of a Viking (*personal name*)

því *n dat of* þat

því *conj* thus, therefore

þvísa (*also* þessu) *n dat sg of* þetta

því at *conj* for, because

því næst thereupon, then

❖ þvílíkr *adj* such

þvít = því at

❖ þykkja <þykkir, þótti, þótt> *vb impers* seem to be, [*w dat subj*] think, seem (to one); **þykkjask** *mid* seem to one, think oneself

þykkr *adj* thick

þykkt *adv* thickly

Þyri *f* Thyri (*personal name*)

þýða (-ddi, -ddr) *vb* explain, interpret; signify; win over; **þýðask [e-n]** (*mid*) associate with [sb]

þær <*acc* þær, *dat* þeim, *gen* þeira~þeirra> *pron* they; those (ones) (*f pl*)

þökk <*gen* þakkar, *pl* þakkir> *f* thanks

Æ

æ *adv* ever, always, forever

æja <ær, áði, áð> *vb* graze; rest

Æsir *m pl of* áss, one of the two major groups of gods

æti *3sg & pl past subjunct of* **eiga**

❖ ætla <-að-> *vb* intend, purpose, mean; think, consider

ætlan *f* intent

ætlat *ppart of* ætla

ætt <*pl* ættir> *f* family, kindred; generation

ættangr *m* family calamity or misfortune

ætti *3sg* & *pl past subjunct* of **eiga**

ævi *f indecl* age, time; **alla ævi** for all time, forever

Œ

œðri *comp adj* higher

œgishjálmr *m* helm of terror

œpa <-ti, -t> *vb* cry, scream, shout

❖ **œrinn** (*also* **ýrinn**) *adj* sufficient

œrit *adv* sufficiently, overly, very

œxla <-ti, -tr> *vb* cause increase, multiply

œztr *superl adj* highest

Ö/Ø

öðlask <-að-> *vb* win, earn

öðru *n dat sg* of **annarr**

øfri *var* of **efri**

øfstr *var* of **efstr**

öfundarorð *n pl* slander, words of envy

öl <*dat* ölvi, *gen pl* ölva> *n* ale, beer

öld <*dat* öldu, *gen* aldar, *pl* aldir> *f* age, time; [*poet*] man *pl* mankind, men

öldnu *wk f acc sg* of **aldinn**

öll *f nom sg* & *n nom/acc pl* of **allr**

öllum *dat pl* of **allr**

Ölvir <*gen* Ölvis> *m* Olvir (*personal name*)

önd<*dat* önd~öndu, *gen* andar, *pl* andir> *f* breath; life; spirit, soul

öndóttr *adj* fearsome, terrifying

Öndóttr kráka *m* Ondott Crow (*personal name*)

önnur *f nom sg* & *n nom/acc pl* of **annarr**

Önundr <-s> *m* Onund (*personal name*)

ör <*gen* örvar> *f* arrow

ørendi *var* of **erendi**

ørendislauss *adj* without effect, purposeless, *lit* errand-less

ørendislaust *adv* without purpose, in vain, for nothing; **fara ørendislaust** go in vain, without a purpose or reason

örlög *n pl* fate

örn <*dat* erni, *gen* arnar; *pl* ernir, *acc* örnu> *m* eagle

øx <*acc/dat* øxi, *gen* øxar, *pl* øxar> *f* axe

Øxarfjörðr *m* Oxarfjord, Axe Fjord (*place name*)

öxl <*gen* axlar, *pl* axlir> *f* shoulder

Øxna-Þórir *m* Oxen-Thorir (*personal name*)

A SELECTION OF BOOKS BY JESSE BYOCK
ABOUT ICELAND AND THE VIKING AGE

Viking Age Iceland

by Jesse Byock
Penguin History, Penguin Books

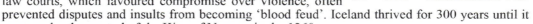

The popular image of the Viking Age is a time of warlords and marauding bands pillaging the shores of Northern Europe.

This deeply fascinating and important history reveals the society founded by Norsemen in Iceland was far from this picture. It was an independent, almost republican Free State, without warlords or kings. Honour was crucial in a world which sounds almost Utopian today. In Jesse Byock's words, it was 'a great village': a self-governing community of settlers, who adapted to Iceland's harsh climate and landscape, creating their own society.

Combining history and anthropology, this remarkable study explores in rich detail all aspects of Viking Age life: feasting, farming, battling the elements, the power of chieftains, the church, marriage, women's roles, and kinship. It shows us how law courts, which favoured compromise over violence, often prevented disputes and insults from becoming 'blood feud'. Iceland thrived for 300 years until it came under the control of the King of Norway in the 1260s.

This was a unique time in history, which has long perplexed historians and archaeologists, and which provides us today with fundamental insights into sometimes forgotten aspects of western society. By interweaving his own original and innovative research with masterly interpretations of the Old Icelandic Sagas, Jesse Byock brilliantly brings it to life.— *from the back cover*

The Saga of King Hrolf Kraki

Translated with an introduction by Jesse Byock
Penguin Classics, Penguin Books

Composed in medieval Iceland, Hrolf's Saga recalls ancient Scandinavia of the Migration Period, when the warrior chieftain King Hrolf ruled in Denmark.

In the Old Norse / Viking world, King Hrolf was a symbol of courage. Sharing rich oral traditions with the Anglo-Saxon epic *Beowulf*, *Hrolf's Saga* recounts the tragedy of strife within Denmark's royal hall. It tells of powerful women and the exploits of Hrolf's famous champions – including Bodvar Bjarki, the 'bear-warrior', who strikingly resembles Beowulf. Combining heroic legend, myth and magic, *Hrolf's Saga* has wizards, sorceresses and 'berserker' fighters, originally members of a cult of Odin. Most startling is the central love triangle: Hrolf's father, a man of insatiable appetites, unknowingly abducts his daughter, who later marries the despised sorcerer King Adils of Sweden.

A powerful human drama with deep historical roots, extraordinary events and fierce battle scenes, *Hrolf's Saga* ranks among the masterworks of the Middle Ages, influencing writers such as J.R.R. Tolkien.— *from the back cover*

www.vikingnorse.com

A SELECTION OF BOOKS BY JESSE BYOCK
ABOUT ICELAND AND THE VIKING AGE

The Saga of the Volsungs: The Norse Epic of Sigurd the Dragon Slayer

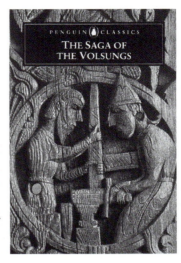

Translated with an introduction and notes by Jesse Byock
Penguin Classics, Penguin Books

An unforgettable tale, the Saga of the Volsungs is one of the great books of world literature. Based on Viking Age poems, the *Volsung* (*Völsunga*) *Saga* combines mythology, legend and sheer human drama. At its heart are the heroic deeds of Sigurd the dragon slayer who acquires runic knowledge from one of Odin's Valkyries. Yet it is set in a human world, incorporating oral memories of the fourth and fifth centuries, when Attila the Hun and other warriors fought on the northern frontiers of the Roman empire. An illuminating Introduction links the historical Huns, Burgundians and Goths with the events of this Icelandic saga, whose author claimed that Sigurd's name was 'known in all tongues north of the Greek Ocean, and so it must remain while the world endures'.

With its ill-fated Rhinegold. the sword reforged, and the magic ring of power, the saga is the Norse version of the *Nibelungenlied* and a primary source for J.R.R. Tolkien's *Lord of the Rings* and for Richard Wagner's *Ring* cycle. — *from the back cover*

The Prose Edda: Norse Mythology

Snorri Sturluson

Translated with Introduction and Notes by Jesse L. Byock
Penguin Classics, Penguin Books

The Prose Edda is the most renowned of all works of Scandinavian literature and our most extensive source for Norse mythology. Written in Iceland, it tells ancient stories of the Norse creation epic and recounts gods, giants, dwarves and elves struggling for survival. It preserves the oral memory of heroes, warrior kings and queens. In clear prose interspersed with powerful verse, the *Edda* provides unparalleled insight into the gods' tragic realization that the future holds one final cataclysmic battle, Ragnarok, when the world will be destroyed. These tales from the pagan era have proved to be among the most influential of all myths and legends, inspiring Wagner's *Ring Cycle* and Tolkien's *The Lord of the Rings*.

This new translation by Jesse Byock captures the strength and subtlety of the original, while his introduction sets the tales fully in the context of Norse mythology. This edition includes detailed notes and appendices. — *from the back cover*

A SELECTION OF BOOKS BY JESSE BYOCK
ABOUT ICELAND AND THE VIKING AGE

Medieval Iceland: Society, Sagas, and Power
Jesse L. Byock
University of California Press

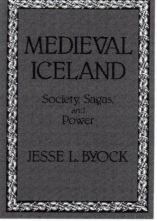

"Byock's book is a tour-de-force of historical argument. He brilliantly reconstructs the inner workings of an intriguing society, not elsewhere to be found in the Western world." — David Herlihy, *History Book Club*

"The first to demonstrate the importance of brokerage, advocacy, and arbitration as a social method of maintaining the governmental system, the balance of power, and the peace." — Helgi Thorláksson, *Skírnir*

"Medieval Iceland was a kind of pure-environment anthropological laboratory... It ought to have been a Utopia. It had: no foreign policy, no defence forces, no king, no lords, no peasants, no dispossessed aborigines, no battles (till late on), no dangerous animals, and no very clear taxes. What could possibly go wrong? Why is their literature all about killing each other? Answers lie, says Byock, in 'the underlying structures and cultural codes' of the island's social order... The most fascinating parts discuss the ways in which saga characters operate within a system of checks and balances to gain their ends." — Tom Shippey, *London Review of Books*

"In this stimulating and important work, Byock has succeeded in rehabilitating the Icelandic sagas as important sources for the social and economic history of the Free State (c. 930s to 1262-64)... Highly recommended." — C.W. Clark, *Choice*

Feud in the Icelandic Saga
Jesse Byock
University of California Press (UCPress)

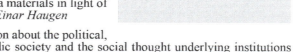

"Byock's thorough inquiry into the Icelandic feud system and its impact on the saga literature is valuable and fruitful in itself. But his specific research work also results in important general conclusions concerning the Icelandic saga as a medieval epic genre... A sound and convincingly motivated statement on the unique character of the Icelandic saga." — Peter Hallberg, *International Journal of Scandinavian Studies*

"Byock has not only succeeded in grounding, in a convincing manner, the social roles of individuals in the sagas but has also laid bare the role of narrative in Old Icelandic society." — Vilhjálmur Árnason, *Skírnir*

"Jesse Byock has here established an admirable basis for further research by clearing away much of the debris of the past. We are now ready for a full-scale reevaluation of saga materials in light of socio-historical and evolutionary views." — *Einar Haugen*

"An admirable study... A wealth of information about the political, social, and economic development of Icelandic society and the social thought underlying institutions and practices." — *The Scandinavian-American Bulletin*

"Jesse Byock's work has illuminated fundamental social concepts better and more clearly than has previously been done because he uses Icelandic sources in a new way." — Helgi Thorláksson, *Ný Saga*

"Boldly imaginative and on the cutting edge of the human sciences." — Dwight Conquergood, *Journal of American Folklore*

www.vikingnorse.com

www.vikingnorse.com

A SELECTION OF BOOKS BY JESSE BYOCK
ABOUT ICELAND AND THE VIKING AGE

Sagas and Myths of the Northmen

Translated by Jesse Byock
Penguin Classics / Penguin Epics XVI
(Penguin Series: The Greatest Stories Ever Told)

A short introductory sampling of selected Norse myths and
legends for beginners to Old Icelandic mythology and sagas
with excerpts from *The Saga of the Volsungs, The Saga of
King Hrolf Kraki* , and *The Prose Edda.*

In a land of ice, great warriors search for glory… when a
dragon threatens the people of the north, only one man can
destroy the fearsome beast. Elsewhere, a mighty leader
gathers a court of champions, including a noble warrior under
a terrible curse. The Earth's creation is described; tales of the
gods and evil Frost Giants are related; and the dark days of
Ragnarok foretold.

Journey into a realm of Old Norse and Viking legend, where
heroes from an ancient age do battle with savage monsters,
and every man must live or die by the sword. — *from the back cover*

Grettir's Saga

Translated with an Introduction and Notes by **Jesse Byock**
Oxford University Press, Oxford World's Classics

*'You will be made an outlaw, forced always to live in the wilds
and to live alone.'*

A sweeping epic of the Viking Age, *Grettir's Saga* follows
the life of the outlaw Grettir the Strong as he battles against
sorcery, bad luck, and the vengefulness of his enemies. Feared
by many, Grettir is a warrior, a poet, and a lover who is afraid
of the dark. Unable to resolve the dispute that has outlawed
him, Grettir lives outside the bounds of family life . He roams
the countryside, ridding Iceland and Norway of berserkers,
trolls, and walking dead. The saga presents medieval Icelandic
life, including love life, food, blood feud, folklore, and legend.
Grettir's Saga, with its scathing humour, explicit verses, and
fantastic monsters, is among the most famous, and widely
read of Iceland's sagas.

Grettir's Saga
A new translation by Jesse Byock

OXFORD WORLD'S CLASSICS

This new translation features extensive maps and illustrative material. — *from the back cover*

www.vikingnorse.com

A SELECTION OF BOOKS BY JESSE BYOCK
ABOUT ICELAND AND THE VIKING AGE

Viking Language 1:
Learn Old Norse, Runes, and Icelandic Sagas
Jesse L. Byock

Viking Language 1: Learn Old Norse, Runes, and Icelandic Sagas is an introduction to the language of the Vikings offering in one book graded lessons, vocabulary, grammar exercises, pronunciation, student guides, and maps. It explains Old Icelandic literature, Viking history, and mythology. Readings include runestones, legends, and sagas.

Viking Language 1 focuses on the most frequently occurring words in the sagas, an innovative method which speeds learning. Because the grammar has changed little from Old Norse, the learner is well on the way to mastering Modern Icelandic. *Viking Language 1* provides a wealth of information about Iceland, where the sagas were written and Old Scandinavian history and mythology were preserved. *Viking Language 1* is accompanied by *Viking Language 2: The Old Norse Reader*.

Viking Language 2:
The Old Norse Reader

Jesse L. Byock

Viking Language 2: The Old Norse Reader is a collection of original texts to accompany *Viking Language 1*. A stand-alone book for classes and the self-learner, *The Old Norse Reader* immerses the learner in Icelandic and Viking Age sources. It provides the tools necessary to read complete sagas and Norse mythic and heroic poetry. *The Reader* includes:

- Sagas of blood feud in Viking Age Iceland accompanied by introductions, notes, maps, and cultural discussions.
- Extensive vocabulary, a comprehensive Old Norse reference grammar and answer key to the exercises in *Viking Language 1*.
- Mythic and heroic poetry teaching eddic, skaldic, and runic verse.
- Selections from Old Norse texts ranging from the doom of the gods at the final battle Ragnarok to descriptions of the ring and the dwarves' gold that inspired Richard Wagner's *Ring Cycle* and J.R.R. Tolkien's *Lord of the Rings*.

www.vikingnorse.com

A SELECTION OF BOOKS BY JESSE BYOCK
ABOUT ICELAND AND THE VIKING AGE

Saga of the Volsungs: The Norse Epic of
Sigurd the Dragon Slayer
Translated with an Introduction and Notes by Jesse L. Byock
University of California Press
The source for Wagner's *Ring* and for Tolkien's *The Lord of the Rings*

A trove of traditional lore, this Icelandic prose epic tells of love, vengeance, war, and the mythic deeds of the dragonslayer, Sigurd the Volsung. Richard Wagner drew heavily upon this Norse source in writing his Ring Cycle. With its magical ring, and the sword to be reforged, the saga was a primary source for J.R.R. Tolkien and romantics such as William Morris. Byock's comprehensive introduction explores the history, legends, and myths contained in the *Volsung (Völsunga) Saga*. It traces the development of a narrative that reaches back to the great folk migrations in Europe when the Roman Empire collapsed.

"Byock extends the background to the saga beyond the interest of 'Wagnerites' to the complex relationship between history and legend in the Middle Ages and the social context of the myths and heroes of the saga... [Byock is] very successful in his adept renderings of Eddic rhythm... The translation of prose is equally fine." — Judy Quinn, *Parergon*

"This is a book of the highest importance. No one should attempt to teach about Viking society or claim to understand it without being familiar with this chilling and enduring myth." — Eleanor Searle, *Medieval Academy of America*

L'Islande des Vikings
Jesse Byock
Traduit de l'anglais (E.-U.) par Béatrice Bonne
Préface de Jacques Le Goff
Aubier Collection historique
Flammarion / Aubier

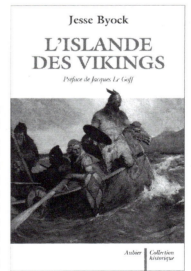

Seigneurs sanguinaires, maraudeurs sillonnant les rivages de l'Europe du Nord et pillant tout sur leur passage, les Vikings n'ont pas bonne réputation. Et pourtant ils ont fondé, en Islande, sur cette île demeurée quasi vierge de toute présence humaine jusqu'au IXe siècle, une société unique : basée sur un État libre et indépendant, elle est en grande partie exempte des hiérarchies sociales habituelles – y compris dans les rapports entre hommes et femmes – et fait reposer le règlement des conflits davantage sur le consensus que sur la violence et la guerre. Entre festins de raie pourrie et manuel de survie en milieu hostile, conflits juridiques et méthode de construction des maisons en mottes de terre herbeuse... c'est la vie quotidienne des Vikings à l'époque médiévale qui nous est ici dévoilée. En entrelaçant ses propres recherches historiques et archéologiques avec ses interprétations magistrales des sagas, ces récits littéraires typiquement islandais, Jesse Byock fait revivre cette civilisation avec brio. — *quatrième de couverture*

www.vikingnorse.com

A SELECTION OF BOOKS BY JESSE BYOCK
ABOUT ICELAND AND THE VIKING AGE

Исландия эпохи викингов

Джесси Байок
Москва, Corpus, 2012
Translated by Ilya Sverdlov (Jesse Byock, *Viking Age Iceland*)

Джесси Л. Байок - специалист по древнеисландскому языку и средневековой Скандинавии, профессор Калифорнийского университета, автор множества книг, переводов и научных статей. Его главный труд, "Исландия эпохи викингов", - это и увлекательное путешествие по исландской действительности в период X-XIII вв., и полезное пособие по чтению саг, и экскурсия в удивительное общество, которое настолько занято делом, что вынуждено вместо междоусобных войн развивать правовую систему.

La Stirpe di Odino: La Civiltà Vichinga in Islanda

Jesse Byock
Traduzione di Marco Federici
Prefazione di Jacques Le Goff
Arnoldo Mondadori Editore

I primi raggiunsero l'Islanda dalla Scandinavia e dalla Brittannia vichinga alla metà del IX secolo e qui diedero vita a uno stato libero, indipendente e non gerarchico, che costituisce un unicum nella storia europea. Le strutture sociali, economiche, politiche e giuridiche, infatti, per quanto ispirate a quelle delle zone d'origine, doveterro essere modellate su una realtà geografica del tutto nuovo, difficile e affascinante, e durarono con minime evoluzioni fino alla conquista norvegese del 1260, dando vita a una civiltà rurale, con una stupefacente cultura del diritto e un forte senso dell'onore.

In questo libro, che il grande medievista Le Goff ha definito "splendido e affascinante", l'autore indaga l'Islanda indipendente in modo globale, facendo ricorso a molteplici tipologie di fonti, da quelle giuridiche a quelle archeologiche, e in particolare analizza le splendide saghe, capolavori letterari dai quali è possibile ricavare la più esatta descrizione di quello che voleva dire vivere nella "terra dei ghiacci" tra IX e XIII secolo.

www.vikingnorse.com

A SELECTION OF BOOKS BY JESSE BYOCK
ABOUT ICELAND AND THE VIKING AGE

アイスランド・サガ
血讐の記号論
Feud in the Icelandic Saga (Japanese edition)

Jesse L. Byock

Translated by Chusaku Shibata and Tomoyuki Inoue

Tokai University Press, Tokyo

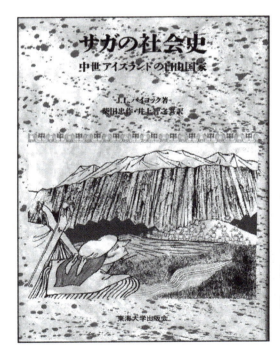

サガの社会史
中世アイスランドの自由国家
Medieval Iceland (Japanese edition)

Jesse L. Byock

Translated by Chusaku Shibata and Tomoyuki Inoue

Tokai University Press, Tokyo

A SELECTION OF BOOKS BY JESSE BYOCK
ABOUT ICELAND AND THE VIKING AGE

Island i sagatiden: Samfund, magt og fejde

Jesse Byock
Oversat av Jon Høyer
C. A. Reitzels forlag

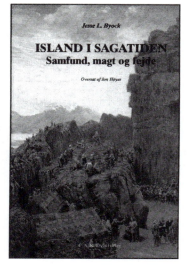

De islandske sagaer udgør i denne bog et vindue ind til et usædvanligt samfund: Uden nogen central og udøvende myndighed formåede denne sociale nyskabelse at inddæmme fejder og konflikter og holde fred og forlig i omkring 300 år. I hele denne tradition, med dens tingsamlinger og kompromisløsninger, har de nordiske samfund dybe rødder.

Sagaerne opfattes i denne bog som et middelalderfolks beretninger om sig selv, fortalt til sig selv, til underholdning og social orientering. De opfattes således som pålidelige gengivelser af sociale mønstre og normer igennem den islandske fristatstid, der var kendetegnet ved en forbavsende kontinuitet. Læst i sammenhæng med anden islandsk middelalderlitteratur kaster sagaerne et gennemtrængende lys over hele dette historiske forløb. — *bagsidetekst*

Island i sagatiden udkom første gang i 1988 i USA og England med titlen *Medieval Iceland* og er en meget benyttet fagbog i mange lande. Denne danske udgave er gennemgribende udvidet siden da og omkring halvanden gang så omfattende. Denne bog kan anbefales til både erfarne forskere og nybegyndere inden for sagastudierne. Byock fremlægger sine undersøgelsesresultater og sine præmisser forbilledligt og klart, og netop derfor vil denne bog stimulere debatten på bedste vis. — Nanna Damsholt, *Scandinavian Journal of History*

Byock er sandsynligvis den første forsker, der viser, hvordan mægling, tredjepartsindgreb og forhandling udgør en vigtig social metode til at sikre statssystemet, magtbalancen og freden. — Helgi Þorláksson, *Skírnir*

Byock's bog er en *tour-de-force* inden for historisk argumentation. På fremragende måde rekonstruerer han de underliggende styringsmekanismer i et fejdesamfund, der ikke findes noget andet sted i den vestlige verden. — David Herlihy, *History Book Club*

De mest fascinerende dele af Byock's bog blotlægger de måder, som sagapersoner handler på for at nå deres mål inden for samfundets kontrol- og balancesystem. — Tom Shippey, *London Review of Books*

Made in the USA
Charleston, SC
12 May 2013